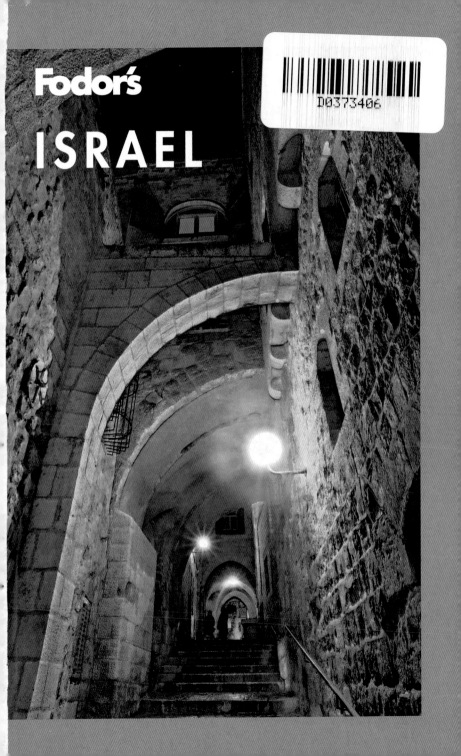

Fodor's
ISRAEL

WELCOME TO ISRAEL

Within its small perimeter Israel packs in abundant riches, from cherished religious sites and well-preserved archaeological treasures to spectacular natural wonders. Holy land to Jews, Christians, and Muslims, this is where biblical place names like Jerusalem and the Galilee come vibrantly alive. Here, too, you can party by the Mediterranean in Tel Aviv, float in the super-salty Dead Sea, and explore cool mountain waterfalls or sweeping desert landscapes. Whether you're in a shrine or on a hiking trail, Israel is a place to renew the spirit.

TOP REASONS TO GO

★ **Jerusalem:** This unique, golden-stone city is the crossroads of three faiths.

★ **Ancient Sites:** Masada, Megiddo, Caesarea, and others reveal millennia of history.

★ **Open-Air Markets:** Bustling crowds, fragrant foods, and colorful artisan gifts beckon.

★ **Desert Adventures:** Memorable camel treks, jeep rides, and hikes await in the Negev.

★ **Local Food:** Falafel, hummus, grilled fish, and Israeli wine tempt the palate.

★ **Biblical Landscapes:** Around the Galilee, scenes evoke New Testament scriptures.

Fodor's ISRAEL

Publisher: Amanda D'Acierno, *Senior Vice President*

Editorial: Arabella Bowen, *Executive Editorial Director*; Linda Cabasin, *Editorial Director*

Design: Fabrizio La Rocca, *Vice President, Creative Director*; Tina Malaney, *Associate Art Director*; Chie Ushio, *Senior Designer*; Ann McBride, *Production Designer*

Photography: Melanie Marin, *Associate Director of Photography*; Jessica Parkhill and Jennifer Romains, *Researchers*

Maps: Rebecca Baer, *Senior Map Editor*; Henry Colomb and Mark Stroud, Moon Street Cartography; David Lindroth, *Cartographers*

Production: Linda Schmidt, *Managing Editor*; Evangelos Vasilakis, *Associate Managing Editor*; Angela L. McLean, *Senior Production Manager*

Sales: Jacqueline Lebow, *Sales Director*

Marketing & Publicity: Heather Dalton, *Marketing Director*; Katherine Fleming, *Senior Publicist*

Business & Operations: Susan Livingston, *Vice President, Strategic Business Planning*; Sue Daulton, *Vice President, Operations*

Fodors.com: Megan Bell, *Executive Director, Revenue & Business Development*; Yasmin Marinaro, *Senior Director, Marketing & Partnerships*

Copyright © 2014 by Fodor's Travel, a division of Random House LLC.

Editor: Linda Cabasin, lead editor; Bethany Beckerlegge, Mark Sullivan

Writers: Benjamin Balint, Judy Balint, Inbal Baum, Daniella Cheslow, Shari Giddens Helmer, Matthew Kalman, Noya Kohavi, Mike Rogoff, Adeena Sussman

Production Editor: Evangelos Vasilakis

Fodor's is a registered trademark of Random House LLC. All rights reserved. Published in the United States by Fodor's Travel, a division of Random House LLC, New York, a Penguin Random House Company, and in Canada by Random House of Canada Limited, Toronto. No maps, illustrations, or other portions of this book may be reproduced in any form without written permission from the publisher.

9th Edition

ISBN 978-0-89141-953-2

ISSN 0071-6588

SPECIAL SALES

This book is available at special discounts for bulk purchases for sales promotions or premiums. For more information, e-mail specialmarkets@randomhouse.com

PRINTED IN COLOMBIA

10 9 8 7 6 5 4 3 2 1

CONTENTS

1 EXPERIENCE ISRAEL 9

Israel Today. 10

What's Where 12

Israel Planner 14

Israel Made Easy 16

Israel Top Attractions. 18

Quintessential Israel 20

If You Like. 22

Israel: People, Religion, and State . .24

Israel's Top Experiences 28

Israel Lodging Primer. 29

Flavors of Israel 30

Israel with Kids 32

Israel's Markets 34

Israel's Best Beaches. 35

Israel and the Performing Arts. . . .36

Israel's Major Holidays 38

Great Itineraries 41

2 JERUSALEM 53

Welcome to
Jerusalem. 54

Holiday Foods in Israel. 56

Jerusalem Planner 59

Exploring Jerusalem 62

Where to Eat. 118

Best Bets for Jerusalem Dining . .120

Where to Stay 135

Best Bets for Jerusalem Lodging. .137

Nightlife and the Arts 145

Shopping 150

**3 AROUND JERUSALEM AND
THE DEAD SEA** 159

Welcome to Around Jerusalem
and the Dead Sea. 160

Around Jerusalem and
the Dead Sea Planner 163

Fodor's Features

Israel Through the Ages 47

Jerusalem: Keeping the Faith 70

The Dead Sea: A Natural Wonder . . . 168

Masada: Desert Fortress 182

Tel Aviv After Dark 261

The Wines of Israel 322

Jesus in the Galilee. 374

Adventures in the Negev 468

Masada and the Dead Sea 165

West of Jerusalem 192

Bethlehem 202

4 TEL AVIV 211

Welcome to Tel Aviv 212

Bauhaus Style in Tel Aviv 214

Tel Aviv Planner 217

Exploring Tel Aviv 219

Where to Eat. 235

Best Bets for Tel Aviv Dining 238

Street Food In Israel 240

Where to Stay 252

Best Bets for Tel Aviv Lodging . . .254

Nightlife and the Arts 259

Sports and the Outdoors 269

Shopping 272

5   HAIFA AND
    THE NORTHERN COAST 277

    Welcome to Haifa
    and the Northern Coast 278

    Haifa and the
    Northern Coast Planner 281

    Haifa 283

    The Northern Coast 303

    The Wine Country and
    Mt. Carmel 315

    Akko to Rosh Hanikra 332

6   LOWER GALILEE 347

    Welcome to Lower Galilee 348

    Lower Galilee Planner 351

    Jezreel and Jordan Valleys 353

    Nazareth and the Galilee Hills . . . 364

    Tiberias and the Sea of Galilee . . 381

7   UPPER GALILEE AND
    THE GOLAN 399

    Welcome to Upper Galilee
    and the Golan 400

    Upper Galilee Planner 403

    Tzfat (Safed) and Environs 405

    Upper Hula Valley 420

    The Golan Heights 426

8   EILAT AND THE NEGEV 435

    Welcome to Eilat and the Negev . . 436

    Eilat and the Negev Planner 439

    Eilat and Environs 441

    The Heart of the Negev 460

    Beersheva 480

    Side Trip to Petra 489

    UNDERSTANDING ISRAEL . . . 500

    Hebrew Vocabulary 500

    Palestinian Arabic Vocabulary . . . 506

    TRAVEL SMART ISRAEL 511

    INDEX 533

    ABOUT OUR WRITERS 544

MAPS

The Old City 64–65

East Jerusalem 98

West Jerusalem 105

Center City 114

Where to Eat and Stay
in Jerusalem 122–123

Masada and the Dead Sea 174

West of Jerusalem 193

Bethlehem 203

Center City & Neveh Tzedek 221

Jaffa 229

Tel Aviv Port and
Northern Tel Aviv 234

Where to Eat in Tel Aviv 239

Where to Stay in Tel Aviv 255

Haifa 288–289

Where to Eat and Stay in Haifa . . 297

The Northern Coast to
Rosh Hanikra 304

Caesarea 306

Akko–Old City 335

Lower Galilee 355

Nazareth 365

Sea of Galilee 381

Where to Eat and Stay in
Tiberias 385

Tzfat (Safed) 406

Tzfat and Environs 414

Upper Hula Valley and
Golan Heights 421

Eilat and Environs 442

Where to Eat & Stay in Eilat 447

The Heart of Negev 461

Beersheva and Environs 481

Petra 491

ABOUT
THIS GUIDE

Fodor's Recommendations

Everything in this guide is worth doing—we don't cover what isn't—but exceptional sights, hotels, and restaurants are recognized with additional accolades. Fodor'sChoice★ indicates our top recommendations; and **Best Bets** call attention to notable hotels and restaurants in various categories. Care to nominate a new place? Visit Fodors.com/contact-us.

Trip Costs

We list prices wherever possible to help you budget well. Hotel and restaurant price categories from **$** to **$$$$** are noted alongside each recommendation. For hotels, we include the lowest cost of a standard double room in high season. For restaurants, we cite the average price of a main course at dinner or, if dinner isn't served, at lunch. For attractions, we always list adult admission fees; discounts are usually available for children, students, and senior citizens.

Hotels

Our local writers vet every hotel to recommend the best overnights in each price category, from budget to expensive. Unless otherwise specified, you can expect private bath, phone, and TV in your room. For expanded hotel reviews, facilities, and deals visit Fodors.com.

Restaurants

Unless we state otherwise, restaurants are open for lunch and dinner daily. We mention dress code only when there's a specific requirement and reservations only when they're essential or not accepted. To make restaurant reservations, visit Fodors.com.

Credit Cards

The hotels and restaurants in this guide typically accept credit cards. If not, we'll say so.

Top Picks
★ Fodor'sChoice

Listings
- ✉ Address
- ✉ Branch address
- ☎ Telephone
- 🖷 Fax
- ⊕ Website
- ✉ E-mail
- ☑ Admission fee
- ◷ Open/closed times
- Ⓜ Subway
- ⊹ Directions or Map coordinates

Hotels &
Restaurants
- 🏨 Hotel
- ↰ Number of rooms
- ⦿Ⅰ Meal plans
- ✕ Restaurant
- ⌂ Reservations
- 👗 Dress code
- ▭ No credit cards
- Ⓢ Price

Other
- ⇨ See also
- ☞ Take note
- 🏌 Golf facilities

EXPERIENCE
ISRAEL

ISRAEL TODAY

Israelis are at once warmly hospitable and feisty. The country's ethnic, religious, and political mix, endlessly fascinating, can be exasperating as well. But, with legendary resilience, Israelis seem to thrive on complexity, and life between the headlines is astonishingly normal.

A Vibrant Economy, and Yet . . .

Israel's founding fathers were socialists and its early economy largely agrarian. That's history, though. Agriculture today is sophisticated and technology-based, but its share of the country's exports is under 3%, as the economy has burgeoned and reinvented itself.

With few natural resources—beyond newly discovered natural gas—the human factor was always crucial. Diamond cutting, an early initiative of Jewish refugees from wartime Holland and Belgium, supplies some 40% of the world's cut and polished stones and 20% of all Israel's exports. And tourism is big, of course, with 3.5 million visitors a year, mostly Holy Land pilgrims and Jewish "roots" travelers.

The real story of the last quarter century is high-tech. Israel is second only to the United States in the number of its start-ups; computer systems, imaging, medical research, and biotech are leading specialties; and Israeli companies with attractive expertise are constantly being snapped up by big foreign corporations.

The country's financial environment, including vigilant bank regulation, has helped it weather global crises better than most. In 2010, Israel was accepted to the Organisation for Economic Co-operation and Development (OECD), yet the gap between the haves and have-nots is high, and one out of every five Israeli families lives below the poverty line. Despite acute public awareness of the problem, global surveys in 2012 show Israel as a conspicuously happy society: the Happy Planet Index, for example, has Israel in 15th place. Go figure.

The Palestine Conundrum

Relations between Israel and the Palestinians, always fraught, have been in crisis for some time. The promising peace talks toward the end of the last decade are a distant memory, with each side blaming the other for the impasse. In a fresh gambit, the Palestinians took their case to the United Nations General Assembly in November 2012, winning overwhelming support for recognition of Palestine as a sovereign but nonmember state. The Israeli government defiantly responded by fast-tracking controversial construction plans in the West Bank. International criticism was unusually strong.

There is mounting concern that time is running out for a "two-state solution," which envisages Israel and a viable sovereign Palestine alongside each other. At this writing, U.S. Secretary of State John Kerry was engaged in high-frequency shuttling between the parties in order to jump-start talks; but faith in the moribund peace process is low, and Palestinians feel that international recognition has given them traction to examine other options. Meanwhile, the credibility of Palestinian leader Mahmoud Abbas has ebbed away, even within his own Fatah faction—let alone his bitter rival, the militantly Islamist Hamas that controls the Gaza Strip.

Beyond the Headlines

Israel is so often a source of breaking news that its life beyond the headlines seems like a well-kept secret. The big cities are very cosmopolitan; a vigorous Israeli film industry has won kudos and awards

at international festivals; and the nation-wide Book Week is a major cultural event. Classical orchestras, ensembles, and solo artists perform in Israel and abroad. Athletes have enjoyed occasional bright moments on the Olympic podium—though Israeli Paralympians are always among the medals—and in European club basketball. And Israel is a world-class chess nation, as Israelis proudly discovered when grandmaster Boris Gelfand challenged the world champion in 2012: the Israeli was just edged out in a sudden-death tiebreaker.

Academia is strong. Six Israelis have been awarded Nobel Prizes since 2002, four in chemistry and two in economics. Innovative research groups continue to make important biological and medical break-throughs—at the conceptual, technological, and pharmacological levels—for the treatment of cancer and many other diseases, in fields like nanotechnology and stem-cell treatment, and much more.

In the important business of Arab-Jewish relations (within Israel), much needs to be done; but there are joint business ventures, bilingual theater groups and bands, and interschool dialogue and collaborative projects.

Greening Israel

Israel's chronic water shortage has spurred the search for creative solutions. Drip irrigation is a clear winner; seawater desalination and wastewater treatment (an extraordinary 75% reclaimed) top up the reserves. Rooftop solar panels for domestic water heaters punctuate city skylines, and small solar-energy plants operate in the Negev Desert. Israel has embraced green concepts, developing and often exporting homegrown environmental products and technologies. Cities are widening their recycling programs, encouraging bikers, and improving public transportation. And organic produce is easier than ever to come by.

Around the Region

Of all the popular uprisings dubbed "the Arab Spring," the most worrying for Israel were those close by. In Egypt, Hosni Mubarak's regime fell and was replaced by the Muslim Brotherhood, which is the mentor of Hamas, the Islamist Palestinian movement that dreams of eliminating Israel.

After one year in office, the Egyptian president, Mohamed Morsi, was deposed by the military, ostensibly because of his failure to deliver on earlier promises. The most important Arab country in the region is seen to be imploding, and the rift between rival factions now threatens its fragile democracy. Israel remains anxious to preserve its peace treaty with Egypt and to see terrorism and arms smuggling in Egyptian Sinai brought under control.

The bloodletting in Syria since 2011 has shocked the world. At this writing, predictions of the imminent fall of the Assad regime seem premature. It may be just a matter of time, however; and Israel's concern is with what will replace it. The alternative to dictatorship is not necessarily Western-style democracy, and another extreme Islamist state on Israel's borders is a distinct possibility.

The year 2012 saw an escalation of rocket attacks from the Hamas-controlled Gaza Strip, and strong Israeli retaliation at year's end. At this writing, the situation had quieted considerably but the Gaza Strip is likely to remain implacably hostile, even if progress is recorded on Palestinian-Israeli issues.

WHAT'S WHERE

Numbers refer to chapters.

2 Jerusalem. The walls of the Old City embrace sites sacred to Judaism, Christianity, and Islam, but Israel's capital is more than its ancient places. Rub shoulders in the vibrant markets, sip coffee in a stone courtyard, and poke around modern museums and malls of a city suspended between East and West, past and present, and (some say) heaven and earth.

3 Around Jerusalem and the Dead Sea. Treat yourself to three very different desert experiences: exploring King Herod's mountaintop palace-citadel of Masada, floating in the supersaline Dead Sea, and frolicking under fresh waterfalls in the Ein Gedi canyon. Day trips to Bethlehem and to wineries west of Jerusalem are other memorable options.

4 Tel Aviv. The beautiful beaches and the seaside promenade alive with cafés and good times hug the Mediterranean. The "city that never sleeps" is Israel's cultural and entertainment center. Don't miss its Bauhaus architecture, charming old neighborhoods, and first-class restaurants and nightlife.

5 Haifa and the Northern Coast. Although you're never far from a Mediterranean beach, take time to see the sights in Haifa, like the Baha'i Shrine and Gardens, and in Akko's medieval Old City. South of Haifa are Roman Caesarea and the Mt. Carmel wine country.

6 Lower Galilee. Verdant valleys, rolling hills, and the freshwater Sea of Galilee are counterpoints to the historical riches in this northern part of Israel. Hike the Arbel cliffs, explore archaeology at Beit She'an and Zippori, and visit Nazareth and the famed sites of Jesus' ministry. At night, enjoy dinner by the lake.

7 Upper Galilee and the Golan. Historical treasures, quaint bed-and-breakfasts, and the great outdoors are some of the best reasons for visiting Israel's northeast corner. The mountaintop city of Tzfat (Safed), cradle of Jewish mysticism, and Rosh Pina, a delightful restored village, are two primary sites.

8 Eilat and the Negev. Visiting the Negev is about experiencing the desert's quiet vistas and remarkable geological treasures, and enjoying Eilat's gorgeous beaches and Red Sea coral reefs. Take a side trip to ancient Petra, in nearby Jordan, to see its temples and tombs carved out of red sandstone cliffs.

ISRAEL PLANNER

Getting Here

International flights land at Ben Gurion International Airport, about 10 miles from Tel Aviv and about 27 miles from Jerusalem.

Security checks on airlines flying to Israel are stringent. Be prepared for what might sound like personal questions about your itinerary, packing habits, and desire to travel to Israel. Remember that the staff is concerned with protecting you, and be patient.

A taxi is the quickest and most convenient way to get to and from the airport. Fares to Jerusalem are NIS 280 ($76) for the 45-minute trip and approximately NIS 170 ($48) to Tel Aviv. Another option is the 10-passenger Nesher that shuttles between Jerusalem and Ben Gurion and costs NIS 62 ($18) per person.

If you depart for the airport from central Tel Aviv by car or taxi at rush hour (7 am–9 am, 5 pm–7 pm), note that the roads can get clogged. Allow 45 minutes for a trip that would otherwise take only about 20 minutes.

The train is a money saver if you're heading for Tel Aviv. A one-way ticket is NIS 15 ($4) and takes under 15 minutes.

Getting Around

You can get almost anywhere in Israel by bus, and the Central Bus Station is a fixture in most towns: ask for the *tahana merkazit*. Egged handles most of the country's bus routes; Dan dominates in Tel Aviv. Both intercity and urban buses run from 5:30 am to 12:30 am Sunday to Thursday.

Note: Public transportation is suspended during the Jewish Sabbath (Shabbat), from about an hour before sundown Friday (depending on the line) until nightfall Saturday, although private minivans ply some lines in Tel Aviv. Haifa has a limited bus service on Shabbat.

Taxis can be a good option on Shabbat—they're plentiful, relatively inexpensive, and can be hailed on the street. Drivers must use the meter according to law. *Sheruts* are shared taxis or minivans that run fixed routes at a set rate; some can be booked in advance.

The train from Tel Aviv to Jerusalem is a scenic, 1¾ hour trip—not the quickest way to travel between the two cities. Commuter trains run efficiently between other cities; the majority of service runs along the coast, from Nahariya south to Tel Aviv, and then inland as far as Beersheva.

For more information on getting here and around, see Travel Smart Israel.

DRIVING DISTANCES/TIMES IN ISRAEL

Eilat to Tel Aviv	223 miles (356 km)	4.5 hrs
Tel Aviv to Jerusalem	36 miles (58 km)	55 mins
Jerusalem to Ben Gurion Airport	27 miles (43 km)	40 mins
Ben Gurion Airport to Tel Aviv	10 miles (16 km)	15 mins
Tel Aviv to Haifa	52 miles (84 km)	1.25 hrs
Haifa to Tiberias	35 miles (56 km)	1.5 hrs
Tiberias to Jerusalem	109 miles (175 km)	2.7 hrs
Jerusalem to Eilat	190 miles (306 km)	4.5 hrs
Jerusalem to Masada	66 miles (106 km)	1.5 hrs
Haifa to Nazareth	23 miles (37 km)	55 mins

Dining

Unless otherwise noted, the restaurants listed in this guide are open daily for lunch (*arukhat tzohorayim*) and dinner (*arukhat erev*), and prices are in Israeli shekels (NIS). Major credit cards are widely accepted; some places accept cash dollars. Recommended tipping ("service") is 12%–15%, usually in cash, though more and more places allow you to include it on your card.

In Israel, many restaurants are *kosher* and will display a dated kosher certificate. These establishments don't serve pork and shellfish, and will either be designated as "meat" restaurants (no dairy products in sight) or "dairy" (which may include fish, but no meat or poultry).

In the cities, cafés are generally open Sunday to Thursday 8 am to midnight. Kosher cafés close two hours before the Sabbath and reopen Saturday night; nonkosher places keep regular hours. Restaurants serving lunch and dinner usually open at noon and close around midnight or 1 am. Israelis eat dinner fairly late, and it's not uncommon to wait for a table at 10 pm.

For details, see Eating Out in Travel Smart Israel.

Lodging

Nearly all hotel rooms in Israel have private bathrooms with a combined shower and tub. The best hotels have a swimming pool, a health club, and occasionally tennis courts; and, with rare exceptions in major cities, most hotels have parking facilities.

Almost all the large Israeli hotels are certified kosher, and include a sumptuous "traditional" Israeli breakfast. The lodgings we list are the cream of the crop in each price category. When pricing accommodations, always ask what's included and what costs extra; if a facility is important to you, ask for details. Prices are in dollars, as paying bills at hotels in foreign currency eliminates the 18% Value-Added Tax (VAT). Unless otherwise noted, all lodgings have a private bathroom, a room phone, and a television.

For details, see the Lodging Primer in this chapter and Accommodations in Travel Smart Israel.

When to Go

Israel has several high seasons, but each attracts different types of visitors. The Jewish New Year (Rosh Hashanah) and Sukkot usually fall in September or October, bringing Jewish travelers wanting to celebrate in the Holy Land. Spring and autumn are favorite times for Christian pilgrims. In April or March, when Passover and Easter generally coincide, Christian and Jewish tourists crowd religious sites in Jerusalem and the Galilee. July and August are the hottest months, and the beaches are buzzing. The weather is perfect in late September and October, and from April to mid-June, when days are warm enough without being too hot, and nights are comfortable. May and June are in between high seasons, and prices are more affordable. The weather is still splendid, and historical sites and other attractions are yet to be filled with tourists.

Renting a Car

Renting a car is a good idea only if you plan to thoroughly explore the country but not within big cities. At the time of this writing, gas costs close to NIS 8 per liter, or $8 per gallon. (Self-service is always cheaper.) Opt for the fullest insurance coverage available, and double check if the coverage applies if you plan to drive in the West Bank. *For more information, see Travel Smart Israel.*

ISRAEL MADE EASY

Customs of the Country

Western-style social graces aren't the strong suit of the average Israeli. But, despite the country's legendary informality, the traditions and customs of its many ethnic and religious communities form an entire corpus of social norms. Sensitivity to those norms can open doors; ignoring them may cause offense. The best example is the modest dress code required (especially for women) in conservative religious environments—Muslim holy places, some churches and monasteries, and (strictest of all) ultra-Orthodox Jewish shrines and neighborhoods. Covered shoulders, modest necklines, and either full-length pants or (safest) skirts below the knees are de rigueur.

Eating Out

Restaurants that abide by kosher dietary regulations, to satisfy a particular clientele, close for Friday dinner and Saturday lunch (Sabbath ends at dark). Kosher hotel eateries remain open, but will not offer menu items that require cooking on the spot. "Kosher" has nothing to do with particular cuisines but with certain restrictions (no pork or shellfish, no dairy and meat products on the same menu, and more). Kosher restaurants today not only have to compete with nonkosher rivals but also must satisfy an increasingly demanding kosher clientele, so the variety of kosher food is growing. Tipping is 12% minimum. Mostly, tips are expected in cash, but adding it to the bill is becoming more common, especially in Tel Aviv.

There's great coffee all over Israel. Latte is called *hafuch*; and if you want black coffee, ask for "filter" coffee or *Americano*. Tap water is safe throughout Israel.

Greetings

Israelis don't stand on ceremony, and greet each other warmly with either a slap on the back (for men) or an air kiss on both cheeks (for women). Tourists are usually greeted with a handshake. Ultra-Orthodox Jewish men won't acknowledge women, and very religious Jews of either gender don't shake hands or mingle socially with members of the opposite sex.

Israelis are known for their bluntness. That openness extends to discussions on religion and politics, too, so don't be afraid to speak your mind (but expect candor in return).

The Jewish Sabbath

The Sabbath extends from sundown Friday until dark on Saturday. Most shops and restaurants in Jewish neighborhoods close, but Arab areas in Jerusalem's Old City, and towns like Nazareth and Akko, will be bustling. While Jerusalem quiets down by Friday afternoon, Tel Aviv remains lively, although bus services are suspended in both cities. Sunday is the first day of the regular work- and school week.

Language

Hebrew is the national language of Israel, but travelers can get by with English. Virtually every hotel has English-speaking staff, as do most restaurants and many shops in the major cities. In smaller towns and rural areas it might be more challenging. A few words of Hebrew, such as *toda* (thank you), *bevakasha* (please), and *shalom* (hello or goodbye) will be warmly appreciated.

Arabic is Israel's other official language, spoken by Arabs, Druze, and a dwindling number of Jews with family roots in Arab lands. Because Israel is a nation of immigrants, mistakes and various accents are tolerated cheerfully.

Israelis use a lot of hand gestures when they talk. A common gesture is to turn the palm upwards and press the thumb and two fingers together to mean "wait a minute"; this has no negative connotations. Just as harmless is the Israeli who says "I don't believe you" to express that something is unbelievably wonderful.

Money and Shopping

The Israeli shekel (designated NIS) is the currency, but the U.S. dollar is accepted in places accustomed to dealing with tourists. At press time, $1 is equal to NIS 3.60. Rates for hotels, guiding services, and car rentals are always quoted and paid for in foreign currency, thus avoiding the 18% local VAT. Many better stores offer a government VAT refund on purchases above NIS 400, claimable at the airport duty-free or at the Jordanian border. Licensed exchange booths on busy streets or in shopping malls are convenient places to change money; banks offer lines, unhelpful hours, and unattractive rates. Although ATM transaction fees may be higher abroad than at home, ATM rates are good because they're based on wholesale rates offered by major banks. Avoid buying gold, silver, gemstones, and antiquities in bazaars (like Jerusalem's Old City souk), where things aren't always what they seem and prices fluctuate wildly.

Safety

Israel is news; it seems—for better or for worse. To be sure, there have been several major security situations over the last decade or so, but intense media coverage has sometimes exaggerated the scope and significance of this or that localized incident. Yet much of the populace seems unmoved. At this writing, the country is entirely calm, though there continue to be security concerns about the Palestinian Territories and some bordering countries. In Jerusalem, the Old City can be thronged during the day and virtually empty at night. Spend your evenings elsewhere. The Arab neighborhoods of East Jerusalem are perhaps not as welcoming as they were once, but unless there's some general security issue at the time, the daytime wanderer shouldn't encounter anything more serious than pickpockets.

At the time of this writing, Israeli authorities were barring their citizens from visiting Palestinian autonomous areas such as Bethlehem and Jericho, but tourists can take an Arab cab. Your concierge or Israeli tour guide may be able to set up a Palestinian guide on the other side. There are standard security checks along the roads to the West Bank, and car-rental companies generally don't allow their vehicles to cross into those areas.

Expect to have your handbags searched as a matter of course when you enter bus and train terminals, department stores, places of entertainment, museums, and public buildings. These checks are usually quick and courteous.

Visiting Sacred Sites

Muslim sites are generally closed for tourists on Friday, the Muslim holy day. Avoid the Muslim Quarter of Jerusalem's Old City between noon and 2 pm on Fridays, when the flow of worshippers in the streets can be uncomfortable or even rowdy. Some Christian sites close on Sunday; others open after morning worship. Many Jewish religious sites, museums, and historical sites close early on Friday; some remain closed through Saturday (the Jewish Sabbath).

ISRAEL
TOP ATTRACTIONS

Old City of Jerusalem

(A) Its golden stones are saturated with history, sanctified by pilgrim prayers, and scarred by war. Explore the exotic medieval Church of the Holy Sepulcher, mingle with Jewish worshippers at the venerated Western Wall, and stroll the Haram esh-Sharif—the Temple Mount plaza—to view the golden Dome of the Rock. Pick your way through the alleyways and markets for great photo ops and a lesson in the challenges of coexistence.

Masada, the Dead Sea, and Ein Gedi

(B) The view and ruins of King Herod's mountaintop palace-fortress are reason enough to climb Masada, as a predawn hike or by swift cable car, but the echoes of the Jewish rebellion against Rome make Masada what it is. Float in the hyperbrine of the nearby Dead Sea, and frolic in the oasis of Ein Gedi, with its waterfalls.

Israel Museum, Jerusalem

(C) This sprawling, world-class museum boasts permanent exhibitions of the Dead Sea Scrolls, a quarter-acre model of ancient Jerusalem, and newly revamped wings of Archaeology, Fine Art, and Jewish Life and Art.

Jordan River Sources

(D) Rushing water and wild vegetation make the Upper Galilee panhandle one of Israel's most beautiful regions. The three-thousand-year-old ruins of biblical Tel Dan overlook the Jordan River's largest tributary; and nearby Banias, with hiking trails alongside spectacular rapids, is Caesarea Philippi of the New Testament.

Tel Aviv-Jaffa

(E) Cosmopolitan and bustling, the city conveys the energy of modern Israel. There's the beach and promenade, a reinvented seaport, culture, great restaurants and nightlife, gentrified old 'hoods, and 1930s Bauhaus architecture.

The Sea of Galilee
(F) This shimmering freshwater lake, known in Hebrew as the *Kinneret*, is linked to many events in the life of Jesus. Pilgrims flock to its shores, sail its waters, and gather for baptism at the River Jordan where it leaves the lake.

Negev Desert Highlands
(G) The Negev highlands are full of surprises. The enormous Ramon Crater and two smaller ones are unique geological phenomena. The ruined town of Avdat pioneered desert water conservation and agriculture two thousand years ago. Ein Avdat is an exquisite spring-fed chalk canyon where ibex are often seen. Modern Israeli history, boutique wineries, and Jeeps and camels complete the picture.

Baha'i Shrine and Gardens
(H) Haifa is the world center for the Baha'i faith, and the magnificent landmark gold-domed Shrine of the Bab caps the tomb of its 19th-century prophet-herald. Free walking tours give the best appreciation of the manicured gardens that cascade down Mt. Carmel.

Caesarea
(I) King Herod built the great port city over two thousand years ago. The renovated Roman theater is back in business; scuba enthusiasts can see elements of the Herodian port; and an ancient aqueduct slices across a beach. Crusader fortifications mix with latter-day restaurants and galleries to create a serene getaway.

Old City, Akko
(J) The picturesque port city has seen it all: Canaanites and Greeks, Crusaders and Napoleon, Turks and Brits. Visit the excellently preserved medieval quarters; browse the copperware shops; eat hummus and seafood; and explore the small port, the Turkish bathhouse, and the British prison from which Jewish resistance fighters broke out in the 1940s.

QUINTESSENTIAL ISRAEL

Falafel and Shawarma

Falafel sandwiches are a fast-food staple in Israel, and stands are found from the busy streets of downtown Tel Aviv to the ultra-Orthodox areas of Jerusalem and the Eilat beach promenade.

It starts with a scoop of seasoned chickpeas ground and formed into small spheres that are quickly fried in oil and then thrust—six or so—into a pita or wrap. Patrons give a nod or a "no thanks" to some hummus or *harif* (hot sauce) and to each of the colorful accompaniments: finely chopped cucumbers and tomatoes, shredded cabbage (white or red), parsley, pickles, and even french fries stuffed on top. Many customers drizzle their creation with self-serve sauces: *amba* (spicy pickled mango) and tahini.

Be sure to have a few extra napkins ready, and assume the falafel position before taking your first bite: leaning forward well away from clothing and shoes. Equally wonderful is shawarma, similar to the Greek gyro (minus the pork). Slices of grilled turkey meat or chicken (or, rarely, the more traditional lamb) are sliced off a vertical rotating rotisserie spit, and served with the same accompaniments as falafel.

The Sabra Personality

The local mythos is that Israelis have prickly personalities. Although you'll hear the word *savlanut* (patience) bandied about, natives don't seem to be blessed with an overabundance of that quality.

The character of Israelis was once compared to a local cactus that produces a "prickly pear" known as the *sabra*. The term "Sabra" has become a sobriquet for the native Israeli: prickly on the outside but sweet on the inside! Fortunately, this national tendency toward abruptness is tempered with a generous dose of Mediterranean warmth.

Israel is more than holy sites and turbulent politics; to get a sense of the country, familiarize yourself with some of the features of daily life.

Markets and Bargaining

Israel's open-air markets are just the place to soak up local culture while shopping for snacks to stock your hotel room. Machaneh Yehuda in Jerusalem and Tel Aviv's Carmel Market are famous. For markets that sell decorative brass, ceramic and glass items, beads, embroidered dresses, and jackets or secondhand funky clothes, head to Jerusalem's Old City (the souk or shouk) or the Jaffa Flea Market.

Bargaining can be fun, but there are some useful pointers. Never answer the question "How much do you want to pay?" When the seller names a price, come back with about half. If the seller balks, be prepared to walk out; if you're called back, they want to make a sale. If you're in a hurry, vendors will know it and won't drop the price. Not every vendor will be in the mood for the bargaining game: don't begin the process unless your intentions are serious.

Café Culture

Café sitting is an integral part of Israeli life, especially in the major cities where it seems as if there's one on every corner. The locals love their *café hafuch* (latte: literally, "upside-down coffee"). In many cafés, a request for cappuccino gets you the same beverage, perhaps with more froth and a shake of cinnamon. Rival Israeli coffee chains have multiplied like crazy across the country since the late '90s. The coffee, invariably made in Italian machines, is usually excellent. Unlike European cafés where the waiters get antsy if you stay too long, in Israel you can sit unhassled for long periods. And free Wi-Fi, while not yet universal, is commonplace. Most cafés offer reasonably priced full breakfasts, sandwiches, salads, pizza, quiches, and soups.

IF YOU LIKE

Archaeology

In an earlier generation, archaeology was something of an Israeli national pastime; but it's still exciting to walk, Bible in hand, in the footsteps of the ancients.

Biblical (Old Testament) sites abound. For starters there's **Megiddo,** with its multiple strata and ancient water system (get the free brochure and visit the tiny museum); Jerusalem's **City of David,** dripping with mystery, deep underground (the 3-D movie is a bonus); and **Tel Dan,** huge and verdant.

Explore Second Temple–period remains at **Masada** (again, take the brochure and find 30 minutes for the wonderful museum), and monumental masonry at the **Jerusalem Archaeological Park** (Davidson Center). On the Mediterranean, explore **Caesarea,** with its Roman theater, hippodrome, sunken harbor, mosaics, and Crusader ruins.

If a hands-on excavation, dirt and all, appeals, Archaeological Seminars has a year-round Dig for a Day program—actually three hours of fun—in the caves of **Beit Guvrin–Maresha National Park.** More heavy-duty digs, mostly in spring or summer, require a one-week minimum commitment from its volunteers; some insist on a month. For a list of expeditions looking for pay-your-own-way labor, browse the Internet; they change from year to year.

Reinforce your newfound archaeological expertise with a visit (best with a docent) to a museum or two: in Jerusalem, there's the **Israel Museum's** excellent Archaeology Wing, and across the street the **Bible Lands Museum.** The less-known Mizgaga Museum on Kibbutz Nahsholim (north of Caesarea) has intriguing artifacts from the ancient port city of Dor nearby.

The Great Outdoors

Israel's nature reserves offer an astonishing diversity, from the lush Upper Galilee to the arid southern deserts. In the north, **Tel Dan** is a fairyland of streams, greenery, and biblical ruins. The **Banias** seeps out softly beneath Mt. Hermon and churns its way south; an easy trail offers great views of waterfalls and cataracts. The **Golan Heights** has more challenging trails, most with running streams and natural pools.

Israel is a major bird migration route, from northern Europe to Africa in the autumn and back again in the spring. Many of the estimated 500 million "frequent flyers" rest awhile in the **Hula** wetlands reserve and nearby Agmon Ha-Hula, popular with pelicans and cranes. On the Golan Heights, eagles and griffon vultures nest in the craggy **Gamla Reserve.**

The **desert** has its space, its silence, and its own subtle beauty. Respect its power: Never hike desert trails alone; avoid intensely hot days; wear a hat and drink copiously. Consider an organized hike with (for example) the **Society for the Protection of Nature in Israel.** In the cool season, the mountains behind Eilat and the deep ravines of the Judean Desert offer serious hikers spectacular canyon trails (pay attention to flood warnings). Off-road trips in the Eilat Mountains and the area of the Ramon Crater are a lot of fun, and camel rides are an option, too.

Running water in the desert is pure magic. The **Ein Avdat canyon** near Sde Boker is easily accessible. The **Ein Gedi** oasis, near the Dead Sea, offers the shorter but often crowded Nahal David, and the much longer, more primeval Nahal Arugot trail. Both have natural freshwater pools and waterfalls, and are home to ibex (wild goats) and hyrax (small furry creatures).

Sacred Spaces

Faith has many voices in the Holy Land, and sanctity wears many different robes. For the uninitiated, it can be a bewildering multisensory experience. Some pilgrims find the hubbub at many sites disconcerting, but keep in mind that most places were not pristine in their day either.

For Christians of every denomination, Israel offers a unique opportunity to follow in the footsteps of Jesus. From the **Sea of Galilee** to the Jordan River and **Nazareth**, scripture comes alive. Ride a boat, explore ancient **Capernaum**, and contemplate the landscape where Jesus preached. In Jerusalem, the **Garden of Gethsemane**, the **Via Dolorosa**, and the **Church of the Holy Sepulcher** evoke the scenes of Jesus' final days. The **Garden Tomb** is a mandatory stop for many Protestants.

For the Jewish faith, the holiest place in the world is the **Western Wall**, a remnant of Jerusalem's ancient Temple Mount. Graves traditionally identified with biblical figures, Talmudic sages, and medieval rabbis dot the Galilee. The tombs of King David in Jerusalem and Rabbi Shimon Bar Yochai on **Mt. Meron** in Upper Galilee are especially famous. But for many Jews, the entire land, rather than individual sites, is biblical and blessed.

The black-domed **al-Aqsa Mosque**, in Jerusalem's Haram esh-Sharif (or Temple Mount), is the third-holiest place in Islam. The golden **Dome of the Rock** nearby is built on the spot where the Prophet Muhammad is believed to have ascended to the heavens to receive the teachings of Islam.

The landmark gold-domed **Baha'i Shrine** on the slopes of Mt. Carmel, in Haifa, covers the tomb of the Bab, the forerunner of Baha'i. Its gardens provide a serene environment for this gentle faith.

Museums

The **Israel Museum** in Jerusalem is regarded as the country's leading cultural institution, with Art, Judaica, and Archaeology wings—and of course the Dead Sea Scrolls. The undervisited **Museum for Islamic Art** has a world-class collection and an unrelated but stunning display of period timepieces. The **Historical Museum of the Holocaust** at Yad Vashem, in Jerusalem, offers a powerful and thought-provoking documentation of a dark period. The nearby **Herzl Museum** uses engaging techniques to re-create the life and times of the founder of the Zionist movement, over a century ago.

The **Tel Aviv Museum of Art** is a don't-miss for aficionados of modern art and architecture. Tel Aviv's **Eretz Israel Museum** (not to be confused with the one in Jerusalem) specializes in glass, ceramics, coins, ethnography, and much more.

Haifa's **National Maritime Museum** is devoted to the thousands of years of maritime history in the Mediterranean basin. The **Tikotin Museum of Japanese Art** on Mt. Carmel is a gem. Located in Haifa's Hadar district is **Technoda** (National Museum of Science and Technology), a delightful interactive exhibition for kids and adults alike.

Guided groups generally skip the **Masada Museum**, but independent travelers will find it helpful in fleshing out their visit to the site.

At the southern end of the country, though not classically a museum, the aquarium section of Eilat's **Coral World Underwater Observatory and Aquarium** provides an explained encounter with the fantastical creatures of the nearby coral reefs (be sure to rent the audio guide).

ISRAEL: PEOPLE, RELIGION, AND STATE

"I could not conceive of a small country having so large a history," wrote Mark Twain after his visit to the Holy Land in 1867. The rich history certainly fascinates, as does the complex political situation despite, or because of, its constant sense of urgency. But beyond that are the people, a varied population of 8 million, representing a startlingly wide array of ethnicities, nationalities, religious beliefs, and lifestyles. The diversity of Israel's population is one of the country's greatest strengths—and one of its essential challenges. It may explain, for example, why defining a national identity is still a work in progress, even after more than sixty years.

Creating a Nation

Israel's founding generation saw the country as a modern reincarnation of the ancient Jewish nation-state. Israel was the "Promised Land" of Abraham and Moses, the Israelite kingdom of David and Solomon, and the home of Jesus of Nazareth and the Jewish Talmudic sages. Although the Jewish presence in the country has been unbroken for more than three thousand years, several massive exiles—first by the Babylonians in 586 BC and then by the Romans in AD 70—created a Diaspora, a dispersion of the Jewish people throughout the world. The sense of historical roots still resonates for many, probably most, Jewish Israelis; and bringing their brethren home has been a national priority from the beginning.

The attachment to the ancient homeland, and a yearning for the restoration of "Zion and Jerusalem," weaves through the entire fabric of Jewish history and religious tradition. Over the centuries, many Jews trickled back to Eretz Yisrael (the Land of Israel), while others looked

forward to fulfilling their dream of return in some future—many felt imminent—messianic age. Not all were prepared to wait for divine intervention, however, and in the late 19th century, a variety of Jewish nationalist organizations emerged, bent on creating a home for their people in Israel (then the district of Palestine in the vast Ottoman Empire). Zionism was created as a political movement to give structure and impetus to that idea.

Some early Zionist leaders, like founding father Theodor Herzl, believed that the urgent priority was simply a Jewish haven safe from persecution, wherever that haven might be. Argentina was suggested, and Great Britain offered Uganda. In light of Jewish historical and emotional links to the land of Israel, most Zionists rejected these "territorialist" proposals.

The establishment of the State of Israel did not, of course, meet with universal rejoicing. To the Arab world, it was anathema, an alien implant in a Muslim Middle East. Palestinian Arabs today mark Israel's independence as the *Nakba*, the Catastrophe, a moment in time when their own national aspirations were thwarted. For many ultra-Orthodox Jews, the founding of Israel was an arrogant preempting of God's divine plan; and to make matters worse, the new state was blatantly secular, despite its concessions to religious interests. This internal battle over the character of the Jewish state, and the implacable hostility of Israel's neighbors—which has resulted in more than six decades of unremitting conflict—have been the two main issues engaging the country since its birth.

The Israeli People

Roughly 6 million of Israel's citizens—a little more than 75%—are Jewish. Some trace their family roots back many generations on local soil; others are first- to fourth-generation *olim* (immigrants) from dozens of different countries. The first modern pioneers arrived from Russia in 1882, purchased land, and set about developing it with romantic zeal. A couple of decades later, inspired by the socialist ideas then current in Eastern Europe, a much larger wave founded the first *kibbutzim*—collective villages or communes. In time, these fiercely idealistic farmers became something of a moral elite, having little financial power but providing a greatly disproportionate percentage of the country's political leadership, military officer cadre, and intelligentsia.

The kibbutz ideology has pretty much run out of steam. A more personally ambitious younger generation has increasingly eschewed the communal lifestyle in favor of the lures of the big city. In the vast majority of the 270 or so kibbutzim across the country, modern economic realities have undermined the old socialist structure, and a high degree of privatization is the order of the day.

The State of Israel was founded in 1948, just three years after the end of World War II and the Holocaust, in which the Nazis annihilated fully two-thirds of European Jewry. In light of the urgency of providing a haven for remnants of those shattered communities, the Law of Return was passed in 1950 granting any Jew automatic right to Israeli citizenship.

Most of the immigrants before Israel's independence in 1948 were Ashkenazi Jews (of Central or Eastern European descent), but the biggest wave in the first decade of statehood came from the Arab lands of North Africa and the Middle East. Israel's Jewish population—600,000 at the time of independence—doubled within 3½ years and tripled within ten.

In the late 1980s and early '90s, a wave of about three-quarters of a million Jews moved to Israel from the former Soviet Union. The Russian influence is felt everywhere in Israel today, not least in the fields of technology and classical music. In the early 1980s, a smaller group of Jews from the long-isolated Ethiopian community trekked across Sudan, on their odyssey to the dreamed-of "Jerusalem." Many perished en route. Another 14,500 were airlifted into Israel over one weekend in 1991. Their challenge—and that of Israeli society—has been their integration into a modern technological society.

The vast majority of Israel's 1.6 million Arabic-speaking citizens are Muslims (among them about 200,000 Bedouin), followed by 130,000 Druze (a separate religious group), and about 125,000 Christian Arabs. Most Israeli Arabs live in the mixed Jewish-Arab towns of Jaffa, Ramla, Lod, Haifa, and Akko; a number of good-sized towns and villages on the eastern edge of the coastal plain; in Nazareth and throughout the Lower Galilee; and, in the case of the Bedouin, in the Negev Desert. The extent to which they're integrated with Israeli Jews often depends on location. In Haifa, for example, there's little tension between the two ethnic groups. On the other hand, Jerusalem's quarter-million Arab residents are Palestinian not Israeli, and the situation is more fraught. All Israeli Arabs are equal under the law and vote for and serve in the *Knesset*, the Israeli parliament.

However, social and economic gaps between the Arab and Jewish sectors do exist, and Arab complaints of government neglect and unequal allocation of resources have sometimes spilled into angry street demonstrations and other antiestablishment activity. The Muslims in Israel are mainstream Sunnis and regarded as both politically and religiously moderate by the standards of the region. Nevertheless, in recent years there has been some radicalization of the community's youth, who identify politically with the Palestinian liberation movement and/or religiously with the Islamic revival that has swept the Middle East.

Of the Christian Arabs, most belong to the Greek Catholic, Greek Orthodox, or Roman Catholic churches; a handful of Eastern denominations and a few small Protestant groups account for the rest. The Western Christian community is minuscule, consisting mainly of clergy and temporary sojourners such as diplomats.

Israel's Druze, though Arabic-speaking, follow a separate and secret religion that broke from Islam about one thousand years ago. Larger kindred communities exist in long-hostile Syria and Lebanon, but Israeli Druze have solidly identified with Israel, and the community's young men are routinely drafted into the Israeli army.

The Arab community itself isn't liable for military service, partly in order to avoid the risk of battlefield confrontations with kinsmen from neighboring countries; between the lines, however, lies the fear that Israeli Arabs in uniform may experience a sense of dual loyalty.

Judaism in Israel

There's no firm separation of religion and state in Israel. Matters of personal status—marriage, divorce, adoption, and conversion—are the preserve of the religious authorities of the community concerned. For this reason there's no civil marriage; if one partner doesn't convert to the faith of the other, the couple must marry abroad. Within the Jewish community, such functions fall under the supervision of the Orthodox chief rabbinate, much to the dismay of members of the tiny but growing Conservative and Reform movements and of the large number of nonobservant Jews.

Almost half of all Israeli Jews call themselves secular. The religiously observant—strict adherence to Sabbath laws and dietary laws, regular attendance at worship services, and so on—account for about 20%. At least another one-third of the Jewish population identify themselves as "traditional," meaning they observe some Jewish customs to some extent, often as a nod to Jewish heritage or out of a sense of family duty. Ultra-Orthodox (*haredi* in Hebrew) is the smaller of the two mainstreams that make up the Orthodox Jewish community; you can easily recognize the men by their black hats and garb. Their parallel universe embraces religion as a 24/7 lifestyle. Their independent school system, 80% government-funded, teaches only religious subjects. While some haredi men do go out to work, many have committed themselves to full-time study.

The confrontation between secular Israelis and the ultra-Orthodox has escalated over the years, as the religious community tries to impose its vision of how a Jewish state should behave. One volatile issue is the Orthodox contention that only someone who meets the Orthodox definition of a Jew (either born of a Jewish mother or converted by strict Orthodox procedures) should be eligible for Israeli

citizenship under the Law of Return. The real resentment, however, is reserved for the political clout and budgets that the haredim have gained as the price of coalition politics, and their almost total refusal to serve in the military on the grounds of continuing religious studies. By contrast, the modern Orthodox—in Israel they prefer to be known as "religious Zionists"—tend to be gung-ho Israeli patriots, serve in the military, and strongly identify with the hard-line settler movement in the West Bank and elsewhere. Unlike the haredim, modern Orthodox men and women are fully immersed in Israeli society. Modern Orthodox men dress in "regular" clothes, but typically wear *kippot* or skullcaps on their heads. Women in both religious communities dress very modestly.

Israeli Government

Israel prides itself on being the only true democracy in the Middle East, but it sometimes seems bent on tearing itself apart politically in the democratic process. This is how the system works (or doesn't): once every four years, prior to national elections, every contesting party publishes a list of its candidates for the 120-member Knesset, in a hierarchy determined by the party's own convention. There are no constituencies or voting districts; each party that breaks the minimum threshold of 2% of the national vote gets in, winning the same percentage of Knesset seats as its proportion of nationwide votes (hence the description of the system as "proportional representation").

The good news is that the system is intensely democratic. A relatively small grouping of like-minded voters countrywide can elect MKs (Members of the Knesset) to represent their views. The largest party able to gain a parliamentary majority through a coalition with other parties forms the government, and its leader becomes the prime minister.

The bad news is that the system spawns a plethora of small parties, whose collective support the government needs in order to rule. Since no party has ever won enough seats to rule alone, Israeli governments have always been based on compromise, with small parties often exerting a degree of political influence quite out of proportion to their actual size. Attempts to change the system have been doomed, because the small parties, which stand to lose if the system is changed, are precisely those on whose support the current government depends.

The religious divide in the Jewish community carries over into the Knesset, where religion is a central plank in the platform of several parties. The other and arguably more active ideological "fault line" divides Israeli society into a dovish liberal left (currently much weakened), a hard-line right wing of ultranationalists, and a fluctuating political center that sometimes knows what it *isn't*, but not too often what it *is*. Where you stand on the left-right spectrum reflects your views on the Israel-Palestinian issue: dovish or hawkish, yea or nay to a Palestinian state, dismantle West Bank settlements or keep building them, divide Jerusalem or keep it all. In a country where security, the Jewishness of Israel, and its democratic character have always been the main issues, these ideological-political distinctions have critical ramifications. Of late, even essential characteristics of a democratic society—the independence of the judiciary, for example—have come under attack from ultraconservatives. Liberals are concerned.

ISRAEL'S TOP EXPERIENCES

Rooftopping in Jerusalem
Historical Jerusalem is about shrines and antiquities, but some thirty-five thousand people live within the Old City walls. From the Ramparts Walk, you can get a look into the courtyards and gardens that lie behind the bolted iron doors you pass on the street. The towers and domes of the city's main faith communities pierce sweeping panoramas.

Shopping in the Market
A walk through a produce market may sometimes feel like a contact sport, but this is hands-down the best way to experience real commerce that combines Middle Eastern–style salesmanship with top-quality products. Spices, dried fruits, nuts, produce, cheeses, and meats are sold from stalls crowded one up against the other. Best are Jerusalem's Machaneh Yehuda and Tel Aviv's Carmel Market.

Floating in the Dead Sea
The Dead Sea is so called for the fact that no living thing can survive in its briny brew. The lake has become a mecca for those who believe in its curative properties; but even if you don't suffer from skin or muscular ailments, bobbing like a cork in the supersaturated water is an utterly relaxing (if slightly bizarre) experience. Reading a newspaper while doing it makes a great photograph as well.

Eating Israeli Breakfast
Israelis don't eat this sumptuously at home, but the "Israeli breakfast" served at most hotels has grown out of local healthy habits of yogurts, fruit, cheeses, eggs, and salads (yes, for breakfast). The often-elaborate hotel buffets began adding baked goods, smoked fish, eggs made to order, a variety of breads and juices, and (Western influence!) cereal and pancakes or waffles. It's a superb way to start your day.

Exploring Tel Aviv's Old Neighborhoods
Tel Aviv's old neighborhoods—situated largely in the south—tell the tale of the development of a modern city that celebrated its 100th anniversary in 2009. Now gentrifying after years of neglect, areas such as Neveh Tzedek fuse architectural preservation and modern progress. There's also plenty of good dining and shopping.

Hiking the Desert
Deserts offer deep silence, minimalist landscapes, sparse vegetation, and rare animal life. Therein lies their magic: the Great Escape. There's a lot of desert in little Israel. Nature reserves like Ein Gedi's two canyons (near the Dead Sea) and Ein Avdat (in the Negev) add the miracle of running water to the enormous crags.

Touring a Winery
Israeli grape growing and wine production can be traced to biblical times. There's no better way to sample the country's vintages than to tour its wineries, from large operations with dozens of varieties to boutique, limited-production establishments. Reservations need to be made for tours and tastings at all but the largest wineries.

Checking Out the Beach Scene in Eilat
The bikinis, the Speedos, the sarongs, the sunglasses—it's the Riviera with local flair. Eilat is a respite for on-the-go Israelis who love nothing more than to spend a few days eating chips (french fries) and dipping into the Red Sea—all set to the *plonk-plonk* soundtrack of *matkot*, the Israeli paddleball game that may as well be a national sport.

ISRAEL LODGING PRIMER

Israel has plenty of hotels belonging to major international hotel chains and smaller national networks, as well as independently run lodgings. Some are utilitarian, but some recent trends are a rise in distinctive boutique hotels and in luxury properties, whether in the cities or the countryside.

In contrast, options such as kibbutz hotels and bed-and-breakfasts (known as *zimmers* in Israel) offer a glimpse into local life and a more leisurely experience. *For specific contacts, see Accommodations in Travel Smart Israel.*

In 2012, Israel approved a one- to five-star ranking system for hotels similar to that used in many places in Europe. The Ministry of Tourism has already rated the country's nine thousand B&Bs. They're ranked A, B, or C, based on size and the facilities offered.

Apartment and House Rentals

Short-term rentals are popular, especially in Jerusalem and Tel Aviv and particularly for families who would otherwise be taking two or three hotel rooms. Options range from basic studios to mansions, and most are privately owned.

Bed-and-Breakfasts

Over the past decade, thousands of zimmers have sprung up, especially in the Galilee and the Golan. These are intimate cabins, usually featuring one or two bedrooms, a kitchenette, a hot tub, and an outdoor lounging area. Prices aren't necessarily lower than hotels, but if it's peace and quiet you're after, these may be just the thing.

Many zimmers are located in *moshavim*—semicommunal rural communities. Private-home owners are also increasingly opening their doors to guests.

Christian Hospices

Lodgings called Christian hospices (meaning hotels) provide accommodations and sometimes meals; these are mainly in and around Jerusalem and the Galilee. Some hospices are real bargains, while others are merely reasonable; facilities range from spare to luxurious. Those in rural settings are often tranquil retreats. Most give preference to pilgrimage groups, but most will accept individual travelers when space is available.

Home Exchanges and Vacation Rentals

With a direct home exchange you stay in someone else's home while they stay in yours. More common in Israel is the vacation rental. You're not actually staying in someone's full-time residence—it's usually his or her investment property.

Kibbutz Hotels

Around the country, kibbutz hotels offer a variety of accommodations in what are often lovely settings. Some kibbutz hotels are luxurious, while others are more basic. Most have large lawns, swimming pools, and athletic facilities. Some offer lectures about the history of kibbutzim and tours of the settlements and the surrounding areas. These kibbutz hotels are popular with large tour groups.

FLAVORS OF ISRAEL

Many Israelis divide the day into at least six excuses to eat. There's breakfast, a 10 am snack, a quick lunch, a 5 pm coffee break (around the time that the Western world is calling for a cocktail), a full dinner, and a snack before bed, just for good measure. Satisfying this appetite is made easier by the great grab-and-go food with soul, including crispy falafel, sold on Israel's streets and in small food joints.

A good number of Israel's restaurants are kosher, and conform to Jewish dietary laws: menus may contain meat or dairy but not both, and pork products and shellfish are out (fish is neutral). Strictly kosher restaurants are closed on the Jewish Sabbath and religious holidays. The majority of hotels countrywide serve kosher food. Bon appétit or, as they say here, *betayavon!*

Israeli Breakfast

The classic Israeli breakfast is legendary, but fewer busy Israelis have time to make it at home these days. You'll mostly find it at hotels, B&Bs, and cafés. Hotel buffets will include bowls of brightly colored "Israeli" salads, platters of cheeses, piles of fresh fruit, granola, hot and cold cereals, baskets of various breads and baked goods ranging from cinnamon or chocolate twists to quiche, smoked fish, fresh fruit juices, made-to-order eggs (*betza ayin*, or "egg like an eye," means a fried egg, *chavitah* is omelet, and *mekushkash* is scrambled), and pancakes (locals pour on maple syrup or chocolate sauce). Country lodgings such as B&Bs offer homemade versions, and city coffeehouses specialize in the Israeli breakfast, accompanied by croissants and cappuccino, often served until 1 pm—and sometimes all day.

The Essential Cup of Coffee

Gone are the days when the only coffee available was instant, tiny cups of Turkish coffee (*café Turki*), or its lazy counterpart, *botz* ("mud": powdered grounds stirred into boiling water). Israel today has a coffee culture on a par with Europe's. Most places use Italian machines; the past decade has seen the advent of Western-style coffee-shop chains, the biggest being Aroma, Café Hillel, Café Joe, Arcaffe, and Café Café. You can have a robust and flavorful latte (known as *hafuch*, or upside-down); an *Americano* should you be homesick; espresso; and in the summer, iced coffee known as *barad*, a slushy chilled confection made with crushed ice. Soy milk is often available, as is decaf (*natoul* in Hebrew). In the Old City of Jerusalem and Arab establishments, coffee is made with the addition of a pinch of cardamom, or *hel*.

Israeli Salad

There are several different kinds of chopped salads in Israel, but there's one classic, and there's no question that this is a trademark dish, with origins in Arab cuisine. Basically it's a combination of fresh cucumbers, tomatoes, and onion, and the secret's in the chopping—each ingredient must be chopped small and evenly. Cooks who fly in the face of tradition might add chopped parsley and mint, and bits of chopped lemon. Then the salad is dashed with quality olive oil and fresh lemon juice and a sprinkle of salt and pepper or *za'atar*, a Middle Eastern herb of hyssop with a sprinkle of sesame seeds. It can be eaten on its own with white cheese and bread before work, spooned into a pita with falafel and hummus at any time of day, and with the main dish at most every meal.

Grilled Meats and Steaks

Virtually every town has at least one Middle Eastern grill restaurant, where you can find kebab, skewered grilled chicken (dark meat baby chicken, or *pargit*, is a favorite), lamb, beef, mixed grill, or spit-grilled shawarma, generally prepared with turkey seasoned with lamb fat, cumin, coriander, and other spices. If you want a good steak, don't worry: order entrecôte and see for yourself. You can even get a good hamburger these days. In Jerusalem, around the open fruit and vegetable market, are grilled-meat eateries famous for chicken and beef on skewers, called *shipudim*, and their *meu'rav Yerushalmi* (Jerusalem mixed grill): chicken hearts, livers, and spleen.

Seafood

There are fish restaurants all over the country, but locals say the best ones are in cities and towns that border the Mediterranean (like Tel Aviv, Jaffa, Ashdod, Haifa, and Akko), around the Kinneret (Sea of Galilee), and in Eilat. In nonkosher restaurants, the chance of finding shrimp, squid, and other nonkosher seafood on the menu has increased substantially.

Salatim

The world *salat* in Hebrew means salad. But many small dishes, served cold, as an appetizer, are called *salatim*. It's basically a mezze. In less fancy restaurants, and often in fish and grilled-meat places, these are slung onto the table along with a basket of pita before you've even managed to get comfortable. They're usually free, but ask. Dig into selections such as two or three types of eggplant, cumin-flecked carrot salad, tahini-enriched hummus, fried cauliflower, pickled vegetables, and cracked-wheat salad (tabbouleh), but leave room for the main course, too.

Cheeses

Holy Land cows are hard at work providing milk for cheeses, and these top the list, followed by goat and sheep milk cheese and, last but not least, the healthy buffalo cheese—mostly mozzarella. Soft, white cheeses reign supreme. An Israeli favorite is *gvina levana*, a spreadable white cheese available in a variety of fat percentages. A few famous cheeses are Bulgarit ("Bulgarian"), a firmer, tangier version of feta (sheep or goat); Brinza (half goat, half sheep); Tzfatit, originally made in the northern city of Tzfat, not too salty; the ubiquitous goat cheese, feta; and Tomme (goat), a zingy white cheese. Hard, yellow cheeses have always been around, but the variety and the quality have soared.

Wines

The excellent wine in Israel is made from major international grape varieties in five main wine regions from north to south. *For more information, see the Wines of Israel feature in Chapter 5.*

World Cuisine

The last decade or so has brought fusion cuisines to Israel—a superb blend of local flavors and ingredients with French-Italian-Asian or Californian influences—designed by young Israeli chefs, many of whom have studied abroad.

Although gourmet restaurants dot the Galilee, Golan, Jerusalem, and other parts of the country, it's definitely worth saving up to eat at one of Tel Aviv's top establishments. These restaurants are most often pricey, and though dressing up is never necessary, feel free. The locals also adore sushi, and Japanese restaurants and fast-food sushi joints abound. If you like to poke around, try some home-cooked ethnic foods—like Moroccan, Persian, Bucharian, or Tripolitan (Libyan) fare.

ISRAEL WITH KIDS

Fortunately, it's easy to keep the kids busy in Israel. Let them expend energy exploring Crusader castles or caves in nature reserves. For fun on the water, try rafting on the Jordan River—and there are the beaches, of course. Check the Friday papers' entertainment guides (they have a children's section) for up-to-date information.

Eating Out

Restaurants are often happy to accommodate those seeking supersimple fare, like pasta, or chicken schnitzel and fries. Fast food is easily accessible and doesn't have to be junk. Falafel or shawarma, kebabs, and cheese- or potato-filled pastries called *bourekas* are very common, and pizza parlors abound.

Nature (and Old Stuff)

Israel's nature reserves and national parks (⊕ *www.parks.org.il*) have plenty for the whole family to do. In the north, you can cycle around a part of the restored Hula Lake (at the site called Agmon Ha'Hula); laugh and learn at the fun 3-D movie about bird migrations at the **Hula Nature Reserve;** kayak or raft the placid waters of the **Jordan River;** and bounce around some awesome landscapes in a Jeep or a 4x4 dune buggy. (The Negev Desert and Eilat Mountains offer comparable off-road experiences.) Explore the medieval **Nimrod's Castle** on the slopes of Mt. Hermon, or **Belvoir** overlooking the Upper Jordan Valley.

Standouts in the south are the oases and walking trails of **Ein Gedi** (with a bonus of bathing under fresh waterfalls) and Ein Avdat. The wondrous **Masada**, Herod's mountaintop palace-fortress, is a real treat and can be reached by foot along the steep Snake Path (recommended for older kids), but there's always the cable car.

Walking is a lively and easy activity to do anywhere. Top in Jerusalem is the Old Testament–period **City of David**, south of the Old City. It's a maze of rock-hewn corridors, ending with a 30-minute wade in the spring water of Hezekiah's Tunnel. (There's a dry exit, too.) The **Ramparts Walk** offers views of the Old City's residential quarters as well as of new Jerusalem outside the walls. Smaller kids can do part of it (with strict adult supervision).

In Tel Aviv, the **Tel Aviv Port** is great for coffee and a stroll—and even little kids can run around (with a bit of adult attention) while you enjoy iced drinks and the balmy weather.

Museums

A dirty word among kids? Maybe so, but the following museums might change some minds.

JERUSALEM. In West Jerusalem, the **Israel Museum's Youth Wing** has outdoor play areas as well as exhibitions, often interactive, and a "recycling room" where children can use their creative energy freely. Great rainy-day options include the **Bloomfield Science Museum** in Givat Ram.

TEL AVIV. The **Eretz Israel Museum** has a series of pavilions on its campus, each with a different theme: pottery, coins, glass, folklore, anthropology, and more. It also has a planetarium—complete with moon rocks.

The **Observatory on the 49th floor of the Azrieli Towers** isn't really a museum, but it offers a cute animated 3-D fantasy movie about Tel Aviv, and a stunning view of the entire metropolis.

HAIFA. The **National Museum of Science and Technology (Technoda)**, the **Railway Museum**, and the **National Maritime Museum** are all geared to young and curious minds—of any age!

THE NEGEV. The **Israel Air Force Museum,** at the Hatzerim Air Force base (west of Beersheva), houses a huge collection of IAF airplanes and helicopters—from World War II Spitfires and Mustangs to contemporary F-16s and Cobras. Each exhibit has a story to tell. There is no English website, but guided tours in English can be arranged (☎ 08/990–6888 ✍ info@iaf-museum.org.il). This could be a stop on the way to or from Eilat, or a doable day trip from Jerusalem or Tel Aviv.

At One with the Animals

In addition to the wonderful **Tisch Family Zoological Gardens** in Jerusalem, with its emphasis on fauna that feature in the Bible or that are native to Israel, the **Ramat Gan Safari** (⊕ www.safari.co.il), near Tel Aviv, and the small but delightful **Haifa Educational Zoo,** offer numerous options for time out with animals.

The **Jerusalem Bird Observatory** (⊕ www.jbo.org.il), perched above the Knesset, offers "close encounters" with ringed birds, bird-watching tours, and other tidbits about bird life; night safaris are recommended.

On the grounds of Kibbutz Nir David, at the foot of Mt. Gilboa, is **Gan Garoo Park,** which specializes in native Australian wildlife—kangaroos and wallabies, cockatoos, and more.

In the high Negev desert, near Mitzpe Ramon, and as far as you can get from their native Andes mountains, gentle alpacas wait for you to hand-feed them. At the **Alpaca Farm** you can learn as well about the whole process of raising them and spinning their marvelously soft wool.

Horseback riding is an option pretty much throughout the country. In the Galilee, end a trail—of a few hours or a couple of days—with hot apple pie at **Vered Hagalil** or with a chunky steak at **Bat Yaar,** in the Biriya Forest near Tzfat (Safed). There are numerous outfits that do camel-hump trails in the Negev (near Beersheva and Arad) and down near **Eilat.**

Beaches

You're never too far from a beach in Israel—but check for a lifeguard. This is a given at city beaches, but not at those off the beaten track.

Considering it's such a tiny country, the range of different beach experiences is amazing, from the Mediterranean to the Red Sea, to the Sea of Galilee and even the supersalty Dead Sea, where you can float but not swim.

And More . . .

The whole family will enjoy getting their hands dirty at the three-hour **Dig for a Day** (⊕ www.archesem.com)—a chance to dig, sift, and examine artifacts.

Off the Tel Aviv–Jerusalem highway at Latrun is **Mini Israel**—hundreds of exact replica models of the main sites around the country, historical, archaeological, and modern. It's great for an all-of-Israel orientation.

In Eilat, venture out to the biblical theme park, **Kings City,** which comes replete with Pharaohs' palaces and temples, Solomon's mines, mazes, and optical illusions.

ISRAEL'S MARKETS

Israel's main markets are found in Jerusalem and Tel Aviv. As for bargaining (not done at produce stalls)—sure, give it a go, but these days it's a hard drive, so decide if you want to have fun playing the game, or not. The difference in price is likely to be less than you think.

Jerusalem

The **Machaneh Yehuda Market** offers produce that's as flavorful as it is colorful. Recent additions to this collection of alleys running off the main market street include a sprinkling of boutique cafés, unusual restaurants, and small stores selling souvenirs, jewelry, and clothes from India. The market, quite a bit cheaper than the supermarket, is a great place to grab some goodies while on the go or for the hotel room later. You can go global—Italian pasta or Indian flavors—but you'll do best with local specialties: *kubeh* soup at Ima's, fresh bourekas or falafel, wonderful fruit and baked goods, and a chunk of sweet sesame *halva*.

Weaving through the **Old City market** (the *souk*) takes you back in time. Lavish rugs and fabrics, oriental ceramics, blown-glass items, not-so-antique antiques, beads, embroidered kaftans, and leather-thong sandals line the stone alleyways. Be cautious about buying items with an intrinsic value: gold, silver, precious stones, and antiquities may not be as advertised. Almost all the salespeople here speak some English, but a polite quip or two thrown at them in Arabic—check the nuances first!—may bring a wonderful smile, and perhaps a little discount. There's hummus and pickles, Arabic coffee, and honey-dripping pastries to buy. A word of caution about having expensive purchases (like olive-wood carvings) shipped by vendors in the market: some

have been known to arrive damaged or not arrive at all. Stick to establishment stores. And beware of pickpockets (your passport is best left in the hotel safe).

Tel Aviv

The **Carmel Market,** or Shuk Hacarmel, begins at its top end (Allenby Road), with stalls of cheap clothes and housewares, and then becomes the city's primary produce market, extending almost down to the sea. The scents are sensational—fresh greens (mint, parsley, basil), lemons and other citrus fruit, salty herring, and more. It can get packed—hold onto your belongings, though pickpocketing isn't usually a problem here. The shuk borders the Yemenite Quarter, with a host of small eateries offering local dishes.

You'll find some true artisans at the **Nahalat Binyamin Pedestrian Mall,** which becomes a crafts market (along with the unsung peddlers of imported goods) on Tuesdays and Fridays. It's a great place to pick up original and reasonably priced gifts. The pedestrian street converges with the Carmel Market at its Allenby Street end. It's lively, with street performers sharing space with shoppers and strollers, and especially crowded on Fridays and as holidays approach.

The **Jaffa Flea Market** has been reinvented. You'll still find the warren of small streets with stands or holes-in-the-wall selling rugs, *finjan* coffee sets, clothes from India, jewelry, retro lamps, and other junk mixed with bargains; however, the city has cleaned up and brought some order to the old chaos. There's a definite appeal to the new good-quality stores offering furnishings, fashion items, jewelry, and crafts. Some great and/or funky eateries and cafés complete the transformation.

ISRAEL'S BEST BEACHES

Whether you'd like to take a dip, jog along the boardwalk at dawn or sunset, have a glass of wine or beer at a beachfront café, or just commune with nature, this little country's beaches have something to offer at the Mediterranean and the Red Sea, and inland at the Dead Sea and on the shores of the Sea of Galilee.

The Med: City Beaches

All the major cities along the coastline like Nahariya, Haifa, Netanya, Herzliya, and Tel Aviv have their own licensed beaches with lifeguards, and varying amenities like showers, changing rooms, beachside cafés, restaurants, and sometimes even a boardwalk.

Tel Aviv's beaches are particularly colorful, with a popular boardwalk for children of all ages, and a diverse local and international crowd of singles and families. Along the way you'll find Chinky Beach (with a retro-hippie crowd), a gay beach (to the right of the Tel Aviv Hilton), and slightly farther north, a segregated beach for those of the religious persuasion with separate days for men and women. In summer, there are free movies, concerts, and meditation and yoga classes right on the beach.

The Red and the Dead

There are beaches and water sports galore in the Red Sea, which laps at the southernmost city of Eilat. The North Beach, near the promenade and the major hotels, is delightfully sandy, and a great place to swim or sunbathe, but don't miss Coral Beach Reserve, with a reef so close that in a minute you can snorkel among a great variety of stony coral and subtropical fish. The Dead Sea—actually a hypersalty lake—draws people from all over the world to luxuriate in its waters, hot springs, and black medicinal mud. The southern shores—the lowest point on the surface of the planet—are filled with hotels that offer spas and beach access. To the north, there are several laid-back beaches—Kalya, Neve Midbar, and Mineral—where you can float.

The Sea of Galilee

Placid and shimmering in the sunlight, the Sea of Galilee, or Lake *Kinneret* in Hebrew, is Israel's only natural freshwater lake, and the backdrop for some of the most important Christian pilgrim sites in the country. Scenery includes the Galilee's lovely mountains and the cliffs of the Golan Heights. Beaches range from rough sand to rocky, many are camper-friendly, and there are large water parks at Gai Beach and Luna Gal.

Beach Basics

■ Sun in this region is stronger than in Europe and most of North America. Don't overdo exposure.

■ Don't leave valuables unattended on blankets, in lockers, or in your car.

■ Observe the flags at the lifeguard stations: white means bathing is safe; red means swim with caution; and black means bathing forbidden. Take them seriously.

■ Don't swim at beaches without lifeguards. In the Mediterranean there are seasons with dangerous undertows, and at times during July and August there's a short jellyfish invasion. Stay out of the water at those times.

The Israeli national beach game is called *matkot,* which uses wood paddles and a small rubber ball. Fervent players often usurp prime territory at the shoreline and are oblivious to passersby, so duck to avoid getting hit with the ball!

ISRAEL AND THE PERFORMING ARTS

Israel has a wealth of cultural activity that reflects both its ethnic diversity and its cosmopolitanism. Innovation and experimentation cross-pollinate traditional forms, creating an exciting Israeli performing-arts scene infused by West and East. Look for listings in sections of the Friday *Haaretz* ("The Guide") and *The Jerusalem Post* ("Billboard"), and in the magazine *Time Out*, all available free in many hotels. The latter now has a Tel Aviv–oriented digital edition (⊕ *www. facebook.com/TimeOutIsrael*).

Music

Classical and Opera Israel's traditionally strong suit was enhanced a generation ago by a wave of immigrant musicians from the former Soviet Union. Apart from the deep reservoir of local talent, a steady stream of visiting artists, ensembles, and even full operatic companies enrich the scene every year. The world-renowned **Israel Philharmonic Orchestra** (⊕ *www. ipo.co.il*) is based in Tel Aviv but plays concert series in Haifa and Jerusalem as well. Look for the **Jerusalem Symphony** (⊕ *www.jso.co.il*) and **Haifa Symphony Orchestras** (⊕ *www.haifasymphony.co.il*) in their respective cities, but they and a host of smaller orchestras and ensembles appear in other, often remote, venues, too. Chamber music listings are full and varied: check out intimate auditoriums like the **Felicja Blumental Center**, the **Israel Music Conservatory** (Stricker) and the **Tel Aviv Museum of Art** in Tel Aviv; the **Jerusalem Music Center** (Mishkenot), the **Eden-Tamir Center (Ein Kerem)**, and various churches in the Holy City; and the **Rappaport Hall** and **Tikotin (Japanese) Museum** in Haifa.

The **Israeli Opera** (⊕ *www.israel-opera. co.il*), resurrected in the mid-1990s, stages up to 10 productions per season (November to July), including a crowd-pleasing extravaganza at the foot of Masada (near the Dead Sea) toward season's end. Its home base, the **Tel Aviv Performing Arts Center (TAPAC)**, hosts smaller operatic and musical events as well.

Noteworthy annual festivals include the multidisciplinary **Israel Festival** (Jerusalem, May to June, ⊕ *www.israel-festival.org.il*), the biannual **Abu Ghosh Vocal Festival** (near Jerusalem, May and October, ⊕ *www. agfestival.co.il*), and three chamber music festivals: **Upper Galilee Voice of Music** (Kibbutz Kfar Blum, July), **Eilat** (Eilat, April to May, ⊕ *www.eilat-festival.co.il*) and **Jerusalem International** (Jerusalem, August to September, ⊕ *www.jcmf.org.il*).

Popular Music Israeli rock bands and pop balladeers fill radio playlists and venues around the country. Popular watering holes are Tel Aviv's **Goldstar Zappa Club** (☏ *03/649–9550*), Barby (☏ *03/518–8123*), and Hangar 22 (in the Port). Big foreign acts like Paul McCartney, Madonna, and Uriah Heep will take over **TAPAC** or the outdoor **Yarkon Park**.

Jerusalem doesn't rock nearly as much as Tel Aviv, but look for cool gigs at **The Lab** (*Hama'abada*) (☏ *02/629–2001*) and **Yellow Submarine** (☏ *02/679–4040*). The weeklong midsummer International Arts and Crafts Fair in **Sultan's Pool**, just outside Jaffa Gate, offers good Israeli acts nightly for no extra charge.

Jazz, Ethnic, and World Music Israeli jazz has come of age with Eilat's **Red Sea Festival** (⊕ *www.redseajazzeilat.com*), a summer fixture on the international calendar, and local artists like trumpeter Avishai Cohen and his siblings crashing the New York scene. Tel Aviv's **Shablul Jazz** is the premier club, but pubs like **Mike's Place** can be hot as well. Middle Eastern influences

are common in Israeli pop songs—that's a given—but even the quintessentially New World genre of jazz hasn't escaped fusion with Yemenite or Ethiopian sounds.

The **Jerusalem International Oud Festival** celebrates a musical tradition that extends from Spain to India (⊕ *www.confederationhouse.org*).

The Upper Galilee mountain town of Tzfat (Safed), home of 16th-century Jewish mysticism, is the setting for the annual **Klezmer Festival** (⊕ *www.safed.co.il*). Three mid-August days of fiddles, clarinets and Eastern European schmaltz.

The veteran **Ein Gev Festival** in April, on the eastern shore of the Sea of Galilee, is devoted to Hebrew songs, much of them in a choral format (⊕ *www.eingev.com*).

Dance

Israel owes its visibility on the world dance radar to modern, not ballet. Still, if tradition speaks to you, check the listings for the Tel Aviv–based **Israel Ballet** (⊕ *www.iballet.co.il*) or the more contemporary Jerusalem Dance Theater (☏ 02/679–5626).

The center of Israeli modern dance is the finely restored **Suzanne Dellal Centre for Dance and Theatre** in Tel Aviv's historic Neveh Tzedek neighborhood (⊕ *www.suzannedellal.org.il*). Its four performance halls are home ground for the veteran and world-renowned **Batsheva Dance Company** (⊕ *www.batsheva.co.il*)—with legendary artistic director Ohad Naharin—and the **Inbal Pinto & Avshalom Pollak Dance Company** (⊕ *www.inbalpinto.com*). The center's season peaks with **Summer Dance,** a two-month feast of top local and international talent. **Tel Aviv Dance** is an autumn festival, while December brings the more intimate yet more intense **International Exposure.**

The field is much wider, however. The **Kibbutz Contemporary Dance Company** (⊕ *www.kcdc.co.il*) has a fine reputation, and the Jerusalem-based **Vertigo Dance Company** (⊕ *www.vertigo.org.il*) takes the audience into new territory. (Ensembles are constantly on the road: regardless of their home base, they might be performing near you.) The **Israel Festival** brings top-class acts to Jerusalem, and the capital now enjoys its own dance festival, **Machol Shalem,** in December.

Theater

Theater in Israel is almost exclusively staged in Hebrew, with the exception of Tel Aviv's **Cameri Theater** (⊕ *www.cameri.co.il*), which presents some of its popular productions with English subtitles.

The **Israel Festival** (⊕ *www.israel-festival.org.il*) in Jerusalem is the place to take in an array of the best of the performing arts over two weeks in May.

Language may not matter at Jerusalem's annual **International Festival of Puppet Theater** (⊕ *www.traintheater.co.il*) in August.

Film

Israel has a thriving film industry. The best movie meccas are the **Cinematheques** in Tel Aviv, Haifa, and Jerusalem (⊕ *www.jer-cin.org.il*). Most Israeli films have English subtitles. Real film buffs note the July dates of the **Jerusalem International Film Festival.** The Haifa Cinematheque has a similar festival in September and October (⊕ *www.haifaff.co.il*).

Tel Aviv celebrates **White Nights** on the last Thursday in June—an all-night bash when most major museums, theaters, and clubs stay open.

ISRAEL'S MAJOR HOLIDAYS

Time is figured in different ways in Israel. The Western Gregorian calendar—the solar year from January to December—is the basis of day-to-day life and commerce, but the school year, for example, which runs from September through June, follows the Hebrew lunar calendar. Jewish religious festivals are observed as national public holidays, when businesses and some museums are closed (on Yom Kippur, the Day of Atonement, *all* sites are closed).

The Muslim calendar is also lunar, but without the compensatory leap-year mechanism of its Hebrew counterpart. Muslim holidays thus drift through the seasons and can fall at any time of the year.

Even the Christian calendar isn't uniform: Christmas is celebrated on different days by the Roman Catholic (Latin) community, the Greek Orthodox Church, and the Armenian Orthodox Church.

Major Jewish Holidays

The phrase "Not religious" in the text indicates that the holiday might be part of the religious tradition, but few or no public restrictions apply. On holy days, when the text indicates "Religious," most of the Sabbath restrictions apply.

Note that in Israel the three festivals of Passover, Shavuot, and Sukkoth/Simhat Torah are observed as prescribed in the Bible: for seven, one, and eight days respectively. Historically, communities outside Israel have added a day to each festival (though many modern liberal communities have adopted the Israeli model).

Shabbat (Sabbath). Religious. The Day of Rest in Israel is Saturday, the Jewish Sabbath, which begins at sundown Friday and ends at nightfall Saturday. Torah-observant Jews don't cook, travel, answer the telephone, or use money or writing materials during the Shabbat, hence the Sabbath ban on photography at Jewish holy sites like the Western Wall. In Jerusalem, where religious influence is strong, the Downtown area clears out on Friday afternoon, and some religious neighborhoods are even closed to traffic.

Kosher restaurants close on the Sabbath, except for the main hotel restaurants, where some menu restrictions apply. In the holy city itself, your dining choices are considerably reduced, but there are more nonkosher eateries open than there used to be. Outside Jerusalem, however, you'll scarcely be affected; in fact, many restaurants do their best business of the week on the Sabbath because nonreligious Israelis take to the roads.

In Arab areas, such as East Jerusalem and Nazareth, Muslims take time off for the week's most important devotions at midday Friday, but the traveler will notice this much less than on Sunday, when most Christian shopkeepers in those towns close their doors. Saturday is market day, and these towns buzz with activity.

There's no public intercity transportation on the Sabbath, although the private *sherut* taxis drive between the main cities. Urban buses operate only in Nazareth and, on a reduced schedule, in Haifa. Shabbat is also the busiest day for nature reserves and national parks—indeed, anywhere the city folk can get away for a day. Keep this in mind if you fancy a long drive; the highways toward the main cities can be choked with returning weekend traffic on Saturday afternoon.

Rosh Hashanah (Jewish New Year), September 25–26, 2014; September 14–15, 2015. **Religious.** This two-day holiday and Yom Kippur are collectively known as the High Holy Days. Rosh Hashanah

traditionally begins a 10-day period of introspection and repentance. Observant Jews attend relatively long synagogue services and eat festive meals, including apples and honey to symbolize the hoped-for sweetness of the new year. Nonobservant Jews often use this holiday to picnic and go to the beach.

Yom Kippur (Day of Atonement), October 4, 2014; September 23, 2015. Religious. Yom Kippur is the most solemn day of the Jewish year. Observant Jews fast, wear white clothing, avoid leather footwear, and abstain from pleasures of the flesh. Israeli radio and television stations shut down. By law, all sites, entertainment venues, and most restaurants must close. Much of the country comes to a halt, and in Jerusalem and other cities the roads are almost completely empty, aside from emergency vehicles. It's considered a privilege to be invited to someone's house to "break the fast" as the holiday ends, at nightfall.

Sukkoth (Feast of Tabernacles), October 9, 2014; September 28, 2015. Religious. Jews build open-roof huts or shelters called *sukkot* (singular *sukkah*) on porches and in backyards to remember the makeshift lodgings of the biblical Israelites as they wandered in the desert. The more observant will eat as many of their meals as possible in their sukkah.

Simhat Torah, October 16, 2014; October 5, 2015. Religious. The last day of the Sukkoth festival season, this holiday marks the end—and the immediate recommencement—of the annual cycle of the reading of the Torah, the Five Books of Moses. Joyful singing and dancing (often in the street) as people carry the Torah scrolls characterize the services.

Hanukkah, November 28–December 5, 2013; December 17–December 24, 2014. Not religious. A Jewish rebellion in the 2nd century BC renewed Jewish control of Jerusalem. In the rededicated Temple, the tradition tells, a vessel was found with enough oil to burn for a day. It miraculously burned for eight days, hence the eight-day holiday marked by the lighting of an increasing number of candles (on a candelabrum called a *hanukkiah*) from night to night. Schools take a winter break. Shops, businesses, and services all remain open.

Purim, March 16, 2014; March 5, 2015 (celebrated one day later in Jerusalem). Not religious. Children dress up in costumes on the days leading up to Purim. In synagogues and on public television, devout Jews read the Scroll of Esther, the story of the valiant Jewish queen who prevented the massacre of her people in ancient Persia. On Purim day, it's customary to exchange gifts of foods with friends. Many towns hold street festivals.

Pesach (Passover), April 15–21, 2014; April 4–10, 2015. First and last days religious; dietary restrictions in force throughout. Passover is preceded by spring-cleaning to remove all traces of leavened bread and related products from the household. During the seven-day holiday itself, no bread is sold in Jewish stores. On the first evening of the holiday, Jewish families gather to retell the ancient story of their people's exodus from Egyptian bondage and to eat a festive and highly symbolic meal called the seder (Hebrew for "order"). Hotels have communal seders.

Yom Ha'atzma'ut (Independence Day), May 5, 2014; April 23, 2015. Not religious. Israel declared independence on May 14, 1948, but the exact date of Yom Ha'atzma'ut every year follows the Hebrew calendar. Although there are gala events, fireworks displays, and military parades all over the country, most Israelis go picnicking or swimming. Stores are closed, but public transportation runs and most tourist sites are open.

Shavuot (Feast of Weeks), June 4, 2014; May 24, 2015. Religious. This holiday, seven weeks after Passover, marks the harvest of the first fruits and, according to tradition, the day on which Moses received the Torah ("the Law") on Mt. Sinai. It's customary to eat dairy products.

Christian Holidays

Easter, April 20, 2014; April 5, 2015. This major festival celebrates the resurrection of Jesus. The nature and timing of its ceremonies and services are colorfully different in each Christian tradition represented in the Holy Land—Roman Catholic (Latin), Protestant, Greek Orthodox, Armenian Orthodox, Ethiopian, and so on. The Western churches—Roman Catholic and Protestant—observe the date above. Check the dates for different groups such as the Armenian Orthodox, Greek Orthodox, and Russian Orthodox churches, who base their holidays on the older Julian calendar.

Christmas. Except in towns with a large indigenous Christian population, such as Nazareth and Bethlehem, Christmas isn't a high-visibility holiday in Israel. The Christmas of the Catholic and Protestant traditions is, of course, celebrated on December 25, but the Greek Orthodox calendar observes it on January 7, and the Armenian Orthodox wait until January 19. Christmas Eve (December 24) is the time for the international choir assembly in Bethlehem's Manger Square, followed by the Roman Catholic midnight mass in the adjacent church. Take a cab to the border crossing (don't forget your passport), and pick up a shared cab to Manger Square on the Palestinian side. Check first with the Israeli Ministry of Tourism information office that the choral event is on schedule.

Muslim Holidays

Muslims observe Friday as their holy day, but it's accompanied by none of the restrictions and far less of the solemnity of the Jewish Shabbat and the Christian Sabbath (in their strictest forms). The noontime prayer on Friday is the most important of the week and is typically preceded by a sermon, often broadcast from mosques' loudspeakers. The dates of Muslim holidays shift each year because of the lunar calendar.

Ramadan, June 28–July 27, 2014; June 18–July 17, 2015. This monthlong fast commemorates the month in which the Qur'an was first revealed to Muhammad. Devout Muslims must abstain from food, drink, tobacco, and sex during daylight hours; the three-day festival of Id el-Fitr then marks the conclusion of the period. The dates are affected by the sighting of the new moon and can change slightly at the very last moment. The Muslim holy sites on Jerusalem's Haram esh-Sharif (the Temple Mount) offer only short morning visiting hours during this time and are closed to tourists during Id el-Fitr.

Eid al-Adha, October 5, 2014; September 24, 2015. This festival commemorating Abraham's willingness to sacrifice his son marks the end of the annual Haj, or pilgrimage to Mecca.

GREAT ITINERARIES

BEST OF ISRAEL, 11 DAYS (WITH OPTIONAL EXTENSIONS)

Israel is a small but varied country. This itinerary lets you see the high points of Jerusalem and the northern half of the country in 11 days; add the desert if you have the time and inclination.

Jerusalem, Days 1–3

You could spend a lifetime in Jerusalem, but three days is probably a good minimum to get a feel for the city and environs. First, spend a day getting an overview of the holy sites of Judaism, Christianity, and Islam. Start with the Western Wall, then go up to the Temple Mount (morning hours) to view the Muslim shrines. Follow the Via Dolorosa to the Church of the Holy Sepulcher. Stop for a Middle Eastern–style lunch in the Christian Quarter before walking down into the Jewish Quarter. (Note: The Temple Mount is closed Friday and Saturday, and some Jewish Quarter sites close early Friday and only reopen Sunday.) Explore the remarkable underworld of biblical (Old Testament) Jerusalem, or if you have a car, pick up one or two of the panoramic views.

On your second day, you can venture farther afield: many consider the Israel Museum and Yad Vashem, including the Holocaust History Museum, essential if you're visiting Jerusalem. Mt. Herzl National Memorial Park is also a meaningful excursion. A good plan is to avoid burnout by doing one of the big museums on Day 2, the other on Day 3. (Note: Yad Vashem and Mt. Herzl are closed Saturday.) Add the Machaneh Yehuda produce market (closed Saturday) and the Knesset menorah.

Your third day can be devoted to the second of the above museums, and sites within an hour of Jerusalem: perhaps a wine tour in the Judean Hills. Or join a dig at Beit Guvrin-Maresha National Park with Archaeological Seminars—and on your way back, visit Mini Israel, with its hundreds of models of Israeli sites.

The Dead Sea region, Days 4 and 5

After getting an early start in your rental car, head east through the stark Judean Desert to Qumran, where the Dead Sea Scrolls were discovered. You can spend an hour (max) touring the ruins and seeing the audiovisual presentation. About 45 minutes south of Qumran along the Dead Sea shore is Ein Gedi, where a leisurely hike to the waterfall and back should take about 1.5 hours, including a dip in a freshwater pool. End the day with a float in the Dead Sea, and spend the night at the Kibbutz Ein Gedi Guest House or one of the fine hotels at Ein Bokek, at the southern end of the lake. The spa treatments featuring the famously curative Dead Sea mud are a highlight for many.

In the morning, hike the Snake Path—or take the cable car—up Masada. The gate to the trail opens before dawn so you can catch the sunrise at the top. Later, head back to Jerusalem to spend the night.

Note: If you don't have a car, one-day bus tours from Jerusalem let you see Masada and the Dead Sea. Or you can also drive to Qumran, Ein Gedi, the Dead Sea, and Masada for the day and return to Jerusalem: that's a full day and you'd need to plan your time carefully.

The Galilee, Days 6–8

From Jerusalem, where you've spent the night, make an early start to allow time for all the sites on today's schedule. Retrace your steps down Route 1 East, stopping just north of the Dead Sea–Jerusalem highway at the oasis town of Jericho, the world's oldest city. It's almost worth a trip through this lush town—with its date palms, orange groves, banana plantations, bougainvillea, and papaya trees—just to be able to say "I was there," but Tel Jericho is also a significant archaeological site. Sample the baklava and orange juice. Jericho is in the Palestinian Authority, so check ahead of time for any entry restrictions. (Most car-rental agencies don't allow their cars into Palestinian areas.)

Take the Jordan Valley route (Route 90) to the Galilee, stopping en route for a swim at the springs of Gan Hashelosha (better known as Sachne); then visit the extensive Roman-Byzantine ruins at Beit She'an, where you can have lunch in town or take a sandwich to the site. The Crusader castle of Belvoir will round out the day, and you can enjoy a lakeside fish dinner in Tiberias, where you'll spend the night.

The next day, spend an hour or two in the far north at the Tel Dan Nature Reserve, with its rushing water and biblical archaeology. Nearby Banias has Roman shrines, a fine walk, and the Suspended Trail overlooking a cauldron of seething white water. Depending on how you spend your day, you can also visit one of the many fine wineries on the Golan Heights, or do some hiking or bird-watching at Gamla. Overnight in Tiberias again, or better yet, farther north in a Hula Valley B&B.

On your third day, you can explore the treasures of Tzfat, with its beautiful vistas, old synagogues, and art and Judaica galleries. Spend the afternoon hiking or horseback riding at Bat Ya'ar (reserve if you want to go trail riding) or kayaking at Hagoshrim or Kfar Blum (seasonal, but no need to reserve). Overnight in Tiberias or at your Hula Valley B&B.

The Mediterranean Coast and Tel Aviv, Days 9–11

From Tiberias or your Hula Valley B&B, head west to the coast. Your first stop can be the cable-car ride to the white sea grottoes of Rosh Hanikra. Then travel to Akko, with its Crusader halls and picturesque harbor. Akko is also an excellent place for a fish lunch. Then drive to Haifa for a view from the Dan Panorama hotel at the top of Mt. Carmel. Spend the night in Haifa.

The next day, visit Haifa's Baha'i Shrine and its magnificent gardens, then continue down the coast to visit the village of Zichron Ya'akov, home of the Carmel Winery and the Beit Aaronsohn Museum. Have lunch and then head to Tel Aviv, stopping at the Roman ruins of Caesarea on the way. In Tel Aviv, you can enjoy a night on the town, perhaps in Neveh Tzedek or Jaffa.

On your third day, take in Tel Aviv's museums, browse Old Jaffa and the flea market, and enjoy a dip in the Mediterranean. From here you can head to the airport if it's time to go home. If you're proceeding on to the desert, spend another night in Tel Aviv.

Extension: The Negev, 2 days

From Tel Aviv, head south toward Beersheva and Route 40. If you're doing this on a Thursday, leave early enough to get to the Beersheva Bedouin market, which is most colorful in the morning. (Beersheva is under two hours' drive from Tel Aviv.) Driving south, stop at Sde Boker, where you can have lunch and see David Ben-Gurion's house and gravesite overlooking the biblical Wilderness of Zin. Near Sde Boker is Ein Avdat, a wilderness oasis that has a trail with stone steps and ladders leading up the magnificent white chalk canyon. This part of the trail is one-way up, so the driver needs to go

back to the car and drive around to meet the others.) Drive on to Mitzpe Ramon, on the edge of the immense Makhtesh Ramon (Ramon Crater). Spend the night here, then enjoy the natural wonders of the Ramon Crater the next day. Spend a second night here as well.

Extension: Eilat and environs, 2 to 5 days

Eilat is under three-hour's drive from Mitzpe Ramon. Drive south on Route 40 to where it joins Route 90 and continue south on the Arava Road, which runs parallel to the border with Jordan. Stop at Hai Bar Nature Reserve, and then at Timna Park for a short walk and a view of Solomon's Pillars, arriving in Eilat in the late afternoon. A minimum of two days here allows you to see all the highlights; in three to five days you can have some serious beach or diving time, and take a side trip to Petra, in Jordan. You'll probably want to pick one hotel in Eilat as a base.

TIPS

In the summer, plan to do most of your walking and hiking by midday to avoid the heat.

Make sure to take lots of water, and a hat, when hiking or walking.

Consider flying back to Tel Aviv from Eilat—or fly round-trip to Eilat if you don't have the time or inclination to drive.

Make your hotel/B&B reservations ahead of time, especially in summer and on weekends year-round, when hotels and B&Bs are crowded with vacationing Israelis.

Most hotels in the Dead Sea area and Eilat have spas with a host of treatments; call ahead or book one when you arrive.

You won't need a rental car in the Old City of Jerusalem; navigating and parking can be a challenge, so save the rental car for trips out of town.

The lunar-like red-rock canyons in the hills behind Eilat are great for hiking (but not alone), and there are also plenty of water-sports options: you can snorkel, parasail, or arrange a boat trip to prime dive spots. Day trips to Petra are available through your hotel concierge. Some like more time to explore that extraordinary site, but since you can't take your rental car across into Jordan, a two-day trip (overnight in Petra) is only doable if you budget for your own guide and car on that side. The return drive from Eilat to Jerusalem via the Arava takes less than five hours, including rest stops.

GREAT ITINERARIES

IN THE FOOTSTEPS OF JESUS, 6 DAYS

Visit the Holy Land, they say, and you'll never read the Bible the same way again; the landscapes and shrines that you'll see, and your encounters with local members of Christian communities at the landmarks of Jesus' life, will have a profound and lasting impact.

Jerusalem and Bethlehem, Days 1 and 2

Spend your first day retracing the climax of the story of Jesus in Jerusalem, starting at the Mt. of Olives. This is where Jesus taught and wept over the city (Luke 19:41), and the tear-shaped Dominus Flevit church commemorates it. The walk down the Mt. of Olives road, also known as the Palm Sunday road, leads to the ancient olive trees in the Garden of Gethsemane, where you can contemplate Jesus' "passion" and arrest.

Follow the Via Dolorosa, stopping at each Station of the Cross, to the Church of the Holy Sepulcher, where most Christians believe Jesus was crucified, buried, and resurrected. The Garden Tomb—the site of Calvary for many Protestants—offers an island of tranquility. Take your time contemplating the sites; this won't be a rushed day.

The next day, you can explore the Southern Wall excavations at the Jerusalem Archaeological Park, adjacent to the Old City's Dung Gate. Scholars believe Jesus could have walked the stones of the ancient street here, and climbed the Southern Steps to the Temple. Down the hill is the City of David, the Old Testament heart of Jerusalem, including the excavated Area G and Warren's Shaft, and King Hezekiah's water tunnel. The

steps of the pool of Siloam, where a blind man had his sight restored (John 9:7–11), were discovered only a few years ago. Add a visit to the Room of the Last Supper on Mt. Zion, near Zion Gate, and then have lunch.

In the afternoon, you can visit Bethlehem, the birthplace of Jesus, to see the Church of the Nativity, one of the oldest churches in the world. Bethlehem is in the Palestinian Authority, so bring your passport. Most car-rental agencies don't allow their cars into Palestinian areas. It's best to take a taxi to the border crossing east of Jerusalem's Gilo neighborhood. The crossing for tourists is usually uncomplicated, and there are Palestinian taxis waiting on the other side to take you to the church. Or you can opt to spend the afternoon in Jerusalem.

On the way to the Galilee, Day 3

Making an early start, head east through the barren Judean Desert to Qumran, where the Dead Sea Scrolls were found. Some scholars believe John the Baptist may have passed through here, and a visit to the site—you can spend an hour here—is an opportunity to learn about the desert in which Jesus sought solitude, purity, and inspiration.

Then head up the Jordan Valley (Route 90), passing through or near Jericho (depending on political conditions). Jesus also healed a blind man here (Mark 10:46), and had a meal with the tax collector Zacchaeus (Luke 19:1–5). If the security situation isn't favorable, the Israeli soldiers at the checkpoint at Jericho won't allow you in (again, read a newspaper and use common sense). If you skip Jericho, Route 90 swings past it to the east. In Jericho, though, a visit to Tel Jericho, the first conquest of the Israelites in

First, and foremost, bring along your Bible; it will get a lot of use.

You won't need a car in Jerusalem, but you will need one for the rest of this itinerary. Your best bet is to pick up a car on the afternoon of the day before you head out of Jerusalem, so that you can make an early start the next day (remember that rental agencies are normally not open on Saturday). The agency will provide you with a basic road map and advice.

Gas stations are numerous, many with convenience stores to stock up on snacks.

the Holy Land (Joshua 6), is a must. You can have lunch at the restaurant next to the tell or at a truck stop on the way north from Jericho.

Then it's on to the ruins at Beit She'an, including the ancient main street, a bathhouse, and mosaics. Not only is this an important Old Testament site, it was also the capital of the Decapolis, a league of 10 Roman cities, among which Jesus taught and healed (Mark 7:31).

Farther north, pilgrims go to Yardenit to be baptized in the Jordan River and remember the baptism of Jesus in these waters. Spend the night in Tiberias.

Sea of Galilee, Day 4

Start the day heading north to the ancient wooden boat at Ginosar, which evokes Gospel descriptions of life on the lake— see, for example, Matthew 9:1. Then, after meditating on Jesus' famous sermon (Matthew 5) in the gardens of the Mt. of

Beatitudes and its chapel (off Route 90 north of the Sea of Galilee), descend to Tabgha to see the mosaics of the Church of the Multiplication of Loaves and Fishes. From a lakeshore perch at the nearby Church of the Primacy of St. Peter, where Jesus appeared to the disciples after the Resurrection (John 21), you can marvel at how Scripture and landscape blend before your eyes.

Farther east, the ruins of ancient Capernaum—the center of Jesus' local ministry—include a magnificent pillared synagogue (partially restored) and Peter's house.

An archaeological mound across the Jordan River, north of the Sea of Galilee, is ancient Bethsaida, where the Gospels say Jesus healed and taught (Luke 9:10, 10:13). To get there, continue east of Capernaum, cross the Jordan River north of the Sea of Galilee, turn left onto Route 888, and a short distance thereafter turn left to Bethsaida in the Jordan River Park. From there, head back down to the lake and continue around its eastern shore to Kursi National Park and the ruins of a Byzantine church where, it's said, Jesus cast out demons into a herd of swine that stampeded into the water (Matthew 8:28–30).

A good idea for lunch is the fish restaurant at Kibbutz Ein Gev. Ask about a cruise on the lake after lunch (the kibbutz also has a boat company). Spend the night in Tiberias or at one of the kibbutz guesthouses or B&Bs in the Hula Valley.

The Hula Valley and Banias (Caesarea Philippi), Day 5

The next day, drive through the Hula Valley; it's especially remarkable in the spring when the flowers bloom and bring alive Jesus' famous teaching from the Sermon on the Mount: "Consider the lilies of the field, how they grow" (Matthew 6:28). At the base of Mt. Hermon (which some scholars see as an alternative candidate for the site of the Transfiguration, as described in Mark 9:2–8), northeast of the Hula Valley, is Banias (Caesarea Philippi), where Jesus asked the disciples, "Who do people say I am?" (Matthew 16:13–20). The remains of a pagan Roman shrine are a powerful backdrop for contemplation of that message. Tel Dan, an important city in the biblical Kingdom of Israel, has a beautiful nature reserve. Stay overnight at your B&B or kibbutz hotel in the Hula Valley.

The Galilee Hills and the Coast, Day 6

Head for the hills, connecting to Route 77 and turning south onto Route 754 to Cana to see the church that commemorates Jesus' first miracle: changing water into wine (John 2:1–11). Continue to Nazareth, Jesus' childhood town. The massive modern Church of the Annunciation is built over a rock dwelling where (Catholics believe) the angel Gabriel appeared to Mary (Luke 1:26–38). The Greek Orthodox tradition is that the event took place at the village well, and their church is built over that site, some distance away. Nazareth's restaurants make tasty lunch stops.

A drive through the lush Jezreel Valley, via Route 60 and then north on Route 65 (the New Testament Valley of Armageddon), brings you to Mt. Tabor, long identified as the Mount of Transfiguration. The valley is named Armageddon (Revelation 16:16), after the archaeological site of Megiddo, now a national park south of Afula on Route 65. The drive back to Jerusalem from Megiddo takes 1½ hours, using the Route 6 toll road, or you can spend the night in Haifa and return to Jerusalem the next day.

ISRAEL
THROUGH THE AGES

Where else in the world can you find the living history of three major religions that have been intertwined for more than 1,000 years? Israel is the crossroads for Christianity, Islam, and Judaism, and many of the remarkable sites here help to tell this country's unique story. One of the best examples can be found in Jerusalem's Old City, where you can visit the Church of the Holy Sepulcher, the Dome of the Rock, and the Western Wall all within a short walk of each other.

| TIMELINE | 1800 BC Beginning of Patriarchal Age | 13th Century BC Israelite exodus from Egypt | 1000 BC David conquers Jerusalem. 950 BC Solomon builds the First Temple |

1800 BC — **1500 BC** — **1200 BC** — **900 BC**

(top left) The Bible—David playing the harp while bringing the Ark of the Covenant from Kirjath-Jearim with other musicians. (bottom) The goddess Asherah was worshipped by some in ancient Israel as the consort of El and in Judah as the consort of Yahweh (some Hebrews baked small cakes for her festival). (right) Artist's depiction of Solomon's court (Ingobertus, c. 880).

Prehistory

1.2 million BC

The land that is now Israel served as a land bridge for Homo Erectus on his epic journey out of Africa. The oldest human remains found outside that continent, 1.4 million years old, were unearthed at Ubediya near Lake Kinneret (Sea of Galilee). It was in the Carmel Caves in northern Israel that the only indication of direct contact between Neanderthal Man and Homo Sapiens, 40,000 years ago, has been found, lending credence to the theory that they lived contemporaneously.

■ Visit: Museum at Degania Alef (⇨ Ch.6), Carmel Caves (⇨ Ch.5)

Early Biblical Period

2000–1000 BC

The arrival of Abraham, Isaac, and Jacob marked the beginning of the Patriarchal Age, dated to around 1800 BC. The Israelite exodus from Egypt took place in the 13th century BC. It was at this time that Israel was divided into Canaanite city-kingdoms. As the Israelites established themselves in the hill country, the Philistines, originating in the Aegean, were landing on the coastal plain. Around 1150, the Philistines invaded. A place name deriving from their presence endures to this day—Palestine.

■ Visit: Valley of Elah (⇨ Ch.3)

United Monarchy

1000–928 BC

David conquered Jerusalem around 1000 BC, united the Israelite tribes into one kingdom, and established his capital here. David's son, Solomon, became king in 968 BC. Around 950 BC, Solomon built the First Temple in Jerusalem, the religious center. Shortly after Solomon's death in 928 BC, the kingdom split in two—the northern tribes, which seceded and formed the Kingdom of Israel, and the southern tribes, now known as the Kingdom of Judah.

■ Visit: City of David (⇨ Ch.2), Temple Mount (⇨ Ch.2)

721 BC Assyrians conquer Israel	586 BC Babylonian rule	538 BC Cyrus the Great of Persia conquers Babylonia. Second Temple rebuilt	AD 27 Jesus' Galilean ministry takes place	AD 70 Romans destroy Second Temple. Masada falls in AD 73.
	600 BC	300 BC	0	AD 300

1

IN FOCUS ISRAEL THROUGH THE AGES

(top left) Hexagonal cylinder of King Sennacherib of Assyria inscribed with an account of his invasion of Palestine and the siege of Jerusalem in the reign of Hezekiah, King of Judah, dated 686 BC. (top center) 1860 engraving of the Western Wall. (top right) Masada. (bottom left) Mosaic in the Church of the Holy Sepulcher, Jerusalem.

928–587 BC

For 200 years, the Kingdom of Israel and the Kingdom of Judah co-existed, though relations were sometimes hostile. But in 721 BC, the Assyrian army, which dominated the region, conquered Israel and took its residents eastward into captivity. The fate of these "ten lost tribes" would be a subject of speculation by scholars thereafter. In 586 BC, the Assyrians were defeated by a new power, the Babylonians. Their king, Nebuchadnezzar, conquered Judah and destroyed Jerusalem and the temple. Those who survived were exiled to the "rivers of Babylon."

538 BC–AD 73

Second Temple Period

This exile ended after only 50 years when Cyrus the Great of Persia conquered Babylonia and permitted the exiles to return to Judah. Jerusalem was rebuilt and a new temple erected. The vast Persian Empire was defeated by Alexander the Great in 333 BC. Judah the Maccabee claimed victory over Hellenistic armies in 165 BC and rededicated the defiled Jewish temple. Judean independence brought the Hasmonean dynasty in 142 BC, which the Romans ended when they annexed the country in 63 BC.

Jesus was born in Bethlehem, and 26 years later began his ministry, teaching mostly around the Sea of Galilee. In AD 29, Jesus and his disciples celebrated Passover in Jerusalem; he was arrested, put on trial, and crucified by the Romans soon after.

In AD 66, the Jews rose up against Roman rule. Their fierce revolt failed and Jerusalem and the temple were destroyed in the process, in AD 70. A vestige of the temple compound, the Western Wall, is venerated by Jews to this day. The last Jewish stronghold, Masada, fell three years later.

▨ Visit: Sea of Galilee (⇨ Ch.6), Via Dolorosa (⇨ Ch.2), Masada (⇨ Ch.3)

325 Constantine
makes Christianity
the imperial religion

622 Muhammad's
hejira and the
beginning of Islam

1099 Crusaders
conquer Jerusalem

500   700   900   1100

(immediate left) Bar Kochba's coin: top, the Jewish Temple facade with the rising star; reverse: A lulav, the text that reads: "to the freedom of Jerusalem." (top left) Saladin, commander of Muslim forces, battles Christians in the 3rd Crusade. (top right) Richard the Lionheart In battle during the Crusades.

Late Roman & Byzantine Period

AD 73–640

In 132, the Roman emperor Hadrian threatened to rebuild Jerusalem as a pagan city and another Jewish revolt broke out, led by Bar-Kochba. In retribution, Hadrian leveled Jerusalem in 135 and changed the name of the country to Syria Palestina. Many of the remaining Jews were killed, enslaved, or exiled.

It wasn't until the 4th century AD that the Roman emperor Constantine made Christianity the imperial religion. This revived life in the Holy Land, making it a focus of pilgrimage and church construction that included the Church of the Nativity in Bethlehem. In spite of persecution, a vibrant Jewish community still existed.

Muhammad's *hejira* (flight) from Mecca to Medina in Arabia took place in 622, marking the beginning of Islam. This became Year One on the Muslim calendar. When Muhammad died in 632, his followers burst out of Arabia and created a Muslim empire that within a century would extend from India to Spain.

■ Visit: Jerusalem's Cardo (⇨ Ch.2); Caesarea (⇨ Ch.5)

Medieval Period

640–1516

The Dome of the Rock was constructed in Jerusalem in 691 by Caliph Abd al-Malik. In 1099, the Crusaders conquered the city and massacred Jews and Muslims there. Cities like Akko (also called Acre) and castles like Belvoir were developed around 1100. Muslim reconquest of the land under the Mamluks began in 1265. In 1291 Akko fell, marking the end of the Crusades. An outstanding period of architecture followed, especially in Jerusalem's Temple Mount (Haram esh-Sharif) and in the Muslim Quarter.

■ Visit: Dome of the Rock (⇨ Ch.2); Al-Aqsa Mosque (⇨ Ch.2); Akko (Ch. 5)

1265 Muslim reconquest begins	Akko falls in 1291, marking the end of the Crusader kingdom	1516 Mamluks defeated in Syria by the Ottoman Turks	1897 First World Zionist Conference
	1300	1500	1700	1900

1

IN FOCUS ISRAEL THROUGH THE AGES

(top left) Jewish settlers known as Biluim, in Palestine, 1880s. The 38th Zionist congress, 1933. (bottom left) *Palestine Post* headline announcing declaration of independence in 1948.

1516–1917 Modern Period

In 1516, the Mamluks were defeated in Syria by the Ottoman Turks. Egyptian nationalists took control of Israel in 1832, but were expelled in 1840 with help from European nations. The country's population shifted in the 19th century, when the steamship made access easy.

The first World Zionist Conference, organized by Theodor Herzl, took place in 1897, fueling the idea of a Jewish homeland. In 1909, Tel Aviv was founded, and Degania, the first kibbutz, was established on the southern shore of the Sea of Galilee.

■ Visit: Akko (⇨ Ch.5); Walls of Jerusalem (⇨ Ch.2)

1917–1948 Creation of a Jewish State

The conquest of Palestine by the British in the First World War ushered in many critical changes. In 1917, the British government expressed support in the Balfour Declaration for creation of a Jewish homeland. Arab nationalism began to rise around 1920 in the post-Ottoman Middle East after Ottoman Turkey, which sided with Germany during the first World War, abandoned Palestine. This marked the point at which tension between Jews and Arabs began to increase, peaking in the massacre of Jews in 1920, 1929, and again in 1936. Various Jewish militias formed to counter the violence.

The British "White Paper" of 1939 restricted Jewish immigration and land purchase in Palestine. Tensions with Britain, and clashes between Arabs and Jews, peaked after World War II. The U.N. Partition Plan of 1947 envisioned two states in Palestine, one Jewish and one Arab. With the end of the British mandate in May 1948, David Ben-Gurion, the Palestinian Jewish leader who would later become Israel's first prime minister, declared Israel a Jewish state. In the following months, Israel survived invasions by the armies of several Arab nations.

■ Visit: Tel Hai (⇨ Ch.7), Independence Hall, Tel Aviv (⇨ Ch.4), Jordan Valley Kibbutzim (⇨ Ch.5), Ben-Gurion's Desert Home (Ch.8)

(left) David Ben-Gurion in 1918. (top right) Knesset, Israeli parliament, Jerusalem. (bottom right) Israeli flag.

The First 50 Years

1948–1998

Fighting ended January, 1949, and a U.N.-supervised cease-fire agreement was signed. Transjordan annexed the West Bank and East Jerusalem; Egypt annexed the Gaza Strip. Palestinian Arabs who fled or were expelled settled in neighboring countries; those who stayed became Israeli citizens. The first elections to the Knesset took place, and David Ben-Gurion was elected prime minister. In 1950, the Knesset enacted the Law of Return, giving any Jew the right to Israeli citizenship.

Around 1964, the Palestine Liberation Organization (PLO) was founded, which sought an independent state for Palestinians and refused to recognize Israel as a state. In 1967, the Six-Day War broke out; Israel occupied territory including the Golan Heights. Egypt and Syria attacked Israel on Yom Kippur in 1973. The Lebanon War in 1982 met with unprecedented Israeli opposition. In 1987, the *intifada* (uprising) brought sustained Palestinian Arab unrest. The Oslo Accords, signed in 1994, involved mutual recognition of Israel and the PLO, as well as Palestinian autonomy in the Gaza Strip and parts of the West Bank.

Israel Today

1998–Present

After Ehud Barak was elected prime minister in 1999, Israel withdrew from Lebanon. The second *intifada* began in 2000 and subsided in 2005, costing more than 3,000 Israeli and Palestinian lives. When Israel withdrew from the Gaza Strip (2005), the Islamist Hamas took over and made it a base for rocket attacks against Israel. Confrontation with the Iran-backed Hamas and Hezbollah continued in those years. In November 2012, the Palestinian Authority won United Nations recognition of Palestine as a sovereign (but non-member) state.

2

JERUSALEM

WELCOME TO JERUSALEM

TOP REASONS TO GO

★ **The Old City:** For an astonishing montage of religions and cultures, the heart of Jerusalem—with the Holy Sepulcher, Arab bazaar, and Western Wall—has few equals anywhere in the world.

★ **Mt. of Olives:** This classic panorama puts the entire Old City, with the golden Dome of the Rock, squarely within your lens. The view is best with the morning sun behind you.

★ **Machaneh Yehuda:** You can munch a falafel as you watch shoppers swirl and eddy through West Jerusalem's outstanding produce market.

★ **Israel Museum:** The museum, fresh from an enormous renewal, is a winner, with its Dead Sea Scrolls, outdoor model, and a stunning collection of fine art, archaeology, and Judaica.

★ **City of David:** Plunge underground to explore Jerusalem's most ancient remains, and wade the 2,700-year-old water tunnel that once saved the besieged city.

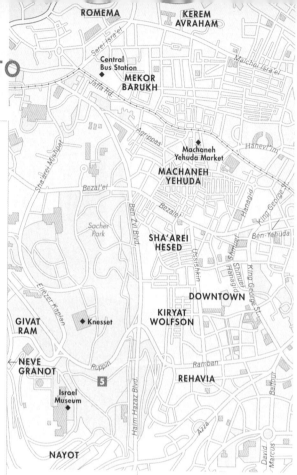

1 **Old City classic sights.** The walled Old City, with its narrow streets, is what Jerusalem is all about. It's a labyrinth of memories, a bewitching flicker show of colors and cultures, best epitomized by the *souk*, or bazaar. But it also has the Holy Sepulcher, the Western Wall, and the Dome of the Rock, redolent with religion and seething with history.

2 **Jewish Quarter.** Excavations since the 1970s have unearthed a cornucopia of interesting ancient sites in and around this reconstructed neighborhood, notably the Herodian Quarter. Another gem is the City of David, located outside the Old City walls. Good stores and lots of eateries complete the picture.

3 **Tower of David and Mt Zion.** Stretching south from Jaffa Gate, this area is a potpourri of interesting minor sights. The Tower of David Museum is the most notable.

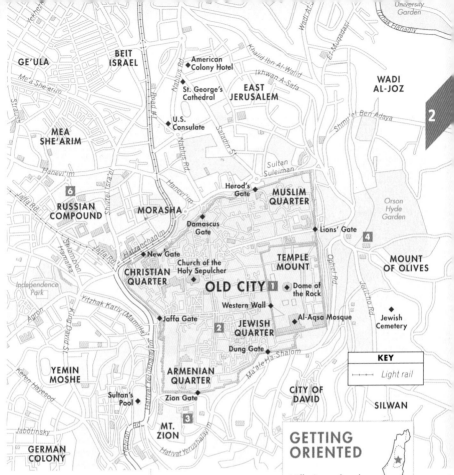

4 Mt of Olives and East Jerusalem. Most visitors, particularly Christians, will identify with two or three particular sites—Gethsemane and the Garden Tomb are the obvious ones. Make your way down the Mt. of Olives. The Rockefeller Museum is a gem.

5 West Jerusalem. Within this extensive side of Jerusalem are several great but unrelated sights, some a few miles apart. Savor the extraordinary Israel Museum and Yad Vashem.

6 Center City. West Jerusalem's Downtown areas have more subtle attractions than the city's postcard snapshots. Check out the Yemin Moshe and Nahalat Shiva neighborhoods, Ben-Yehuda Street, and the Machaneh Yehuda market.

GETTING ORIENTED

Hilly Jerusalem has two centers of gravity—the Old City, on the east side; and the modern Downtown triangle of King George, Ben-Yehuda, and Jaffa streets on the west. Jerusalem is Israel's capital and home to its national institutions, most in Jewish West Jerusalem. East Jerusalem, including the Old City, is largely (but not entirely) Arab. Coexistence is sometimes fragile, and the two communities tend to keep to themselves.

HOLIDAY FOODS IN ISRAEL

PASSOVER MATZOH

The journey from slavery in Egypt to freedom, remembered during the weeklong Passover holiday each spring, inspires the preparation of unleavened bread called matzoh. Why unleavened? The Hebrew people left Egypt in a hurry and had no time for bread to rise. Today it's rare to find bread or any foods made with leavening agents for sale during Passover, especially in Jerusalem. Matzoh is a flat, crisp—and bland on its own—square of crunchiness. Modern times have produced matzoh flavored with onion and made richer with eggs. Cooks get creative with fried matzoh and baked treats.

You know it's a holiday when special treats suddenly appear in bakeries, street stalls, supermarkets, and restaurants. Round doughnuts dabbed with jelly at Hanukkah, cheese blintzes bursting with raisins at Shavuot, or triangles of filled pastry at Purim: foods symbolize each holiday's historical event or theme.

On holidays, families and friends sit down to festive meals of favorite foods eaten in time-honored tradition. Tu b'Shevat, the winter New Year of Trees celebration, has everyone munching juicy dried fruit such as tart apricots, golden raisins, and sweet dates and figs, accompanied by nuts and pumpkin or sunflower seeds. On Independence Day in spring, people barbecue, and the scent of sizzling meat wafts throughout Israel.

Shabbat, the Jewish Sabbath, is observed each Friday night and Saturday. Pride of place goes to a golden-crusted, braided, soft *challah* bread; look for these in bakeries each week.

ROSH HASHANAH

During the New Year holiday each fall, *sweet* is the byword, indicating wishes for a sweet year: apple slices dipped in honey are nibbled, and ruby-red pomegranate seeds decorate salads and are eaten with the hope that good deeds performed in the coming year will be as plentiful as the seeds of this fruit. Plump dates hang in bunches at markets; Sephardic Jews end the holiday meal with them. Bakeries and restaurants feature dark-honey cake enhanced with ginger and cinnamon.

HANUKKAH

As winter approaches, Hanukkah celebrates a 2nd-century BC victory over the Greeks; the story includes a miraculous amount of oil for the Temple menorah, or candelabrum. Foods fried in oil are the order of the day. Round, deep-fried jelly doughnuts called *sufganiyot*—browned to a crisp on the outside and pillowy soft inside—appear all over town. Fillings get more creative every year, from caramel or chocolate to lemon cream or halvah.

PURIM

This early-spring holiday commemorates a victory in which food helped win the day, the 6th-century BC triumph over the evil Haman. On Purim, everyone eats triangular pastries called *hamantaschen* or, in Hebrew, *oznai Haman*—Haman's ears. The treats are

filled with jam, poppy seeds, dates, or chocolate. It's a tradition, known as *mishloach manot*, to exchange gifts of foods, and you'll see children on the streets carrying little baskets of goodies as well as the ubiquitous "ears."

SHAVUOT

The Feast of Weeks, a spring holiday, marks the giving of the Torah at Mt. Sinai. Explanations for the connection with eating dairy foods are many; one is that just as milk sustains the body, so the Torah provides spiritual nourishment for the soul. Look for rich, creamy cheesecakes with sour-cream toppings and cheese blintzes with raisins. Try cheeses from Israel's goat and sheep farms, from cottage cheese to sharp blue and chunky tomme (a goat cheese).

RAMADAN

The holiest month of the Islamic year is Ramadan, when believers fast from sunrise to sunset every day. Special sweets are enjoyed at family meals in the evening and at the feast of Eid el-Fitr, at the end of Ramadan. A favorite delicacy is *attayif*, puffy little pancakes folded over a filling of cheese or nuts and doused in syrup. Look for these at bakeries or on outdoor griddles in the Old City of Jerusalem, Nazareth, Haifa, and Akko's Old City.

—*by Judy Stacey Goldman*

By Matthew Kalman and Mike Rogoff

Jerusalem is a city suspended between heaven and earth, East and West, past and present—parallel universes of flowing caftans and trendy coffee shops. For some people, Jerusalem is a condition, like being in love; for others, it is a state of mind, a constant tension between rival flags and faiths, or members of the same faith. You may feel moved, energized, or swept into the maelstrom of contemporary issues—but the city will not leave you unaffected.

The word *unique* is easy to throw around, but Jerusalem has a real claim on it. The 5,000-year-old city is sacred to half the human race, and its iconic Old City walls embrace primary sites of the three great monotheistic religions. For Jews, Jerusalem has always been their spiritual focus and historical national center; the imposing Western Wall is the last remnant of the ancient Temple Period complex. For almost 2,000 years, Christians have venerated Jerusalem as the place where their faith was shaped—through the death, burial, and resurrection of Jesus of Nazareth—and the candlelit Church of the Holy Sepulcher is where the greater part of Christendom recognizes those events. Islamic tradition identifies Jerusalem as the *masjid al-aqsa*, the "farthermost place," from which Muhammad ascended to Heaven for his portentous meeting with God: the dazzling, gold-top Dome of the Rock marks the spot.

The Old City is far more than shrines, however. Its arches, hidden courtyards, and narrow cobblestone alleyways beckon you back in time. The streets are crowded with travelers, pilgrims, and vendors of everything from tourist trinkets and leather sandals to fresh produce, embroidered fabrics, and dubious DVDs. Your senses are assaulted by intense colors and by the aromas of turmeric, fresh mint, wild sage, and cardamom-spiced coffee. The blare of Arabic music and the burble of languages fill the air.

Step outside the Old City and you'll be transported into the 21st century—well, at least the 20th: quaint neighborhoods, some restored, embody an earlier simplicity. West Jerusalem forms the bulk of a modern metropolis of 800,000, Israel's largest city. It's not as cosmopolitan as Tel Aviv, but it does have good restaurants, fine hotels, vibrant markets, and upscale neighborhoods. The Downtown triangle of Jaffa Street, King George Street, and Ben-Yehuda Street, and the elegant Mamilla Mall outside Jaffa Gate, are natural gathering places.

The city prides itself on its historical continuity. A municipal bylaw dating back to 1918 makes it mandatory to face even high-rise commercial buildings with the honey-colored "Jerusalem stone," the local limestone that has served Jerusalem's builders since, well, forever. Watch the stone walls glow at sunset—the source of the by-now clichéd but still compelling phrase "Jerusalem of Gold"—and understand the mystical hold Jerusalem has had on so many minds and hearts for so many thousands of years.

JERUSALEM PLANNER

WHEN TO GO

Jerusalem, like Israel in general, is a year-round destination, but the very best months are late March through April, and October through November, when prices are lower and the weather is good, even warm. Winter is colder than in Tel Aviv, but sunny days often follow gloomy ones. Jerusalem gets its own back in the hot, rainless summer months; the inland capital is dry and cools off toward evening. Avoid the main Jewish holidays, when hotels charge peak prices and many tourist attractions change schedules.

PLANNING YOUR TIME

Israel itineraries tend to favor Jerusalem. The Old City alone offers an absorbing two days. Beyond its religious shrines are ancient sites, panoramic walks, and museums. Allow time for poking around the Arab market and the stores of the Jewish Quarter. The immediate environs—the City of David, Mt. of Olives, Mt. Zion, and a few sites north of the Old City walls—can add a day or more. West Jerusalem's spread-out attractions take patience to explore. Add time for shopping and you're quickly up to a five- to six-day stay. Jerusalem is also a convenient base for day trips to Masada and the Dead Sea, and even Tel Aviv.

A few tips for maximizing your time: Make a list of must-see sights. Pay attention to opening times and plot out your day's destinations to minimize backtracking. Mix experiences each day, to avoid overdosing on museums, shrines, or archaeology. Above all, take time to let your senses absorb the city. Take time to walk around and sip a coffee at a sidewalk café. Jerusalem is as much about atmosphere as it is a checklist of world-class sights.

TRAVEL PRECAUTIONS

Violence against individuals is rare and tourists aren't specific targets. Nevertheless, avoid Muslim Quarter backstreets, and be cautious walking around the Old City at night (when almost everything is closed anyway). The important weekly Muslim prayers around midday Friday sometimes get passionate if there's a hot Palestinian-Israeli issue in the news. Emotions can spill into the streets of the Muslim Quarter as the crowds leave the al-Aqsa Mosque.

As in any major tourist destination, pickpockets can be a problem: keep purses closed and close to you, and wallets in less accessible pockets. Don't leave valuables in parked cars, and use hotel safes.

GETTING HERE AND AROUND

AIR TRAVEL

See Getting Here and Around in Travel Smart Israel for information about air travel to Israel.

BUS TRAVEL

Taking the bus from Ben Gurion Airport to Jerusalem is cheap but slow. Board the Egged shuttle (line 5, fare NIS 5.5) for a 10-minute ride to the Ben Gurion Airport El Al Junction, and wait for the Egged bus (line 947, fare NIS 24). It drops you off at Jerusalem's Central Bus Station. An easier, but often tediously long, alternative is taking one of the 10-seat *sherut* taxis (limo-vans). They depart from Ben Gurion Airport as soon as they fill up and drop you at any Jerusalem address for NIS 62.

Egged operates the extensive bus service within Jerusalem. The fare is NIS 6.60 for 90 minutes of travel on all buses and the light rail within the city; you don't need exact change. A cab is more time-effective and for a group often more cost-effective as well. Egged operates Route 99, a two-hour circle tour of Jerusalem for visitors with 24 stops. The route begins at the Central Bus Station; the cost is NIS 60 for one full trip or NIS 80 for hop on/hop off. Intercity buses travel all over the country from the Central Bus Station. Buses leave every 10 minutes for Tel Aviv and the fare is NIS 30.60 round-trip. ■TIP➜ Buying tickets at the counter is time-consuming and confusing. Buy your ticket or round-trip to Tel Aviv at the platform or on the bus.

Bus Contacts **Egged** ☎ *2800 ⊕ www.egged.co.il/eng.

CAR TRAVEL

By car, Route 1 is the chief route to Jerusalem. Route 443 via Modi'in is often quicker, although it passes through the West Bank and you must stop at an Israeli army checkpoint.

Walking and taking cabs or a guide-driven tourist limo-van are often more time-effective than a car in the city.

LIGHT RAIL TRAVEL

Jerusalem's single light rail line, an efficient way to navigate parts of central Jerusalem, begins at Pisgat Zeev in the north and runs via French Hill and the Damascus Gate along Jaffa Street to the Central Bus Station. It then heads southwest over the Bridge of Strings and terminates at Mt. Herzl. The trains operate Sunday to Thursday between

5:30 am and midnight; service ceases Friday at 2:15 pm, resuming on Saturday at 6 pm. A single ticket can be purchased from machines at each station and allows unlimited rides on city buses and trains for 90 minutes. However, there aren't enough machines, and they're difficult to use. It's easier to purchase a ticket on a bus and then use it for the train as well. If you're staying for more than a couple of days, buy a Rav-Kav multiticket for bus and train from the Central Bus Station. A photo ID is required for purchase.

Information CityPass ☎ *073/210–0601* ⊕ *www.citypass.co.il/english.*

TAXI TRAVEL

There's a flat fare for taxis from the airport, currently NIS 262 during the day and NIS 312 at night.

Taxis can be flagged on the street, ordered by phone, or picked up at a taxi stand or at major hotels. The law requires taxi drivers to use their meters.

TRAIN TRAVEL

Train service from Jerusalem's Malcha Train Station to Tel Aviv is infrequent—just five trains daily, with none between Friday afternoon and Saturday afternoon—and takes about 80 minutes. The round-trip fare to Tel Aviv is NIS 40.50.

RESTAURANTS

While the range of Jerusalem eateries will never rival that of cosmopolitan Tel Aviv, you can eat very well in the holy city. Middle Eastern food is a strong suit. Modern Israeli fare draws on the plethora of fresh produce and the local emphasis on seasonal fruits and vegetables. Proportionately, there are far more kosher establishments than in Tel Aviv, but fear not: the food can be just as varied and delicious, and the dietary restrictions often hardly noticeable.

HOTELS

Accommodations range from cheap and simple to high-end deluxe in a variety of settings, from the city center to the almost-rural periphery. Where possible, avoid Jewish holidays—especially the one-week holidays of Passover (March or April) and Sukkot (September or October), when hotels are full and prices peak.

TOURS

BIKE TOURS

Fodor's Choice ★ **Midnight Biking Through Jerusalem.** Tour guide Moshe Gold runs this venture, which features two- to three-hour tours through the streets of Jerusalem. The rides, beginning at 9:30 pm, are for ages 12 and up. Led by licensed English and Hebrew-speaking guides, they can be customized according to your interests. ⊠ *Yanovsky St., Haas Promenade parking lot, Talpiot Industrial Zone* ☎ *054/636–2884* ⊕ *www.jerusalembiking.com.*

ORIENTATION TOURS

Veteran nationwide tour operators Egged Tours and United Tours offer similar half-day Jerusalem orientation tours, including a panoramic view and Old City highlights. Except for Saturday, full-day tours usually add Yad Vashem. Some itineraries have a particular Christian orientation. Prices are usually quoted in U.S. dollars. The approximate cost is $46 for a half-day tour and $68 for a full day, though some run as much as $89. The price includes pick-up from major hotels.

Tour Contacts Egged Tours ☎ *03/694–8888* ⊕ *www.egged.co.il/eng.* **United Tours** ☎ *03/617–3315* ⊕ *www.unitedtours.co.il.*

PRIVATE GUIDES

The daily rate for a private guide with an air-conditioned car, limousine, or seven-passenger van is $500 to $650; add another $100 for bigger vans. Many guides will offer their services without a car for $300 to $400 per day. For a private tour, approach Genesis 2000.

Contacts Genesis 2000 ☎ *052/286–2650, 052/381–4484, 02/676–5868* ⊕ *www.genesis2000.co.il.*

WALKING TOURS

Zion Walking Tours is best known for its topic-focused Old City walking tours, but some of its eight routes venture well beyond the walls. Another option is Egged's Route 99 bus, a two-hour circle tour of Jerusalem.

Contacts Zion Walking Tours ✉ *Inside Jaffa Gate, opposite police station, Jaffa Gate* ☎ *02/627–7588* ⊕ *zionwt.dpages.co.il.*

VISITOR INFORMATION

Jerusalem's Tourist Information Office is open Saturday to Thursday 8:30 to 5 and Friday 8:30 to 1:30. The Christian Information Centre is open weekdays 8:30 to 5:30 and Saturday 8:30 to 12:30.

Contacts Christian Information Centre ✉ *Jaffa Gate, Armenian Patriarchate St., Jaffa Gate* ☎ *02/627–2692* ⊕ *www.cicts.org.* **Tourist Information Office** ✉ *Jaffa Gate, Omar Ben el-Hatab St., Jaffa Gate* ☎ *02/627–1422* ⊕ *tour.jerusalem.muni.il.*

EXPLORING JERUSALEM

Immerse yourself in Jerusalem. Of course, you can see the primary sights in a couple of days—some visitors claim to have done it in less—but don't short-change yourself if you can help it. Take time to wander where the spirit takes you, to linger longer over a snack and people-watch, to follow the late Hebrew poet, Yehuda Amichai, "in the evening into the Old City / and . . . emerge from it pockets stuffed with images / and metaphors and well-constructed parables . . ." The poet struggled for breath in an atmosphere "saturated with prayers and dreams"; but the city's baggage of history and religion doesn't have to weigh you down. Decompress in the markets and eateries of the Old City, and the jewelry and art stores, coffee shops, and pubs of the New.

Jerusalem beyond its ancient walls is a city of neighborhoods. Several are picturesque or quaint enough to attract the casual daytime visitor, but hold little interest once the sun goes down: the upscale Talbieh–Yemin Moshe area is a good example. Two hives of activity after dark are the Downtown complex of the Ben-Yehuda Street pedestrian mall (*midrachov*) and Nahalat Shiva, and Emek Refa'im, the main artery of the German Colony.

The city is built on a series of hills, part of the country's north–south watershed. To the east, the Judean Desert tumbles down to the Dead Sea, the lowest point on Earth, less than an hour's drive away. The main highway to the west winds down through the pine-covered Judean Hills toward the international airport and Tel Aviv. North and south of the city—Samaria and Judea, respectively—is what is known today as the West Bank. Since 1967, this contested area has been administered largely by Israel, though the major concentrations of Arab population are currently under autonomous Palestinian control.

OLD CITY: THE CLASSIC SIGHTS

Drink in the very essence of Jerusalem as you explore the city's primary religious sites in the Muslim and Christian quarters, and at the Western Wall, and touch the different cultures that share it. The Old City's 35,000 inhabitants jostle in the cobblestone lanes with an air of ownership, at best merely tolerating the "intruders" from other quarters. Devout Jews in black and white scurry from their neighborhoods north and west of the Old City, through the Damascus Gate and the Muslim Quarter, toward the Western Wall. Arab women in long, embroidered dresses flow across the Western Wall plaza to Dung Gate and the village of Silwan beyond it. It's not unusual to stand at the Western Wall, surrounded by the sounds of devotions, and hear the piercing call to prayer of the Muslim *muezzin* above you, with the more distant bells of the Christian Quarter providing a counterpoint.

Sites such as the Western Wall, Calvary, and the Haram esh-Sharif bring the thrill of recognition to ancient history. The devout can't fail to be moved by the holy city, and its special, if sometimes dissonant, moods and modes of devotion tend to fascinate the nonbeliever as well.

GETTING HERE AND AROUND

To explore the key sites in one day, keep in mind opening times and geography, and plan accordingly. Heading to Dung Gate first thing in the morning will get the Western Wall area and the Temple Mount (Muslim shrines) off the list. Exit the northern end of the mount to the Via Dolorosa and Holy Sepulcher. Jaffa Gate will take you right to the Holy Sepulcher and on to the Western Wall but poses a problem of timing for the Temple Mount. Lions' Gate is best for beginning with the Via Dolorosa, and fine for everything else except the Temple Mount. With some initial walking through the bazaar, Damascus Gate allows you to choose your preferred sequence of sights. Of course, you can spread your visit over more than one day.

TIMING AND PRECAUTIONS

Avoid the Via Dolorosa, much of which runs through the Muslim Quarter, between noon and 2 pm Fridays, the time of important weekly Muslim prayers. All the holy places demand modest dress: no shorts and no sleeveless tops.

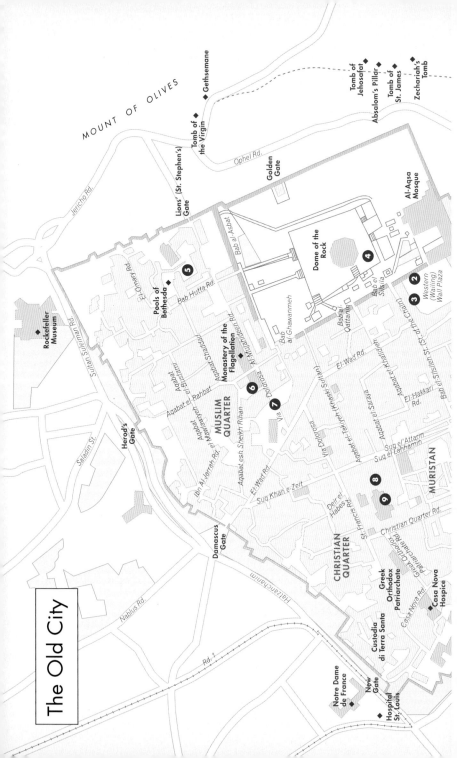

The Old City

MOUNT OF OLIVES

Tomb of Jehosafat

Absalom's Pillar

Tomb of St. James

Zechariah's Tomb

Gethsemane

Tomb of the Virgin

Jericho Rd.

Ophel Rd.

Lions' (St. Stephen's) Gate

Golden Gate

Al-Aqsa Mosque

Bab al-Asbat

Dome of the Rock

4

Rockefeller Museum

Sultan Suleiman Rd.

Pools of Bethesda

5

El-Omary Rd.

Bab Hutta Rd.

Bab el-Silsila

2

3

Western (Wailing) Wall Plaza

Monastery of the Flagellation

Al Mujahideen Rd.

Aqabat Shaddad

Aqabat el-Bustami

Bab al-Ghawanmeh

Bab el-Silsileh St. (St. of the Chain)

Bab Qattanin

Herod's Gate

Aqabat el-Mawianyeh

Aqabat el-Rahbat

6

Via Dolorosa

7

El-Wad Rd.

Aqabat el-Khalidieh

El-Hakkari Rd.

Saladin St.

MUSLIM QUARTER

Ibn Al-Jarrah Rd.

Aqabat esh Sheikh Rihan

Via Dolorosa

Aqabat el-Takiyeh (Khaski Sultan)

Aqabat el-Saraya

El-Wad Rd.

Suq el'Attarin

Suq el Lahhamin

Damascus Gate

Suq Khan E-Zeit

Deir el Habes Rd.

St. Francis Rd.

8

9

MURISTAN

CHRISTIAN QUARTER

Hatzanhanim

Christian Quarter Rd.

Greek Orthodox Patriarchate

Greek Orthodox Patriarchate Rd.

Casa Nova Rd.

Casa Nova Hospice

Nablus Rd.

Custodia di Terra Santa

Notre Dame de France

New Gate

Hospital St. Louis

Rd. 1

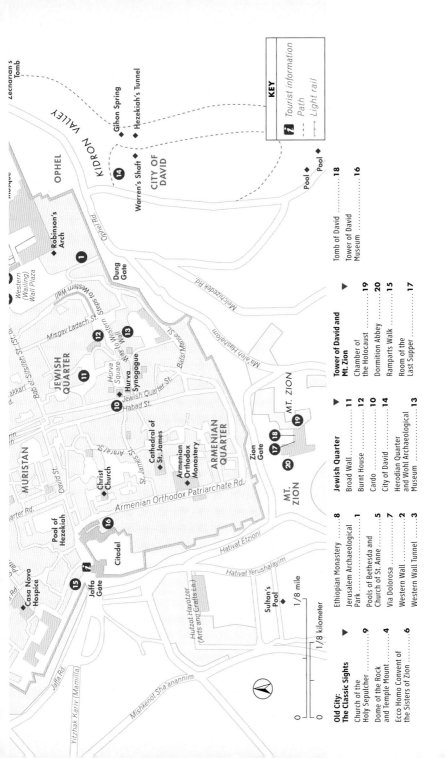

Old City:
The Classic Sights ▶

Church of the
Holy Sepulcher 9
Dome of the Rock
and Temple Mount 4
Ecco Homo Convent of
the Sisters of Zion 6

Ethiopian Monastery 8
Jerusalem Archaeological
Park 1
Pools of Bethesda and
Church of St. Anne 5
Via Dolorosa 7
Western Wall 2
Western Wall Tunnel 3

Jewish Quarter ▶

Broad Wall 11
Burnt House 12
Cardo 10
City of David 14
Herodian Quarter
and Wohl Archaeological
Museum 13

Tower of David and
Mt. Zion ▶

Chamber of
the Holocaust 19
Dormition Abbey 20
Ramparts Walk 15
Room of the
Last Supper 17

Tomb of David 18
Tower of David
Museum 16

KEY

🛈 *Tourist information*
-- - *Path*
── *Light rail*

TOP ATTRACTIONS

Fodor's Choice ★　**Church of the Holy Sepulcher.** *For information about the church, see the feature "Jerusalem: Keeping the Faith" in this chapter.*

Fodor's Choice ★　**Dome of the Rock and Temple Mount.** *For information about these sites, see the feature "Jerusalem: Keeping the Faith" in this chapter.*

Jerusalem Archaeological Park. A gold mine for Israeli archaeologists, this site's most dramatic and monumental finds were from the Herodian period, the late 1st century BC. The low-rise, air-conditioned **Davidson Visitors Center** (on your right as you enter the site) offers visual aids, some artifacts, two interesting videos (which alternate between English and Hebrew), and restrooms. It's a good place to start your visit if you're on your own. Allow 30 minutes for the center and another 40 minutes for the site.

The best place to start a tour is the high corner facing you. King Herod the Great rebuilt the Second Temple on the exact site of its predecessor, where the Dome of the Rock now stands. He expanded the sacred enclosure by constructing a massive, shoebox-shaped retaining wall on the slopes of the hill, the biblical Mt. Moriah. The inside was filled with thousands of tons of rubble to create the huge plaza, the size of 27 football fields, known today as the Temple Mount. The stones near the corner, with their signature precision-cut borders, aren't held together with mortar; their sheer weight gives the structure its stability. The original wall was at least a third higher than it is today.

To the left of the corner is the white pavement of an impressive main street and commercial area from the Second Temple period. The protrusion high above your head is known as **Robinson's Arch,** named for a 19th-century American explorer. It's a remnant of a monumental bridge to the Temple Mount that was reached by a staircase from the street where you now stand: look for the ancient steps. The square-cut building stones heaped on the street came from the top of the original wall, dramatic evidence of the Roman destruction of AD 70. A piece of Hebrew scriptural graffiti (Isaiah 66:14) was etched into a stone, possibly by a Jewish pilgrim, some 15 centuries ago.

Climb the wooden steps and turn left. A modern spiral staircase descends below present ground level to a partially reconstructed labyrinth of Byzantine dwellings, mosaics and all; from here you reemerge outside the present city walls. The broad, impressive **Southern Steps** on your left, a good part of them original, once brought hordes of Jewish pilgrims through the now-blocked southern gates of the Temple Mount. The rock-hewn ritual baths near the bottom of the steps were used for the purification rites once demanded of Jews before they entered the sacred temple precincts. ▮ TIP➡ April to September, this section of the site closes at noon; October to March it closes at 11 am. ⊠ *Dung Gate, Old City* ☎ *02/627-7550* ⊕ *www.archpark.org.il* ⌑ *NIS 30* ☾ *Sun.– Thurs. 8–5, Fri. and Jewish holiday eves 8–2.*

Via Dolorosa. Commonly called the "Way of the Cross" in English, *Via Dolorosa* literally translates as "the Way of Suffering." It's venerated as the route Jesus walked, carrying his cross, from the place of his trial and condemnation by Pontius Pilate to the site of his crucifixion and burial. (Stations I and II are where the Antonia fortress once stood, widely regarded as the site of the "praetorium" referred to in the Gospels.) The present tradition jelled no earlier than the 18th century, but it draws on much older beliefs. Some of the incidents represented by the 14 Stations of the Cross are scriptural; others (III, IV, VI, VII, and IX) aren't. Tiny chapels mark a few of the stations; the last five are inside the Church of the Holy Sepulcher. Catholic pilgrim groups, or the Franciscan-led Friday afternoon procession, take about 45 minutes to wind their way through the busy market streets of the Muslim and Christian quarters, with prayers and chants at each station.

Here are the 14 stations on the Via Dolorosa that mark the route that Jesus took, from trial and condemnation to crucifixion and burial. *For a map of the Via Dolorosa, see the feature "Jerusalem: Keeping the Faith" in this chapter.*

Station I. Jesus is tried and condemned by Pontius Pilate.

Station II. Jesus is scourged and given the cross.

Station III. Jesus falls for the first time. (Soldiers of the Free Polish Forces built the chapel after World War II.)

Station IV. Mary embraces Jesus.

Station V. Simon of Cyrene picks up the cross.

Station VI. A woman wipes the face of Jesus, whose image remains on the cloth. (She is remembered as Veronica, apparently derived from the words *vera* and *icon,* meaning "true image.")

Station VII. Jesus falls for the second time. (The chapel contains one of the columns of the Byzantine Cardo, the main street of 6th-century Jerusalem.)

Station VIII. Jesus addresses the women in the crowd.

Station IX. Jesus falls for the third time.

Station X. Jesus is stripped of his garments.

Station XI. Jesus is nailed to the cross.

Station XII. Jesus dies on the cross.

Station XIII. Jesus is taken down from the cross.

Station XIV. Jesus is buried.

✉ *Muslim and Christian Quarters.*

NEED A BREAK?

Holy Rock Café. Between the Stations VI and VII of the Via Dolorosa is the very good Holy Rock Café. The name may be a little hokey, but there's nothing wrong with its freshly squeezed orange and pomegranate juice (in season), Turkish coffee, mint tea, and superb *bourma,* a round Arab confection filled with whole pistachio nuts. ✉ *Via Dolorosa, Between Stations VI and VII, Muslim Quarter.*

CLOSE UP

A Walk on the Via Dolorosa

The Old City's main Jewish and Muslim sites can be visited individually, but the primary Christian shrines—the **Via Dolorosa** (or Way of the Cross) and the Holy Sepulcher—are best experienced in sequence. This walk will keep you oriented in the confusing marketplace through which the Via Dolorosa winds its way. (Beware of slick pickpockets.) The route takes a leisurely 30 minutes; plan additional time if you want to linger at specific sites. About 200 yards up the road from St. Anne's Church (near Lions' Gate), look for a ramp on your left leading to the dark metal door of a school. This is the site of the ancient Antonia fortress. On Friday afternoons at 4 (April to September; at 3 from October to March), the brown-robed Franciscans begin their procession of the Via Dolorosa outside the metal door. This is Station I; Station II is across the street. Just beyond it, on the right, is the entrance to the **Ecce Homo Convent of the Sisters of Zion**, with a Roman arch in the chapel. The continuation of the arch crosses the street outside; just beyond it, a small vestibule on the right has a view of the chapel's interior.

The Via Dolorosa runs down into El-Wad Road, one of the Old City's most important thoroughfares. To the right, the street climbs toward the Damascus Gate; to the left, it passes through the heart of the Muslim Quarter and reaches the Western Wall. Black-hatted Hasidic Jews hurry on divine missions, nimble local Muslim kids in T-shirts and jeans play in the street, and Christian pilgrims pace out ancient footsteps.

As you turn left onto El-Wad Road, Station III is on your left. Right next to it is Station IV and, on the next corner, 50 yards farther, Station V. There the Via Dolorosa turns right and begins its ascent toward Calvary. Halfway up the street, a brown wooden door on your left marks Station VI.

Facing you at the top of the stepped street, on the busy Suq Khan e-Zeit, is Station VII. The little chapel preserves one of the columns of the Byzantine Cardo (street). Step to the left, and walk 30 yards up the street facing you to Station VIII, marked by nothing more than an inscribed stone in the wall on the left. Return to the main street and turn right. (If you skip Station VIII, turn left as you reach Station VII from the stepped street.) One hundred yards along Suq Khan e-Zeit from Station VII, turn onto the ramp on your right that ascends parallel to the street. (The clutter of market merchandise makes it easy to miss.) At the end of the lane is a column that represents Station IX.

Step through the open door to the left of the column into the courtyard of the **Ethiopian Monastery** known as Deir es-Sultan. From the monastery's upper chapel, descend through a lower one and out a small wooden door to the court of the **Church of the Holy Sepulcher.** Most Christians venerate this site as that of the death, burial, and resurrection of Jesus—you'll find Stations X, XI, XII, XIII, and XIV within the church. A good time to be here is in the late afternoon, after 4 pm, when the different denominations in turn chant their way between Calvary and the tomb. *For more information on the sights in bold type, see the listings in the Old City section; see the feature "Jerusalem: Keeping the Faith" for a map.*

Fodor's Choice   **Western Wall.** *For information about this sight, see the "Jerusalem: Keep-*
★   *ing the Faith" feature in this chapter.*

Western Wall Tunnel. The long tunnel beyond the men's side of the Western Wall isn't a rediscovered ancient thoroughfare but was deliberately dug in recent years with the purpose of exposing a strip of the
2,000-year-old Western Wall along its entire length. The massive construction, part of a retaining wall of King Herod's Temple Mount,
includes two building stones estimated to weigh an incredible 400
tons and 570 tons, respectively. Local guided tours are available and
are recommended—you can visit the site only as part of an organized
tour—but the times change from week to week (some include evening
hours). The tour takes about 75 minutes; among the attractions are a
kinetic model of the Western Wall and some of the mammoth building
stones. During daylight hours, tours end at the beginning of the Via
Dolorosa, in the Muslim Quarter. After dark, that exit is closed, and
the tour retraces its steps through the tunnel. The ticket office is under
the arches at the northern end of the Western Wall plaza. ⊠ *North
of Western Wall, Western Wall* ☎ *02/627–1333* ⊕ *english.thekotel.org*
⊠ *NIS 30* ⊙ *Sun.–Thurs. 7 am–late evening (changing schedules), Fri.
and Jewish holiday eves 7–noon. Call ahead for exact times of tours.*

WORTH NOTING

Ecce Homo Convent of the Sisters of Zion. The arch that crosses the Via
Dolorosa, just beyond Station II, continues into the chapel of the adjacent convent. It was once thought to have been the gate of Herod's
Antonia fortress, perhaps the spot where the Roman governor Pontius Pilate presented Jesus to the crowd with the words *"Ecce homo!"*
("Behold, the man!"). Recent scholarship has determined otherwise:
it was a triumphal arch built by the Roman emperor Hadrian in the
2nd century AD.

The basement of the convent has several points of interest: an impressive reservoir with a barrel-vault roof, apparently built by Hadrian in
the moat of Herod's older Antonia fortress; a small but attractive collection of ancient artifacts found on site; and the famous *lithostratos*,
or stone pavement, etched with games played by Roman legionnaires.
The origin of one such diversion—the notorious Game of the King—
called for the execution of a mock king, a sequence tantalizingly reminiscent of the New Testament description of the treatment of Jesus by
the Roman soldiers. Contrary to tradition, however, the pavement of
large, foot-worn brown flagstones is apparently not from Jesus' day, but
was laid down a century later. Allow 30 minutes for the visit. ⊠ *41 Via
Dolorosa, Muslim Quarter* ☎ *02/627–7292* ⊕ *www.eccehomoconvent.
org* ⊠ *NIS 9* ⊙ *Daily 8–5.*

Ethiopian Monastery. Stand in the monastery's courtyard beneath the
medieval bulge of the Church of the Holy Sepulcher, and you have a
cross-section of Christendom. The adjacent Egyptian Coptic monastery peeks through the entrance gate, and a Russian Orthodox gable,
a Lutheran bell tower, and the crosses of Greek Orthodox, Armenian
Orthodox, and Roman Catholic churches break the skyline.

Continued on page 86

JERUSALEM: KEEPING THE FAITH

Unforgotten and unforgettable, the city of Jerusalem is holy ground for the three great monotheistic religions, whose numbers embrace half the world's population. Its Old City is home to some of the most sacred sites of Judaism, Christianity, and Islam: the Western Wall, the Temple Mount/Haram esh-Sharif, the Church of the Holy Sepulcher, and the Dome of the Rock and Al-Aqsa Mosque. Some travelers visit them to find their soul, others to seek a sense of communion with ancient epochs. Whether pilgrim or tourist, you'll discover that history, faith, and culture commingle here as perhaps nowhere else on earth.

By Mike Rogoff

(right) The Western Wall, (opposite left) Dome of the Church of the Holy Sepulcher, (opposite right) The Dome of the Rock

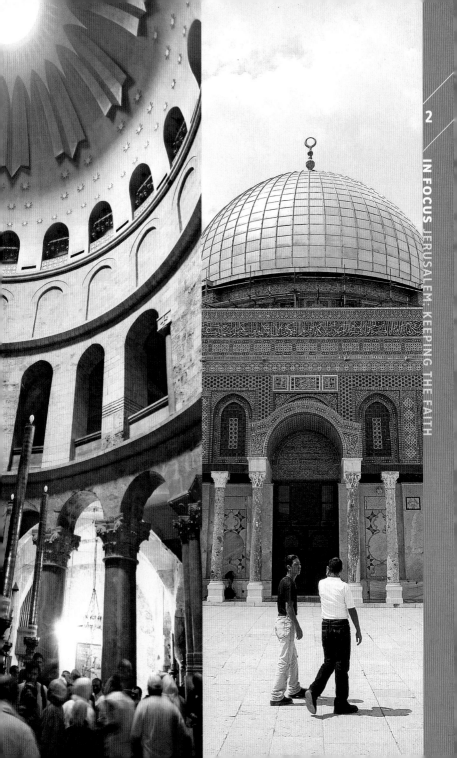

ONE CITY UNDER GOD

Jerusalem is a composite of three faith-civilizations: Jewish, Christian, and Muslim. They cohabit the Old City uneasily, burdened by centuries of struggle with each other for rights and real estate. But at the level of day-to-day routine, each draws its adherents to, respectively, the Western Wall, the Church of the Holy Sepulcher, and the Al-Aqsa Mosque. To the visitor, the collage of spiritual traditions is often bewildering, sometimes alien, always fascinating. The intricate choreographies of devotion have been known to move nonbelievers as well as the devout.

HISTORY AND HOLY STONES

Wander the cobblestone lanes of historical Jerusalem and you can hear in your mind's ear the echoes of King David's harp, trace the revered footsteps of Jesus of Nazareth, and sense

(left) Woman praying, (top right) Miracle of Holy Fire, Church of the Holy Sepulcher, (bottom right) Men praying near the Dome of the Rock

the presence of the Prophet Muhammad. In the space of just a few hours, you can visit Golgotha and the tomb of Jesus, gaze at the shrine that caps "the farthermost place" from which Islam's founder rose to heaven, and stand before the only extant remnant of the Second Temple compound. Not without reason do some visitors imagine their fold-out atlases to be road maps leading to heaven itself.

Great dramas played out on these stones—occasionally, it is claimed, on the very same stone. The rock capped by the gold dome is the summit of Mt. Moriah, identified in Jewish tradition with the biblical site where Abraham erected an altar and prepared to sacrifice his son Isaac. It was here on the Temple Mount that the "First" and "Second" Jewish Temples stood for a total of one thousand years. In the same rock, devout Muslims point to the imprint of a foot, regarded as that of Muhammad himself, as evidence that it was here that the Prophet ascended to heaven for his meeting with God. The Dome of the Rock and the nearby Al-Aqsa Mosque enshrine that tradition.

On the one hand, Jerusalem is a layer-cake of time, each period leaving distinct strata. The biblical kings David and Solomon transformed a small and already-ancient Jebusite town into an important metropolis. The march of history proceeded through destruction and the Babylonian captivity, Hellenization, Roman rule and another destruction, Byzantine Christianity, the Muslim invasions, the 12th-century Crusades, the Muslim reconquest, European rediscovery of the Holy Land and British control, and down to Jerusalem's contemporary status as the capital (though some dispute it) of the State of Israel.

At another level—change the metaphor—Jerusalem is a complex tangle, a Gordian knot of related but competing faith traditions, historical narratives, and national dreams. The knot seems fated to be around for a while yet, with

no hero in sight to slice it through with one bold stroke.

FINDING YOUR FEET

Each of the three religious sites is infused with its own unique tradition. Making a connection between these stone structures of the past and the wellsprings of religious faith or cultural identity can be uplifting. Many pilgrims focus on their own shrines; some take the time to explore the others so close at hand. The Western Wall is just steps from the Jerusalem Archaeological Park, where excavations turned up remnants of King Herod the Great's grand structures that Jesus almost certainly knew. The ramp between the Western Wall and the park leads up to the vast plaza—the Temple Mount or Haram esh-Sharif—now dominated by the Muslim shrines. Any of the gates at its far northern end will deposit you on the Via Dolorosa. A twenty-minute stroll through the bustling bazaar brings you to the Church of the Holy Sepulcher, revered as the site of Jesus' death and burial.

Whichever site you start with (this feature lists them in historical order: Wall, Church, Dome), a tour of all three unfailingly provokes a powerful appreciation of Jerusalem as an epicenter of faith.

Israelites enslaved during the Babylonian Captivity after the fall of Jerusalem in 586 BC

THE WESTERN WALL

No Jewish shrine is holier than the Western Wall, the remains of the ancient Second Temple compound, whose stones are saturated with centuries of prayers and tears.

 The status of the Western Wall as the most important existing Jewish shrine derives from its connection with the ancient Temple, the House of God. The 2,000-year-old Wall was not itself part of the Temple edifice, but of the massive retaining wall King Herod built to create the vast plaza now known as the Temple Mount.

After the destruction of Jerusalem by the Romans in AD 70, and especially after the dedication of a pagan town in its place 65 years later, the city became off-limits to Jews for generations. The precise location of the Temple—

in the vicinity of today's Dome of the Rock—was lost. Even when access was regained, Jews avoided entering the Temple Mount out of fear of trespassing on the most sacred, and thus forbidden, areas of the ancient sanctuary. With time, the closest remnant of the period took on the aura of the Temple itself, making the Western Wall a kind of holy place by proxy.

Jewish visitors often just refer to the site as "the Wall" (*Kotel* in Hebrew); "Wailing Wall" is a Gentile term, describing the sight—once more common—of devout Jews grieving for God's House. For many Jews, the ancient Temple was as much a national site as a religious one, and its destruction as much a national trauma as a religious cataclysm.

(top) Jewish man praying at the Western Wall, (right) Western Wall

VISITING THE WALL

The swaying and praying of the devout reveal the powerful hold this place has on the hearts and minds of many Jews.

On Monday and Thursday mornings, the Wall bubbles with colorful bar-mitzvah ceremonies, when Jewish families celebrate the coming of age of their 13-year-old sons. The excitement is still greater on Friday evenings just after sunset, when the young men of a nearby yeshiva, a Jewish seminary, often come dancing and singing down to the Wall to welcome in the "Sabbath bride." The fervor reaches its highest point three times a year during the three Jewish pilgrimage festivals—Passover, Sukkot (Feast of Tabernacles), and Shavuot (Feast of Weeks), when many Jews come to pray. But many people find that it's only when the crowds have gone (the Wall is floodlit at night and always open), and you share the warm, prayer-drenched stones with just a handful of bearded stalwarts or kerchiefed women, that the true spirituality of the Western Wall is palpable.

The Wall precinct functions under the aegis of the rabbinic authorities, with all the trappings of an Orthodox synagogue. Modest dress is required (men must cover their heads in the prayer area), there is segregation of men and women in prayer, and smoking and photography on the Sabbath and religious holidays are prohibited. Expect a routine check of your bags. ✉ In the southeast corner of the Old City; accessible from Dung Gate, the Jewish Quarter, and the Muslim Quarter's El-Wad St. and the Street of the Chain ⊕ http://english.thekotel. org ⊘ 24 hrs daily.

NOTES IN THE WALL

The cracks between the massive stones of the Western Wall are stuffed with slips of paper bearing prayers and petitions. "They reach their destination more quickly than the Israeli postal service," it has been said, with a mixture of serious faith and light cynicism. The cracks are cleared several times a year, but the slips are never simply dumped. Since they often contain God's name, and are written from the heart, the slips are collected in a sack and buried with reverence in a Jewish cemetery.

THE TEMPLE MOUNT, OR HARAM ESH-SHARIF

The size of 27 football fields, the Temple Mount is the vast plaza constructed around the Second Temple in the late 1st century BC by King Herod the Great.

In order to rebuild the Temple on a grand scale, and significantly expand the courts around it, Herod leveled off the top of Mt. Moriah with thousands of tons of rubble. The massive retaining walls include some of the largest building stones known. Structurally, the famous Western Wall is simply the western side of the huge shoebox-like project.

Some scholars regard the Temple Mount as perhaps the greatest religious enclosure of the ancient world, and the

(top) Aerial view of the Jewish Quarter and the Temple Mount, (top left) Al-Aqsa Mosque, (top right) Drawing of a reconstruction of the First Temple

splendid Temple, the one Jesus knew, as an architectural wonder of its day. The Romans reduced the building to smoldering ruins in the summer of AD 70, in the last stages of the Great Revolt of the Jews (AD 66–73). Many of its treasures, including the gold menorah, were carried off to Rome as booty.

Jewish tradition identifies the great rock at the summit of the hill—now under the golden Dome of the Rock—as the foundation stone of the world, and the place where Abraham bound and almost sacrificed his son Isaac (Genesis 22). With greater probability, this was where the biblical King David made a repentance offering to the Lord (II

Samuel 22), and where his son Solomon built "God's House," the so-called First Temple. The Second Temple stood on the identical spot, but the precise location of its innermost holy of holies is a question that engages religious Jews and archaeologists to this day.

Christian tradition adds the New Testament dimension. Here Jesus disputed points of law with other Jewish teachers, angrily overturned the tables of money changers, and, looking down at the Temple precinct from the Mount of Olives, predicted its destruction. The Byzantines seem to have neglected the place (perhaps believing it cursed); the medieval Templars took their name from the area in which they set up their headquarters.

Muslims identify it as "the farthermost place," from which Muhammad rose to heaven, and call this area Haram esh-Sharif, the Noble Sanctuary. (*See section on the Muslim shrines in this feature.*)

✉ Access between the Western Wall and Dung Gate, Temple Mount ☎ 02/662-6250 ☉ Apr.–Sept., Sun.–Thurs. 7:30 AM–11 AM and 1:30 PM–2:30 PM; Oct.–Mar., Sun.–Thurs. 7:30 AM–10 AM and 12:30 PM–1:30 PM, subject to change.

THE JERUSALEM ARCHAEOLOGICAL PARK

Immediately south of the Western Wall, in the shadow of the Temple Mount, is an important archaeological site, still popularly known as the Western and Southern Wall excavations. The dominant monumental structures were the work of King Herod the Great, some 2,000 years ago, though there are some Byzantine and early Arab buildings of interest. Robinson's Arch, named for a 19th-century American explorer, once supported a monumental stairway leading up to the Temple Mount. Also discovered were numerous "mikva'ot" (singular "mikveh," a Jewish ritual bath) and a Herodian street, once lined with shops. In the southern part of the site is the low-rise Davidson Visitors Center; its exhibits range from ancient artifacts to computer-animated recreations of the Second Temple. *For complete information, see the separate entry for Jerusalem Archaeological Park in this chapter.*

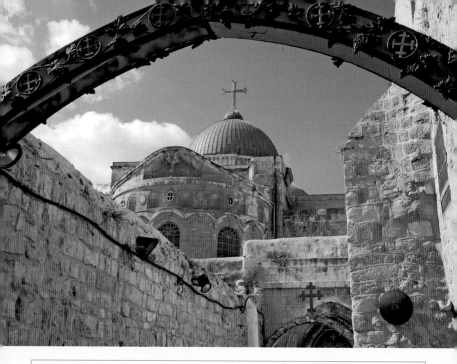

THE CHURCH OF THE HOLY SEPULCHER

Follow the footsteps of Jesus along the Via Dolorosa to the hallowed church that enshrines Golgotha—the hillside of Jesus' crucifixion, burial, and resurrection.

Vast numbers of Christians, especially adherents of the older "mainstream" churches, believe that this church marks the place where Jesus was crucified by the Romans and buried by his followers, and where he rose from the dead three days later. Some claim that the antiquity of the Holy Sepulcher tradition argues in favor of its authenticity, since the fervent early Christian community would have striven to preserve the memory of such an important site. The church is outside the city walls of Jesus' day—a vital point, for no executions or burials took place within Jerusalem's sacred precincts.

The site was officially consecrated, and the first church built here, following the visit in AD 326 by Helena, mother of the Byzantine emperor Constantine the Great. The present imposing structure, the fourth church on the site, was built by the Crusaders in the 12th century. Interior additions over the years have distorted the Gothic plan, but look for the Norman-style vault at the far end of the Greek Orthodox basilica (facing the tomb), and the ceiling of the dim corridor leading to the adjacent Catholic chapel. After a fire in 1808, much of the church was rebuilt in 19th-century style.

(top) Church of the Holy Sepulcher, (top right) Greek Orthodox chapel, Calvary, (bottom right) Monk kissing the Stone of Unction

HOLIEST LANDMARKS

On the floor just inside the entrance of the church is the rectangular pink **Stone of Unction**, where, it is said, the body of Jesus was cleansed and prepared for burial. Pilgrims often rub fabric or religious trinkets on the stone to absorb its sanctity, and take them home as mementos. Nearby steep steps take you up to **Golgotha**, or Calvary, meaning "the place of the skull," as the site is described in the New Testament. Up the steps, the chapel on the right is Roman Catholic: a window looks out at Station X of the Via Dolorosa, a wall mosaic at the front of the chapel depicts Jesus being nailed to the cross (Station XI), and a bust of Mary in a cabinet to the left of it represents Station XIII where Jesus was taken off the cross. The central chapel—all candlelight, oil lamps, and icons—is Greek Orthodox. Under the altar, and capping the rocky hillock on which you stand, is a silver disc with a hole, purportedly the place—Station XII—where the cross actually stood.

The **tomb** itself (Station XIV), encased in a pink marble edifice, is in the rotunda to the left of the main entrance of the church, under the great dome that dominates the Christian Quarter. The only hint of what the tomb must have been like 2,000 years ago is the ledge in the inner chamber (now covered with marble) on which Jesus' body would have been laid. You can see a more pristine example of an upscale Jewish tomb of the period in the gloomy Chapel of St. Nicodemus, opposite the Coptic chapel in the back of the sepulcher.

SHARING THE CHURCH

An astonishing peculiarity of the Holy Sepulcher is that it is shared, albeit unequally and uncomfortably, by six Christian denominations. Centuries of sometimes-violent competition for control of key Christian sites culminated in the Status Quo Agreement of 1852.

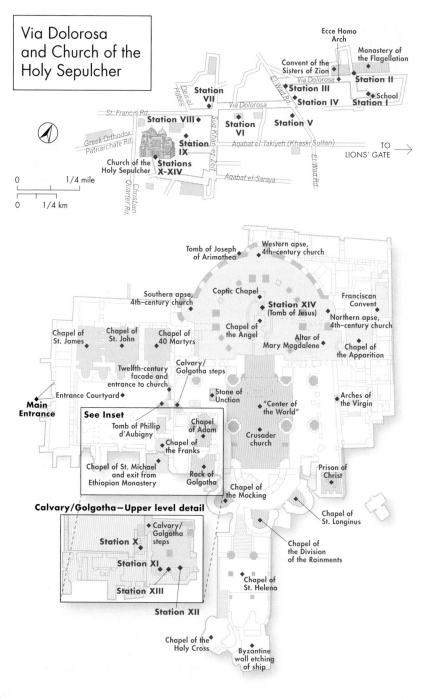

Via Dolorosa and Church of the Holy Sepulcher

Ecce Homo Arch

Monastery of the Flagellation

Convent of the Sisters of Zion

Station II

Station III

Station VII

Station IV

School

Station I

Via Dolorosa

Station VIII

Station VI

Station V

TO LIONS' GATE

St. Francis Rd.

Deir el-Habes

El Wad Rd.

Greek Orthodox Patriarchate Rd.

Station IX

Aqabat el-Takiyeh (Khaski Sultan)

Suq Khan-ez-Zeit

Church of the Holy Sepulcher

Stations X–XIV

Aqabat el-Saraya

Christian Quarter Rd.

0   1/4 mile

0   1/4 km

Tomb of Joseph of Arimathea

Western apse, 4th-century church

Southern apse, 4th-century church

Coptic Chapel

Station XIV (Tomb of Jesus)

Franciscan Convent

Chapel of St. James

Chapel of St. John

Chapel of 40 Martyrs

Chapel of the Angel

Northern apse, 4th-century church

Altar of Mary Magdalene

Chapel of the Apparition

Twelfth-century facade and entrance to church

Calvary/ Golgotha steps

Stone of Unction

"Center of the World"

Arches of the Virgin

Main Entrance

Entrance Courtyard

See Inset

Tomb of Phillip d'Aubigny

Chapel of Adam

Crusader church

Prison of Christ

Chapel of the Franks

Chapel of St. Michael and exit from Ethiopian Monastery

Rock of Golgotha

Chapel of the Mocking

Chapel of St. Longinus

Calvary/Golgotha—Upper level detail

Station X

Calvary/ Golgotha steps

Chapel of the Division of the Rainments

Station XI

Chapel of St. Helena

Station XIII

Station XII

Chapel of the Holy Cross

Byzantine wall etching of ship

Mosaic of Jesus near the Stone of Unction

Under the pressure of Orthodox Russia, the Ottoman Turks recognized the precedence of the Greek Orthodox as on-the-ground representatives of the Eastern Rite churches.

Each denomination guards its assigned privileges, and minor infringements by one of its neighbors can flare up into open hostility. At the same time, the phenomenon gives the place much of its color. Try visiting in the late afternoon (the exact time changes with the seasons), and watch the groups in turn— Greek Orthodox, Latins (as Roman Catholics are known in the Holy Land), Armenian Orthodox, and Egyptian Copts—in procession from Calvary to the tomb. The candlelight and swinging censers are passingly similar; the robes and lusty hymn-singing are different.

A modern agreement among the Greeks, the Latins, and the Armenians on the interior restoration of the great dome was hailed as a breakthrough in ecumenical relations, and it was rededicated in January, 1997 in an unprecedented interdenominational service. ✉ Between Suq Khan e-Zeit and Christian Quarter Rd., Christian Quarter ☎ 02/627-3314 ☜ Free ☉ Apr.–Sept., daily 5 AM–9 PM; Oct.–Mar., daily 4 AM–7 PM

SUGGESTIONS FOR YOUR VISIT

While the first nine Stations of the Cross are to be found along the Way of the Cross—the Via Dolorosa—the final and most holy ones are within the Church of the Holy Sepulcher itself. The best time to visit may be around 4PM when many denominations are found worshipping. *For more information, see the separate entry for the Via Dolorosa elsewhere in this chapter.*

As in many religious sites, modest dress and discreet behavior are required here, but it's difficult for the clergy of any particular community to assert authority. Come early or late to avoid the worst crowds; be patient, too. A small flashlight or some candles will help you explore the small tomb of St. Nicodemus, an authentic Jewish tomb of the period.

Entrance of the Church of the Holy Sepulcher

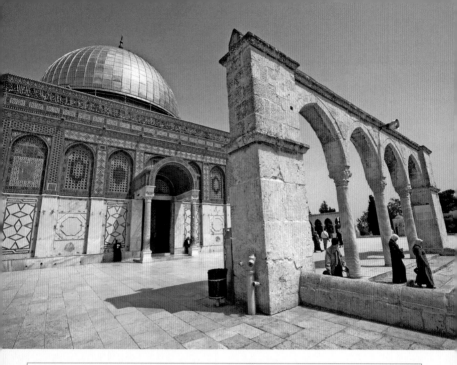

THE DOME OF THE ROCK AND AL-AQSA MOSQUE

The focal point of these sanctuaries, whose interiors are currently open only to Muslims, is the Rock—the place from which Muhammad is believed to have ascended to heaven to be given the divine precepts of Islam.

The magnificent golden **Dome of the Rock** dominates the vast 35-acre Temple Mount, the area known to Muslims as Haram esh-Sharif (the Noble Sanctuary). This is the original octagonal building, completed in AD 691. It enshrines the great rock—the summit of Mt. Moriah—from which the prophet Muhammad is said to have risen to heaven. Jerusalem is not mentioned in the Koran, but Muhammad's "Night Ride" is. Awakened by the archangel Gabriel, he was taken on the fabulous winged horse el-Burak to the *masjid al-aqsa*, the "farthermost place." From there he rose to heaven, met God face to face, received the teachings of Islam, and returned to Mecca the same night. Tradition has it that the *masjid al-aqsa* was none other than Jerusalem, and the great rock the very spot from which the prophet ascended.

To be sure, Muhammad's triumphant successors venerated Jerusalem's biblical sanctity; but some modern scholars suggest they did not like the feeling of being Johnnies-come-lately in the

(top) Eight *qanatirs* (arcades) stand by sets of steps leading to the Dome of the Rock, (top right) The rock, the Dome's central shrine

holy city of rival faiths. The impressive Dome of the Rock, built by the Ummayad caliph Abd el-Malik, was almost certainly intended to proclaim the ascendancy of the "true faith."

A SPLENDID SHRINE

Considering the original builders and craftsmen adopted the artistic traditions of their Byzantine predecessors, it's hardly surprising that the plan of the shrine resembles those of its Christian contemporaries, like the Byzantine Church of San Vitale in Ravenna, Italy. Take a close look at the bright exterior tiles in variegated shades of blue. The marvelous gold dome was restored in the 1990s, with 176 pounds of 24-carat gold electroplated on copper.

At the time of this writing, non-Muslims were denied entry to the interior of the building, with its beautiful granite columns supporting arches, some of which bear the original green-and-gold mosaics set in arabesque motifs. In obedience to Islamic religious tradition, no human or animal forms appear in the artwork. The mosaics were restored in 1027, but preserved much of the original work.

All this splendor was designed to emphasize the importance of the rock itself, directly under the great dome. The faithful reach out and touch an inden-

tation which, they believe, was nothing less than the Prophet's footprint, left there as he ascended to heaven.

THE THIRD-HOLIEST OF ALL

At the southern end of the Haram, immediately in front of you as you enter the area from the Western Wall plaza (the only gate for non-Muslims), is the large, black-domed **Al-Aqsa Mosque**. The Dome of the Rock is a shrine, the place where a hallowed event is believed to

THE DOME'S MOSAICS

Some of the Arabic inscriptions in the mosaics are quotations from the Koran; others are dedications. One of the latter originally lauded Abd el-Malik, caliph of the Damascus-based Ummayad dynasty, who built the shrine. Some 140 years later, the caliph of a rival dynasty removed el-Malik's name and replaced it with his own, but he neglected to change the date.

have taken place. Individuals go there to pray, but Al-Aqsa is a true mosque, attracting thousands of worshippers on Fridays and Muslim holidays. It is third in holiness for Muslims everywhere, after the great mosques of Mecca and Medina, both in Saudi Arabia.

Built by the Ummayad dynasty in the early 8th century AD, it has been destroyed and restored several times. In the 12th century, the Al-Aqsa Mosque became the headquarters of the Templars, a Crusader monastic order that took its name from the ancient temple that once stood nearby. The spot has been the setting for more recent dramas, most importantly the assassination of King Abdullah I of Jordan (the present king's great-grandfather) in 1951.

EXPLORING THE HARAM

The Haram today is a Muslim preserve, a legacy that dates back to AD 638, when the Arab caliph Omar Ibn-Khatib

seized Jerusalem from the Byzantines. At the time of this writing, the Muslim shrines were closed to non-Muslims indefinitely, leaving the faithful alone to enjoy their wondrous interiors.

Even if you can't get inside, the vast plaza is visually and historically arresting, and worth a visit. Fifteenth-century Mamluk buildings line the western edge. Overlooking the plaza at its northwestern corner is a long building, today an elementary school, built on the artificial scarp that protected Herod's Antonia fortress. Christian tradition, very possibly accurate, identifies the site as the praetorium where Jesus was tried.

Security check lines to enter the Haram esh-Sharif are often long; it's best to come early. Note that the Muslim attendants prohibit Bibles in the area. ✉ Access between the Western Wall and Dung Gate, Haram esh-Sharif, Temple Mount ☎ 02/622–6250 ☉ Apr.–Sept., Sun.–Thurs. 7:30 AM–11 AM and 1:30 PM–2:30 PM; Oct.–Mar., Sun.–Thurs. 7:30 AM–10 AM and 12:30 PM–1:30 PM, subject to change. Last entry 1 hr before closing.

(top) Parts of columns on the Haram, (right) Mosaics and arches grace the Dome's interior

The robed Ethiopian monks live in tiny cells in the rooftop monastery. One of the modern paintings in their small, dark church depicts the visit of the Queen of Sheba to King Solomon. Ethiopian tradition holds that more passed between the two than is related in the Bible— she came to "prove" his wisdom "with hard questions" (I Kings 10)— and that their supposed union produced an heir to both royal houses. The prince was met with hostility by Solomon's legitimate offspring, says the legend, and the king was compelled to send him home—with the precious Ark of the Covenant as a gift. To this day (say the Ethiopians), it remains in a sealed crypt in their homeland. The script in the paintings is Gehz, the ecclesiastical language of the Ethiopian church. Taking in the rooftop view and the church will occupy about 15 minutes. The exit, via a short stairway to a lower level, deposits you in the courtyard of the Church of the Holy Sepulcher. ⊠ *Suq Khan e-Zeit, on the roof of the Church of the Holy Sepulcher, Christian Quarter* 🖃 *Free* ☉ *Daily during daylight.*

Pools of Bethesda and Church of St. Anne. The transition is sudden and complete, from the raucous cobbled streets and persistent vendors to the pepper trees, flower beds, and birdsong of this serene Catholic cloister. The Romanesque **Church of St. Anne** was built by the Crusaders in 1140, and restored in the 19th century. Its austere and unadorned stone interior and extraordinarily reverberant acoustics make it one of the finest examples of medieval architecture in the country. According to local tradition, the Virgin Mary was born in the grotto over which the church is built, and the church is named after her mother. In the same compound are the excavated **Pools of Bethesda,** a large public reservoir in use during the 1st century BC and 1st century AD. The New Testament speaks of Jesus miraculously curing a lame man by "a pool, which is called in the Hebrew tongue Bethesda" (John 5). The actual bathing pools were the small ones, east of the reservoir, but it was over the big pools that both the Byzantines and the Crusaders built churches, now ruined, to commemorate the miracle. A visit to both sites will take no more than 30 minutes. ⊠ *Al-Mujahideen Rd., near Lions' Gate, Muslim Quarter* 🕿 *02/628–3285* 🖃 *NIS 7* ☉ *Apr.–Sept., daily 8–12 and 2–6; Oct.–Mar., daily 8–12 and 2–5.*

JEWISH QUARTER

This is at once the Old City's oldest quarter and its newest neighborhood. Abandoned for a generation, the quarter was restored and resettled after the Six-Day War of 1967. The subsequent archaeological excavations exposed artifacts and structures that date back 27 centuries and more. If you have a photographer's eye, get off the main streets and stroll at random. The limestone houses and alleys—often counterpointed with a shock of bougainvillea or palm fronds and ficus trees—offer pleasing compositions.

If you like to people-watch, find a shaded café table and sip a good latte while the world jitterbugs by. The population of the Jewish Quarter is almost entirely religious, roughly split between "modern" Orthodox (devout, but integrated into contemporary Israeli society at every level)

The Via Dolorosa often teems with pilgrims but can sometimes offer a quiet path.

and the more traditional ultra-Orthodox (men in black frock coats and black hats, in many ways a community apart). The locals, especially the women, tend to dress very conservatively. Several religious-study institutions attract a transient population of young students, many of them from abroad. Religious Jewish families tend to have lots of kids, and little ones here are given independence at an astonishingly early age. It's quite common to see three- and four-year-olds toddling home from preschool alone or shepherded by a one-year-more-mature brother or sister. And if you see a big group of Israeli soldiers, don't assume the worst. The army maintains a center for its educational tours here, and the recruits are more likely than not boisterously kidding around with each other as they follow their guide. Shopping is good here—especially jewelry and Judaica—and there are decent fast-food options when hunger strikes.

A renewed landmark of the quarter is the high, white-domed Hurva Synagogue. It was built and soon destroyed in the 18th century, rebuilt in the 19th, and blown up when the Jordanian Arab Legion captured the area in the 1948 war. The current building, rededicated in spring 2010, is a faithful reconstruction of its predecessor.

The biblical City of David, just 10 minutes away, is an adventure-filled adjunct to the Jewish Quarter. It's in the City of David that archaeologists have discovered the real meat of biblical Jerusalem.

GETTING HERE AND AROUND
It's best to approach the Jewish Quarter on foot. From Jaffa Gate, you can plunge into the Arab bazaar and follow David Street until it becomes a T-junction: the right turn becomes Jewish Quarter Street.

Alternatively, after you enter Jaffa Gate, follow the vehicle road to the right and through a small tunnel, then turn left (on foot) onto St. James Street and down to the quarter. A third idea is to begin your tour on Mt. Zion, and then continue to the Jewish Quarter through Zion Gate.

TIMING AND PRECAUTIONS

Allow at least two hours to explore the Jewish Quarter, not counting shopping and eating. If you're pressed for time, absorb the scene over the rim of a glass or mug, and take time to visit the Herodian Quarter. Exploring the City of David, outside the city walls, will take anywhere from 1½ to 2½ hours, depending on how adventurous (and able-bodied) you are. Avoid visiting on Saturday, when everything is closed, and some religious locals may resent you taking pictures on their Sabbath. Sites with entrance fees close by midday Friday.

TOP ATTRACTIONS

Burnt House. "We could almost smell the burning and feel the heat of the flames," wrote archaeologist Nahman Avigad, whose team uncovered evidence of the Roman devastation of Jerusalem in AD 70 at this house site, part of a larger, unexcavated complex under the Jewish Quarter. Charred cooking pots, sooty debris, and—most arresting—the skeletal hand and arm of a woman clutching a scorched staircase recaptured the poignancy of the moment. Stone weights inscribed with the name Bar Katros—a Jewish priestly family whose name is known from ancient sources—suggested that this might have been a basement industrial workshop, possibly for the manufacture of sacramental incense used in the Temple. A video presentation recreates the bitter civil rivalries of the period and the city's tragic end. ⊠ *Tiferet Israel St., Jewish Quarter* ☎ *02/626–5922* ☎ *NIS 20; combined ticket with Herodian Quarter NIS 25* ⊙ *Sun.–Thurs. 9–5, Fri. and Jewish holiday eves 9–noon (last entry 40 mins before closing).*

Fodor's Choice ★ **City of David.** For a time-travel adventure, plunge underground to where landscape, archaeology, and biblical history intersect. Just south of the Old City walls, the City of David is the very heart of Old Testament Jerusalem, built more than four millennia ago over the vital Gihon Spring. It was given its royal Israelite sobriquet one thousand years later, when the legendary King David conquered the city and made it his capital.

Begin with the great rooftop observation point above the visitor center, and take in the 15-minute 3-D movie (call ahead for reservations). A few flights of steps down from the center is Area G, uncovered between 1978 and 1985. The sloping structure you see, possibly a support ramp for a palace or fort, dates back to at least the 10th century BC. The most intriguing artifacts found here were 51 *bullae*, clay seal impressions no bigger than a fingernail, used for sealing documents. Some were inscribed with biblical names.

Head down the steps, where a small sign a third of the way down points to Warren's Shaft and the descent to the spring. Charles Warren was the British army engineer who discovered the spacious, sloping access tunnel—note the ancient chisel marks and rough-cut steps—in 1867. The vertical shaft that drops into the Spring of Gihon

Early Jerusalem: The Spring of Gihon

Today at the City of David archaeological site south of the Old City wall, you can explore part of the Spring of Gihon, the lifeblood of the ancient city and the primary reason for its settlement over four millennia ago. It gushed into the Kidron Valley until the local Canaanites carved out channels to divert much of the water into a large reservoir. According to the Bible, King Hezekiah attempted to protect Jerusalem's precious water supply in the face of an imminent Assyrian assault on the capital (701 BC). Racing against time, his men dug the so-called Siloam or Hezekiah's Tunnel through solid rock, one team starting from the Gihon Spring and the other from a new inner-city reservoir. Miraculously, considering the serpentine course of the third-of-a-mile-long tunnel, the two teams met in the middle. The chisel marks, the ancient plaster, and the zigzags near the halfway point as each team sought the other by sound, bear witness to the remarkable project. With the water now diverted into the city, the original opening of the spring was blocked to deny the enemy access.

wasn't the actual biblical "gutter" through which David's warriors penetrated the city three thousand years ago, as it was hewn in a later era. (A different access to the spring has been discovered elsewhere, so the biblical story remains.) The underground path and steps lead down to the spring.

Waders need water-shoes or sandals, a flashlight (cheap LED ones are on sale at the visitor center) and appropriate clothing: the water is below the knees for almost the entire length of the tunnel (a 30-minute walk), but thigh-deep for the first few minutes. The visitor center has lockers for your unnecessary gear. In this very conservative neighborhood, it's advisable for women to wear covering over their swimsuits when walking outside. The wade isn't recommended for very small children.

If you don't fancy getting wet, you can still view the spring, and then continue through the dry Canaanite tunnel, returning aboveground, still within the park but some distance from the Pool of Siloam. It's a steep climb back up to the visitor center, but there's a shuttle van: ask the guard. When you buy your entrance ticket, check that the shuttle is running.

The tunnel emerges in the Pool of Siloam, mentioned in the New Testament as the place where a blind man had his sight restored (John 9). The current exit takes you down modern steps and over the large flagstones of a 1st-century-BC commercial street until you reach a pool unearthed in 2004 by city workers repairing a sewage pipe. Archaeologists exposed finely cut steps and two corners of the pool, possibly a large public *mikveh*, or Jewish ritual bath, for pilgrims who flocked to the Temple two thousand years ago.

An underground Roman-period drainage tunnel is the new adventurous route back up the hill. A small additional fee, paid with your general ticket, allows you to continue north, and emerge in the Jerusalem

Archaeological Park, inside Dung Gate. Allow 2 1/2 hours for a full unhurried tour of the City of David (though you can cover a lot of ground in less time). Guided tours in English are available. ⊠ *Off Ophel Rd., Silwan* ☏ *02/626–8700* ⊕ *www.cityofdavid.org.il* ⊠ *NIS 27 for City of David, NIS 12 for just Siloam Pool and ancient street; NIS 13 for 3-D film; NIS 5 shuttle-van; guided tour NIS 60 (includes admission and film)* ⊙ *Apr.–Sept., Sun.–Thurs. 8–7, Fri. and Jewish holiday eves 8–4; Oct.–Mar., Sun.–Thurs. 8–5, Fri. and Jewish holiday eves 8–2, last entrance 2 hrs before closing.*

Herodian Quarter and Wohl Archaeological Museum. Excavations in the 1970s exposed the Jewish Quarter's most visually interesting site: the remains of sumptuous mansions from the late Second Temple period. Preserved in the basement of a modern Jewish seminary—but entered separately—the geometrically patterned mosaic floors, still-vibrant frescoes, and costly glassware and ceramics provide a peek into the life of the wealthy in the days of Herod and Jesus. Several small stone cisterns have been identified as private *mikvehs* (Jewish ritual baths); holograms depict their use. Large stone water jars are just like those described in the New Testament story of the wedding at Cana (John 2). Rare stone tables resemble the dining-room furniture depicted in Roman stone reliefs found in Europe. On the last of the site's three distinct levels is a mansion with an estimated original floor area of some 6,000 square feet.

None of the upper stories have survived, but the fine, fashionable stucco work and the quality of the artifacts found here indicate an exceptional standard of living, leading some scholars to suggest this may have been the long-sought palace of the high priest. The charred ceiling beam and scorched mosaic floor and fresco at the southern end of the reception hall bear witness to the Roman torching of the neighborhood in the late summer of AD 70, exactly one month after the Temple itself had been destroyed. Allow about 45 minutes to explore the site. ⊠ *Hakara'im Rd., Jewish Quarter* ☏ *02/626–5922* ⊠ *NIS 18; NIS 35 combined ticket with Burnt House* ⊙ *Sun.–Thurs. 9–5, Fri. and Jewish holiday eves 9–1 (last entry 30 mins before closing).*

WORTH NOTING

Broad Wall. The discovery in the 1970s of the rather unobtrusive 23-foot-thick foundations of an Old Testament city wall was hailed as one of the most important archaeological finds in the Jewish Quarter. Hezekiah, King of Judah and a contemporary of the prophet Isaiah, built the wall in 701 BC to protect the city against an impending Assyrian invasion. The unearthing of the Broad Wall—a biblical name—resolved a long-running scholarly debate about the size of Old Testament Jerusalem: a large on-site map shows that the ancient city was more extensive than was once thought. ⊠ *Off Jewish Quarter St., Jewish Quarter.*

Cardo. Today it's known for shopping, but the Cardo has a long history. In AD 135, the Roman emperor Hadrian built his town of Aelia Capitolina on the ruins of Jerusalem, an urban plan essentially preserved in the Old City of today. The *cardo maximus,* the generic

Jews in the Old City

The history of Jewish life in the Old City has been marked by the trials of conflict and the joys of creating and rebuilding community. Here are some highlights from the medieval period on.

1099. Crusaders conquer Jerusalem, followed by wholesale massacre. Jews lived at the time in today's Muslim Quarter.

1267. Spanish rabbi Nachmanides ("Ramban") reestablishes Jewish community. (His synagogue is on Jewish Quarter Street.)

1517. Ottoman Turks conquer Palestine and allow Sephardic Jews (expelled from Spain a generation earlier) to resettle the country. They develop four interlinked synagogues in the quarter.

1700. A large group of Ashkenazi Jews from Eastern Europe settles in Jerusalem.

1860. The first neighborhood is established outside the walls (Mishkenot Sha'ananim). Initially, very few Old City Jews had the courage to move out.

1948. Israel's War of Independence. Jewish Quarter surrenders to Jordanian forces and is abandoned. By then, the residents of the quarter represent only a tiny percentage of Jerusalem's Jewish population.

1967. Six-Day War. The Jewish Quarter, much of it ruined, is recaptured. Archaeological excavations and restoration work begin side by side.

1980s. Section after section of the Jewish Quarter becomes active again as the restoration work progresses—apartments and educational institutions, synagogues and stores, restaurants and new archaeological sites.

name for the city's main north–south street, began at the present-day Damascus Gate, where sections of the Roman pavement have been unearthed. With the Christianization of the Roman Empire in the 4th century, access to Mt. Zion and its important Christian sites became a priority, and the main street was eventually extended south into today's Jewish Quarter. The original width—today you see only half—was 73 feet, about the width of a six-lane highway. A strip of good stores (jewelry, art, and Judaica) occupies the Cardo's medieval reincarnation. ⊠ *Jewish Quarter St., Jewish Quarter.*

TOWER OF DAVID AND MT. ZION

When you've "done" the main sights, take a leisurely few hours to dip into lesser-known gems on the periphery of the Old City. Most of the city walls were built in the 16th century by the Ottoman sultan Suleiman the Magnificent. According to legend, his two architects were executed by order of the sultan himself and buried behind the railings just inside the imposing Jaffa Gate. One version relates that they angered Suleiman by not including Mt. Zion and the venerated Tomb of David within the walls. Others say that the satisfied sultan wanted to make sure they would never build anything grander for anyone else.

Jaffa Gate got its name from its westerly orientation, toward the once-important Mediterranean harbor of Jaffa, now part of Tel Aviv. Its Arabic name of Bab el-Khalil, "Gate of the Beloved," points you south, to the city of Hebron, where the biblical Abraham, the "Beloved of God" in Muslim tradition, is buried. The vehicle entrance is newer, created by the Ottoman Turks in 1898 for the visit of the German emperor, Kaiser Wilhelm II. The British general, Sir Edmund Allenby, took a different approach when he seized the city from the Turks in December 1917: he and his staff officers dismounted from their horses to enter the holy city with the humility befitting pilgrims.

The huge stone tower on the right as you enter Jaffa Gate is the last survivor of the strategic fortress built by King Herod 2,000 years ago. Today it's part of the so-called citadel that houses the Tower of David Museum—well worth your time as the springboard for exploring this part of the historical city. Opposite the museum entrance (once a drawbridge) is the neo-Gothic Christ Church (Anglican), built in 1849 as the first Protestant church in the Middle East. Directly ahead is the souk (Arab bazaar), a convenient route to the Christian and Jewish quarters. To reach Mt. Zion, follow the vehicle road inside the walls to Zion Gate, or take the Ramparts Walk.

GETTING HERE AND AROUND
Jaffa Gate, the logical entry point for this area and tour, is an easy walk from the Downtown or King David Street areas. City bus routes 20, 38, and 99, as well as the light rail, take you right there, but any Downtown stop is within striking distance.

TIMING AND PRECAUTIONS
Sunday through Thursday is when everything is open. Some sites have limited hours or are closed Friday or Saturday. Modest dress is required at shrines.

TOP ATTRACTIONS

Fodor'sChoice ★ **Ramparts Walk.** The narrow stone catwalks of the Old City walls provide great panoramic views and interesting perspectives of this intriguing city. But they also offer an innocent bit of voyeurism as you look down into gardens and courtyards and become, for a moment, a more intimate partner in the secret domestic life of the different quarters you pass. Across the rooftops, the domes and spires of the three religions that call Jerusalem holy compete for the skyline, just as their adherents jealously guard their territory down below. Peer through the shooting niches, just as the long-ago watchmen did. The hotels and high-rises of the new city dominate the skyline to the west and south; the bustle of East Jerusalem is almost tangible to the north; and the churches and cemeteries quietly cling to the Mt. of Olives to the east. There are many high steps on this route; the railings are secure, but small children shouldn't walk alone.

The two sections of the walk are disconnected from each other (though the same ticket covers both). The shorter southern section (taking 30 minutes) is accessible only from the end of the seemingly dead-end terrace outside Jaffa Gate at the exit of the Tower of David Museum. Descent is at Zion Gate or just before Dung Gate. The longer and more varied walk begins at Jaffa Gate (up the stairs immediately on the left as you enter the Old City),

CLOSE UP

The Quarters of the Old City

Today the third of a square mile within the Old City walls is home to some 35,000 Jerusalemites, representing a babel of languages, a plethora of religious rites, and a potpourri of ethnicities. Different sections, or quarters, within the walls have distinct characters. Here's a brief guide to the highlights.

The **Muslim Quarter**, located between Damascus Gate and the Western Wall, and east to Lions' Gate, is the largest in both area and population. The famous Via Dolorosa (Way of the Cross) that winds through this quarter offers an illusory universalism: the side streets, with their busy grocery stores, neighborhood mosques, and stenciled pictures of Mecca, bespeak the real character of this residential area. The enormous Haram esh-Sharif (the Jewish Temple Mount), with the gold Dome of the Rock and the black-domed Al-Aqsa Mosque, is its natural extension.

Fragmented into a dozen denominational domains, the **Christian Quarter** is capped by the gray dome of the Church of the Holy Sepulcher. (The struggle for visibility in the holy city seems to be as much about dominating the skyline as about controlling real estate.) The numerous churches and religious institutions in this quarter, which is west of the Muslim Quarter, make for low population density.

The **Jewish Quarter** lies to the west of the Western Wall. Shattered in the 1948 war, it was revived in aesthetic stone in the 1970s and is home largely to religious Jews. Archaeological finds and the neighborhood's contemporary tale have given the area a character all its own.

The heart of the **Armenian Quarter**, the Old City's smallest, is the monastery, in the southwest corner within the walls. The closed enclave perpetuates the life and faith of a far-off land, the first to embrace Christianity.

with descent at New, Damascus, Herod's, or Lions' gates. In terms of timing, allow 40 minutes for the shorter section, south-southeast to Zion Gate, with an extra 10 to 15 minutes to Dung Gate. For the longer section, it takes 20 minutes to walk north-northeast to New Gate, another 20 minutes east to Damascus Gate, 15 minutes from there to Herod's Gate, and about 20 minutes more to Lions' Gate. ⊠ *Jaffa Gate* ☎ *02/625–4403* 🎫 *NIS 16; NIS 55 combined ticket with Ophel Archaeological Garden, Damascus Gate, and Zedekiah's Cave* ✆ *Apr.–Sept., Sat.–Thurs. 9–5; Oct.–Mar., Sat.–Thurs. 9–4. Short route also open Fri. 9–2.*

Room of the Last Supper. Tradition has enshrined this spare, 14th-century second-story room as the location of the "upper room" referred to in the New Testament (Mark 14). About two thousand years ago, when Jesus and his disciples celebrated the ceremonial Passover meal that would become known in popular parlance as the Last Supper, the site was *inside* the city walls. Formally known as the Cenacle or the Coenaculum, the room is also associated with a second New Testament tradition (Acts 2), as the place where Jesus' disciples, gathered on Pentecost seven weeks after his death, were "filled with the Holy Spirit," and began to speak in foreign "tongues."

A bicycle is one way anyone can avoid Jerusalem's often intense traffic.

A little incongruously, the chamber has the trappings of a mosque as well: restored stained-glass Arabic inscriptions in the Gothic windows, an ornate *mihrab* (an alcove indicating the Muslim direction of prayer, toward Mecca), and two Arabic plaques in the wall. The Muslims weren't concerned with the site's Christian traditions but with the supposed Tomb of King David—the "Prophet" David in their tradition—on the level below. Allow 10 minutes to imbibe the atmosphere. ⊠ *Mt. Zion* ⛱ *Free* ☉ *Sat.–Thurs. 8–5, Fri. 8–1.*

Fodor's Choice ★ **Tower of David Museum.** Many visitors find this museum invaluable in mapping Jerusalem's often-confusing historical byways. Housed in a series of medieval halls, known locally as the Citadel (*Hametzuda* in Hebrew), the museum tells the city's four-millennia story through models, maps, holograms, and videos. The galleries are organized by historical period around the Citadel's central courtyard, where the old stone walls and arches add an appropriately antique atmosphere. Walking on the Citadel ramparts provides unexpected panoramas. The basement has a model of 19th-century Jerusalem. Be sure to inquire at the ticket office about the next screening of the animated introductory film (which has English subtitles), and don't miss the spectacular view from the top of the big tower. Guided tours in English are offered at 11. You'll need at least 90 minutes to do justice to this museum.

The stunning outdoor "Night Spectacular" is a 45-minute sound-and-light pageant of historical images played onto the ancient stone walls and towers. The outdoor event runs throughout the year (unless it rains) on Monday, Wednesday, Thursday, and Saturday nights, with anywhere from two to four shows a night. ⊠ *Jaffa Gate* ☎ *02/626–5333,*

02/626–5310 for recorded info ⊕ www.towerofdavid.org.il ✉ NIS 36 for museum, NIS 55 for night show, NIS 70 for combined ticket ⊙ Sept.–June, Mon.–Thurs. 9–4, Sat. and holiday eves 9–2; July and Aug., Sat.–Thurs. 9–5, Fri. 9–2.

ALSO WORTH NOTING

Chamber of the Holocaust. This small museum is also dedicated to the memory of the 6 million European Jews annihilated by the Nazis in the Second World War. Among the artifacts salvaged from the Holocaust are items that the Nazis forced Jews to make out of sacred Torah scrolls. One Jewish tailor fashioned a vest for his Nazi "customer" out of the inscribed parchment, but with grim humor he chose sections that contained the worst of the biblical curses. Plaques commemorate many of the 5,000 European Jewish communities destroyed from 1939 to 1945. ⊠ *Mt. Zion, near Tomb of David* ☎ *02/671–5105* ✉ *NIS 12* ⊙ *Sun.–Thurs. 9–3:45, Fri. 9–1:30.*

Dormition Abbey. The large, round Roman Catholic church, with its distinctive cone-shaped roof, ornamented turrets, and landmark clock tower, is a Jerusalem landmark. It was built on land bought by the German emperor, Kaiser Wilhelm II, when he visited Jerusalem in 1898. The German Benedictines dedicated the echoing main church, with its Byzantine-style apse and mosaic floors, in 1910. The lower-level crypt houses a cenotaph with a carved-stone figure of Mary in repose (*dormitio*), reflecting the tradition that she fell into eternal sleep. Among the adjacent little chapels is one donated by the Ivory Coast, with wooden figures and motifs inlaid with ivory. The premises include a bookstore and a coffee shop. A visit takes about 20 minutes. ⊠ *Near the Room of the Last Supper, Mt. Zion* ☎ *02/565–5330* ⊕ *www.cicts.org* ✉ *Free* ⊙ *Weekdays 8:30–11:45 and 12:40–5:30; Sat. 8:30–11:45, 12:40–2:45, and 3:30–5:30; Sun. 10:30–11:45 and 12:30–5:30.*

Tomb of David. According to the Bible, King David, the great Israelite king of the 10th century BC, was buried in "the City of David," one of the contemporary names for his capital, Jerusalem. Medieval Jewish pilgrims erroneously placed the ancient city on this hill, where they sought—and supposedly found—the royal tomb. Its authenticity may be questionable, but a millennium of tears and prayers has sanctified the place.

A cenotaph, a massive stone marker draped with velvet cloth and embroidered with symbols and Hebrew texts traditionally associated with David, caps the tomb itself. Behind it is a stone alcove, which some scholars think may be the sole remnant of a synagogue from the 5th century AD, the oldest of its kind in Jerusalem. Religious authorities have divided the shrine, already cramped, into two tiny prayer areas to separate men and women. Modest dress is required; men must cover their heads. ⊠ *Mt. Zion* ☎ *02/671–9767* ✉ *Free* ⊙ *Apr.–Sept., Sun.–Thurs. 8–6, Fri. and Jewish holiday eves 8–2; Oct.–Mar., Sun.–Thurs. 8–5, Fri. and Jewish holiday eves 8–1.*

Jerusalem Through the Ages

The first known mention of Jerusalem is in Egyptian "hate texts" of the 20th century BC, but many archaeologists give the city a considerably earlier founding date. Abraham and the biblical Joshua may have been here, but it was King David, circa 1000 BC, who captured the city and made it his capital, thus propelling it onto the center stage of history.

FIRST AND SECOND TEMPLES

King David's son Solomon built the "First" Temple, giving the city a preeminence it enjoyed until its destruction by the Babylonians, and the exile of its population, in 586 BC. The Israelites returned 50 years later, rebuilt the Temple (the "Second"), and began the slow process of revival. By the 2nd century BC, Jerusalem was again a vibrant Jewish capital, albeit one with a good dose of Hellenistic cultural influence. Herod the Great (who reigned 37 BC–4 BC) revamped the Temple on a magnificent scale and expanded the city into a cosmopolis of world renown.

This was the Jerusalem Jesus knew, a city of monumental architecture, teeming—especially during the Jewish pilgrim festivals—with tens of thousands of visitors. It was here that the Romans crucified Jesus (circa AD 29), and here, too, that the Great Jewish Revolt against Rome erupted, ending in AD 70 with the destruction (once again) of the city and the Temple.

ROMANS AND OTTOMANS

The Roman emperor Hadrian redesigned Jerusalem as the pagan polis of Aelia Capitolina (AD 135), an urban plan that became the basis for the Old City of today. The Byzantines made it a Christian center, with a massive wave of church building (4th–6th centuries AD), until the Arab conquest of AD 638 brought the holy city under Muslim sway. Except during the golden age of the Ummayad Dynasty, in the late 7th and early 8th centuries, Jerusalem was no more than a provincial town under the Muslim regimes of the early Middle Ages. The Crusaders stormed it in 1099 and made it the capital of their Latin Kingdom. With the reconquest of Jerusalem by the Muslims, the city again lapsed into a languid provincialism for 700 years under the Mamluk and Ottoman empires. The British conquest in 1917 thrust the city back into the world limelight as rising Jewish and Arab nationalisms vied to possess it.

DIVIDED AND REUNITED

Jerusalem was divided by the 1948 war: the larger Jewish western sector became the capital of the State of Israel, while Jordan annexed the smaller, predominantly Arab eastern sector, which included the Old City. The Six-Day War of 1967 reunited the city under Israeli rule, but the concept of an Arab "East" Jerusalem and a Jewish "West" Jerusalem remains, even though new Jewish neighborhoods in the northeastern and southeastern sections have made the distinction oversimplified.

The holy city continues to engage the attention of devotees of Christianity, Islam, and Judaism. Between Jews and Arabs it remains the subject of debate and occasional violence as rival visions clash for possession of the city's past and control of its future. It's widely recognized that any peace negotiations between Israel and the Palestinians will fail unless the issue of sharing Jerusalem is resolved.

MT. OF OLIVES AND EAST JERUSALEM

Loosely speaking, East Jerusalem refers to the Arab neighborhoods controlled by Jordan in the years when the city was divided (1948–1967). That includes Mt. of Olives, the areas north of the Old City.

The sights in this area are for the most part distinctly Christian. A few are a little off the beaten path, and the best way to explore them—if you're energetic enough—is on foot. If you're driving, however, you can find parking at the Seven Arches Hotel on the Mt. of Olives, and at the cluster of large hotels near the American Colony; or take a cab.

GETTING HERE AND AROUND

The Route 99 circle bus tour has a stop near Hebrew University's Mt. Scopus campus. If you enjoy a bit of a walk and the weather is fine, it's no more than 20 minutes across to the Mt. of Olives (with a bonus of a panoramic view of the Judean Desert to the east). A cab ride is an alternative, but if you skip the top of the mountain, the rest of the sights are accessible by foot from the Old City.

TIMING AND PRECAUTIONS

Morning views are best from the Mt. of Olives. Some of the sites are closed on Sunday. Watch out for pickpockets on the Mt. of Olives and the road down to Gethsemane, and on Nablus Road outside the Garden Tomb.

TOP ATTRACTIONS

Fodor'sChoice
★

Garden of Gethsemane. After the Last Supper, the New Testament relates, Jesus and his disciples walked to the Mt. of Olives, to a "place" called Gethsemane, where he was betrayed and arrested. Gethsemane derives from the Aramaic or Hebrew word for "oil press," referring to the precious olive that has always flourished here. The enormous, gnarled, and still-productive olive trees on the site may be older than Christianity itself, according to some botanists. They make a fine picture, but a fence prevents pilgrims from taking home sprigs as a more tangible souvenir.

The **Church of All Nations,** with its brilliantly colorful, landmark mosaic facade, was completed in 1924 on the scanty remains of its Byzantine predecessor. The prolific architect, Antonio Barluzzi, filled the church's interior domes with mosaic symbols of the Catholic communities that contributed to its construction. The windows are glazed with translucent alabaster in somber browns and purples, creating a mystical feeling in the dim interior. At the altar is the so-called Rock of the Agony, where Jesus is said to have endured his Passion; this is the source of the older name of the church, the **Basilica of the Agony.**

A popular approach to Gethsemane is walking down the steep road from the top of the Mt. of Olives, perhaps stopping in on the way at the Dominus Flevit church where, tradition has it, Jesus wept as he foretold the destruction of the city (Luke 19). The entrance to the well-tended garden at the foot of the hill is marked by a small platoon of vendors outside. ✉ *Jericho Rd., Kidron Valley* ☎ *02/626–6444* ✆ *Free* ☼ *Apr.–Sept., daily 8–noon and 2–6; Oct.–Mar., daily 8–noon and 2–5.*

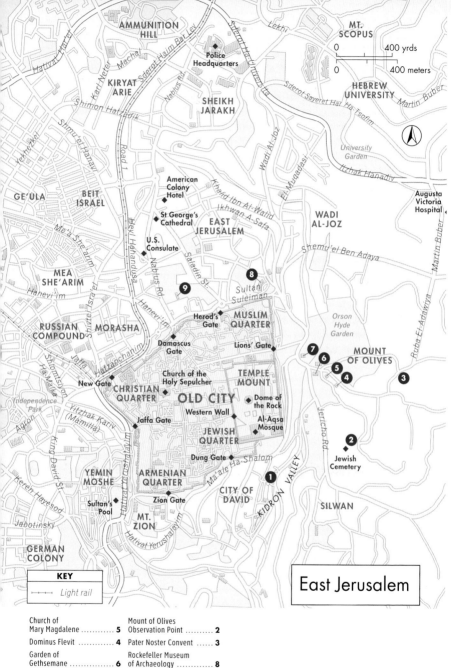

East Jerusalem

AMMUNITION HILL

MT. SCOPUS

Police Headquarters

KIRYAT ARIE

SHEIKH JARAKH

HEBREW UNIVERSITY

0   400 yrds
0   400 meters

University Garden

GE'ULA

BEIT ISRAEL

American Colony Hotel

St George's Cathedral

EAST JERUSALEM

WADI AL-JOZ

Augusta Victoria Hospital

U.S. Consulate

MEA SHE'ARIM

Shemu'el Ben Adaya

RUSSIAN COMPOUND

MORASHA

Herod's Gate

MUSLIM QUARTER

Sultan Suleiman

8

9

Orson Hyde Garden

MOUNT OF OLIVES

Damascus Gate

Lions' Gate

7 **6** **5** **4**

3

Church of the Holy Sepulcher

TEMPLE MOUNT

New Gate

CHRISTIAN QUARTER

OLD CITY

Independence Park

Jaffa Gate

Western Wall

Dome of the Rock

Al-Aqsa Mosque

JEWISH QUARTER

2

Jewish Cemetery

YEMIN MOSHE

Dung Gate

ARMENIAN QUARTER

CITY OF DAVID

Sultan's Pool

Zion Gate

MT. ZION

1

KIDRON VALLEY

SILWAN

GERMAN COLONY

KEY

—+— Light rail

Church of
Mary Magdalene **5**

Dominus Flevit **4**

Garden of
Gethsemane **6**

Garden Tomb **9**

Kidron Valley **1**

Mount of Olives
Observation Point **2**

Pater Noster Convent **3**

Rockefeller Museum
of Archaeology **8**

Tomb of the Virgin **7**

2

Garden Tomb. A beautifully tended English-style country garden makes this an island of tranquillity in the hurly-burly of East Jerusalem. What Christian pilgrims come for, however, is an empty ancient tomb, and a moving opportunity to ponder the Gospel account of the death and resurrection of Jesus. It's a favorite site for the many Protestant visitors who respond less or not at all to the ornamentation and ritual of the Holy Sepulcher.

In 1883, British general Charles Gordon spent several months in Jerusalem. From his window looking out over the Old City walls, he was struck by the skull-like features of a cliff face north of the Damascus Gate. He was convinced that this, rather than the Church of the Holy Sepulcher, was "the place of the skull" (Mark 15) where Jesus was crucified. An ancient rock-cut tomb had already been uncovered there, and subsequent excavations exposed cisterns and a wine press, features typical of an ancient garden.

According to the New Testament, Jesus was buried in the fresh tomb of the wealthy Joseph of Arimathea, in a garden close to the execution site, and archaeologists identified the tomb as an upper-class Jewish burial place of the Second Temple period. Recent research has shown that this tomb might be from the Old Testament period, making it too old to have been that of Jesus. The gentle guardians of the Garden Tomb don't insist on the identification of the site as that of Calvary and the tomb of Christ, but are keen to provide a contemplative setting for the pilgrim, in a place that just might have been historically significant. ⊠ *Conrad Schick St., East Jerusalem* ☎ *02/627–2745* ⊕ *www.gardentomb.com* ▱ *Free* ☽ *Mon.–Sat. 9–noon and 2–5:30.*

■ NEED A
BREAK?

American Colony Hotel. The upscale American Colony Hotel is an elegant 19th-century limestone building with cane furniture, Armenian ceramic tiles, and a delightful courtyard. The food is generally very good, and a light lunch or afternoon tea in the cool lobby lounge, at the poolside restaurant, or on the patio under the trees can make for a well-earned break. ⊠ *1 Louis Vincent St., at Nablus Rd., American Colony* ☎ 02/627–9777.

Fodor'sChoice
★

Mt. of Olives Observation Point. The Old City, with its landmark domes and towers, is squarely within your lens in this classic, picture-postcard panoramic view. It's best in the early morning, with the sun at your back, or at sunset on days with some clouds, when the golden glow and sunbeams more than compensate for the glare.

The magnificent, gold Dome of the Rock and the black-domed al-Aqsa Mosque to the left of it dominate the skyline; but look behind them for the large gray dome of the Holy Sepulcher and (farther left) the white one of the Jewish Quarter's Hurva Synagogue for a hint of the long-running visibility contest among faiths and nations. To the left of the Old City, the cone-roof Dormition Abbey and its adjacent clock tower crown Mt. Zion, today outside the walls but within the city of the Second Temple period.

The Mt. of Olives has been bathed in sanctity for millennia. On the slope beneath you, and off to your left, is the vast Jewish cemetery, reputedly the oldest still in use anywhere in the world. For more than

DID YOU KNOW?

Many graves in the Jewish cemetery on the slope of the Mt. of Olives have small stones placed on the marker by visitors (burial is below-ground). The ancient custom is a way of paying your respects to the deceased.

two thousand years, Jews have been buried here to await the coming of the Messiah and the resurrection to follow. The raised structures over the graves are merely tomb markers, not crypts; burial is belowground.

Camel and donkey drivers (usually one of each) are always pushing to give you a short ride (not cheap!), and the vendors can be persistent, but a polite "no thank you" is sometimes enough for them to go bother someone else. ▨ **TIP→** Beware of pickpockets here and on the road down to Gethsemane. Fairly good bathrooms are a welcome addition. ⊠ *E-Sheikh St., opposite Seven Arches Hotel, Mt. of Olives.*

Rockefeller Museum of Archaeology. This museum's octagonal white stone tower is an East Jerusalem landmark. Built in the 1930s, it has echoing stone halls and somewhat old-fashioned displays that recall the period of the British Mandate. Among the most important exhibits are cultic masks from Neolithic Jericho, ivories from Bronze-Age Megiddo, the famous Israelite "Lachish Letters" (6th century BC), Herodian inscriptions, and decorative reliefs from the Church of the Holy Sepulcher. This branch of the Israel Museum has some parking on Saturday only. ▨ **TIP→** For winter visitors, note that the buildings have no heating. ⊠ *27 Sultan Suleiman St., East Jerusalem* ☎ *02/670–8811* ⊕ *www.english.imjnet.org.il* ⊠ *Free* ⊘ *Sun., Mon., Wed., and Thurs. 10–3, Sat. 10–2.*

WORTH NOTING

Church of Mary Magdalene. With its sculpted white turrets and gold onion domes, this Russian Orthodox church looks like something out of a fairy tale. It was dedicated in 1888, when the competition among European powers for influence in this part of the world was at its height. Princess Alice, the mother of Prince Philip, Duke of Edinburgh, is buried here, near her aunt, the martyred Russian Grand Duchess Elizabeth.

The church has limited hours, but its icon-studded interior and tranquil garden are well worth a visit if your plans bring you to the area at the right time. ⊠ *E-Sheikh St., above the Garden of Gethsemane, Mt. of Olives* ☎ *02/628–4371* ⊠ *Free* ⊘ *Tues. and Thurs. 10–noon.*

Dominus Flevit. Designed by Antonio Barluzzi in the 1950s, the tear-shaped church—its name means "the Lord wept"—preserves the New Testament story of Jesus' sorrowful prediction of the destruction of Jerusalem (Luke 19). The remarkable feature of its simple interior is a picture window facing west, the iron cross on the altar silhouetted against a superb view of the Old City. Many archaeological items were unearthed here, including a group of ancient ossuaries, or bone boxes, preserved in a grotto on the right as you enter the site. The courtyard is a good place to enjoy the view in peace between waves of pilgrim groups. (Equally worthy of mention are the restrooms, rare in this area.) The church is about one-third of the way down the steep road that descends to Gethsemane from the Mt. of Olives Observation Point. Beware of pickpockets on the street outside. ⊠ *E-Sheikh St., below Mt. of Olives Observation Point, Mt. of Olives* ☎ *02/626–6450* ⊠ *Free* ⊘ *Daily 8–11:45 and 2–5.*

Kidron Valley. This deep valley separates the Old City and the City of David from the high ridge of the Mt. of Olives and the Arab neighborhood of Silwan. In the cliff face below the neighborhood are the symmetrical openings of tombs from both the First Temple (Old Testament) and

Second Temple (Hellenistic-Roman) periods. You can view the impressive group of 2,200-year-old funerary monuments from the lookout terrace at the southeast corner of the Old City wall, down and to your left, or wander down into the valley itself and see them close up. The huge, square, stone structure with the conical roof is known as **Absalom's Pillar.** The one crowned by a pyramidal roof, a solid block of stone cut out of the mountain, is called **Zachariah's Tomb.** The association with those Old Testament personalities was a medieval mistake, and the structures more probably mark the tombs of wealthy Jerusalemites of the Second Temple period who wished to await the coming of the Messiah and the resurrection to follow in the style to which they were accustomed. ⊠ *Jericho Rd., south of the Garden of Gethsemane, Kidron Valley.*

Pater Noster Convent. The focal point of this Carmelite convent is a grotto, traditionally identified as the place where Jesus taught his disciples the Lord's Prayer (Matthew 6). The site was purchased by the Princesse de la Tour d'Auvergne of France in 1868, and the convent stands on the site of earlier Byzantine and Crusader structures. An ambitious basilica, begun in the 1920s, was designed to follow the lines of a 4th-century church, but was never completed: its aisles, open to the sky, are now lined with pine trees. The real attractions of the site, however, are the many large ceramic plaques adorning the cloister walls and the small church, with the Lord's Prayer in more than 100 different languages. (Look for the high wall, metal door, and French flag on a bend 200 yards before the Seven Arches Hotel.) ⊠ *E-Sheikh St., Mt. of Olives* ☎ *02/626–4904* 🕾 *NIS 7* ⊙ *Mon.–Sat. 8:30–noon and 2:30–4:30.*

Tomb of the Virgin. The Gothic facade of the underground Church of the Assumption, which contains this shrine, clearly dates it to the Crusader era (12th century). Tradition has it that this is where the Virgin Mary was interred and then "assumed" into heaven. In an otherwise gloomy church—hung with age-darkened icons and brass lamps—the marble sarcophagus, apparently medieval, remains illuminated. The Status Quo Agreement in force in the Church of the Holy Sepulcher and Bethlehem's Church of the Nativity pertains here, too: the Greek Orthodox, Armenian Orthodox, and even the Muslims control different parts of the property. The Roman Catholic Franciscans were expelled in 1757, a loss of privilege that rankles to this day. ⊠ *Jericho Rd., adjacent to the Garden of Gethsemane, Kidron Valley* ☎ *02/628–4613* 🕾 *Free* ⊙ *Daily 5–noon and 2:30–5.*

WEST JERUSALEM

Visitors tend to focus, naturally enough, on the historical and religious sights on the eastern side of town, especially in the Old City; but West Jerusalem houses the nation's institutions, is the repository for its collective memory, and—together with the Downtown—gives more insight into contemporary life in Israel's largest city. The world-class Israel Museum and Yad Vashem are located here, as well as poignant Mt. Herzl and the picturesque neighborhood of Ein Kerem. These attractions, which are spread out over a number of West Jerusalem neighborhoods such as Givat Ram, are most easily accessed by car or by a combination of buses, light rail, and short cab rides.

On the Mt. of Olives, the stunning mosaic facade of the Church of All Nations is a city landmark.

GETTING HERE AND AROUND

There are good city bus services and the single-line light rail in this part of town (ask at each site how to get to the next), but a few cab rides (most under $10 on the meter) will be a much better use of limited time. Remember that Egged bus Route 99 serves a good number of sights as well.

TIMING AND PRECAUTIONS

Pay attention to the closing times of sites: several aren't open on Saturdays and close early on Fridays. Some museums have evening hours on particular days—a time-efficient option. Avoid burnout by staggering visits to the museums, and combining them with different kinds of experiences.

TOP ATTRACTIONS

Bible Lands Museum. Most archaeological museums group artifacts according to their place of origin, but the curators here have abandoned this method in favor of a chronological display. Exhibits cover a period of more than six thousand years—from the prehistoric Neolithic period to that of the Byzantine Empire—and sweep geographically from Afghanistan to Nubia (present-day Sudan). Rare clay vessels, fertility idols, cylinder seals, ivories, and sarcophagi fill the soaring, naturally lighted galleries. Look for the ancient Egyptian wooden coffin, in a stunning state of preservation.

The concept of the museum is intriguing, but some have criticized its methodology. A concept was imposed on a largely preexisting collection, rather than a collection being created item by selected item to illustrate a concept. Plan on an hour to see the permanent exhibition—a guided tour will enhance the experience—and check out the interesting (and sometimes spectacular) temporary exhibitions downstairs. ⊠ *25 Granot St., Givat Ram* ☎ *02/561–1066* ⊕ *www.blmj.org* 💲 *NIS 40* ⊙ *Sun.–Tues. and Thurs. 9:30–5:30, Wed. 9:30–9:30, Fri. and Jewish holiday eves 10–2, Sat. 10–2. English guided tours Sun.–Tues, Thurs., and Fri. at 10:30, Wed. at 10:30 and 5:30.*

Chagall Windows and Hadassah Hospital. Marc Chagall's vibrant stained-glass windows draw visitors to Hadassah Hospital's huge Ein Kerem campus. When the U.S.–based Hadassah organization began planning this hospital on the western edge of town, it asked the Russian-born Jewish artist to adorn the small synagogue. Chagall was reportedly so delighted that he created the windows for free. Taking his inspiration from the Bible—Jacob's deathbed blessings on his sons and, to a lesser extent, Moses' valediction to the tribes of Israel—he created 12 windows in luminous primary colors, with an ark full of characteristically Chagallian beasts and a bag of Jewish and esoteric symbols. The innovative techniques of the Reims glassmakers give the wafer-thin windows a convincing illusion of depth. Recorded explanations in the synagogue are available in several languages. Buses 12, 19, 27, and 42 head to the Ein Kerem campus. ⊠ *Hadassah Hospital, Henrietta Szold Rd., Ein Kerem* ☎ *02/677–6271* ⊕ *www.hadassah-med.com* 💲 *NIS 10* ⊙ *Sun.–Thurs. 8–12:45 and 2–3:30.*

Ein Kerem. The neighborhood of Ein Kerem (sometimes spelled Ein Karem) still retains much of its old village character. A couple of hours is enough time to explore it, though you could spend more if you take time out for a coffee. Tree-framed stone houses are strewn across its hillsides with a pleasing Mediterranean nonchalance. Artists and professionals who have joined the older working-class population over the last 40 years have marvelously renovated many homes. Back alleys provide an off-the-beaten-path feel, and occasionally a serendipitous art or craft studio. The neighborhood is served by city Bus 17 and is 5 minutes from Mt. Herzl or Yad Vashem and less than 10 minutes from the Hadassah Hospital. There's free underground parking. ⊠ *Ein Kerem.*

FAMILY
Fodor's Choice
★

Israel Museum. An essential stop in Jerusalem, this eclectic treasure trove and world-class museum focuses on three main specialties: fine art, archaeology, and Jewish life and art. All the exhibits are enhanced by state-of-the-art presentations. Some strategy notes: if you like museums, plan on two visits. The vegetarian/dairy café, Mansfeld, is a good place for a light meal or coffee. The more expensive Modern has tempting meat and fish combinations and remains open beyond museum hours. The lockers and an ATM in the museum's entrance hall are useful.

BRIDGE OF STRINGS

The "Bridge of Strings" (or "Cords") was designed by Spanish architect Santiago Calatrava to suspend the new light rail over the busy intersection at Jerusalem's western entrance (Tel Aviv Highway, Route 1). The commission was intended to provide the city with a contemporary icon. "What do we need it for?" complained some residents. Judge for yourself from the best angle: not as you enter the city but from the sidewalk outside the International Convention Center (⊠ *Binyanei Ha'ooma, Zalman Shazar Blvd.*).

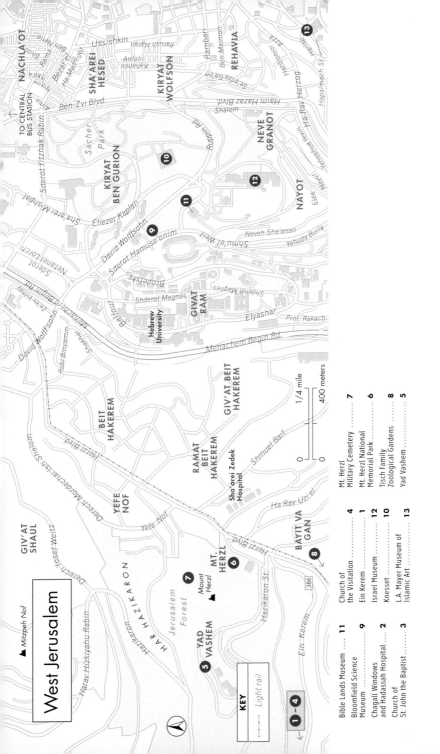

West Jerusalem

KEY

Light rail

1–4

Bible Lands Museum **11**	
Bloomfield Science Museum **9**	
Chagall Windows and Hadassah Hospital **2**	
Church of St. John the Baptist......... **3**	

Church of the Visitation **4**	
Ein Kerem **1**	
Israel Museum **12**	
Knesset **10**	
L.A. Mayer Museum of Islamic Art **13**	

Mt. Herzl Military Cemetery **7**	
Mt. Herzl National Memorial Park **6**	
Tisch Family Zoological Gardens **8**	
Yad Vashem **5**	

1/4 mile

0

0   400 meters

The **Dead Sea Scrolls** are certainly the Israel Museum's most famous—and most important—collection. A Bedouin boy discovered the first of the two-thousand-year-old parchments in 1947 in a Judean Desert cave, overlooking the Dead Sea. Of the nine main scrolls and bags full of small fragments that surfaced over the years, many of the most important and most complete are preserved here; the Antiquities Authority holds the rest of the parchments, and a unique copper scroll is in Jordan. (⇨ *See Masada and the Dead Sea in Chapter 3*). The white dome of the Shrine of the Book, the separate pavilion in which the scrolls are housed, was inspired by the lids of the clay jars in which the first ones were found.

The scrolls were written in the Second Temple period by a fiercely zealous separatist Jewish sect, widely identified as the Essenes, a group described by contemporary historians. Archaeological, laboratory, and textual evidence dates the earliest of the scrolls to the 2nd century BC; none could have been written later than AD 68, the year in which their home community, known today as Qumran, was destroyed by the Romans. The parchments, still in an extraordinary state of preservation because of the dryness of the Dead Sea region, contain the oldest Hebrew manuscripts of the Old Testament ever found, authenticating the almost identical Hebrew texts still in use today. Sectarian literature includes "The Rule of the Community," a sort of constitution of this ascetic group, and "The War of the Sons of Light and the Sons of Darkness," an account of a future cataclysmic conflict that would, they believed, presage the messianic age.

The medieval Aleppo Codex, on display in the small lower gallery under the white dome, is considered the most authoritative text of the Hebrew Bible in existence. If this speaks to you, the excellent website ⊕ *www.aleppocodex.org* will have you impatient to see the real thing.

The quarter-acre **1:50 scale model,** adjacent to the Shrine of the Book, represents Jerusalem as it was on the eve of the Great Revolt against Rome (AD 66). Until 2006, the huge, intricate reconstruction was a popular attraction in its original home, on the grounds of the former Holyland Hotel in West Jerusalem. The outdoor model was originally designed and built in the mid-1960s by the late Professor Michael Avi-Yonah. He relied on considerable data gleaned from Roman-period historians, important Jewish texts, and even the New Testament, and based some of his generic reconstructions (villas, a theater, markets, etc.) on Roman structures that have survived across the ancient empire, from France to Turkey. Later archaeological excavations have sometimes confirmed and sometimes challenged Avi-Yonah's sharp intuition, and the model has been updated occasionally to incorporate new knowledge. The available audio guide is a worthwhile aid in deciphering the site.

Taken together, the Dead Sea Scrolls, the huge model, and certain Roman-period exhibits in the Archaeology Wing evoke the turbulent and historically momentous Second Temple period. That was the era from which Christianity emerged; and when the Romans razed the Temple in Jerusalem, it compelled a slow revolution in Jewish life and religious practice that has defined Judaism to this day.

The Shrine of the Book at the Israel Museum dramatically displays delicate sections of the Dead Sea Scrolls.

The **Archaeology Wing** has been reorganized to highlight particular treasures in galleries that follow a historical sequence. If you know a bit of the Bible, many artifacts in the Canaanite, Israelite, and Hellenistic-Roman sections offer evocative illustrations of familiar texts. Don't miss the small side rooms devoted to glass, coins, and the Hebrew script.

Jewish Art and Life is the new name for the wing made up mostly of finely wrought Jewish ceremonial objects (Judaica) from widely disparate communities. The "synagogue route" with its reconstructed old synagogues from Cochin (India), Germany, and Venice (Italy) has acquired an addition from the Caribbean community of Suriname.

The **Art Wing** is a slightly confusing maze spread over different levels, but if you have patience and time, the payoff is great. Older European art rubs shoulders with modern works, contemporary Israeli, design, and photography. The flyer available at the museum entrance lists new and temporary exhibitions. Landscape architect Isamu Noguchi designed the open-air **Art Garden.** Crunch over the gravel amid works by Daumier, Rodin, Moore, Picasso, and a number of less-legendary local luminaries.

The **Youth Wing** mounts one new exhibition a year, delightfully interactive and often adult-friendly, designed to encourage children to appreciate the arts and the world around them, or be creative in a crafts workshop. Parents with restless kids will also be grateful for the outdoor play areas. ⊠ *Ruppin Rd., Givat Ram* ☎ *02/670–8811* ⊕ *www. imj.org.il* ⊠ *NIS 50 (includes audio guide); half price for return visit within three months (keep your ticket); free entrance for young visitors (under 18) on Tues. and Sat.* ☉ *Sun., Mon., Wed., Thurs., Sat., and Jewish holidays 10–5, Tues. 4–9, Fri. and Jewish holiday eves 10–2.*

Knesset. Both the name of Israel's one-chamber parliament and its number of seats (120) were taken from *Haknesset Hagedolah*, the Great Assembly of the Second Temple period, some two thousand years ago. The 40-minute public tour includes the session hall and three enormous, brilliantly colored tapestries designed by Marc Chagall on the subjects of the Creation, the Exodus, and Jerusalem. On other days, when in session, Knesset proceedings (conducted in Hebrew, of course) are open to the public—call ahead to verify. Arrive at least 30 minutes before the tour (especially in summer, when the lines are longer), and be sure to bring your passport. Bags and cameras have to be deposited with security.

Across the road from the Knesset main gate is a 14-foot-high, 4-ton bronze menorah, based on the one that once stood within the sanctuary of the ancient temple in Jerusalem. The seven-branch candelabrum was adopted soon after independence as the official symbol of the modern State of Israel. This one, designed by artist Bruno Elkin, and given as a gift by British parliamentarians to the Knesset in 1956, is decorated with bas-relief depictions of events and personages in Jewish history, from biblical times to the modern day. Behind the menorah is the Wohl Rose Garden, which has hundreds of varieties of roses, many lawns for children to romp on, and adult-friendly nooks in its upper section. ✉ *Kiryat Ben-Gurion, Givat Ram* ☎ *02/675-3337* ⊕ *www.knesset.gov. il* ◷ *Free* ☉ *English guided tours Sun. and Thurs. at 8:30, noon, and 2.*

Mt. Herzl National Memorial Park. Cedars of Lebanon and native pine and cypress trees surround the entrance to Mt. Herzl National Memorial Park, the last resting place of Zionist visionary Theodor Herzl and many Israeli leaders.

In 1894, the Budapest-born Herzl was the Paris correspondent for a Vienna newspaper when he covered the treason trial of Alfred Dreyfus, a Jewish officer in the French army. Dreyfus was later exonerated, but Herzl was shocked by the anti-Semitic outbursts that accompanied the trial. He devoted himself to the need for a Jewish state, convening the first World Zionist Congress in Basel, Switzerland, in 1897. That year Herzl wrote in his diary: "If not in five years, then in 50, [a Jewish state] will become reality." True to his prediction, the United Nations approved the idea exactly 50 years later, in November 1947. Herzl died in 1904, and his remains were brought to Israel in 1949. His simple grave marker, inscribed in Hebrew with just his last name, caps the hill.

To the left (west) of his tomb, a gravel path leads down to a section containing the graves of Israeli national leaders, among them prime ministers Levi Eshkol, Golda Meir, and Yitzhak Rabin, and presidents Zalman Shazar and Chaim Herzog. Bear down and right through the military cemetery, exiting back on Herzl Boulevard, about 250 yards below the parking lot where you entered. The main gate closes at set times; the exit via the military cemetery is always open. ✉ *Herzl Blvd., Mt. Herzl* ☎ *02/643-3266* ◷ *Free* ☉ *Apr.–Sept., Sun.–Thurs. 8–6:45, Fri. and Jewish holiday eves 8–12:45; Oct.–Mar., Sun.–Thurs. 8–4:45, Fri. and Jewish holiday eves 8–12:45.*

Israel's Electoral System

"Take two Israelis," runs the old quip, "and you've got three political parties!" The saying isn't without a kernel of truth in a nation where everyone has a strong opinion, and usually won't hesitate to express it. The Knesset, Israel's parliament, reflects this rambunctious spirit, sometimes to the point of paralyzing the parliamentary process and driving the public to distraction.

Israel's electoral system is based on proportional representation. In contrast with the winner-takes-all approach of the constituency system, any Israeli party that wins 2% of the national vote gets the number of seats in the 120-member Knesset to which its share of the ballot entitles it. The system is a legacy of the dangerous but heady days of Israel's War of Independence, in 1948–49. To avoid an acrimonious and divisive election while the fledgling state was still fighting for its life, the founding fathers developed a one-body parliamentary system that gave representation to rival ideological factions in proportion to their comparative strength in the country's *pre*-State institutions.

The good news is that it's wildly democratic: even relatively small fringe groups can have their voices heard.

The bad news is that the system spawns a plethora of political parties, making it virtually impossible for one party to get the majority needed to govern alone. (The past phenomenon of single-member parties was curbed by the introduction of the threshold: a party that wins that share of the vote automatically gets two seats, and more often than not a third one as well.) Consequently, Israeli governments have always consisted of a coalition of parties, inevitably making them governments of compromise. The smaller coalition partners have been able to demand a price for their crucial parliamentary support—influential political positions, budgets for pet projects, and so on—that's often beyond what a minor party deserves, and is sometimes at odds with the good of the nation at large.

Israel also has a president—not a political leader—chosen by the members of the Knesset for one term of seven years. After the Knesset elections, the president consults with every party that made the 2% cut, and entrusts the party leader who seems to have the best coalition options with the job of forming a government. If successful within a designated period, he or she becomes prime minister.

Herzl Museum. On the left as you enter Mt. Herzl National Memorial Park, the Herzl Museum is a strongly engaging, multimedia introduction to the life, times, and legacy of Israel's spiritual forebear, Theodore Herzl. Tours take 50 minutes and cost NIS 25. Call ahead for tours in English. ⊠ *Mt. Herzl National Memorial Park, Herzl Blvd., Mt. Herzl* ☎ *02/632–1515* ⊕ *www.herzl.org* ☉ *Sun.–Thurs. 8:30–5 (later tours possible Apr.–Sept.), Fri. 8:30–1, last tour 1 hr before closing, closed Jewish religious holidays eves.*

OFF THE
BEATEN
PATH

Tisch Family Zoological Gardens. Spread over a scenic 62-acre ridge in the Judean Hills, this zoo has many of the usual species that delight zoo visitors everywhere: monkeys and elephants, snakes and birds, and all the rest. But it goes much further, focusing on two groups of wildlife.

In Yad Vashem's Holocaust History Museum, the Hall of Names includes 600 photos of Jews who perished.

The first is creatures mentioned in the Bible that have become locally extinct, some as late as the 20th century. Among these are Asian lions, bears, cheetahs, the Nile crocodile, and the Persian fallow deer. The second focus is on endangered species worldwide, among them the Asian elephant and rare macaws.

This is a wonderful place to let kids expend some energy—there are lawns and playground equipment as well—and allow adults some downtime from regular touring. Early morning or late afternoon are the best hours in summer; budget 2½ hours to see everything. A wagon train does the rounds of the zoo, at a nominal fee of NIS 2 (not on Saturdays and Jewish holidays). The Noah's Ark Visitors Center has a movie and computer programs. The zoo is served by the Circle Tour bus (line 99), and by city routes 26A (from Central Bus Station) and 33 (from Mt. Herzl). The ride is about 30 minutes; a cab would take 15 minutes from Downtown hotels. ⊠ *Derech Aharon Shulov, near the Jerusalem Mall, Malcha* ☎ *02/675–0111* ⊕ *www.jerusalemzoo.org. il* ⊠ *NIS 49* ⊙ *June–Aug., Sun.–Thurs. 9–7, Fri. 9–4:30, Sat. 10–6; May, Sun.–Thurs. 9–6, Fri. and Jewish holiday eves 9–4:30, Sat. 10–6; Sept.–Apr., Sun.–Thurs. 9–5, Fri. and Jewish holiday eves 9–4:30, Sat. 10–5. Closing times in Apr. and Sept. are sometimes late; call ahead. Last entrance 1 hr before closing.*

Fodor's Choice **Yad Vashem.** The experience of the Holocaust—the annihilation of 6 million Jews by the Nazis during World War II—is so deeply seared into the Jewish national psyche that understanding it goes a long way toward understanding Israelis themselves. The institution of Yad Vashem, created in 1953 by an act of the Knesset, was charged with preserving a record of those times. The name Yad Vashem—"a memorial and a name (a memory)"—comes from the biblical book of Isaiah (56:5). The Israeli government has made a tradition of bringing almost all high-ranking official foreign guests to visit the place.

The riveting **Holocaust History Museum**—a well-lit, 200-yard-long triangular concrete "prism"—is the centerpiece of the site. Powerful visual and audiovisual techniques in a series of galleries document Jewish life in Europe before the catastrophe and follow the escalation of persecution and internment to the hideous climax of the Nazi's "Final Solution." Video interviews and personal artifacts individualize the experience. ■ TIP→ Note that children under 10 aren't admitted, photography isn't allowed in the exhibition areas, and large bags have to be checked.

The small **Children's Memorial** is dedicated to the 1.5 million Jewish children murdered by the Nazis. Architect Moshe Safdie wanted to convey the enormity of the crime without numbing the visitor's emotions or losing sight of the victims' individuality. The result is a single dark room, lit by five candles infinitely reflected in hundreds of mirrors. Recorded narrators intone the names, ages, and countries of origin of known victims. The effect is electrifying. Also focusing on children is a poignant exhibition called "No Child's Play," about children's activities during the Holocaust. It's in an art museum beyond the exit of the Holocaust History Museum.

The **Avenue of the Righteous** encircles Yad Vashem with several thousand trees marked with the names of Gentiles in Europe who risked and sometimes lost their lives trying to save Jews from the Nazis. Raoul Wallenberg, King Christian X of Denmark, Corrie ten Boom, Oskar Schindler, and American journalist Varian Fry are among the more famous honorees. The **Hall of Remembrance** is a heavy basalt-and-concrete building that houses an eternal flame, with the names of the death camps and concentration camps in relief on the floor.

At the bottom of the hill, large rough-hewn limestone boulders divide the **Valley of the Communities** into a series of small, man-made canyons. Each clearing represents a region of Nazi Europe, laid out geographically. The names of some five thousand destroyed Jewish communities are inscribed in the stone walls, with very large letters highlighting those that were particularly important in prewar Europe.

There's an information booth (be sure to buy the inexpensive map of the site), a bookstore, and a cafeteria at the entrance to Yad Vashem.

Allow about two hours to see the Holocaust History Museum, more if you rent an audio guide. If your time is short, be sure to see the Children's Memorial and the Avenue of the Righteous. To avoid the biggest crowds, come first thing in the morning or noon to two. The site is an easy 10-minute walk or a quick free shuttle from the Mt. Herzl intersection, which in turn is served by many city bus lines. The Egged sightseeing Bus 99 takes you right into Yad Vashem. ⊠ *Hazikaron St., near Herzl Blvd., Mt. Herzl* ☎ *02/644-3565* ⊕ *www.yadvashem.org* ▢ *Free* ☉ *Sun.–Wed. 9–5, Thurs. 9–8 (late closing for history museum, art gallery, and synagogue only), Fri. and Jewish holiday eves 9–2. Last entrance 1 hr before closing.*

WORTH NOTING

FAMILY **Bloomfield Science Museum.** For kids, this may be the city's best rainy-day option, but don't wait for a rainy day to enjoy the museum. Along with a range of intriguing, please-touch interactive equipment that demonstrates scientific principles in an engagingly fun environment, there's lots of innovation and creativity—not least of all in the changing exhibits. Explanations are in English, and Hebrew University science students, as many as 20 at a time on busy weekends, are on hand to explain stuff. ⊠ *Museum Blvd., Givat Ram* ☎ *02/654–4888* ⊕ *www.mada.org. il* 🗐 *NIS 37–NIS 45* ⊘ *Mon.–Thurs. 10–6; Fri. and Jewish holiday eves 10–2; Sat. 10–3 (10–4 Apr.–Sept.); last entrance 30 mins before closing.*

Church of St. John the Baptist. The village of Ein Kerem isn't mentioned by name in the New Testament, but its identification as the birthplace of John the Baptist is a tradition that apparently goes back to the Byzantine period (5th century AD). The grotto associated with that event is enshrined in the large, late-17th-century Franciscan church that bears his name, its orange tile roof a prominent landmark in Ein Kerem. The church's old paintings and glazed tiles alone make it worth a visit. ⊠ *Ein Kerem St., Ein Kerem* ☎ *02/632–3000* 🗐 *Free* ⊘ *Apr.–Sept., daily 8– noon and 2:30–5:45; Oct.–Mar., daily 8–noon and 2:30–4:45.*

Church of the Visitation. Built over what is thought to have been the home of John the Baptist's parents, Zechariah and Elizabeth, this church sits high up the hillside in Ein Kerem, with a wonderful view of the valley and the surrounding wooded hills. It's a short but stiff walk up from the spring at the center of the village. When Mary, pregnant with Jesus, came to visit her cousin, the aging Elizabeth, who was also with child, "the babe leaped in [Elizabeth's] womb" with joy at recognizing the unborn Jesus. Mary thereupon pronounced the paean to God known as the Magnificat ("My soul doth magnify the Lord" [Luke 1]). One wall of the church courtyard is covered with ceramic tiles quoting the Magnificat in 41 languages. The upper church is adorned with large wall paintings depicting the mantles with which Mary has been endowed—Mother of God, Refuge of Sinners, Dispenser of All Grace, Help of Christians—as well as the Immaculate Conception. Other frescoes depict Hebrew women of the Bible also known for their "hymns and canticles," as the Franciscan guide puts it. ⊠ *Madreigot Habikur, at end of Hama'ayan St., Ein Kerem* ☎ *02/641–7291* 🗐 *Free* ⊘ *Apr.– Sept., daily 8–11:45 and 2:30–6; Oct.–Mar., daily 8–11:45 and 2:30–5. Gates closed Sat., ring bell.*

L.A. Mayer Museum for Islamic Art. This institution prides itself on being a private Jewish initiative (opened 1974) that showcases the considerable and diverse artistic achievements of Islamic culture worldwide. Its rich collections—ceramics, glass, carpets, fabrics, jewelry, metalwork, and painting—reflect a creativity that spanned half a hemisphere, from Spain to India, and from the 7th century to modern times. Unconnected to the main theme is a unique collection of rare (some priceless) antique European clocks and watches, the pride of the founder's family. ⊠ *2 Hapalmach St., Hapalmach* ☎ *02/566–1291* ⊕ *www.islamicart.co.il/ en* 🗐 *NIS 40* ⊘ *Sun., Mon., Wed. 10–3; Tues., Thurs. 10–7; Fri. and Jewish holiday eves 10–2; Sat. and Jewish holidays, 10–4.*

Mt. Herzl Military Cemetery. The tranquillity and well-tended greenery of Israel's largest military cemetery almost belie its somber purpose. Different sections are reserved for the casualties of each war the nation has fought. The large number of headstones, all identical, are a sobering reminder of the price Israel has paid for its national independence and security. Note that officers and privates are buried alongside one another—lost lives are mourned equally, regardless of rank. ⊠ *Herzl Blvd., Mt. Herzl* 📞 *02/643-7257* 💳 *Free* 🕙 *Always open.*

CENTER CITY

West Jerusalem's Downtown and near-Downtown areas, just west of the Old City, are a mix of old neighborhoods, new limestone edifices, monuments, and markets. There are plenty of hotels and restaurants here, too. Few of the attractions appear on a Jerusalem don't-miss checklist, but you'll rub shoulders with the locals in the Machaneh Yehuda produce market, breathe the atmosphere of day-to-day life on Ben-Yehuda and Jaffa streets, get a feel for the city's more recent history in Nahalat Shiva and Yemin Moshe—in short, for a few brief hours you can be a bit less of a tourist.

GETTING HERE AND AROUND

There's paid parking in the center city, but you're better off walking, grabbing a cab, or riding the light rail. The area is served by bus lines 18, 20, 21, and 23 from Mt. Herzl via the Central Bus Station (where other lines join the route); 4, 18, and 21 from the German Colony and Talbieh; and 9 from the Knesset and the Israel Museum.

TIMING AND PRECAUTIONS

Jaffa Street, Ben-Yehuda Street, and Machaneh Yehuda are ghostly quiet from Friday afternoon until Saturday night because of the Jewish Sabbath. Morning through midday Friday is the most bustling, as Jerusalemites meet friends for coffee or lunch, and do their weekend shopping.

TOP ATTRACTIONS

Ben-Yehuda Street. Most of the street is an open-air pedestrian mall, in the heart of Downtown, forming a triangle with King George Street and Jaffa Street. It's known locally as the **Midrachov,** a term concocted from two Hebrew words: *midracha* (sidewalk) and *rechov* (street). The street is named after the brilliant linguist Eliezer Ben-Yehuda, who in the late 19th century almost single-handedly revived Hebrew as a modern spoken language; he would've liked the clever new word. Cafés have tables out on the cobblestones; vendors display cheap, arty items like funky jewelry and prints; and buskers are usually out in good weather, playing

Ben-Yehuda
Street **8**

Bet Ticho **9**

Hinnom Valley ...**4**

Independence
Park **5**

Machaneh
Yehuda **10**

Montefiore's
Windmill **1**

Nahalat Shiva ...**6**

Umberto Nahon
Museum of
Italian Art **7**

Yemin Moshe **3**

YMCA **2**

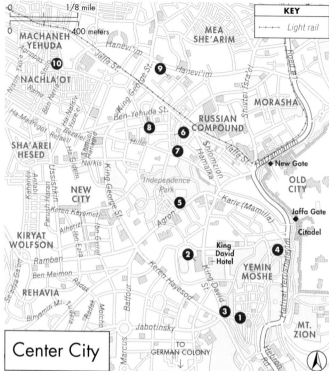

tunes old and new. It's a great place to sip coffee or munch falafel and watch the passing crowd. However, on Saturday and Jewish holidays only a few restaurants are open but nothing else. ✉ *Downtown.*

Fodor's Choice   **Machaneh Yehuda.** For a unique local experience, head to this block-
★   long alley and a parallel wider street filled with the brilliant colors of the city's best-quality and lowest-priced produce, cheeses, and baked goods. It's fun to elbow your way through this decidedly unslick market anytime, but it's riotously busy on Thursday and Friday, when Jewish Jerusalem shops for the Sabbath. The hawkers' cries get more passionate as closing time approaches. Look for the excellent eatery called Mizrachi, down the third lane on the left as you enter from Agrippas Street. The market links Jaffa Street and Agrippas Street, parallel to and just a five-minute walk up from King George Street. Many of the Downtown bus lines stop on King George, and several on Agrippas itself, while the light rail runs the length of Jaffa Street (which is otherwise closed to traffic). There's paid parking close to the market. ✉ *Machaneh Yehuda* ☉ *Sun.–Thurs. 8 am–sunset Fri. and Jewish holiday eves 8 am–2 hrs before sunset.*

Montefiore's Windmill. Sir Moses Montefiore had this limestone windmill built in 1857 to provide a source of income for his planned neighborhood of Mishkenot Sha'ananim. In 2012, with Dutch and English

GERMAN COLONY

Israelis have discovered the old-world charms of "the Moshava" (the German Colony), and so should you. This isn't the place to go for big sights; instead, take in the pleasant eateries, cafés, and stores that proliferate in this neighborhood a mile or so south of Downtown. It's a good place to relax along with the residents. Come during daytime Friday or on warm evenings (except Friday). Look for the (irregular) Friday food and flea market at the Adam School on the main drag (⊠ 22 Emek Refai'm Street).

German inscriptions on 19th-century stone houses along the same street recall the Templers (not medieval, spelled with an e), breakaway Lutherans who believed their presence in the Holy Land would hasten the Second Coming. Jerusalem's German Colony was one of half a dozen communities established in the 1860s and '70s under extremely trying conditions.

Feelings of German patriotism ran high in World War I, and many were interned as enemy aliens in 1918, in the wake of the British conquest of Palestine. Some of their pro-Nazi descendants were exiled during World War II.

expertise, the windmill was restored to working order and will mill wheat again as soon as the interior has been renovated. Montefiore was a prominent figure in the financial circles of mid-19th-century London—a rare phenomenon for a Jew at the time. It didn't harm his fortunes that he married into the legendary Rothschild family, and became the stockbroker of its London branch. The larger-than-life philanthropist—he stood a remarkable 6 feet 3 inches tall—devoted much of his long life, and his wealth, to aiding fellow Jews in distress, wherever they might be. To this end he visited Palestine, as this district of the Ottoman Empire was then known, seven times. ⊠ *Yemin Moshe St., Yemin Moshe.*

Nahalat Shiva. This small neighborhood has a funky feel, with worn flagstones, wrought-iron banisters, and defunct water cisterns. Its name translates roughly as "the Estate of the Seven," so called by the seven Jewish families that founded the quarter in 1869. The alleys and courtyards have been refashioned as a pedestrian district, offering equal opportunities to the keen photographer, the eager shopper, and the gastronome. An eclectic variety of eateries, from Israeli to Italian, Asian to Arabic, tempt you to take a break from the jewelry and ceramics. ⊠ *Bordered by Salomon, Rivlin, Jaffa, and Hillel Sts., Nahalat Shiva.*

YMCA. A high-domed landmark bell tower thrusts out of the palatial white-limestone facade of the YMCA, offering superb views in all directions. For NIS 10, you can ride the small elevator to the balconies, where you can gaze out over the Old City. A bit of trivia: the building, dedicated in 1933, was designed by Arthur Loomis Harmon, one of the architects of New York City's Empire State Building. ⊠ *26 King David St., Downtown* ☎ *02/569–2692* ⊕ *www.jerusalemymca.org* ⊡ *Free; NIS 10 for the elevator* ☼ *Tower: Sun.–Thurs. 8–8, Fri.–Sat. 8–5.*

WORTH NOTING

Bet Ticho (*Ticho House*). Set among pine trees, this handsome two-story historical building is part museum, part restaurant, and part concert venue. Dr. A. A. Ticho was a renowned Jewish ophthalmologist who emigrated from Austria to Jerusalem in 1912. His cousin, Anna Ticho, a trained nurse, followed the same year, to assist him in his pioneering struggle against the endemic scourge of trachoma. They were soon married, and in 1924 bought and renovated this fine 19th-century stone house. Anna's artistic talent gradually earned her a reputation as a brilliant chronicler—in charcoal, pen, and brush—of the landscape around Jerusalem. Bet Ticho displays a selection of her works, offers changing intimate art and photography exhibitions, and has a very good vegetarian restaurant. ⊠ *9 Harav Kook St., Downtown* ☎ *02/624–5068* ⊕ *www.imj.org.il* ⊡ *Free* ⊙ *Sun., Mon., Wed., and Thurs. 10–5, Tues. 10–10, Fri. and Jewish holiday eves 10–2.*

OFF THE BEATEN PATH

Haas Promenade. Get your bearings in Jerusalem by taking in the panorama from the Haas Promenade, an attractive 1-km (2/3-mile) promenade along one of the city's highest ridges. Hidden behind a grove of trees to the east (your right as you pan the view) is a turreted limestone building, the residence of the British High Commissioner for Palestine in the 1930s and 1940s. In Hebrew, the whole ridge is known as Armon Hanatziv, the Commissioner's Palace. The building became the headquarters of the U.N. Truce Supervision Organization (UNTSO), charged with monitoring the 1949 armistice line that divided the city. It remained a neutral enclave between Israeli West Jerusalem and Jordanian-controlled East Jerusalem until the reunification of the city in the Six-Day War of 1967. You can reach the promenade by car from Hebron Road—consult a map, and look for signs to East Talpiot and the Haas Promenade—by Bus 8 or by cab. If the traffic flows well, it's a 10-minute drive from Downtown or 5 minutes from the German Colony. There are restrooms just off the sidewalk at the "city" end of the promenade. ⊠ *Daniel Yanovsky St., East Talpiot.*

Hinnom Valley. The Hinnom Valley achieved notoriety in the 7th century BC during the long reign of the Israelite king Menasseh (697–640 BC). He was an idolater, the Bible relates, who supported a cult of child sacrifice by fire in the Valley of the Son of Hinnom. Over time, the biblical Hebrew name of the valley—*Gei Ben Hinnom*, contracted to *Gehennom* or *Gehenna*—became a synonym for hell in both Hebrew and New Testament Greek.

In the late 1970s, Israeli archaeologist Gabriel Barkai discovered a series of Old Testament–period rock tombs at the bend in the valley, below the fortress-like St. Andrew's Scots Church. A miraculously unplundered pit yielded "grave goods" like miniature clay vessels and jewelry. The most spectacular finds, however, were two tiny rolled strips of silver designed to be worn around the neck as amulets. When unrolled, the fragile pieces revealed a slightly condensed version of the biblical priestly benediction, inscribed in the ancient Hebrew script. (The original, in Numbers 6, begins: "The Lord bless you and keep you.") The 7th-century BC text is the oldest biblical passage ever found. The tombs are an open site, behind the Menachem Begin Heritage Center. Access

Me'a She'arim

The name of this neighborhood just north of Downtown is the biblical "hundredfold," describing the bountiful blessing God gave Isaac (Genesis 26). The appearance of that verse in the cyclical Torah reading the very week the neighborhood was founded, in 1874, was regarded as a good omen. This is 24/7 ultra-Orthodox Judaism. The community is insular and uncompromising and clings to an old-world lifestyle: residents have no TVs; some reject the legitimacy of modern Israel; and people speak Yiddish rather than the "sacred" Hebrew as the conversational language.

Modesty in dress and behavior is imperative for anyone entering the neighborhood. Visitors (best in tiny groups) must avoid male-female contact; women should wear long skirts, long sleeves, and nothing exposed below the neck. It's a voyeuristic experience, but avoid the Sabbath and photograph discreetly at other times if you choose to go.

Me'a She'arim is traversed by Me'a She'arim Street, and most of the historic neighborhood is on the slope above it (in the direction of Hanevi'im Street and the Downtown area). To the west it's more or less bounded by Strauss Street; to the east it almost touches Road No. 1.

is through the center, but only when it's open for business. ✉ 6 *Nahon St., below St. Andrew's Scots Church, Hinnom Valley* ☎ *02/565–2020* 🎫 *Free* ☉ *Sun., Mon., Wed., and Thurs. 9–4:30; Tues. 9–7; Fri. and Jewish holiday eves 9–12:30.*

Independence Park. This is a great area for lounging around, throwing Frisbees, or eating a picnic lunch in warm weather. Some of the Muslim graves at the bottom of the park date from the 13th century. The large defunct reservoir nearby, known as the Mamilla Pool, is probably late medieval, though it may have much earlier Roman origins. ✉ *Between Agron and Hillel sts., Downtown.*

Yemin Moshe. This now-affluent neighborhood, with its attractive old stone buildings, bursts of greenery and bougainvillea, and well-kept cobblestone streets, grew up a century ago alongside the older Mishkenot Sha'ananim, and was named for that project's founder, Sir Moses (*Moshe* in Hebrew) Montefiore. In the 1950s and '60s, the area overlooked the nervy armistice line that gashed through the city, and was dangerously exposed to Jordanian sniper positions on the nearby Old City walls. Most families sought safer lodgings elsewhere, leaving only those who couldn't afford to move, and the neighborhood ran to seed. The reunification of Jerusalem under Israeli rule after the Six-Day War in 1967 changed all that. Developers bought up the area, renovated old buildings, and built new and spacious homes in a compatible style. Yemin Moshe is now a place to wander at random, offering joy to photographers and quiet nooks for meditation. A couple of restaurants are added bonuses. ✉ *Yemin Moshe.*

WHERE TO EAT

Jerusalem is less chic and cosmopolitan than Tel Aviv—no question about it—but you can still eat very well in the holy city. Inexpensive eateries serving Middle Eastern standards, fast-food favorites, or sandwiches and salads remain popular; but travel abroad by Israelis has whetted the appetite of both cooks and customers for more interesting food. The excellence of local produce that is still, by and large, eaten seasonally and the endurance of ethnic or family culinary traditions have been fertilized by imported new ideas and individual inspiration.

The result—common enough to sniff a trend in it—is a joyfully rich menu of palate pleasers. Some of the new restaurants clearly identify themselves by cuisine—French or Spanish, for example—while others defy easy labeling. Not quite Mediterranean, not quite European (though clearly influenced by both), they're, well, Israeli enough to deserve a new sobriquet: modern Israeli. How groundbreaking the trend is remains to be seen—categorizing cuisines isn't an exact science—but there's no doubt that new restaurants have markedly changed the culinary map of Jerusalem.

Some cuisine designations are self-explanatory, but other terms may be less so. A restaurant advertising itself as "dairy" will serve meals without meat; many such places do serve fish, in addition to pasta, soup, and salads. "Oriental" on a sign is usually a literal translation of *mizrachi,* suggesting Middle Eastern (in contrast to Western).

The term *kosher* doesn't imply a particular style of cooking, only that certain religious restrictions are adhered to in the selection and preparation of the food. In Jerusalem, where there are many kosher standards from which to choose, the selection can be dizzying. But unless specific kosher standards apply to your eating habits, don't worry. You can find plenty of fine steaks and some fish fillets. Remember that most kosher restaurants are closed for Friday dinner and Saturday lunch in observation of the Jewish Sabbath. A generous handful of kosher cafés, bars, and restaurants remain open, and most nonkosher establishments remain open all weekend.

Dress codes are pretty much nonexistent in Jerusalem's restaurants (as in the rest of Israel). People tend to dress very casually—jeans are perfectly appropriate almost everywhere anytime. A modicum of neatness and modesty (trousers instead of jeans, a button-down shirt instead of a T-shirt) might be expected in the more exclusive establishments. If you brought the kids, you're in luck: nearly every Israeli restaurant is kid-friendly, and many have special menus and high chairs.

Prices in the reviews are the average cost of a main course at dinner or, if dinner isn't served, at lunch. Use the coordinates at the end of each listing (✢ 2A) to locate a site on the corresponding map.

CENTER CITY

The area extends from the Machaneh Yehuda market and Nachla'ot neighborhood, through the central Downtown triangle, to Nahalat Shiva and the junction with King David Street and then through the Mamilla Mall up to the Jaffa Gate, a walk of 20 minutes from end to end. The range is vast, from funky budget or takeaway joints to upscale fine-dining specialists, from Middle Eastern food to European cuisine, and several surprises in between. Nonkosher restaurants do a roaring trade on Friday night, after the Sabbath begins, when their kosher counterparts are closed and the city streets quiet.

$$$
MIDDLE EASTERN

✕ **Barood.** Jerusalemite Daniella Lerer combines her family's Sephardic culinary traditions with modern Israeli cooking techniques. Starters include fried eggplant with yogurt and falafel filled with labaneh cheese. For your main course, try *pastilla* (meat pies filled with beef, pine nuts, and grilled eggplant); *sufrito* (braised dumplings cooked with Jerusalem artichokes); beef and leeks in lemon juice; and shrimp in wine and lemon. For dessert, look for the traditional *sutlach,* a cold rice pudding topped with cinnamon, nuts, and jam. Barood's other face is its well-stocked bar serving more familiar fare like spareribs and sausages. Reservations are a must for dinner Friday night. $ *Average main: NIS 88* ⊠ *Feingold Courtyard, 31 Jaffa St., Downtown* ☎ *02/625–9081* ☾ *Closed Sun.* ✛ *C2.*

$$$
AMERICAN

✕ **Black.** Some may find the black-and-crimson decor, mirrored ceilings, large screens showing sport events, and illuminated liquor bottles a little macho, but Black is wildly popular with younger folks looking for a party atmosphere and a menu that includes more than just burgers. Entrées like schnitzel (breaded cutlets of turkey or chicken) are available, as are plenty of beef and lamb dishes. If you're in the market for a burger, try the Popeye, made with beef and spinach. All are served with a range of toppings including sunny-side-up eggs and goose breast. Gluten-free options are available, as is a takeout option. The bar, with its good range of drinks, exudes youthful cool. $ *Average main: NIS 85* ⊠ *18 Shlomzion Hamalka St., Downtown* ☎ *02/624–6767* ☾ *No dinner Fri. No lunch Sat.* ✛ *C2.*

$$
FAST FOOD
FAMILY

✕ **Burgers Bar.** The menu bears a passing resemblance to that of the big hamburger chains, but the product is a different creature altogether. Hamburgers of different weight are more like cakes than patties, come with tasty sauces, and all are made to order. Lamb and chicken wraps and robust salads reflect Israeli tastes. Popular with local youngsters are the house french fries, more like sautéed potatoes. $ *Average main: NIS 62* ⊠ *12 Shammai St., Downtown* ☎ *02/622–1555* ☾ *No dinner Fri. No lunch Sat.* ✛ *B1.*

$
MODERN ISRAELI
Fodor'sChoice
★

✕ **Café Mizrachi.** Established by Eli Mizrachi, who once sold dried beans in a stall at Machaneh Yehuda, and run by his pastry-chef daughter Moran, this café was created to add a more sophisticated flavor to the beloved market. Expanded to the size of three market stalls, the café is known for its excellent local fare, including fresh pasta with Jerusalem artichokes and leeks; four-cheese ravioli with a cherry tomato and pepper confit; and the wondrously sinful ricotta and raisin brioche. The coffee is also excellent. This is a worthwhile stop on summer evenings, when Mizrachi stays open late to serve drinks, light dishes, and

BEST BETS FOR JERUSALEM DINING

With hundreds of restaurants to choose from, how will you decide where to eat? Fodor's writers and editors have selected their favorite restaurants by price, cuisine, and experience in the lists below. In the first column, Fodor's Choice properties represent the "best of the best" across price categories. You can also search by area for excellent eats—just check out our complete reviews in the following pages.

Fodor's Choice ★

Café Mizrachi, $, p. 119

Chakra, $$$$, p. 121

Eucalyptus, $$$$, p. 124

HaChazer, $$$$, p. 130

Ima, $$$, p. 125

Little Jerusalem, $$, p. 126

Machneyuda, $$$$, p. 126

Mona, $$$$, p. 127

By Price

$

Abu Shukri, p. 131

Café Mizrachi, p. 119

Pinati, p. 127

Te'enim, p. 134

Village Green, p. 128

$$

Baba Israeli Kitchen, p. 129

Café Paradiso, p. 132

Little Jerusalem, p. 126

Spaghettim, p. 127

T'mol Shilshom, p. 128

$$$

Angelica, p. 132

Focaccia Bar, p. 130

Ima, p. 125

$$$$

Canela, p. 121

Chakra, p. 121

Darna, p. 121

Dolphin Yam, p. 124

Eucalyptus, p. 124

HaChazer, p. 130

Mona, p. 127

By Cuisine

MEAT LOVERS

Angelica, $$$, p. 132

Black, $$$, p. 119

Burgers Bar, $$, p. 119

El Gaucho, $$$$, p. 124

HaChazer, $$$$, p. 130

Joy, $$$$, p. 130

Machneyuda, $$$$, p. 126

MIDDLE EASTERN

Baba Israeli Kitchen, $$, p. 129

Ima, $$$, p. 125

Nafoura, $$, p. 131

MODERN ISRAELI

Angelica, $$$, p. 132

Chakra, $$$$, p. 121

HaChazer, $$$$, p. 130

Mona, $$$$, p. 127

Scala, $$$$, p. 134

DAIRY AND FISH

Little Jerusalem, $$, p. 126

T'mol Shilshom, $$, p. 128

VEGETARIAN

Te'enim, $, p. 134

Village Green, $, p. 128

By Experience

CHILD-FRIENDLY

Baba Israeli Kitchen, $$, p. 129

Burgers Bar, $$, p. 119

Keshet Hahurva, $$, p. 131

Little Jerusalem, $$, p. 126

Luciana, $$, p. 130

Spaghettim, $$, p. 127

OUTSIDE DINING

Barood, $$$, p. 119

Chakra, $$$$, p. 121

Colony, $$$, p. 129

Keshet Hahurva, $$, p. 131

Little Jerusalem, $$, p. 126

Nafoura, $$, p. 131

Village Green, $, p. 128

LOCAL FAVORITES

Abu Shukri, $, p. 131

Caffit, $$, p. 129

Focaccia Bar, $$$, p. 130

Ima, $$$, p. 125

Joy, $$$$, p. 130

Pinati, $, p. 127

GREAT VIEWS

Chakra, $$$$, p. 121

Lavan, $$$, p. 134

Rooftop, $$$$, p. 127

Te'enim, $, p. 134

sometimes jazz. [$] *Average main: NIS 49* ✉ *12 HaShezif St., Machaneh Yehuda* ☎ *02/624–2105* ⏲ *No dinner Fri. No lunch Sat.* ✥ *D3.*

$$$$ FRENCH FAMILY

🍴 **Canela.** The parquet floors, white baby grand piano, diaphanous drapes, and flower arrangements suggest class, and rightly so. Canela helped pioneer kosher fine dining in Jerusalem, and its French cuisine is still among the city's finest. Great starters include the sea bream ceviche, smoked goose and asparagus, and a chicken liver with almonds and berries that melts on your tongue. The deliberately restrained list of entrées includes a fine salmon with gnocchi, but meat rules. Try chicken breast stuffed with smoked goose breast or the particularly good fillet with wild rice. There's also a good children's menu. Kosher rules don't allow for dairy desserts, but the chocolate ganache will leave you wondering where they hid the milk. [$] *Average main: NIS 164* ✉ *8 Shlomzion Hamalka St., Downtown* ☎ *02/622–2293* 🌐 *www.canela.rest-e.co.il* ✍ *Reservations essential* ⏲ *Closed Fri. No lunch Sat.* ✥ *C2.*

$$$$ MODERN ISRAELI Fodor's Choice ★

🍴 **Chakra.** Despite being known as one of the city's best restaurants, Chakra still pretends to be anonymous: its name is nowhere in sight. It draws a lively thirtysomething crowd of hip Jerusalemites that appreciate the sophisticated decor and tasty fare from the open kitchen. Tables are arranged around the striking semicircular bar. The patio, perfect for fine-weather dining, enjoys a park view. Daily specials enhance the expansive menu, and some good starters include beef or red-tuna carpaccio, grilled eggplant with pine nuts, or shrimp with sea salt; ask for bread and baba ghanoush dip. Try the lamb osso buco or the gray mullet, which comes grilled to perfection on a slice of black slate. Share a dessert of ice cream in a tahini-and-date sauce. [$] *Average main: NIS 105* ✉ *41 King George St., Downtown* ☎ *02/625–2733* 🌐 *www.chakra-rest.com* ✍ *Reservations essential* ✥ *E4.*

$$$$ ITALIAN

🍴 **Cielo.** Chef Adi Cohen maintains his family's tradition of good Italian fare from Lombardy. The soft lighting is easy on the eyes, and the lack of decoration isn't a shortcoming in the very intimate setting: large, tastefully framed wall mirrors add depth to the room. The service is professional and friendly. A starter menu includes great traditional dishes like ravioli (the stuffings change: look for seafood or truffles), and a superb lasagna and cannelloni combination. Especially interesting among the entrées are the tender *piccatina con funghi* (thinly sliced veal with lemon and mushrooms), *tournedo dello chef* (beef fillet with white wine, truffles, and porcini mushrooms) and *tournedo Modena* (beef fillet with balsamic vinegar and leek sauce). The house red wine is excellent. [$] *Average main: NIS 112* ✉ *18 Ben Sira St., Downtown* ☎ *02/625–1132* 🌐 *www.cielo.rest-e.co.il* ✍ *Reservations essential* ⏲ *No lunch Fri.* ✥ *E4.*

$$$$ MOROCCAN

🍴 **Darna.** A vaulted tunnel sets you down in a corner of Morocco, complete with imported floor tiles and inlaid chairs. The fixed-price menus are a veritable banquet; ordering à la carte, though, offers more flexibility. The salads are quite different from the local Arab *mezze* (salads), but don't miss the *harira* soup of meat, chickpeas, and lentils flavored with cumin, or the *pastilla fassia,* phyllo dough stuffed with almonds, cinnamon, and Cornish hen (vegetarian versions are usually available). The *tagines,* or Moroccan stews, are excellent, but the house specialty is the more expensive roast baby-lamb shoulder with almonds, served on

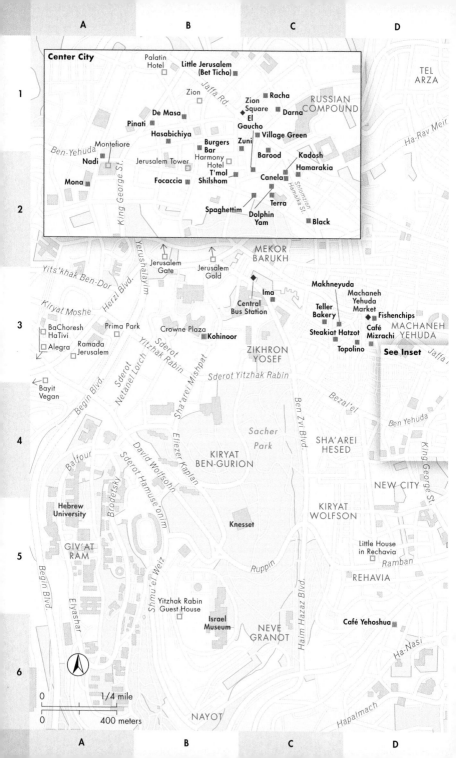

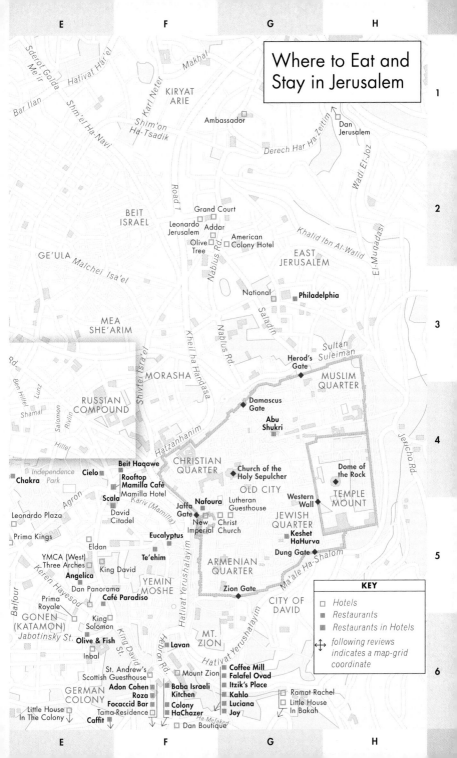

Where to Eat and Stay in Jerusalem

E **F** **G** **H**

1

Bar Ilan
Sderot Golda Me'ir
Hativat Har'el
Shm'el Ha-Navi
Karl Neter
Makhal
KIRYAT ARIE
Shim'on Ha-Tsadik
Ambassador
Derech Har Ha-Zeitim
Dan Jerusalem
Wadi El-Joz

2

Road 1
BEIT ISRAEL
Grand Court
Leonardo Jerusalem
Addar
Olive Tree
American Colony Hotel
Khalid Ibn Al-Walid
EAST JERUSALEM
El-Muqadasi

GE'ULA
Malchei Isa'el
Nablus Rd.

3

MEA SHE'ARIM
Kheil ha Handasa
Nablus Rd.
Saladin
National
Philadelphia
Sultan Suleiman

Rd.
Ben Hillel
Lunz
Shamal
Salomon
Rivlin
Hillel
RUSSIAN COMPOUND
Shivtei Isra'el
MORASHA
Hatzanhanim
Herod's Gate
MUSLIM QUARTER

4

Independence Park
Cielo
Beit Haqawe
Damascus Gate
Abu Shukri
Jericho Rd.

Chakra
Agron
Rooftop
Mamilla Café
Mamilla Hotel
Scala
Kariv (Mamilla)
David Citadel
CHRISTIAN QUARTER
Church of the Holy Sepulcher
OLD CITY
Dome of the Rock
TEMPLE MOUNT

Leonardo Plaza
Prima Kings
Nafoura
Jaffa Gate
New Imperial
Lutheran Guesthouse
Christ Church
Western Wall
JEWISH QUARTER
Keshet
HaHurva
Dung Gate
Ma'ale Ha-Shalom

5

Balfour
Keren Hayesod
Eldan
YMCA (West)
Three Arches
Angelica
King David
Eucalyptus
Te'ehim
Dan Panorama
ARMENIAN QUARTER
Zion Gate
CITY OF DAVID
Prima Royale
Café Paradiso
GONEN (KATAMON)
King Solomon
Jabotinsky St.
Olive & Fish
Inbal
YEMIN MOSHE
MT. ZION
Hativat Yerushalayim

6

St. Andrew's
Scottish Guesthouse
Lavan
Mount Zion
Coffee Mill
Falafel Ovad
Itzik's Place
Ramat Rachel
GERMAN COLONY
Adon Cohen
Roza
Focaccid Bar
Tama-Residence
Baba Israeli Kitchen
Colony
HaChazer
Kahlo
Luciana
Joy
Little House In Bakah
Little House In The Colony
Caffit
Dan Boutique
Ha-Mefaked

KEY
☐ Hotels
■ Restaurants
■ Restaurants in Hotels
↔ following reviews indicates a map-grid coordinate

couscous. Finish with refreshing mint tea (served with fine ceremony) and the wonderful *toubkal* delight, sweet phyllo dough with cinnamon and almond milk. $ *Average main: NIS 130* ⊠ *3 Horkonos St., Downtown* ☏ *02/624–5406* ⊕ *www.darna.co.il* ⟋ *Reservations essential* ⊘ *Closed Fri. No lunch Sat.* ✛ *C1.*

$$
ITALIAN

✕ **De Masa.** A welcome oasis of calm and sophistication among the frenzied fast-food joints and simple eateries of Ben-Yehuda Street, the elegant De Masa is the place for coffee accompanied by one of the fine selection of pastries, or perhaps a light meal. Appetizers include pesto with crispy Manchego cheese and an enticing range of focaccia. For your main course, try the salad of seared tuna with chili aioli or the ravioli with sheep's milk cheese. If you get there early, six different breakfasts are on offer. The upstairs gallery is quiet and cosy. $ *Average main: NIS 69* ⊠ *7 Ben-Yehuda St., Downtown* ☏ *054/232–8861* ⊘ *No dinner Fri. No lunch Sat.* ✛ *B1.*

$$$$
SEAFOOD

✕ **Dolphin Yam.** Hebrew for "Sea Dolphin," this eatery serves some of the city's best seafood in one of the liveliest parts of Downtown. The decor is pleasant enough—pale yellow stucco walls, recessed wine racks, and arched windows—but it's not a place for intimacy. Food is what draws the mixed clientele, including plenty of families. Start with a selection of refillable dishes; the wild roasted eggplant with tahini and pine nuts is excellent. Move on to the shrimp in a cream-and-mushroom sauce or the *musar baladi* (drum fish) in fish broth and dried tomato sauce. You can also experiment with the generous seafood platter for two. $ *Average main: NIS 101* ⊠ *9 Ben Shetach St., Downtown* ☏ *02/623–2272* ⟋ *Reservations essential* ✛ *C2.*

$$$$
ARGENTINE

✕ **El Gaucho.** Red meat reigns at this Argentinian grill, and the chef here knows how to cook it. The stone building is a little hard to find, but once you're inside you'll find a cozy space with dramatic arches, flagstone floors, beamed ceilings, and wooden tables. Nibble on juicy chicken wings or flaky empanadas while you wait for your steak: try the entrecote or the chorizo (don't confuse this tender sirloin with the spicy sausage of the same name, which is also available) with a parsley-based *chimichurri* sauce. A house specialty is the slow-cooked *asado*, grilled boneless beef ribs. There's a children's menu, as well as several dishes to make vegetarians happy. $ *Average main: NIS 114* ⊠ *22 Rivlin St., Nahalat Shiva* ☏ *02/624–2227* ⊕ *www.elgaucho.co.il* ⊘ *Closed Fri. No lunch Sat.* ✛ *C2.*

$$$$
MIDDLE EASTERN
Fodor's Choice
★

✕ **Eucalyptus.** Owner-chef Moshe Basson, repeated winner of international couscous contests, has explored the kitchens and fields of older Jewish and Arab women to revive antique recipes and unfashionable ingredients. The result is a delicious and intriguing feast. Appetizers are all tasty, but try the figs stuffed with chicken breast in a tamarind sauce and the extraordinary stuffed mallow leaves (instead of conventional *dolmades*, or stuffed grape leaves). Two exquisite mains include the traditional *makhloubeh* with chicken and rice, and the clay-baked lamb in pastry with okra. Finish with unusual desserts and herbal tea. If you're in the mood, ask Basson to share some of his culinary lore. $ *Average main: NIS 105* ⊠ *14 Hativat Jerusalem St., Hutzot Hayotzer* ☏ *02/624–4331* ⊕ *www.the-eucalyptus.com* ⟋ *Reservations essential* ⊘ *No dinner Fri. No lunch Sat.* ✛ *F5.*

2

$ × **Fishenchips.** Shlomi Ohana's tiny fish-and-chips emporium in the heart
BRITISH of the vegetable market offers fresh selections direct from his father
FAMILY Haim's seafood stall down the alleyway. Everything is garnished with
a range of tasty dressings and accompanied by great fries. Try classic
British-style cod in batter, or a range of interesting dishes including
tuna, salmon, and "today's fresh catch from my father's stall." There
are also good beers on tap. Ohana has tripled the seating area because
of the huge demand, so there's plenty of space. $ *Average main: NIS 49*
⊠ *10 HaEgoz St., Machaneh Yehuda* ☎ *02/624–9503* ⌁ *Reservations
not accepted* ⊙ *No dinner Fri. No lunch Sat.* ✛ *D3.*

$$ × **Focaccia.** The smallish interior in an old stone building is pleasant
ITALIAN enough, but the spacious enclosed patio overlooking the street is much
livelier. A popular haunt for twenty- and thirtysomethings (and also
popular with families), this restaurant has the feel of a neighborhood
brasserie. There are many toppings (don't miss the black-olive spread),
and some tasty starters (try the fried mushrooms stuffed with goat
cheese or the fried calamari). The chicken livers stir-fried with apples,
shallots, and nuts are delicious. There are great sandwich options, like
sirloin strips, and several salads and pasta dishes. It's worth making a
reservation on weekends, when it's packed with regulars. $ *Average
main: NIS 75* ⊠ *4 Rabbi Akiva St., Downtown* ☎ *02/625–6428* ⊕ *www.
fucaccia-bar.rest-e.co.il* ✛ *B2.*

$ × **Hamarakia.** Housed in a slightly dilapidated old building, this funky
ISRAELI hangout draws young, impecunious students. The name means "soup
pot," and a cheap, ever-changing menu of hearty soups and stews, served
with half loaves of crusty bread, butter, and pesto, make it a satisfying
alternative to the conventional three-course meal. *Shakshuka* (a tangy,
simmering dish of eggs, tomatoes, and onions), interesting salads, and
other vegetarian and vegan options complete the menu. There's a piano
in the corner, a box of old records, and a chandelier made of spoons.
Late-evening drinkers can listen to jazz two nights a week, usually Mon-
days and Wednesdays. When the weather permits, you can sprawl on the
couches and pillows arranged out back. $ *Average main: NIS 28* ⊠ *4
Koresh St., Downtown* ☎ *02/625–7797* ⊙ *No lunch. Closed Fri.* ✛ *C2.*

$ × **Hasabichiya.** The sign is only in Hebrew at Hasabichiya, a hole-in-the-
ISRAELI wall stand featuring what many say is the best sabich in the city. Thin
slices of fried eggplant are combined with a mix of salads and wrapped
in a laffa or stuffed into a pita. The hours? Until the eggplant runs out.
$ *Average main: NIS 18* ⊠ *9 Shamai St., Downtown* ☎ *no phone* ✛ *B1.*

$$$ × **Ima.** It's pronounced *ee*-mah, means "Mom," and is named for the
MIDDLE EASTERN owner's Kurdish-Jewish mother, who inspired many of the excellent tra-
Fodor's Choice ditional Middle Eastern offerings. At the end of Agrippas Street, in walk-
★ ing distance from Machaneh Yehuda, the restaurant has a more diverse
clientele than the fast-food places up the street—you'll rub shoulders
with diplomats, lawyers, and politicians. The century-old stone house,
with its arched doorways and niched windows, create different-size
dining areas that bestow a feeling of intimacy. Avoid the glassed-in terrace during the summer. The modest array of salads includes hummus
and baba ghanoush, as well as stuffed grape leaves and the wonderful
kibbeh (seasoned ground meat deep-fried in a jacket of bulgur wheat).

A selection of stuffed vegetables is an excellent choice if you're sharing. The tangy kibbeh soup full of dumplings is almost a meal in itself. Entrées are often accompanied by *majadra* (rice and lentils). $ *Average main: NIS 77* ✉ *55 Shmuel Baruch, Nachla'ot* ☎ *02/624–6860* ☽ *No dinner Fri. Closed Sat.* ✛ *C3.*

$$
ISRAELI
FAMILY
Fodor's Choice
★

✕ **Little Jerusalem.** This imposing stone building called Bet Ticho was once the home of artist Anna Ticho, whose evocative drawings of Jerusalem adorn its walls. House specialties include excellent salmon blintzes, savory quiches, onion soup served inside crusty loaves of bread, and sea bream in a fresh ginger sauce. The generous portions are often large enough to share, and the desserts are sinful. On Tuesday night, there's a wine-and-cheese buffet accompanied by live jazz. Friday morning you can hear chamber-music concerts in the upstairs gallery. Angle for a table on the patio in warm weather. A good children's menu makes this a good spot for families. $ *Average main: NIS 70* ✉ *9 Harav Kook St., Downtown* ☎ *02/624-4186* ⊕ *www.go-out.com/ticho* ⚞ *Reservations essential* ☽ *No dinner Fri. No lunch Sat.* ✛ *B1.*

$$$$
ISRAELI
FAMILY
Fodor's Choice
★

✕ **Machneyuda.** This hot spot is named for the way Israelis pronounce the name of Machaneh Yehuda. On the edge of its namesake market, this restaurant is considered one of the best in Jerusalem, possibly the country. With ample seating at the busy kitchen bar and at the rustic tables scattered throughout the two-level dining room, there's plenty of opportunity to watch the efficiently exuberant chefs slice, dice, and sauté your meal. The menu—composed of fresh, seasonal ingredients—changes daily, but nearly always includes *chamshuka*, a fusion of chopped meat and hummus; a dreamily creamy polenta topped with crisp asparagus, mushroom ragout, and shaved Parmesan; and a flavorful bouillabaisse. Reserve at least two weeks in advance. $ *Average main: NIS 124* ✉ *10 Beit Yaakov St., Machaneh Yehuda* ☎ *02/533-3442* ⚞ *Reservations essential* ☽ *No dinner Fri. No lunch Sat.* ✛ *C3.*

$$
CAFÉ

✕ **Mamilla Café.** The Mamilla Hotel has added more than one option to the Jerusalem dining scene, and this café on Mamilla Avenue is the latest. With a dining room with long, marble tabletops and a spacious, outdoor patio, it's an appealing space. The tapas-style menu is geared toward sharing. The bulgur salad is delicious, as are the pumpkin-and-anchovy pizza and the ricotta ravioli with tomatoes and capers. The fruit tart is worth the calories. $ *Average main: NIS 60* ✉ *Mamilla Hotel, Mamilla Ave., Mamilla* ☎ *02/548-2230* ⊕ *www.mamillahotel. com/mamillacafe* ☽ *No dinner Fri. No lunch Sat.* ✛ *E4.*

FAST FOODS TO TRY

Falafel and hummus are ubiquitous in Jerusalem, as is the **sabich**, a pita stuffed with deep-fried eggplant and hard-boiled eggs. Tasty **shawarma** is grilled lamb or turkey, also served in pita bread. Try the stands in the Ben-Yehuda Street open-air mall, and near the Machaneh Yehuda produce market.

If you crave meat, **me'oorav Yerushalmi** (Jerusalem-style mixed grill) is a specialty of the eateries on Agrippas Street, near the Machaneh Yehuda market. It's a deliciously seasoned meal of pitas stuffed with grilled chicken hearts and other organ meats.

$$$$ MODERN ISRAELI Fodor's Choice ★ 🍴 **Mona.** A gate through an old wall leads you into the stone hall of the Artists' House. The atmosphere envelops you at the door—flagstone floors, an open fire in winter, yesteryear artifacts, and a great bar. Start your exploration of modern Israeli fare with the calamari with scorched onions or the tasty beef carpaccio. Meat eaters have plenty to choose from; vegetarians have a variety of large salads (perfect to share) and a couple of pasta dishes (try the ravioli). Wonderful mains include the richly flavored butcher's cut with bone marrow and herb butter, and the well-blended spiciness of the calamari and shrimp in ginger, chili, and sesame oil. Desserts change but are always dependably good. Wait until later in the evening if you just want to order drinks at the see-and-be-seen bar. [$] *Average main: NIS 112* ✉ *12 Shmuel Hanagid, Downtown* ☎ *02/622–2283* ✍ *Reservations essential* ⏲ *No lunch Fri.* ✥ *A2.*

$ MIDDLE EASTERN 🍴 **Pinati.** When aficionados of local standards like garlicky hummus, skewered shish kebab, schnitzel, and bean soup argue hotly about the merits of their favorite eateries, Pinati comes up as a leading contender. In the very heart of Downtown, this is the original location of Pinati, which means "corner" in Hebrew. It's now a chain, but this simple spot remains a convenient place to take the weight off your feet and rub shoulders with the locals. Not for long, though: your table will soon be in demand, and you'll have to share at peak times. [$] *Average main: NIS 30* ✉ *13 King George St., Downtown* ☎ *02/625–4540* ✍ *Reservations not accepted* 💳 *No credit cards* ⏲ *No dinner Fri. Closed Sat.* ✥ *B1.*

$$ RUSSIAN FAMILY 🍴 **Racha.** This lively and welcoming Downtown venue has quickly gained a reputation for its live music and authentic Georgian food and atmosphere. Lily and her brother Israel gave up their day jobs to recreate the recipes handed down by their mother, Tina, who hails from the Racha region in the Caucasus. Most nights there's a traditional banquet, or *supras*, that culminates in the *tamada*, or toast over a ram's horn filled with wine. For starters, try the strips of chicken breast in a ground nut sauce, or the roasted eggplant with onion and pomegranate. Distinctive pastries include pancakes stuffed with meat and served with a spicy green plum sauce. For your main course, try the traditional goulash. [$] *Average main: NIS 72* ✉ *6 Havatselet St., Downtown* ☎ *02/537–6600* 🌐 *www.racha.rest-e.co.il* ✍ *Reservations essential* ⏲ *No dinner Fri. No lunch Sat.* ✥ *C1.*

$$$$ MODERN ISRAELI 🍴 **Rooftop.** On the top of the Mamilla Hotel, this open-air restaurant lays claim to one of the best views of Jerusalem, and you can enjoy it from a cushioned chair as you dine on spiked iced tea and roast beef or lamb focaccia. The brasserie-style menu includes beef carpaccio served with creamed apples and balsamic vinegar, and tortellini with goose confit and foie gras accompanied by vegetable cream. The extensive wine list features 20 local boutique labels. If you're on a budget, opt for a hamburger at the bar. The atmosphere is lovely and the view is unbeatable, so reservations are a must in summer. [$] *Average main: NIS 114* ✉ *Mamilla Hotel, 11 King Solomon St., Mamilla* ☎ *02/548–2230* 🌐 *www.mamillahotel.com/rooftop* ✍ *Reservations essential* ✥ *C2.*

$$ ITALIAN FAMILY 🍴 **Spaghettim.** Although the menu includes other Italian dishes, spaghetti is the thing here—the name weds the Italian term to a Hebrew plural form—with more than 40 sauces using olive oil, tomato, cream, and

butter. Look for traditional combinations as well as variations like the carbonara, a tempting mixture of smoked meat, sausage, white wine, butter, nutmeg, ground pepper, and cream. Among the reasonably priced meat and fish options, try the salmon grilled in a brick oven with garlic confit and sun-dried tomatoes. Whole-wheat pasta and tofu substitutes are available, as are simple pastas for kids. The high ceiling and sleek metallic lines are trendy elements; the clientele here is a mix of families and young people. $ *Average main: NIS 70* ⊠ *35 Hillel St., Downtown* ☎ *02/623–5547* ⊕ *www.spaghettim.co.il* ✛ *C2.*

$$$$
MIDDLE EASTERN

✕ **Steakiat Hatzot.** Agrippas Street, down the block from the Machaneh Yehuda produce market, has some of Jerusalem's best-known blue-collar *mizrahi* (Middle Eastern) diners. Loyalists claim that Steakiat Hatzot, which means "midnight grill," actually pioneered the *me'orav Yerushalmi*—Jerusalem mixed grill—a substantial and delicious meal-in-a-pita of cumin-flavored bits of chicken hearts and other organ meats. For a late-night snack, there's no equal to a sandwich eaten on the sidewalk in front of the street-side grill. Make sure you want the extras before you order to avoid unasked-for side dishes. $ *Average main: NIS 116* ⊠ *121 Agrippas St., Machaneh Yehuda* ☎ *02/624–4014* ⌣ *Reservations not accepted* ▬ *No credit cards* ☉ *Closed Fri. and Sat.* ✛ *C3.*

$$
ISRAELI

✕ **T'mol Shilshom.** The name—a Hebrew literary phrase that translates roughly as "yesteryear"—is a clue to the character of the place. A tiny passageway leads to a rear courtyard and an iron stairway up to this funky restaurant and bookstore in two separate rooms on the top floor of a 19th-century house. Hosting Hebrew (and occasionally English) poetry readings and modest book parties, T'mol Shilshom has long been a popular spot with intellectuals and folks who just enjoy lingering over a novel. No meat is served, but choose from a tempting selection of salads, pastas, and fish dishes like salmon in a white wine and fig sauce. Desserts are luscious, and the array of hot drinks is always welcome on a cold, rainy day. $ *Average main: NIS 69* ⊠ *5 Yoel Salomon St., Nahalat Shiva* ☎ *02/623–2758* ⊕ *www.tmol-shilshom.co.il* ☉ *No dinner Fri. No lunch Sat.* ✛ *B2.*

$$
ITALIAN

✕ **Topolino.** Israelis love anything Italian, so it's not surprising that on Agrippas Street you'll find this cozy trattoria offering a well-honed selection of traditional fare. Try the smattering of seats outside for a quick espresso or plate of homemade pasta after buying your fruits and vegetables in the nearby Machaneh Yehuda market. In the evening, be prepared to wait for one of the closely grouped tables inside, where the house specialties include figs baked in goat cheese, sardine bruschetta, or creamy chestnut gnocchi, all made with fresh ingredients from the market stalls. $ *Average main: NIS 64* ⊠ *62 Agrippas St., Machaneh Yehuda* ☎ *02/622–3466* ✛ *D3.*

$
VEGETARIAN
FAMILY

✕ **Village Green.** Near Zion Square, this airy vegetarian restaurant prides itself on the quality of its offerings. There's a good variety of soups, quiches, and salads. Many ingredients are organic, making this a great choice for vegans as well. The hot buffet is self-service (charged by weight), and every meal comes with a choice of homemade rolls. For a coffee-time option, take a fine latte and a slice of home-baked cake or pie (gluten-free and sugar-free options available) out to a table on the shaded sidewalk. $ *Average main: NIS 27* ⊠ *33 Jaffa St., Downtown* ☎ *02/625–3065* ⊗ *No dinner Fri. Closed Sat.* ⊹ *C1.*

$$$ ✗ **Zuni.** In this elegantly clubby version of the 24-hour diner, you can
AMERICAN enjoy cappuccino and croissants in the morning (or opt for the clas-
FAMILY sic Israeli breakfast of eggs, cheeses, and fresh vegetables), a BLT with Gouda or a burger with Gorgonzola for lunch, or pork sausages with Pecorino and black beans for dinner. You can also take advantage of the free Wi-Fi as you linger over a cup of coffee. The vibe is more of a gentleman's (or lady's) club than café, but there's a good kids' menu that's served fast to keep little ones happy. $ *Average main: NIS 99* ⊠ *15 Yoel Salomon St., Nahalat Shiva* ☎ *02/625–7776* ⊹ *C2.*

GERMAN COLONY AND BAKA

South of Downtown, the German Colony is a hot spot for eateries, cafés, and little shops. It's a fun spot to pass a morning, afternoon, or evening. Cross the nearby railway tracks (being converted into a bike path) to reach the neighborhood of Baka. With its own set of quirky cafés, it's worth the 10-minute walk.

$$ ✗ **Adon Cohen.** Levana Cohen has transformed the local grocery store
MODERN ISRAELI owned by her parents in the grungy Talpiot neighborhood into one of the city's most talked-about lunchtime eateries. This spot is squeezed between an audio store and a driving school. Delicious salads with fresh vegetables and herbs prepare you for a selection of home-cooked meat dishes with a Mediterranean flavor. Try the moussaka, stuffed artichokes, or Cohen's signature meat patties with Swiss chard and mango. $ *Average main: NIS 74* ⊠ *124 Hebron Rd., at Hatenufah St., Talpiot Industrial Zone* ☎ *02/566–5077* ⌲ *Reservations not accepted* ⊗ *No dinner. Closed Fri. and Sat.* ⊹ *F6.*

$$ ✗ **Baba Israeli Kitchen.** This popular *chummousiya*, as restaurants serving
MIDDLE EASTERN hummus-based dishes are called, is a worthwhile stop for a quick lunch
FAMILY or dinner. Try the hallmark dish with minced lamb, grilled tomato, and roasted pine nuts. Marinated slices of boneless chicken thighs are also tasty, as is the spicy merguez sausage. If you're not in the mood for hummus, there's also grilled chicken and finely chopped salad served on a grilled half pita. $ *Average main: NIS 64* ⊠ *31 Emek Refaim St., German Colony* ☎ *02/671–9922* ⊗ *No dinner Fri. Closed Sat.* ⊹ *F6.*

$$ ✗ **Caffit.** This German Colony institution is as well-known for its famed
CAFÉ Oreganatto salad (made with sweet potatoes) as it is for the sweet
FAMILY potato pancakes and salmon burgers. One of the few local cafés serving a Friday morning breakfast buffet—although you may want to order the usual eggs, cheeses, and salad—it's a warm, welcoming place with a personable staff. It's a favorite spot for locals, both for the excellent coffee and the full meals. The Botanical Gardens branch has the same menu, but a different view: lily pads, flittering birds, and lots of flow-ers. $ *Average main: NIS 72* ⊠ *36 Emek Refa'im St., German Colony* ☎ *02/563–5284* ⊗ *No dinner Fri. No lunch Sat.* ⊹ *E6.*

$$$ ✗ **Colony.** Once used by the British Railroad Company, this vast space
ECLECTIC has tables scattered through the inside dining areas and out onto the balcony. There's a lengthy bar with comfortable couches for those

seeking more of a salon vibe. A hangout for foreign journalists, diplomatic corps, and in-the-know locals, Colony offers a familiar but tasty menu of steaks, pastas, and salads, including the highly recommended roasted eggplant and marinated chicken. The extensive drink menu is worth a gander, especially the Sabra cactus cocktail. Be sure to order dessert, which usually includes a divine strawberry cassata and flavorful tahini ice cream. $ *Average main: NIS 86* ⊠ *7 Bethlehem Rd., Baka* ☎ *02/671–9922* ⊕ *www.2eat.co.il/colony* ✛ *F6.*

$$$
ITALIAN
FAMILY

✕ **Focaccia Bar.** This kosher cousin of the popular Downtown restaurant is a welcome addition to the burgeoning culinary scene in the German Colony. The large display of fresh vegetables and open *taboon* oven add to the lively and informal atmosphere. The inventive menu offers nine different focaccia starters, including an excellent kebab variety. Try the Peruvian-style chicken strips blanched with mint and seasoned with lime and cilantro or the veal ragout in tomato and herb salsa. Other good choices include the chicken legs baked with figs and beef meatballs in a honey-mustard marinade. $ *Average main: NIS 83* ⊠ *35 Emek Refaim St., German Colony* ☎ *02/538–7182* ⊘ *No dinner Fri. No lunch Sat.* ✛ *F6.*

$$$$
ISRAELI
Fodor's Choice
★

✕ **HaChazer.** In a former train station, this spacious eatery's dark-wood tables and white cloth napkins might be unremarkable, but the interesting menu, with its welcome departure from the standard Jerusalem dishes, more than makes up for it. The chef takes meat eating seriously, adding Mediterranean, South American, and Asian touches to the menu. There's a fine selection of house stews—including some made with oxtails, beef cheeks, and grilled veal—and a selection of juicy steaks. Specialties include beef carpaccio in truffle oil, broiled sweetbreads served on eggplant cream, and lamb brain with an aioli sauce. The desserts change according to season and are eminently worthwhile. $ *Average main: NIS 106* ⊠ *7 Bethlehem Rd., Baka* ☎ *02/671–9922* ⊕ *www.2eat.co.il/eng/hachazer* ⚑ *Reservations essential* ⊘ *No dinner Fri. Closed Sat.* ✛ *F6.*

$$$$
ECLECTIC

✕ **Joy.** In the heart of busy Emek Refa'im, the main drag of the German Colony, this is a popular spot for a family meal, quiet time for two, or a get-together with a large group. With stone walls, dramatic arches, and subdued lighting, the decor is classic. The menu emphasizes meat dishes, so be sure to try the tangy chicken wings, beef carpaccio with garlic fries, or savory sweet potato fries before digging into one of the excellent hamburgers, lamb kebabs, or steaks. For the diet-conscious diner, there's a classic salad with chicken slices and grilled chicken liver. The solid bar has some excellent beers on tap. $ *Average main: NIS 116* ⊠ *24 Emek Refa'im St., German Colony* ☎ *02/625–3065* ⊘ *No dinner Fri. Closed Sat.* ✛ *F6.*

$$
ITALIAN
FAMILY

✕ **Luciana.** Perfect for open-air dining, this Italian-style trattoria has a spacious deck with a good view of bustling Emek Refa'im. Late at night you'll spot locals sipping glasses of wine and nibbling at eggplant rolls. In the dining room, the glass walls offer ample light and a feeling of spaciousness. With a meatless menu, Luciana offers flavorful pasta dishes, including the signature tortellini with beets and sheep's milk cheese, and the root-vegetable risotto with poached eggs and Parmesan. For dessert, try the tiramisu served in a screw-top jar. Luciana is a good choice if you have kids in tow, as it offers plenty of simple pizzas and pasta dishes. [$] *Average main: NIS 74* ✉ *27 Emek Refa'im St., German Colony* ☎ *02/563–0111* ⏲ *No dinner Fri. Closed Sat.* ✣ *F6.*

$ ITALIAN 🍴 **Roza.** The tasty and sophisticated menu, together with helpful service from young staff, has made this restaurant an instant hit with locals in the German Colony. The servings are generous and very reasonably priced. Start with one of nine choices of focaccia—the sliced roast beef with arugula or the smoked goose breast are popular—before moving on to a mouthwatering selection of entrées like fettuccini with chicken and cilantro. The tasty tortilla wraps are a lighter option. Decorated with cobalt blue tiles, the dining room is friendly and informal. [$] *Average main: NIS 48* ✉ *2 Rachel Imenu St., German Colony* ☎ *02/563–8000* ⏲ *No dinner Fri. No lunch Sat.* ✣ *F6.*

OLD CITY

The walled Old City pretty much shuts down at night, so most watering holes cater to the lunch customer. There are several falafel-and-shawarma places and Middle Eastern eateries in the Muristan area of the Christian Quarter, very few in the Muslim Quarter, and a more numerous and broader range of stands and restaurants (falafel, pizza, sandwiches, burgers, and some fuller-menu options) in and near the Jewish Quarter's Hurva Square and on the route to the Western Wall.

$ MIDDLE EASTERN 🍴 **Abu Shukri.** In the heart of the Old City, this place has an extraordinary and well-deserved reputation for having the best hummus in town. Don't expect much in the way of decor. This is a neighborhood eatery, and a look at the clientele confirms that you've gone local. Enjoy the excellent fresh falafel balls, baba ghanoush, tahini, and *labaneh* (a slightly sour cheese served with olive oil and spices). Eat family style, and don't overorder: you can get additional portions on the spot. [$] *Average main: NIS 30* ✉ *63 El-Wad Rd., Muslim Quarter* ☎ *02/627–1538* ✍ *Reservations not accepted* 💳 *No credit cards* ⏲ *No dinner* ✣ *G4.*

$$ MODERN ISRAELI FAMILY 🍴 **Keshet HaHurva.** With wooden tables in the tile-floored dining room and under the trees in the nearby square, this pleasant eatery in the Jewish Quarter's central plaza has continued to grow under new proprietors Nissim and Veronique Avershai. The menu offers fresh salads, crepes, pasta, pizza, and trademark potato latkes. Try the salad with mozzarella or the Moroccan Nile perch, one of several fish dishes. Or just have a cold drink or coffee while you rest from your tour of the Old City. [$] *Average main: NIS 74* ✉ *2 Tiferet Israel St., Jewish Quarter* ☎ *02/628–7515* 🌐 *www.keshethahurva.com* ⏲ *Closed Sat. No dinner Fri.* ✣ *G5.*

$$ MIDDLE EASTERN FAMILY 🍴 **Nafoura.** Just inside the Jaffa Gate (up the first street on the left), Nafoura offers a tranquil courtyard for alfresco lunchtime dining. Your table might lean against the Old City's 16th-century wall. The pleasant if unremarkable interior is a comfortable refuge in inclement weather. Start with the traditional array of salads, enough for two people to share. Focus on the excellent local dishes (hummus, baba ganoush, tahini, and so on) and skip the mushrooms and corn. Ask for the *kibbeh,* delicacies of cracked wheat and ground beef, or the *lahmajun,* the meat-topped "Armenian pizza." From the typical selection of entrées, try the lamb cutlets or the sea bream. The NIS 50 buffet is an excellent

value. [$] *Average main: NIS 54* ✉ *18 Latin Patriarchate Rd., Christian Quarter* ☎ *02/626–0034* ⏲ *No dinner* ✣ *F5.*

$$$ MIDDLE EASTERN FAMILY

🍴 **Philadelphia.** Through an arched entryway and down some steps off the main drag through East Jerusalem, you'll find the Ottoman-style domed dining rooms of Philadelphia. (The name comes from the Greek word for Petra in Jordan.) The traditional fare includes such local favorites as St. Peter's fish or red snapper, as well as stuffed vegetables. Good choices include the chicken fried with onions in a beet and lemon sauce, or the stuffed neck of lamb. In business for more than a quarter century, it's a comfortable place to kick back. [$] *Average main: NIS 85* ✉ *9 A-Zahra St., Salah A-Din* ☎ *02/532–2626* ✣ *F5.*

REHAVIA, TALBIEH, KING DAVID STREET, AND YEMIN MOSHE

These upscale, classic Jerusalem neighborhoods, some of them an easy walk south from Downtown, are home to most of the city's top hotels. While that fact explains the presence of at least some of the restaurants, don't write them off as tourist traps: some have a very good local reputation. Pay particular attention to Aza Street, Rehavia's main drag, where a number of solid restaurants and cafés are patronized all day and evening by locals of all ages.

$$$ MODERN ISRAELI

🍴 **Angelica.** Running what many Israeli foodies describe as "one of the best restaurants in Israel," proprietor-chef Erez Margi trained in fine dining, and it shows. Wonderfully fresh and perfectly cooked ingredients mean great textures and an explosion of great flavors. Try not to fill up on the wonderfully crusty bread while you sample such starters as homemade merguez sausage, beef fillet tartare, or foie gras tortellini. Main courses are carnivore heaven: superb lamb stew, tender steaks, and goose leg confit with apples and chestnuts. If that's not your style, choose one of the tempting fish or pasta dishes. An array of fruit tarts is the house dessert specialty. The clean lines of Angelica's aqua-hued dining room add an extra touch of class, as does the excellent service. [$] *Average main: NIS 90* ✉ *Washington St., King David St.* ☎ *02/623–0056* ✍ *Reservations essential* ⏲ *Closed Fri. No lunch* ✣ *E5.*

$$ MEDITERRANEAN

🍴 **Café Paradiso.** You may be suspicious of this café's strategic location near the major hotels, but the food is excellent and much of the clientele local. Although the white stucco and dark-wood accents are pleasant, the decor isn't the big attraction. The menu tempts with flavorful appetizers (dolmades and stuffed vegetables; a salad of fresh figs, blue cheese, and greens), grilled steaks, and tasty pasta dishes. Mullet baked with rosemary, olive oil, and white wine is recommended, but ask about other seafood dishes on the constantly changing menu. There are child-friendly options, too. For fine-weather dining, there's a small deck over the sidewalk. Reservations are essential Friday night but aren't accepted otherwise. [$] *Average main: NIS 72* ✉ *36 Keren Hayesod St., Talbieh* ☎ *02/563–4805* ⏲ *Closed Sun.* ✣ *E5.*

$$ AMERICAN FAMILY

🍴 **Café Yehoshua.** One of the restaurants that locals flock to for breakfast, lunch, or dinner, Café Yehoshua offers an Israeli take on American diner food. The menu includes everything from steak sandwiches to shrimp

JERUSALEM'S CAFÉS

Sitting down for coffee and cake in one of Jerusalem's fine cafés is something of a tradition. Yeast cakes and strudels recall the past, but today's palate craves flaky brioches and savory tarts. Italian coffee machines have driven a rise in quality and a demand for the perfect *hafuch*, the strong Israeli version of a cappuccino.

Two Jerusalem coffee chains have expanded across the country. Aroma has excellent coffee and fresh sandwiches and salads. Hillel is a favorite with locals for breakfast, with its good food and good prices.

In Jerusalem, the open-air mall of Ben-Yehuda Street has several venerable hangouts, but the newer cafés along the bars and restaurants of Shlomzion Hamalka Street offer more sophisticated menus—and better coffee. The Mamilla Mall, outside Jaffa Gate, is known for its coffee places, but don't overlook Emek Refa'im Street in the German Colony or Bethlehem Road in Baka.

Most popular watering holes serve decent light, affordable meals for lunch and dinner as well, and courtyard seating gets full in fine weather and on summer evenings. Coffee and a pastry are about NIS 30 to NIS 40; sandwiches, salads, quiche, and pasta will cost NIS 16 to NIS 46. If you're not a coffee drinker, consider trying a *gazoz*, a fizzy drink.

Coffee Mill. This place is a must for coffee devotees, with its dizzying selection of blends. You can opt for a light meal, too. ⊠ *23 Emek Refa'im St., German Colony* ☎ *02/566–1665.*

Grand Cafe. A large sidewalk terrace, breakfast served all day, and good coffee have made this newcomer an instant success with both locals and visitors. ⊠ *70 Bethlehem Rd., Baka* ☎ *02/570–2702.*

Itzik's Place. In the middle of the Bethlehem Road shopping district, this tiny shop is known for its coffee, sandwiches, and salads. ⊠ *33 Bethlehem Rd., Baka* ☎ *02/561–2054.*

Kadosh. This is one place locals are reluctant to share, lest it lose its "Jerusalemite" character. Baked goods, generous breakfasts, and '30s-style decor are all part of the draw. ⊠ *6 Shlomzion Hamalka St., Downtown* ☎ *02/625–4210* ⊕ *www.kadoshcafe.rest-e.co.il.*

Kahlo. The famous shabby-chic decor has been updated, but Kahlo remains popular with both locals and tourists alike. Try the generous sandwiches. ⊠ *31 Bethlehem Rd., Baka* ☎ *02/673–6365.*

Modus. This cozy spot on Jerusalem's main drag has a loyal following for its homemade sandwiches, apple strudel, and bourekas. ⊠ *31 King George St., Downtown* ☎ *02/624–4215.*

Nadi. The solid menu focuses on artisanal Israeli cheeses and fabulous sourdough bread. ⊠ *10 Shatz St., Downtown* ☎ *02/625–1737.*

Teller Bakery. This bakery has decent coffee and pastries, but don't miss the sourdough breads. ⊠ *74 Agrippas St., Machaneh Yehuda* ☎ *02/622–3227.*

cocktail. Grab a seat in one of the booths and linger over comfort food, particularly the Roquefort schnitzel. Evening is a great time to stop by for a drink and a bite-sized burger. $ *Average main: NIS 60* ⊠ *17 Aza St., Rehavia* ☎ *02/563–2898* ⊕ *www.yehoshua.rest-e.co.il* ⊹ *D6.*

$$$

CAFÉ

✕ **Lavan.** At the in-house eatery of the popular Cinematheque, coffee and other beverages satisfy film buffs. The superb view of Old City walls from the glassed-in patio makes this a destination for locals as well as tourists. (The fact that it's open Saturday is another plus.) The fare is light: fresh fish of the day, pizza, and salads. The chef's more inventive dishes have mixed success, but one winner is gnocchi with chestnuts and sautéed onions. Do try the unusual ice cream made with tahini and halva. $ *Average main: NIS 88* ⊠ *Cinematheque, 11 Hebron Rd., Yemin Moshe* ☎ *02/673–7393* ⊹ *F6.*

$$$$

MODERN ISRAELI

✕ **Olive & Fish.** Its location near many of the major hotels is part of the appeal, but Olive & Fish also pleases locals with its contemporary Israeli dishes. The glass-enclosed front porch is popular; the interior, with pale yellow walls, framed prints, and unintrusive lighting, is warm and inviting. For starters, try the tasty grilled eggplant with tahini, or the excellent hot salmon salad. Great fish options include sea bass or St. Peter's fish with artichokes, sun-dried tomatoes, white wine, and lemon. Other temptations include delectable chicken and beef kebabs, or tender *pargiyot* (spring chicken chunks) in a date-honey sauce. Save room for one of the pies or chocolate creations. $ *Average main: NIS 101* ⊠ *2 Jabotinsky St., Talbieh* ☎ *02/566–5020* ⚱ *Reservations essential* ⊗ *Closed Fri. No lunch Sat.* ⊹ *E6.*

$$$$

MODERN ISRAELI

✕ **Scala.** Dark wood, atmospheric lighting, and jazzy background music enhance the sophisticated feel of this restaurant in the David Citadel Hotel. For starters, try the sirloin carpaccio or caramelized veal short ribs. Chef Oren Yerushlami's menu features slow-cooked lamb osso buco with Jerusalem artichoke purée, beef medallions with smoked duck breast, and pan-seared bream fillets with kalamata olives. The lighter bar menu is also worth a look. The desserts are delicious. The service at this kosher dining room is informed and attentive. $ *Average main: NIS 140* ⊠ *David Citadel Hotel, 7 King David St., King David St.* ☎ *02/621–1111* ⊕ *www.scala-rest.com* ⚱ *Reservations essential* ⊗ *No lunch. Closed Fri. and Sat.* ⊹ *E5.*

$

VEGETARIAN

✕ **Te'enim.** In the classic limestone Confederation House—with stone arches, flagstone floors, and tantalizing views of the Old City walls—Te'enim finds a delicate balance between traditional and innovative in its vegetarian fare. Great choices include the spinach salad with ricotta or the endive salad with grilled goat cheese and roasted almonds. Standard main dishes include a mushroom, polenta, olive, garlic, and red wine bake, as well as the successful *Maharajah majadra,* with bulgur, onion, ginger chutney, and yogurt. Daily specials at Te'enim ("Figs") include such unusual offerings as Mexican chili. The homemade sorbets and unusually flavored ice creams are excellent, but try the surprising mini eggplant in date honey and almonds. $ *Average main: NIS 49* ⊠ *12 Emile Botta St., Yemin Moshe* ☎ *02/625–1967* ⊕ *www.teenim. rest-e.co.il* ⊗ *No dinner Fri. Closed Sat.* ⊹ *F5.*

WEST JERUSALEM

The "cultural mile" in West Jerusalem isn't known for fine dining—lunchtime cafeterias are the best you can hope for—but one superb Indian restaurant is a shining exception.

$$ INDIAN 🍴 **Kohinoor.** Moghul-influenced design elements immediately set a tone of quiet, informal elegance at this hotel restaurant. Naan breads, piquant dips, and slightly spicy lamb samosas are great starters. The cuisine is the less-fiery northern Indian: among the best entrées are the superb lamb *rogan gosht* and the subtle, tender, tandoori-baked chicken tikka. Curries or the flavorsome *dhal makham* (beans, lentils, and onions in a spicy sauce) are vegetarian options. Finish with fragrant *kulfi* ice cream or the exotic *elaichi kheer* rice pudding. The lunch buffet is an excellent value. [$] *Average main: NIS 70* ✉ *Crowne Plaza Hotel, 1 Ha'aliyah St., Givat Ram* ☎ *02/658–8867* 🌐 *www.tandoori.co.il* ✍ *Reservations essential* 🕒 *No dinner Fri. No lunch Sat.* ✥ *B3.*

WHERE TO STAY

Some travelers insist on a hotel in a central location; others prefer to retreat to a haven at the end of the day, with atmosphere more important than accessibility. Jerusalem has more of the first kind than the second, and even hotels once considered remote are really no more than 10 minutes by cab from the city center. Most hotels are contemporary and modern, but a few have retained an old-world charm. There are also guesthouses, B&Bs, and other lodgings that offer more of the local charm coupled with often-cheaper prices.

The majority of Jerusalem's better hotels are in West Jerusalem, the Israeli side of the old Green Line that divided the city between 1948 and 1967. Some Israelis still avoid Arab East Jerusalem, but the term is as much a matter of perception as of political geography: three large Israeli-run hotels (Olive Tree, Grand Court, and Leonardo Jerusalem) are just over the old line, sharing the seam where East meets West with the Palestinian-run American Colony and Addar.

The less-expensive hotels in East Jerusalem were seriously affected by Palestinian street violence between the late 1980s and the early 2000s. The ensuing shrinkage of hotel occupancy led to a widespread decline in standards as well.

Defining high season is not an exact science. Some hotels may talk about peak periods in addition to or instead of high season, typically the week-long Jewish holiday of Passover (March or April), and a similar period around Sukkot (September or October). Depending on the hotel, rates may go up during other Jewish holidays, as well as around Christmas. Because of variations in hotel policy, and because the dates of Jewish holidays shift annually in accordance with the Hebrew calendar, the difference in room rates can be significant.

New construction in Jerusalem tends to be high-end (the Harmony Hotel is a refreshing exception). The luxurious Waldorf Astoria, being built in the shell of a historic building on Agron Street, is due to open in 2014.

Almost all West Jerusalem hotels are kosher.

Prices in the reviews are the lowest cost of a standard double room in high season.Use the coordinates at the end of each listing (✢ 2A) to locate a site on the corresponding map.

CENTER CITY

This section embraces an area from the Rehavia neighborhood northeast down to Zion Square in the heart of Downtown. It's more about central locations than leafy retreats. Parking is at a premium: this is discouraging territory for those with rental cars.

$ HOTEL Fodor's Choice ★ 🏨 **Harmony Hotel.** The appearance of a boutique hotel in the historic Nahalat Shiva neighborhood, in the heart of Downtown Jerusalem, created a buzz in tourism circles. **Pros:** free Wi-Fi; heart of where it's happening; free leaflets for self-guided tours. **Cons:** Downtown noise when you open windows. [$] *Rooms from: $194* ✉ *14 Shammai St., Yoel Salomon St., Downtown* ☎ *02/621–9999* 🌐 *www.atlas.co.il/harmony-hotel-jerusalem* ↳ *48 rooms* 🍴 *Breakfast* ✢ *B2.*

$ HOTEL 🏨 **Jerusalem Tower.** The prime location, in the middle of Downtown and a 10-minute walk from the Old City, makes this hotel a great option if you want to be close to the action. **Pros:** good value; in the heart of things; free Wi-Fi. **Cons:** not many amenities; no room to spread out. [$] *Rooms from: $155* ✉ *23 Hillel St., Downtown* ☎ *02/620–9209* 🌐 *www.jerusalemtowerhotel.com* ↳ *120 rooms* 🍴 *Breakfast* ✢ *B1.*

$$ HOTEL 🏨 **Leonardo Plaza.** Overlooking Independence Park, the 22-story Leonardo Plaza is a Jerusalem landmark with terrific views, especially from upper floors. **Pros:** 10-minute walk from the Old City; good restaurants; up-to-date gym. **Cons:** business hotel feel; paid parking. [$] *Rooms from: $250* ✉ *47 King George St., Downtown* ☎ *02/629–8666* 🌐 *www.leonardo-hotels.com* ↳ *300 rooms* 🍴 *Breakfast* ✢ *E5.*

$ HOTEL 🏨 **Montefiore.** The side-street location in the center of town—on a pedestrian-only block with shops and restaurants just outside the front door—adds to the serenity of this reasonably priced hotel. **Pros:** 10-minute walk from Old City; interesting shops nearby; free Wi-Fi. **Cons:** a bit old-fashioned. [$] *Rooms from: $150* ✉ *7 Shatz St., Downtown* ☎ *02/622–1111* 🌐 *www.montefiorehotel.com* ↳ *47 rooms, 1 suite* 🍴 *Breakfast* ✢ *A2.*

$ B&B/INN 🏨 **Palatin Hotel.** Proprietor Tody Warshavsky's grandfather built the Palatin Hotel in 1936, and members of the Knesset, which used to be just up the road, stayed here when parliament was in session. **Pros:** central location; multilingual staff; free coffee all day. **Cons:** no elevator; no restaurant. [$] *Rooms from: $125* ✉ *4 Agrippas St., Downtown* ☎ *02/623–1141* 🌐 *www.hotel-palatin.co.il* ↳ *28 rooms* 🍴 *Breakfast* ✢ *B1.*

$ B&B/INN 🏨 **Zion.** With little balconies overlooking a pedestrian-only street off Ben-Yehuda Street, this 19th-century stone building has an old-world feel. **Pros:** Downtown location; inexpensive rates; European character. **Cons:** slightly dingy; not for those with mobility issues. [$] *Rooms from: $100* ✉ *10 Dorot Rishonim St., Downtown* ☎ *02/623–2367* 🌐 *www.hotelzion.com* ↳ *25 rooms* 🍴 *Multiple meal plans* ✢ *B1.*

BEST BETS FOR JERUSALEM LODGING

2

Fodor's writers and editors have selected their favorites hotels and other lodgings by price and experience. Fodor's Choice properties represent the "best of the best" across price categories. You can also search by area for excellent places to stay—just check out our complete reviews on the following pages.

Fodor's Choice

American Colony Hotel, $$, p. 144

David Citadel, $$$$, p. 138

Harmony Hotel, $, p. 136

Inbal, $$$, p. 139

Mamilla Hotel, $$$$, p. 139

Mount Zion, $$, p. 143

Ramat Rachel, $$, p. 143

By Price

$

Addar, p. 144

Ambassador, p. 144

Harmony Hotel, p. 136

Little House in the Colony, p. 142

Lutheran Guesthouse, p. 143

Prima Royale, p. 139

St. Andrew's Scottish Guesthouse, p. 143

Zion, p. 136

$$

American Colony Hotel, p. 144

Dan Boutique, p. 142

Dan Jerusalem, p. 144

Dan Panorama, p. 138

Mount Zion, p. 143

Ramada Jerusalem, p. 142

Ramat Rachel, p. 143

$$$

Inbal, p. 139

$$$$

Crowne Plaza, p. 140

David Citadel, p. 138

King David, p. 139

Mamilla Hotel, p. 139

By Experience

BEST ISRAELI BREAKFAST

American Colony Hotel, $$, p. 144

Inbal, $$$, p. 139

King David, $$$$, p. 139

Mamilla Hotel, $$$$, p. 139

Leonardo Plaza, $$, p. 136

BEST SPA

Dan Jerusalem, $$, p. 144

David Citadel, $$$$, p. 138

Inbal, $$$, p. 139

Ramada Jerusalem, $$, p. 142

BEST FOR KIDS

David Citadel, $$$$, p. 138

Inbal, $$$, p. 139

Ramada Jerusalem, $$, p. 142

Ramat Rachel, $$, p. 143

Yitzhak Rabin Guest House, $, p. 142

YMCA Three Arches, $, p. 139

BEST VIEWS

Crowne Plaza, $$$$, p. 140

Dan Jerusalem, $$, p. 144

Leonardo Plaza, $$, p. 136

Mamilla Hotel, $$$$, p. 139

Ramat Rachel, $$, p. 143

BEST POOL

King David, $$$$, p. 139

Mount Zion, $$, p. 143

Ramada Jerusalem, $$, p. 142

Ramat Rachel, $$, p. 143

BEST FOR HISTORY BUFFS

American Colony Hotel, $$, p. 144

Christ Church, $, p. 143

King David, $$$$, p. 139

BEST HOTEL BAR

American Colony Hotel, $$, p. 144

King David, $$$$, p. 139

Mamilla Hotel, $$$$, p. 139

BEST ROOF DECK

Dan Boutique, $$, p. 142

Lutheran Guesthouse, $, p. 143

Mamilla Hotel, $$$$, p. 139

Prima Royale, $, p. 139

BEST FOR ROMANCE

Alegra, $$$, p. 140

American Colony Hotel, $$, p. 144

Little House in the Colony, $, p. 142

Mamilla Hotel, $$$$, p. 139

Mount Zion, $$, p. 143

Both ancient arches and minarets are part of the distinctive landscape of the Old City.

REHAVIA, TALBIEH, AND KING DAVID STREET

These are desirable residential neighborhoods, good for jogging and after-dinner strolls. A 10- or 20-minute walk takes you to the Old City and Downtown. Alongside the city's high-end hotels are several budget-friendly options.

$$
HOTEL
Dan Panorama. The guest rooms at this this 11-story landmark in the middle of the hotel district are a bit compact, but thoughtful lighting, well-placed furnishings, and interesting artwork make a difference. **Pros:** excellent location; pleasant staff; thoughtful renovations. **Cons:** not as deluxe as it would like to be. *Rooms from: $220 ⊠ 39 Keren Hayesod St., Talbieh ☎ 02/569-5695 ⊕ www.danhotels.com ⤵ 283 rooms, 9 suites ⓞ Breakfast ✛ E5.*

$$$$
HOTEL
FAMILY
Fodor's Choice
★
David Citadel. Talk about a great first impression—this hotel's lobby, by noted Italian architect Piero Lissoni, is elegant and welcoming, as is the soothingly decorated lounge and terrace one floor above. **Pros:** five minutes from Jaffa Gate; welcomes families; year-round outdoor pool. **Cons:** feels like a business hotel; events sometimes intrusive. *Rooms from: $480 ⊠ 7 King David St., King David St. ☎ 02/621-1111 ⊕ www. thedavidcitadel.com ⤵ 381 rooms ⓞ Breakfast ✛ E5.*

$$
HOTEL
Eldan. The address in the heart of a prestigious hotel district—just a five-minute walk from Downtown or from Jaffa Gate—is a major draw here. **Pros:** prime location; cheerful rooms; some nice views. **Cons:** few frills; no pool; busy street. *Rooms from: $200 ⊠ 24 King David St., King David St. ☎ 02/567-9777 ⊕ www.eldanhotel.com ⤵ 76 rooms ⓞ Breakfast ✛ E5.*

$$$
HOTEL
FAMILY
Fodor'sChoice
★

Inbal. Jerusalem stone lends a warm glow to this low-slung hotel, which is wrapped around a central courtyard and atrium. **Pros:** excellent location; free parking; relaxing lobby. **Cons:** smallish bathrooms; can be noisy. $ *Rooms from: $350* ✉ *3 Jabotinsky St., Talbieh* ☎ *02/675–6666* ⊕ *www.inbalhotel.com* ⚲ *282 rooms, 26 suites* ❙❍❙ *Breakfast* ✛ *E6.*

$$$$
HOTEL

King David. The grande dame of Israeli luxury hotels opened in 1931 and has successfully (and self-importantly) defended its title ever since. **Pros:** great pool and garden; terrific location and views; historic building. **Cons:** reputation for snobbish staff; limited parking. $ *Rooms from: $470* ✉ *23 King David St., King David St.* ☎ *02/620–8888* ⊕ *www.danhotels.com* ⚲ *198 rooms, 35 suites* ❙❍❙ *Breakfast* ✛ *E5.*

$
HOTEL

King Solomon. The centerpiece of the marble-floored lobby at the King Solomon is a huge, spherical sculpture of Jerusalem by renowned sculptor Frank Meisler. **Pros:** reasonable rates; close to Old City; great views. **Cons:** few balconies; limited parking; reception sometimes understaffed. $ *Rooms from: $190* ✉ *32 King David St., Talbieh* ☎ *02/569–5500* ⊕ *www.kingsolomon-hotel.com* ⚲ *142 rooms, 6 suites* ❙❍❙ *Breakfast* ✛ *E6.*

$
B&B/INN

Little House in Rechavia. For quick walks to the Old City, the Little House in Rechavia is a good choice. **Pros:** nice location; neighborhood feel; reasonable rates. **Cons:** no restaurant. $ *Rooms from: $129* ✉ *20 Ibn Ezra St., Rehavia* ☎ *02/563–3344* ⊕ *www.jerusalem-hotel.co.il* ⚲ *27 rooms* ❙❍❙ *Breakfast* ✛ *D5.*

$$$$
HOTEL
Fodor'sChoice
★

Mamilla Hotel. With clever and soaring architectural flourishes by Moshe Safdie and restrained yet luxurious interior design by Piero Lissoni, the Mamilla Hotel is a sleek and comfortable haven. **Pros:** contemporary design; most central location; good service. **Cons:** some may not like the glass-walled bathrooms. $ *Rooms from: $480* ✉ *11 King Solomon St., Mamilla* ☎ *02/548–2222* ⊕ *www.mamillahotel.com* ⚲ *194 rooms, 33 suites* ❙❍❙ *Breakfast* ✛ *E5.*

$$
HOTEL

Prima Kings. "The Kings"—the name by which it's still known—sits on a busy intersection, less than a 10-minute walk from the city center. **Pros:** 10 minutes from Downtown and the Old City; adjacent late-night supermarket. **Cons:** a bit overpriced; traffic noise when windows are open. $ *Rooms from: $210* ✉ *60 King George St., Rehavia* ☎ *02/620–1201* ⊕ *www.prima.co.il* ⚲ *217 rooms* ❙❍❙ *Breakfast* ✛ *E5.*

$
HOTEL

Prima Royale. The centerpiece of this centrally located boutique hotel is a spectacular rooftop deck where you can sip cocktails, listen to classical or jazz music on summer evenings, or gaze through telescopes at the 360-degree panorama. **Pros:** live music; tasteful decor; quiet location. **Cons:** no pool; limited parking. $ *Rooms from: $172* ✉ *3 Mendele St., off Keren Hayesod, Talbieh* ☎ *02/560–7111* ⊕ *www.prima.co.il* ⚲ *126 rooms, 7 suites* ❙❍❙ *Breakfast* ✛ *E6.*

$
HOTEL
FAMILY

YMCA Three Arches. Built in 1933, this limestone building with its famous domed bell tower has long been a Jerusalem landmark. **Pros:** great location; free sports facilities; free Wi-Fi. **Cons:** poor restaurant. $ *Rooms from: $155* ✉ *26 King David St., King David St.* ☎ *02/569–2692* ⊕ *www.ymca3arch.co.il* ⚲ *52 rooms, 4 suites* ❙❍❙ *Breakfast* ✛ *E5.*

WEST JERUSALEM

This cluster of hotels in Givat Ram and Romema is near the point where the Tel Aviv Highway (Route 1) enters Jerusalem. Some properties are near the Central Bus Station, others closer to the Israel Museum and the Knesset. Ein Kerem, a leafy enclave, is included here, too, along with Mt. Herzl. Downtown is some distance away, the Old City even farther—a long walk, but 10 to 15 minutes by cab or bus, and bus lines are plentiful. If it's hotel deals you're after or if other places in town are booked, this area makes a great option.

$$$ **Alegra.** In the picturesque village of Ein Kerem, this new boutique
B&B/INN hotel occupies a century-old house famous for the true-life-Romeo-and-Juliet story of a Jewish-Arab couple. **Pros:** modern design; gorgeous rooms; the perfect setting for romance. **Cons:** far from attractions; not for families; limited public spaces. $ *Rooms from: $315* ⊠ *13 Derech HaAchayot, Ein Kerem* ☎ *02/650–0506* ⊕ *www.hotelalegra.co.il* ⤵ *7 rooms* |◎| *Breakfast* ✛ *A3.*

$ **BaChoresh HaTivi.** The exuberantly lush garden and sweeping view of
B&B/INN the valley are your first hint that you've found the perfect hideaway; the well-appointed pine-and-tile suites confirm it. **Pros:** quiet setting; whirlpool baths in suites; massage available. **Cons:** parking can be remote; far from central Jerusalem; steps to climb. $ *Rooms from: $145* ⊠ *12 Madregot HaRoma'im, at Ein Kerem St. G/7, Ein Kerem* ☎ *02/643–6586* ⊕ *www.bachti.co.il* ⤵ *3 suites* |◎| *Breakfast* ✛ *A3.*

$ **Bayit Vegan.** Opposite Mt. Herzl in West Jerusalem, this lodging has
B&B/INN sweeping views of the Judean Hills; despite the away-from-it-all setting, it's only a 15-minute taxi ride from Downtown. **Pros:** Internet access is on the house; reasonable rates; close to light rail station. **Cons:** remote location; sometimes noisy. $ *Rooms from: $130* ⊠ *8 HaPisga St., Mt. Herzl* ☎ *02/642–0990* ⊕ *www.bvh.co.il* ⤵ *115 rooms* |◎| *Breakfast* ✛ *A4.*

$$$$ **Crowne Plaza.** Although this gleaming white tower with sweeping city
HOTEL views is a classic business hotel, it's also a comfortable option when you're on vacation. **Pros:** away from city noise; nice spa and sports facilities; great views. **Cons:** few attractions within walking distance; limited parking. $ *Rooms from: $440* ⊠ *1 HaAliyah St., Givat Ram* ☎ *02/658–8888* ⊕ *www.crowneplaza.com* ⤵ *375 rooms, 21 suites* |◎| *Breakfast* ✛ *B3.*

$ **Jerusalem Gate.** Tour groups are this hotel's bread and butter, but its
HOTEL reasonably priced rooms and middle-of-it-all address attract budget-minded couples and families as well. **Pros:** a spacious place to stay; direct access to shopping; on major bus routes. **Cons:** far from Downtown; attracts large groups; charge for Wi-Fi. $ *Rooms from: $97* ⊠ *43 Yirmiyahu St., Romema* ☎ *02/500–8500* ⊕ *www.jerusalemgatehotel.com* ⤵ *294 rooms, 4 suites* |◎| *Breakfast* ✛ *B2.*

$ **Jerusalem Gold.** Owner-manager Ariella Shmida Doron's personal
HOTEL touch is felt in this hotel's well-coordinated guest rooms, some of which are done in a rich burgundy, others in bottle green. **Pros:** handy location; bus lines to everywhere; reasonable rates. **Cons:** crowded seating in lounge; grungy neighborhood; extra charge for Internet and parking. $ *Rooms from: $120* ⊠ *234 Jaffa St., Romema* ☎ *02/501–3333* ⊕ *www.jerusalemgold.com* ⤵ *163 rooms, 35 suites* |◎| *Breakfast* ✛ *B2.*

Inbal

American Colony Hotel

Mamilla Hotel

David Citadel

$ ⬛ **Prima Park.** This West Jerusalem hotel has a good local reputation
HOTEL thanks to its tastefully decorated rooms and comfortably furnished
lounge. **Pros:** friendly staff; intimate atmosphere; close to light rail.
Cons: far from Dowtown; small rooms; area dead at night. *$ Rooms
from: $120 ✉ 2 Vilnai St., Givat Ram ☎ 02/658–2222 ⊕ www.prima-
hotels-israel.com/jerusalem-hotels/prima-park-jerusalem-hotel ⤴ 210
rooms, 7 suites ⊙ Breakfast ✦ A3.*

$$ ⬛ **Ramada Jerusalem.** This massive hotel's marble lobby, with its reflect-
HOTEL ing copper ceiling, clubby leather chairs, and frilly potted palms, has a
FAMILY feeling of grandeur. **Pros:** good value; great gym; wonderful for families.
Cons: neighborhood is dead at night. *$ Rooms from: $236 ✉ Ruppin
Bridge at Herzl Blvd., Givat Ram ☎ 02/659–9999 ⊕ www.ramada.com
⤴ 350 rooms, 10 suites ⊙ Breakfast ✦ A3.*

$ ⬛ **Yitzhak Rabin Guest House.** Although it's part of the Youth Hostel
B&B/INN Association, this guest house is a great choice for couples and families.
FAMILY **Pros:** big on aesthetics; great place to meet fellow travelers; handy snack
bar. **Cons:** no-frills rooms; remote location. *$ Rooms from: $110 ✉ 1
Nahman Avigad St., Givat Ram ☎ 02/594–5511 ⊕ www.iyha.org.il/eng
⤴ 77 rooms ⊙ Breakfast ✦ B6.*

GERMAN COLONY, HEBRON ROAD, AND ENVIRONS

This area lies in Jerusalem's southeast quadrant, due south of Jaffa
Gate. Baka is some distance away, but all other listed properties are a
fairly easy walk from the Old City. The German Colony has become
a popular leisure-time neighborhood, with numerous restaurants and
coffee shops.

The slightly rustic kibbutz location of Ramat Rachel is technically south
of the city limits, but geographically part of Jerusalem—enjoying the
best of both worlds, as locals would say.

$$ ⬛ **Dan Boutique.** A streamlined reception area, circular wooden bar, and
HOTEL lobby lounge with funky furnishings welcome you to this contempo-
rary lodging. **Pros:** great design; inviting public area; close to new train
station. **Cons:** limited free parking; slightly remote location; charge for
Wi-Fi. *$ Rooms from: $236 ✉ 31 Hebron Rd., Hebron Rd. ☎ 02/568–
9999 ⊕ www.danhotels.com ⤴ 123 rooms, 6 suites ⊙ Breakfast ✦ F6.*

$ ⬛ **Little House in Bakah.** This handsome Ottoman-style mansion with
B&B/INN dramatic arched windows sits on the edge of a residential neighborhood near public transportation and many shops and restaurants. **Pros:**
intimate vibe; good value; nice neighborhood. **Cons:** a bit dowdy; no
elevator; traffic noise. *$ Rooms from: $119 ✉ 1 Yehuda St., corner of
80 Hebron Rd., Bakah ☎ 02/673–7944 ⊕ www.jerusalem-hotel.co.il
⤴ 34 rooms ⊙ Breakfast ✦ G6.*

$ ⬛ **Little House in the Colony.** On a quiet street just steps away from the
B&B/INN bubbling main drag of the German Colony, this tiny B&B shares its historic setting with a landmark cinema and a restaurant. **Pros:** quiet and
intimate feel; reasonable rates; shops and eateries nearby. **Cons:** a bit
expensive for what you get; no restaurant. *$ Rooms from: $119 ✉ 4a
Lloyd George St., German Colony ☎ 02/566–2424 ⊕ www.jerusalem-
hotel.co.il ⤴ 22 rooms ⊙ Breakfast ✦ E6.*

$$ · **HOTEL** · **Fodor's Choice** · ★ · 🛏 **Mount Zion.** Arched doorways and windows in golden-hued Jerusalem stone frame this hotel's ethereal views of the Hinnom Valley. **Pros:** wonderful mix of old and new; inviting pool area; easy walk to Old City. **Cons:** staff could be cheerier; area dead at night. $ *Rooms from: $250* ✉ *17 Hebron Rd., Hebron Rd.* ☎ *02/568–9555* ⊕ *www.mountzion.co.il* ⤵ *117 rooms, 20 suites* ⊙ *Breakfast* ✛ *F6.*

$$ · **RESORT** · **FAMILY** · **Fodor's Choice** · ★ · 🛏 **Ramat Rachel.** The relaxed, informal atmosphere is a big part of this hotel's appeal. **Pros:** quiet atmosphere; children's playground; petting zoo. **Cons:** a little pricey; remote location; sometimes crowded with tour groups. $ *Rooms from: $236* ✉ *Kibbutz Ramat Rachel, Ramat Rachel* ☎ *02/670–2555* ⊕ *www.ramatrachel.co.il* ⤵ *164 rooms* ⊙ *Breakfast* ✛ *G6.*

$ · **B&B/INN** · 🛏 **St. Andrew's Scottish Guesthouse.** Built in the early 1930s as part of St. Andrew's Church, the guesthouse is as much a retreat as a place to stay overnight—"feeling like you're home" is the way they like to put it. **Pros:** serene atmosphere; free Wi-Fi; close to the German Colony. **Cons:** slightly remote location; steps to climb; no restaurant. $ *Rooms from: $150* ✉ *1 David Remez St., Hebron Rd.* ☎ *02/673–2401* ⊕ *www.scotsguesthouse.com* ⤵ *18 rooms, 1 suite, 1 apartment* ⊙ *Breakfast* ✛ *F6.*

$ · **RENTAL** · 🛏 **Tamar Residence.** In the heart of trendy Baka, this hotel offers mostly two-room suites with well-equipped kitchenettes and extra space for the kids. **Pros:** great value for families; modern vibe; underground parking. **Cons:** far from Downtown; breakfast is extra. $ *Rooms from: $150* ✉ *70 Bethlehem Rd., Baka* ☎ *077/270–5555* ⊕ *www.tamarsuites.com* ⤵ *33 rooms* ⊙ *No meals* ✛ *F6.*

OLD CITY

The Old City, the historic walled heart of Jerusalem, includes the Armenian Quarter, the Christian Quarter, the Jewish Quarter, and the Muslim Quarter. Lodging options here are limited.

$ · **B&B/INN** · 🛏 **Christ Church.** Inside the Jaffa Gate, this guesthouse is part of the oldest Protestant church in the Middle East. **Pros:** tranquil haven; excellent for sightseeing. **Cons:** not always comfortable for non-Christian guests. $ *Rooms from: $142* ✉ *Armenian Orthodox Patriarchate Rd., Jaffa Gate* ☎ *02/627–7727* ⊕ *www.cmj-israel.org* ⤵ *32 rooms* ⊙ *Breakfast* ✛ *G5.*

$ · **B&B/INN** · 🛏 **Lutheran Guesthouse.** Tucked into an alleyway behind the souk in the Armenian Quarter, this Old City guesthouse is a maze of stone buildings and courtyards. **Pros:** free Internet access; leaf-framed panoramas; free hot drinks. **Cons:** Old City atmosphere not for everyone. $ *Rooms from: $130* ✉ *St. Mark's Rd., Old City* ☎ *02/626–6888* ⊕ *www.luth-guesthouse-jerusalem.com* ⤵ *36 rooms* ⊙ *Breakfast* ✛ *G5.*

$ · **B&B/INN** · 🛏 **New Imperial.** This rambling, century-old stone building is identifiable by its iron balconies overlooking the busy square just inside the Jaffa Gate. **Pros:** good value; great location; authentic feel. **Cons:** can be noisy; room modernization not very aesthetic. $ *Rooms from: $85* ✉ *Omar Ibn El-Khattib St., inside the Jaffa Gate, Old City* ☎ *02/628–2261* ⤵ *45 rooms* ⊙ *Breakfast* ✛ *F5.*

EAST JERUSALEM AND THE "SEAM LINE"

The cluster of hotels here, some Israeli-run, some Palestinian, are within yards of each other, and of the old "seam" (as it's sometimes called) that once divided Jerusalem into East and West. At some levels, the old divisions remain, but the seam area itself has become a comfortable middle ground.

In splendid isolation on the northeast side of town, with long views southwest toward the Old City, Mt. Scopus is home to the original Hebrew University and Hadassah Hospital campuses. The Regency Jerusalem hotel here abuts the French Hill neighborhood, at the northern end of the ridge.

$ ☷ **Addar.** This elegantly intimate boutique hotel sits on the seam between
HOTEL   East and West Jerusalem, just a 10-minute walk from the Old City. **Pros:** English-speaking manager; reasonably priced meals; near the Old City. **Cons:** not an inviting neighborhood in which to stroll. [$] *Rooms from: $100* ✉ *53 Nablus Rd., Seam Line* ☎ *02/626–3111* ⊕ *www.addar-hotel. com* ⤳ *7 rooms, 23 suites* ⏐◯⏐ *Breakfast* ✛ *F2.*

$ ☷ **Ambassador.** One of East Jerusalem's longtime favorites, the Ambas-
HOTEL   sador has been thoroughly transformed by tasteful renovations and the liberal use of Jerusalem limestone. **Pros:** outdoor dining; lovely views; comfortable rooms. **Cons:** far from attractions; area dead at night. [$] *Rooms from: $180* ✉ *56 Nablus Rd., Sheikh Jarrah, East Jerusalem* ☎ *02/541–2222* ⊕ *www.jerusalemambassador.com* ⤳ *115 rooms* ⏐◯⏐ *Breakfast* ✛ *E1.*

$$ ☷ **American Colony Hotel.** Once a pasha's palace, this cool limestone oasis
HOTEL   with its flower-filled inner courtyard and gorgeous garden is in a class
Fodor's Choice   of its own—no wonder it's a favored haunt of statesmen, stars, and
★   spies. **Pros:** free Internet access; atmospheric cellar bar; good English bookstore. **Cons:** dead neighborhood at night; a cab ride from most attractions. [$] *Rooms from: $299* ✉ *1 Saint Vincent St., Seam Line* ☎ *02/627–9777* ⊕ *www.americancolony.com* ⤳ *96 rooms, 24 suites* ⏐◯⏐ *Breakfast* ✛ *G2.*

$$ ☷ **Dan Jerusalem.** Cascading down Mt. Scopus, the sprawling Dan
HOTEL   Jerusalem has spectacular views and a bold design. **Pros:** impressive architecture; memorable lobby; great panoramic views. **Cons:** remote location; charge for Internet access. [$] *Rooms from: $212* ✉ *32 Lehi St., Mt. Scopus* ☎ *02/533–1234* ⊕ *www.danhotels.com* ⤳ *455 rooms, 50 suites* ⏐◯⏐ *Breakfast* ✛ *H1.*

$ ☷ **Grand Court.** This huge hotel is a celebration of light and space: from
HOTEL   the large, airy lobby, with its limestone walls and marble arches, to the well-lighted, comfortable guest rooms, with their soft decor and bright bathrooms. **Pros:** 10-minute walk from Damascus Gate; cheerful natural lighting; well-decorated rooms. **Cons:** neighborhood dead at night. [$] *Rooms from: $162* ✉ *15 St. George St., Seam Line* ☎ *02/591–7777* ⊕ *www.grandcourt.co.il* ⤳ *439 rooms, 15 suites* ⏐◯⏐ *Breakfast* ✛ *F2.*

$ ☷ **Leonardo Hotel Jerusalem.** A huge circular skylight in the middle of
HOTEL   the lobby gives this hotel a sense of light and space. **Pros:** comfortable rooms; lots of space; 10-minute walk from Damascus Gate. **Cons:** neighborhood dead at night; no distinctive character. [$] *Rooms from:*

$150 ☒ 9 St. George St., Seam Line ☎ *02/532–0000* ⊕ *www.leonardo-hotels.com* ⤳ *382 rooms, 18 suites* ⦿ *Breakfast* ⊹ *F2.*

$
HOTEL ⛢ **National.** Five minutes from the Old City, this hotel is once again attracting the diplomats and government officials who patronized it during its glory days. **Pros:** free Wi-Fi. **Cons:** a bit out of the way. ⓢ *Rooms from: $185* ☒ *4 Al Zahra St., Salah A-Din* ☎ *02/627–6663* ⊕ *www.nationalhotel-jerusalem.com* ⤳ *99 rooms* ⦿ *No meals.* ⊹ *G3.*

$$
HOTEL ⛢ **Olive Tree.** The stone arches, lacey latticework, and bronze ornaments in the reception area help to create a distinctly regional atmoshere, as do the old flagstones in the skylit atrium and polished floorboards in the comfortable lounge. **Pros:** 10-minute walk from Damascus Gate; superior sports facilities; elegant atmosphere. **Cons:** neighborhood is dead at night. ⓢ *Rooms from: $250* ☒ *23 St. George St., Seam Line* ☎ *02/541–0410* ⊕ *www.olivetreehotel.com* ⤳ *300 rooms, 4 suites* ⦿ *Breakfast* ⊹ *F2.*

NIGHTLIFE AND THE ARTS

The holy city isn't as staid as you might think, even though more than half its residents—ultra-Orthodox Jews and the Arab community—don't partake in Western-style entertainment and arts. You can combine a great meal or tasty snack with a concert, pub, or dance bar for a lively evening out on the town. Thursday and Friday nights are the hot times for bars and clubs and late-night shows; classical music and dance performances tend to avoid Friday nights, and take place over the rest of the week. Check out listings in English-language publications you find in hotels.

NIGHTLIFE

Although Jerusalem can't compete with Tel Aviv in terms of the number of nightlife attractions, what the city lacks in quantity it more than makes up for in quality. Pubs, bars, and nightclubs in Jerusalem tend to be more relaxed than those in Tel Aviv—they're friendlier, more informal, and often less expensive. As in Tel Aviv, the nightlife scene in Jerusalem starts very late: some places only begin to fill up after midnight, and most pubs are open until the early hours of the morning. Given the university presence in the city, there's often a younger crowd at many places.

CENTER CITY

BARS AND PUBS

HaTaklit. The name means "The Record," a nostalgic tribute by the three young, musically inclined owners to the vinyl predecessor to CDs and MP3s. This is a great place for beer, live music, occasional dance parties, and a back room where international soccer games are screened. ☒ *7 Helene Hamalka St., Downtown* ☎ *02/624–4073.*

Mirror Bar. This chic hotel bar appeals to a cross section of travelers, locals, and expats. The intimate space is perfect for a nightcap or a table of excellent tapas. ☒ *Mamilla Hotel, 11 King Solomon St., Mamilla* ☎ *02/548–2222* ⊕ *www.mamillahotel.com/mirrorbar.*

You can join Jerusalemites as they unwind at the movies at the popular Jerusalem Cinematheque.

Tuvia. This popular spot offers a wide variety of imported beers, tasty food, and good background music that appeals to a slightly older crowd. ⊠ *4 Shushan St., Downtown* ☎ *02/624–0949.*

Uganda. As a sort of inside joke, this ramshackle, überhip dive is named for the African country once proposed as an alternative site for the Jewish state. Palestinian beer is on tap, and is accompanied by tasty hummus. Live music, comic books, and vinyl records make this place quite popular with art students. ⊠ *4 Aristobulus St., Downtown* ☎ *02/623–6087* ⊕ *www.ugandajlm.com.*

Yudaleh. This wine and tapas bar is good for a drink before dinner or a light meal before hitting the town. ⊠ *10 Beit Yaacov St., Machaneh Yehuda* ☎ *02/533–3442.*

DANCE CLUBS

HaTza'atzua. Named for a beloved toy store that previously occupied this space, Toy Bar is a multilevel club with cozy couches for drinking and nibbling, massive flat-screen televisions for live performance broadcasts and keeping an eye on the game, and a great selection of local DJs. ⊠ *6 Dhu Nuwas St., Downtown* ☎ *02/623–6666* ⊕ *www.toybar.com.*

Sira. A great watering hole with a small dance floor, Sira features a variety of music spun by DJs. The late hours make this one of the most fun places in the city to dance. Here you'll find a Bohemian hodgepodge of students and internationals. ⊠ *4 Ben-Sira St., Downtown* ☎ *02/623–4366.*

RESTAURANT BARS

Adom. Lively, popular, and always open late, this bistro has a reputation for good shrimp and other seafood. ✉ *Feingold Courtyard, 31 Jaffa St., Downtown* ☎ *02/624–6242.*

Casino de Paris. Owned by Israeli rock star Shaanan Streett, this bar in the heart of the vegetable market occupies what was once a British Army brothel. The hippest place in town, it boasts a fine selection of original cocktails and beers from local microbreweries. ✉ *Georgian Market, 3 Machaneh Yehuda St., Downtown* ☎ *02/650–4235.*

Link. Popular with a professional crowd, this place has a deck that's a great spot on warm evenings. The grilled chicken wings are terrific. ✉ *3 Hama'alot St., Downtown* ☎ *02/625–3446.*

Zuni. The Jerusalem version of a gentleman's club, Zuni fills up with a young crowd after midnight. ✉ *15 Yoel Salomon St., Nahalat Shiva* ☎ *02/625–7776.*

WEST JERUSALEM

DANCE CLUBS

Ha'Oman 17. Veteran dance club Ha'Oman 17 is a hip, stylish place open only on the weekend. ✉ *17 Ha'oman St., Talpiot Industrial Zone* ☎ *02/678–1658.*

JAZZ CLUBS

Yellow Submarine. A not-for-profit music center, Yellow Submarine offers free jazz concerts one night a week, popular sing-along evenings, and performances by major Israeli and international rock and pop artists. A decent bar serves salads and other light fare. A varied schedule of gigs by top performers at reasonable prices makes it a venue worth checking out. ✉ *13 HaRechavim St., Talpiot Industrial Zone* ☎ *02/679–4040* ⊕ *www.yellowsubmarine.org.il.*

EAST JERUSALEM

BARS AND PUBS

Cellar Bar. This place has the feel of an intimate wine cellar, with small tables, quiet corners, and a mix of languages that makes you feel far away from all the political problems of the day. ✉ *American Colony Hotel, 1 Louis Vincent St. at Nablus Rd., East Jerusalem* ☎ *02/627–9777* ⊕ *www.americancolony.com.*

THE ARTS

Classical music is the capital's strong suit. Artists in other musical genres pass through from time to time, but Jerusalem is seldom their main focus. Dance performances are more infrequent, and professional English theater is very rare, although amateurs are often worthwhile.

For English-language schedules of performances and other cultural events, consult the Friday weekend section of the *Jerusalem Post* and its insert "In Jerusalem," Friday's "The Guide" of *Haaretz*'s English edition, *Time Out Jerusalem*, and the free weekly and monthly booklets available at hotels and information bureaus.

Bimot. This is the main ticket agency for performances in Jerusalem. Student discounts are sometimes available. ⊠ *8 Shammai St., Downtown* ☎ *02/623–7000* ⊕ *www.bimot.co.il/eng.*

DANCE

Gerard Behar Center. Look out for two excellent Jerusalem-based contemporary dance companies, Vertigo and Kolben, both of which are based at the Gerard Behar Center. ⊠ *11 Bezalel St., Downtown* ☎ *02/625–1139* ⊕ *gerard-behar.jerusalem.muni.il.*

FESTIVALS

Fodor's Choice
★

Israel Festival. Top national and international orchestras, theater companies, choirs, dance troupes, and street entertainers participate in this festival, usually held in late May or early June. Styles range from classical to avant-garde. The Jerusalem Theatre is the main venue, but a dozen secondary locations around the city get some of the smaller acts. ☎ *02/560–5755* ⊕ *www.israel-festival.org.il.*

Fodor's Choice
★

Hutzot Hayotzer Arts and Crafts Festival. The fine crafts and lively concerts presented at this festival are a highlight of August. Located in the Sultan's Pool, an ancient reservoir in the Hinnom Valley beneath the walls of the Old City, the 10-day event showcases crafts by Israeli and international artisans and features open-air concerts by top Israeli rock and pop performers. Arrive early for the best seats. ⊠ *Hativat Yerushalayim, Hutzot Hayotzer* ☎ *02/623–7000* ⊕ *www.artfair.jerusalem.muni.il.*

International Festival of Puppet Theater. The creation of Jerusalem's Train Theater, this festival is dedicated to the art of puppeteering. Each August, puppeteers from around the globe bring their productions to theaters and street venues around the city. Shows are generally geared toward youngsters, although some are entertaining for the whole family. ☎ *02/561–8514* ⊕ *www.traintheater.co.il/puppets_festival/english.*

Jerusalem Season of Culture. Held from May to July each year, this diverse selection of events highlights local and international artists, musicians, dancers, and other types of performers. Many of the offerings are delightfully offbeat. ⊠ *7 Bethlehem Rd., German Colony* ☎ *02/653–5880* ⊕ *www.jerusalemseason.com.*

Jerusalem Wine Festival. Held in August, this event presents the latest vintages from the country's vineyards, showcasing the best of Israel's 200 boutique wineries alongside major producers from around the world. For the price of a wineglass, you can sample all you want. The Israel Museum is the main venue, and it's very pleasant to wander through the sculpture garden with a glass of fine wine. ⊠ *Israel Museum, Ruppin Blvd., Givat Ram* ☎ *02/670–8811* ⊕ *www.imj.org.il.*

Oud Festival. Held each November, this festival paying homage to the Arabic lute presents a range of ethnic music from Turkey, Iraq, India, and a host of other cultures, often including Israeli rock. Performances are held at various concert halls around town. ☎ *02/624–5206* ⊕ *www.confederationhouse.org/english.*

FILM

Many new films, American and otherwise, reach Israel's screens very quickly, while some are mysteriously delayed. Israeli films have been garnering international praise in recent years; they and other non-English-speaking movies are almost always subtitled in English. Check newspaper listings for showtimes.

Jerusalem Cinematheque. Specializing in old, rare, and art films, this complex has four theaters, a restaurant, and splendid views of the Old City and the Hinnom Valley from the terrace. Its monthly programs focus on specific directors, actors, or subjects. The annual Jerusalem Film Festival, held in July, attracts large crowds, as does December's Jewish Film Festival. ⊠ *11 Hebron Rd., Hinnom Valley* ☎ *02/565–4356* ⊕ *www.jer-cin.org.il.*

Lev Smadar. In the German Colony, this venue is a bit of a throwback to yesteryear's movie atmosphere. It's a single-screen cinema with its own café and bar in an older building on a narrow lane. Its local following watches European and independent films, as well as the occasional blockbuster. ⊠ *4 Lloyd George St., German Colony* ☎ *02/561–8168* ⊕ *www.lev.co.il.*

MUSIC

Classical music abounds in Jerusalem, with Israeli orchestras and chamber ensembles performing year-round and a trickle of international artists passing through. There's other interesting programming around town, too.

Beit Avi Chai. This 270-seat auditorium hosts lectures, concerts, and theater in Hebrew and English throughout the year. ⊠ *44 King George St., Downtown* ☎ *02/621–5300* ⊕ *www.bac.org.il.*

Beit Shmuel. Musical and theatrical performances fill the season at this theater. Most of the plays are in Hebrew, but some are in English. ⊠ *6 Eliyahu Shama'a St., King David St.* ☎ *02/620–3455* ⊕ *www. beitshmuel.co.il.*

Bet Ticho. This place hosts evenings of song on Sundays and Thursdays, jazz on Tuesdays, and light classical music on Saturdays. ⊠ *9 Harav Kook St., near Zion Sq., Downtown* ☎ *02/624–4186.*

International Convention Center. Opposite the Central Bus Station, the center is the local venue for the world-renowned Israel Philharmonic Orchestra. ⊠ *1 Zalman Shazar Blvd., Givat Ram* ☎ *02/623–7000* ⊕ *www.ipo.co.il/eng.*

Jerusalem Theatre. This venue is officially named the Jerusalem Centre for the Performing Arts, though nobody calls it that. The 750-seat Henry Crown Auditorium is the home base of the Jerusalem Symphony Orchestra, and the venue for the popular Etnachta series of free concerts produced by Israel Radio's classical station and broadcast live Mondays at 5 pm, generally from October through June. The Israel Philharmonic Orchestra stages its Intermezzo concerts here at noon on Fridays. ⊠ *20 Marcus St., Talbieh* ☎ *02/560–5755* ⊕ *www.jerusalem-theatre.co.il.*

YMCA Concert Hall. This 500-seat concert hall is the main venue for the much-acclaimed Jerusalem International Chamber Music Festival, held each year in late August or early September. It hosts rousing Israeli singing and folk dancing on Monday, Thursday, and Saturday evenings. Reservations are advised, as is getting there early for the best seats. ⊠ *26 King David St., King David St.* ☎ *02/569-2692* ⊕ *www.jcmf.org.il/en* ✉ *About NIS 100.*

Zappa at the Lab. This popular music venue hosts the country's top jazz, rock, and pop performers. Small and intimate, it's a great place to see Israel's best musicians close up. Dinner and drinks are usually available. Posters around town announce upcoming concerts. ⊠ *28 Hebron Rd., JVP Media Quarter* ☎ *03/762-6666* ⊕ *www.zappa-club.co.il.*

MUSIC IN CHURCHES

Church of the Redeemer. In the Christian Quarter of the Old City, this church hosts occasional concerts. ⊠ *Muristan, Christian Quarter* ☎ *02/626-6800* ⊕ *www.evangelisch-in-jerusalem.org.*

Dormition Abbey. On Mt. Zion, this abbey hosts occasional concerts. ⊠ *Hativat Etsiyoni, Mt. Zion* ☎ *02/565-5330* ⊕ *www.dormitio.net.*

Jerusalem Center. This center at Brigham Young University hosts a Sunday evening classical concert. ⊠ *Hadassa Lampel St., Mt. Scopus* ☎ *02/626-5666* ⊕ *www.ce.byu.edu/jc.*

THEATER

The Israel Festival, held in May or June in the Jerusalem Theatre, is your best bet for quality English-language productions.

Khan Theater. Set in a former coaching inn and silk factory, this atmospheric venue has some performances and special events in English. ⊠ *2 David Remez Sq., Hebron Rd.* ☎ *02/671-8281* ⊕ *www.khan.co.il.*

Hebrew University at Mt. Scopus. The Hebrew University at Mt. Scopus has 10 lighted courts and rental equipment. Courts go for NIS 20 an hour during the day and NIS 25 an hour in the evening. You can rent a racket for NIS 20, and buy three balls for NIS 30. Call ahead to book, especially during campus recess. ⊠ *1 Churchill St., Mt. Scopus* ☎ *02/588-2796* ⊕ *www.cosell.co.il.*

SHOPPING

Jerusalem offers distinctive ideas for gifts—for yourself or others—from jewelry and art to traditional crafts, items of a religious nature, and souvenirs. The several shopping areas make it easy to plan expeditions. Prices are generally fixed in the center city and the Jewish Quarter of the Old City, though you can sometimes negotiate for significant discounts on expensive art and jewelry. Shopping in the Old City's colorful Arab bazaar, or souk (pronounced "shook" in Israel—rhymes with "book"), is fascinating but can be a trap for the unwary.

Young fashion designers, often graduates of Jerusalem's Bezalel Academy of Arts and Design, have opened a stream of shops and boutiques. They're scattered throughout the city. Several galleries representing Israeli artists are close to the hotels on King David Street.

2

Jewelry in Israel is of a high international standard. You can choose between conservative styles; sleek, modern pieces inspired by different ethnicities; and the increasingly popular bead jewelry of Michal Negrin and other current Israeli stars of both the local and international scene.

Stores generally open by 8:30 am or 9 am, and some close between 1 pm and 4 pm. A few still close on Tuesday afternoon, a traditional but less and less observed half day. Jewish-owned stores (that is, all of West Jerusalem—the "New City"—and the Old City's Jewish Quarter) close on Friday afternoon by 2 pm or 3 pm, depending on the season and the kind of store (food and souvenir shops tend to stay open later), and reopen on Sunday morning. Some stores geared to the tourist trade, particularly Downtown, reopen on Saturday night after the Jewish Sabbath ends, especially in summer. Arab-owned stores in the Old City and East Jerusalem are busiest on Saturday and quietest on Sunday, when many (but not all) Christian storekeepers close for the day.

CENTER CITY
SHOPPING STREETS AND MALLS
Midrachov. This pedestrian-only strip of Ben-Yehuda Street is the heartbeat of West Jerusalem. The selection of clothing, shoes, jewelry, and souvenir stores makes for a fun shopping experience. Street musicians serenade passersby and those seated at the many outdoor cafés. Summer evenings are lively, as the mall fills with peddlers of cheap jewelry and crafts. ⊠ *Downtown.*

Yoel Salomon Street. In the old neighborhood of Nahalat Shiva, just off Zion Square, is the pedestrian-only Yoel Salomon Street. Between the restaurants on the main drag and in the adjacent alleys and courtyards, you'll find several crafts galleries and artsy jewelry and clothing shops. ⊠ *Nahalat Shiva.*

STREET MARKETS
Fodor's Choice ★ **Machaneh Yehuda.** This block-long alleyway market becomes a blur of brilliant primary colors as the city's best-quality fruit and vegetables, pickles and cheeses, fresh fish and poultry, confections, and falafel await inspection. The busiest days are Thursday and Friday, when Jews shop for the Sabbath; the market is closed on Saturday, along with the rest of Jewish West Jerusalem. Combine your visit with a meal at one of the many Middle Eastern restaurants in the neighborhood or grab a cup of excellent coffee at a Western-style café. Before you fill your baskets and bags, stop in at the wonderful boutiques and shops scattered throughout the market. On summer evenings, there's also live music. ⊠ *Off Jaffa St., Machaneh Yehuda.*

SPECIALTY STORES
BEAUTY PRODUCTS **Ahava Center.** The Ahava Center stocks all the company's products using minerals from the Dead Sea, but at less attractive prices than elsewhere. ⊠ *5 Ben-Yehuda St., Downtown* ☎ *02/625–2592.*

Dead Sea Gallery. This tiny store offers big discounts on Ahava skincare products. The company's Dermud line featuring Dead Sea minerals is particularly worth trying. The helpful staff and the competitive prices make this visit a particular pleasure. Mail-order service is also available. ⊠ *17 Jaffa St., corner of King Solomon St., Downtown* ☎ *02/622–1451.*

Ceramic creations large and small are among the many lovely crafts worth seeking out around Jerusalem.

CLOTHING **Adi Kilav.** This shop sells striking, handmade leather shoes in bright colors at reasonable prices. Adi Kilav's classic lines reflect his training in architecture. ⊠ *6 Shatz St., Downtown* ☎ *02/563–3701* ⊕ *www.adikilav.com.*

Haegoz 30. This shop offers a monochromatic selection of Israeli designer clothing and offbeat accessories, chosen by an owner who knows what looks good on her customers. ⊠ *30 Haegoz St., Machaneh Yehuda* ☎ *02/623–2467.*

Him with the Shirts. Here's where to find a great array of T-shirts with clever slogans and designs, primarily in Hebrew. ⊠ *3 Ben Sira St., Downtown* ☎ *077/783–3499* ⊕ *www.h-i-h.co.il.*

Kedem Sasson. This Israeli fashion designer caters to the fuller figure, with clothes in soft fabrics, some of them in decidedly quirky styles. ⊠ *21 King George St., Downtown* ☎ *02/625–2602* ⊕ *www.kedem-sasson.com.*

Lord Kitsch. This local chain stocks a range of casual clothes, including T-shirts in a rainbow of colors. There are other branches at 42 Jaffa Street in Downtown, in Achim Yisrael Mall, and on Alrov Mamilla Avenue. ⊠ *1 King George St., Downtown* ☎ *02/625–8120.*

Naama Bezalel. Naama Bezalel specializes in decidedly feminine lines for a range of ages, as well as a selection of distinctly beautiful bridal dresses. The second store across the street carries discounted leftovers from past seasons. ⊠ *27 King George St., Downtown* ☎ *02/625–5611.*

Poenta. This store has two locations in Jerusalem. One is in Nahalat Shiva, selling unique bags, jewelry, and crafts. A second outpost at 6 Shatz Street in Downtown has a distinctive selection of Israeli designer clothing, as well as bags and jewelry. ⊠ 21 Yoel Salomon St., Nahalat Shiva ☎02/624–0383.

Sofia. Owner Miri Ashur Zuta offers a well-honed selection of Israeli designer clothing and accessories. ⊠ 2 Bezalel St., Downtown ☎02/625–2765.

Sweet-T. Head here for a good selection of T-shirts ready for custom decoration. ⊠ 2 Ben-Yehuda St., Downtown ☎02/625–4835 ⊕ www. jerusalemtshirts.com.

Tashtari. This exclusive boutique features handmade evening bags, including a line made of recycled materials. Owner Amos Sadan's outstanding "wearable art"—much of which is influenced by Japanese aesthetics—includes hats, scarves, and shawls. ⊠ 25 King George St., Downtown ☎02/625–3282 ⊕ www.tashtari.com.

CRAFTS **Barbara Shaw.** Australian immigrant Barbara Shaw has put her colorful, contemporary stamp on a selection of household gifts, from crisp dish towels and whimsical aprons to pillows and tote bags. There's another branch on Emek Refa'im Street in the German Colony. ⊠ 2 Bezalel St., Downtown ☎02/625–7474 ⊕ www.barbarashawgifts.com.

Cadim. A decidedly contemporary selection of ceramics is on view at this shop. ⊠ 4 Yoel Salomon St., Nahalat Shiva ☎02/623–4869 ⊕ www. cadimceramicsgallery.com.

Charlotte. This shop carries colorful ceramics, weavings, painted silks, jewelry, and fashion accessories. ⊠ 4 Coresh St., Downtown ☎02/625–1632.

Danny Azoulay. These delicate items in fine porcelain are all hand-painted in rich shades of blue, red, and gold. Traditional Jewish ritual objects include fine paper cuts and a range of ornamental ketubot (wedding contracts). Less expensive items include napkin rings and bottle stoppers. ⊠ 5 Yoel Salomon St., Nahalat Shiva ☎02/623–3918 ⊕ www. artofketubot.com.

Darian Armenian Ceramics. This is the only Armenian gallery in West Jerusalem. Besides ceramic pieces with Jewish themes, the shop carries hand-painted tables and mirrors and has a plentiful selection of bargain-priced seconds. You can often catch Arman Darian and his staff working on new designs. ⊠ 12 Shlomzion Hamalka, Downtown ☎057/470–2582 ⊕ www.darianart.com.

Gans. This shop sells good-quality Judaica, all of it made in Israel. Choose from glassware, jewelry, painted silk, and ceramic pieces in both traditional and modern designs. There are many moderately priced options. ⊠ 8 Rivlin St., Nahalat Shiva ☎02/625–1159 ⊕ www.gans.co.il.

Guild of Ceramicists. This shop beckons with its delightfully colorful tiled steps. The functional and ornamental pottery is made by 12 Israeli artists, and it looks more whimsical than usual. ⊠ 27 Yoel Salomon St., Nahalat Shiva ☎02/624–4065.

Jerusalem Experience. This is the place for items of religious interest and handmade Judaica. The friendly staff is happy to show you Israeli perfumes, skincare products, ceramics, glassware, and textiles, but also books about Jerusalem and other aspects of Israel. ⊠ 17 Jaffa St., opposite Safra Square, Downtown ☎02/622–3030.

Judaicut. This shop sells traditional and affordable papercuts, a traditional and well-established Jewish art form. These pieces make unusual gifts—to say nothing of being both light and easy to pack. They can be customized with your name. ⊠ *21 Yoel Salomon St., Nahalat Shiva* 🕾 *02/623–3634* ⊕ *www.judaicut.co.il.*

Shemonah Beyachad. Roughly translated as "Altogether Eight," this enterprise has grown to become a group of 11 ceramicists, at least one of whom is usually on duty in the store. ⊠ *11 Yoel Salomon St., Nahalat Shiva* 🕾 *02/624–7250.*

JEWELRY **Hedya.** This boutique carries the collections of both Ze'ev and Sharon Tammuz. Necklaces and earrings are made from antique gold, silver, amber, and other materials that retain a feel of the past. ⊠ *23 Hillel St., Downtown* 🕾 *02/622–1151.*

Idit. Offering an intriguing range of in-house designs, this family business is still run by the children of the founder, craftsman Chaim Paz. ⊠ *23 King George St., Downtown* 🕾 *02/622–1911* ⊕ *www.iditjewelry.com.*

GERMAN COLONY AND BAKA
SHOPPING STREETS AND MALLS
Emek Refa'im. This is a popular area in which to shop, dine, and people-watch from early morning to late at night. Gifts and jewelry are easy to find in a rainbow of styles and tastes to meet different budgets. ⊠ *German Colony.*

SPECIALTY STORES
BEAUTY PRODUCTS **Sabon Shel Paam.** Herb-infused soaps, creams, lotions, and scrubs are available at this shop. ⊠ *35 Emek Refa'im St., German Colony* 🕾 *02/650–6644* ⊕ *www.sabon.ro.*

CLOTHING **Osfa.** With well-chosen pieces by local designers, this small but well-stocked boutique has a friendly staff that knows its wares. ⊠ *53 Bethlehem Rd., Baka* 🕾 *052/423–7410* ⊕ *www.osfacollect.com.*

Pashmina. Here you'll find a wonderful selection of Israeli-designed clothing, jewelry, shoes, belts, and bags. Let the owner, Michal, or her skilled assistants advise you; they know their inventory and are helpful without being pushy. ⊠ *4 HaMelitz St., German Colony* 🕾 *02/561–0567.*

CRAFTS **Hoshen.** Attractive items in wood, ceramics, fabric, and jewelry are available at Hoshen. ⊠ *32 Emek Refa'im, German Colony* 🕾 *02/563–0966* ⊕ *www.hoshenshop.com.*

Nisha. This shop displays an ample selection of well-priced Israeli crafts, from clay jewelry to whimsical pottery. ⊠ *31 Bethlehem Rd., Baka* 🕾 *02/672–5630.*

JEWELRY **Keo.** This shop specializes in delicate, modern pieces at reasonable prices. ⊠ *25 Emek Refa'im, German Colony* 🕾 *02/563–7026.*

Sheshet. Sheshet has a solid selection of contemporary Israeli gold and silver pieces, as well as locally designed leather bags, belts, and wallets. ⊠ *34 Emek Refa'im, German Colony* 🕾 *02/566–2261.*

Stav. Exquisite (and expensive) pieces in a graceful mix of both ethnic and modern influences are on sale at Stav. ⊠ *40 Emek Refa'im, German Colony* 🕾 *02/563–7059* ⊕ *www.stavjewelry.com.*

OLD CITY

SHOPPING STREETS AND MALLS

Cardo. In the Old City's Jewish Quarter, the Cardo began life as the main thoroughfare of Byzantine Jerusalem. It was a commercial street during the Crusader era, and has now been converted into an attractive shopping area. Beyond souvenirs and Judaica, you'll find good-quality jewelry and artwork. ⊠ *Jewish Quarter St., Jewish Quarter.*

STREET MARKETS

Fodor's Choice ★

Souk. Jerusalem's main market is the souk in the Old City, spread over a warren of intersecting streets. This is where much of Arab Jerusalem shops. It's awash with color and redolent with the clashing scents of exotic spices. Baskets of produce vie for attention with hanging shanks of lamb, fresh fish on ice, and fresh-baked delicacies. Food stalls are interspersed with purveyors of fabrics and shoes. The baubles and trinkets of the tourist trade often seem secondary, except along the well-trodden paths of the Via Dolorosa, David Street, and Christian Quarter Road.

Haggling with merchants in the Arab market—a time-honored tradition—isn't always the good-natured experience it once was. It's not always easy to identify the honest merchants among the many whose jewelry, antiquities, leather, and embroidery are often not what they claim. Unless you know what you want, know how much it's *really* worth, and enjoy the sometimes aggressive give-and-take of bargaining, you're better off just enjoying the local color and doing your shopping in the less crowded New City. ■ TIP→ Women should watch their purses and dress discreetly. ⊠ *Christian and Muslim Quarters.*

SPECIALTY STORES

ART GALLERIES

Blue and White Art Gallery. Udi Merioz, the artist and owner of Blue and White Art Gallery, does "soft painting," a special appliqué technique that uses synthetic fibers on canvas. The gallery also represents Israeli artist Yaacov Agam. ⊠ *1 Cardo St., Jewish Quarter* ☎ *02/628–8464* ⊕ *www.blueandwhiteart.com.*

Elia Photo Service. Kevork Kahvedjian's collection of 3,500 photographic prints of Jerusalem and the Holy Land dating back to 1860 provides a window into a vanished world. Many of them have been published in history books and adorn the walls of local hotels and restaurants. All are available as high-quality prints in various sizes, mounted and ready for framing. ⊠ *14 Al-Khanka St., Christian Quarter* ☎ *02/628–2074* ⊕ *www.eliaphoto.com.*

CLOTHING

Bilal Abu Khalaf. Patronized by embassies, upscale hotels, and fashionable cogniscenti, the family of Bilal Abu Khalaf has been trading in fine fabrics for Jerusalem's elite for three generations. The shop is an Aladdin's cave of Damascene silks woven with golden thread, Moroccan brocade set with semiprecious stones, and the finest fabric from Kashmir. Christian, Muslim, and Jewish clerics all purchase their robes here. Phone ahead to arrange a riveting 20-minute presentation of the shop's most beautiful treasures, and an explanation of the Crusader church visible through the glass floor. ⊠ *164 Suq Aftimus, Muristan, Christian Quarter* ☎ *02/626–1718.*

Stores along the narrow streets of the souk in the Old City tempt passersby with food, fabrics, and ceramics.

CRAFTS

Hagop Antreassian's. The standouts in Armenian Hagop Antreassian's studio are his wonderful large bowls. They won't fit in your carry-ons, but Antreassian ships. You can often find him painting or firing his clay creations in his studio just inside Zion Gate. ⊠ *Armenian Patriarchate, opposite Zion Gate, Armenian Quarter* ☎ *02/626–3871.*

Jerusalem Pottery. Through a tiny passageway opposite the sixth Station of the Cross is the store of two fine local artisans, Stefan Karakashian and his son Hagop. Their particularly high-quality work includes plates, bowls, tiles, and plaques. ⊠ *15 Via Dolorosa, Muslim Quarter* ☎ *02/626–1587* ⊕ *www.jerusalempottery.biz.*

Sandrouni. This shop stocks a variety of utilitarian pieces in many colors and styles. ⊠ *Armenian Orthodox Patriarchate Rd., opposite entrance to St. James Convent, Armenian Quarter* ☎ *02/628–3567.*

REHAVIA, TALBIEH, KING DAVID STREET, AND YEMIN MOSHE

SHOPPING STREETS AND MALLS

Arts and Crafts Lane. Downhill from the Jaffa Gate, Hutzot Hayotzer is home to goldsmiths and silversmiths specializing in jewelry, fine art, and Judaica, generally done in an ultramodern, minimalist style. The work is of extremely high quality and priced accordingly. ⊠ *Hutzot Hayotzer, Hinnom Valley.*

King David Street. This avenue is lined with prestigious stores and galleries, most with an emphasis on art, antiquities, or high-end jewelry. ⊠ *King David St.*

2

Mamilla Mall. Bordered by Old City's Jaffa Gate on one end and the upscale Mamilla Hotel on the other, this open-air mall features such familiar clothing chains as Ralph Lauren and Tommy Hilfiger. There's also a growing number of independent Israeli fashion, crafts, and jewelry designers, and restaurants and cafés, all with a spectacular view. ⊠ *Alrov Mamilla Ave., Mamilla* ⊕ *www.alrovmamilla.com.*

SPECIALTY STORES

ART GALLERIES **Motke Blum.** On Arts and Crafts Lane, Motke Blum does fine soft-colored oils and minimalist landscapes. ⊠ *Hutzot Hayotzer, Hinnom Valley* ☎ *02/623–4002* ⊕ *www.motke.com.*

BEAUTY PRODUCTS **Laline.** This shop is known for its trademark white-and-black setting for luxe creams and soaps. ⊠ *Alrov Mamilla Ave., Mamilla* ☎ *054/334– 5032* ⊕ *www.laline.co.il.*

CLOTHING **Ronen Chen.** Simple, classic styles in very comfortable fabrics are the hallmark of Ronen Chen. ⊠ *Alrov Mamilla Ave., Mamilla* ☎ *02/624–2881* ⊕ *www.ronenchen.com.*

CRAFTS **Jerusalem House of Quality.** Here you'll discover the work of some excellent Israeli craftspeople working in ceramics, glass, jewelry, sculpture, and wood. You can often see them at work in their studios on the second floor. ⊠ *12 Hebron Rd., Hebron Rd.* ☎ *02/671–7430* ⊕ *www. art-jerusalem.com.*

JEWELRY **Dan Alsberg.** With a shop on Arts and Crafts Lane, Dan Alsberg is a particularly outstanding and original craftsman of modern pieces, mostly in gold and silver. ⊠ *Hutzot Hayotzer, outside Jaffa Gate, Hinnom Valley* ☎ *02/627–1430* ⊕ *www.studioalsberg.com.*

H. Stern. The Jerusalem flagship store of this international company offers high-quality, expensive pieces. ⊠ *Alrov Mamilla Ave., Alrov Mamilla* ☎ *02/624–2855* ⊕ *www.hstern.co.il.*

Michal Negrin. Whimsical, vintage-inspired jewelry and fashion accessories have made Michal Negrin a remarkable success story. ⊠ *Alrov Mamilla Ave., Mamilla* ☎ *02/624–2112* ⊕ *www.michalnegrin.com.*

Sari Srulovitch. This shop's award-winning hand-crafted silver tableware and Jewish ceremonial objects combine traditional and modern themes in distinctive designs with a clean, contemporary feel. ⊠ *7 Hutzot Hayotzer, opposite Jaffa Gate, Hinnom Valley* ☎ *02/628–6699* ⊕ *www. sarisrulovitch.com.*

WEST JERUSALEM

SHOPPING STREETS AND MALLS

Malcha Mall. Known locally as Kenyon Malcha, this huge shopping mall is—at 500,000 square feet—one of the largest in the Middle East. It includes a department store, a supermarket, and almost 200 shops and eateries. The interior is an attractive mix of arched skylights and wrought-iron banisters. ⊠ *Derech Agudat Sport Maccabi, Malcha* ☎ *02/679–1333.*

SPECIALTY STORES

CLOTHING **Tali Imbar.** This Israeli designer creates casually elegant clothes that are a pleasure to wear. ⊠ *Alrov Mamilla Ave., Malcha* ☎ *02/679–3890* ⊕ *www.talimbar.com.*

CRAFTS **House of Harrari.** In the village of Ramat Raziel, a 25-minute drive from Downtown Jerusalem, you'll find this house of musical instruments. The Bible inspired the small decorative door harps and graceful 10- and 22-string folk instruments. The workshop displays the instruments in different stages of production. The gallery will ship your purchase home. Call for directions. ⊠ *52 Brosh St., Ramat Raziel* ☎ *02/570–9075* ⊕ *www.harrariharps.com.*

Klein. Check here for some of the highest-quality olive-wood objects in Israel. This is the factory showroom, off the tourist route. It stocks everything the company makes, from bowls and yo-yos to attractive trays decorated with Armenian pottery tiles, picture frames, boxes, and desktop paraphernalia. ⊠ *3 Ziv St., at Bar Ilan St., Tel Arza* ☎ *02/538–9992.*

Ruth Havilio. Artist Ruth Havilio makes hand-painted tiles with a more modern feel, for both decorative and practical purposes. Her sense of color and fun (whimsical clay animals, for instance) plays alongside more traditional styles. You can have tiles personalized, but keep in mind that this can't be done on the spot. To get there, take the alley to the left of St. John's Church. Part of the charm of the gallery is its evocative courtyard setting. ⊠ *Ein Kerem St. D/4, Ein Kerem* ☎ *02/641–7912.*

JEWELRY **Adipaz.** This shop cuts diamonds and makes its own jewelry, much of it without precious stones. ⊠ *20 Pierre Koenig St., Talpiot Industrial Zone* ☎ *02/678–3887.*

AROUND JERUSALEM AND THE DEAD SEA

With Masada and Bethlehem

WELCOME TO AROUND JERUSALEM AND THE DEAD SEA

TOP REASONS TO GO

★ **Ein Gedi:** This oasis rich in flora, fauna, and archaeology—praised in the Bible for its beauty and today one of Israel's most impressive national parks—offers spectacular hiking near waterfalls and canyons.

★ **Masada:** The awe-inspiring remains of this mountaintop palace overlooking the Dead Sea recall its history as a retreat for Herod the Great and as the last stand of the Jewish rebels against Rome in AD 73.

★ **Dead Sea:** At the lowest point on Earth, float effortlessly on one of the world's saltiest bodies of water, renowned for its therapeutic qualities. In Ein Bokek, cover yourself with the mud, exported as a beauty treatment.

★ **Bethlehem:** Follow in the footsteps of Jesus from the Church of the Nativity to the grotto where Mary nursed him.

★ **Judean Hills wineries:** Close to Jerusalem, this area is home to more than two dozen wineries that produce some excellent and highly prized wines.

Map labels:
Neot Kedumim, TO TEL AVIV, Modi'in, Horon Junction, Beit Horon, 463, 431, 3, 1, 443, Givat Ze'ev, Latrun Armored Corps Museum, Mini Israel, Sha'ar Hagai, Nataf, Kubeibe, 436, Latrun Neve Shalom, Ma'aleh Hahamisha, Abu Ghosh, Hulda, Trappist Abbey of Latrun, Shoresh, Neve Ilan, 3, 44, Eshta'ol, Kesalon, Tzuba, Ein Hemed, Kibbutz Tzora, 2, Ya'aran Farm, 386, Beit Shemesh, Tel Beit Shemesh, Sorek Cave, Beit Jala, SHEFELAH, 38, Beit Jimal, Solomon's Pools, 375, 367, Elazar, Alon Shevut, Kfar Etzion, Efrat, Beit Guvrin, 35, Alon Shevut, Elazar, Kfar Etzion, 60, Efrat, Tel Maresha, Beit Fajjar, 356, Halhul, 35, Hebron, Kiryat Arba, Bani Na'im

1 **Masada and the Dead Sea.** Herod the Great's desert retreat would be an extraordinary archaeological site even if it had never made it into the history books. But Masada is also famous for being where hundreds of Jews committed suicide rather than surrender to Rome. Hike (or take the cable car) to the top of the plateau for sunrise over the Dead Sea, then take a relaxing dip in this saltiest of all lakes. Combine a visit with a trip to Ein Gedi or Ein Bokek, both near the Dead Sea, for unforgettable desert adventures.

2 **West of Jerusalem.** The picturesque Judean Hills west of Jerusalem are dotted with natural springs and forested nature reserves, as well as outstanding wineries, boutique breweries, and farms making great goat cheese. Pack a picnic and take the winding road to visit Soreq Cave and Beit Guvrin National Park.

3 **Bethlehem.** Just a few miles south of Jerusalem in the West Bank, visit the birthplace of Jesus, today marked by the Church of the Nativity on Manger Square.

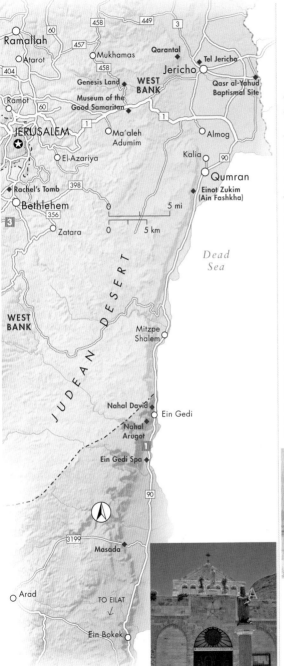

Ramallah
60
457
458
449
3
Atarot
Mukhamas
Qarantal
404
458
Jericho
Tel Jericha
Genesis Land
WEST
BANK
Qasr al-Yahud
Baptismal Site
Ramot
60
Museum of the
Good Samaritan
1
JERUSALEM
1
Ma'aleh
Adumim
Almog
El-Azariya
Kalia
90
Rachel's Tomb
398
Qumran
Bethlehem
356
Einot Zukim
(Ain Fashkha)
0   5 mi
Zatara
0   5 km
Dead
Sea

JUDEAN DESERT

WEST
BANK
Mitzpe
Shalem

Nahal David
Ein Gedi
Nahal
Arugot
Ein Gedi Spa
90

3199
Masada
Arad
TO EILAT
Ein Bokek

GETTING ORIENTED

3

The wealth of beautiful landscapes, historical treasures, and biblical sites within an easy drive of Jerusalem makes a number of good day trips. To the west lie the Judean Hills, covered with vineyards and farms. To the south is Bethlehem, an age-old pilgrimage site for Christians. And to the east is the Judean Desert, graced with fertile oases like Jericho and Ein Gedi. Descending from Jerusalem's peaks, you quickly arrive at the Dead Sea—the lowest point on the face of Earth. Ein Bokek, near the Dead Sea's southern end, is a good place to float in its warm, salty water.

סכנת טביעה
خطر الغرق
DANGER OF
DROWNING

Updated
by Daniella
Cheslow

The Judean Hills that encircle Jerusalem, together with the wilderness that slopes precipitously eastward to the Dead Sea, offer an astonishing range of scenery: springs and oases, forests and fields, caves, hiking trails, and impressive archaeological sites such as Masada. West of the city, farmers are coaxing grapes from the valley where David once battled Goliath. The area is becoming more popular with a wide range of travelers, thanks to its wineries, breweries, and boutique cheese and olive oil producers.

The Judean Desert–Dead Sea area—little changed from when Abraham wandered here with his flocks—contrasts sharply with the lush greenery of the oases of Ein Gedi, Ein Fashkha, and the verdant fields of Jericho. Nomadic Bedouin still cling to their ancestral way of life, herding sheep and goats, though you'll notice some concessions to modernity: pickup trucks are parked beside camels.

The route along the Dead Sea shore is hemmed in by towering brown cliffs fractured by *wadis*, or dry riverbeds. Ein Gedi has two of the most spectacular of these wadis, Nahal David and Nahal Arugot. In Ein Bokek, near the southern end of the Dead Sea, you can settle into one of the numerous health and beauty spas that make use of the Dead Sea's saline waters and medicinal mud.

Just to the north is Masada, Herod the Great's mountaintop palace-fortress built over 2,000 years ago, which is a UNESCO World Heritage site. Overlooking the Dead Sea, the king's extravagant architectural feat still displays ingenious water systems, elaborate frescoes and mosaic floors, and bathhouses. Add the human drama of the last Jewish stand against Rome during the Great Revolt, and it's easy to understand why this is one of the most visited sights in Israel.

Just south of Jerusalem, Bethlehem is a major site of Christian pilgrimage. The Church of the Nativity, the oldest church in the country, erected in the 4th century, is built over the grotto where Christian tradition holds Jesus was born. The West Bank Palestinian city of almost 40,000 sits on the ancient highway through the rocky Judean Hills. Farmers tend century-old terraces of olives, figs, and grapes all around the ancient city.

AROUND JERUSALEM AND THE DEAD SEA PLANNER

WHEN TO GO

The Dead Sea region is pleasant between October and April, but suffers from searing dry heat during the summer. Beginning the day with a tour of Masada can help beat the heat and the crowds. Ein Bokek, with its unique hotels and spas by the Dead Sea, attracts visitors even in broiling hot summer. Bethlehem is best early or late in the day if you want to avoid the crowds. Before you set out, check the hours for the Church of the Nativity. The area to the west of Jerusalem is agreeable any time of the year.

Some advanced planning pays off if you want to visit this region during a religious holiday, since transportation can be difficult during Jewish holidays like Yom Kippur and the Muslim observance of Ramadan. On Passover, Israelis tend to mob the Dead Sea. Similarly, Christmas is celebrated three times in Jerusalem and Bethlehem, according to the Western, Orthodox, and Armenian rites. Visit Manger Square on Christmas Eve for an unforgettable holiday, but book hotels far in advance.

PLANNING YOUR TIME

The Dead Sea can be a great day trip from Jerusalem, but you'll have a richer experience if you spend a few nights in Ein Bokek. An ideal itinerary might be: On the first morning, climb Masada and marvel at the views, then head to your Ein Bokek hotel for an afternoon at the Dead Sea; watch the hills of Jordan redden as the sun sets. On the second day, drive to Ein Gedi (½ hour north of Ein Bokek) for the waterfalls and a dip in the pools. On the third day, stop in Jericho on the way back to Jerusalem.

When traveling to Bethlehem, Jericho, and other areas under Palestinian control, you'll need to present your passport at the checkpoint. This usually just takes a minute. There can be traffic crossing back from Bethlehem to Jerusalem, so allow extra time.

GETTING HERE AND AROUND

BUS TRAVEL

Egged buses are modern, air-conditioned, and reasonably priced. Service is dependable on main routes but infrequent to outlying rural districts. Egged buses don't run from sunset Friday to sunset Saturday.

From the Beersheva Central Bus Station, buses depart four times a day for Arad, Ein Bokek, and other southern points. For Ein Bokek, there's also a daily 8:40 am bus from Tel Aviv's Arlozorov Bus Station (a three-hour ride) and several buses, departing on the hour, from Jerusalem (a two-hour journey). Buses can be crowded, especially on Friday and Sunday. You can't buy tickets or reserve seats by phone for the above routes; go to the bus station, and arrive early.

CAR TRAVEL

Driving is preferable to relying on public transportation here, as some sights are on secondary roads where bus service is scarce. Highway conditions are good, and most destinations are signposted in both Hebrew and English. The steep road between Arad and Ein Bokek has one hairpin turn after another. Unless otherwise posted, stick to the intercity speed of 90 kph (56 mph). Budget extra time for leaving Jerusalem during rush hours. Gas stations are plentiful; some are open 24 hours, but play it safe and keep the tank at least half full.

If you plan to drive to areas controlled by the Palestinian Authority, several East Jerusalem car-rental companies offer insurance to the West Bank. Always check whether there's political unrest that could make roads unsafe. Throw a *kefiyya*, the traditional checkered headscarf, onto your dashboard for extra security.

SHERUT TRAVEL

Sheruts, or shared taxis seating up to 10 passengers, run set routes (usually along major bus routes) and charge a nominally more expensive fare. These run on Saturdays between Tel Aviv and Jerusalem. Known in Arabic as *serveeses*, they run to Bethlehem and Jericho from East Jerusalem's Damascus Gate, though an Arab taxi may be delayed at military checkpoints.

TRAIN TRAVEL

Israel Railways has regular—but slow—train service between Jerusalem and Tel Aviv, hourly from 6 am to 8 pm, from the southern neighborhood of Malcha; there are occasional departures from the Jerusalem Biblical Zoo. The beautiful 40-minute ride through forested hills to the Judean lowlands is spectacular for the scenery alone.

For more information on getting here and around, see Travel Smart Israel.

DINING

Some Judean Hills wineries offer fancy meals along with their tastings, but these should be reserved in advance. Abu Gosh, on the way to Latrun, is known for its hummus and kebab restaurants. There are also some passable cafeterias west of Jerusalem and a handful of excellent restaurants set in the hills. An alternative is to take a packed lunch or have a picnic west of Jerusalem with wine and cheese. At the Dead Sea, it's always a good idea to make reservations in Ein Bokek restaurants, especially on Friday and Saturday night.

Prices in the reviews are the average cost of a main course at dinner or, if dinner isn't served, at lunch.

LODGING

Visitors, both national and international, who come to "take the waters" and enjoy the serene desert scenery, heavily use the lodgings in the Dead Sea region. On the northern shore, facilities range from youth hostels to kibbutz inns. Although they might conjure up visions of spartan plainness, the kibbutz inns are surprisingly comfortable. They also offer a chance to see life on the communal settlements firsthand.

Along the southern shore, hotels in sunny Ein Bokek run from family-style simplicity to pampering luxury. Shuttle buses link hotels with each other and the center of town. A beautiful and luxurious spa with a wide range of facilities is an important feature of each large hotel, and many smaller hotels as well. The high seasons are mid-March to mid-June, and mid-September to the end of November.

Since visitors typically explore the area west of Jerusalem on a day trip, lodgings are few and far between. The exceptions are some fine bed-and-breakfast–style guesthouses known as *zimmers*.

Prices in the reviews are the lowest cost of a standard double room in high season.

3

TOUR OPTIONS
Bus tours pick you up and return you to your hotel in Jerusalem: very convenient. Egged and United have full-day tours of Masada, the Dead Sea, and Ein Gedi, daily for about $100 per person from Jerusalem. The Jerusalem-based Eshcolot runs private tours. Abraham Tours also offers packages to Masada and the Dead Sea, as well as to the West Bank.

Abraham Tours ☎ *02/566–0045* ⊕ *www.abrahamtours.com.* **Egged Tours** ☎ *03/694–8888* ⊕ *www.egged.co.il.* **Eshcolot Tours** ☎ *02/566–5555, 02/676–3866.* **United Tours** ☎ *03/617–3315* ⊕ *www.unitedtours.co.il*

MASADA AND THE DEAD SEA

The 4,000-foot descent from Jerusalem to the Dead Sea is only 24 km (15 miles), but takes you on a journey from one climate to another. Annual precipitation plummets from 22 inches in Jerusalem to 2 inches at the Dead Sea. Still, the desert's proximity has always made it part of that city's consciousness. Refugees fled here, hermits sought its solitude; and when the Temple stood, on the Day of Atonement a scapegoat bearing the sins of the Jewish people was symbolically driven off its stark precipices.

INN OF THE GOOD SAMARITAN

20 km (13 miles) east of Jerusalem on Route 1 and 500 yards east of the junction with Route 458.

GETTING HERE AND AROUND
Follow Route 1 east from Jerusalem for 20 km (13 miles). The site is clearly signposted on the south side of the road. You'll need your own car, as buses do not stop here.

EXPLORING
FAMILY **Genesis Land.** On the scrubby mountains where Abraham likely walked, ride camels with actors dressed up as the patriarch and his manservant Eliezer. Young children will find the reenactment of Biblical stories enchanting, especially when they can enjoy making pita bread or eating lunch in a Bedouin-style tent overlooking the desert. Older children will roll their eyes at the actors wearing simple robes over jeans and sneakers. ⊠ *Off Rte. 1, Alon* ☎ *02/997–4477* ⊕ *www.genesisland.co.il* 🎫 *NIS 85* ☉ *Sun.–Fri., call for appointment.*

Museum of the Good Samaritan. About 2,000 years ago, thieves ambushed a man traveling the Jerusalem–Jericho road, and only one passing Samaritan bothered to help him, dragging him to a nearby inn (Luke 10). Today, on what may be the same spot, is the Museum of the Good Samaritan, housed in a restored Ottoman inn. It's an extensive collection of intricate mosaics scraped off the floors of churches, synagogues, and Samaritan houses of worship in Gaza and the West Bank. When you visit, ask to see the silent film about the parable dating from the 1920s, filmed on the very same arid hills that stretch for miles from the museum. The staff here has plenty of information and maps about nearby sites and trails as well.

If you're feeling energetic, drive over the bridge that crosses the highway and climb the dirt track to the top of the hill. Amid the scanty ruins of a small 12th-century Crusader fort—from which the outskirts of Jerusalem and Jericho are visible—the Gospel passage comes alive. The museum is 5 miles east of Maaleh Adumim. ⊠ *Rte 1., Maaleh Adumim* ☎ *02/633–8230* ⊕ *www.parks.org.il* 🖃 *NIS 22* ☉ *Oct.–Mar., Sun.–Thurs. 8–4, Fri. 8–3; Apr.–Sept., Sun.–Thurs. 8–5, Fri. 8–4.*

JERICHO

35 km (22 miles) east of Jerusalem on Route 1 and 5 km (3 miles) north on Route 90.

The sleepy oasis of Jericho—adorned with date palms, orange groves, banana plantations, bougainvillea bushes, and papaya trees—is aptly called *Ariha*, or "fragrant," in Arabic. This oldest continuously inhabited city in the world, Jericho is immortalized as the place where "the walls came tumblin' down" at the sound of Joshua's trumpets. Those ramparts haven't been found, but the ruins of Hisham's Palace will give you an idea of the devastating power of an earthquake at a time when cities were built of mud, wood, and stone.

The Palestinian population of about 25,000 is mostly Muslim, but the tiny Christian minority is well represented by a number of landmark churches and monasteries. These biblical and archaeological sites are what draw most tourists today.

GETTING HERE AND AROUND

Follow Route 1 east from Jerusalem for 35 km (13 miles), then turn north on Old Route 90. Jericho is clearly signposted. Egged bus drivers will drop you off at the side of Route 1, but it's still 5 km (3 miles) to Jericho. Arab serveeses from Damascus gate go to Azariya (Abu Dis); another shared taxi goes from there to Jericho. Serveeses also travel from Bethlehem to Jericho.

TIMING

Jericho is very pleasant during the winter months but swelteringly hot in the summer.

SAFETY AND PRECAUTIONS

As always, it's wise to check on the political situation before venturing into the Palestinian Authority. There are seldom problems in Jericho, however. Although there are no restrictions on tourists in private cars visiting the town, you will need to present your foreign passport to reenter Israeli-controlled territory. Only Palestinian car-rental companies offer insurance for driving in the West Bank. You might prefer to hire a driver or visit with a tour group.

EXPLORING

TOP ATTRACTIONS

Hisham's Palace. Known as Khirbet al-Mafjar in Arabic, the recently restored Hisham's Palace has exquisite stonework and a spectacular mosaic floor. Hisham was a scion of the Ummayad dynasty, which built the Dome of the Rock and al-Aqsa Mosque in Jerusalem. Although the palace was severely damaged by the great earthquake of AD 749 while still under construction, the surviving mosaics and stone and plaster reliefs are evidence of its splendor.

A small gatehouse leads into a wide courtyard dominated by a star-shape stone window that once graced an upper floor. Several sections of the fine geometric mosaics have been left exposed; others are covered by sand. The most impressive part of the complex is the reception room, off the plaza. Its intricate mosaic floor, depicting a lion hunting gazelles, is one of the most beautiful in the country. The balustrade of an ornamental pool reflects the artistic influences of both East and West. Fragments of ornate stucco reliefs are still visible on some of the walls.

To get here go north from the traffic circle that constitutes downtown Jericho, follow Hisham's Palace Road for 4 km (2½ miles), turn right at the sign to Hisham's Palace after the Police Intelligence Building, and then take an immediate left down a 1-km (½-mile) access road. ⊠ *Hisham's Palace Rd.* ☎ *02/232–2522* ⊠ *NIS 10* ☉ *Daily 8–5.*

Fodor'sChoice ★ **Jericho Cable Car.** To the west of Tel Jericho is the Mt. of Temptation, identified by tradition as the "exceedingly high mountain" from which Satan tempted Jesus with dominion over "all the kingdoms of the world" (Matthew 4). Halfway down the mountain sits the remarkable Greek Orthodox monastery of Qarantal, the name being a corruption of *quarantena*—a period of 40 days (the source of the English word *quarantine*)—the period of Jesus' temptation. Built into the cliff face in 1895 on Byzantine and Crusader remains, it's flanked by caves that once housed hermits. Departing from a ticket booth facing Tel Jericho, a cable car offers rides up and down the mountain. You can see all of Jericho and parts of Jordan from the restaurant at the cable car's upper station. ⊠ *Ain as-Sultan St.* ☎ *02/232–1590, 02/232–2240* ⊕ *www.jericho-cablecar.com* ⊠ *Round-trip NIS 55* ☉ *Daily 8–8.*

Qasr Al Yahud. This is the site where Jesus is said to have been baptized (Matthew 3:13–17), and where the Israelites crossed the Jordan River to enter the Promised Land (Joshua 3). Back then, the Jordan was a mighty, roaring river; today, it is little more than a silty creek. A recent renovation has added a wooden deck, changing rooms, and an inexpensive gift shop. You can almost shake hands with the Jordanian soldier guarding the opposite bank. The route to the water is lined on either side by mines and barbed wire, but old monasteries lend a holy air to the place. Bring modest clothing if you plan to go under. ⊠ *Off Rte. 90* ☎ *02/650–4844* ⊕ *www.parks.org.il* ⊠ *Free* ☉ *Apr.–Sept., Sun.–Thurs. 8–5; Oct.–Mar., Sun.–Thurs. 8–4, Fri. 8–4.*

Continued on page 173

DID YOU KNOW?

The Dead Sea's salt and concentration of thick, black mud enriched with organic elements are sought after for their curative properties and beautifying elements.

THE DEAD SEA
A NATURAL WONDER

The Dead Sea at Ein Bokek

Taking a dip in the Dead Sea is a must-do experience in Israel. This unique body of water—the shores of which are the lowest point of dry land on Earth—was a resort for King Herod in the 1st century BC and the site of Queen Cleopatra's cosmetics empire.

The Dead Sea is slowly dying. A combination of less rainfall in the region and Israeli and Jordanian diversion of the Jordan river for irrigation has caused its waters to recede at a rapid rate, threatening the area's ecology.

Israel started developing the Dead Sea as a tourist destination in the 1950s. Today, more than a dozen hotels in the area take advantage of the Dead Sea's mineral-rich mud and waters, known for nourishing, cleansing, and stimulating the skin, as well as for therapeutic benefits for treating medical conditions.

Spas offer an array of services: body wraps, mud massages, facial peels, and the like, in addition to general amenities such as Jacuzzis and saunas.

It's an easy day-trip from Jerusalem, but spending the night allows you to watch the sun rise over Jordan. After a day on the beach, you can head back to your hotel for lunch and a spa treatment, followed by a Turkish bath or a dip in a warm sulfur pool.

by Sarah Bronson

THE DEAD SEA: PAST AND PRESENT

The stark, beautiful shores of the Dead Sea are literally the lowest point of dry land on Earth, at 1,373 feet below sea level. It's called the Dead Sea because virtually nothing can live in it; with a salt concentration of about 32%, the water is almost 9 times saltier than the ocean.

WHY IS THE DEAD SEA SALTY?

The Dead Sea is salty because water flows in from the Jordan River and other sources, but has no way of flowing out. Evaporation leaves a massive amount of salt behind. Beaches here aren't sandy—they're caked with hardened crystals of salt. The consistently dry air surrounding the Dead Sea has a high oxygen content, low pollution and allergen levels, and weakened ultraviolet radiation.

HOW DID THE DEAD SEA FORM?

The high mesas of the Judean desert nearby, also below sea level, bear testimony to the millions of years of geological changes that created this unique place. The Dead Sea was formed by fault lines shifting in the Earth's crust, a process that began about 15 million years ago and created the basin where the Dead Sea is now located.

WHY IS THE DEAD SEA IN DANGER?

Since it receives a maximum of 2 to 4 inches of rain per year, the Dead Sea's main source of water is the Jordan River, and by extension, the Sea of Galilee to the north.

The Dead Sea's water levels have fluctuated greatly over the last 10,000 years. However, its shores have significantly receded in the past few decades—about one meter per year—due to the lack of rainfall in Israel's north and human activity. Israel, Jordan, and Syria all divert water away from the Jordan River for drinking and irrigation. Less than 7% of the river's original flow reaches the Dead Sea.

WHAT'S BEING DONE TO STOP IT?

Israel and Jordan have been in talks for years to seek a solution to this pressing environmental problem. Currently the countries hope to build a canal to pump water into the Dead Sea from the Red Sea. Environmentalists are concerned about the possible negative impacts of such a canal both on the Dead Sea and on the Arava region. No firm plans to move forward have been announced. To find out more, visit www.foeme.org.

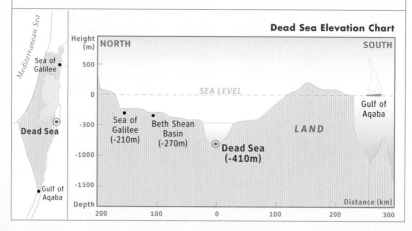

Dead Sea Elevation Chart

EXPERIENCING THE SPAS AND BEACHES

Before booking at a hotel or spa, carefully check what services it offers and whether any particular areas are closed for the season or for repairs. Quality of treatments at the spas can vary widely.

ENJOYING THE WATER

When entering the Dead Sea, wear flip flops or waterproof sandals, as the sea's floor has a rough, rock salt surface. Before getting in the water, check for the nearest source of fresh water, in case you get painful salt water in your eyes. (Note: The Ein Gedi spa provides freshwater spigots in the Dead Sea itself, floating on buoys). Lean back slowly and rise gently, and be careful not to splash water toward yourself or others.

Small wounds such as scratches will burn for a few moments, but avoid getting salt water in any deep or open wounds. Don't stay in the Dead Sea (or in the spas' warmed mineral pools) for more than 15 minutes at a time, and drink plenty of water afterward.

GETTING MUDDY

It can be surprisingly difficult to find free Dead Sea mud. Some hotels pump the mud to their grounds, or provide vats of it at their beach. You can also purchase

(top) People sunbathing on the shores of the Dead Sea. (bottom) Covered in Dead Sea mud

more refined mud in packets and apply it at the beach for your photos.

Bring a friend to the mudbaths so that you can help each other slather the dark goo on every inch of exposed skin. Cake it on evenly but thinly, so that it will dry within 15-20 minutes in the sun. You might need a third person to take pictures, unless you want mud on your camera!

Dead Sea products, including salts and mud, make great gifts and are available at all the spas, but note that similar items may be available at your local health food store at home.

PLANNING YOUR VISIT

(left) Dead Sea. (right) Artist creating salt sculptures in the Dead Sea

GETTING HERE FROM JERUSALEM

By car: Take Route 1 east past Jericho to Route 90 south along the Dead Sea shore. Continue about an hour to reach Ein Gedi or Ein Bokek. Total driving time is about 90 minutes.

By public transportation: Egged Bus Lines run buses from Jerusalem's Central Bus Station along the Dead Sea shore every hour or so Sun.–Thurs. from 8 AM to 4:15 PM, and return buses from 8:15 AM to 7:30 PM. Just tell your driver which hotel or spa you're visiting. On Fridays bus service is more limited. To check schedule updates, call Egged at 03/694-8888 or see egged.co.il/Eng.

By guided tour: Hotel staff can help you join a group tour to the Dead Sea. Or contact United Tours (02/625-2187 www.unitedtours.co.il) for daily, English-language trips from Jerusalem.

WHEN TO GO

In fall (Oct.-Nov.) and spring (Mar.–May) it's almost always sunny and pleasant. In winter temperatures are 68°–74°, and there's consistent sun. In summer it's usually an uncomfortable 90°–102° and scorching.

BEACH AND SPA TIPS

■ The Dead Sea has several public beaches, sometimes with a token fee for use of the showers or for lawn chair rental. "Private" hotel beaches are, by law, open to anyone, though only hotel guests will receive amenities.

■ Inquire carefully when booking your hotel if the cost of meals is included. There are few restaurants in the area.

■ For non-guests, some hotels offer day rates of about NIS 100 to use their spas and saunas. Other hotels include meals for a fee. Extra charges apply for facials and massages.

WHAT ELSE IS NEARBY

■ Combine a visit to Ein Bokek with visits to Ein Gedi and Qumran, which also have Dead Sea beaches and nature reserves.

■ To arrange a Dead Sea cruise, desert hike, overnight camping trip, or group event, call the Dead Sea Tourist Information Center at 08/997-5010.

■ Ask your concierge about visiting the tiny town of Ein Tamar, just south of Ein Bokek, home to many artists and craftspeople.

Russian Museum. Russian funding has given a glorious status to the gnarled sycamore that tradition identifies as the Tree of Zaccheus, which the chief tax collector climbed to get a better look at Jesus (Luke 19:1–4). The Russian Museum was built as a Greek-style palace just behind the tree, and it houses an extensive collection of Russian art and ancient Palestinian artifacts. Behind the museum is a sprawling garden complex with lush green lawns and towering palm trees. ⊠ *Medvedev St.* ⊹ *As you reach Jericho via Route 1, take the left fork at the traffic island. When the road swings to the left, look for the museum on the right.* ☎ *02/231–3006* ⊠ *NIS 20* ⊙ *Mon.–Sat. 9–5.*

Tel Jericho. Also called Tel es-Sultan (Sultan's Hill), Tel Jericho covers the legendary ancient city. Nearly 200 years of excavations have still not uncovered the walls that fell when Joshua stormed the city in the mid-13th century BC. The most impressive ruins that have been unearthed are a massive tower and wall, remains of the world's oldest walled city. Little is known about these early urbanites, who lived here in the Neolithic period between 7800 and 6500 BC, or why they needed such fortifications thousands of years before they became common in the region.

Across the road is **Ain as-Sultan,** or the Sultan's Spring. The name comes from the prophet Elijah's miracle of sweetening the water with a bowl of salt (II Kings 2:19–22). The waters are still eminently drinkable if you wish to refill your bottles. To the east in Jordan are the mountains of the biblical kingdoms of Ammon and Moab, among them the peak of Mt. Nebo, from which Moses viewed the Promised Land before dying at the ripe old age of 120.

To get to Tel Jericho by car, drive along Old Route 90, the main road through Jericho, and turn left at the traffic circle onto Ain as-Sultan Street. The parking lot is about 2 km (1 mile) down the road. ⊠ *Ain as-Sultan St.* ☎ *02/232–4815* ⊠ *NIS 10* ⊙ *Oct.–Mar., daily 8–5; Apr.– Sept., daily 8–6.*

Telul Abu'Alayiq. The remains of the royal palace of the Hasmonean dynasty (2nd–1st centuries BC) have been uncovered at Telul Abu'Alayiq. In the 1st century BC, Mark Antony gave the valuable oasis of Jericho to his beloved Cleopatra; the humiliated King Herod, Antony's local vassal, was then forced to lease the property back from the Egyptian queen. Herod the Great expanded and improved the palace, turning it into a winter retreat. He died there in 4 BC. The site isn't developed; there's no entrance fee, and you can wander here during daylight. It's located about 3 km (2 miles) south of Tel Jericho. ⊠ *Off Rte. 90* ⊠ *Free* ⊙ *Open 24 hrs.*

WORTH NOTING

FAMILY **Auja Eco Center.** This tiny Palestinian village north of Jericho has turned an acute water shortage into an ecotourism opportunity. Established by Friends of the Earth Middle East, Auja Eco Center brings together Israeli, Palestinian, and Jordanian environmentalists. The knowledgeable staff leads hikes in the surrounding areas, including a moonlit trek in the stark desert and visits to nearby Bedouin communities that are also suffering from diminished water supplies. A rooftop restaurant

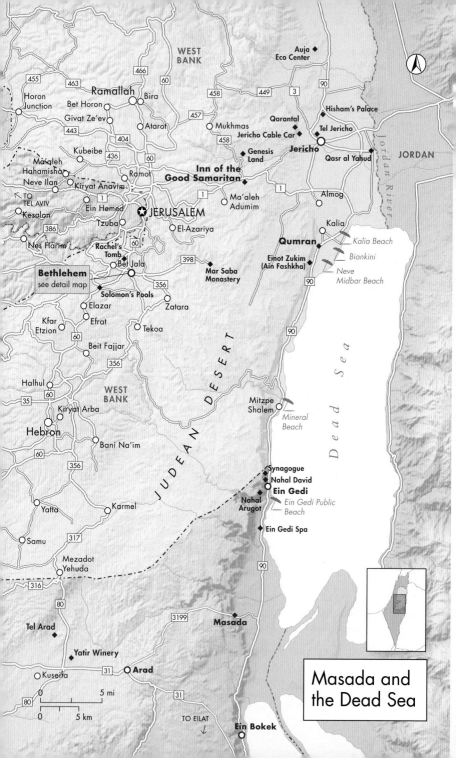

Masada and
the Dead Sea

offers traditional food with lovely views of the area. Curious teens will enjoy the displays on recycling, while younger children can enjoy the playground. There's a B&B should you wish to sleep over. ✉ *Rte. 90, 13 km (9 miles) north of Jericho, Auja* ☎ *02/231–0424* 🌐 *www.aujaecocenter.org.*

FAMILY **Banana Land.** This is the only water park in the West Bank. Around the swimming pools you'll encounter Palestinian families enjoying a day off. ✉ *Canaanite Dulok St., 4 km (2½ miles) north of Tel Jericho* ☎ *02/232–0445* 🎟 *NIS 10* 🕒 *Daily 8:30 am–11 pm.*

3

WHERE TO EAT

$$ MIDDLE EASTERN 🍴 **Abu Omar Shaabi Restaurant.** Sheets of golden baklava line the walls of this bakery, steps from Jericho's main square. The *bourma*, a sugary rope of angel hair–like dough wrapped around whole pistachios, is the ideal complement to strong, black Arabic coffee. Locals flock to the restaurant for grilled chicken or lamb served with fresh salads and hummus. [$] *Average main: NIS 50* ✉ *Arrasheed St., off main square* ☎ *02/232–3429* 💳 *No credit cards.*

$$ MIDDLE EASTERN FAMILY Fodor's Choice ★ 🍴 **Limonah.** Sun-dappled tables under green palm leaves and passion-fruit plants provide a delightful setting for Palestinan basics done right on Jericho's main restaurant street. The minty lemonade is a revelation after a hot day. *Mezze* (Middle Eastern salads) are delicious, as is the whole grilled fish drenched in a garlicky lemon sauce. For dessert, there's an attached ice cream shop, or you can ask for sweets like baklava. Kids can escape to an on-site playground while parents enjoy beer or a waterpipe. Look for the giant lemon outside the entrance. [$] *Average main: NIS 70* ✉ *Muntazahat St.* ☎ *02/231–2977.*

$$ MIDDLE EASTERN FAMILY 🍴 **Sultan.** Reached by cable car, this restaurant has tables scattered on different levels down a hillside, so you can usually find a quiet spot. Try sipping a cup of coffee or a fresh fruit juice while taking in the views of the oasis below. There's a buffet on offer, as well as Western-style dishes like grilled chicken. [$] *Average main: NIS 60* ✉ *Qarantal St.* ☎ *02/232–1590.*

$$ MIDDLE EASTERN 🍴 **Temptation.** The closest restaurant to Tel Jericho (they share a parking lot), this touristy spot serves tasty meat dishes, Palestinian standards like hummus and salads, and a wide range of mezze. Lunches are a good value. [$] *Average main: NIS 70* ✉ *Ain as-Sultan St.* ☎ *02/232–2614.*

WHERE TO STAY

$$ HOTEL 🏨 **InterContinental Jericho.** A Moorish-inspired lobby decorated with soaring stone arches lets you know that you've arrived at this sumptuous desert resort, as do the the four pools that sparkle in the arid valley. **Cons:** smoking allowed in some public areas; not within walking distance of downtown. [$] *Rooms from: $205* ✉ *Jerusalem–Jericho Rd.* ☎ *02/231–1200* 🌐 *www.intercontinental.com* 🛏 *181 rooms, 14 suites* 🍽 *No meals.*

The dryness of Qumran helped preserve the Dead Sea Scrolls stored in caves in the sculpted rock.

QUMRAN

13 km (8 miles) south of the Almog Junction on Route 90, 20 km (13 miles) south of Jericho, 50 km (31 miles) east of Jerusalem.

GETTING HERE AND AROUND

Follow Route 1 east from Jerusalem for 50 km (31 miles), turning south on Route 90. Qumran is on the right. Not far from Qumran are some Dead Sea beaches worth a stop if you have a car, including Mineral Beach. Qumran is in the West Bank, but cars are routinely waved through the checkpoints.

SAFETY AND PRECAUTIONS

Check the weather forecast before hiking in the winter. On rare occasions, flash floods cause closures on Route 90.

EXPLORING

Qumran. The sandy caves in the cliffs north of the Dead Sea yielded the most significant archaeological find ever made in Israel: the Dead Sea Scrolls. These biblical, apocryphal, and sectarian religious texts were found under extraordinary circumstances in 1947 when a young Bedouin goatherd stumbled on a cave containing scrolls in earthen jars. Because the scrolls were made from animal hide, he first went to a shoemaker to turn them into sandals. The shoemaker alerted a local antiquities dealer, who brought them to the attention of Professor Eliezer Sukenik of the Hebrew University of Jerusalem. Six other major scrolls and hundreds of fragments have since been discovered in 11 of the caves, and some are on display in Jerusalem's Israel Museum.

Most scholars believe that the Essenes, a Jewish separatist sect that set up a monastic community here in the late 2nd century BC, wrote the scrolls. During the Great (Jewish) Revolt against Rome (AD 66–73), they apparently hid their precious scrolls in the caves in the cliffs before the site was destroyed in AD 68. Others contend the texts were brought from libraries in Jerusalem, possibly even the library of the Jewish Temple.

Almost all books of the Hebrew Bible were discovered here, many of them virtually identical to the texts still used in Jewish communities today. Sectarian texts were also found, including the constitution or "Community Rule," a description of an end-of-days battle ("The War of the Sons of Light Against the Sons of Darkness"), and the "Thanksgiving Scroll," containing hymns reminiscent of biblical psalms.

A short film at the visitor center introduces the mysterious sect that once lived here. Climb the tower for a good view, and note the elaborate system of channels and cisterns that gathered precious floodwater from the cliffs. Just below the tower is a long room some scholars have identified as the **scriptorium**. A plaster writing table and bronze and ceramic inkwells found here suggest that this may have been where the scrolls were written. You shouldn't need more than an hour to tour this site. ⊠ *Rte. 90, 13 km (8 miles) south of Almog Junction, Kibbutz Kalia* ☎ *02/994–2235* ⊕ *www.parks.org.il* ✉ *NIS 22* ☉ *Apr.–Sept., daily 8–5; Oct.–Mar., daily 8–4.*

BEACHES AND POOLS

Qumran is conveniently located near some beaches on the Dead Sea. You can't actually swim in the briny water; you take a leisurely float in its incredible salinity, about 10 times that of the ocean. Anyone can enjoy the benefits of the mineral concentration in the Dead Sea water and mud, and the oxygen-rich atmosphere at the lowest point on Earth. Beach shoes or rubber sandals are a must, as the salt in the hypersaturated water builds up into sharp ridges that are hard to walk on. Any open cuts on your body will sting when they encounter the briny water, so avoid shaving the day you go to the sea.

Biankini Beach. Beautiful Biankini Beach has a spa offering mineral treatments and massages and a Moroccan restaurant featuring couscous served on imported crockery. The beach also has a modest collection of cabins for overnighters. Kids can splash in a freshwater wading pool. **Amenities:** food and drink; parking (free); showers; toilets. **Best for:** walking; swimming. ⊠ *Off Rte. 90, 3 km (2 miles) north of Qumran* ☎ *02/940–0266* ⊕ *www.biankini1.com* ✉ *Fri.–Sat., NIS 80; Sun.–Thurs, NIS 60* ☉ *Oct.–Mar., daily 8–5; Apr.–Sept., daily 8–6.*

FAMILY **Einot Zukim.** Known for its freshwater springs, Einot Zukim (also called Ein Fashkha) is a nature reserve with many species of trees and reeds not often found in the arid Judean Desert. You can swim in two shallow spring-fed pools and visit an archaeological site from the Second Temple period and a manor from the Herodian period. Call ahead for free English-language tours on Thursdays. **Amenities:** food and drink; lifeguards; parking; showers; toilets. **Best for:** walking; swimming. ⊠ *Rte. 90, 3 km (2 miles) south of Qumran* ☎ *02/994–2355* ⊕ *www.parks.org.il* ✉ *NIS 29* ☉ *Oct.–Mar., daily 8–4; Apr.–Sept., daily 8–5.*

Kalia Beach. On the Dead Sea, Kalia Beach (the name derives from *kalium*, the Latin name for potassium, found in abundance here) is the place to go for a free mud bath. Slather your whole body with the mineral-rich black mud and let it dry before showering. The beach also has chair and towel rentals, a gift shop, and a snack bar, and the adjacent kibbutz has a swimming pool and guest rooms. **Amenities:** food and drink; lifeguards; parking; showers; toilets. **Best for:** swimming; walking. ⊠ *Off Rte. 90, 3 km (2 miles) north of Qumran* 🕾 *02/994–2391* 🖾 *NIS 35* ☼ *Oct.–Mar., daily 8–5; Apr.–Sept., daily 8–6:30.*

Fodor'sChoice ★ **Mineral Beach.** Less touristy and more serene than some of the other beaches, Mineral Beach is a great place to unwind and mingle with Israelis. There's a warm sulfur pool fed by a natural thermal spring, a freshwater wading pool for kids, free pots of Dead Sea mud, and plenty of shade for relaxing on the sand. Reserve massages in advance. **Amenities:** food and drink; lifeguards; parking; showers; toilets. **Best for:** swimming; walking. ⊠ *Rte. 90, 20 km (12½ miles) south of Qumran* 🕾 *02/994–4888* ⊕ *www.dead-sea.co.il* 🖾 *Sun.–Thurs. NIS 50, Fri. and Sat. NIS 60* ☼ *Sun.–Thurs. 9–6, Fri. and Sat. 8–6.*

Neve Midbar Beach. South of Biankini Beach, Neve Midbar Beach is open late, when boisterous young Israelis come to party. **Amenities:** food and drink; lifeguards; parking; showers; toilets. **Best for:** partiers; sunset; swimming. ⊠ *Rte. 90, 3 km (2 miles) north of Qumran* 🕾 *02/994–2781* ⊕ *www.nevemidbar-beach.com* 🖾 *NIS 50* ☼ *Oct.–Mar., daily 8–5; Apr.–Sept., daily 8–7.*

EN ROUTE **Kibbutz Mitzpe Shalem.** This kibbutz manufactures the excellent Ahava skin- and hair-care products based on (but not smelling like) Dead Sea minerals. The factory outlet here is open Sunday to Thursday 8 to 5, Friday 8 to 4, and Saturday 8:30 to 5. It's 20 km (12½ miles) south of Qumran. ⊠ *Rte. 90* 🕾 *02/994–5123* ⊕ *www.ahavaus.com.*

EIN GEDI

33 km (21 miles) south of Qumran, 20 km (12½ miles) north of Masada, 83 km (52 miles) southeast of Jerusalem.

After miles of burnt brown and beige desert rock, the green lushness of the Ein Gedi oasis leaps out in vivid and unexpected contrast. This nature reserve is one of the most beautiful places in Israel—with everything from hiking trails to ancient ruins. Settled for thousands of years, it inspired the writer of the *Song of Songs* to describe his beloved "as a cluster of henna in the vineyards of Ein Gedi." Loads of waterfalls and gurgling springs make this an option for summer hiking, too.

GETTING HERE AND AROUND

Follow Route 1 east from Jerusalem for 50 km (31 miles), turning south on Route 90. Ein Gedi is on the right. Egged bus drivers will drop you off at the side of Route 90. From there, it's a short walk to the gate of the national park.

SAFETY AND PRECAUTIONS

Check the weather forecast before hiking in the winter. Flash floods are an occasional danger.

Waterfalls, pools, and desert landscapes are among the pleasures awaiting hikers in Ein Gedi's nature reserve.

EXPLORING

FAMILY

Fodor's Choice
★

Ein Gedi Nature Reserve. This beautiful nature reserve is home to **Nahal David** (David's Stream). The cave at Nahal David is believed to be the place where David hid while Saul hunted him down three thousand years ago (I Samuel 24:1–22). When Saul stepped into the cave, David resisted the urge to kill the king. He cut off a piece of his robe instead as an act of reconciliation.

The clearly marked trail rises past several pools and small waterfalls to the beautiful upper waterfall. There are many steps, but it's not too daunting. Allow at least 1¼ hours to include a refreshing dip under one of the lower waterfalls. Look out for ibex (wild goats), especially in the afternoon, and for the small, furry hyrax, often seen on tree branches. Leopards here face extinction because of breeding problems; they're seldom seen nowadays.

If you're a more serious hiker who is interested in further adventure, don't miss the trail that breaks off to the right 50 yards down the return path from the top waterfall. It passes the remains of Byzantine irrigation systems and offers breathtaking views of the Dead Sea. The trail doubles back on itself toward the source of Nahal David. Near the top, a short side path climbs to the remains of a 4th-millennium BC Chalcolithic temple, the treasures of which can be seen in Jerusalem's Israel Museum. The main path leads on to the streambed, again turns east, and reaches **Dudim Cave**, formed by boulders and filled with crystal clear spring-water. Swimming in "Lover's Cave" is one of the most refreshing and romantic experiences in Israel. Since this trail involves a considerable climb (and hikers invariably take time to bathe in the "cave"), access to the trail is permitted only up to 3½ hours before closing time. Reaching Ein Gedi from the north, the first turnoff to the right is the parking lot at the entrance to Nahal David. ⊠ *Rte. 90* 🕾 *08/658–4285* ⊕ *www.parks. org.il* 🖃 *NIS 29, includes Nahal Arugot and synagogue* ☉ *Oct.–Mar., Sat.–Thurs. 8–4, Fri. 8–3; Apr.–Sept., Sat–Thurs. 8–5, Fri. 8–4. Last admission 1 hour before closing.*

Nahal Arugot. Although not as lush as Nahal David, the deep canyon of Nahal Arugot is perhaps more spectacular. Enormous boulders and slabs of stone on the opposite cliff face seem poised in midcataclysm. The hour-long hike to the **Hidden Waterfall** (not too difficult) passes by beautiful spots where the stream bubbles over rock shelves and shallow pools offer relief from the heat. If you're adventurous and have water shoes, you can return through the greenery of the streambed, leaping the boulders and wading the pools. Experienced hikers can ascend the Tsafit Trail to Mapal Hachalon, or the Window Waterfall. It offers stunning views over the Dead Sea. To get here from the Nahal David parking lot, continue south through the date orchards and follow signs to Nahal Arugot. ⊠ *Off Rte. 90* 🕾 *08/658–4285* ⊕ *www.parks.org.il* 🖃 *NIS 29, includes Nahal David and synagogue* ☉ *Oct.–Mar., Sat.–Thurs. 8–4, Fri. 8–3; Apr.–Sept., Sat–Thurs. 8–5, Fri. 8–4. Last admission 1 hour before closing.*

Synagogue. A Jewish community lived in Ein Gedi for more than 1,200 years, beginning in the 7th century BC. In the 3rd century AD, they built a synagogue nestled between Nahal David and Nahal Arugot whose beautiful mosaic floor is a highlight worth seeing. The mosaic includes an inscription in Hebrew and Aramaic invoking the wrath of heaven on various troublemakers, including "whoever reveals the secret of the town." The secret is believed to refer to a method of cultivating a now-extinct balsam tree, which was used to make the prized perfume for which Ein Gedi was once famous. To get here from Nahal David parking lot, continue south a few hundred yards through the date orchards. ⊠ *Off Rte. 90* 🕾 *08/658–4285* ⊕ *www.parks.org.il* 🖃 *NIS 15; NIS 29 includes Nahal Arugot and Nahal David* ☉ *Oct.– Mar., Sat.–Thurs. 8–4, Fri. 8–3; Apr.–Sept., Sat.–Thurs. 8–5.*

SPORTS AND THE OUTDOORS

There's no problem hiking the area alone, on well-marked trails. Be sure to ask for a trail map at the admission booth to the national park.

BEACHES AND POOLS

Ein Gedi Public Beach. The somewhat rocky Ein Gedi Public Beach gives you free access to the Dead Sea. Freshwater showers (absolutely essential) by the water's edge and basic changing facilities are NIS 2. There's also a snack bar and a gift shop. ■TIP➔ Don't leave valuables unguarded. **Amenities:** food and drink; lifeguards; parking; showers; toilets. **Best for:** sunrise; sunset; swimming. ⊠ *Rte. 90* 🕾 *08/659–4761* 🖃 *Free* ☉ *Oct.–Mar., daily 8–5; Apr.–Sept., daily 8–6.*

Ein Gedi Spa. With access to the Dead Sea, Ein Gedi Spa lets you soak in one of six covered pools whose water is rich in sulfur, magnesium, calcium, sodium, and potassium. You can also relax in a freshwater pool or slather yourself in mud. The place has good facilities, including

A DRIVE TO THE DEAD SEA

From Arad, you can make the steep, 24-km (15-mile) descent to the Dead Sea and on to Ein Bokek via the sharp curves of Route 31. The stunning canyons and clefts that unfold on every side enhance the drama of the drive.

On the way out of town, you can pause at the Moav observation point, which features an impressive sculpture by the artist Yigal Tumarkin. Watch for the sign on the right indicating that you've reached sea level. Two more observation points soon appear on the left. You can't cross to the first—Metsad Zohar—from your side of the road. The second—Nahal Zohar—looks down on an ancient, dry riverbed, the last vestige of an eons-old body of water that once covered this area. The Dead Sea lies directly east, with the Edom Mountains of Jordan on the other side. To the right (south) is Mt. Sodom. You'll soon see, from above, the southern end of the Dead Sea, sectioned off into the huge evaporation pools of the Dead Sea Works, where potash, bromine, and magnesium are extracted.

The road ends where it joins Route 90; once there, you're at 1,292 feet below sea level, the lowest point on Earth.

indoor showers, lockers, and changing rooms. Massages (NIS 300 for 50 minutes) and treatments are available; advance reservations are recommended. A snack bar and restaurant are here, too. ✉ *Rte. 90* ☎ *08/659–4813* 🎫 *Sun.–Fri. NIS 79, Sat. NIS 89* 🕒 *Oct.–Mar., daily 8–5; Apr.–Sept., daily 8–6.*

WHERE TO EAT AND STAY

$ FAST FOOD 🍴 **Pundak Ein Gedi.** Take a break from the blistering desert sun at this casual eatery. The outdoor kiosk is open around the clock, while the air-conditioned dining room is open from 9:30 to 4:30. The sandwiches and cold drinks are nothing fancy, but after a morning of hiking they hit the spot. [$] *Average main: NIS 18* ✉ *Rte. 90* ☎ *08/659–4761.*

$$ HOTEL 🏨 **Ein Gedi Guest House.** Surrounded by a spectacular botanical garden with baobab trees, cacti, and hundreds of species of topical flora, this inn is nestled between 1,600-foot-high cliffs and the Dead Sea. **Pros:** informative staff; serene oasis atmosphere; soothing spa. **Cons:** some dingy rooms; pricey. [$] *Rooms from: $285* ✉ *Rte. 90* ☎ *08/659–4220, 08/659–4221* 🌐 *www.ein-gedi.co.il/en* 🛏 *166 rooms* 🍽 *Some meals.*

ARAD

20 km (12½ miles) west of Masada, 25 km (15½ miles) west of Ein Bokek and the Dead Sea, 45 km (28 miles) east of Beersheva.

Breathe deeply: Arad sits 2,000 feet above sea level and is famous for its dry, pollution-free air and mild climate, ideal for asthma sufferers. The modern town was established by ex-kibbutzniks as a planned community in 1962. Its population of nearly 25,000 now includes immigrants from Russia and Ethiopia, as well as the acclaimed Israeli writer Amos Oz.

Continued on page 188

MASADA: DESERT FORTRESS

The isolated flattop rock of Masada commands the surrounding desert, its ancient remains bearing witness to long-ago power and conflict. One of Israel's most stunning archaeological sites, Masada earned fame and a place in history first as one of King Herod's opulent palace-fortresses and later as the site of the last stand of Jewish rebels against the legions of Rome, almost 2,000 years ago.

A KING'S PALACE

Surrounded by steep cliffs and with spectacular views of the Dead Sea and the desert, the Masada plateau offers nearly impregnable natural protection.

Herod the Great, the brilliant builder and paranoid leader who reigned over Israel as king of the Jews by the grace of the Roman Empire in the 1st century BC, developed the 18-acre site. Both for his relaxation and as a possible refuge from his enemies (including Cleopatra) and hostile subjects, Herod built atop Masada a fantastic, state-of-the-art complex of palaces, storehouses, and water systems.

THE REVOLT OF THE JEWS

Herod died around 4 BC, and the Jews rebelled against Rome in AD 66. By AD 70, the Roman Empire had destroyed Jerusalem and crushed the Jewish revolt there. Around AD 72, the last Jewish rebels took refuge at Masada. For at least a year, 960 Israelite men, women, and children lived here, protected from thousands of Roman soldiers by cliffs more than 1,400 feet high.

The Roman general and governor Flavius Silva, determined to end the rebellion, built eight legionnaire camps around the mountain. Silva's forces gradually erected an assault ramp on Masada's western side.

THE REBELS' "TERRIBLE RESOLVE"

According to a few survivors who related the story to the 1st-century historian Flavius Josephus, the night before the Romans reached Masada's walls, the rebel leader Elazar Ben-Yair gave a rallying speech. He reminded his community that they had resolved "neither to serve the Romans nor any other save God." After discussion, the Jews agreed to commit suicide rather than be taken captive.

The men drew lots to choose the ten who would kill the others. Those ten, having carried out "their terrible resolve," Josephus wrote, drew additional lots to select the one who would kill the other nine and then himself. When the Romans breached the walls the next morning, they found hundreds of corpses. The zealots' final action made the Roman victory at Masada a hollow one.

Although Josephus' physical description of Masada is accurate, some historians doubt his narrative. Several artifacts, including pottery shards bearing names (the lots, perhaps?), support the accuracy of Josephus' text, but no one can be sure what happened at the end. Masada continues to inspire debate.

TOURING MASADA'S TOP SIGHTS

Ride the cable car up Masada, hike the Snake Path, or walk the easier Ramp Path. Take in these highlights of Herod's buildings and the Jewish rebels' presence—and awesome desert views.

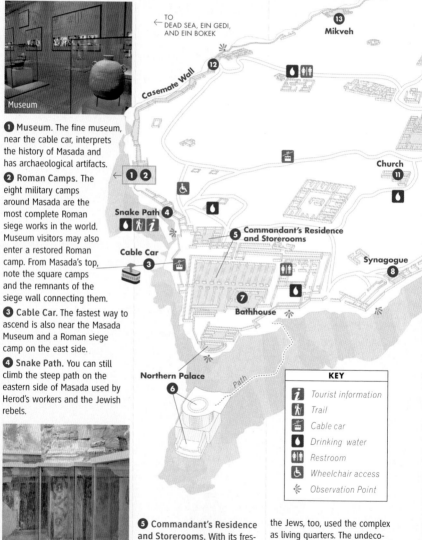

Museum

1 Museum. The fine museum, near the cable car, interprets the history of Masada and has archaeological artifacts.

2 Roman Camps. The eight military camps around Masada are the most complete Roman siege works in the world. Museum visitors may also enter a restored Roman camp. From Masada's top, note the square camps and the remnants of the siege wall connecting them.

3 Cable Car. The fastest way to ascend is also near the Masada Museum and a Roman siege camp on the east side.

4 Snake Path. You can still climb the steep path on the eastern side of Masada used by Herod's workers and the Jewish rebels.

TO
← DEAD SEA, EIN GEDI,
AND EIN BOKEK

13 Mikveh

12

Casemate Wall

11 Church

Snake Path **4**

Cable Car

3

5 Commandant's Residence and Storerooms

Synagogue **8**

7

Bathhouse

Northern Palace

6

Path

KEY

🛈	Tourist information
🚶	Trail
🚠	Cable car
💧	Drinking water
🚻	Restroom
♿	Wheelchair access
🔭	Observation Point

Frescoed walls

5 Commandant's Residence and Storerooms. With its frescoed walls, this area may have housed Herod's commanders. Simple ovens here indicate that the Jews, too, used the complex as living quarters. The undecorated rooms stored grain, dry fruit, and wine.

Inauguration of the synagogue: blowing the shofar (2005)

7 Bathhouse. This spa on a desert cliff demonstrates Herod's grandiosity, his dedication to Roman culture, and the success of Masada's water systems. The building has cold and lukewarm baths, a sauna, frescoes, and tile work. Jewish rebels incorporated a ritual bath.

8 Synagogue. Built into the wall, the synagogue is oddly shaped, but its benches and geniza (burial for damaged scrolls) indicate its function. Here, perhaps, the rebels agreed to die at their own hands. Today the synagogue is used for bar and bat mitzvahs.

9 Roman Ramp. You can stand on the western edge where Romans breached Masada's defenses. The original ramp is below, as well as a modern path for walkers.

10 Western Palace. Believed to have been an administrative base and a guest house, this palace retains frescoed walls and mosaics in Greek style; unusual for Herodian mosaics, one has a fruit motif.

11 Church. During the 5th to 7th centuries, monks lived at Masada, choosing it for its isolation. This 5th-century chapel is Byzantine in design, with mosaic floors.

12 Casemate Wall. Despite Masada's strategic advantages, Herod built a casemate (double-layered) wall around the oblong flattop rock, including offices

Bathhouse

Roman Ramp on the western slopes of Masada

and storerooms. The Jewish rebels used these rooms as dwellings.

13 Mikveh. In Jewish culture, the mikveh, or ritual bath, is a symbol of life and purity. Two found on Masada were built in accordance with Jewish laws still followed today. The presence of mikvehs indicates the rebels' religious piety.

14 Water Cistern. Like other cisterns at Masada, the southern cistern—into which you may descend—was built underground to prevent evaporation. Also make your way to see the spectacular canyon view to the south, and test the echoes.

Mikveh

Northern Palace

6 Northern Palace. Herod's personal living quarters is an extraordinary three-tiered structure that seems to hang from the cliffs. The amazing, terraced buildings feature colorful frescoes, Greek-inspired architecture, and Herod's personal bathhouse.

Water Cistern

Casemate Wall

Western Palace

Western gate

Ramp path

Roman Ramp

TO ARAD →

Casemate Wall

MASADA FROM JERUSALEM

Masada lookout

BY CAR

For Masada's eastern side, take Route 1 east to Route 90 south along the Dead Sea. Masada is off Route 90, about 15 minutes south of Ein Gedi (it's also near Ein Bokek). One-way driving time is about 80 minutes; add time to get out of Jerusalem.

For Masada's western side and the Roman Path entrance, head to Route 6 south, which merges with Route 40; continue on Route 31 to Arad and Route 3199/Masada. It takes about 2.5 hours one way from southern Jerusalem. Avoid Route 60 and Hebron, and take a good map.

Note: There is no direct car access from the west side of Masada to the east. Those wishing to ascend on one side and descend on the other must arrange for their car to meet them on the other side; the drive is about 30 minutes.

BY GUIDED TOUR OR BUS

Your hotel can help you join a group tour to Masada, or contact **United Tours** (☎ 02/625–2187, ⊕ www.unitedtours. co.il) for daily, English-language trips from Jerusalem to Masada and other sites in the Judean Desert and the Dead Sea.

Egged Bus Lines (☎ 03/694–8888) runs buses for the two-hour trip from Jerusalem's Central Bus Station to Masada approximately every hour Sunday through Thursday from 8 AM to 4:15 PM; return buses leave 8:30 AM to 7:50 PM. Friday service ends earlier.

THREE WAYS TO GET UP AND DOWN MASADA

On Masada's east side, the cable car takes only three minutes. The quickest way up, the **cable car** is convenient to the Masada Museum and a restored Roman siege camp. The long, steep **Snake Path** up the east side is an arduous but rewarding one-hour hike, recommended for visitors who are fit or determined to ascend Masada the same way the Jewish rebels did. Accessible from Arad on the west side, the **Ramp Path** is less grueling and takes fifteen to thirty minutes to ascend; it's equivalent to climbing about twenty flights of stairs.

MAKING THE MOST OF YOUR VISIT

WHEN TO VISIT

The weather at Masada is fairly consistent year-round; it's hot during the day. Visit in the early morning or late afternoon, when the sun is weakest. ■ TIP→ It's popular to hike up before dawn via the Snake or Ramp Path, and watch the sun rise from behind Jordan and the Dead Sea. After 9 or 10 AM, extreme heat may dictate that you use the cable car.

WHAT TO WEAR AND BRING

Layered clothing is recommended, as cool early-morning temperatures rise to uncomfortable heat. Good walking shoes and hats or bandanas are musts. Free drinking water is available at Masada, but bring plenty to start with. Food is not sold atop the site. The museum cafeteria sells lunch after 11 AM. Sunscreen and a camera are essential.

TIMING AND HIGHLIGHTS

Visiting Masada, a UNESCO World Heritage Site, can take three to seven hours, depending on your interest. The museum takes about an hour. Going up can take from three minutes (cable car) to sixty minutes (Snake Path). Your tour at the top might take ninety minutes or up to three hours.

The **Masada Museum**, near the cable car, offers an excellent combination of life-size scenes depicting the history of Masada; archaeological artifacts; and audio guide (available in English). Watch the short English-language film near the cable-car entrance. Atop Masada, many highlights such as Herod's **Northern Palace** and the **bathhouse** are toward the site's

Cable car heading down from Masada

northern end. On the sparser southern side, the views and echo point near the southern **water cistern** are notable.

OTHER THINGS TO DO

If you're traveling or staying overnight on the Dead Sea side, combine your excursion with a hike in **Ein Gedi** or a visit to a spa in **Ein Bokek**. If you're staying in Arad, check out the Masada **Sound-and-Light Show** (☎ 08/995-9333) Tuesday and Thursday evenings at 8:30 PM from March through October. To arrange a bar mitzvah at Masada, contact the **Israel Parks Service** at ✉ info@parks.org.il.

VISITOR INFORMATION

Masada National Park: Off Rte. 90 (east) or Rte 3199 (west), ☎ 08/658-4207, ⊕ www.parks.org.il **Note:** Most of Masada is wheelchair accessible.

☉ **Park and cable car hours:** Apr.–Sept., daily 8-5; Oct.–Mar., daily 8–4; closes 1 hour earlier on Fri. and Jewish holiday eves. Closed Yom Kippur.

☉ **Pre-dawn entrance for walkers:** Snake Path opens 1 hour before sunrise; Ramp Path opens 45 minutes before sunrise.

🎫 **Admission:** NIS 29 park, via Snake or Roman paths; NIS 58 park plus cable car one-way; NIS 76 park plus round-trip cable car; NIS 20 museum (includes audio guides for museum and site); NIS 20 audio guide to park (includes museum entrance).

Cooking pots at Masada

Arad is often used as a base for excursions to sites in the Dead Sea area. It has an archaeological site and is also near Yatir, one of the country's finest desert wineries. You can also take a stroll through the galleries and workshops of Eshet Lot, the artist's quarter.

GETTING HERE AND AROUND

Arad is accessible by Route 31; the city is 45 km (28 miles) east of Beersheva. Driving from Jerusalem by Route 40 will take about 2½ hours; avoid Route 60 and Hebron in the West Bank. Egged bus lines run to Arad from Beersheva and Tel Aviv. The tourist office is behind the Paz gas station opposite the entrance to Arad; you'll see a yellow sign with "i" for information. A small supply of maps, brochures, and hiking information is available; a simple 24/7 café called Yellow sits next to the gas pumps.

ESSENTIALS

Visitor Information Arad Tourist Information Center ⊠ *Near Paz gas station* ☎ *08/995–1871* ⊕ *www.deadsea.co.il.*

EXPLORING

Glass Art Museum. This gallery displays the exciting creations of artist Gideon Fridman, who uses recycled glass to create "talking glass" sculptures in ovens he built himself. Works by other artists are also on display. The gallery is on the road to the tourist information center. Pass the gas station on your left, turn right at the roundabout, take the second right onto Sadan Street, go to the end of the street, and it's on the left. A trip here is worth the effort. ⊠ *11 Sadan St.* ☎ *08/995–3388* ⊕ *www.warmglassil.com/english* ⊠ *NIS 30* ⊙ *Sun.–Wed. 10–1, Thurs. and Sat. 10–2.*

Tel Arad. The 250-acre site of the biblical city of Arad (to the northwest of the modern city) contains the remains of a major metropolis from the Bronze Age and the Israelite period. The lower city, with its meticulously planned streets and plazas, was inhabited in the Early Bronze Age (3150–2200 BC), when it was one of the largest cities in this region. Here you can walk around a walled urban community and enter the carefully reconstructed dwellings, whose style became known as the "Arad house."

After the Early Bronze Age, Arad was abandoned. The book of Numbers (21:1–3) relates that the Canaanite king of Arad battled the Israelites during the exodus from Egypt but that his cities were "utterly destroyed." The upper city was first settled in the Israelite period (1200 BC). It's worth the trek up the somewhat steep path to see the Israelite temple, a miniature version of Solomon's Temple in Jerusalem.

At the entrance, pick up a free pamphlet explaining the ongoing excavations and purchase the plan of the Canaanite city of Arad (NIS 8), with a map, recommended walking tour, and diagrams of a typical Arad house. Tel Arad is 8 km (5 miles) west of Arad. At the Tel Arad Junction on Route 31, turn north on Route 80 for 3 km (2 miles). ⊠ *Rte. 80* ☎ *057/776–2170* ⊕ *www.parks.org.il* ⊠ *NIS 15* ⊙ *Apr.–Sept., Sun.–Thurs. 8–5, Fri. and Jewish holiday eves 8–2; Oct.–Mar., Sun.–Thurs. 8–4, Fri. and Jewish holidays eves 8–2.*

Yatir Winery. At the foot of the ancient Tel Arad, this boutique vineyard was established in 2000. Yatir Forest (a Cabernet Sauvignon blend) is the premier label. The adjacent Yatir Forest, after which the winery is named, is the largest planted forest in Israel. Call ahead for a visit and tasting. ✉ *Rte. 80* ☎ *08/995–9090* 🌐 *www.yatir.net* 🕒 *Sun.–Fri., hrs vary.*

WHERE TO EAT AND STAY

$$ MIDDLE EASTERN 🍴 **Muza.** With chunky wood furniture, soccer scarves draped along one wall, and a bar lined with beer bottles, this is a classic pub. It's on Route 31, at the entrance to Arad. The place is warm and cozy, staffed by smiling servers and filled with locals and travelers enjoying skewered meat, burgers, hummus, and "toast," the Israeli term for a grilled cheese sandwich. A big-screen TV is always tuned to a soccer match, and the covered terrace allows for open-air dining. [$] *Average main: NIS 50* ✉ *Rte. 31, near the Alon gas station* ☎ *08/997–5555* 🌐 *www.muza-arad.co.il.*

$$ B&B/INN Fodor's Choice ★ 🏨 **Yehelim Boutique Hotel.** The stunning desert views from this award-winning hotel take full advantage of the pristine surroundings. **Pros:** lovely views; friendly staff; delicious breakfast. **Cons:** books up fast; no pool. [$] *Rooms from: $240* ✉ *72 Moav St.* ☎ *077/563–2806, 052/652–2718* 🌐 *www.yehelim.com* 🛏 *10 rooms, 2 suites* 🍽 *Breakfast.*

EIN BOKEK

40 km (25 miles) east of Arad, 8 km (5 miles) north of Zohar–Arad Junction on Route 90.

Fodor's Choice ★ The sudden and startling sight, in this bare landscape, of gleaming, ultramodern hotels surrounded by waving palm trees signals your arrival at the spa-resort area of Ein Bokek, near the southern tip of the Dead Sea. According to the Bible, it was along these shores that the Lord rained fire and brimstone on the people of Sodom and Gomorrah (Genesis 19:24) and turned Lot's wife into a pillar of salt (Genesis 26). Here, at the lowest point on Earth, the hot, sulfur-pungent air hangs heavy, and a haze often shimmers over the water. You can float, but you can't sink, in the warm, salty water.

Once upon a time, Ein Bokek comprised a handful of hotels, each with a small "spa," with a pebbly beach out front. Today, it's a collection of luxurious hotels with curvy pools and landscaped outdoor areas; each has a rooftop solarium and a state-of-the-art spa equipped to provide beauty and health treatments, and some have private beaches. Each hotel has a decent restaurant. There are no full-service restaurants outside the hotels, although a few casual eating places are set along the beach and in two tiny shopping centers. The central cluster of hotels is linked by a promenade to two hotels at the very southern end of the area.

GETTING HERE AND AROUND

To drive to Ein Bokek from Jerusalem, take Route 1 eastbound, marked Jericho–Dead Sea. At the Dead Sea, Take Route 90 south, passing Qumran, Ein Gedi, and Masada, until you reach Ein Bokek. Egged buses run between Jerusalem and Ein Bokek several times a day. The trip is 1½ hours.

EXPLORING

Arava Road. Traversing the Arava Valley from Ein Bokek to Eilat, the 177-km (111-mile) Route 90 parallels the Israel-Jordan border, almost touching it at some points. To the east rise the spiky, red-brown mountains of Moab, in Jordan. The road follows an ancient route mentioned in biblical descriptions of the journeys of the Children of Israel.

The *Arava* (meaning "wilderness") is part of the Great Rift Valley, the deep fissure in the earth stretching from Turkey to East Africa, the result of an ancient shift of landmasses. Just south of Ein Bokek, you'll pass signs for the settlements **Neot HaKikar** and **Ein Tamar** (home to many craftspeople), whose date palms draw water from underground springs rather than irrigation.

With the Edom Mountains rising in the east, the road continues along the southern Dead Sea valley. You'll cross one of the largest dry riverbeds in the Negev, Nahal Zin, and you'll pass several sprawling date orchards that belong to neighboring kibbutzim.

WHERE TO STAY

$$$$
RESORT

☆ Crowne Plaza Dead Sea. This 12-story hotel may not be as flashy as some of its neighbors, but its waterfront location and direct beach access make it ideal. **Pros:** perfect location; good service; free Wi-Fi. **Cons:** noisy dining room; average food; dated rooms. $ *Rooms from: $450 ✉ Off Rte. 90 ☎ 08/659–1919 ⊕ www.crowneplaza.com ⤳ 304 rooms, 14 suites* ⦿ *Some meals.*

$$$
HOTEL
ALL-INCLUSIVE

☆ Daniel Dead Sea. At this upscale lodging, an undulating front wall swirls around a huge flower-shaped pool. **Pros:** lovely pool; near the beach; video games for kids. **Cons:** drab decor; staff can be brusque. $ *Rooms from: $359 ✉ Off Rte. 90 ☎ 08/668–9999 ⊕ www. tamareshotels.co.il/e/daniel_dead_sea ⤳ 302 rooms, 4 suites* ⦿ *Multiple meal plans.*

$$$$
RESORT
Fodor's Choice
★

☆ Isrotel Dead Sea. The nine-story Isrotel wants to set a new standard for the area's luxury hotels, and mostly achieves its goals. **Pros:** sparkling pool; beer and wine on tap for dinner; good business lounge. **Cons:** expensive Internet access; in summer, can be overrun with kids; service can be brusque. $ *Rooms from: $600 ✉ Off Rte. 90 ☎ 08/668– 9666 ⊕ www.isrotel.com/isrotel_dead_sea ⤳ 290 rooms, 7 suites* ⦿ *Breakfast.*

$$$$
RESORT
Fodor's Choice
★

☆ Le Meridien. Reached via a trail of baby palm trees, this hotel stands out for its cavernous lobby, wonderful views, delightful spa, and endless swimming pool. **Pros:** lovely rooms; pretty grounds; the area's largest outdoor pools. **Cons:** up a steep hill; inconsistent food; occasional poor service. $ *Rooms from: $480 ✉ Off Rte. 90 ☎ 08/659– 1234 ⊕ www.fattal-hotels.com ⤳ 603 rooms, 24 suites* ⦿ *Multiple meal plans.*

$$$ 🏨 **Leonardo Club.** Bring the whole family to this all-inclusive property,
RESORT where adults can enjoy a midnight supper and kids can cool off with ice
FAMILY pops around the clock. **Pros:** the area's only all-inclusive hotel; excellent kids' programs; nice views. **Cons:** small rooms; drab entry; noisy
lobby; far from center of Ein Bokek. $ *Rooms from: $346* ✉ *Off Rte.
90* ☎ *08/668–9444* ⊕ *www.fattal-hotels.com* ↪ *388 rooms, 14 suites*
🍴 *Multiple meal plans.*

$ 🏨 **Masada Guest House.** This moderately priced guesthouse at the foot of
HOTEL Masada is the most convenient lodging for those intent on watching the
spectacular sunrise over the Dead Sea. **Pros:** convenient to Masada; nice
swimming pool; air-conditioned rooms. **Cons:** rowdy teenage groups;
no evening entertainment; minimalist beds. $ *Rooms from: $148* ✉ *Off
Rte. 90, at the entrance to Masada* ☎ *08/995–3222* ⊕ *www.youth-
hostels.org.il* ↪ *88 rooms* 🍴 *Breakfast.*

$$$ 🏨 **Royal Rimonim.** A crown topped with the letter R marks this glass-
RESORT encased tower, where the pool is immense, the restaurant serves excellent seafood, and the lavish spa has 32 deluxe treatment rooms. **Pros:**
large and luxurious spa; plentiful buffet; wheelchair accessible. **Cons:**
tiny balconies offer little privacy; outdated carpets; deposit required
for bathrobes. $ *Rooms from: $345* ✉ *Off Rte. 90* ☎ *08/668–8555*
⊕ *www.rimonim.com* ↪ *387 rooms, 20 suites* 🍴 *Some meals.*

$$$ 🏨 **Spa Club.** The lovely Moroccan-style spa is the main draw of this
RESORT adults-only hotel, especially the heated indoor pool, Turkish-style steam
bath, and elegant spa suites with private whirlpool tubs big enough
for couples. **Pros:** extraordinary spa treatments; quiet atmosphere;
unlimited tea bar in lobby. **Cons:** beach is across the road; cafeteria
has little natural light; guest-room windows are small. $ *Rooms from:
$358* ✉ *Off Rte. 90* ☎ *08/668–8000* ⊕ *www.prima.co.il* ↪ *98 rooms*
🍴 *Breakfast.*

SPORTS AND THE OUTDOORS

The beaches of Ein Bokek are free to the public and are usually fairly
crowded. A lifeguard is on duty year-round, and there's ample parking
alongside the promenade. Most don't have facilities.

Dead Sea Divers. In the sea, where everyone floats, diving requires lots
of weights just to keep you below the surface. Under the sea is another
world of rocky, white salt crystals. A day's training and diving costs
NIS 2,400. Avi Bresler will pick you up from your hotel in Ein Bokek.
☎ *03/540–7638, 052/259–0014* ⊕ *deadseadivers.com.*

SHOPPING

Several companies manufacture excellent Dead Sea skin and beauty
products made from mud, salts, and minerals; the actual mud is
sold in squishy, leak-proof packages. Ahava and Jericho are popular
brands sold at the shopping centers of Ein Bokek and at the shops
in most hotels.

Dead Sea Diamond Center. Unique, handcrafted jewelry by Israeli designers is sold at this establishment opposite Le Meridien hotel. Call for a
shuttle to pick you up. ✉ *Rte. 90* ☎ *08/995–8777.*

WEST OF JERUSALEM

The rugged Judean Hills tumble down from Jerusalem to the west, eventually easing into the gentler terrain of the coastal lowlands (known in Hebrew as the *Shfela*). This is a region of forests, springs, monasteries, battlefields, national parks, and archaeological treasures. It's the fastest-growing wine-producing area in the country, encompassing more than two-dozen vineyards. A number of locals also produce goat and sheep cheese, as well as craft beers. For Jerusalemites, the Judean Hills are a place to hike and picnic. For many visitors, this sparsely populated region with its ancient terraced hills evokes the landscape of the Bible with none of the distractions of a big city.

LATRUN

25 km (16 miles) west of Jerusalem on Route 1.

Latrun is the ridge that projects into and dominates the western side of the Ayalon Valley. A natural passage between the coastal plain and the Judean Hills, the strategic valley has served as a battleground throughout history, from the conquests of the biblical Israelite leader Joshua in the 13th century BC, through the Hasmonean campaigns of the 2nd century BC, to the bloody defeat of the newly established Israel Defense Force by Jordan's Arab Legion in 1948. Today, the Trappist monastery is known for its olive oil and wine, and Mini Israel is a favorite for children of all ages.

GETTING HERE AND AROUND

Coming from Jerusalem on Route 1, exit onto Route 3 (the Modi'in and Ashkelon–Beersheva road), about 5 km (3 miles) west of the Sha'ar Hagai gas station. At the T-junction, turn left for the Trappist Abbey of Latrun, the Latrun Armored Corps Museum, and Mini Israel. There are no good public transportation options.

EXPLORING

TOP ATTRACTIONS

Fodor's Choice ★ **Abu Gosh.** The picturesque Arab community of Abu Gosh is renowned for its hummus, the tasty blend of chickpeas, sesame paste, olive oil, lemon juice, and garlic. In 2010, 50 chefs prepared over four tons of hummus, beating the world record set the month before in Lebanon. Abu Gosh also hosts a vocal music festival every summer and autumn; classical concerts take on a special character in the old village churches. ⊠ *Rte. 425, Abu Gosh* ⊕ *www.agfestival.co.il/en.*

FAMILY **Latrun Armored Corps Museum.** The name Latrun is thought to derive from "La Toron de Chevaliers" (the Tower of the Knights), the French name of the Crusader castle that occupied the crest of the hill in the 12th century. Eight centuries later, in 1940, the British erected the concrete fortress that today holds the museum. In the 1948 War of Independence, Israeli forces attempted five times to capture the fortress from Jordanian soldiers. The names of 142 Israeli soldiers who fell in these unsuccessful attempts are engraved on the walls. There are more than 100 assorted antique tanks on which children love to climb. ⊠ *Rte. 3, 1 km (½ mile) south of Rte. 1* ☎ *08/978-4351* ⊕ *www.yadlashiryon.com* ⊠ *NIS 30* ☉ *Sun.–Thurs. 8:30–4:30, Fri. 8:30–12:30, Sat. and holidays 9–4:30.*

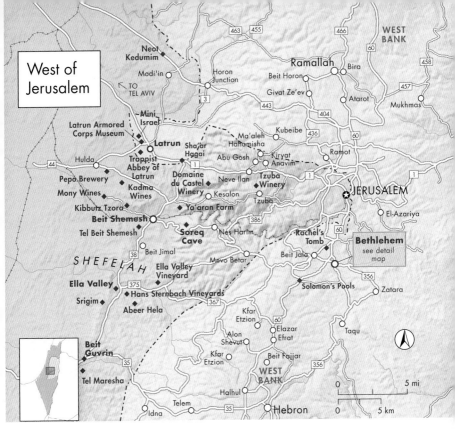

West of Jerusalem

FAMILY
Fodor's Choice
★

Mini Israel. One of the most popular attractions in Israel, this theme park spreads over 13 acres and contains nearly 400 models of the most important historical, national, religious, and natural sites in the country. Worth an hour's visit, the site is especially fun for children. About 25,000 miniature "residents" have been meticulously created to present not just the physical, but also the cultural, religious, and social aspects of contemporary Israel. A walk through the park lets you see and hear the people of different faiths and cultures that make up the country's human landscape. ⊠ *Rte. 424, 1 km (½ mile) south of Latrun* ☎ *700/559–559* ⊕ *www.minisrael.co.il* ☒ *NIS 69* ☉ *Sept.–June, Sat.–Thurs.10–6; Fri. 10–2; July–Aug., Sat.–Thurs. 5–10, Fri. 10–2.*

FAMILY
Fodor's Choice
★

Sataf. Just outside Jerusalem, Sataf was one of many Arab villages that were abandoned in the 1948 War of Independence. You can hike here on well-marked trails amid ancient terraces shaded with pine, fig, and almond trees. Hikes last two or four hours, and pass springs where you can get your feet wet. On weekends, follow the pictures of goats to get to **Shai Seltzer,** who raises goats in the forest and ages unique and delicious cheese in an old Byzantine cave. You can walk to Sataf from Ein Kerem. ⊠ *Sataf Junction, intersection of Rtes. 395 and 3965, Sataf* ☎ *054/440–3762* ☒ *Free* ☉ *Daily, during daylight hours.*

WORTH NOTING

OFF THE BEATEN PATH

Neot Kedumim. At the 625-acre Oases of Antiquity, ancient terraces and wine and oil presses were excavated and restored, thousands of trees and shrubs were planted, and pools and cisterns were dug. A network of roads and walking paths (most of them paved and wheelchair accessible) allows for a leisurely exploration of the site. Take one of the self-guided tours (maps available in English) or inquire ahead about times of guided tours. Allow two hours minimum for the visit. ✉ *Rte. 443, 20 km (12 miles) north of Latrun* ☎ *08/977–0777* 🌐 *www.neot-kedumim.org.il* 🎫 *NIS 25* 🕒 *Sun.–Thurs. 8:30–4, Fri. 8:30–1.*

Pepo Beer. Moti Bohadana named his brewery for his father and the eight beers for all the women in his life. Elisheva, named after his grandmother, is a bitter, hoppy IPA. Tamara is a red, flowery ale, and Tirza is an Irish stout. Ask about the delicious local bread and cheese. Music events are held Thursday nights. To get here from Latrun, take Route 3 toward Ashkelon and turn left on Route 44. Follow signs for the Navot Winery. ✉ *Rte. 44, Moshav Tzlafon* ☎ *054/530–4576* 🕒 *Fri. 9:30–1 hr before sunset. Call ahead other days.*

Trappist Abbey of Latrun. Trappist monks have been producing wine here since the 1890s. The interior of the 19th-century abbey is an odd mix of round neo-Byzantine arches and apses and the soaring ceiling that seems Gothic in inspiration. Survivors of the Cistercian Order suppressed in the French Revolution, the Trappists keep a vow of silence. But you needn't worry about making a faux pas by talking; the staff in the shop will address you—in English, French, Hebrew, or Arabic. The setting in the foothills is lovely. ✉ *Rte. 3, 2 km (1 mile) off Rte. 1* ☎ *08/922–0065* 🎫 *Free* 🕒 *Apr.–Sept., Mon.–Sat. 8:30–11:30 and 3–5; Oct.–Mar., Mon.–Sat. 8:30–11 and 2:30–4.*

WHERE TO EAT

$$$ DINER

🍴 **Elvis Inn.** At the entrance to Neve Illan, this American-style diner has the largest collection of Elvis memorabilia this side of Graceland. This kitschy place is probably the only Elvis-souvenir shop in the world where you can get *shawarma* (spit-grilled meat). Don't worry, there's also traditional roadhouse fare that the King would love. Serious fans should come on the anniversary of his birth (August 16) or death (January 8), when Israel's Elvis impersonators come to get all shook up. [$] *Average main: NIS 80* ✉ *Rte. 4115, Neve Illan* ☎ *02/534–1275* 🕒 *No Friday dinner.*

$$ FAST FOOD

🍴 **Nof Latrun.** At this self-service cafeteria, with an air-conditioned dining room and outdoor picnic tables, enjoy the basics: schnitzel (breaded chicken breast), grilled meats, or fresh salads. Sandwiches and ice cream are available at the take-out window. The cafeteria is across the parking lot from the Latrun Armored Corps Museum. [$] *Average main: NIS 56* ✉ *Rte. 3, 1 km (½ mile) south of Rte. 1* ☎ *08/920–1670* 🕒 *No dinner Fri. Closed Sat.*

ISRAELI
Fodor's Choice ★

🍴 **Rama's Kitchen.** Chef Rama Ben Zvi combines local cheeses and meats with wild herbs gathered from as far away as the Dead Sea, for a meal that could easily last hours amid the gorgeous Judean Hills. The menu changes at this spot open only a couple of days a week, but the beet hummus is outstanding, and the lamb kebabs come skewered on an olive branch or a cinnamon stick. Desserts like pistachio ice cream are delightfully executed. The prices are upscale, but the handmade wood furniture and gravel floor mean you don't have to dress to impress. Drinks include an apple-and-honey cocktail, and the wine list offers a long list of Israeli bottles. [$] *Average main: NIS 100* ✉ *Off Rte. 1, Nataf* ☎ *02/570–0954* 🌐 *ramak.co.il/en* ✍ *Reservations essential* 🕒 *Closed Sun.–Thurs.*

SOREQ CAVE

25 km (17 miles) southwest of Jerusalem on Rtes. 386 and 3866, 12 km (7½ miles) east of Beit Shemesh on Route 3855.

GETTING HERE AND AROUND

Follow Route 1 west from Jerusalem, then head south on Route 38 and east on Route 3855. Turn northwest on Route 3866, continuing up the mountain for about 5 km (3 miles) to a junction with a large sculpture commemorating the Challenger spacecraft. Turn left and continue for about 2 km (1 mile) to the parking lot.

EXPLORING

Soreq Cave. At the heart of the Avshalom Nature Reserve on the western slopes of the Judean Hills, the Soreq Cave contains a wondrous variety of stalactites and stalagmites. Some formations are at least three hundred thousand years old and allow scientists to track climate changes over the millennia. It was discovered in 1968 when a routine blast in the nearby Har-Tuv quarry tore away the rock face, revealing a subterranean wonderland.

Colored lights are used to highlight the natural whites and honey browns of the stones. Local guides have given the stalactite forms nicknames like "macaroni," "curtains," and "sombreros." In a series of "interfaith" images, some find rocky evocations of Moses, the Madonna and Child, Buddha, and the Ayatollah Khomeini. Photography is allowed only on Friday morning, when there are no guided tours. Despite the high humidity, the temperature in the cave is comfortable year-round.

The 150 steps down to the cave mean it's not ideal for visitors with mobility concerns. Local guides take groups as they arrive into the cave every 15 minutes for a 30-minute tour (English tours on request). An English-language video explains how the cave was formed. ✉ *Rte. 3866, Avshalom Nature Reserve* ☎ *02/991–1117* 🌐 *www.parks.org.il* 🎟 *NIS 29* 🕒 *Apr.–Sept., Sat.–Thurs. 8–5, Fri. 8–4; Oct.–Mar., Sat.–Thurs. 8–4, Fri. 8–3; last entry 1¼ hr before closing.*

Tzuba Vineyard. Part of the eponymous kibbutz, this winery produces excellent red dessert wines as well as a blend of Cabernet Sauvignon and Cabernet Franc. ✉ *Rte. 395, 12 km (7½ miles) west of Jerusalem, Kibbutz Tzuba* ☎ *02/534–7678* 🌐 *www.tzubawinery.co.il* 🕒 *Sun.–Thurs. 9–1 and 2–4, Fri. 9–2.*

WHERE TO STAY

There are some very good kibbutz guesthouses in wooded enclaves of the Judean Hills, a 15- to 20-minute drive west of Jerusalem. All have commanding hilltop views, quiet surroundings, very comfortable if not luxurious accommodations, and good swimming pools.

$$ HOTEL FAMILY **Hotel Tzuba.** Nice views, delicious brunches, and a popular children's park make this hotel a good choice for families. **Pros:** great place for young children; interesting tours; panoramic views. **Cons:** no evening entertainment; meals eaten in the kibbutz dining hall; minimum stays on weekends. [$] *Rooms from: $242* ✉ *Rte. 39, 12 km (7½ miles) west of Jerusalem, Tzuba* ☎ *02/534–7000* 🌐 *www.belmont.co.il* 🛏 *64 suites* 🍴 *Breakfast.*

$$ HOTEL **Ma'aleh Hahamisha.** This large guesthouse, spread over beautifully landscaped gardens, is ideal for nature lovers. **Pros:** panoramic views; indoor pool; park-like setting. **Cons:** some rooms dated; no evening entertainment; can get crowded with tour groups; rooms in older wings have twin beds instead of queen-sized mattresses. [$] *Rooms from: $250* ✉ *Rte. 1, 14 km (9 miles) west of Jerusalem, Kibbutz Maaleh Hahamisha* ☎ *02/533–1331* 🌐 *www.inisrael.com/maale5* 🛏 *230 rooms* 🍴 *Breakfast.*

$$ HOTEL FAMILY **Neve Ilan.** A cut above its neighbors, this hotel has spacious, nicely furnished rooms, a sparkling heated pool, and a well-equipped exercise room. **Pros:** panoramic views; beautiful swimming pool; childrens' activities. **Cons:** no evening entertainment. [$] *Rooms from: $206* ✉ *North of Rte. 1, 15 km (10 miles) west of Jerusalem, Neve Illan* ☎ *02/533–9339* 🌐 *www.c-hotels.co.il* 🛏 *160 rooms, 4 suites* 🍴 *Breakfast.*

SHOPPING

Ya'aran Farm. This small but popular farm, run by Yavshi and Bar Ya'aran, produces more than 10 types of hard and soft goat cheese. It's best to come on a Saturday, when the couple bakes their own bread. If Bar isn't too busy, she'll explain to you her vision of living off the land, using only rainwater and solar power and windmills for energy. The Jewish National Fund hired the couple in 1995 as fire watchers for the newly replanted forest. Since grazing animals keep down the brush, the Ya'arans began herding goats. The farm is 5 miles east of Beit Shemesh. ✉ *On Rte. 3866, Beit Shemesh* ☎ *02/999–7811* 🕓 *Fri. and Sat. 9–4 in winter, 9–5 in summer. Weekdays, call in advance.*

BEIT SHEMESH

12 km (7½ miles) west of Soreq Cave on Rtes. 3855 and 38, 35 km (22 miles) west of Jerusalem.

The modern town of Beit Shemesh, Hebrew for "House of the Sun," takes its name from an ancient city now entombed by the tell on a rise on Route 38, 2 km (1 mile) south of the main entrance. Nearby are a number of wineries and breweries worth exploring.

This is Samson country. Samson, one of the judges of Old Testament Israel, is better known for his physical prowess and lust for Philistine women than for his shining spiritual qualities, but it was here, "between

WINERIES IN THE JUDEAN HILLS

For years, good Israeli wine was an oxymoron, but the days of producing only sweet sacramental wines are long gone. In the past few decades, a viniculture revolution has yielded an abundance of wines that easily compete against those from older vineyards. The Judean Hills area is now home to more than two-dozen vineyards, the majority of them close to Route 38, north and south of Beit Shemesh. Since most vineyards are "boutique"—producing fewer than 100,000 bottles per year—few have visitor centers that encourage drop-in visits or have regularly scheduled tours, so call ahead. The wineries are convenient to Tel Aviv (40 minutes away) as well as Jerusalem (about 20 minutes). Every October, the area's more than 20 wineries sponsor a wine festival at Ein Hemed National Park. Check out regional events at ⊕ *www.touryoav.org.il.*

Tzorah and Eshta'ol," that "the Spirit of the Lord began to stir him" (Judges 13). Today, Eshta'ol is a *moshav* (a cooperative settlement composed of individual farms) a few minutes' drive north, and Tzora is the wine-producing kibbutz immediately to the west.

GETTING HERE AND AROUND

Follow Route 1 west from Jerusalem, then head south on Route 38 to Beit Shemesh. Israel Railways provides regular train service between Jerusalem and Tel Aviv via Beit Shemesh on an hourly basis from 6 am to 8 pm.

EXPLORING

TOP ATTRACTIONS

Fodor'sChoice ★ **Abeer Haela.** Aram Dekel was the first to brew beer in this picturesque setting, and some of his bottles evoke biblical recipes with date syrup and honey. The allspice beer stays on your tongue with its crisp and potent flavor. Also, make sure to ask about the mead and ginger liqueur. The homemade goat cheese and sausages are just as special, and all are served in an airy, shaded pub. ⊠ *Farm 25, Rt. 3554, Tzafririm* ☏ *054/700–0512* ⊙ *Fri. 10–3, Sat. 10–5.*

Domaine du Castel. This vineyard consistently produces some of the country's best wines. The small winery—and its exquisite cellar—offers tours and tastings of wine and cheese by appointment, Sunday to Thursday. ⊠ *Rte. 395, Moshav Ramat Raziel* ☏ *02/534–2249* ⊕ *www.castel.co.il.*

Fodor'sChoice ★ **Ella Valley Vineyards.** In Kibbutz Netiv Halamed Hey, the vineyards are a "stone's throw" from where David slew Goliath (I Samuel 17). Under the supervision of French-trained winemaker Doron Rav Hon, this young winery produced its first harvest in 2002, but ancient winepresses from the Byzantine period attest to the region's historical wine production. Their top-quality wines include Cabernet, Merlot, Chardonnay, and Muscat. ⊠ *Rte. 38, 10 km (6½ miles) south of Beit Shemesh, Kibbutz Netiv Halamed Hey* ☏ *02/999–4885* ⊕ *www.ellavalley.com* ⊙ *Sun.–Thurs. 8:30–4:30, Fri. 8:30–12:30.*

WORTH NOTING

Kadma Wines. Born in the Republic of Georgia, former software engineer Lina Slutzkin remembers how wine was once made there in egg-shaped clay casks. At Kadma Wines, she uses these unusual vessels to produce a wide range of red wines. Don't forget to sample the fresh goat cheese and tasty bread. ✉ *Rte. 44, 9 miles northwest of Beit Shemesh, Kfar Uriya* ☎ *02/999–2732, 054/919–5156* ⊕ *www.kadma-wine.co.il* ☉ *Fri. and Sat. 11–3, Sun.–Thurs. call ahead.*

Kibbutz Tzora. Overlooking the Soreq Valley, this kibbutz produces some excellent red wines, as well as homemade olive oil, honey, and cheese. ✉ *Rte. 3835, just northwest of Beit Shemesh* ☎ *02/990–8261* ⊕ *www. tzorawines.com* ☉ *Sun.–Thurs. 10–5, Fri. 10–2.*

Mony Wines. On the grounds of the Deir Rafat monastery, this winery is family-run but supervised by Sam Soroka, one of the most experienced winemakers in Israel. The shop sells the wines, mostly reds, but also Chardonnay and Muscat, as well as olives and olive oil. ✉ *Rte. 3856, 4 km (2½ miles) west of Kibbutz Tzora, Deir Rafat* ☎ *02/991–6629* ☉ *Daily 9–5.*

Shapiro Beer. "Jerusalem's Beer" is actually brewed in Beit Shemesh, but brothers Dani, Itzik, and Avi learned how to brew in their Jerusalem basement. The three main beers are an oatmeal stout, a wheat beer, and a pale ale, all labeled with a Jerusalem lion downing a bottle. Call in advance to tour the brewery and sip a few samples in the tiny kitchen overlooking the floor. ✉ *Off Rte. 38* ☎ *02/561–2622* ⊕ *shapirobeer. co.il* ☉ *Call ahead, as hrs vary.*

Srigim Brewery. Ohad Ayalon and Ofer Ronen take great care when crafting their fantastic Bavarian-style wheat beer, dark ale, and Indian ale, which you can sip on a balcony overlooking the Ella Valley. ✉ *Rte. 353, Srigim* ☎ *052/622–7679, 052/593–8287* ⊕ *www.srigim-beer.co.il* ☉ *Fri. 10:30–4.*

Tel Beit Shemesh. This low-profile archaeological site has fine views of the fields of Nahal Soreq, where Samson dallied with Delilah (Judges 16). When the Philistines captured the Israelite Ark of the Covenant in battle (11th century BC), they found that their prize brought divine retribution with it, destroying their idol Dagon and afflicting their bodies with tumors and their cities with rats (I Samuel 5). The Philistines rid themselves of the jinxed ark by sending it back to the Israelites at Beit Shemesh. The stone ruins of the tell—including the oldest iron workshop in the world—are hard to interpret without an archaeologist on hand. ✉ *Rte. 38, 2 km (1 mile) from Tzora turnoff* ▨ *Free* ☉ *Open 24 hrs.*

ELLA VALLEY

10 km (6 miles) south of Beit Shemesh, 42 km (26 miles) west of Jerusalem.

The Ella Valley is one of those delightful places—not uncommon in Israel—where you can relate the scenery to a specific biblical text and confirm the maxim that once you've visited this country, you'll never read the Bible in quite the same way again. Beyond the junction of Route 38 with Route 383, and up to the right above the pinewood slopes of Park Britannia, is a distinctively bald flattop hill, **Tel Azekah,** the site of an ancient Israelite town. The hills are especially delightful in March and April when the wildflowers are out, and hiking paths are plentiful.

In the Ella Valley, the southernmost of the great valleys that cut from the Judean highlands toward the coast, Route 38 crosses a usually dry streambed; 200 yards beyond it is a place to pull off and park. If you have a Bible, open it to I Samuel 17 and read about the dramatic duel between the Israelite shepherd David and the Philistine champion Goliath. The battle probably took place close to where you're standing:

And Saul and the men of Israel were gathered, and encamped in the valley of Ella, and drew up in line of battle against the Philistines. And the Philistines stood on the mountain on the one side, and Israel stood on the mountain on the other side, with a valley between them.

Look east up the valley to the mountains of Judah in the distance and the road from Bethlehem—the same road by which David reached the battlefield. The white northern ridge, a spur of the mountains of Judah, may have been the camp of the Israelite army. The southern ridge (where the gas station is today) is where the Philistines gathered. The creek, the only one in the valley, is where David "chose five smooth stones." The rest, as they say, is history: Goliath was slain, the Philistines were routed, and David went on to become the darling of the nation and eventually its king.

MICROBREWERIES IN ISRAEL

In the last decade, microbreweries have taken off in Israel. Importers are bringing in more exotic varieties of barley and hops, and well-traveled Israelis are recreating favorites they sipped in Belgium, Germany, England, and the United States. The area around the Ella Valley, Beit Shemesh, and Latrun is especially easy to tour because most breweries are a short distance from each other. It's worth calling in advance, as the hours change frequently.

GETTING HERE AND AROUND

Follow Route 1 west from Jerusalem, then head south on Route 38, passing Beit Shemesh on your left.

WHERE TO EAT

$$ MODERN ISRAELI Fodor's Choice ★

🍴 **Hans Sternbach Vineyards.** It's worth the drive here to sample the rustic and delicious creations by vintner Gadi Sternbach, who makes nearly everything on the menu, from the outstanding cured beef to the smoked salmon to the freshly baked bread. The succulent beef stew and unforgettable glazed onions are cooked in a sauce that uses the winery's own red wines. Seating is in the dining room or on a terrace shaded by leafy trees and flowers. Sternbach is a former tour guide and can explain the biblical history of the surrounding hills. Vineyard tours are available. [$] *Average main: NIS 70* ✉ *Farm 83, Rte. 3544, Givat Yeshayahu* ☎ *02/999–0162* 🌐 *www.hsw.co.il* ✍ *Reservations essential* 🕒 *Fri. and Sat. 10–6.*

BEIT GUVRIN

21 km (13 miles) south of Beit Shemesh, 52 km (33 miles) southwest of Jerusalem.

GETTING HERE AND AROUND

Follow Route 1 west from Jerusalem, then head south on Route 38 through Beit Shemesh until the end of the road. At Nehushga Junction, turn west on Route 35. The park is off Route 35 opposite Kibbutz Beit Guvrin.

EXPLORING

FAMILY
Fodor'sChoice
★

Beit Guvrin. This national park encompasses some 1,250 acres of rolling hills in the Judean lowlands. For thousands of years people here have been digging quarries, burial caves, storerooms, hideouts, and dovecotes—a subterranean labyrinth of unparalleled complexity. In the Second Temple period, millions of pilgrims ascended to Jerusalem to offer animal sacrifices. At Beit Guvrin, doves were raised on a vast scale to supply the pilgrims' need. Unlike many ruins, this national park allows you to readily envision life two thousand years ago, both above and under the ground.

The antiquities sprawl around the kibbutz of Beit Guvrin, just beyond the junction of Routes 38 and 35. These are bits and pieces of the 2nd- to 3rd-century AD Beit Guvrin, renamed (around the year 200) *Eleuthropolis*, "the city of free men." The amphitheater—an arena for Roman blood sports and mock sea battles—is one of only a few discovered in Israel.

After entering the park, drive toward the flattop mound of ancient Maresha, known today as **Tel Maresha.** King Rehoboam of Judah fortified it, but it was during the Hellenistic period (4th–2nd centuries BC) that the city reached its height and the endless complexes of chalk caves were dug. Maresha was finally destroyed by the Parthians in 40 BC and replaced by the nearby Roman city of Beit Guvrin. The view from the tell is worth the short climb.

Ancient Mareshans excavated thousands of underground chambers to extract soft chalk bricks, with which they built their homes above ground. Residents then turned their "basement" quarries into industrial complexes, including water cisterns, olive-oil presses, and **columbaria** (derived from the Latin word *columba,* meaning dove or pigeon). The birds were used in ritual sacrifice and as food, producers of fertilizer, and message carriers.

The most interesting and extensive cave system is just off the road on the opposite side of the tell (the trail begins at a parking lot). It includes water cisterns, storerooms, and a restored ancient olive press. The excitement of exploration makes this site a must for kids (with close parental supervision, though the safety features are good), but the many steps are physically demanding.

The great "bell caves" of **Beit Guvrin** date from the Late Roman, Byzantine, and even Early Arab periods (2nd–7th century AD), when the locals created a quarry to extract lime for cement. At the top of each bell-shaped space is a hole through the four-foot-thick stone crust of

Beit Guvrin-Maresha National Park preserves ancient caves used for storage, industry, and tombs.

the ground. When the ancient diggers reached the soft chalk below, they began reaming out their quarry in the structurally secure bell shape, each bell eventually cutting into the one adjacent to it. Although not built to be inhabited, the caves may have been used as refuges by Early Christians. In the North Cave, a cross high on the wall, at the same level as an Arabic inscription, suggests a degree of coexistence even after the Arab conquest of the area in AD 636. More recently, Beit Guvrin was an Arab village, depopulated in 1948.

After leaving this system, make sure to continue walking down the hill to visit the **Sidonian Burial Caves.** These magnificent 3rd- to 2nd-century BC tombs—adorned with colorful, restored frescoes and inscriptions—offer important archaeological evidence as to the nature of the town's ancient Phoenician colonists.

The undeveloped complexes of caves near the tell are off-limits to visitors. Keep to the marked sites only. The brochure at the entrance has a good map of the site. ⊠ *Off Rte. 35, 21 km (13 miles) south of Beit Shemesh* 🕾 *08/681–1020* ⊕ *www.parks.org.il* 🖃 *NIS 29* ⊙ *Apr.–Sept., Sat.–Thurs. 8–5, Fri. 8–4; Oct.–Mar., Sat.–Thurs. 8–4, Fri. 8–3. Last entrance 1 hr before closing.*

Dig for a Day. Archaeological Seminars, in Jerusalem, runs a program at Beit Guvrin called Dig for a Day. The three-hour activity includes supervised digging in a real excavation inside a cave, into which local inhabitants dumped earth and artifacts 21 centuries ago. Participants then sift the buckets of dirt they've hauled out of the cave, looking for finds. Some museum-quality artifacts of the 3rd to 2nd centuries BC (Hellenistic period) have been uncovered here. (No, you can't take home what you find!) You're then led on a fun 30-minute exploration through caves not yet open to the public. This involves some crawling, because some spaces are too tight or too low for walking upright. The tour ends with a short talk in the pottery shed about how clay vessels are reconstructed. ☎ 02/586–2011 ⊕ *www.archesem.com.*

EN ROUTE Instead of the Tel Aviv–Jerusalem expressway, an attractive alternative route back to Jerusalem is Route 375 through the Ella Valley, past Israel's main satellite communications receiver, and up through wooded hill country to Tzur Hadassah (look out for the rock-hewn Roman road on the right). Route 386 heads off to the left and runs north to Jerusalem through rugged mountain scenery, emerging in the Ein Kerem neighborhood on the city's western edge.

BETHLEHEM

8 km (5 miles) south of Jerusalem.

Fodor's Choice
★
Even from a distance, it's easy to identify the minarets and steeples that symbolically vie for control of the skyline of Bethlehem, home to one of the oldest Christian communities in the world. Although a few decades ago most residents were Christians, today the great majority of Bethlehem's 38,000 residents are Muslim, as elsewhere in the West Bank.

For Christians the world over, the city is synonymous with the birth of Jesus, and the many shrines that celebrate that event. Bethlehem is also the site of the Tomb of Rachel, Jacob's wife, who died in childbirth here. Rachel's Tomb today lies in Israeli-controlled territory, immediately to the north of the wall that divides the area.

GETTING HERE AND AROUND

The birthplace of Jesus is 15 minutes south of Jerusalem. Bethlehem is part of the Palestinian Authority, and is set off from Jerusalem by the controversial security wall that snakes through the Judean Hills. The wall is especially intimidating around the Bethlehem border crossing, as it stands taller than most of the surrounding buildings and is constructed of solid concrete. Graffiti artists have covered the Bethlehem side with demands for rights for Palestinians. British artist Banksy also left his mark, inspiring a falafel stand and souvenir stand named after him. As daunting as it seems, tourists with a foreign passport will have no difficulty visiting Bethlehem. Simply show the cover of your passport and you'll be whisked through, usually without a single question.

About a dozen new hotels have sprouted up in the last few years, proving that the city has more to offer than day trips to religious sites.

At the moment, Israelis are not allowed across the border. Your tour guide or the concierge at your hotel will be able to arrange for Palestinian guides to meet you across the border. If you're a more independent traveler, you can take one of the Palestinian taxis at the border. If you're taking a taxi, *servees* (shared taxi), or bus from East Jerusalem, you must change to a local bus or taxi from the Bethlehem side of the terminal to Manger Square.

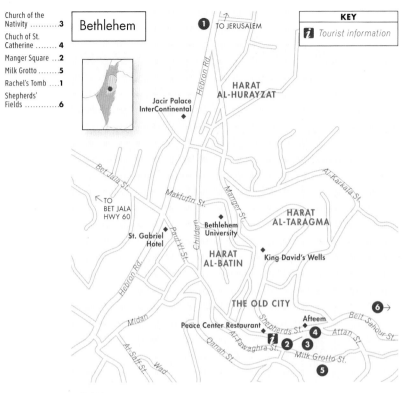

Church of the
Nativity **3**
Chuch of St.
Catherine **4**
Manger Square ...**2**
Milk Grotto **5**
Rachel's Tomb **1**
Shepherds'
Fields **6**

TIMING

Allow at least two hours for a visit to the Church of the Nativity and Manger Square.

SAFETY AND PRECAUTIONS

Tourists are unlikely to be bothered in Bethlehem, but ask your hotel concierge if there have been any recent issues.

TOURS

In recent years Bethlehem has made a concerted effort to woo tourists. Several companies like Alternative Tourism Group offer people-to-people meetings and unusual hiking trips through farming villages. The visitor information center on Manger Square has lots of great information.

ESSENTIALS

Visitor Information Alternative Tourism Group ☎ *02/277–2151* ⊕ *www.atg.ps.* **Bethlehem Tourist Information Office** ✉ *Peace Center, Manger Sq.* ☎ *02/276–6677* ⊕ *travelpalestine.ps.* **Visitor Information Center** ✉ *Manger Sq.* ☎ *02/275–4235* ⊕ *vicbethlehem.wordpress.com.*

EXPLORING

TOP ATTRACTIONS

Church of St. Catherine. Adjacent to the Church of the Nativity, and accessible by a passage from its Armenian chapel, is Bethlehem's Roman Catholic parish church. Built by Franciscans in 1882, the church incorporates remnants of its 12th-century Crusader predecessor. Note the bronze doors with reliefs of St. Jerome, St. Paula, and St. Eustochium. From this church, the midnight Catholic Christmas mass is broadcast around the world. Steps descend from within the church to a series of dim grottoes, clearly once used as living quarters. Chapels here are dedicated to Joseph; to the Innocents killed by Herod the Great; and to the 4th-century St. Jerome, who wrote the Vulgate, the Latin translation of the Bible, supposedly right here. Adjacent to the church is a lovely cloister, restored in 1949. A small wooden door (kept locked) connects the complex with the Grotto of the Nativity. Call ahead to check hours, as they change frequently. ⊠ *Manger Sq.* ☎ *02/274–2425* ☉ *Apr.–Sept., daily 6 am–7:30 pm; Oct.–Mar., daily 5 am–6 pm.*

Fodor's Choice ★ **Church of the Nativity.** At this church marking the traditional site of the birth of Jesus, the stone exterior is crowned by the crosses of the three denominations sharing it: the Greek Orthodox, the Latins (Roman Catholic, represented by the Franciscan order), and the Armenian Orthodox. The blocked, square entranceway dates from the time of the Byzantine emperor Justinian (6th century), the arched entrance (also blocked) within the Byzantine one is 12th-century Crusader, and the current low entrance was designed in the 16th century to protect the worshippers from attack by hostile Muslim neighbors.

The church interior is vast and gloomy. In the central nave, a large wooden trapdoor reveals a remnant of a striking mosaic floor from the original basilica, built in the 4th century by Helena, mother of Constantine the Great, the Roman emperor who first embraced Christianity. Emperor Justinian's rebuilding two centuries later enlarged the church, creating its present-day plan and structure, including the 44 red-stone columns with Corinthian capitals that run the length of the nave in two paired lines.

This is the oldest standing church in the country. When the Persians invaded in 614, they destroyed every Christian church and monastery in the land except this one. Legend holds that the church was adorned with a wall painting depicting the Nativity tale, including the visit to the infant Jesus by the Three Wise Men of the East. For the local artist, "east" meant Persia, and he dressed his wise men in Persian garb. The Persian conquerors didn't understand the picture's significance, but "recognized" themselves in the painting and so spared the church. In the 8th century, the church was pillaged by the Muslims and was later renovated by the Crusaders. Patches of 12th-century mosaics high on the walls, the medieval oak ceiling beams, and the figures of saints on the Corinthian pillars hint at its medieval splendor.

The elaborately ornamented front of the church serves as the parish church of Bethlehem's Greek Orthodox community. The right transept is theirs, too, but the left transept belongs to the Armenian Orthodox. The altar in the left transept is known as the altar of the kings, because

Christmas in Bethlehem includes a colorful Greek Orthodox procession in Manger Square.

tradition holds this to be the place where the three magi dismounted. For centuries, all three "shareholders" in the church have vied for control of the holiest Christian sites in the Holy Land. The 19th-century Status Quo Agreement that froze their respective rights and privileges in Jerusalem's Church of the Holy Sepulcher and the Tomb of the Virgin pertains here, too: ownership, the timing of ceremonies, the number of oil lamps, and so on are all clearly defined.

From the right transept at the front of the church, descend to the **Grotto of the Nativity**, encased in white marble. Long lines can form at the entrance to the grotto, making the suggestion of spending just an hour to see the church an impossibility. Once a cave—precisely the kind of place that might have been used as a barn—the grotto has been reamed, plastered, and decorated beyond recognition. Immediately on the right is a small altar, and on the floor below it is the focal point of the entire site: a 14-point **silver star** with the Latin inscription "*hic de virgine maria jesus christus natus est*" (Here of the Virgin Mary, Jesus Christ was born). The Latins placed the original star here in 1717 but lost control of the altar 40 years later to the more influential Greek Orthodox. In 1847 the star mysteriously disappeared, and pressure from the Turkish sultan compelled the Greeks to allow the present Latin replacement to be installed in 1853. The Franciscan guardians do have possession, however, of the little alcove a few steps down on the left at the entrance to the grotto, said to be the manger where the infant Jesus was laid. ⊠ *Manger Sq.* ☎ *02/274-2440* ✉ *Free* ⊘ *Church: Apr.–Sept., daily 6:30 am–7:30 pm; Oct.–Mar., daily 5:30 am–5:30 pm. Grotto: Apr.–Sept., Mon.–Sat. 9–7:30, Sun. noon–7:30; Oct.–Mar., Mon.–Sat. 9–5:30, Sun. noon–5:30.*

CLOSE UP

The West Bank

The West Bank is that part of the onetime British Mandate of Palestine, west of the Jordan River, that was occupied by the Kingdom of Transjordan in its war with the nascent State of Israel in 1948 and annexed shortly afterward. That country then changed its name to the Hashemite Kingdom of Jordan to reflect its new geopolitical reality. The territory was lost to Israel in the Six-Day War of 1967.

Following the Oslo Accords in 1993, much of the West Bank has been turned over to the Palestinian Authority. In Israel itself, the region is often referred to as "the territories," "over the Green Line" (a term denoting the 1949 armistice line between the West Bank and Israel), or by its biblical names of Judea (the area south of Jerusalem) and Samaria (the much larger area north of Jerusalem).

The West Bank is a kidney-shape area, a bit larger than the U.S. state of Delaware. The large majority of the approximately 2 million Palestinians are Muslim, with the Christian minority living mostly in the greater Bethlehem area and Ramallah, and a tiny community of Samaritans living on Mt. Gerizim near Nablus.

While the Oslo Accords promised peace and final status discussions, a comprehensive agreement has proven elusive due to seemingly irreconcilable differences on the thorny issues of land, refugees, and Jerusalem. In late 2000, the simmering crisis exploded with lethal ferocity as young Palestinians took to the streets in riots known as the Second Intifada. In 2002, Israel began building a separation barrier roughly along the 1967 border. In 2005, Israel unilaterally withdrew from the Gaza Strip and four remote settlements in northern Samaria. Although violence has subsided significantly, some visitors still avoid the West Bank. Others, while exercising caution, visit such worthwhile West Bank sites as Bethlehem and Jericho.

In addition to the 2 million Arabs in the West Bank, half a million Israelis also live there in hundreds of small settlements and a number of cities. Although the cities and bigger towns are really suburbs of Jerusalem and Tel Aviv, nationalist Israelis who see the region as an integral and inalienable part of the biblical homeland set up other settlements.

With its prime location within 14 km (9 miles) of the Mediterranean Sea, and its mountain heights—dominating Israel's main population centers—the West Bank has a strategic value that has convinced even many Israelis that it would be folly to relinquish it to potentially hostile Arab control. Other Israelis favor some kind of two-state solution.

A person's attitude toward the questions of continuing settlement in the West Bank and the ultimate status of the region is an important touchstone of political affiliation in Israel. The country remains completely divided on these issues.

Tourists can travel to Bethlehem and Jericho as security conditions permit; they need to take passports with them. At this writing, Israeli citizens are prohibited from entering areas under full Palestinian control. Please check your government's travel advisory before visiting these areas.

Manger Square. Bethlehem's central plaza and the site of the Church of the Nativity, Manger Square is built over the grotto thought to be the birthplace of Jesus. The end of the square opposite the church is the Mosque of Omar, the city's largest Muslim house of worship. The square occupies the center of Bethlehem's Old City and has a tourist information office, several good souvenir shops, and restaurants where you can drink a coffee while people-watching.

Shepherds' Fields. Just east of Bethlehem is the town of Beit Sahour, famous in Christian tradition as home of the Shepherd's Field where herdsmen received "tidings of great joy" that Jesus was born in Bethlehem (Luke 2). The same fields are also said to be where the Biblical Ruth the Moabite, daughter-in-law of Naomi, "gleaned in the field" (Ruth 2:2). Local Christians disagree about where the real Shepherd's Fields are, and two chapels and gardens offer rival interpretations, complete with rival Byzantine relics. Entrance is free to both.

> ## CHRISTMAS IN BETHLEHEM
>
> In Bethlehem, Christmas is celebrated three times: December 25 by the Roman Catholics and Protestants; January 6 by the Greek, Coptic, and Russian Orthodox; and January 19 by the Armenian Orthodox. For nearly a month, Manger Square is brilliantly illuminated and bursting with life. On December 24, choirs from around the world perform carols and sacred music in the square between 8:30 pm and 11:30 pm, and at midnight at the Franciscan Church of St. Catherine. That service is relayed on closed-circuit television onto a large screen in Manger Square and, via satellite, to all parts of the globe.

The Greek Orthodox Der El Rawat Chapel is a small white building with a charming red dome; inside, bright paintings of the Stations of the Cross cover the walls and soaring ceilings. A mosaic dating to a 5th-century Byzantine church lies just outside. It's open Monday to Saturday 9 to 3. A Catholic church is a short walk away. This tiny, minimalist chapel is tucked away in a lush garden, with walking paths surrounded by soaring pines and bright aloe plants. Outside are a number of souvenir stores and coffee shops. It's open Monday to Saturday 8 to 5:30, Sunday 8 to 11 and 2 to 5:30. ⊠ *Beit Sahour.*

WORTH NOTING

Milk Grotto. Legend has it that when Mary stopped here to nurse the baby Jesus, a drop of milk fell on the floor in this cave-like grotto and the walls turned white. The grotto and the church above are beautiful, especially just before sunset when the light catches the stained-glass windows. ⊠ *Milk Grotto St.* ☎ *02/274–3867* ⛫ *Free* ☉ *Daily 8–5.*

Rachel's Tomb. This Israeli enclave in a Palestinian area is on the right shortly after passing through the border. The Bible relates that the matriarch Rachel, second and favorite wife of Jacob, died in childbirth on the outskirts of Bethlehem, "and Jacob set up a pillar upon her grave" (Genesis 35:19–20). There's no trace of that pillar, but observant Jews for centuries have hallowed the velvet-draped cenotaph inside the building as the site of Rachel's tomb. People come to pray here for good health, fertility, and a safe birth. Some pilgrims wind a red thread seven times around the tomb, and give away snippets of it as talismans to cure all ills.

Islam as well venerates Rachel. Next to the tomb is a Muslim cemetery, reflecting the Middle Eastern tradition that it's a special privilege to be buried near a great personage. Note that men and women are segregated here and have different entrances. Egged Bus 163 runs from Jerusalem to the tomb. The site is surrounded by a concrete barrier, so for access from Bethlehem you must return to Jerusalem. ✉ *Rte. 60* 🎟 *Free* 🕒 *Sun.–Wed., 12:30 am–10:30 pm, Thurs. 24 hrs., Fri. midnight–sunset; Sat. opens after nightfall.*

WHERE TO EAT

$ MIDDLE EASTERN Fodor's Choice ★

🍴 **Afteem.** Just off Manger Square, Afteem draws locals and tourists alike for its falafel, hummus, and chicken platters. Enjoy them sitting inside a stone cave or standing on the steps outside. Taybeh beer, local wine, and fresh fruit juices are available to wash it all down. The best part: the prices are unbeatable. [$] *Average main: NIS 25* ✉ *Manger Sq.* ☎ *02/274–7940* 💳 *No credit cards* 🕒 *Closed Sun.*

$$ MIDDLE EASTERN

🍴 **Ka'bar.** Just west of Bethlehem in Beit Jala, this flourescent-lit hole-in-the-wall has perfected the art of grilled chicken—a good thing, since it's the only item on the menu. The birds are butterflied and charred on a six-foot-long grill outside. Half or whole chickens are served with colorful salads, creamy hummus, and an unforgettable light garlic sauce whipped with olive oil. Taxi drivers can take you here from Manger Square, and it's worth the trip. [$] *Average main: NIS 50* ✉ *Near Municipality Bldg., Beit Jala* ☎ *02/274–1419* 💳 *No credit cards* 🕒 *Closed Sun.*

$ MIDDLE EASTERN Fodor's Choice ★

🍴 **Peace Center Restaurant.** Palestinian classics are the main draw at this eatery steps from the Church of the Nativity. Try the *maqloubeh,* a perfectly spiced and baked chicken leg served with a colorful pilaf of yellow rice and eggplant, cauliflower, and carrots. Another great option is *mensaf,* pieces of lamb in an aromatic goat yogurt sauce served over rice. Palestinian Taybeh beer is on tap, and the tiramisu is a refreshing treat to enjoy in Bethlehem's busiest square. [$] *Average main: NIS 40* ✉ *20 Manger Sq.* ☎ *059/518–7622.*

$ MIDDLE EASTERN

🍴 **Tent Restaurant.** Slip into a bright red chair, order an *argileh* water pipe, and wait for waiters in white shirts and black vests to bring out well-spiced grilled meats, hummus, and salads. This massive restaurant with wide windows is a great way to end a day of sightseeing. [$] *Average main: NIS 45* ✉ *Shepherd's Field St., Beit Sahour* ☎ *02/277–3875.*

$ MIDDLE EASTERN

🍴 **Wall Lounge.** The Israeli-built separation barrier can be a forboding presence in Bethlehem, but at this restaurant it's the canvas for the menu, a screen for outdoor movies, and the backdrop for sipping a beer on warm summer nights. It's especially lively here during soccer season. The simple menu includes hummus, hamburgers, and grilled meats. [$] *Average main: NIS 40* ✉ *Caritas St.* ☎ *02/745–4551* 💳 *No credit cards.*

WHERE TO STAY

$ HOTEL Fodor's Choice ★ **Jacir Palace InterContinental Bethlehem.** Bethlehem's most luxurious accommodation is in a century-old mansion, and the stunning stone building and five-star service will make you feel like a sultan. **Pros:** amazing atmosphere; excellent service; swimming pool. **Cons:** navigating the hallways can be tough; long walk to main Bethlehem sites. [$] *Rooms from: $190* ✉ *Jerusalem-Hebron Rd.* ☎ *02/276–6777* 🌐 *www.ihg.com* 🛏 *250 rooms, 5 suites* 🍴 *No meals.*

$ HOTEL **Saint Gabriel Hotel.** In the center of Bethlehem, this gleaming 10-story hotel offers great views of Bethlehem from the rooms and from the rooftop. **Pros:** comfortable rooms; affordable prices; great location. **Cons:** rooms can lack character; few amenities; double beds are two mattresses pressed together. [$] *Rooms from: $150* ✉ *Pope Paul VI St.* ☎ *02/275–9990* 🌐 *www.st-gabrielhotel.com* 🛏 *136 rooms* 🍴 *No meals.*

SHOPPING

In the city's 300 workshops, Bethlehem craftspeople make carved olive-wood and mother-of-pearl objects, mostly of a religious nature, but the many stores along the tourist route in town sell jewelry and trinkets. For quality and reliability, most of the large establishments on Manger Street are worth investigating, but some of the merchants near the Church of the Nativity, on Manger Square, have good-quality items as well.

Christmas House. At this olive-wood factory, Palestinian craftsmen whittle away at elaborate Nativity sculptures. The gracious owner is proud to show you exactly how the well-known souvenirs are made. Ask to go up to the roof, which offers a great view of Manger Square. The shop ships worldwide. Don't forget to bargain. ✉ *74 Milk Grotto St.* ☎ *02/275–7233* 🌐 *mychristmashouse.com.*

4

TEL AVIV

WELCOME TO TEL AVIV

TOP REASONS TO GO

★ **Exploring the neighbor-hoods:** Check out Neveh Tzedek's pastel-colored homes and boutiques, Jaffa's jumble of a flea market, Tel Aviv Port's undulating board-walk, and Florentine's urban hipster feel.

★ **Mediterranean beaches:** Hit the sand, walk along the promenade, or watch the sun dip into the Mediterranean with the locals in the evening.

★ **Bauhaus architecture:** Tel Aviv is also known as "The White City" because it is home to the largest concentration of Bauhaus architecture in the world. Explore it on a walking tour.

★ **Nahalat Binyamin Pedestrian Mall:** Stalls of this twice-weekly street fair offer a range of handmade crafts from pottery to jew-elry at reasonable prices.

★ **Israel's best modern cuisine:** Inventive chefs have put the city on the gastronomic map—all good news for the hun-gry traveling gourmet.

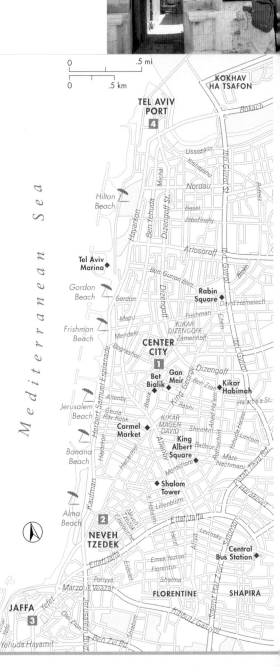

1 Center City. Most of Tel Aviv's major sites can be found in this warren of small side streets and hidden parks. Look for Rothschild Boulevard brimming with Bauhaus buildings, Carmel Market, and the Nahalat Binyamin Pedestrian Mall.

2 Neveh Tzedek. Restoration has meant a renaissance for this neighborhood of narrow roads lined with boutiques, galleries, and cafés. The Suzanne Dellal Centre for Dance and Theatre, with its orange-tree-studded square, is magical.

3 Jaffa. This port—where a certain whale is said to have swallowed Jonah—is one of the oldest in the world. Here you'll find a flea market crammed with antique furniture and a growing number of trendy boutiques and restaurants.

4 The Tel Aviv Port and Northern Tel Aviv. The abandoned warehouses of the Tel Aviv Port have been transformed into upscale restaurants, cafés, and clubs. Cyclists and strolling families pack the undulating boardwalk.

GETTING ORIENTED

Tel Aviv's compact size and flat landscape make it easy to get around on foot. The city's main north–south thoroughfares of Hayarkon, Ben Yehuda (which becomes Allenby), Dizengoff, and Ibn Gvirol streets run more or less parallel to the Mediterranean shoreline. Closest to the water is Hayarkon and the beachfront Tayelet (promenade). At the northern end of Hayarkon is the Tel Aviv Port. Most hotels are on the beachfront along Hayarkon.

4

BAUHAUS STYLE IN TEL AVIV

Viewing Bauhaus, the defining architectural style of Tel Aviv, is a great way to explore the city. The geometric forms and pastel colors of this modern design ethos, transplanted in the 1930s by Jewish architects fleeing Europe, fit both the landscape and Zionist notions of a socialist Utopia.

The rounded corner balconies, rooftop garden, and staircase with windows are classic Bauhaus elements in this restored building at 17 Emile Zola Street.

The so-called "White City," the central part of Tel Aviv that is home to the largest concentration of Bauhaus buildings, was named a World Cultural Heritage Site by UNESCO in 2003. Bauhaus-inspired architecture, more accurately referred to as the Modern or International Style, was based on the idea that art should serve society and that form should also have function. For example, balconies were not designed to be merely decorative but to serve as a source of shade, fresh air, and a place from which to interact with neighbors. Today conservation efforts are making headway, but many classic buildings need repair, their beauty lost under peeling paint and cracked concrete. It's a work in progress as the city offers incentives to owners to restore their properties.

STYLE ELEMENTS

Signature **vertical staircases** offset horizontal lines and are recognizable by the steel-frame windows that provide light. **Roof gardens**, identifiable by pergolas of beams and columns, were designed with the expectation that neighbors would socialize on their rooftops. **Balconies** can be curved or square or rectangular in shape, and are often overhung with ledges that provide shade.

A BAUHAUS WALK

The city's Bauhaus bounty is best discovered by foot. A good place to stroll is along **Rothschild Boulevard** and its side streets, which also have pleasant cafés and restaurants. A walking tour can begin at **No. 90**, at the corner of Balfour Street. Here a three-story, mustard-colored building, with the clean lines that are a trademark of the style, stands in contrast to the highly decorated building next door. Note the front door with horizontal strips of wood inlaid in the glass. Its wooden shutters aren't necessarily an element that would be seen in European Bauhaus examples, but here became a necessity because of the sun. Walk to **Nos. 89 and 91**, twin buildings in need of renovation, and see the small vertical windows indicating the placement of a central staircase and the two main styles of balcony, rounded and rectangular.

Walk back across the boulevard and look for **Engel Street**, a pedestrian-friendly lane lined with Bauhaus buildings. **No. 7** features horizontal bands of balconies and windows. The front door has an asymmetrical overhang and canopy. For an example of the city's restoration efforts, look up to its top floor, which continues the horizontal theme.

Returning to Rothschild Boulevard, walk to **Nos. 113 and 115**. Here again you can see the "thermometer" staircase and its small, elegant windows. On the right-hand side the balconies wrap around the building, mimicking the corner of the street; on the left-hand side the balconies are aligned with the side of the building.

SEEING MORE

Check the city tourist office for free Bauhaus walking tours. The **Bauhaus Center** at 99 Dizengoff Street sells books and more, and offers excellent walking tours. Another resource is the **Bauhaus Foundation Museum** at 21 Bialik Street, open Wednesday and Friday. Bialik Street has many attractive older buildings. Exploring on your own? Here are a few key buildings around the city.
9 Gordon St., 1935. Take in its elegant cube-within-a-cube design, wooden shutters, and rooftop pergola.
Haaretz Print Works, 56 Mazeh St., 1934. The building where *Haaretz* newspaper was once printed has steel-framed glass windows and balconies with rounded railings and cantilevered roofs.
25 Idelson St., 1931. Designed as a family villa: note a mix of balconies, the asymmetric form, and the mix of small horizontal and vertical windows.

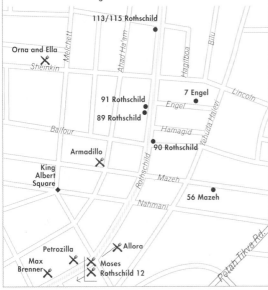

Updated by
Inbal Baum

Tel Aviv, Israel's ever-growing metropolis, would be unrecognizable to its founders, a small group of Jewish immigrant families in what was then Ottoman-ruled Palestine. A skyline of shimmering skyscrapers has replaced the towering sand dunes of just over a century ago. The city is now known for its boxy Bauhaus apartment buildings, theaters, and concert halls, as well as its legions of sidewalk cafés that host overflowing crowds every night of the week.

The city manages to pull off the seemingly impossible task of being both hip and homey: witness the happy mix of wine bars, clothing boutiques, hardware shops, and greengrocers—often on the same block. High-end restaurants mingle with old-school eateries where elderly men hold noisy court about the issues of the day over black coffee and apple turnovers.

Sometimes described as an urban village, Tel Aviv is made for walking (or biking, now that it has an extensive network of more than 100 km [62 miles] of bike paths and a bike-share system). From most parts of the city, the sea is never more than a 20-minute walk. In this combination beach town, business center, and arts mecca, people spend Friday afternoons bumping into friends, wandering from café to café, and pausing to hear live jazz trios, all the while strolling with their dogs down boulevards lined with 1940s-era newspaper kiosks that have been transformed into gourmet sandwich stands.

Tel Aviv isn't the most beautiful of cities, although its charms have a way of making you forgive its aesthetic shortcomings. It was declared a UNESCO World Cultural Heritage Site in 2003 because its collection of International-Style architecture, known more commonly as Bauhaus, is the largest in the world. Although restoration efforts are moving along, many of these buildings are in need of a face-lift. It might take an hour or two of wandering on the tree-lined side streets for you to appreciate their graceful lines and subtle architectural flourishes.

There's a spirit of freedom in Tel Aviv, where it's possible to escape from the difficult political realities that are closer to the surface in places like Jerusalem. After all, the city's nickname among Israelis is "the Bubble." Residents tend to be politically and socially liberal. The gay scene is thriving, as are the arts and music communities. It's an exciting city, one that newcomers, returning visitors, and longtime residents all find captivating.

TEL AVIV PLANNER

WHEN TO GO

Tel Aviv's mild Mediterranean climate means that any time is a good time to visit. Nevertheless, midday summer temperatures in the 90s may mean choosing museums and other air-conditioned sites until the sun dips and the sea breeze stirs. Weekends (in Israel this means Thursday nights, Fridays, and Saturdays) are the busiest times, but also the most fun in terms of people-watching and special events.

PLANNING YOUR TIME

With two to four days, you can explore most of Tel Aviv and still have time for the beach. Although it's not a huge area to cover, see the city in geographical order. Start with Old Jaffa in the south, and amble through the art galleries, flea market, and fishing port. Jaffa's a good choice in the evening for strolling, low-key restaurants, and wine bars. From here, it's a quick walk north to see Neveh Tzedek. Check out the well-restored buildings, and catch a performance at the Suzanne Dellal Centre at night. In the center of town, don't miss the Bauhaus buildings of the White City or the Nahalat Binyamin market (on Tuesday or Friday). With more time, explore the north, and see the Diaspora, the Palmach, and the Eretz Israel museums, as well as Hayarkon Park for boating or cycling. The Tel Aviv Port is a good place for trendy dining and nightlife.

GETTING HERE AND AROUND

BIKE TRAVEL

Tel Aviv has more than 100 km (62 miles) of designated bike lanes and a user-friendly bike rental system called Tel-O-Fun. Look for the bright green bike stands throughout the city. The basic access fee is NIS 17 Sunday through Friday, NIS 23 on Saturday and on holidays. There's even a weekly basic access fee of NIS 70. Beyond the access fee, you pay an extra fee based on how long you keep the bike: NIS 10 for up to 90 minutes, NIS 70 for 3.5 hours, for example.

BUS TRAVEL

Buses are run primarily by Dan, and also by Egged. The fare is a fixed NIS 6.60 within the city center, and you buy your tickets on the bus. There's a small discount for a 10-ride card. Combined train-and-bus tickets are also available. Privately run minibuses, called "service taxis," run along two of the major lines: Bus 4 (Ben Yehuda and Allenby streets) and Bus 5 (Dizengoff Street and Rothschild Boulevard). You can flag these down and ask to get off at any point along their routes; the fare is the same as on regular buses. Minibuses also run on Saturday, when regular buses don't. Buses leave for Jerusalem every 15 minutes throughout most of the day.

Bus Contacts Dan ☏ *03/639–4444* ⊕ *www.dan.co.il.*
Egged ☏ *03/694–8888* ⊕ *www.egged.co.il.*

CAR TRAVEL

Driving in Tel Aviv isn't for the fainthearted; Israeli drivers are aggressive, and motorbikes weave in and out of traffic. Major highways lead in and out of Tel Aviv: Route 1 from Jerusalem, Route 4 from the northern coast, and Route 5 from the east. Take advantage of Tel Aviv's belt road, the Ayalon Freeway, to access various parts of the city.

TAXI TRAVEL

From the airport, the fastest and easiest way into the city is by taxi, and costs NIS 140. During rush hour, allow 45 minutes for a trip that would otherwise be 20 minutes.

Taxis can be any car model or color and have lighted signs on top. They're plentiful, even in bad weather; drivers honk to catch your attention, even if you're not trying to catch theirs. If traveling within the metropolitan area, make sure the driver turns the meter on when you get in. Rates are NIS 11.10 for the first 18 seconds and 30 *agorot* in increments thereafter. *Sherut* taxis consist mainly of a fleet of vans at the Central Bus Station that run the same routes as the buses, at comparable one-way prices. They run on Saturday at a higher charge.

TRAIN TRAVEL

From the airport, the train is a money saver for NIS 15 and takes about 20 minutes.

The train is an excellent way to travel between Tel Aviv and cities and towns to the north, such as Netanya, Hadera, Haifa, and Nahariya. To Jerusalem, buses are a better option until the high-speed line is completed. Northbound trains depart from the Central Railway Station and the Azrieli Station. Trains run roughly every hour on weekdays from between 5 am and 6 am to between 10 pm and 11 pm depending on the destination; there are fewer trains on Friday and Jewish holiday eves and no service on Saturday or on holidays. There's also a line to Beersheva. The information office is open Sunday to Thursday 6 am to 11 pm and Friday 6 to 3.

Train Contacts Central Railway Station ✉ *Arlozoroff St.* ☏ *03/611–7000* ⊕ *www.rail.co.il/en.*

RESTAURANTS

Tel Aviv is very much a café society. Locals of all ages love their morning, afternoon, and evening coffee time—so much so that it's often hard to get a seat. The city's cosmopolitan character is reflected in its restaurants, which offer cuisines from around the world. Still occupying many street corners are stands selling delicious Middle Eastern fast food—such as falafel (patties made from chickpeas) and shawarma (spit-grilled meat).

HOTELS

The major hotels along Hayarkon Street are right on the Tayelet next to the beach. Staying at a boutique hotel in a restored historic building adds a wonderful accent to the Tel Aviv experience. Most of the city's hotels are only a short distance from most major attractions.

TOURS

The Tel Aviv–Jaffa Municipality has laid out three self-guided tours. The White Route relates Tel Aviv's history, the Blue Route its coastline, and the Green Route its natural wonders. Free, city-sponsored walking tours sponsored by the Tel Aviv–Jaffa Municipality are available as follows: Old Jaffa, beginning at the clock tower on Wednesday at 10 am; neighborhood evening historical tour beginning at the corner of Rothschild Boulevard and Herzl Street, Tuesday at 8 pm; and the Bauhaus White City, Saturday at 11 am, beginning at 46 Rothschild Boulevard. No prior registration is required.

Twelve Tribes provides personal guides, usually with a car, who will take you anywhere in the city and even around the country. Personal guides can also be arranged through most hotels. Kefland runs a half-hour boat tour on Saturday year-round, from the Jaffa Port along the Tel Aviv waterfront and back. The fare is NIS 25. Another great way to learn about Tel Aviv is through its food. The culinary tour company Delicious Israel offers private walking tours that let you experience the food and the history of the city.

Tour Information Delicious Israel ☎ *052/569–9499* ⊕ *www.deliciousisrael.com.* **Kefland** ✉ *Jaffa Port* ☎ *03/682–9070* ⊕ *www.kefland.co.il.* **Tel Aviv–Jaffa Municipality** ☎ *03/516–6188* ⊕ *www.tel-aviv.gov.il.* **Twelve Tribes** ✉ *29 Hamered St.* ☎ *03/510–1911* ⊕ *www.twelve-tribes.co.il.*

VISITOR INFORMATION

The Israeli Government Tourist Office operates a 24-hour information desk in the arrivals hall at Ben Gurion Airport that will make same-day reservations. The city tourist office, on the oceanfront promenade, stocks maps of walking tours around the city and is open Sunday to Thursday 9:30 to 5:30, Friday 9:30 to 1.

Information Israel Government Tourist Office ☎ *03/975–4260* ⊕ *www.goisrael.com.* **Tel Aviv Tourist Information Office** ✉ *46 Herbert Samuel St.* ☎ *03/516–6188.*

EXPLORING TEL AVIV

From the city center, it's easy to head south to Jaffa and its ancient port and lively flea market—to get there the scenic way, saunter along the seaside promenade overlooking the beach—and the other southern neighborhoods like the gentrified Neveh Tzedek and the more rough-edged Florentine.

Even farther north, at the edge of Tel Aviv proper, lies the sprawling green lung of Tel Aviv, Hayarkon Park. You'll also discover the city's recently renovated port area, an ideal setting for a seaside breakfast or a toast at sunset with which to usher in Tel Aviv's infamous inexhaustible nightlife.

CENTER CITY

Think of downtown Tel Aviv as a cat's cradle of boulevards and side streets leading to all of the city's great sights. These few square miles are the heart and soul of the city. Swirling around you might be surfers heading up from the beach, film crews shooting commercials, and couples walking their dogs along leafy boulevards. At Hayarkon Park, a welcome swath of green on the Yarkon River, families picnic not far from joggers and bikers on well-paved paths.

GETTING HERE AND AROUND

Most of the main bus lines travel through the center of the city, but two in particular are of interest to travelers: Bus 4 on Ben Yehuda Street and Bus 5 on Dizengoff Street. Both run at frequent intervals. Both of these thoroughfares also have minibuses that can be hailed like taxis and are often an even faster option for getting around. The flat landscape makes strolling along streets like Dizengoff, King George, Rothschild, and Ibn Gvirol very easy.

TIMING AND PRECAUTIONS

Give yourself the better part of a day to savor this part of the city, as there is a lot to see. It's well lighted at night and is considered safe for evening strolls.

TOP ATTRACTIONS

Bauhaus Foundation Museum. Those who love architecture won't want to miss this one-room museum on historic Bialik Street. It occupies the ground floor of an original Bauhaus building, built in 1934 and home to the Bauhaus Foundation. Visitors discover that the pristine lines and basic geometric forms typical of the Bauhaus school extend to everyday objects as well, from furniture to light fixtures to glazed stoneware. There's even a door handle designed by Walter Gropius (1883–1969), founder and first director of the Bauhaus. ⊠ *21 Bialik St., Center City* ☎ *03/620–4664* ⊠ *Free* ☉ *Wed. 11–5, Fri. 10–2.*

Fodor's Choice ★ **Beit Ha'ir.** Catch up on Tel Aviv's remarkable history at this historical museum in the original 1924 municipal building, an architectural masterpiece that has been lovingly restored. Among the exhibits highlighting the progress of the last century is a brief film tracing the city's development from huts in the sand to gleaming apartment towers. There's also a pretty patchwork floor made up of colorful tiles typical of vintage Tel Aviv buildings and the restored office of the city's first mayor, Meir Dizengoff, with the original map of Tel Aviv hanging on a wall. ⊠ *27 Bialik St., Center City* ☎ *03/525–3403* ⊕ *www.beithair. org* ⊠ *NIS 20* ☉ *Mon. and Tues. 9–5, Thurs. 9–8, Fri. and Sat. 10–2.*

Fodor's Choice ★ **Carmel Market.** The first section of Carmel Market (commonly referred to as the *shuk*) consists of cheap clothing, but continue farther down to the fruit and vegetable section, where the real show begins. Vendors loudly hawk their fresh produce, and the crowded aisles reveal Israel's incredible ethnic mix. Don't pass by the small side streets filled with unusual treats. The market is the most fun on Tuesday or Friday, when it can be combined with a visit to the Nahalat Binyamin Pedestrian Mall's crafts fair. ⊠ *Along Hacarmel St., Center City* ☉ *Sun.–Thurs. 7am–sunset; Fri. 7 am–2 hrs before sunset.*

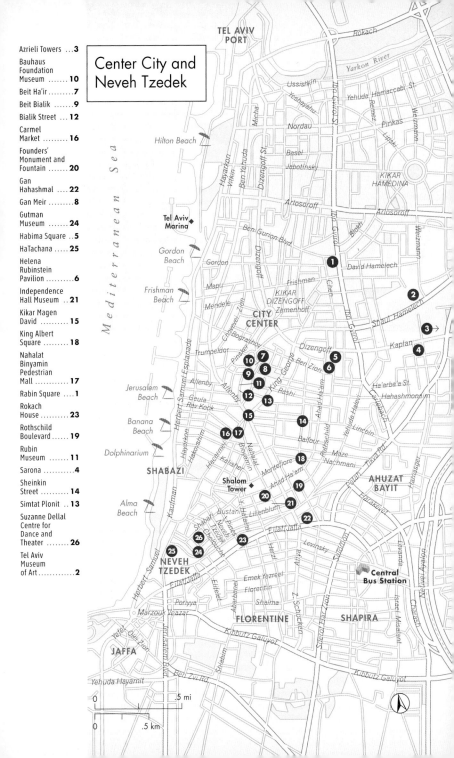

Azrieli Towers ...**3**

Bauhaus Foundation Museum **10**

Beit Ha'ir **7**

Beit Bialik **9**

Bialik Street ...**12**

Carmel Market **16**

Founders' Monument and Fountain **20**

Gan Hahashmal **22**

Gan Meir **8**

Gutman Museum **24**

Habima Square ..**5**

HaTachana **25**

Helena Rubinstein Pavilion **6**

Independence Hall Museum ..**21**

Kikar Magen David ...**15**

King Albert Square **18**

Nahalat Binyamin Pedestrian Mall **17**

Rabin Square **1**

Rokach House **23**

Rothschild Boulevard **19**

Rubin Museum **11**

Sarona **4**

Sheinkin Street **14**

Simtat Plonit ..**13**

Suzanne Dellal Centre for Dance and Theater **26**

Tel Aviv Museum of Art **2**

Center City and Neveh Tzedek

A crowd enjoys the folk music and the sunshine on the Promenade Tayelet.

Gan Hahashmal. This hip neighborhood—great for window-shopping—started with a collective of designers who settled into what was then a rundown area and spruced it up with boutiques, restaurants, cafés, and bars. Surrounding a former power plant that's been transformed into a small park, this is where you'll find the country's best up-and-coming designers. ⊠ *Barzilai St. at HaHashmal St., Center City.*

NEED A BREAK?

Yemenite Quarter. The Carmel Market and Allenby Road border the Yemenite Quarter, which hides several cheap and satisfying kosher restaurants offering shawarma and skewered meats. Wash your meal down with a beer as you gaze out onto the neighborhood's warren of cobblestone lanes. Some streets that are nice to stroll include Nahliel and Haim Havshush, lined with restaurants serving tasty hummus and Yemenite flatbread. This is a soothing place for a stroll on a Friday afternoon, when all the eateries are closing for the Sabbath.

FAMILY **Habima Square.** Here you'll find a number of cultural institutions, including the Habima Theatre, Mann Auditorium, and the Helena Rubinstein Pavilion for Contemporary Art. A great place for kids to run around, the square also has a relaxation garden with music wafting from the ecologically designed seating. ⊠ *Rothschild Blvd. at Marmorek St., Center City.*

Independence Hall Museum. This impressive building was originally the home of the city's first mayor, Meir Dizengoff. The country's leaders assembled here on May 14, 1948, to announce to the world the establishment of the State of Israel. Today the museum's **Hall of Declaration** stands as it did on that dramatic day, with the original microphones on the long table where the dignitaries sat. Behind the table is a portrait of the Zionist leader Theodor Herzl. ✉ *16 Rothschild Blvd., Center City* ☎ *03/517–3942* 🎫 *NIS 20* ⏰ *Sun.–Thurs. 9–5, Fri. 9–2.*

Fodor'sChoice ★ **Nahalat Binyamin Pedestrian Mall.** Everything from plastic trinkets to handmade silver jewelry can be found at this bustling street market, open on Tuesday and Friday. A profusion of buskers compete to entertain you. For a finishing touch of local color, cafés serving cakes and light meals line the street. At the end of the fair is a large Bedouin tent, where you can treat yourself to a *laffa* with *labaneh* and *za'atar* (large pita bread with tangy sour cream, sprinkled with hyssop, an oregano-like herb). ✉ *Nahalat Binyamin St., off Allenby St., Center City* ⏰ *Tues. and Fri. until sundown.*

> **WORD OF MOUTH**
>
> "Be sure to go to Independence Hall. There was a well-done movie there that gave an overview of the history of Tel Aviv, and an excellent docent who gave a talk on why Independence Hall in Tel Aviv was chosen to announce the Independence of Israel, and details about that day."
>
> —jgg

Fodor'sChoice ★ **Rothschild Boulevard.** Half a century ago, this magnificent tree-lined boulevard was one of the most exclusive streets in the city. Today it's once again what visionaries at the beginning of the 20th century meant it to be—a place for people to meet, stroll, and relax. Alongside the street are some of the city's best restaurants and bars, and many Bauhaus gems are on or just off the street.

Rubin Museum. Recognized as one of Israel's major painters, Reuven Rubin (1893–1974) bequeathed his house to Tel Aviv along with 45 of his works, which make up the permanent collection. The house, built in 1930, is now an art gallery, with changing exhibits by Israeli artists. Upstairs is a small but well-stocked art library where you can pore over press clippings and browse through art books. A moving audiovisual presentation tells the story of Rubin's life, and his original studio can still be seen on the third floor. ✉ *14 Bialik St., Center City* ☎ *03/525–5961* ⊕ *www.rubinmuseum.org.il* 🎫 *NIS 20* ⏰ *Mon., Wed., and Thurs. 10–3, Tues. 10–8, Sat. 11–2.*

Sarona. Shaded by leafy trees, this area was formerly an agricultural colony established by German Templars in 1871. The picturesque houses are being transformed into a complex with a visitor center, restaurants, bars, boutiques, and cultural institutions. ✉ *Kaplan St., near Begin Rd., Center City* ☎ *03/609–9028* ⊕ *www.saronatlv.co.il.*

Tel Aviv Museum of Art. This museum houses a fine collection of national and international art, including works by prominent Jewish artists like Marc Chagall and Roy Lichtenstein. There's also an impressive French impressionist collection and many sculptures by Aleksandr Archipenko. A bright and airy wing opened in 2011, doubling the exhibition space. The gift shop sells unique pieces of jewelry and other items that make memorable souvenirs. ✉ *27 Shaul Hamelech Blvd., Center City* ☎ *03/607–7020* ⊕ *www.tamuseum.com* 🎫 *NIS 42* ⏰ *Mon., Wed., and Sat. 10–4, Tues. and Thurs. 10–10, Fri. 10–2.*

Low-rise Bauhaus-style buildings are common in parts of central Tel Aviv.

WORTH NOTING

Azrieli Towers. A spectacular 360-degree view of Tel Aviv and beyond awaits on the 49th-floor observation deck of this office building and mall complex, which consists of three buildings—one triangular, one circular, and one square. Call ahead, as it sometimes closes early for special events. ✉ *Ayalon Fwy., Hashalom Exit West, Center City* ☎ *03/608–1179* ⊕ *www.mitzpe49.co.il* ⊠ *NIS 22 for observatory* ⊗ *Sun.–Fri. 9:30 am–10 pm.*

Beit Bialik (*Bialik House*). Spiffed up for the city's centennial, Bialik House is the charming two-story home of Chaim Nachman Bialik (1873–1934), considered the father of Hebrew poetry. The original bold colors were restored, as were many of the original furnishings. Bialik was already a respected poet and publisher by the time he moved to Tel Aviv from Russia in 1924; in the remaining 10 years of his life, his house, built in 1927, became the intellectual center of Tel Aviv. It's said that when Bialik lived here, the street was closed to traffic in the afternoon in order to let him write in peace and quiet. English-language tours can be arranged in advance. ✉ *22 Bialik St., Center City* ☎ *03/525–3403* ⊗ *Mon. and Tues. 9–5, Thurs. 9–8, Fri. and Sat. 10–2.*

Bialik Street. This area has been more successful than many other Tel Aviv neighborhoods in maintaining its older buildings. Bialik has long been a popular address with many of the city's artists and literati, so it's not surprising that some of the houses have been converted into small museums, including Beit Ha'ir, Beit Bialik, the Rubin Museum, and the Bauhaus Foundation Museum. Here you'll find a **mosaic**, designed by artist Nahum Gutman, which depicts the history of the city from the ancient days of Jaffa to the rise of Tel Aviv. Gutman was among the elite group of Tel Aviv's first artists.

Founders' Monument and Fountain. Dedicated in 1949, the Founders' Monument honors those who founded Tel Aviv. This large slab of stone also encapsulates the city's past in three copper bas-relief panels representing the earliest pioneer days of planting and building as well as modern architecture. ⊠ *Rothschild Blvd., at Nahalat Binyamin St., Center City.*

FAMILY **Gan Meir.** You're virtually guaranteed a traffic jam on this section of King George Street not far from Dizengoff Center, but you can get a respite by sitting on one of Gan Meir's benches, shaded by beautiful old trees. The first trees were planted in 1936 when the city offered to name the park after its first mayor, Meir Dizengoff, in honor of his 70th birthday. The feisty Dizengoff objected, so the park only got its official name in 1944, years after he passed away. There's a large playground for kids and an enclosed dog run. ⊠ *King George and Hashmonim Sts., Center City.*

Helena Rubinstein Pavilion. This annex of the Tel Aviv Museum of Art houses changing contemporary exhibits in an intimate space that's perfect for one-person shows. It's also a great escape from the midday sun. ⊠ *6 Tarsat St., Center City* 🕾 *03/528–7196* ⊕ *www.tamuseum.com* 🎫 *Free* 🕙 *Mon., Wed., and Sat. 10–4, Tues. and Thurs. 10–10, Fri. 10–2.*

Kikar Magen David. This meeting point of six streets is named for the six-point Magen David, or Star of David. Faded historic buildings flank it on one side, shops and eateries on the other. It's the gateway to the Carmel Market, the open-air fruit and vegetable market. Musicians and street performers find their way to the open area in the middle of the hustle and bustle. ⊠ *King George and Allenby Sts., Center City.*

King Albert Square. Named for the Belgian monarch who was a personal friend of Mayor Dizengoff, this prominent square is surrounded by some interesting monuments. The Bauhaus-style Pagoda House, now a luxury apartment building, was built as a private home in 1924. The rooftop ornament gives the building its name. Inside the elegant stairwell of Shifrin House, at 2 Melchett Street, are crumbling remnants of frescoes of the Western Wall and Rachel's Tomb. ⊠ *Nahmani and Montefiore Sts., Center City.*

Rabin Square. The square was renamed for Prime Minister Yitzhak Rabin after he was assassinated here on November 4, 1995. Passersby often pause at the small monument of black stones, rippled and uneven as if after an earthquake. This quiet memorial is the work of Israeli artist Danny Karavan. The southeast corner of the square is a great place to grab a coffee and enjoy the interesting people-watching. ⊠ *Ibn Gvirol St., Center City.*

Sheinkin Street. This popular thoroughfare off Allenby Street has plenty of cafés and restaurants where you can watch passersby. This is where young people shop for the latest fashions: the sizes are tiny, the favored color is black, and some of the boutiques are so miniscule you'll think you walked straight into the dressing room. Street performances add to the boisterous fun (though it's hard to see much through the crowds).

Simtat Plonit. Wander down this alley to see old Tel Aviv decorative architecture at its best. Two plaster obelisks at the entrance mark the city's first "gated" community. Note the stucco lion in front of **Number 7,** which used to have glowing eyes fitted with lightbulbs. The original apartment house is painted pale yellow with garish orange trim. An outspoken builder named Meir Getzel Shapira bought Simtat Plonit in the 1920s and insisted that this pint-size street be named after him. Tel Aviv's first mayor, Meir Dizengoff, argued that another street already had that name. The mayor emerged victorious and named it Simtat Plonit, meaning "John Doe Street."

NEVEH TZEDEK

Neveh Tzedek is a prime tourist destination because of its restaurants, cafés, cultural life, and historic buildings. Not surprisingly, it's where you'll find the fantastic dance and theater complex, the Suzanne Dellal Centre, as well as a growing number of trendy galleries and boutiques. Though bordered on three sides by major thoroughfares (Eilat Road to the south, Herzl Street to the west, and Kaufman Street along the sea), this quarter is very tranquil.

Made up of about a dozen tiny streets crammed with one- and two-story dwellings in various stages of renovation, Neveh Tzedek is rich with history. This is where the saga of Tel Aviv began, when a small group of Jewish families from Jaffa laid the cornerstone for their new neighborhood, naming it Neveh Tzedek (Dwellings of Justice). When Tel Aviv was busy expanding to the north and the east in the early days of the state, Neveh Tzedek was allowed to deteriorate. But in recent years the beautiful old buildings were rediscovered, and the lovingly restored homes here are now among the most prestigious addresses in the city.

GETTING HERE AND AROUND

The spine of Neveh Tzedek is Shabazi Street, which runs the length of the neighborhood. Most shops and restaurants are either on or near Shabazi Street. The roads here are notoriously narrow, and pedestrians have the right of way.

TIMING AND PRECAUTIONS

Neveh Tzedek is the perfect place to spend a few leisurely hours exploring the interesting shops and tasty eateries. The neighborhood can get pretty crowded on weekends, and most of the action is in the bars and restaurants along and around Shabazi Street.

TOP ATTRACTIONS

HaTachana. On the edge of Neveh Tzedek, this Turkish-era train station is where travelers once embarked to Jerusalem on the first piece of railroad in the Middle East. Even Theodor Herzl, founder of modern Zionism, passed through here. Dubbed HaTachana, Hebrew for "The Station," it recently reopened to the public after a NIS 100 million renovation.

If you're looking for a "bird's-eye" view of the city, it doesn't get better than from the top of the Azrieli Towers.

Situated on 49 acres, the complex includes 22 different buildings, among them the former station that now houses art exhibits. A pair of restored train cars tells the story of the station's days as a major travel hub in the region. You'll also find restaurants, cafés, and boutiques peddling handcrafted jewelry and homegrown designer clothes. At the entrance is a tourist information stand. ⊠ *Koifman and Ha'Mered Sts., Neveh Tzedek* ⊕ *www.hatachana.co.il* ✉ *Free* ☉ *Sat.–Thurs. 10–10; Fri. 10–5.*

Fodor's Choice
★
Suzanne Dellal Centre for Dance and Theatre. A pair of whitewashed buildings—one built in 1892, the other in 1908—make up this attractive complex. The square, designed by foremost landscape designer Shlomo Aronson, has hints of a medieval Middle Eastern courtyard in its scattering of orange trees connected by water channels. One side of the square is decorated with a tile triptych, which illustrates the neighborhood's history and famous people who lived here in the early years, including S. Y. Agnon, who went on to win the Nobel Prize in Literature. There's a café-bar on the premises and a number of great restaurants nearby for pre- or postperformance meals. ⊠ *6 Yehieli St., near Shabazi St., Neveh Tzedek* ☎ *03/510–5656* ⊕ *www.suzannedellal.org.il.*

WORTH NOTING

Gutman Museum. In the 1920s, a number of Tel Aviv's most famous writers lived in this building, whose renovations have somewhat obscured its original look. One of the first houses in Neveh Tzedek, the building now displays the art of Nahum Gutman, colorful chronicler of early Tel Aviv. Tours in English are available by prearrangement. ⊠ *21 Rokach St., Neveh Tzedek* ☎ *03/510–8554* ⊕ *www.gutmanmuseum.co.il* ✉ *NIS 24* ☉ *Mon.–Thurs. 10–4, Fri. 10–2, Sat. 10–3.*

A Focus on the Arts

For a tiny nation, Israel has a thriving and abundant arts scene. The country is home to thousands of classical musicians—many of whom emigrated from the former Soviet states—and the Israel Philharmonic Orchestra has a world-class reputation.

A number of music festivals are held annually, drawing international crowds—from the Red Sea Jazz Festival, in the south, to the Voice of Music chamber music event and Jacob's Ladder Folk Festival, in the north.

Israeli theater, too, enjoys a significant following. There are six professional repertory theaters—including the Habima and the Cameri in Tel Aviv—and dozens of regional and amateur companies performing throughout the country. They perform almost exclusively in Hebrew.

Professional dance companies also abound in Israel today. The Suzanne Dellal Centre for Dance and Theatre in Tel Aviv is the primary venue and home to the Batsheva Dance Company, the national dance troupe.

Folk dancing has always been popular in Israel—in fact, it's an evolving art form. As well as "Israeli" folk dancing (really a blend of Jewish and non-Jewish folk dance forms from around the world), some of Israel's different ethnic groups have preserved their traditional dances.

Enthusiasm for the visual arts can be seen in all walks of Israeli life, including the burgeoning gallery scene and extensive amount of street graffiti. A wide range of Israeli art can be viewed at the Israel Museum in Jerusalem, the Tel Aviv Museum of Art, and the Ramat Gan Art Museum. Small galleries abound; a large concentration can be found on Gordon Street in Tel Aviv and in Old Jaffa.

Rokach House. The home of Neveh Tzedek founder Shimon Rokach had fallen into disrepair and was slated for demolition before being reclaimed and restored by his grandaughter, artist Leah Majaro-Mintz. It now houses an exhibit of items from the quarter's early days, as well as pieces of her own art. Guided tours in English are available by calling ahead. A cabaret-style performance (in Hebrew) showcasing Neveh Tzedek's history, preceded by samples of the period's cuisine, is offered on Thursday and Friday evening at 8:30 pm. ⊠ *36 Rokach St., Neveh Tzedek* ☎ *03/516–8042* ⊕ *www.rokach-house.co.il* ✉ *NIS 10* ۝ *Sun.– Thurs. 10–4, Fri. and Sat. 10–2.*

JAFFA

Part of the sprawling municipality of Tel Aviv, the ancient port city of Jaffa is a mix of Jews, Christians, and Muslims. It's an ideal place for strolling down cobblestone streets and for dining at one of the no-frills fish restaurants that line the quay. Don't miss the Old City, where art galleries and shops occupy the centuries-old buildings along the narrow roads. At the Jaffa Flea Market, you can be part of the trading and bargaining for treasures—real and perceived—that are a hallmark of the Middle East.

Andromeda's
Rock 1

Clock Tower
Square 7

Design Museum
Holon 12

El-Mahmoudiye
Mosque 6

Ilana Goor
Museum 8

Jaffa Flea
Market 10

Jaffa Port 2

Kedumim
Square 3

St. Peter's
Monastery 4

San Antonio
Roman Catholic
Church 11

Summit Park 5

Weizmann Institute
of Science 13

Yefet Street 9

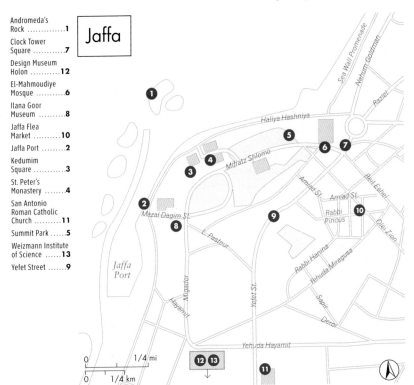

The streets around Clock Tower Square bustle on weekday afternoons, when schoolchildren stop by the open-air eateries for flaky pastries, and weekend evenings, when the bars empty out and their patrons are in search of a late-night bite. An oceanfront promenade connects Tel Aviv with Jaffa. The sprawling park that runs parallel to the promenade was once a landfill, but is now one of the city's greenest areas. Kids love the playgrounds and vast stretches of grass.

South of Jaffa are two worthwhile excursions. Design Museum Holon, in the suburb of that name, is an exciting contemporary art museum. A bit farther south, in Rehovot, is the Weizmann Institute of Science.

Some historians claim that Jaffa was named after its founder, Japhet, son of Noah; others think its name is from the Hebrew *yafeh* (beautiful). What's certain is its status as one of the world's oldest ports—perhaps the oldest. The Bible says the cedars used in the construction of the Holy Temple passed through Jaffa on their way to Jerusalem; the prophet Jonah set off from Jaffa before being swallowed by the whale; and St. Peter raised Tabitha from the dead here. Napoléon was but one of a succession of invaders who brought the city walls down; these walls were rebuilt for the last time in the early 19th century by the Turks and torn down yet again as recently as 1879.

GETTING HERE AND AROUND

From central Tel Aviv, Dan Buses 18 and 10 take you to Jaffa. You can also walk or bike along the seafront promenade to get here. A cab ride costing about 50 shekels will also get you to Jaffa.

TIMING AND PRECAUTIONS

Some areas in Jaffa can feel deserted at night. Although the flea market and the port area are safe, at night you should stay away from dark streets and avoid walking alone.

TOP ATTRACTIONS

Jaffa Flea Market. One of many small bazaars surrounding the clock tower in the mid-19th century, the Jaffa Flea Market is the only survivor of that era. Along the cobblestone streets you can find everything from European antiques to Israeli memorabilia. Clothing designers have opened boutiques on its alleys. The market's main street is **Olei Zion**, but there are a number of smaller streets and arcades to explore at your leisure, so take your time. Watch the locals bargain, and do what they do: *never* agree to the first price a seller demands. ⊠ *Olei Zion St., Jaffa* ⊗ *Sun.–Fri. 9–4.*

NEED A BREAK?

Capitolina Ice Cream. An artisanal ice-cream shop in every sense of the word, this shop makes everything using fresh ingredients from the nearby markets. A cool haven in the hubbub of the bustling Jaffa Flea Market, it's the place to treat yourself to a taste of *malabi* (rose-water), pistachio, or other flavors. ⊠ *Jaffa Flea Market, 9 Olei Tzion, Jaffa* ☎ *03/603–6275.*

Fodor's Choice ★

Jaffa Port. This small, intimate-feeling marina (one of the most ancient ports in the world) is home to bobbing wooden fishing boats, and a waterfront of restaurants, cafés, boutiques, and a small number of art galleries. Some of its warehouses have been converted into public space for rotating art exhibits. From here, enjoy a fish lunch or a snack from one of the food stalls, and then hop on a boat for a cruise along the city's coastline. ⊠ *Retsef Aliyah Ha'Shniyah, Jaffa* ⊕ *www.jaffamarket.co.il.*

Kedumim Square. The focus of Kedumim Square is an archaeological site that exposes 3rd-century-BC catacombs; the site has been converted into a free underground visitor center with large, vivid, illustrated descriptions of Jaffa's history. A labyrinthine network of tiny alleys snakes in all directions from Kedumim Square down to the fishing port; a good selection of galleries and jewelry stores can be found south of the square around Mazal Dagim Street. ⊠ *Kedumim Square St., Jaffa.*

St. Peter's Monastery. Jaffa is famous as a meeting point of East and West, and as soon as you step into this century-old Franciscan church you'll find yourself steeped in a European atmosphere. St. Peter's was built over the ruins of a citadel dating from the Seventh Crusade, led by King Louis IX of France. A monument to Louis stands at the entrance to the friary. Napoléon is rumored to have stayed here during his Jaffa campaign of 1799. To enter, ring the bell on the right side of the door; you'll probably be greeted by one of the custodians, most of whom speak Spanish and some English. ⊠ *Kedumim Sq., Jaffa* ☎ *03/682–2871.*

Old Town Jaffa

Summit Park. Seven archaeological layers have been unearthed in a part of this park called Ramses II Garden. The oldest sections of wall (20 feet thick) have been identified as part of a Hyksos city dating from the 17th century BC. Other remains include part of a 13th-century-BC city gate inscribed with the name of Ramses II; a Canaanite city; a Jewish city from the time of Ezra and Nehemiah; Hasmonean ruins from the 2nd century BC; and traces of Roman occupation. At the summit is a stone sculpture called *Faith*, in the shape of a gateway, which depicts biblical stories. ⊠ *Kedumim Square St., Jaffa.*

WORTH NOTING

Andromeda's Rock. From Kedumim Square, a number of large boulders can be seen out at sea not far from shore. Greek mythology says one of these (pick your own, everyone does) is where the people of Jaffa tied the virgin Andromeda in sacrifice to a sea monster to appease Poseidon, god of the sea. But Perseus, riding the winged horse Pegasus, soared down from the sky to behead the monster, rescue Andromeda, and promptly marry her. ⊠ *Jaffa.*

Clock Tower Square. Completed in 1906, in time to mark the 30th anniversary of the reign of Sultan Abdul Hamid II, this clock tower is the center of Jaffa. The stained-glass windows from 1965 depict events in Jaffa's history. The centuries-old buildings have been carefully restored, preserving their ornate facades. Since Jaffa was a major port in Turkish times, it's not surprising to find the Turkish Cultural Center here. ⊠ *Clock Tower Square, Yefet St., Jaffa.*

OFF THE
BEATEN
PATH

Design Museum Holon. Israeli-born architect Ron Arad designed this striking, much-acclaimed structure made of rounded ribbons of orange-and-red steel that rises off a drab street like a modernist mirage. Inside is a two-story space with changing exhibits on contemporary design, including fashion, jewelry, and textiles. English language recorded tours are available for free. A good café known for tasty pastries and cakes is located at the entrance. The museum is in Holon, a suburb south of Tel Aviv that's easily reachable by Egged Buses 90 or 97 or Dan Bus 3. ⊠ *8 Pinhas Eilon St., Holon* ☎ *073/215–1515* ⊕ *www.dmh.org.il* ✉ *NIS 35* ⊙ *Mon. and Wed. 10–4, Tues. and Thurs. 10–8, Fri. 10–2, Sat. 10–6.*

El-Mahmoudiye Mosque. When Turkish governor Muhammed Abu Najat Aja built the fountain here in the early 19th century, it had six pillars and an arched roof, providing shade as well as refreshment. The fountain's foundation is still visible in the parking lot west of the minaret. It's closed to the public, as is the rest of the mosque, but if its ornate carved doors on the western side are open, you can peek into the spacious restored courtyard surrounded by arches. The archway on the south side formed the entrance to the *hammam*, or old Turkish bath. In the late 19th century, a separate entrance was built into the east wall to save the governor and other dignitaries the bother of having to push through the market-square crowds at the main entrance, on the south wall. ⊠ *Yefet St., at Mifratz Shlomo St., Jaffa.*

NEED A
BREAK?

Abulafia Bakery. There's always a line outside Abulafia Bakery, south of Jaffa's clock tower. For a simple snack with an exquisite flavor, order a pita topped with *za'atar* (a mixture of herbs, spices, and seeds), or stuffed with salty cheese, calzone-style. In winter, Abulafia is a good place to try *sachlab*, a warm drink sprinkled with coconut and cinnamon. ⊠ *7 Yefet St., Jaffa.*

Ilana Goor Museum. Veteran Israeli artist Ilana Goor works and resides in this restored 18th-century house with its romantic stone arches and high ceilings. She's turned part of it into a museum of her sculptures in wood, stone, and metal, some reminiscent of the "found-art" genre. A gift shop occupies part of the complex. ⊠ *4 Mazal Dagim St., Jaffa* ☎ *03/683–7676* ⊕ *www.ilanagoor.com* ✉ *NIS 32* ⊙ *Sun.–Fri. 10–4, Sat. and Jewish holidays 10–6.*

San Antonio Roman Catholic Church. Although its white bricks look new, this church actually dates from 1932, when it was built to accommodate the growing needs of Jaffa's Roman Catholic community. The church is named for St. Anthony of Padua, friend and disciple of St. Francis of Assisi. ⊠ *51 Yefet St., Jaffa* ☎ *03/513–3800.*

OFF THE
BEATEN
PATH

Weizmann Institute of Science. On the grounds of one of Israel's finest science centers, the Weizmann Institute is educational and fun for kids of all ages. A highlight is the open-air Clore Garden of Science, where you can experience how it feels to walk on the moon and climb on or through dozens of other interactive exhibits that explain various scientific phenomena. Also worth a visit is the glass-and-steel Eco-Sphere, which houses educational exhibits on the environment. Call ahead for reservations. ⊠ *1 Herzl St., Rehovot* ☎ *08/934–4500* ⊕ *www. weizmann.ac.il* ✉ *NIS 40* ⊙ *Sun.–Thurs. 9–4.*

The colorful Design Museum Holon hosts changing exhibits that explore the importance of design in daily life.

Yefet Street. Think of Yefet as a sort of thread between eras: beneath it is the old market area, while all around you stand schools and churches of the 19th and 20th centuries. Several deserve mention. At Number 21 is the Tabitha School, established by the Presbyterian Church of Scotland in 1863. Behind the school is a small cemetery where some fairly prominent figures are buried, including Dr. Thomas Hodgkin, the first to define Hodgkin's disease. Number 23 was once a French Catholic school, and it still carries the sign "Collège des Frères." At Number 25, the fortresslike Urim School was set up as a girls' school in 1882.

TEL AVIV PORT AND NORTHERN TEL AVIV

While still considered center city, from the east–west cross street of Arlozoroff north, Tel Aviv flows into blocks of tranquil residential streets of small apartment houses, up to the banks of the Yarkon River and its beautiful park. The Tel Aviv Port is one of the city's hottest places to eat, shop, and stroll. Just north of the river are three important museums. The Eretz Israel Museum is close to Tel Aviv University; the Palmach Museum is next door to it; and the Diaspora Museum is farther north.

GETTING HERE AND AROUND

Dan Bus Company's Route 4 is an easy way to reach the port. The museums are about 8 km (5 miles) from the downtown hotels; Dan Buses 7, 25, and 45 will take you to the area. Allow at least two hours to visit each museum.

Diaspora
Museum 5

Eretz Israel
Museum 2

Ganei Yehoshua
(Hayarkon
Park) 4

Palmach
Museum 3

Tel Aviv Port 1

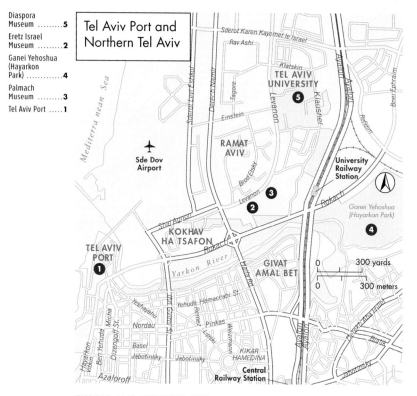

Tel Aviv Port and Northern Tel Aviv

TIMING AND PRECAUTIONS

The port area can feel a bit overrun on the weekends, especially with families and young children. Northern Tel Aviv tends to be bustling by day, sleepy at night.

NORTHERN TEL AVIV

TOP ATTRACTIONS

Diaspora Museum. Presented here are 2,500 years of Jewish life in the Diaspora (the settling of Jews outside Israel), beginning with the destruction of the First Temple in Jerusalem and chronicling such major events as the exile to Babylon and the expulsion from Spain in 1492. Photographs and text labels provide the narrative, and films and music enhance the experience. One highlight is a replica collection of miniature synagogues throughout the world, both those destroyed and those still functioning. Another is the computerized genealogy section, where it's possible to look up Jewish family names to determine their origins. There's a music center with Jewish music from around the world and a children's gallery with interactive exhibits. ⊠ *Tel Aviv University, Klausner St., Northern Tel Aviv* ☎ *03/745–7800* ⊕ *www.bh.org.il* ☒ *NIS 42* ⊘ *Sun.–Thurs. 10–7, Fri. 9–1.*

Eretz Israel Museum. This museum's eight pavilions span 3,000 years of Israeli life, covering everything from ethnography and folklore to ceramics and other handicrafts. In the center is the ancient site of Tel Kassile, where archaeologists have uncovered 12 layers of settlements. There's also a daily sound-and-light show in the adjacent planetarium. ✉ *2 Levanon St., Northern Tel Aviv* ☎ *03/641–5244* ⊕ *www. eretzmuseum.org.il* ✉ *Museum NIS 42, planetarium NIS 74* ⊙ *Sun.– Wed. 10–4, Thurs. 10–8, Fri. and Sat. 10–2.*

FAMILY **Ganei Yehoshua.** Hayarkon Park is where Tel Avivians go to stretch out on the grass for a picnic or a nap in the shade. For those seeking more activity, a bike ride on one of its paths can be combined with a visit to the tropical garden and the rock garden. Or you can rent a pedal boat, rowboat, or motorboat to ply Yarkon Stream. There's even a pleasure boat, which takes up to 80 people for 20-minute rides. ✉ *Rokach Blvd., Northern Tel Aviv* ☎ *03/642–2828* ⊕ *www.park.co.il* ✉ *Free* ⊙ *Garden Sun.–Thurs. 10–2:30, Fri. 10–1:30, Sat. 10–3:30.*

WORTH NOTING

Palmach Museum. This museum makes you feel as if you were back in the days of the Palmach, the pre-State underground, with a group of young defenders. Visitors are led through rooms, each of which encompasses one part of the Palmach experience. There's the "forest," which has real-looking trees; a room with a falling bridge and faux explosions; and a chilling mock-up of an illegal-immigrants' ship. Call ahead for reservations. ✉ *10 Levanon St., Northern Tel Aviv* ☎ *03/643–6393* ⊕ *www. palmach.org.il* ✉ *NIS 30* ⊙ *Sun. and Mon. 9–4:30, Tues. 9–8, Wed. 9–1:30, Thurs. 9–4, and Fri. 9–11:30.*

TEL AVIV PORT

TOP ATTRACTIONS

Tel Aviv Port. A little over a decade ago, this was a cluster of decrepit warehouses, but now the port is buzzing with cafés and restaurants. It ends where the pavement gives way to a wooden platform designed with moderate dips and curves, pleasing to the eye and fun for roller skaters. Also here is Bayit Banamal, a small mall with eclectic boutiques. On weekends, when restaurants are all packed by 1 pm, there's a very appealing farmers' market and a small swap meet good for finding handmade jewelry, old books, and Israeli memorabilia. ✉ *Hayarkon and Dizengoff Sts., Tel Aviv Port.*

WHERE TO EAT

The city's cosmopolitan character is happily represented in its food, although stands selling Middle Eastern fast food for which this part of the world is famous—such as falafel and shawarma—still occupy countless street corners. You'll find restaurants serving everything from American-style burgers to sushi and chili con carne. In contrast to Jerusalem, diners who keep kosher have to search for a kosher restaurant, aside from those in the hotels. A spate of new kosher establishments caters to a significant slice of the discerning dining market, but with the fairly rapid turnover of some Tel Aviv eateries, the concierge is still the best person to ask about the latest in kosher restaurants.

Most Tel Aviv restaurants, except those that keep kosher, are open seven days a week. Many serve business lunches at reasonable prices, making them less-expensive options than the price categories suggest. As elsewhere in the Mediterranean, Israelis dine late; chances are there will be no trouble getting a table at 7 pm, whereas past 10, diners may face a long line. Casual attire is always acceptable in Tel Aviv, even in the poshest restaurants.

Tel Aviv's restaurants are concentrated in a few areas: Sheinkin and Rothschild streets, Basel, Ibn Gvirol Street, and the Tel Aviv Port. Herzliya Pituach, a seaside suburb north of Tel Aviv, has a cluster of good restaurants in the upscale Arena Mall at the marina, with a picturesque view of the yachts at anchor.

Prices in the reviews are the average cost of a main course at dinner or, if dinner is not served, at lunch.

Use the coordinate (✛ A1) at the end of each listing to locate a site on the corresponding map.

CENTER CITY

$$$$
ISRAELI
✕ **Abraxas North.** For one of the best meals in the city, take your place at one of the tables spilling out onto the sidewalk or alongside the small, chic bar. The menu changes daily, depending on what Eyal Shani, its celebrity chef, finds to be the freshest produce or catch of the day. A couple of delectable dishes are often featured, including lamb shawarma marinated overnight in wine grapes from the Judean Hills, and cold shrimp with green onions and tomatoes served in piping-hot homemade pita. If you arrive without reservations, you may be able to find room at the bar. $ *Average main: NIS 129* ⊠ *40 Lilienblum St., Center City* ☎ *03/516–6660* ⊕ *www.abraxas.co.il* ⌦ *Reservations essential* ✛ *B5.*

$$
ITALIAN
✕ **Allora.** The well-stocked wooden bar is the centerpiece of this tiny eatery, where the roaring brick oven and pizza-dough kneaders are in full view. The focaccia makes a great starter, served with a variety of dips including Clemente-olive spread, garlic confit, and, for Middle Eastern good measure, *labaneh* (yogurt cheese). The Balkan pizza, topped with grilled eggplant, peppers, and feta cheese, is especially tasty. The narrow porch is your perch to watch the people strolling and cycling along the tree-lined center of Rothschild Boulevard. $ *Average main: NIS 70* ⊠ *60 Rothschild Blvd., Center City* ☎ *03/566–5655* ⊕ *allora.co.il* ✛ *B5.*

$$
CAFÉ
✕ **Ashtor.** This small corner café, a neighborhood favorite, is where you can catch a glimpse of the beauty of European café culture. Coffee is the main event, over which you can linger for hours along with your newspaper, computer, or friends from the neighborhood. Because it's in the heart of the upscale Basel area, patrons include celebrities that live nearby. The menu includes everything from sandwiches and salads to pastas and schnitzel. $ *Average main: NIS 56* ⊠ *37 Basel St., Center City* ☎ *03/546–5318* ✛ *B2.*

$$$
EASTERN
EUROPEAN
✕**Baba Yaga.** A pleasant lawn and wooden deck front this small restaurant at the slightly shabbier end of Hayarkon Street. Black tablecloths, high-backed chairs, and old-fashioned light fixtures give the place a touch of elegance. Baba Yaga is a notorious witch in Russian folk tales, and there's a collection of witch dolls behind the bar. Try the seafood dishes and Russian favorites like borscht and Stroganoff (made with sweet cream rather than sour). There's a good selection of Israeli boutique wines, along with an interesting mix of foreign beers. Every evening at 7:30, there's live international music. $ *Average main: NIS 98* ✉ *12 Hayarkon St., Center City* ☎ *03/516–7305* ⊕ *babayagarest.com* ✛ *B4.*

$$
CAFÉ
✕**Benedict.** Celebrating the love that Israelis have for breakfast, this restaurant with simple and sunny decor features many variations on the morning meal, served around the clock. Choose the classic Israeli breakfast with all the trimmings, the Mexican egg scramble, or several different styles of eggs Benedict. French toast and pancakes satisfy anyone's sweet tooth. Despite the dish's unusual name, it's worth tasting the signature "egg balls," cooked omelet style, formed into a dumpling shape, and served with a choice of sauces such as spinach and cream. $ *Average main: NIS 67* ✉ *29 Rothschild Blvd., Center City* ☎ *03/686–8657* ⊕ *www.benedict.co.il* ✛ *B5.*

$$
FRENCH
✕**Brasserie.** The dark upholstery, mustard-colored walls, and menu in French (as well as Hebrew and English) are all meant to recall Paris, and the wide selection of excellently prepared food is a credit to French cuisine. It's open around the clock, and always seems to have a crowd. Brunch is popular, with dishes like eggs Creole and eggs Norwegian style (poached with salmon and spinach), as well as pancakes and club sandwiches. For lunch or dinner, try the ravioli with crab, steak tartare, or the salade Nicoise. $ *Average main: NIS 65* ✉ *70 Ibn Gvirol, Center City* ☎ *03/696–7111* ⊕ *www.brasserie.co.il* ✛ *C3.*

$$
ASIAN FUSION
✕**The Bun.** The Asian-influenced fare at this tiny casual eatery at the entrance to the Carmel Market is some of the freshest you'll find in Israel. Each dish is made on the spot in an open kitchen by friendly brothers Shai and Ayal. The creative steamed buns veer from tradition, and the result is innovative without reaching too far—try the ones with braised short ribs, pickles, and miso barbecue sauce. The great Vietnamese salad with green papayas, green beans, cherry tomatoes, and chili is a healthy addition alongside a steaming bowl of ramen or udon noodle soups. Finish off with the crème caramel miso, a smooth dessert with the consistency of flan, combining both salty and sweet flavors. $ *Average main: NIS 56* ✉ *18 Hillel Hazaken, Center City* ☎ *03/604–4725* ✛ *B4.*

$$
EASTERN
EUROPEAN
✕**Café Batia.** Although it's moved from its decades-old location, the café has kept its menu full of old-fashioned Eastern European favorites. Try a bowl of matzoh-ball soup, leg of goose, or stuffed cabbage for a taste of what Grandma used to prepare. If you're adventurous, sample some of the less well-known dishes, such as *pupiks,* which is Yiddish for gizzards. Vegetarians can enjoy everything from egg salad to cabbage salad. $ *Average main: NIS 62* ✉ *95 HaHashmonaim, Center City* ☎ *03/522–1335* ✛ *B2.*

4

BEST BETS FOR TEL AVIV DINING

With hundreds of restaurants to choose from, how will you decide where to eat? Fodor's writers and editors have selected their favorite restaurants by price, cuisine, and experience in the lists below. In the first column, Fodor's Choice properties represent the "best of the best" across price categories. You can also search by area for excellent eats—just check out our complete reviews in the following pages.

Fodor's Choice

Abraxas North, $$$$, p. 236
Ha'Basta, $$$$, p. 242
Herbert Samuel, $$$$, p. 247
Kalamata, $$, p. 251
Messa, $$$$, p. 244
Montefiore, $$$$, p. 244
Orna and Ella, $$, p. 245

Best By Price

$

Café Mersand, p. 242
Lilush, p. 243
Sabich, p. 246
Sonya Getzel Shapira, p. 246

$$

Abdu Hadayag, p. 248
The Container, p. 248
Moses, p. 244
Orna and Ella, p. 245

$$$

Manta Ray, p. 250
Yaffo Caffe, p. 251

$$$$

Abraxas North, p. 236
Herbert Samuel, p. 247
Messa, p. 244
Montefiore, p. 244
Mul Yam, p. 251

Best By Cuisine

ITALIAN

Bellini, $$$, p. 247
Pronto, $$$$, p. 245

MEDITERRANEAN

Abraxas North, $$$$, p. 236
Herbert Samuel, $$$$, p. 247
Suzanna, $$, p. 247

MIDDLE EASTERN

Abu Hassan, $, p. 248
Dr. Shakshuka, $, p. 248

Falafel Benin Johnny, $, p. 242
Sabich Tchernikovsky, $, p. 246

Best By Experience

BRUNCH

Brasserie, $$, p. 237
Dallal, $$$$, p. 247
Puaa, $, p. 251
Yaffo Caffe, $$$, p. 251

HOT SPOTS

Herbert Samuel, $$$$, p. 247
Kitchen Market, $$$, p. 251
Oasis, $$$$, p. 244
Orna and Ella, $$, p. 245

CHILD-FRIENDLY

Dr. Shakshuka, $, p. 248
Max Brenner, $, p. 244
Shalvata, $$, p. 252

Sonya Getzel Shapira, $, p. 246
Yaffo Caffe, $$$, p. 251

OUTSIDE DINING

Café Metzada, $$, p. 242
Ha'Basta, $$$$, p. 242
Manta Ray, $$$, p. 250
Margaret Tayar, $$$, p. 250
Shalvata, $$, p. 252
Sus Etz, $, p. 246

MOST ROMANTIC

The Container, $$, p. 248
Kalamata, $$, p. 251
Montefiore, $$$$, p. 244
Mul Yam, $$$$, p. 251

SEAFOOD

Abdu Hadayag, $$, p. 248
The Container, $$, p. 248
Margaret Tayar, $$$, p. 250
Mul Yam, $$$$, p. 251
Shtsupak, $$$, p. 246

VIEWS

Allora, $$, p. 236
comme il faut, $$$, p. 251
Kalamata, $$, p. 251
Manta Ray, $$$, p. 250
Margaret Tayar, $$$, p. 250
Raphael, $$$$, p. 245

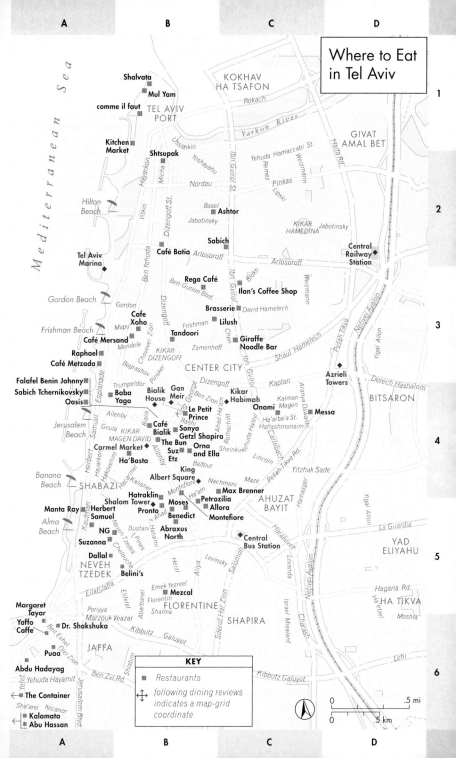

STREET FOOD IN ISRAEL

Fast, faster, fastest! If you're hungry right now, the streets of the Holy Land await your eating pleasure. Israel has a refined culture of noshing on the run, since everyone is always in a hurry and apparently hungry most of the time. Put food and drink in hand and join the locals.

To find the goods from falafel to papayas, look for the food stalls and kiosks that line Israel's main streets and shopping areas. Fruit and vegetable markets, notably Carmel Market in Tel Aviv and Machaneh Yehuda in Jerusalem, offer snack opportunities. In Tel Aviv, Rothschild Boulevard and Ben-Gurion Boulevard have popular food kiosks offering made-to-order sandwiches and fresh-squeezed juices. In Jerusalem, try the Old City's hummus spots or home-style restaurants. Most fast-food stalls serve lunch only. The outdoor markets in Tel Aviv and Jerusalem close in late afternoon and on Shabbat. In Jerusalem, no food stalls open on Shabbat, but in the Old City (except the Jewish Quarter) hummus and falafel joints do business.

GRAB IT AND GO

Some street fare is substantial, whether it's falafel or the sandwiches on five-nut artisanal breads that are edging out traditional favorites in Tel Aviv. Other choices are lighter. Sold in markets, in bakeries, and on street stands are sweet pastries called *rugelach*: these two-bite-size twists are rolled up with cinnamon or oozing with chocolate. Just-roasted nuts or sunflower seeds are a quick pick-me-up; or sip fresh-squeezed fruit juices such as pomegranate or carrot. Frosty frozen yogurt and rich ice creams are perfect on hot days. A frothy cappuccino is always good; in winter, try a cup of hot custard-like *sahlab*, perhaps sprinkled with cinnamon.

FALAFEL

The region's ultimate fast-food snack consists of deep-fried chickpea balls—the best are crispy outside with soft centers. "Falafel" also refers to the whole production of the balls served in pita pockets with an array of chopped vegetable salads plus hummus, tahini, and pickles that you add yourself and then eat (watch for drips!) with a waxed paper napkin for further refinement. Vendors compete with extra touches such as free salads. It's filling, nutritious, and cheap.

HUMMUS

Ubiquitous in the Middle East, hummus is a creamy paste made from mashed chickpeas, olive oil, garlic, and *tahini* (a sesame sauce). You eat it in a pita or scoop it up from a plate with the same. In Hebrew, there's a verb for this action specifically related to hummus: *lenagev*, which means "to wipe." Heartfelt arguments prevail among Israelis over where to find the best hummus, but eat it at a Middle Eastern specialty place; some of the best are on market alleys and side streets—even at gas stations.

SHAWARMA

For this fast-food favorite, marinated lamb or turkey slices are stacked and grilled on a vertical spit, then sliced off and stuffed into a pita. Accompaniments are usually the same choice as for falafel, though onion rings and

french fries are other extras. Jerusalem mixed grill (*me'oorav Yerushalmi*) is unique to the Holy City; look for it on Agrippas Street, alongside the outdoor fruit and vegetable market. It's a well-seasoned meal of grilled chicken hearts and other organ meats eaten in a pita with grilled onions.

TAHINI

Silky in texture, this sauce with a nutty, slightly sweet taste is made from ground sesame seeds, fresh lemon juice, and sometimes garlic. The tasty green variety has parsley chopped in. Tahini is used as a sauce and is the main ingredient in halva, the famous Middle Eastern sweet. A popular dessert—among nondieters—is a dish of vanilla ice cream topped with tahini and crumbled halva and flooded with date syrup.

BOUREKAS

From the Balkans comes Israel's favorite snack: flaky, crispy, golden-brown *bourekas*. Best eaten warm, these pastry triangles, squares, or crescents are deliciously filled with tangy cheese or mashed potato or creamy spinach and sometimes mushrooms. Small (two bites) or large (four bites), they can be made of several kinds of dough: puff pastry, phyllo, and short pastry. Bourekas are especially fine when topped with toasted sesame seeds.

—*by Judy Stacey Goldman*

$ CAFÉ 🍴 **Café Bialik.** This veteran of Tel Aviv café culture is the perfect complement to a stroll down historic Bialik Street. Plenty of restaurants serve more or less the same menu as Café Bialik—an "Israeli breakfast," which is a wide selection of chopped salads with eggs done in a variety of ways, toast, coffee, and juice, and sometimes smoked salmon and small sandwiches. But it's the neighborhood-hangout feel and the old-fashioned chrome bar stools and wooden tables that make this place stand out. Evenings ring with live music. [$] *Average main: NIS 46* ✉ *2 Bialik St., Center City* ☎ *03/620–0832* 🌐 *www.cafebialik.co.il* ⊕ *B4.*

$ CAFÉ 🍴 **Café Mersand.** For a taste of the best of the local hipster scene, score a table in the wood-paneled dining room or on the sunny sidewalk. The older customers, some of whom have been coming since the place opened its doors in 1955, mingle unusually well with the younger crowd. Everyone enjoys the specials from the original menu, including the poppy seed cake and the brownie cheesecake. In the morning, try the Turkish breakfast, which includes couscous, cheese, a hard-boiled egg, and halva. [$] *Average main: NIS 40* ✉ *18 Frishman St., Center City* ☎ *03/523–4318* ⊕ *B3.*

$$ CAFÉ 🍴 **Café Metzada.** A varied but simple menu—including steak, salads, sandwiches, and pasta—makes this a good place to recharge after a day at the beach or a nice spot to relax with a glass of wine at sunset. The highlight of this café isn't the food but the indoor or outdoor seating with fabulous Mediterranean views. [$] *Average main: NIS 60* ✉ *83 Hayarkon St., Center City* ☎ *03/510–3353* ⊕ *A3.*

$ CAFÉ 🍴 **Café Xoho.** Doubling as an art-and-music haven for locals, this inviting neighborhood café will make you feel as if you're in someone's fun and relaxing living room. The service is personal, the patrons are friendly (you'll most likely end up in a conversation with many of them), and the extensive menu has options for everyone. The in-house baked goods including homemade bagels and an ever-changing array of muffins make for a light breakfast or afternoon snack. The salads and sandwiches are made fresh, so you can choose any toppings you like. [$] *Average main: NIS 35* ✉ *18 Mapu St., Center City* ☎ *072/249–5497* ⊕ *B3.*

$ MIDDLE EASTERN 🍴 **Falafel Benin Johnny.** Passed down from father to son, this local landmark has been serving some of the best falafel for more than 50 years. For a few shekels, you'll get a pita filled with plentiful, perfectly prepared falafel balls, fried potatoes (called "chips" here) and just the right amount of salad. Sit on the outdoor bench or stand and enjoy this classic Israeli street food done right. [$] *Average main: NIS 14* ✉ *3 Tchernikovsky, Center City* 💳 *No credit cards* ⊕ *B4.*

$ ASIAN 🍴 **Giraffe Noodle Bar.** Generous portions of noodles in a variety of Japanese, Thai, and other Asian styles attract a loyal clientele. There's a selection of soups and sushi for starters. Save room for the meringue-based, berry-topped pavlova for dessert. Lunch is a particularly good bargain. [$] *Average main: NIS 49* ✉ *49 Ibn Gvirol St., Center City* ☎ *03/691–6294* 🌐 *www.giraffe.co.il* ⊕ *C3.*

$$$$ MEDITERRANEAN Fodor's Choice ★ 🍴 **Ha'Basta.** This tiny restaurant and wine bar, just a clutch of round tables on an alley just off Carmel Market, draws its inspiration from the market's fresh offerings. (The name is Hebrew for "market stall.") The dishes change daily, and the kitchen is well known for dishing out

Most Israeli food is kid-friendly. This little one is trying pita and hummus. —photo by rooneyroo, Fodors.com member

organ meats you might not see much back home. For the less adventurous, the seafood and pork dishes are sure to be fresh and aesthetically appealing. Try also the white pizza with black truffles when in season. The paella with bacon, sausage, shrimp, and mussels is about as nonkosher as it gets for a place whose chef refers to the nearby market as the "Holy of Holies," a Biblical reference to where the Ark of the Covenant was kept. $ *Average main: NIS 169* ✉ *4 Ha'Shomer St., Center City* 🕾 *03/516–9234* ✍ *Reservations essential* ✛ *B4.*

$$$
STEAKHOUSE
✕ **Hatraklin.** At this bistro in the heart of Nahalat Binyamin Street, the warm environment, hearty food, fine wine, and excellent service will leave you feeling satisfied. The wine menu boasts over 160 Israeli boutique wines, and the friendly owner-sommelier, Yossi Ben Odis, will let you know exactly which wine pairs well with your meal. The house special is the "seared sirloin" that you cook yourself at the table on a specially heated rock. The menu is mostly meat and chicken dishes complemented with a few options for vegetarians. $ *Average main: NIS 98* ✉ *41 Nahalat Binyamin St., Center City* 🕾 *03/566–0013* ⊕ *www. hatraklin.co.il* ✛ *B5.*

$
MEDITERRANEAN
✕ **Lilush.** At this cozy neighborhood bistro, the portions are generous, the prices extremely reasonable, and the atmosphere a friendly hubbub of clattering dishes and animated conversations. Tables are packed close together, both in the small dining room and on the sidewalk. The thick menu is filled with hearty salads and pastas, as well as the signature paninis. In the warmer months, there are creative daily specials like tasty risotto. During the winter, there's a daily selection of 12 soups. The all-day happy hour will keep your mouth and wallet smiling. $ *Average main: NIS 42* ✉ *73 Frishman St., Center City* 🕾 *03/529–1852* ✛ *B3.*

$ ECLECTIC FAMILY 🍴 **Max Brenner.** Chocolate lovers should run, not walk, to this eatery for a mouthwatering, *Charlie and the Chocolate Factory* experience. Beneath pipes of imaginary chocolate crisscrossing the ceiling, children of all ages can order the likes of chocolate pizza—topped with chocolate chips, of course—or chocolate fondue for dipping toasted marshmallows and fruit like melon, dates, and bananas. There's even chocolate soup! For a souvenir, take home some hand-stenciled pralines in artfully designed tins. And yes, there are nonchocolate options, including pastas and salads. [$] *Average main: NIS 49* ✉ *45 Rothschild Blvd., Center City* ☎ *03/560–4570* 🌐 *www.max-brenner.co.il* ✣ *B4.*

$$$$ MODERN ISRAELI Fodor's Choice ★ 🍴 **Messa.** Chef Aviv Moshe serves traditional dishes like the shredded-wheat type of pastry called *kadaif,* but his method of preparation is in a class of its own. This Mediterranean–Middle Eastern haute cuisine is enlivened with French and Italian touches. White is the dominant color in the lavish dining room, with marble floors and tented ceiling lamps on which video art is projected. A long, central table with stylish high-back chairs is the room's centerpiece, perfect for mingling with fellow diners while the attentive staff serves such dishes as seared red tuna over an eggplant-and-goat-cheese roll with pomegranate dressing, or sea bass with shallot ravioli. Adjacent to the restaurant is the bar, a much more chaotic affair done up in stark black. [$] *Average main: NIS 148* ✉ *19 Ha'arbaa St., Center City* ☎ *03/685–8001* 🌐 *www.messa.co.il* ✍ *Reservations essential* ✣ *C4.*

$$$$ FRENCH Fodor's Choice ★ 🍴 **Montefiore.** The restaurant at the Hotel Montefiore serves modern brasserie fare, throwing in a few Vietnamese touches for good measure. For starters, sample the raw tuna with yuzu or the mussels with lemongrass. Main dishes include baked drumfish with tomatoes and olive oil, grilled lamb chops, and sirloin steak with wild mushrooms. The dining room is in a lovingly restored home on Montefiore Street in the heart of historic Tel Aviv. The white walls, potted plants, and slatted wooden blinds, and even the silver-plated sugar servers selected by co-owner Ruthie Brouda, evoke old-world colonial days. The impeccable service, well-prepared food, and interesting wine list compare very favorably with the city's more expensive restaurants. [$] *Average main: NIS 110* ✉ *Hotel Montefiore, 36 Montefiore St., Center City* ☎ *03/564–6100* 🌐 *www.hotelmontifiore.co.il/restaurant* ✍ *Reservations essential* ✣ *B4.*

$$ AMERICAN FAMILY 🍴 **Moses.** This bar and grill is part retro lounge, part bistro. The extensive menu has everything from shish kebabs to calamari and quesadillas. It's good for the whole family, with children's dishes like hamburgers and, for the adults, an interesting selection of cocktails. The ribs in molasses are a real treat, as is the chicken Caesar salad. Drop by after midnight, when late-night specials add to the mix. [$] *Average main: NIS 60* ✉ *35 Rothschild Blvd., Center City* ☎ *03/566–4949* 🌐 *www.mosesrest.co.il* ✣ *B4.*

$$$$ CONTEMPORARY 🍴 **Oasis.** Chef Rima Olivera's 30 years of experience in the world's best kitchens and her principles of cooking set this eatery apart from the rest of the Tel Aviv food scene. The menu changes constantly based on the choicest seasonal ingredients, including those that are locally grown and those hand-picked from abroad. Every detail of the intimate 30-seat restaurant, including the soothing green decor and the open kitchen,

has Rima's personal touch. The natural tastes emanating from dishes have just a hint of butter or cream, if any at all. You won't find the standard plate of bread on the table, as Olivera wants you to leave the meal feeling sated, not stuffed. Taste the gently seasoned zucchini salad with truffle oil for starters. Be sure to end the meal with a perfectly balanced ice cream (flavors change with the menu) made in-house. $\boxed{S}$ *Average main: NIS 145 $\boxtimes$ 1 Tchernichovsky, Center City $\textcircled{a}$ 03/620–6022 $\textcircled{a}$ Reservations essential $\oplus$ B4.*

$$$
JAPANESE

$\times$ **Onami.** This distinguished Japanese restaurant is consistently ranked among the best in a city with no shortage of sushi. The expansive bar is the restaurant's centerpiece, and the surrounding tables are filled with all sorts of locals, from extended families enjoying an early meal to young people who arrive in clusters later in the evening. Onami presents a large variety of tastefully presented Japanese dishes, including *agedashi* tofu (fried and served with a sweet soy sauce), that can be combined with sushi or sashimi. $\boxed{S}$ *Average main: NIS 78 $\boxtimes$ 18 Ha'arba'a, Center City $\textcircled{a}$ 03/562–1172 $\textcircled{w}$ www.onami.co.il $\textcircled{a}$ Reservations essential $\oplus$ C4.*

$$
MODERN ISRAELI
Fodor's Choice
$\star$

$\times$ **Orna and Ella.** As the loyal clientele will attest, Orna and Ella is worth the trip because of its comfort-food-with-a-twist menu. Entrées might be anything from moussaka to a tomato-and-cucumber salad piled high with feta cheese and topped with a yogurt-mint dressing. The house specialty, a mound of sweet-potato pancakes, is not to be missed. Desserts include a scrumptious pear-and-almond-cream tart. Innovative vegan offerings, such as macadamia nut dip, are worth a taste. There's often a long wait, especially Friday afternoons and weekday evenings. $\boxed{S}$ *Average main: NIS 56 $\boxtimes$ 33 Sheinkin St., Center City $\textcircled{a}$ 03/620–4753 $\textcircled{w}$ www.ornaandella.com $\oplus$ B4.*

$$$$
ITALIAN

$\times$ **Pronto.** Pronto's owner was made a Knight of the Italian Republic for his contribution to Italian culture outside Italy with this small oasis of Roman cuisine. Dishes are imaginative yet uncomplicated and served in an elegant, quiet dining room. The menu, which changes seasonally, includes favorites like a cold antipasti platter appetizer and lamb osso buco. The homemade pastas are delicate and seasoned to highlight the high-quality ingredients. Finish off the meal with one of the interesting house-made ice-cream flavors such as salted caramel. $\boxed{S}$ *Average main: NIS 128 $\boxtimes$ 4 Herzl St., Center City $\textcircled{a}$ 03/566–0915 $\textcircled{w}$ www.pronto.co.il $\oplus$ B4.*

$$$$
MEDITERRANEAN

$\times$ **Raphael.** This place bills itself as a bistro (to be exact, a "resto-bistro"), but that term doesn't begin to conjure up the elegant setting with touches of the Far East. The Mediterranean (framed by picture windows) is the perfect backdrop for the sophisticated cuisine. Try a first course like market vegetables stuffed with lamb, goat cheese, and basmati rice, then move on to main dishes like swordfish accented with white Madagascar pepper and tomato confit. The service is particularly attentive and pleasant. $\boxed{S}$ *Average main: NIS 125 $\boxtimes$ 87 Hayarkon St., Center City $\textcircled{a}$ 03/522–6464 $\textcircled{w}$ raphaeltlv.co.il $\textcircled{a}$ Reservations essential $\oplus$ A3.*

$
CAFÉ

$\times$ **Rega Café.** Tel Aviv's boulevards are characterized by kiosks in the center of the street such as the Rega Café that serves simple food alongside excellent barista-crafted coffee beverages that are eaten outside on small benches and tables. Enjoy the people-watching along the boulevard as you sip your coffee or cold beverage and snack on the made-to-order salads, sandwiches, and breakfast foods. The Greek salad and Philly cheese steak are particularly good choices to go along with the afternoon latte. $ *Average main: NIS 30* ✉ *76 Shlomo Hamelech, at Ben Gurion Blvd., Center City* ☎ *03/523–1997* ✛ *B3.*

$

MIDDLE EASTERN

✕ **Sabich.** This hole-in-the-wall eatery on Ibn Gvirol Street specializes in *sabich*, a meal-in-a-pita popular in the region. It's considered a breakfast food (the word comes from the Arabic for "morning") because it includes a hard-boiled egg, in addition to hummus, tomatoes, peppers, and spices. It's a filling snack any time of day, however. Another popular menu item is the platter of meatballs served in a light tomato sauce. The indoor dining area consists of three or four stools at a counter, and there are a few tables outside as well. $ *Average main: NIS 16* ✉ *99 Ibn Gvirol, Center City* ☎ *03/523–1810* ▭ *No credit cards* ☉ *No dinner.* ✛ *C2.*

$

ISRAELI

✕ **Sabich Tchernikovsky.** This food stand is one of the best spots to sample the Iraqi-Israeli street food called *sabich*. The Zen-like concentration of the owner results in a hearty and thoughtful dish consisting of fried eggplant, hard-boiled eggs, potatoes, and tahini—a perfect combination of flavors. Here you have the rare option of a whole-wheat pita. $ *Average main: NIS 17* ✉ *2 Tchernichovsky, Center City* ▭ *No credit cards* ✛ *B4.*

$$$

SEAFOOD

✕ **Shtsupak.** Diners crowd the tables inside and out at this simple seafood place. They've been doing so for years, despite the fact that the trendy Tel Aviv Port, with several fish places of its own, is a few steps away. Locals agree that the fish here is reasonably priced, well prepared, and always fresh. For the main course, there's a catch of the day, which may include whole trout, fried calamari, or oysters in cream sauce. All the entrées come with an assortment of salads. $ *Average main: NIS 90* ✉ *256 Ben Yehuda St., Center City* ☎ *03/544–1973* ⊕ *www.shtsupak.co.il* ✛ *B2.*

$

CAFÉ

✕ **Sonya Getzel Shapira.** This quirky café, decorated with antique glass lamps and other flea market finds, has a refreshingly relaxed feel. A black-and-white checked floor adds to the retro vibe. Regulars ask for the *shakshuka*, a North African dish of pan-fried tomatoes and spices topped with an egg, as well as the market salad with sweet potatoes and feta cheese with a roasted pepper dressing. If the weather is pleasant, you can sit in the garden and let the kids roam. $ *Average main: NIS 45* ✉ *1 Simta Almonit St., Center City* ☎ *077/526–1234* ⊕ *www.cafesonya.co.il* ✛ *B4.*

$

CAFÉ

✕ **Sus Etz.** If you're hungry after shopping on Sheinkin Street, this simple café is great for taking a load off. The menu is extensive, including a tempting array of sandwiches served alongside generous salads, pastas, and main dishes like breast of chicken with rosemary. Average folks as well as lunching ladies come here, and the people-watching in the dining room and at sidewalk tables is part of the fun. $ *Average main: NIS 42* ✉ *20 Sheinkin St., Center City* ☎ *03/528–7955* ✛ *B4.*

$$$

INDIAN

✕ **Tandoori.** This longtime favorite—which introduced Israelis to fine Indian cuisine—has maintained the high quality of its food and service over the years. There are all the standard curries, but tandoori chicken is the specialty. It comes to the table sizzling hot, and finger bowls of rose water mean you can dig in with abandon. The spicy dishes are toned down, yet still go well with a glass of mango lassi. A luncheon buffet offers a good selection from the menu. [$] *Average main: NIS 79* ✉ *2 Zamenhoff St., Center City* ☎ *03/629–6185* 🌐 *tandoori.co.il* ✣ *B3.*

NEVEH TZEDEK

$$$ ITALIAN 🍴 **Bellini.** With indoor and outdoor seating, this Tuscan-style establishment facing the open square across from the Suzanne Dellal Centre is perfect for a pre- or postperformance nosh. For a special treat, try the gnocchi with truffle oil accompanied by the namesake beverage. The service is friendly and helpful, and the Italian house wine is a break from the usual. [$] *Average main: NIS 80* ✉ *Suzanne Dellal Centre, 6 Yehieli St., Neveh Tzedek* ☎ *03/517–8486* 🌐 *www.bellini.co.il* ✣ *B5.*

4

$$$$ MEDITERRANEAN 🍴 **Dallal.** Inside a beautifully restored historic building, this bistro has a rarified atmosphere and an on-the-premises bakery that turns out a luscious array of French-style pastries. The breakfast menu highlights some of the baked delights, including the smoked-salmon croissants and the indulgent strawberry French toast sandwich. The enclosed patio, with its wrought-iron tables and chairs, is a lovely place to enjoy a late afternoon coffee among a mixed crowd of business executives, surfers, and families. The business lunch is a good value while the dinner menu offers more extensive fish and meat options. [$] *Average main: NIS 110* ✉ *10 Shabazi St., Neveh Tzedek* ☎ *03/510–9292* 🌐 *www.dallal.info* ✣ *B5.*

$$$$ MEDITERRANEAN Fodor's Choice ★ 🍴 **Herbert Samuel.** Walking through the door of this understated but elegant dining room, you hear the energetic hum of good conversation. The upscale but very accessible menu has a strong Mediterranean influence and changes every season. Leave room for the luscious house-made desserts. A glass-enclosed kitchen is on full view for those seated upstairs, which is a must-see for anyone who loves to cook. If you're seeking a cool vibe, a seat at the downstairs bar is preferable. The extensive wine list and refreshing cocktails are professionally created. [$] *Average main: NIS 120* ✉ *6 Koifman St., Neveh Tzedek* ☎ *03/516–6516* 🌐 *www.herbertsamuel.co.il* ✍ *Reservations essential* ✣ *A5.*

$$$$ CONTEMPORARY 🍴 **NG.** Tucked away in a quiet corner of the city, this small, elegant bistro specializes in fine cuts of expertly prepared meat. It's purported to be the only place in Israel where you can enjoy a real porterhouse steak. And for dessert? That depends on the time of year. Tangy strawberry-vanilla pie is a winter specialty, and fig-vanilla pie is a summer favorite. The building is historic, yet the interior is contemporary, with Mediterranean tile floors in geometric patterns. [$] *Average main: NIS 150* ✉ *6 Ahad Ha'am St., Neveh Tzedek* ☎ *03/516–7888* ✍ *Reservations essential* ⏲ *No lunch Sun., Mon., Wed., and Thurs.* ✣ *B5*

$$ MEDITERRANEAN 🍴 **Suzanna.** In a century-old building near the Suzanne Dellal Centre for Dance and Theatre, this popular eatery bustles day and night. Sample the Kurdish *kibbeh* (meat-filled semolina dumplings) and pumpkin soup, or the Moroccan *harira*, a thick soup with chickpeas, veal, and coriander. To start things off, the savory antipasti platter is a welcome sight for the hungry traveler. Opt for a table on the terrace beneath the massive branches of an old ficus tree. [$] *Average main: NIS 69* ✉ *9 Shabazi St., Neveh Tzedek* ☎ *03/517–7580* ✣ *B4.*

FLORENTINE

$$ ✕**Mezcal.** This lively neighborhood restaurant and bar hits the spot with
MEXICAN refreshing margaritas and straightforward, tasty Mexican fare. Share a
few plates from the "street food" menu of tostadas, tacos, chimichan-
gas, and enchiladas. A multicourse tasting menu on Sunday night is an
opportune time to sample the chef's favorites. Happy hour starts every
day at 6 pm, a good time to try the Bloody Maria, chili martini, or
classic margarita. Try the *churros*—sweet tubes of fried dough—if you
have room for dessert. $ *Average main: NIS 52* ✉ *2 Vital St., Florentine*
☎ *03/518–7925* ✛ *B5.*

JAFFA

$$ ✕**Abdu Hadayag.** Neighborhood lore says that Abdu, who is usually
SEAFOOD on hand to greet you at the door, was a fisherman in his early years.
His simple establishment has long been a fixture of Jaffa's main street.
The fishing nets, lanterns, and other marine accoutrements are refresh-
ingly down-to-earth in a city where the interior design of restaurants
has sometimes become as important as its menu. The menu includes
grouper, red snapper, gray mullet, and mackerel, as well as melita, an
Israeli fish in the barracuda family. $ *Average main: NIS 75* ✉ *37 Yefet,
Jaffa* ☎ *03/518–2595* ✛ *A6.*

$ ✕**Abu Hassan.** This shop serves what's often called the country's best
MIDDLE EASTERN hummus, which isn't an easy task with so many places serving this
addictive chickpea dish. For something quite different, order the *masa-
bacha* with chunks of chickpeas served in warm hummus, or the hummus *ful*, made from Egyptian fava beans. Get here early and expect to
wait in line, because once the pot is empty the restaurant closes (usually around 2:30 pm). $ *Average main: NIS 25* ✉ *1 Dolphin St., Jaffa*
☎ *03/682–0387* ▬ *No credit cards* ✛ *A6.*

$$ ✕**The Container.** The surprises at Jaffa Port include this waterfront eat-
SEAFOOD ery, whose name and decor are inspired by the shipping containers
once unloaded along this dock. In fact, its sleek bar is fashioned from
the metal shell of one discarded container. Steps away from bobbing
fishing boats, diners feast on a mostly fish and seafood menu on high
tables made from wooden crates. The menu varies, but red snapper
with horseradish and Jerusalem artichokes with truffles are among its
delights. Local art graces the walls and live music reverberates through-
out the week. $ *Average main: NIS 75* ✉ *Jaffa Port, Warehouse 2, Jaffa*
☎ *03/683–6321* ⊕ *www.container.org.il* ✛ *A6.*

$ ✕**Dr. Shakshuka.** For quick, simple, and tasty kosher North African fare,
MEDITERRANEAN visit this eatery on the edge of the Jaffa Flea Market. Seating is at the
long communal tables set up in rows in an airy courtyard between two
stone buildings. Sample the namesake dish, *shakshuka*, a sizzling mix-
ture of tomatoes, peppers, and spices topped with a sunny-side-up egg
and served in a metal pan. Also on offer are chicken and lamb kebabs
and large bowls of couscous served with rich, chunky vegetable or meat
soups and small plates of Middle Eastern salads. $ *Average main: NIS
42* ✉ *3 Beit Eshel, Jaffa* ☎ *03/518–6560* ▬ *No credit cards* ✛ *A6.*

DID YOU KNOW?

The bountiful spread that is the traditional Israeli breakfast can include everything from salads to omelets to baked goods. But not all are served alfresco!

If you visit Jaffa, sit at the old port and watch the sun dip down into the Mediterranean.

$$ ✕ **Kalamata.** With an unbeatable view of the Mediterranean Sea on one
MEDITERRANEAN side and the Old City on the other, this Greek-influenced eatery will
Fodor'sChoice add a romantic touch to your visit to Jaffa. Sip ouzo or *arak* (a locally
★ produced anise-flavored liqueur) alongside fresh-baked kalamata olive
bread and colorful small dishes like grilled artichokes over lentils or
fish kebabs with cilantro-mint salad. The small dining space is set in
an old stone building on the water, so be sure to request one of the
few tables by the window to watch a special sunset accompanied by
your favorite glass of wine. $ *Average main: NIS 66* ⊠ *10 Kedu-
mim Sq., Jaffa* ☎ *03/681–9998* ⊕ *www.kalamata.co.il* ⌂ *Reservations
essential* ✛ *A6.*

$$$ ✕ **Manta Ray.** This boisterous restaurant has a relaxed atmosphere, a
SEAFOOD great beach view, and indoor and outdoor dining. It appeals to every-
one from families to couples looking for romance, and attracts a loyal
clientele from as far away as Jerusalem. The filling, imaginative appetizers vary from day to day; some standards include the shrimp with
spinach, mango, and cracked wheat, or the goat cheese with beets.
The baked sea bream with rosemary and olive oil is simple Mediterranean fare at its best, especially with a spicy chili and pepper sauce
on the side. $ *Average main: NIS 90* ⊠ *Alma Beach, near the Dolphi-
narium, Jaffa* ☎ *03/517–4773* ⊕ *www.mantaray.co.il* ⌂ *Reservations
essential* ✛ *A5.*

$$$ ✕ **Margaret Tayar.** A Jaffa institution, this slightly ramshackle spot treats
SEAFOOD you to a view of the city's coastline. Mediterranean-style grilled fish is
the specialty, but the menu also includes favorites like fried sardines
stuffed with caviar. Owner Margaret Tayar is a gregarious presence,
serving up steaming plates from her tiny kitchen off a small wooden

bar topped with jars of pickled red peppers and kumquats. The snug interior is fine for cold winter days, but when the weather is fine, opt for a spot on the garden patio overlooking the sea. $ *Average main: NIS 90* ⊠ *8 Razif Ha'Aliyah Ha'Shnia, at Clock Tower Square, Jaffa* 🕾 *03/682–4741* ⊟ *No credit cards* ✛ *A6.*

$ × **Puaa.** In the heart of the Jaffa Flea Market, Puaa's lumpy sofas and
CAFÉ   slightly battered tables and chairs make for a kick-your-shoes-off atmosphere—and some patrons oblige. It's a popular gathering place for thirtysomething Tel Avivians, as well as young families. All the cakes, cookies, and croissants are baked fresh on the premises. There's a good selection of vegetarian dishes, including the Middle Eastern favorite *majadarah* (rice with lentils), served with salad and yogurt. One of the prize meat dishes is sautéed chicken with mushrooms, onions, shatta peppers, and pieces of apple. $ *Average main: NIS 46* ⊠ *8 Rabbi Yohanan St., Jaffa* 🕾 *03/682–3821* ⊕ *www.puaa.co.il* ✛ *A6.*

$$$ × **Yaffo Caffe.** The Italian-style ice creams and sorbets prepared daily
ITALIAN   by chef Ronnie Rivlin are the highlight of this light, airy corner café in the middle of the Jaffa Flea Market. Apple pie and berry frozen yogurt are among the most popular choices. The Kosher Italian menu also includes an extensive list of pastas and pizzas, making it a good choice for families when the little ones begin to clamor for a break. The Friday brunch buffet is a good value and will fill you up for the day. $ *Average main: NIS 84* ⊠ *11 Olei Tzion St., Jaffa* 🕾 *03/518–1988* ⊕ *www. caffeyaffo.com* ✛ *A6.*

TEL AVIV PORT

$$$ × **comme il faut.** This trendy and sunny eatery opens onto the Tel Aviv
CAFÉ   Port boardwalk on one side and the Bayit Banamal ("House on the Port") shopping center on the other. Enjoy the cool sea breeze over coffee or a glass of wine. Light offerings include polenta with mushrooms and HaMeiri cheese or fried whole artichokes. Breakfast for two includes a morning cocktail and fresh Israeli cheeses. $ *Average main: NIS 78* ⊠ *1 Bayit Banamal, Tel Aviv Port* 🕾 *03/717–1550* ⊕ *www. comme-il-faut.com/cafe* ✛ *B1.*

$$$ × **Kitchen Market.** In the farmers' market at Tel Aviv Port, this place has
MODERN ISRAELI   stellar views of the sea, making it an ideal rendezvous for a romantic lunch or dinner. Because of the location, you can bet that the ingredients are as fresh as possible. With a menu full of modern Israeli dishes to choose from, the restaurant makes it hard for you to pick just one, but you almost can't lose. For a few lighter dishes, try the mushroom ragout with boiled egg and truffle oil or the colorful tomato, mozzarella, and labaneh salad. $ *Average main: NIS 98* ⊠ *Hangar 12, Tel Aviv Port* 🕾 *03/544–6669* ⊕ *www.kitchen-market.co.il* ✛ *B1.*

$$$$ × **Mul Yam.** The seafood here is flown in fresh from abroad—Nova
SEAFOOD   Scotia lobsters, red snapper from New Zealand, turbot from the North Sea, and clams from Brittany. Also arriving by air are purple-hued rice from China and wild berries from Provence. The owners have selected an extensive list of fine wines from Israel and around the world that complement dishes whose complex seasonings and lovely presentation put Mul Yam in a class of its own. Watch a slice of life at the trendy Tel

Aviv Port through a glass wall. Summer lunches let you sample some of the gastronomic delights at lower prices. Indulge in the desserts. [$] *Average main: NIS 160* ✉ *Hangar 24, Tel Aviv Port* ☎ *03/546–9920* 🌐 *www.mulyam.com* ✍ *Reservations essential* ✥ *B1.*

$$ MIDDLE EASTERN 🍴 **Shalvata.** By day this Middle Eastern favorite is where Tel Aviv parents take their kids to run around while they eat, but by night it's one of the city's better-known watering holes. Come winter, the fireplace offers a cozy escape from the cold. Menu favorites include crispy calamari, as well as Greek salad with squares of tangy feta drizzled with olive oil and fresh herbs. [$] *Average main: NIS 54* ✉ *Near Hangar 25, Tel Aviv Port* ☎ *03/544–1279* 🌐 *www.shalvata.co.il* ✥ *B1.*

WHERE TO STAY

Nothing stands between Tel Aviv's luxury hotels and the Mediterranean Sea except the golden beach and a promenade outfitted with chairs and gazebos. Tel Aviv's hotel row is on Hayarkon Street, which becomes Herbert Samuel Esplanade as you proceed south between the Tel Aviv Port area and Jaffa. Across the street from the luxury hotels are a number of more economical ones. Boutique hotels are becoming more popular and are also centrally located, so you're never far from the trendy shops and outdoor cafés of Ben Yehuda and Dizengoff streets.

Don't want to stay in a city? Herzliya Pituach is a resort area 12 km (7½ miles) up the coast from Tel Aviv. It has a number of beachfront hotels, a public square with outdoor cafés that's a short walk from the beach, and a marina and adjacent Arena Mall with a selection of high-end shops, restaurants, and pubs. The area has a cosmopolitan air, as affluent suburbanites live here, as do diplomats and foreign journalists.

Hotel reservations are essential during all Jewish holidays and are advised throughout the year. Some hotels have parking lots, but a few rely on public lots that can be at least a short walk away.

Prices in the reviews are the lowest cost of a standard double room in high season. Use the coordinate (✥ A1) *at the end of each listing to locate a site on the corresponding map.*

CENTER CITY

$$ HOTEL Fodor's Choice ★ 🏨 **ArtPlus Hotel Tel Aviv.** Designed as a showcase of modern Israeli art, this boutique hotel manages to pull off the look of a gallery and the feel of a homey oasis. **Pros:** a fun happy hour for guests; friendly atmosphere; chic but accessible style. **Cons:** small rooms; on a slightly run-down section of Ben Yehuda Street. [$] *Rooms from: $250* ✉ *35 Ben Yehuda St., Center City* ☎ *03/797–1700* 🌐 *www.atlas.co.il* 🛏 *62 rooms* 🍽 *Breakfast* ✥ *B3.*

$$ HOTEL Fodor's Choice ★ 🏨 **Brown TLV.** As hip as the city around it, this fun boutique hotel offers luxurious pampering at a remarkably reasonable price, making it a great find. **Pros:** warm and attentive service; terrific value; walk to the beach. **Cons:** small rooms. [$] *Rooms from: $280* ✉ *25 Kalisher St., Center City* ☎ *03/717–0200* 🌐 *www.browntlv.com* 🛏 *30 rooms* 🍽 *Breakfast* ✥ *B4.*

$$$ HOTEL 🏨 **Carlton.** The lobby of this massive hotel has intimate sitting areas, each of which features the work of a different artist. **Pros:** homey feel; great service; close to public beach. **Cons:** location near Atarim Square, which is rather shabby. [$] *Rooms from: $350* ✉ *10 Eliezer Peri St., Center City* ☎ *03/520–1818* 🌐 *www.carlton.co.il* 🛏 *280 rooms* 🍴 *Breakfast* ⊕ *B4.*

$$ HOTEL 🏨 **Center Chic.** This hotel has a cozy lobby filled with books about Tel Aviv and a lounge area that screens vintage black-and-white films about Israel. **Pros:** free bicycles for guests; trendy Bauhaus design; rooftop view. **Cons:** small rooms. [$] *Rooms from: $200* ✉ *2 Zamenhoff St., Center City* ☎ *03/526–6100* 🌐 *www.atlas.co.il* 🛏 *56 rooms* 🍴 *Breakfast* ⊕ *B3.*

$$ HOTEL 🏨 **Cinema.** In the 1930s this was the Esther Cinema, one of the first movie theaters in Tel Aviv. **Pros:** a sense of history and style; careful renovation; complimentary afternoon coffee. **Cons:** outside the main tourist area. [$] *Rooms from: $245* ✉ *1 Zamenhoff St., Center City* ☎ *03/526–7100* 🌐 *www.atlas.co.il* 🛏 *82 rooms* 🍴 *Breakfast* ⊕ *B3.*

$$ HOTEL 🏨 **City.** A block from the beach, this six-story hotel on a street lined with small apartment houses has a light, airy lobby with a small sitting area on one side and a cozy restaurant on the other. **Pros:** friendly staff; adjoining rooms for families; kosher restaurant offers special meals. **Cons:** rooms are a bit small. [$] *Rooms from: $200* ✉ *9 Mapu St., Center City* ☎ *03/524–6253* 🌐 *www.atlas.co.il* 🛏 *96 rooms* 🍴 *Multiple meal plans* ⊕ *B3.*

$$$$ HOTEL 🏨 **Dan Tel Aviv.** Return visitors say they love the sense of history at the Dan, built in 1953 and billed as Tel Aviv's very first hotel. **Pros:** historic premises; close to the beach; suites have stereo systems. **Cons:** guest lounge bans children. [$] *Rooms from: $475* ✉ *99 Hayarkon St., Center City* ☎ *03/520–2525* 🌐 *www.danhotels.com* 🛏 *280 rooms, 49 suites* 🍴 *Breakfast* ⊕ *A3.*

$ HOTEL 🏨 **Grand Beach.** There's a small but inviting rooftop pool and sundeck at this basic hotel, located less than five minutes from the beach. **Pros:** close to many restaurants; comfortable lobby bar; reasonable rates. **Cons:** many tour groups. [$] *Rooms from: $190* ✉ *250 Hayarkon St., Center City* ☎ *03/543–3333* 🌐 *www.grandbeach.co.il* 🛏 *212 rooms* 🍴 *Breakfast* ⊕ *B2.*

$$$$ HOTEL 🏨 **Hilton Tel Aviv.** Perched on a cliff, this sprawling hotel is buffered on three sides by Independence Park. **Pros:** the lap of luxury; quiet location; separate shower stalls in many rooms. **Cons:** at the end of the hotel strip, somewhat detached from the city. [$] *Rooms from: $560* ✉ *Hayarkon St., at Independence Park, Center City* ☎ *03/520–2222* 🌐 *www.hilton.com* 🛏 *584 rooms* 🍴 *Breakfast* ⊕ *B2.*

$ HOTEL 🏨 **Hotel de la Mer.** Dating from the 1930s, this historic Bauhaus building is now a lovely boutique hotel. **Pros:** warm service; address near the beach; around-the-clock tea and coffee service. **Cons:** rooms on the small side; on an unattractive side street. [$] *Rooms from: $167* ✉ *62 Hayarkon, off Nes Tziona St., Center City* ☎ *03/510–0011* 🌐 *www.delamer.co.il* 🛏 *26 rooms, 1 suite* 🍴 *Breakfast* ⊕ *B4.*

$$$$ HOTEL Fodor's Choice ★ 🏨 **Hotel Montefiore.** This stunning boutique hotel shows off what restoration can bring to the historic buildings of Tel Aviv. **Pros:** crisp service; historic building; excellent breakfast. **Cons:** in a congested area. [$] *Rooms from: $500* ✉ *36 Montefiore St., Center City* ☎ *03/564–6100* 🌐 *www.hotelmontefiore.co.il* 🛏 *12 rooms* 🍴 *Breakfast* ⊕ *B4.*

BEST BETS FOR TEL AVIV LODGING

Fodor's writers and editors have selected their favorite hotels and other lodgings by price and experience. Fodor's Choice properties represent the "best of the best" across price categories. You can also search by area for excellent places to stay—just check out our complete reviews on the following pages.

Fodor's Choice

ArtPlus Hotel Tel Aviv, $$, p. 252

Brown TLV, $$, p. 252

David Intercontinental, $$$, p. 258

Hotel Montefiore, $$$$, p. 253

The Rothschild 71, $$, p. 257

Shalom & Relax, $$, p. 257

Best By Price

$

Maxim, p. 257

$$

ArtPlus Hotel Tel Aviv, p. 252

Brown TLV, p. 252

Cinema, p. 253

The Rothschild 71, p. 257

Shalom & Relax, p. 257

$$$

Carlton, p. 253

David Intercontinental, p. 258

Renaissance Tel Aviv, p. 257

Sheraton Tel Aviv Hotel and Towers, p. 257

$$$$

Daniel Herzliya Hotel, p. 258

Hotel Montefiore, p. 253

Best By Experience

BEST CONCIERGE

Carlton, $$$, p. 253

David Intercontinental, $$$, p. 258

Hilton Tel Aviv, $$$$, p. 253

Shalom & Relax, $$, p. 257

BEST ISRAELI BREAKFAST

Dan Tel Aviv, $$$$, p. 253

David Intercontinental, $$$, p. 258

Hilton Tel Aviv, $$$$, p. 253

Shalom & Relax, $$, p. 257

BEST HOTEL BAR

Brown TLV, $$, p. 252

Hilton Tel Aviv, $$$$, p. 253

Hotel Montefiore, $$$$, p. 253

The Rothschild Hotel, $$$, p. 257

Sheraton Tel Aviv Hotel and Towers, $$$, p. 257

BEST ROOF DECK

ArtPlus Hotel Tel Aviv, $$, p. 252

Brown TLV, $$, p. 252

Carlton, $$$, p. 253

Grand Beach, $, p. 253

Shalom & Relax, $$, p. 257

BEST HOTEL SPA

Dan Accadia, $$$$, p. 258

Hilton Tel Aviv, $$$$, p. 253

Sheraton Tel Aviv Hotel and Towers, $$$, p. 257

BEST FOR KIDS

Dan Accadia, $$$$, p. 258

Sharon, $$$, p. 258

BEST FOR ROMANCE

David Intercontinental, $$$, p. 258

Hotel Montefiore, $$$$$, p. 253

Neve Tzedek Hotel, $$$$, p. 258

BEST VIEWS

Dan Panorama, $$, p. 258

David Intercontinental, $$$, p. 258

Sheraton Tel Aviv Hotel and Towers, $$$, p. 257

BEST BEACH

Dan Tel Aviv, $$$$, p. 253

Hilton Tel Aviv, $$$$, p. 253

Renaissance Tel Aviv, $$$, p. 257

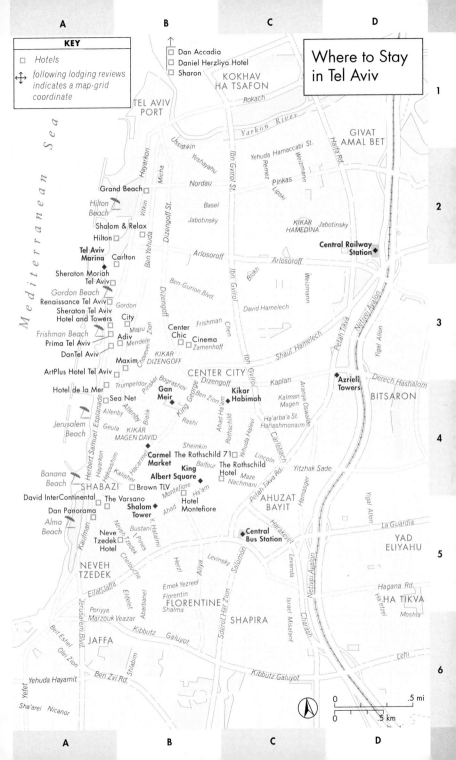

Where to Stay in Tel Aviv

KEY

☐ Hotels

⬌ following lodging reviews indicates a map-grid coordinate

■ Dan Accadia
■ Daniel Herzliya Hotel
■ Sharon

KOKHAV HA TSAFON

TEL AVIV PORT

Rokach

Yarkon River

GIVAT AMAL BET

Mediterranean Sea

Ussishkin

Yeshayahu

Ibn Gvirol St.

Yehuda Hamaccabi St.

Remez

Weizmann

Halfa Rd.

Grand Beach

Micha

Nordau

Basel

Jabotinsky

Pinkas

Lipski

Hilton Beach

Vitkin

Dizengoff St.

Ben Yehuda

KIKAR HAMEDINA

Jabotinsky

Shalom & Relax

Hilton

Arlosoroff

Central Railway Station

Tel Aviv Marina

Carlton

Ben Yehuda

Arlosoroff

Sheraton Moriah Tel Aviv

Ben-Gurion Blvd.

Blokh

Ibn Gvirol

David Hamelech

Weizmann

Petah Tikva

Netivei Ayalon

Yigal Allon

Gordon Beach

Renaissance Tel Aviv

Sheraton Tel Aviv Hotel and Towers

Gordon

City

Mapu

Frishman

Chen

David Hamelech

Shaul Hamelech

Dizengoff

Center Chic

Derech Hashalom

Frishman Beach

Prima Tel Aviv

Adiv

Mendele

Cinema

Zamenhoff

DanTel Aviv

Chovevei Zion

KIKAR DIZENGOFF

Maxim

ArtPlus Hotel Tel Aviv

Trumpeldor

Dizengoff

CENTER CITY

Kaplan

Azrieli Towers

BITSARON

Hotel de la Mer

Sea Net

Esplanade

Pinsker

Bograshov

King George

Ben Zion

Gan Meir

Kikar Habimah

Kalman Magen

Aranya Oswaldo

Allenby

Bialik

Rashi

Ahad Ha'am

Rothschild

Ha'arba'a St. Hashashmonaim

Jerusalem Beach

Herbert Samuel

Hayarkon

Allenby

Geula

KIKAR MAGEN DAVID

Ahad Ha'am

Yehuda Halevi

Carlebach

Lincoln

Yitzhak Sade

Sheinkin

Banana Beach

Kalisher

Hacarmel

Carmel Market

The Rothschild 71

Balfour

King Albert Square

Brown TLV

The Rothschild Hotel

Maze Nachmani

Petah Tikva Rd.

La Guardia

SHABAZI

David InterContinental

The Varsano

Montefiore

Ahad Ha'am

Hotel Montefiore

AHUZAT BAYIT

Harakevet

Hamasger

Yigal Allon

YAD ELIYAHU

Dan Panorama

Shalom Tower

Neveh Tzedek

Pines

Netivei Ayalon

HA TIKVA

Alma Beach

Kaufman

Neve Tzedek Hotel

Bustani

Y. Halami

Central Bus Station

Salomon

Levanda

Ha etzel

Moshia

NEVEH TZEDEK

Chelouche

Herzl

Aliya

Hagana Rd.

Eilat/Jaffa

Elifelet

Abarbanel

Levinsky

Israel Misalant

Charash

Porivya

Shalma

Emek Yezreel

Florentin

Sderot Har Zion

Lehi

Marzouk Veazar

Kibbutz

FLORENTINE

SHAPIRA

JAFFA

Galuyot

Ben Zvi Rd.

Shabim

Kibbutz Galuyot

Beit Eshel

Olei Zion

Jerusalem Blvd.

Yehuda Hayamit

Yefet

Sha'arei Nicanor

0   .5 mi
0   .5 km

David Intercontinental

Hotel Montefiore

The Rothschild 71

ArtPlus Hotel Tel Aviv

Brown TLV

$ HOTEL **Maxim.** Located across from the beach, Maxim has simply decorated rooms, many with sea views. **Pros:** complimentary coffee and cake in lobby; free parking; across from beach. **Cons:** small rooms; not much character. [$] *Rooms from: $120* ✉ *86 Hayarkon St., Center City* ☎ *03/517–3721* 🌐 *www.maxim-htl-ta.co.il* ⇨ *71 rooms* 🍴 *Breakfast* ✢ *B3.*

$$ HOTEL **Prima Tel Aviv.** Excellent views of the sea are available from many of the nicely decorated rooms at the Prima Tel Aviv. **Pros:** near the sea; cozy rooms; lots of interesting art. **Cons:** charge for Wi-Fi. [$] *Rooms from: $205* ✉ *105 Hayarkon St., at Frishman St., Center City* ☎ *03/520–6666* 🌐 *www.prima.co.il* ⇨ *55 rooms* 🍴 *Breakfast* ✢ *B3.*

$$$ HOTEL **Renaissance Tel Aviv.** All the rooms and suites have spectacular sea-facing balconies at this comfortable luxury hotel with a geometric facade. **Pros:** pretty sun decks; beautiful indoor pool; top-notch eateries. **Cons:** business lounge closes at midnight. [$] *Rooms from: $321* ✉ *121 Hayarkon St., Center City* ☎ *03/521–5555* 🌐 *www.marriott.com* ⇨ *342 rooms, 4 suites* 🍴 *Breakfast* ✢ *B3.*

$$ HOTEL Fodor's Choice ★ **The Rothschild 71.** When you enter this nicely renovated International-Style building you'll feel right at home, thanks to a living room–style lobby where you can enjoy coffee and tea. **Pros:** personal service; espresso machine in each room; good value for space; living room–style lobby with coffee/tea, cookies, and Lambrusco. **Cons:** the included breakfast is in a restaurant under the hotel that has very unfriendly service (hotel is working on this issue). [$] *Rooms from: $260* ✉ *71 Rothschild Blvd., Center City* ☎ *03/629–0555* 🌐 *www.the-rothschild.com* ⇨ *30 rooms* 🍴 *Breakfast* ✢ *C4.*

$$$ HOTEL **The Rothschild Hotel.** One of the latest boutique hotels to open along Rothschild Street, this one has a color scheme and design aesthetic intended to evoke the feeling of the Tel Aviv of days gone by. **Pros:** free Wi-Fi; top-notch restaurant; espresso machine in each room. **Cons:** on a busy street. [$] *Rooms from: $300* ✉ *96 Rothschild Blvd., Center City* ☎ *03/957–8888* 🌐 *www.the-rothschild-hotel.com* ⇨ *29 rooms* ✢ *C4.*

$ HOTEL **Sea Net.** Offering simple, clean rooms, this hotel has an informal atmosphere that appeals to European travelers—French and German are frequently heard in the small lobby. **Pros:** warm service; sea views; good location. **Cons:** rooms are a bit worn; roof terrace can be noisy. [$] *Rooms from: $160* ✉ *6 Nes Tsiona St., Center City* ☎ *03/517–1655* 🌐 *www.seanethotel.com* ⇨ *70 rooms* 🍴 *Breakfast* ✢ *B4.*

$$ HOTEL Fodor's Choice ★ **Shalom & Relax.** The newest addition to the Atlas Hotel chain, the Shalom & Relax is a great place to stay. **Pros:** rooftop lounge with sea view; complimentary Wi-Fi access; free use of bikes. **Cons:** no pool. [$] *Rooms from: $280* ✉ *216 Hayarkon St., Center City* ☎ *03/762–5400* 🌐 *www.atlas.co.il* ⇨ *51 rooms* 🍴 *No meals* ✢ *B2.*

$$$ HOTEL **Sheraton Tel Aviv Hotel and Towers.** Combining a personal touch with the efficiency of an international chain, this hotel is an attractive option on the beach of Tel Aviv. **Pros:** fine restaurant; espresso machines in every room; dog beds for visiting canines. **Cons:** pool area needs updating. [$] *Rooms from: $390* ✉ *115 Hayarkon St., Center City* ☎ *03/521–1111* 🌐 *www.sheratontelaviv.com* ⇨ *325 rooms, 24 suites* 🍴 *Breakfast* ✢ *B3.*

NEVEH TZEDEK

$$
HOTEL

Dan Panorama. This high-rise near the southern end of the beach is a short walk to Jaffa and Neveh Tzedek. **Pros:** across the street from the beach; handy location; efficient service. **Cons:** staid atmosphere; feels more business hotel than luxury vacation spot. $ *Rooms from: $290* ✉ *10 Y. Koifman St., Neveh Tzedek* ☎ *03/519–0190* ⊕ *www.danhotels. com* ⇗ *500 rooms* ⦿ *Breakfast* ⊹ *A5.*

$$$
HOTEL
Fodor'sChoice
★

David InterContinental. At the southern end of the beach, this luxurious hotel is a magnet for celebrities—and with gorgeous views of the sea, it's easy to understand why. **Pros:** ocean views; tasty restaurant; near Neveh Tzedek. **Cons:** beach is across a busy avenue. $ *Rooms from: $395* ✉ *12 Kaufman St., Neveh Tzedek* ☎ *03/795–1111* ⊕ *www. ichotelsgroup.com* ⇗ *516 rooms, 39 suites* ⦿ *Breakfast* ⊹ *A5.*

$$$$
B&B/INN

Neve Tzedek Hotel. Brothers Golan Dor and Tomi Ben-David came up with the plan to restore the faded elegance of this historic building: the wooden doors and cabinets in these five luxury suites are among some of the appointments that were hunted down in flea markets, and the sinks are constructed out of halved wine barrels.**Pros:** innovative design; homey feel; free Wi-Fi. **Cons:** no lobby; on a slightly shabby street; uninspiring views. $ *Rooms from: $680* ✉ *4 Degania St., Neveh Tzedek* ☎ *054/207–0706* ⊕ *www.nevetzedekhotel.com* ⇗ *5 suites* ⦿ *Breakfast* ⊹ *B5.*

$$$$
B&B/INN

The Varsano. In the heart of Neveh Tzedek, this cozy boutique hotel offers a bit of luxury in a bustling neighborhood. **Pros:** trendy location; spacious rooms; free Wi-Fi. **Cons:** ground-floor rooms lack a view. $ *Rooms from: $410* ✉ *16 Hevrat Shass St., Neveh Tzedek* ☎ *077/554–5500* ⊕ *www.varsano.co.il* ⇗ *7 suites, 3 rooms* ⦿ *Breakfast* ⊹ *B5.*

HERZLIYA PITUACH

$$$$
HOTEL

Dan Accadia. The three buildings of this seaside hotel are surrounded by plant-filled gardens, which in turn surround a pool overlooking the sea. **Pros:** lovely views; gorgeous grounds; dinner buffets on summer nights. **Cons:** little local atmosphere. $ *Rooms from: $600* ✉ *22 Ramat Yam St., Herzliya Pituach* ☎ *09/959–7070* ⊕ *www.danhotels. com* ⇗ *209 rooms* ⦿ *Breakfast* ⊹ *B1.*

$$$$
HOTEL

Daniel Herzliya Hotel. The high-ceilinged lobby at the Daniel Herzliya Hotel has a glass wall that lets you gaze out at the Mediterranean—and the rooms have even better views. **Pros:** in-house spa. **Cons:** some rooms are small and plain; public parking is first-come, first-served. $ *Rooms from: $440* ✉ *60 Ramot Yam, Herzliya Pituach* ☎ *09/952–8282* ⊕ *english.tamareshotels.co.il* ⇗ *200 rooms* ⦿ *Breakfast* ⊹ *B1.*

$$$
HOTEL

Sharon. The northernmost hotel on the strip overlooking the water is close to numerous shopping and dining options. **Pros:** homey atmosphere; nice location; sense of local color. **Cons:** rooms on lower floors have uninspiring views; noisy lobby. $ *Rooms from: $320* ✉ *5 Ramat Yam, Herzliya Pituach* ☎ *09/957–5777* ⊕ *www.sharon.co.il* ⇗ *173 rooms* ⦿ *Breakfast* ⊹ *B1.*

See art that reflects aspects of Jewish life, past and present, at the Diaspora Museum on the Tel Aviv University campus.

NIGHTLIFE AND THE ARTS

"When do they sleep?" That's what visitors tend to ask about Tel Avivians because they always seem to be out and about, coming or going from a bar, restaurant, or a performance. Tel Aviv's reputation for having the some of the world's best nightlife is well deserved, and the city is also Israel's cultural center.

NIGHTLIFE

On Lilienblum and Allenby streets, and in Florentine, where many of the pubs and bars are clustered, things don't really get started until at least 10 pm, especially on Friday night. Most places stay open "until the last customer," which means at least 3 am when things finally begin to wind down, although some are still crowded at 5 am.

For those who want to start and finish the evening early, some night spots—particularly wine bars—open before the night owls descend. Happy hours are becoming more and more popular.

CENTER CITY

BARS AND CLUBS

223. This stylish neighborhood has the feel of Prohibition-era New York City. The suspender-wearing bartenders specialize in excellent mixed drinks. Order a spicy apple martini to go alongside the expertly crafted bar food. ✉ *223 Dizengoff St., Center City* ☎ *03/544–6537* ⊕ *www.223.co.il.*

Abraxas. A hot spot frequented by local celebrities, Abraxas gets a little wild on weekends when it becomes a dance bar popular with students. ⊠ *40 Lilienblum St., Center City* ☎ *03/510–4435.*

Armadillo. Billed as one of Tel Aviv's first neighborhood bars, Armadillo's beer is cold and its vibe is friendly. It's a good choice if you're looking for a mellow crowd. ⊠ *51 Ahad Ha'am St., Center City* ☎ *03/620–5573.*

Bar Barbunia. Aptly named for a small fish that's a staple of the city's old-time restaurants, Bar Barbunia draws a mixed crowd that ranges from fishermen to financial planners. It manages to be both smoky and cheerful, and the music tends toward classics from the '70s. ⊠ *192 Ben Yehuda St., Center City* ☎ *03/524–0961.*

Café Europa. A place to see and be seen, especially in summer evenings, Café Europa's sparkling cocktails and creative small plates draw attractive customers to a packed outdoor patio. Be adventurous and taste one of the cocktails made with a local product, such as the anise-flavored *arak.* ⊠ *9B Rothschild Blvd., Center City* ☎ *03/525–9987.*

Cafe Noga. This Tel Aviv institution doubles as a pool hall, with 19 tables drawing a fun-loving crowd. If darts is your sport, stop in on Wednesday nights for the weekly contest. The music runs from oldies to hip-hop, depending on which staff member is working. ⊠ *4 Pinsker St., near Allenby St., Center City* ☎ *03/629–6457* ⊕ *www.cafenoga.co.il.*

Deli. The clandestine entrance—through the back of a nondescript sandwich shop—leads in-the-know partiers to a lounge where house music DJs spin into the wee hours. The bartenders know how to serve up the right mixtures to get people dancing. ⊠ *47 Allenby St., Center City* ☎ *03/642–5738.*

Evita. One of Tel Aviv's best gay bars, Evita is a small, classy place with some of the city's best DJs. The long line outside in the later hours attests to its popularity. ⊠ *31 Yavne St., Center City* ☎ *03/566–9559* ⊕ *www.evita.co.il.*

HaMaoz. The quirky interior of this bar resembles someone's apartment, down to the black-and-white family photos on the walls. There's even a refrigerator in the kitchen and a working shower in the bathroom. There's always a crowd in the living room, where there's a flat-screen TV and a collection of DVDs. The place is geared toward the twenty- and thirty-something crowd. ⊠ *32 King George St., Center City* ☎ *03/620–9458.*

HaMinzar. One of the oldest bars in Tel Aviv, "The Monastery" is a gritty, down-to-earth pub that's popular with a slightly older after-work crowd, as well as with students later in the evening and on weekends. Happy hour runs until 8 pm. The kitchen serves up some fine food, too. ⊠ *60 Allenby St., Center City* ☎ *03/517–3015.*

Hashoftim. A neighborhood tavern rich with history, Hashoftim's regulars tend to be older and mellower. Groups of friends congregate outside in the beer garden or inside at the small bar while enjoying jazz or blues. ⊠ *39 Ibn Gvirol, at Hashoftim St., Center City* ☎ *03/695–1153* ⊕ *www.hashoftim.com.*

Jimmy Who?. In an old bank building, this place creatively uses the space for three connected bars that each have a different feel. Push your way through the turnstile in the middle, and you'll find yourself dancing

Continued on page 265

The Bat Sheva Dance Company from Tel Aviv is well known for exceptional modern dance.

TEL AVIV AFTER DARK

Settling in at your hotel after dinner isn't an option if you want to truly experience Tel Aviv like a local. In this city famous for its nightlife, dusk is the catalyst that propels the day's steady buzz of activity into high gear. Restaurants fill to max capacity, bars become packed, and people rush to dance and musical performances. Generally speaking, southern Tel Aviv—where you'll find Florentine and Jaffa—has a mellow, low-key vibe with a bohemian flavor. Areas farther north, along Rothschild Boulevard and the Tel Aviv Port, tend to have pricier places frequented by movers and shakers. In the middle is newly hip Neveh Tzedek, where everyone mixes.

JAFFA

Jaffa at night

A winding, cobblestone street in Jaffa

An ancient port, mentioned in the Bible, this is one of the few examples of Jewish and Arab citizens living side-by-side. Like the Old City in Jerusalem, this area of winding stone alleyways retains its historic feel, and is today a serene spot perched on a hill in the southern end of Tel Aviv with promenades that afford alluring nighttime views of the twinkling coastline.

THE SCENE
With its tranquil vibe, Jaffa is the city's least fast-paced night spot. It's preeminently a romantic place to spend the evening to stroll, eat, and shop, where you'll find a relatively mature crowd of tourists and locals alike.

LOCATION LOWDOWN
Amble along the streets of the artist's quarter to Kedumim Plaza, and you'll find yourself at the top of the hill in the heart of Jaffa. There's live music offered here on Saturday evenings. Or catch a classical quartet at the Franciscan Church of St. Peter, a 17th-century building where Napoleon stayed after capturing the city.

NEIGHBORHOOD KNOW-HOW
If you're in the mood to learn something before going out, the Association for Tourism–Tel-Aviv-Jaffa (☎ 03/516–6188 ⊕ www.visit-TLV.co.il) offers free evening walking tours every Wednesday at 9:30 PM.

TOP PICKS

Try the romantic **Kalamata** (10 Kedumim Sq., ☎ 03/681–7998) in the center of Old Jaffa.

Jaffa Bar (Yeffet 30, ☎ 03/518–4668) draws an older, sophisticated clientele.

Saloona (Tirza 17, in the Noga Compound, ☎ 03/518–1719) is Jaffa's sexiest lounge-bar with a hip, artistic feel.

Roam the **Jaffa Flea Market** (Olei Zion St.) and around Rabbi Yohanan Street. Have a drink in one of many great bars.

NEVEH TZEDEK

The Mann Auditorium

After many years of neglect, Neveh Tzedek has been rediscovered, becoming Tel Aviv's most popular neighborhood day or night. It brims with laid-back wine bars, galleries, boutiques, and restored two-storey houses painted in warm pastels.

THE SCENE
The first Jewish neighborhood outside of Jaffa was once home to Israeli artists and writers, and still attracts a trendy, avant-garde crowd mixed with nouveau-riche locals.

LOCATION LOWDOWN
The most scenic way to reach Neveh Tzedek is to walk from Jaffa, past the Valhalla neighborhood, across the Shlush Bridge. Neveh Tzedek centers around the Suzanne Dellal Center, Tel Aviv's modern dance hub and headquarters of internationally acclaimed dance companies such as Bat-Sheva, Inbal, and Vertigo.

NEIGHBORHOOD KNOW-HOW
After watching a contemporary dance performance, walk through the Dellal Center's beautiful piazza, with its burbling fountains and orange trees, to the neighborhood's main thoroughfare, Shabazi Street, which intersects Neveh Tzedek's charming smaller lanes.

TOP PICKS

Chill at one of the neighborhood's tiny but classy wine bars, like **Jajo** (Shabazi 47), or on the terrace at **Suzanna** (Shabazi 9).

Neveh Tzedek also happens to be a short walk from **Manta Ray** (☎ 03/517–4773, ⊕ www.mantaray.co.il), the quintessential Tel Aviv restaurant, and the perfect place to sip an aperitif on the curving terrace overlooking Alma Beach.

TEL AVIV PORT

The Tel Aviv Port

Chin-Chin

Tel Aviv's hottest, loudest, most throbbing nightlife spot is the Tel Aviv Port (in Hebrew, the *Namal*) in the city's northern reaches (www.namal.co.il). With its cutting edge music, DJ-spun grooves, and raucous crowds, the Port has contributed in no small measure to Tel Aviv's newly-acquired fame as a major player in the clubbing world.

THE SCENE
Luckily for some, clubs here come alive only on weekends, when they house churning thickets of stylish club crawlers. During the week, it's all about trying the latest trendy restaurant.

LOCATION LOWDOWN
Restaurants and clubs here were built above a small, artificial harbor which stands beside the Yarkon River's estuary. Over the last decade, the port was transformed into a chic waterfront area that includes a wooden boardwalk, the largest in Israel, its undulating shape inspired by the sand dunes of Tel Aviv's early days.

NEIGHBORHOOD KNOW-HOW
Long, disorganized lines form at club entrances, so do your best to catch the doorman's eye. Speaking English sometimes helps. The Port's clubs only warm up at 2 AM, so fortify yourself with a disco nap. And most clubs won't take plastic for cover charges or drinks.

TOP PICKS

Two of the Port's most flamboyant clubs are the **TLV** (☎ 03/541–0222), with a state of the art speaker system, and the split-level **Chin-Chin** (☎ 03/544–0633), where willowy women dance on the bar.

If clubs aren't your scene, satisfy your musical appetite and catch a trio at the first-rate **Shablul Jazz Club** (⊕ www.shabluljazz.com), housed in spacious quarters at the Port's Hangar 13.

through this dimly lighted maze. ✉ *24 Rothschild Blvd., Center City* ☎ *050/666–7337* ⊕ *www.jimmywho.co.il.*

Levontin 7. This is a vibrant spot to experience the local music scene. Two shows every night feature the widest possible mix of musical offerings, from solo singers to bands blasting indie rock in Arabic. There's a cozy bar upstairs. ✉ *7 Levontin St., Center City* ☎ *03/560–5084* ⊕ *www.levontin7.com.*

M.A.S.H. A sports bar catering to soccer and rugby fans (that is, mostly Brits and Aussies), M.A.S.H. is the place to go when you want to see a live event on satellite TV. ✉ *275 Dizengoff St., Center City* ☎ *03/605–1007.*

Mike's Place. This well-stocked bar has live music that appeals to the over-30 crowd. Its location, on the promenade facing the beach, makes it popular with tourists. ✉ *86 Herbert Samuel, Center City* ☎ *03/510–6392* ⊕ *www.mikesplacebars.com.*

Molly Bloom. This is the country's most authentic Irish pub—no surprise, as it's run by Irishman Robert Segal. Live music reverberates on Monday and Friday afternoons. There's a full menu, including such Emerald Isle favorites as shepherd's pie and beef stew. ✉ *100 Hayarkon St., Center City* ☎ *03/522–1558* ⊕ *www.molly-blooms.com.*

Fodor'sChoice **Nanutchka.** This ornate bistro and bar occupies a courtyard and a large
★ interior space adorned with tapestries and paintings. The dancing gets going around 10 pm every night. Drinks include specialties of the house—a selection of sweet but light wines from the country of Georgia. The menu is delicious, featuring divine appetizers like *tinakali* (cheese dumplings with yogurt). ✉ *30 Lilienblum St., Center City* ☎ *03/516–2254.*

Par Derriere. Don't let the entrance—an obscure passageway off Allenby Street—turn you off from this relaxed courtyard bar. Customers engage in close conversation over tables dotted with candles in a romantic courtyard. The Parisian-born owner has stocked the bar with an array of wines from Israel and elsewhere. Tapas, such as delectable carpaccio topped with thin slices of Parmesan, are tasty, as are the cheese plates. Tuesday night you can watch live concerts. ✉ *4 King George St., Center City* ☎ *03/629–2111.*

Pavella. With a patio that opens onto lively King George Street, this Caribbean-themed cocktail bar draws happy-hour crowds for inexpensive drinks and oysters. For an Israeli-inspired taste, try the Halva Martini or their version of a "Dr. Pepper" with black pepper for spice. More than 10 types of ceviche keep your taste buds busy. ✉ *79 King George St., Center City* ☎ *03/544–9807* ⊕ *www.pavella.co.il.*

Rothschild 12. This hipster hangout hosts live music most nights. Things can get very loud under the exposed concrete ceiling, so you may want to escape to the cozy courtyard. The front section of the bar is a café that's open all day. ✉ *12 Rothschild St., Center City* ☎ *03/510–6430.*

Shesek. You'll be enveloped with a cool vibe even on the hottest nights at Shesek Bar. The range of alternative music changes nightly, sometimes veering toward hip-hop, funk, or even swing. The young regulars—many of them musicians, journalists, and film-industry types—sit under retro orange light fixtures at the bar or slide into beige leather booths. ✉ *17 Lilienblum St., Center City* ☎ *03/516–9520.*

Bistro-bars, such as Nanutchka, are all the rage in Tel Aviv. Many have DJs and dancing nightly.

Vicky Cristina. In a renovated railroad station, this tapas bar evokes a Latin atmosphere with its sultry mood music. Sangria and other Spanish-style beverages are the theme of the large outdoor bar, where you may be lucky enough to catch some live music. ✉ *1 Y. Koifman St., Hatachana Complex, Building 17, Center City* ☎ *03/736–7272.*

Wine Bar. Sitting at one of the four tables on the street of this neighborhood wine bar will make you feel as if you're in Paris. There's a varied selection of Israeli wines and food, so you'll also experience the essence of Tel Aviv. ✉ *36 Nahalat Binyamin St., Center City* ☎ *03/510–2923* ⊕ *www.wine-bar.co.il.*

Zizi Trippo. This hot club's focus is on dancing, but some secluded corners can be found for quiet conversation. Bartenders wave their hands in the air to the beat of the music, adding to the feel of escapist abandon. ✉ *7 Carlebach, Center City* ☎ *03/561–1597.*

NEVEH TZEDEK
BARS AND CLUBS
Jajo. The elegant Jajo Vino and Jajo Bar are situated across from each other in the heart of Neveh Tzedek, and both are designed with an elegant character. Each location seats only about 20 people, but these dimly lit jewels are as chic as could be. The chandeliers dropping from the high ceiling, the flickering candles on the tables, the gracefully arched windows, and the oh-so-hip clientele all make both Jajo Vino and Jajo Bar ideal for intimate conversation. ✉ *44 Shabazi St., Neveh Tzedek* ☎ *03/510–0620.*

FLORENTINE
BARS AND CLUBS

Hudna. This place attracts students and young professionals who lean toward the left on the political spectrum. The bar is split in two, with an alley down the middle that's ideal for kicking back and enjoying a pint. Gobble up a burger and fries, or try some of the excellent homemade hummus. ⊠ *13 Abarbanel St., Florentine* ☎ *03/518–4558.*

Metushelah. This wine bar on the edge of the funky Florentine neighborhood draws a mixed crowd. Named for the Biblical Noah's grandfather, a winemaker of note, Metushelah stocks over 140 wines, the majority of them Israeli. ⊠ *16 Uriel Acosta St., Florentine* ☎ *03/681–1018* ⊕ *metushelach.co.il.*

Norma Jean. With an attractive brick facade, this bistro and bar on the edge of the Florentine quarter serves more than 200 kinds of whiskey, said to be the biggest collection in the country. The kitchen serves full meals, with a focus on pleasing the carnivorous. ⊠ *23 Elifelet St., Florentine* ☎ *03/683–7383* ⊕ *www.normajean.co.il/english.*

JAFFA
BARS AND CLUBS

Jaffa Bar. This bar is a good choice if you're looking for space to breathe and lower decibel levels. The place, which tends to attract an older, more sophisticated clientele, is spacious, with a sleek bar and an eclectic decor. ⊠ *30 Yefet, Jaffa* ☎ *03/518–4668* ⊕ *www.cordelia.co.il.*

Fodor'sChoice
★
Saloona. In the Noga neighborhood of Jaffa, this swank bar retains a hip, artistic feel that draws people to the area. Enjoy a drink under the gigantic chandeliers while you listen to live music. ⊠ *17 Tirza St., Jaffa* ☎ *03/518–1719.*

TEL AVIV PORT
BARS AND CLUBS

Chin-Chin. At this massive dance club, the crowds groove to house music. There's lots of dancing on the bar and in every corner. ⊠ *3 Hataarucha St., Tel Aviv Port* ☎ *03/544–0633* ⊕ *www.chinchin.co.il.*

TLV. This megaclub doesn't start jumping until around 2 am. The state-of-the-art speaker system keeps the young crowd moving until sunrise. ⊠ *3 Hataarucha St., Tel Aviv Port* ☎ *03/544–4194.*

THE ARTS

Tel Aviv is Israel's cultural capital, and it fulfills this role with relish. The Tel Aviv Museum of Art, the city's major artistic venue (for concerts and lectures as well as the fine arts) is complemented by a host of galleries, especially along Gordon Street. Tel Aviv is also home to a dynamic dance scene, including the iconic Batsheva Dance Company.

The Friday editions of the English-language *Jerusalem Post* and *Haaretz* contain extensive entertainment listings for the entire country. There are a handful of mostly online ticket agencies for performances in Tel Aviv.

Hadran ☎ *03/521–5200* ⊕ *www.hadran.co.il.* **Castel** ☎ *03/604–5000* ⊕ *www.eventim.co.il.* **Leaan** ☎ *03/524–7373* ⊕ *www.leaan.co.il.*

DANCE

Fodor'sChoice
★

Suzanne Dellal Centre for Dance and Theatre. Most of Israel's dance groups, including the contemporary Batsheva Dance Company and Inbal Pinto, perform in the Suzanne Dellal Centre for Dance and Theatre. The complex itself is an example of new Israeli architectural styles used to restore some of the oldest buildings in Tel Aviv. ⊠ *5 Yehieli St., Neveh Tzedek* ☎ *03/510–5656* ⊕ *www.suzannedellal.org.il.*

MUSIC

Enav Cultural Center. Run by the city, the Enav Cultural Center is a 300-seat venue offering eclectic music and theater. ⊠ *71 Ibn Gvirol St., Center City* ☎ *03/521–7760, 03/521–7763.*

Mann Auditorium. Israel's largest concert hall, Mann Auditorium is the home of the Israel Philharmonic Orchestra, led by maestro Zubin Mehta. The low-slung gray building, among the most architecturally sophisticated cultural buildings in the country when it was completed in 1957, has excellent acoustics and a seating capacity of three thousand. It also hosts pop and rock concerts. ⊠ *1 Huberman St., Center City* ☎ *03/528–9163* ⊕ *www.hatarbut.co.il.*

Mayumana. This exciting troupe of drummers bangs in perfect synchronicity on anything from garbage pails to the floor. It also plays actual drums from cultures all over the world. ⊠ *15 Louis Pasteur St., Jaffa* ☎ *03/681–1787* ⊕ *www.mayumana.com.*

Shablul Jazz Club. This intimate jazz club presents everything from hip-hop to ethno jazz Monday through Saturday nights. Performers range from veteran jazz artists to up-and-coming young talents. ⊠ *Hangar 13, Tel Aviv Port* ☎ *03/546–1891* ⊕ *www.shabluljazz.com.*

Zappa Club. One of Tel Aviv's best venues for live music, the Zappa Club is in the Ramat HaHayal neighborhood, just a short cab ride away from downtown. ⊠ *24 Raoul Wallenberg St., Northern Tel Aviv* ☎ *03/762–6666* ⊕ *www.zappa-club.co.il.*

OPERA

Tel Aviv Performing Arts Center. The Tel Aviv Performing Arts Center is home to the Israeli Opera, as well as the Israel Ballet and the Cameri Theatre. It's possible to book a behind-the-scenes tour 75 minutes prior to the performance. ⊠ *19 Shaul Hamelech St., Center City* ☎ *03/692–7777* ⊕ *www.israel-opera.co.il.*

THEATER

While there are a few exceptions, theater performances are almost always in Hebrew, so inquire before booking.

Beit Lessin Theatre. Israel's second largest repertory theater, the Beit Lessin Theatre hosts works by Israeli playwrights in Hebrew. ⊠ *101 Dizengoff St. at Frishman, Center City* ☎ *03/725–5333* ⊕ *www.lessin.co.il.*

Fodor'sChoice
★

Cameri Theatre of Tel Aviv. This theater offers an interesting "See it in Hebrew, Read it in English" program in which, three times a week, the most popular productions are simultaneously translated into English. ⊠ *19 Shaul Hamelech St., Center City* ☎ *03/606–1900* ⊕ *www.cameri.co.il.*

Habima National Theater. This troupe is rooted in the Russian Revolution, when a group of young Jewish artists established a theater company that performed in Hebrew—this at a time when Hebrew was barely a living language. Subsequent tours through Europe and the United States in the 1920s won wide acclaim. Many of the group's members moved to Israel and helped establish a theater company that now inhabits multiple spaces, including a newly renovated complex at Habima Square. ⊠ *Habima Sq., end of Rothschild Blvd., Center City* ☎ *03/629–5555, 03/526–6666* ⊕ *www.habima.co.il.*

HaSimta Theatre. In Old Jaffa, HaSimta Theatre features avant-garde and fringe performances in Hebrew (or sometimes without words at all). ⊠ *8 Mazal Dagim St., Jaffa* ☎ *03/681–2126* ⊕ *www.hasimta.com.*

Nalaga'at Center. This cultural and entertainment center features deaf and blind performers. Shows can be combined with a preperformance snack at the BlackOut Restaurant (eating in the dark) or Café Kapish (ordering in sign language). ⊠ *Retsif Haaliya Hashniya, Jaffa* ☎ *03/633–0808* ⊕ *www.nalagaat.org.il.*

SPORTS AND THE OUTDOORS

Almost all outdoorsy activity in Tel Aviv centers on its gorgeous beaches, from boating to scuba diving to surfing, or relaxing by spreading out a towel in the sand to get some sun.

BEACHES

Tel Aviv's western border, an idyllic stretch of Mediterranean sand, has miles of beaches and a beachfront promenade. Just after dawn, it's the territory of joggers, cyclists, and yoga enthusiasts. As the sun rises, so do the number of beach goers, from bikini-clad young women to middle-aged men playing the ever-popular (and noisy) ball-and-paddle game called *matkot*. Sunsets here are spectacular.

The city beaches have many of the same amenities: restrooms, changing areas, towel and umbrella rentals, and restaurants or cafés. Beaches are generally named after something nearby—a street or a hotel, for example. They're hugely popular, especially on weekends. If you'd rather not battle the crowds, come during the week. The lapping of gentle waves offers respite and relaxation for most of the year. There's a strong undertow on these beaches, so exercise caution.

Dolphinarium Beach. At the southern end of Hayarkon Street, Dolphinarium Beach (sometimes known as Aviv Beach) has a festive atmosphere, especially on Friday around sunset. Young Israelis, many of whom have returned from post-army trips to Asia or South America, gather for drumming circles and other group activities. **Amenities:** food and drink; lifeguards; showers; toilets; water sports. **Best for:** partiers; sunset. ⊠ *Shlomo Lahat Promenade, facing the David InterContinental Hotel, Center City.*

Surfers line the beach in Herzliya, a resort area less than ten miles up the coast from downtown Tel Aviv.

Frishman Beach. Facing a strip of restaurants and cafés on the seaside promenade, Frishman Beach is across from many of the large hotels and gets its fair share of tourists. Saturday morning it attracts Israeli dancing circles. Lounge chairs are available for a fee, but there's not much quiet because of the lifeguards constantly screeching over the loudspeaker. **Amenities:** food and drink; lifeguards; showers; toilets. **Best for:** sunset. ⊠ *Frishman St. and Hayarkon St., Center City.*

Gordon Beach. At the end of Gordon Street, this wide beach is popular with local families because of its calm water and tidal pool. Weekends you'll find both sunbathing travelers and youngsters lining the beach with sand castles. Gordon Pool, just north of the beach, is a saltwater pool that's good for lap swimming. **Amenities:** food and drink; lifeguards; toilets. **Best for:** swimming. ⊠ *Gordon St., at Hayarkon St., Center City.*

Herzliya Pituach Beach. About 10 km (7 miles) north of Tel Aviv is the Herzliya Pituach Beach, a white-sand beach lined by well-manicured lawns. Nearby are restaurants, cafés, and a handful of luxury high-rise hotels. From central Tel Aviv, Dan's Bus 90 heads to this beach. **Amenities:** food and drink; lifeguards; toilets; water sports. **Best for:** snorkeling; swimming; walking. ⊠ *Ramat Yam St., at Medinat Hayehudim St., Herzliya Pituach.*

Hilton Beach. In front of the hotel of the same name, Hilton Beach is very popular, especially with enthusiastic *matkot* players. The northern end of Hilton Beach is a gay-friendly area known as Gay Beach, which can get packed on sunny summer afternoons. Here you'll also find Dog Beach, which got its name because pampered pooches are let off their leashes to play. There is no car access, so walk or bike down the promenade to reach this stretch of sand. **Amenities:** food and drink; lifeguards; showers; toilets; water sports. **Best for:** surfing, swimming; windsurfing. ⊠ *North of Tel Aviv Marina, Shlomo Lahat Promenade, Center City.*

Jerusalem Beach. At the bottom of Allenby Road, Jerusalem Beach is known for its beachside café featuring Brazilian bands that get the crowd dancing. **Amenities:** food and drink; showers; toilets; water sports. **Best for:** partiers. ⊠ *Allenby Rd., at Retsif Herbert Samuel, Center City.*

Metzizim Beach. This stretch of sand near the Yarkon River attracts a younger crowd. It's an especially good choice for families because it has a long sandbar that keeps the waves gentle. Many people nurse a beer at the nearby pub and watch the sunset. Just south of Metzizim Beach is a private area for Orthodox Jews who prefer gender-separated swimming. Women come on Sunday, Tuesday, and Thursday, while men are here on Monday, Wednesday, and Friday. Everyone is welcome on Saturday, and it's one of the area's mellowest beaches. **Amenities:** food and drink; lifeguards; parking (paid); showers, toilets. **Best for:** partiers; swimming. ⊠ *Havakuk Ha'navi St., near Tel Aviv Port, Northern Tel Aviv.*

Tel Baruch Beach. In the northern reaches of Tel Aviv, Tel Baruch Beach is popular among families with young children because it has a breakwater that softens the waves. Because it's the farthest beach from downtown, it can often be less crowded. The section to the north has an unsavory reputation after dark. **Amenities:** food and drink; lifeguards; parking (paid); showers; toilets; water sports. **Best for:** swimming; walking. ⊠ *Propes St., Northern Tel Aviv.*

BIKING

EcoBike. This place offers fun cycling trips around Tel Aviv—choose from among the classic bike tour, the electric bike tour, and the "bikes and beer" excursion, which includes a stop at a bar for a frosty cold one at the end. ⊠ *9 Hebron St., Ramat Gan* ☎ *077/450–1650* ⊕ *www. ecobike.co.il.*

Fodor'sChoice ★ **Tel-O-Fun.** Tel Aviv runs this convenient bike-sharing system—pick up a bike at one station and return it there or at any other station around the city. The fees (23 NIS daily/70 NIS weekly for access, plus additional charges based on how many hours you use the bike) must be paid by credit card at the pick-up bike station. The bikes are quite heavy and are useful for getting from point to point throughout the city or for riding along the promenade. ⊠ *Center City* ☎ **6070* ⊕ *www.tel-o-fun.co.il/en.*

BOATING

Ganei Yehoshua (*Hayarkon Park*). In the northern part of the city, Ganei Yehoshua rents pedal boats and rowboats (NIS 95 per hour) and motorboats (NIS 140 per half hour). ⊠ *Rokach Blvd., Center City* ☎ *03/642–0541.*

Sea Kayak Club. This club offers two-hour kayaking tours of the coastline throughout the year. Beginners are welcome when conditions are calm. The cost is NIS 150. ⊠ *Jaffa Port, Jaffa* ☎ *03/681–4732* ⊕ *www. kayak4all.com.*

SAILING

Derech Hayam. At Herzliya Marina, Derech Hayam is the place to charter a sailboat or other vessel. ⊠ *1 Yordei Hayam, Herzliya* ☎ *09/957–8811* ⊕ *www.yamclub.co.il.*

Ofek Yachts. You can charter a yacht with a skipper at Ofek Yachts at the Tel Aviv Marina. ⊠ *Tel Aviv Marina, 14 Eliezer Peri St.* ☎ *03/529–9988* ⊕ *www.ofek-yacht.co.il.*

Sea Tel Aviv. You can charter a variety of boats here for daytime excursions or romantic sunset sails leaving from Tel Aviv Marina. It's also possible to arrange scuba diving, snorkeling, and other activities. ⊠ *Tel Aviv Marina, 10 Eliezer Peri* ☎ *052/869–8080* ⊕ *www.seatelaviv.co.il.*

SCUBA DIVING

Dugit Diving Center. This water-sports center is a popular meeting place for veteran divers. Although the view beneath the surface of the Mediterranean Sea doesn't offer as breathtaking an array of fish and coral as the Red Sea, it's a good place to start. Dugit can also make arrangements for diving courses in Herzliya. ⊠ *250 Ben-Yehuda St., Center City* ☎ *03/604–5034* ⊕ *www.dugit.co.il.*

SURFING

Topsea. Teaching surfing at every level, Topsea offers both private and group courses, as well as surfboard rentals for those with previous experience. Scope out the online surfcam to know if the waves are worth the rental. ⊠ *Kikar Atarim, 165 Hayarkon St., Northern Tel Aviv* ☎ *050/432–9001* ⊕ *www.topsea.co.il.*

SWIMMING

FAMILY **Gordon Pool.** Reopened after an extensive renovation, Gordon Pool includes an Olympic-size swimming pool, dressing rooms, and lounge chairs. The pool has a separate section for kids. ⊠ *14 Eliezer Peri, Center City* ☎ *03/762–3300* ⊕ *www.gordon-pool.co.il* ☉ *Sun.–Thurs. 6–7, Fri. 6–6, Sat. 8–6.*

FAMILY **Meymadiyon.** Open from June to September, Meymadiyon is a 25-acre water park featuring a swimming pool, waterslides, a wave pool, a kiddie pool, and lawns dotted with plastic chairs. ⊠ *Ganei Yehoshua, Northern Tel Aviv* ☎ *03/642–2777* ⊕ *www.meymadion.co.il.*

SHOPPING

The Tel Aviv shopping scene is the most varied in the country. It's Israel's fashion capital, and you'll find styles quite different from what you might see back home in terms of design and color. The real pleasure of shopping in Tel Aviv is access to the exciting creations of its cadre of young designers that have made waves around the world. Dizengoff Street, north of Arlozoroff Street, is where you'll find the shops of many of Israel's best-known designers.

If it's crafts and jewelry you're shopping for, Neveh Tzedek is the place to go, especially along the main drag of Shabazi Street. Local crafts and jewelry also star in the Tuesday and Friday Nahalat Binyamin

Pedestrian Mall, where prices can be lower than at regular stores and you can almost always meet the artist who made them. As for Judaica, there are a number of stores on Ben Yehuda and Dizengoff streets.

CITY CENTER

CLOTHING

Bingo. This shoe shop specializes in high-end Italian and Spanish brands and offers a wide selection of Israeli designer shoes for all ages. ⊠ *24 Hey B'Iyar St., Kimar Hamedina, Center City* ☎ *03/641–4915* ⊕ *www. bingo-shoes.co.il.*

Carmen Miranda. Bringing Brazilian fashion to Tel Aviv, this store sells imported swimwear, flip-flops, and jewelry. ⊠ *20 Sheinkin, Center City* ☎ *055/663–2100* ⊕ *www.carmenmiranda.co.il.*

Couple Of. This shop is known for making beautiful and comfortable shoes for hard-to-fit feet. ⊠ *144 Dizengoff St., Center City* ☎ *03/529–1098* ⊕ *www.coupleof.co.il.*

Frau Blau. The designer couple, Helena Blaunstein and Philip Blau, make clothing that's part of their avant-garde artistic vision. The collections are loud and humorous, and the fashion-forward pieces use the innovative technique of printing on fabric called "trompe l'oeil," which makes images appear three-dimensional. The store is in the Gan Hahashmal area of Center City. ⊠ *8 HaHashmal St., Center City* ☎ *03/560–1735* ⊕ *www.fraublau.com.*

Gideon Oberson. Sexy and stylish beach apparel is the focus of Gideon Oberson's boutique. The vibrant and colorful swimsuits are meant to complement the skin and figure of each person. ⊠ *36 Gordon St., Center City* ☎ *03/524–3822* ⊕ *www.gideonobersonswim.com.*

Ido Recanati. Making tailored but casual clothes for women, this designer has a talent for creating clothing that's flattering for everyone, including those with fuller figures. ⊠ *13 Malchei Yisrael St., Center City* ☎ *03/529–8481.*

Kisim. This designer is influenced by Japanese origami, which you'll notice in the handbags, clutches, and wallets. The designer's informal style has an elegant twist. One of the bags was famously used by Sarah Jessica Parker in *Sex and the City.* ⊠ *8 HaHashmal St., Center City* ☎ *03/560-4890* ⊕ *www.kisim.com.*

Mandinka. This shop sells modern, sophisticated clothing in light fabrics that are perfect for Tel Aviv's steamy climate. ⊠ *105 King George St., Center City* ☎ *03/624–1431* ⊕ *www.mandinka.co.il.*

Maya Bash. These designer clothing collections made from wearable cottons and other light materials are great for the Tel Aviv climate. The unique cuts and comfortable materials are making Maya Bash a hit in Germany and Japan. ⊠ *13 Barzilay St., Center City* ☎ *03/560–0305* ⊕ *www.mayabash.com.*

Rina Zin. This designer's chic styles with a European cut appeal to older women. ⊠ *216 Dizengoff St., Center City* ☎ *03/523–5746* ⊕ *www. rinazin.com/en.*

Jaffa is the place to browse in shops and galleries, as the neighborhood has a slow-paced, mellow vibe.

CRAFTS

Olia. Look for Israeli-made olive oils, pomegranate- or date-flavored vinaigrettes, and herbs from the Galilee at this shop. There's a branch in the Carmel Market on Friday. ✉ *73 Frishman St., Center City* ☎ *03/522–3235* ⊕ *www.olia.co.il.*

Raphael. One of the most pleasant shopping experiences in Tel Aviv, this shop carries a large selection of Judaica, jewelry, and handicrafts by some of the best Israeli artists. ✉ *94 Ben Yehuda St., Center City* ☎ *03/527–3619* ⊕ *www.raphaels.co.il.*

JEWELRY

Hagar Satat. Mixing leather with gold and silver, Hagar Satat's jewelry is great for special occasions or everyday wear. Pick up a well-priced piece from this studio store. ✉ *13 Levontin St., Center City* ☎ *03/560–6095* ⊕ *www.hagarsatat.com.*

JUDAICA

Miller. Specializing in Judaica, Miller has a particularly wide selection of silver items. This shop is also home to a good jewelry collection. ✉ *157 Dizengoff St., Center City* ☎ *03/524–9383.*

LOCAL SPECIALTIES

The Bauhaus Center. This display of books, maps, posters, furnishings, dishes, and even Judaica, all inspired by Bauhaus design, is a reminder that this school of design embraced more than buildings. ✉ *99 Dizengoff St., Center City* ☎ *03/522–0249* ⊕ *www.bauhaus-center.com.*

Kelim Shloovim. This stylish store, run by the nonprofit organization Shikum Acher (A Different Rehabilitation), sells high-quality housewares made by various nonprofit organizations. Handmade candles, soaps, jewelry, and toys are just some of the creative and chic products you'll find on the shelves. ⊠ *229 Dizengoff St., Center City* ☎ *03/535–3810* ⊕ *www.kelimshloovim.org.il.*

Made in TLV. This fun-spirited souvenir shop sells all locally designed items like postcards, stationery, T-shirts, and large photos depicting both old and modern Tel Aviv. ⊠ *HaTachana, Hangar 5, near the entrance, Neveh Tzedek* ☎ *03/510–4333.*

MARKETS

Fodor's Choice
★
Carmel Market. Beginning at Allenby Road, Carmel Market is the city's primary produce market, but it also has stalls selling inexpensive clothing and housewares. ⊠ *Along Hacarmel St., Center City* ☉ *Sun.–Thurs. 7 am–sunset; Fri. 7 am–2 hrs before sunset.*

Nahalat Binyamin Pedestrian Mall. At the street fair along Nahalat Binyamin Pedestrian Mall, held Tuesday and Friday, local crafts ranging from handmade puppets to olive-wood sculptures and silver jewelry attract throngs of shoppers. ⊠ *Nahalat Binyamin St., off Allenby St., Center City* ☉ *Tues.–Fri. 9–4.*

JAFFA

JEWELRY

Adina Plastelina. This gallery and jewelry studio in the heart of Old Jaffa sells hand-crafted jewelry in sterling silver and gold that's combined with polymer clay in the ancient technique called *millefiori*, which means "a thousand flowers" in Italian. The combination of metals and modern materials creates an innovative and classy look. ⊠ *23 Netiv Hamazalot St., Jaffa* ☎ *03/518–7894* ⊕ *www.adinaplastelina.com.*

JUDAICA

Dar-Fez. This shop has an extensive and colorful selection of Judaica adorned with silver and copper and inlaid with mother-of-pearl. ⊠ *23 Raziel St., Clock Tower Sq., Jaffa* ☎ *03/518–1417.*

Frank Meisler. A specialist in Jewish fine art and a pioneer in pewter pieces, Frank Meisler has a magical studio and gallery located in the heart of the artist's quarter in Old Jaffa. Here you'll find regal Judaica as well as a display of caricature sculptures. ⊠ *25 Simtat Mazal Arie, Jaffa* ☎ *03/512–3000* ⊕ *www.frank-meisler.com.*

LOCAL SPECIALTIES

Galilee's. Agricultural and artistic products made in the north—wines and liqueurs, herbs and spices, and health and beauty products—are on offer at this Jaffa favorite. You can taste many of the products before purchasing. ⊠ *Clock Tower Square House, 22 David Raziel St., Jaffa* ☎ *03/544–2834* ⊕ *www.galilees.co.il.*

MARKETS

Jaffa Flea Market. A mix of junk, fine antiques, and designer clothing, Jaffa Flea Market has something for everyone. There's a wide selection of reasonably priced Middle Eastern–style jewelry with small silver coins and imitation stones. Many interesting restaurants have popped up in this area. ⊠ *Olei Zion St., Jaffa* ☉ *Sun.–Fri. 9–4.*

NEVEH TZEDEK

CRAFTS

Chomer Tov Ceramics Gallery. This ceramics gallery, a cooperative of 14 artists, is on Neveh Tzedek's main drag. ⊠ *27 Shabazi St., Neveh Tzedek* ☎ *03/516–6229* ⊕ *www.chomertov.co.il.*

JEWELRY

Ayala Bar. Israeli designer Ayala Bar's sparkling, multicolored bracelets, earrings, and necklaces, now famous around the world, can be seen from time to time in shops throughout the country, but the best selection is at this flagship store. ⊠ *36 Shabazi St., Neveh Tzedek* ☎ *03/510–0082* ⊕ *www.ayalabar.com.*

Dave + Etsy. This talented husband-and-wife team work together to create playful and memorable jewelry pieces. Their whimsical take on pomegranates and Jewish stars result in gentle Israel-inspired pieces that make meaningful gifts. The store is filled with charms, so take your time while searching, as there's something for everyone. ⊠ *67 Shabazi St., Neveh Tzedek* ☎ *054/442–2204* ⊕ *www.davesty.com.*

LOCAL SPECIALTIES

SOHO Design Center. Carrying pieces by Israeli and international designers, this store is filled to the brim with interesting items, from kitchen accessories to handbags to children's toys. ⊠ *HaTachana, Hangar 12, in the center, Neveh Tzedek* ☎ *03/716–7010* ⊕ *www.sohocenter.co.il.*

TEL AVIV PORT

MARKETS

Tel Aviv Port Farmers' Market. After wandering through the stalls selling organic produce, sample the fresh offerings at eateries like the in-house pasta bar or the specialty-sandwich stand. Don't miss the just-squeezed pomegranate juice. ⊠ *Hangar 12, Tel Aviv Port* ⊕ *www.shukhanamal.co.il* ☉ *Mon.–Thurs. and Sat. 9–8, Fri. 7–4.*

FLORENTINE

MARKETS

Levinsky Market. In the gritty Florentine area, Levinsky Market is known as a spice-and-herb market but it also has wonderful Mediterranean delicacies. Nearby you'll find good Persian eateries. Once considered off the beaten path, the Levinsky Market is now a central destination for foodies. ⊠ *Levinsky St.* ☉ *Sun.–Fri. 8–5.*

5

HAIFA AND THE NORTHERN COAST

With Caesarea, Akko, and Rosh Hanikra

WELCOME TO HAIFA AND THE NORTHERN COAST

TOP REASONS TO GO

★ **Caesarea:** Originally built by Herod the Great, these 2,000-year-old Roman ruins occupy a strategic spot on the sea. They include Byzantine bathhouses and Crusader moats.

★ **Baha'i Gardens:** In Haifa, this unforgettable series of gardens tumbles down from Mt. Carmel into 19 terraces that enclose a gold-domed shrine.

★ **Underground Akko:** At this fascinating archaeological site, you can descend into Crusader knights' halls, navigate a secret tunnel toward the sea, and rest in a Turkish bathhouse.

★ **Glorious beaches:** The coast means beaches, and this is Israel's finest stretch of golden sand. Haifa's beaches are particularly beautiful. Scuba diving or para-gliding are options.

★ **Great wine:** Taste and toast internationally known wines at the many wineries nestled into the hillsides of the northern coast. Tishbi and Carmel are especially worth visiting.

LEBANON

Ma'alot-Tarshiba 899 89 864 854

Shagor 85
Karmi'el

G A L I L E E

70 Sakhnin
Tamra Arraba

Kafar Manda

Shefar'am

79

754

77

Nazareth 75

JEZREEL VALLEY 73 Mizra 60

Afula

65 675

2 The Northern Coast.
Besides an especially lovely string of beaches, the Mediterranean coast south of Haifa offers wonderfully preserved archaeological sites at Caesarea and Nahsholim-Dor.

3 The Wine Country and Mt Carmel. The quality of Israeli wines has risen to heady heights on the international scene. One of the country's very first wineries is here, along with two others of equal stature. They're in or near charming towns such as Zichron Ya'akov, making access as easy as saying "l'chaim."

4 Akko to Rosh Hanikra.
The northern coast is known for its fine-sand beaches and nature reserves. You'll also find upscale bed-and-breakfast lodgings tucked away in long-established rural agricultural settlements. The sea-battered caves at Rosh Hanikra are worth the trip north.

1 Haifa. This steep-sloped port city, the largest in northern Israel, rewards you at every turn with hillside breezes and breathtaking vistas of the Mediterranean. At the base of the hill are the beaches, some of the area's best.

GETTING ORIENTED

Two seaside cities anchor this stretch of coastline. Haifa, a hilltop city on a peninsula jutting into the Mediterranean, offers the magnificent Baha'i Shrine and Gardens, the bustling German Colony, fine restaurants, the Carmelite Monastery, maritime museums, and more. The ancient port of Akko features underground ruins dating from the era of the Crusaders. Many people come to this area for the beaches, but the coastal Route 2 and the slightly more inland Route 4 can whisk you to such sites as King Herod's port city of Caesarea, the 19th-century town of Zichron Ya'akov, and the artists' colony of Ein Hod. Farther to the north are the cliffs and grottoes of Rosh Hanikra.

5

Updated by
Benjamin
Balint

Stretched taut on a narrow coastal strip between Tel Aviv and the Lebanese border, this gorgeous region offers a rare blend of Mediterranean beaches, fertile fields and citrus groves of the Sharon Plain, and seaside historical sights. Whether you succumb to the delights of the ancient port of Caesarea with its spectacularly restored Roman ruins, to the alleyways and beautifully vaulted Crusader halls of the old city of Akko, or to the vistas and gardens of modern Haifa, this lovely part of Israel won't disappoint.

It was in the softly contoured foothills of Mt. Carmel that the philanthropist Baron Edmond de Rothschild helped found the country's wine industry in the 19th century, now one of the region's most successful enterprises. The Carmel range rises dramatically to its pine-covered heights over the coast of Haifa, an amiable and thoroughly modern port city. Across the sweeping arc of Haifa Bay lies Akko, a jewel of a Crusader city that combines Romanesque ruins, Muslim minarets, and swaying palms. To the north, the resort town of Nahariya draws droves of vacationing Israelis. And just south of the Lebanese border, don't miss the amazing seaside coves of Rosh Hanikra, which have been scooped from the cliffs by the pounding surf.

As the scenery changes, so does the ethnic mix of the residents: Druze, Carmelite monks, Baha'is, Christian and Muslim Arabs, and Jews. Paleontologists continue to study on-site the artifacts of the most ancient natives of all, the prehistoric people of the caves of Nahal Me'arot, on Mt. Carmel. The Baha'is, dedicated to the idea that all great religions teach the same fundamental truths about an unknowable God, dominate Haifa's mountainside. Their terraced gardens spill down the slope toward a gleaming golden-domed shrine. White Friars of the Carmelite order preside over their serene monasteries in Haifa and in Mukhraka, on Mt. Carmel, next door to the Druze villages. The Druze of the Galilee and Carmel, now numbering more than 125,000, have lived here for a thousand years. Although they consider themselves an integral part of Israeli society, they maintain a unique cultural and religious enclave on Mt. Carmel, with the esoteric rites and rituals of their faith and the distinctive handlebar moustaches and white head scarves favored by the older men. Akko's vast subterranean Crusader vaults and halls, Ottoman skyline of domes and minarets, and outdoor *shuk* (market) are enchanting.

As you drive north, you'll enjoy long stretches of unimpeded views of the sparkling blue Mediterranean. Beautiful beaches lie beside Netanya, Haifa, and Achziv (and in between), with soft sand, no-frills hummus joints, and seaside restaurants. You can learn to scuba dive or explore underwater shipwrecks, hike the pine-scented slopes of Mt. Carmel, tread the winding lanes of Ein Hod artists' village, and taste local wines and tangy cheeses at some excellent wineries.

HAIFA AND THE NORTHERN COAST PLANNER 5

WHEN TO GO

There's really no bad time to visit this region. Spring (April and May) and fall (October and November) are balmy and crisp, making them the most pleasant seasons for travelers. Summer (June to September) is hot, but humidity remains low, and soft sea and mountain breezes cool things down. Winter (December to March) brings cold weather (sun interspersed with rain) and chilly sea winds.

As in the rest of Israel, hotels are often booked solid on weekends. On Saturdays and national holidays, Israelis hit the road, so north-to-south traffic out of Tel Aviv can be heavy. If you're taking a few days to explore the region, traveling Sunday to Thursday will guarantee you plenty of peace and quiet. If you can only go on Friday and Saturday, make reservations well in advance, and be prepared for crowds at the beaches and tourist sights.

PLANNING YOUR TIME

Haifa, the country's third-largest city, can be a useful base for exploring sights both to the south (Caesarea and the wine country) and north (the Crusader city in historic Akko and the coast up to Rosh Hanikra). Ein Hod, an artists' colony, and the Carmel Caves are also nearby. Haifa itself is notable for the Baha'i Gardens and Germany Colony. However, the coast's southern sights can also be seen easily if you're staying in Tel Aviv. Several companies offer day tours to Caesarea and Akko from Jerusalem, Tel Aviv, and Netanya; this may be a useful option.

Not counting time in Haifa, you could see the area's highlights in a couple of days, starting with King Herod's port city, Caesarea, and the wine country in the Carmel Hills. Check tour information for the wineries in Benyamina and Zichron Ya'akov. The picturesque Druze villages of Daliyat el Carmel and Isfiya are well worth a visit, too. You can also spend a full day exploring Akko, to the north; the grottoes at Rosh Hanikra are lovely, but far north. Plan time for swimming or hiking; the Mediterranean coast has great beaches and scenic trails.

GETTING HERE AND AROUND

AIR TRAVEL

Ben Gurion International Airport, the country's main gateway, is 105 km (65 miles) south of Haifa, about a 90-minute drive. A convenient *sherut* (shared taxi minibus) service to Haifa costs NIS 88, and runs 24 hours a day, 7 days a week.

BUS TRAVEL

Egged serves the coastal area from Jerusalem Central Bus Station to Tel Aviv Central Station. There's service to Netanya, Hadera, Zichron Ya'akov, and Haifa from both cities. From Jerusalem, a direct bus to Haifa takes one hour and 40 minutes. Getting to Caesarea requires a change at Hadera. To get to Akko, change at Haifa. Crowds are heavy at bus stations on Thursday night and Sunday morning. Buses don't operate from Friday evening to Saturday evening; in Haifa, select buses run on Saturday.

CAR TRAVEL

Driving is the most comfortable and convenient way to tour this region. You can take Route 2 (the coastal road) or Route 4 (parallel to Route 2, but slightly inland) north along the coast from Tel Aviv to Haifa, continuing on Route 4 up to the Lebanese border. From Jerusalem follow Route 1 to Tel Aviv; connect via the Ayalon Highway to Herzliya and Route 2.

TAXI TRAVEL

In towns, taxis can be hailed on the street day or night. Ask the driver to turn on the meter, or *moneh*.

TRAIN TRAVEL

The northern coast is one part of Israel where train travel is both practical and scenic. As always, remember that service is interrupted Friday evening to Saturday evening. Israel Railways trains from Jerusalem and Tel Aviv travel several times a day to Netanya, Benyamina, Caesarea, Haifa, Atlit, Akko, and Nahariya. You'll have to change trains in Tel Aviv when coming from Jerusalem.

The train line from Ben Gurion Airport travels to Tel Aviv, Benyamina, Atlit, Haifa, Akko, and Nahariya. The trip from Tel Aviv to Haifa takes about one hour. Sunday to Thursday, trains depart every 20 minutes from 6:20 am until 9:30 pm; on Friday they run from 6 am until an hour before sundown. On Saturday there are four departures after 7:30 pm. Train travel from Jerusalem to Haifa is feasible only if you have plenty of time, as you have to change in Tel Aviv.

RESTAURANTS

You won't have to look hard for a restaurant, whether simple or fancy, with a striking view of the Mediterranean. Fish, served with a variety of sauces, is usually grilled or baked. The most common types are *locus* (grouper), *mulit* (red mullet), *churi* (red snapper), and *farida* (sea bream). Also fresh, but from commercial ponds and the Sea of Galilee, are the ubiquitous tilapia, *buri* (gray mullet), and *iltit* (a hybrid of salmon and trout). Fresh seafood, such as shrimp and calamari, is available in abundance. Many casual restaurants serve schnitzel (breaded and fried chicken cutlets) with french fries, which kids often love.

Until recently, coastal restaurants weren't as refined as those in Tel Aviv. No longer. Haifa now has several first-class restaurants with creative chefs. The artists' village of Ein Hod offers sumptuous Argentinean dining, and there's locally famous falafel in the Druze village of Daliyat el Carmel. Netanya boasts the area's highest concentration of kosher establishments. Dress is always informal. *Prices in the reviews are the average cost of a main course at dinner or, if dinner isn't served, at lunch.*

HOTELS

Options range from small inns to luxury hotels, though the selection and quality of accommodations doesn't equal that of, say, Tel Aviv. Gracious bed-and-breakfasts (known in Israel as *zimmers*) are tucked into coastal rural settlements, mostly north of Nahariya. The splendid spa hotel in the Carmel Forest near Haifa deserves its reputation. In some places, such as Zichron Ya'akov, pickings are slim; but because this region is so compact, you can cover many coastal sights from one base, such as Haifa. *Prices in the reviews are the lowest cost of a standard double room in high season.*

HAIFA

Spilling down from the pine-covered heights of Mt. Carmel, Haifa is a city with a vertiginous setting that has led to comparisons with San Francisco. The most striking landmark on the mountainside is the gleaming golden dome of the Baha'i Shrine, set amid utterly beautiful garden terraces. The city is the world center for the Baha'i faith, and its members provide informative walking tours of the flower-edged 100-acre spot, a UNESCO World Heritage Site. At the top of the hill you'll find some small but interesting museums, the larger hotels, and two major universities. At the bottom is the lovingly restored German Colony, a perfect area for strolling.

Israel's largest port and third-largest city, Haifa was ruled for four centuries by the Ottomans and gradually spread its tendrils up the mountainside into a cosmopolitan city whose port served the entire Middle East. The climate is gentle, the beaches beautiful, and the locals friendly.

You won't see the religious garb of Jerusalem or the tattoos and piercings of Tel Aviv in this diverse but fairly conservative city. In fact, you can't always tell at a glance who is part of an Arab or Jewish Israeli family, or if someone is a more recent immigrant from the former Soviet Union.

GETTING HERE AND AROUND

A direct bus operated by Egged leaves Tel Aviv for Haifa every 20 minutes between 5:20 am and 11 pm; travel time is one hour. Trains from Tel Aviv to Haifa also take one hour and cost NIS 30.50. Trains depart every half hour from 6 am until 10:30 pm; on Friday from 6 am until an hour before sundown. During the day on Saturdays trains don't run, but there are four departures after 7:30 pm.

There are plenty of nice walks in the city, but to see the sights, a car or a taxi is required; another option is the local buses. The Carmel Tunnels, which bypass the most congested parts of Haifa by boring below Mt. Carmel, cuts a 30- to 45-minute drive down to less than 10. The toll is NIS 6, and can be paid with cash at the tollbooths. The tunnels aren't much use to visitors, but if you're just passing through, they could save you time. Coming north from Tel Aviv, the entrance is at the end of Route 2. From the north, it's off Route 4 near the Checkpoint Interchange.

Haifa has the six-station Carmelit subway—actually a funicular railway—that runs from Gan Ha'em Park on Hanassi Boulevard (adjacent to the Dan Panorama) in Central Carmel down to Kikar Paris in the port area in six minutes. The fare is NIS 6.60 for a single ticket (NIS 15 for a day pass), and the train operates Sunday to Thursday 6 am to midnight, Friday 6 to 3, and Saturday sundown to midnight.

Thirty-minute boat rides operate twice daily in each direction between Haifa and Akko.

The Haifa Cable Car travels from the lower station at Bat Galim to the upper station at Stella Maris, and offers panoramic views of the bay. It's accessible by bus routes 41 and 42 from Bat Galim and 25, 26, 27, 30, and 31 from Stella Maris. Free parking is available at both ends.

TOURS

Three times a week, Carmelit Cruiser offers boat tours of Haifa Bay. The ride, which leaves from Kishon dock, lasts one hour and costs NIS 30. Call ahead for departures.

ESSENTIALS

Boat Contact Carmelit Cruiser ☎ 04/841–8765.

Bus Contact Egged ☎ 03/694–8888 ⊕ www.egged.co.il/eng/.

Taxi Contacts Carmel ☎ 04/838–2727, 04/838–2626. **Horev** ☎ 04/888-8888.

Train Contact Israel Railways ☎ 03/611–7000 ⊕ www.rail.co.il.

Visitor Information Haifa Tourist Board ✉ 48 Ben Gurion Blvd., German Colony ☎ 04/853–5606 ✍ info@tour-haifa.co.il ⊕ www.tour-haifa.co.il ⊕ Sun.–Thurs. 9–5, Fri. 9–1.

EXPLORING HAIFA

Israel's "city on the hill" is divided into three main levels, each crisscrossed by parks and gardens: the port down below; Hadar, a commercial area in the middle; and Merkaz Carmel (known as "the Merkaz"), with the posher hotels and many restaurants, on the crest of Mt. Carmel.

Thanks to the beneficence of the Baha'is, you can enjoy a walking tour that takes you through the stunning terraces that lie like multicolored jewels from the crest of the city at Mt. Carmel to the German Colony below.

WORD OF MOUTH

"Shrine of the Bab is one of many holy sites in Israel. Perched on the slopes of Mt. Carmel, the Baha'i Gardens pay homage to Baha'i's founders."

—photo by GeneZ, Fodors.com member

TOP ATTRACTIONS

Fodor's Choice ★   **Baha'i Shrine and Gardens.** The most striking feature of the stunning gardens that form the centerpiece of Haifa is the Shrine of the Bab, whose brilliantly gilded dome dominates the city's skyline. The renovated shrine gleams magnificently with 11,790 gold-glazed porcelain tiles.

Haifa is the world center for the Baha'i faith, founded in Iran in the 19th century. It holds as its central belief the unity of mankind. Religious truth for Baha'is consists of progressive revelations of a universal faith. Thus the Baha'is teach that great prophets have appeared throughout history to reveal divine truths, among them Moses, Zoroaster, Buddha, Jesus, Muhammad, and most recently, the founder of the Baha'i faith, Mirza Husayn Ali, known as Baha'u'llah—"the Glory of God." The Shah and then the Ottomans exiled Baha'u'llah (1817–92) from his native Persia to Akko, where he lived as a prisoner for almost 25 years. The Baha'is' holiest shrine is on the grounds of Baha'u'llah's home, where he lived after his release from prison and where he's now buried, just north of Akko.

Here in Haifa, at the center of the shrine's pristinely manicured set of 19 garden terraces, is the mausoleum built for the Bab (literally, the "Gate"), the forerunner of this religion, who heralded the coming of a new faith to be revealed by Baha'u'llah. The Persian authorities martyred Bab in 1850. Baha'u'llah's son and successor built the gardens and shrine and had the Bab's remains reburied here in 1909. The building, made of Italian stone and rising 128 feet, gracefully combines the canons of classical European architecture with elements of Eastern design and also houses the remains of Baha'u'llah's son. The dome glistens with some 12,000 gilded tiles imported from the Netherlands. Inside, the floor is covered with rich Oriental carpets, and a filigree veils the serene inner shrine.

The magnificent gardens, with their gravel paths, groomed hedges, and 12,000 plant species, are a sight to behold: stunningly landscaped circular terraces extend from Yefe Nof Street for 1 km (½ mile) down the hillside to Ben Gurion Boulevard, at the German Colony. The terraces are a harmony of color and form—pale pink-and-gray-stone flights of stairs and carved urns overflowing with red geraniums set off the perfect cutouts of emerald green grass and floral borders, dark green trees, and wildflowers, with not a leaf out of place anywhere. The gardens, tended by 120 dedicated gardeners, are one of Israel's 11 UNESCO World Heritage Sites.

Three areas are open to the public year-round, except on Baha'i holidays: the shrine and surrounding gardens (*80 Hatzionut Avenue, near Shifra Street*); the upper terrace and observation point (*Yefe Nof Street*); and the entry at the lower terrace (*Hagefen Square, at the end of Ben Gurion Boulevard*). Free walk-in tours in English are offered at noon every day except Wednesday. These depart from 45 Yefe Nof Street, near the top of the hill. Note: the Shrine of the Bab is a pilgrimage site for the worldwide Baha'i community; visitors to the shrine are asked to dress modestly (no shorts). ⊠ *80 Hatzionut Ave., Merkaz Carmel* ☎ *04/831–3131* ✉ *ganbahai@bwc.org* ⊕ *www.ganbahai.org.il/en/ haifa/* 💲 *Free* ☉ *Shrine, daily 9–noon; gardens, daily 9–5.*

Fodor's Choice **German Colony.** Although it runs along a single boulevard, "The Colony"
★ packs in history (with explanatory placards), interesting architecture,
great restaurants, and wonderful spots for people-watching. Ben Gurion
Boulevard was the heart of a late-19th-century colony established by
the German Templer religious reform movement. Along either side are
robust two-story chiseled limestone houses with red-tile roofs. Many
bear German names, dates from the 1800s, biblical inscriptions on the
lintels, and old wooden shutters framing narrow windows.

Neglected for years, the German Colony is now one of the city's loveliest (and flattest) strolls. It's best to start your exploration around Yaffo
(Jaffa) Street so that you're walking toward the stunning Baha'i Gardens. Along the way you can have a meal or a cup of coffee, explore
the shops in the City Centre Mall, and learn about the history of the
Templers. Any time of day is pleasant, but evening, when the cafés and
restaurants are brimming with people, is best.

The Templers' colony in Haifa was one of seven in the Holy Land. The
early settlers formed a self-sufficient community; by 1883 they'd built
nearly 100 houses and filled them with as many families. Industrious
workers, they introduced the horse-drawn wagon—unknown before
their arrival—to Haifa. They also built with their own funds a pilgrimage road from Haifa to Nazareth. The Germans' labors gave rise to
modern workshops and warehouses, and it was under their influence
that Haifa began to resemble a modern city, with well-laid-out streets,
gardens, and attractive homes.

Haifa's importance to Germany was highlighted in 1898, when Kaiser
Wilhelm II sailed into the bay, on the first official visit to the Holy Land
by a German emperor in more than 600 years. In the 1930s, many
Templers began identifying with German nationalism and the Nazi
party, and during World War II the British deported them as nationals
of an enemy country.

Tikotin Museum of Japanese Art. Established in 1957 by renowned collector Felix Tikotin, this graceful venue on the crest of Mt. Carmel
adheres to the Japanese tradition of displaying beautiful objects that
are in harmony with the season, so exhibits change every three months.
The Japanese atmosphere, created in part by sliding doors and parti-
tions made of wood and paper, enhances a display of scrolls, screens,
pottery and porcelain, lacquer and metalwork, paintings from several
schools, and fresh-flower arrangements. The library, the largest of its
kind in Israel, houses some three-thousand volumes related to Japanese
art. ⊠ *89 Hanassi Blvd., Merkaz Carmel* ☎ *04/838–3554* ⊕ *www.tmja.
org.il* ⊠ *NIS 50* ☸ *Sun.–Wed. 10–4, Thurs. 10–7, Fri. 10–1, Sat. 10–5.*

Yefe Nof Street. Also known as Panorama Road, this gently curving
street high above the city skirts behind Haifa's biggest hotels, providing
remarkable views. Enjoy the beauty of the lushly planted Louis Promenade, with shaded benches along the way, beginning behind the Dan
Carmel Hotel. On a clear day, from any of several lookouts you can see
the port below, Akko across the bay, and the cliffs of Rosh Hanikra,
with Lebanon in the distance. Panorama Road is spectacular during
both day and night. ⊠ *Merkaz Carmel.*

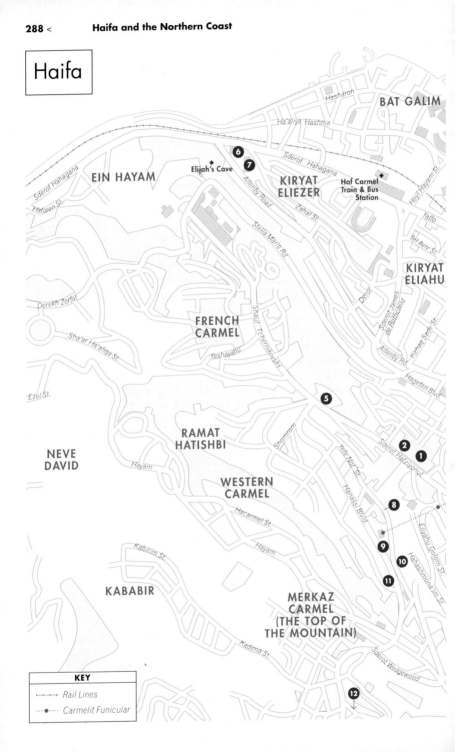

Haifa

BAT GALIM

Hasharoni

Ha'aliya Hashnia

Sderot Hahagana

EIN HAYAM

Elijah's Cave

KIRYAT ELIEZER

Haf Carmel Train & Bus Station

Hey'l Hayam St.

Sderot Hahagana

Haforen St.

Allenby Road

Zahal St.

Yaffo

Tel Aviv St.

KIRYAT ELIAHU

Stella Maris Rd.

Derekh Zorfat

Derot

Sderot James de Rothschild

FRENCH CARMEL

Shaul Tchernikovsky

Yizhar Sade St.

Sha'ar Ha'aliya St.

Yeshayahu

Allenby Rd.

Hagefen Blvd.

Ezel St.

5

RAMAT HATISHBI

Shomrom

2 1

NEVE DAVID

Hayam

Yefe Nof St.

WESTERN CARMEL

Hanassi Blvd.

8

Hacarmel St.

Eliyahu Golomb St.

Hayam

9

Kabirim St.

10

KABABIR

11

Hahashmona Im St.

MERKAZ CARMEL (THE TOP OF THE MOUNTAIN)

Kadima St.

Sderot Wedgewood

12

KEY

———— *Rail Lines*

····•···· *Carmelit Funicular*

Baha'i Shrine
and Gardens **1**

Carmelite Monastery
and Stella Maris Church **5**

Clandestine Immigration
and Naval Museum **6**

German Colony **3**

Haifa Museum of Art **4**

Haifa Zoo **9**

Hecht Museum **12**

Mané Katz
Museum **10**

National Maritime
Museum **7**

National Museum of
Science, Technology, and Space
(MadaTech) **13**

Technion **14**

Tikotin Museum
of Japanese Art **11**

Vista of Peace
Sculpture Garden **2**

Yefe Nof Street **8**

Haifa's History

First mentioned in the Talmud, the area around Haifa had two settlements in ancient times. To the east, in what's today a congested industrial zone in the port, lay Zalmona, and 5 km (3 miles) west around the cape was Shiqmona. The city was under Byzantine rule until the Arab conquest in the 7th century, when it became a center of glass production and dye making from marine snails.

CRUSADERS AND OTTOMANS

In 1099, the Crusaders conquered the city and maintained it as a fortress along the coastal road to Akko for 200 years. In the 12th century, a group of hermits established the Order of Our Lady of Mt. Carmel (the Carmelite order) over Elijah's Cave. After Akko and Haifa succumbed to the Mamluk Sultan Baybars in 1265, Haifa was destroyed and left derelict. It was a sleepy fishing village for centuries.

The city reawakened under the rule of the Bedouin sheikh Dahr el-Omar, who in 1750 ordered the city to be demolished and moved about 3 km (2 miles) to the south. The new town was fortified by walls and protected by a castle, and its port began to compete with that of Akko across the bay.

From 1775 until World War I, Haifa remained under Turkish control with a brief interruption: Napoléon came to Haifa en route to ignominious defeat at Akko during his Eastern Campaign. General Bonaparte left his wounded at the Carmelite Monastery when he beat a retreat in 1799, but the French soldiers there were killed and the monks driven out by Ahmed el-Jazzar, the victorious pasha of Akko. A small memorial stands before the monastery to this day.

THE 19TH CENTURY

The religious reform movement known as the Templers founded Haifa's German Colony in 1868, and in 1879 European Jews settled in the city.

Under the auspices of Sultan Abdul Hamid II, Haifa was connected to the legendary Hejaz railway through the Jezreel Valley to Damascus. Although the line is long dormant, a Turkish-built monument to the sultan stands in Haifa to this day.

MODERN TIMES

After World War I, Haifa was taken from the Turks by the British, and during the British Mandate period, was the scene of many dramatic confrontations between the British who sought to keep Jews from entering Palestine and the clandestine efforts of the Haganah to smuggle in immigrants and the survivors of the Holocaust. One of the ships used to run the British blockade, an old American craft called the *Af-Al-Pi-Chen*, can be seen in the Clandestine Immigration and Maritime Museum.

The city became the center of the Baha'i faith in the early 20th century. With the creation of a deep-water port in 1929, Haifa's development as a modern city began. By the time the State of Israel was declared in 1948, Haifa had a population of more than 100,000. Today it's the country's third-largest city, home to 270,000 Jews and Arabs.

Haifa's restored, 19th-century German Colony is a relaxing place to dine or spend an evening.

WORTH NOTING

Carmelite Monastery and Stella Maris Church. The imposing Stella Maris (Latin for "Star of the Sea") is graced by wall and ceiling paintings that bring to life the dramatic story of the prophet Elijah, the patron of the Carmelite order, and that depict King David, the Holy Family, and the four evangelists. During the Crusader period, hermits emulating Elijah's ascetic life lived in caves on this steep mountain slope. In the early 13th century, they united under the leadership of Saint Berthold, who petitioned the patriarch of Jerusalem for a charter. Thus was born the Carmelite order, which spread across Europe. The Carmelite monks were forced to leave their settlements on Mt. Carmel at the end of the 13th century and couldn't return for nearly four centuries. When they found Elijah's cave inhabited by Muslim dervishes, they set up a monastery nearby.

The church of the present monastery dates from 1836 and was built with the munificence of the French monarchy, hence the name of the surrounding neighborhood: French Carmel. A small pyramid memorial topped with an iron cross commemorates those French who were slaughtered here by the Turks in 1799 after the retreating Napoléon left his ailing troops behind at the monastery. Inside, paintings in the dome depict Elijah in the chariot of fire in which he ascended to heaven, and other biblical prophets. The small grotto a few steps down at the end of the nave is traditionally associated with Elijah and his pupil, Elisha. ⊠ *Stella Maris Rd., French Carmel* ☎ *04/833–7758* ▢ *Free* ☉ *Daily 8–12:30 and 3–6.*

Clandestine Immigration and Naval Museum. The rather dull name of this museum belies the dramatic story it tells of the heroic efforts to bring Jewish immigrants to Palestine from war-torn Europe in defiance of British policy. In 1939, on the eve of World War II, the British issued the so-called White Paper, which effectively strangled Jewish immigration to Palestine. Out of 63 clandestine ships that tried to run the blockade after the war's end, all but five were intercepted, and their passengers were deported to Cyprus. The museum—full of moving stories of courage and tenacity—is centered around the *Af Al Pi Chen* (Hebrew for "Nevertheless"), a landing craft which attempted to bring 434 Jewish refugees ashore. A photomural and model of the celebrated ship the *Exodus* recalls the story of the 4,530 refugees aboard who were forcibly transferred back to Germany in 1947, but not before the British forces opened fire on the ship. The history of Israel's navy, told here in impressive detail, begins with the transformation of these clandestine immigration craft into warships. ✉ *204 Allenby Rd., Kiryat Eliezer* ☎ *04/853–6249* 🎫 *NIS 15* ⊙ *Sun.–Thurs. 8:30–4.*

Elijah's Cave. This site is considered sacred by Jews, Christians, and Muslims; an early Byzantine tradition identified it as the cave in which Elijah found refuge from the wrath of Ahab, king of Israel from 871 to 853 BC. Graffiti from pilgrims of various faiths and centuries is scrawled on the right wall, and written prayers are often stuffed into crevices. Modest dress is required. The cave is a pretty 20-minute walk down the fairly steep path that begins across from the entrance to the Stella Maris Carmelite Monastery and church and descends past the lighthouse and World War II fortification. It is more easily accessible by a short flight of stairs that rises from Allenby Road not far from the Bat Galim cable-car station. ✉ *230 Allenby Rd., Ein Hayam* 🎫 *Free* ⊙ *Sun.–Thurs. 8–5, Fri. and Jewish holiday eves 8–1.*

Haifa Museum of Art. This museum, on the southern edge of the Wadi Nisnas neighborhood, displays artwork from all over the world, dating from the mid-18th century to the present. But it serves as a special repository of contemporary Israeli art: included are 20th-century graphics and contemporary paintings, sculptures, and photographs. The print collection is of special note, as are frequent solo exhibitions by young Israeli artists. The museum also houses an interactive children's wing. ✉ *26 Shabbtai Levy St., Hadar* ☎ *04/911–5911* ⊕ *www.hma.org.il* 🎫 *NIS 50* ⊙ *Sun.–Wed. 10–4, Thurs. 10–7, Fri. 10–1, Sat. 10–5.*

NEED A BREAK?

falafel joints. In a city known for its falafel, the universally beloved Israeli food, check out the falafel joints called Michel and Hazkenim at **18 and 21 Wadi Street**, the circular street in the Wadi Nisnas market, and George's at **26 Yohanan Hakadosh**. You'll get plenty of fresh steaming chickpea balls stuffed into warm pita bread with crunchy cucumber and tomato. ✉ *Wadi Nisnas.*

FAMILY **Haifa Zoo.** Amid masses of trees and lush foliage in the Gan Ha'Em park is a seemingly happy collection of roaring lions and tigers, big brown bears, chattering monkeys, stripe-tailed lemurs, a placid camel,

$ HOTEL **Crowne Plaza.** Catering to a business crowd, this well-designed hotel is built into a pine-shaded slope. **Pros:** indoor pool and Jacuzzi open until 9 pm; free Wi-Fi in rooms. **Cons:** mediocre breakfast by Israeli standards. [$] *Rooms from: $145* ✉ *111 Yefe Nof St., Merkaz Carmel* ☎ *04/835–0835* 🌐 *www.ihg.com* 🛏 *100 rooms* 🍴 *Breakfast* ⊕ *B6.*

$$$ HOTEL **Dan Carmel.** The Dan Carmel, beautifully situated on the heights of Merkaz Carmel, is a longtime favorite with stately charm and devoted staff. **Pros:** superb views; attentive staff. **Cons:** outdated decor; pool closed in winter. [$] *Rooms from: $330* ✉ *87 Hanassi Blvd., Merkaz Carmel* ☎ *04/830–3030* 🌐 *www.danhotels.com* 🛏 *204 rooms, 18 suites* 🍴 *Breakfast* ⊕ *B6.*

$$ HOTEL **Dan Panorama.** The glitzier younger sister of the Dan Carmel up the road, this 21-story hotel is popular with business executives (especially the comfortable second-floor lobby with its circular bar). **Pros:** welcoming staff; splendid views; large fitness center. **Cons:** no balconies; dated decor. [$] *Rooms from: $220* ✉ *107 Hanassi Blvd., Merkaz Carmel* ☎ *04/835–2222* ✉ *panoramahaifa@danhotels.com* 🌐 *www.danhotels.com* 🛏 *266 rooms* 🍴 *Breakfast* ⊕ *A5.*

$ HOTEL **Nof.** On Merkaz Carmel, these modest guest rooms take full advantage of the setting, with large windows facing the sea. **Pros:** central location; modest prices; excellent buffet breakfasts. **Cons:** basic rooms; lobby can be noisy; no pool. [$] *Rooms from: $155* ✉ *101 Hanassi Blvd., Merkaz Carmel* ☎ *04/835–4311* 🌐 *www.nofhotel.co.il* 🛏 *80 rooms, 6 suites* 🍴 *Breakfast* ⊕ *A6.*

$ B&B/INN **Port Inn Hostel Guest House.** A haven for budget travelers, this inn is in a neighborhood filled with interesting shops. **Pros:** cheerful garden; good for single travelers. **Cons:** far from tourist sites; not a lot of privacy. [$] *Rooms from: $90* ✉ *34 Yaffo St., Downtown* ☎ *04/852–4401* 🌐 *www.portinn.net* 🛏 *10 rooms, 9 with bath* 🍴 *Breakfast* ⊕ *C4.*

$$ HOTEL **Villa Carmel.** The facade may look ordinary, but this boutique hotel's interior is unlike anything else you'll find in Haifa. **Pros:** chic atmosphere; attention to detail; on a quiet street. **Cons:** no pool; no room service. [$] *Rooms from: $210* ✉ *1 Heinrich Heine, off 30 Moriah Blvd., Merkaz Carmel* ☎ *04/837–5777* 🌐 *www.villacarmel.co.il* 🛏 *16 rooms* 🍴 *Breakfast* ⊕ *A6.*

NIGHTLIFE AND THE ARTS

Haifa at night may not pulse like Tel Aviv, but there are more than a few things to do after dark. For information on performances and other special events in and around Haifa, check Friday's *Jerusalem Post* or the *Haaretz* newspaper; both publish separate weekend entertainment guides. In balmy weather, a stroll along the Louis Promenade and then along Panorama Road, with lovely views of nighttime Haifa, is a relaxing way to end the day.

NIGHTLIFE

For a festive evening, try the restaurants and cafés-cum-pubs in the German Colony. Night spots in Haifa come and go, and some open only on certain evenings, so call ahead if possible.

Barbarossa. The bar at Barbarossa is on the balcony, where you can enjoy happy hour while soaking up the great view from 6:30 to 9. The bar swings all night, aided by skilled bartenders, fine cognacs, and more than 100 whiskeys to choose from. There's free private parking for customers. ✉ *8 Pica St., next to Horev Center, Horev* ☎ *04/811–4010.*

Duke. The lovely Duke is a civilized old-world Irish pub with good draft beers and fish-and-chips. ✉ *107 Moriah Blvd., Merkaz Carmel* ☎ *04/834–7282.*

Frangelico. With the unlikely name of Frangelico, Haifa's first sushi bar turns into an attractive pub at night—the kind of place where everyone seems to know everyone else. A side room with sofas lends to the casual ambience. ✉ *132 Moriah Blvd., Merkaz Carmel* ☎ *04/824–8839.*

Pundak HaDov. One of Haifa's oldest and most reliable pubs and sports bars, the cozy Pundak HaDov (The Bear Inn) has live music weekly and tends to fill up with enthusiastic revelers. ✉ *135 Hanassi Blvd., Merkaz Carmel* ☎ *04/838–1703.*

THE ARTS

Haifa Symphony Orchestra. Under the direction of acclaimed maestro Noam Sheriff, the Haifa Symphony Orchestra performs at the Haifa Auditorium (Krieger Center) four to five times a month from October through July. For ticket and performance information, contact the box office. ✉ *6 Eliyahu Hakim St., French Carmel* ☎ *04/859–9499.*

Israel Philharmonic Orchestra. The world-class Israel Philharmonic Orchestra gives 20 concerts at the Haifa Auditorium (Rappaport Hall) from October through July. ✉ *138 Hanassi Blvd., Merkaz Carmel* ☎ *04/810–1558.*

SPORTS AND THE OUTDOORS

BEACHES

Haifa's coastline is one fine, sandy public beach after another. They span 5 km (3 miles) of coast and have lifeguard stations, changing rooms, showers, toilets, refreshment stands, sports areas, restaurants, and a winding stone promenade. In the north are the Bat Galim and Surfers Beaches. Moving south, you'll come across the Carmel Beach, Nirvana, Zamir, Dado, Dado South, and the Student's Beach. To be on the safe side, never swim when a lifeguard isn't on duty. There's parking at every beach, and all are free. All city beaches are reachable by local buses.

Carmel Beach. With its attractive boardwalk and beachside kiosks, Carmel Beach sits in front of the Leonardo Hotel at the southern entrance to Haifa. Although there are two lifeguard stations, it doesn't have the amenities of Dado and Zamir. ✉ *Access via Andrei Sakharov St., South Haifa.*

Dado Beach. On Saturday at Dado Beach, Haifa's longest stretch of sandy beach, Israelis of all ages come and folk dance, to the delight of onlookers. You'll also find exercise equipment, picnic areas, showers, and a small bathing pool for young children. ✉ *David Elazar St., South Haifa.*

Hof HaShaket. North of the Leonardo Hotel, and next to the Rambam Medical Center, the quiet Hof HaShaket offers separate gender days: Sunday, Tuesday, and Thursday for women; Monday, Wednesday, and Friday for men; Saturday for everyone. ⊠ *Entrance from Cheyl HaYam St., South Haifa.*

Zamir Beach. Zamir Beach, just next to Dado Beach, is regarded as one of the best Haifa beaches, with fine golden sand and many amenities, including coffeehouses, restaurants, access for the disabled and even Wi-Fi. ⊠ *David Elazar St., South Haifa.*

DIVING

Ze'ev HaYam. At Ze'ev HaYam, named after the captain who was instrumental in founding Haifa's shipping industry, you can sign up for a half-day introductory class or rent equipment and sail out to a dive site where you'll see underwater caves and a shipwreck. The staff is happy to pick you up at your hotel. ⊠ *Kishon Fishing Harbor, Haifa Port* ☎ *04/832–3911.*

> **BEACH BASICS**
>
> Between Tel Aviv and the Lebanese border are miles of beautiful sandy beaches, most of them public and attended by lifeguards from early May to mid-October. Many Israeli beaches are left untended off-season, but they're generally cleaned up and well maintained once warm weather returns. Beachside restaurants can make for rough-and-tumble eating because of loud music, but it's fun to eat fresh food by the beach. *Never* swim in the absence of a lifeguard, as undertows can be dangerous.

SHOPPING

Haifa is studded with modern shopping malls with boutiques, eateries, and movie theaters, not to mention drugstores, photography stores, and money-exchange desks.

Castra. Near the Hof Carmel railway station, a popular mall called Castra features three floors of jewelry and clothing boutiques and art workshops. It's easily spotted by Eric Brauer's large ceramic-tile mural outside depicting Old Testament themes. ⊠ *4 Fliman St., South Haifa* ☎ *04/859–0000.*

Panorama Center. Located in the heart of the Carmel Center next to the Dan Panorama hotel, the Panorama Center offers everything from a pharmacy and newspaper stand to a wine outlet and clothing shops. ⊠ *109 Hanassi Blvd., Merkaz Carmel* ☎ *04/837–5011.*

Sara's Gift Shop. Sara's Gift Shop in the Dan Carmel Hotel is crammed with jewelry made exclusively for this boutique, including silver inlaid with Roman glass, gold Baha'i pendants, and art-deco earrings. ⊠ *Dan Carmel Hotel, 85–87 Hanassi Blvd., Merkaz Carmel* ☎ *04/830–3098.*

THE NORTHERN COAST

Beaches abound, the sea sparkles, and skies are sunny most of the year in the coastal area south of Haifa. Archaeological sites, such as the outstanding Roman, Byzantine, and Crusader ruins at Caesarea, house beautiful restored treasures, and historical museums are fun and not fusty. Netanya and Nahsholim-Dor have plenty for seekers of sun and fun, including paragliding and other adventures. Fresh fish, seafood, and good local wine please every palate.

NAHSHOLIM-DOR

29 km (19 miles) south of Haifa.

The beautiful beach at Dor is fit for a king—not surprising since it has a royal history. Founded 3,500 years ago, biblical Dor was once the maritime capital of the Carmel coast. The best harbor between Jaffa and Akko, it was a target for many an imperial ambition, from the ancient Egyptians and the "Sea Peoples" through to King Solomon and on down. It was renowned in antiquity for its precious purple dye; reserved for royalty, this hue was extracted from a mollusk that was abundant along the coast. Today, as you watch fishing boats bob in the sheltered bays, you can complement your sun tanning with a swim to a small offshore island, a visit to the diving site, or a break at a pub.

GETTING HERE AND AROUND

Take Route 2, getting off at the Zichron Ya'akov exit. At the Fureidis Junction, travel north about 1 km (½ mile) until you reach the small sign for Nahsholim-Dor. There's no public transportation here.

EXPLORING

FAMILY **Mizgaga Museum.** Well worth a visit, this museum next to the Nahsholim Hotel holds a rich trove of finds from both local nautical digs and excavations at nearby Tel Dor. It's in the partly restored former glass factory opened by Baron Edmond de Rothschild in 1891 to serve the wineries of nearby Zichron Ya'akov. The sequence of peoples who settled, conquered, or passed through Dor—from the Canaanites to Phoenicians to Napoléon—can be traced through these artifacts. Of particular interest is the bronze cannon that Napoléon's vanquished troops dumped into the sea during their retreat from Akko to Egypt in May 1799. An informative film in English illuminates the history of the ancient port city of Dor. ✉ *Kibbutz Nahsholim, Rd. 7011* ☎ *04/639–0950* 🌐 *www.mizgaga.com/eng* 🎫 *NIS 18* 🕒 *Sun.–Thurs. 9–2, Fri. 9–1, Sat. 10:30–3.*

WHERE TO STAY

$ HOTEL FAMILY 🏨 **Nahsholim Hotel.** Low-slung buildings separated by lawns with hammocks and just steps from the beach contain standard rooms (many with sea views) and apartments that accommodate up to five people**Pros:** fabulous beach; family-friendly vibe. **Cons:** expensive for what you get. [$] *Rooms from: $170* ✉ *Kibbutz Nahsholim, Rd. 7011* ☎ *04/639–9533* 🌐 *www.nahsholim.co.il* 🛏 *41 rooms, 48 apartments* 🍴 *Breakfast.*

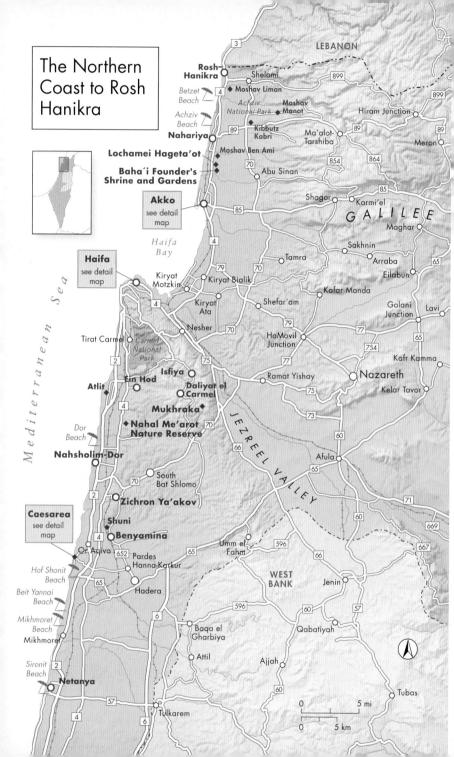

The Northern Coast to Rosh Hanikra

Rosh-Hanikra
Shelomi
Moshav Liman
Betzet Beach
Achziv National Park
Achziv Beach
Moshav Manot
Nahariya
Kibbutz Kabri
Ma'alot-Tarshiba
Lochamei Hageta'ot
Moshav Ben Ami
Baha'i Founder's Shrine and Gardens
Abu Sinan
Shagor
Karmi'el
Akko
see detail map
Haifa Bay
Maghar

LEBANON
Hiram Junction
GALILEE
Sakhnin
Tamra
Arraba
Eilabun
Haifa
see detail map
Kiryat Motzkin
Kiryat Bialik
Shefar'am
Kafar Manda
Kiryat Ata
Golani Junction
Lavi
Nesher
HaMovil Junction
Kafr Kamma
Tirat Carmel
Carmel National Park
Isfiya
Daliyat el Carmel
Ramat Yishay
Nazareth
Atlit
Ein Hod
Kelar Tavor
Mukhraka
Nahal Me'arot Nature Reserve
Dor Beach
JEZREEL VALLEY
Nahsholim-Dor
South Bat Shlomo
Afula
Zichron Ya'akov
Caesarea
see detail map
Shuni
Benyamina
Umm el Fahm
Or Aqiva
Pardes Hanna-Karkur
Hof Shonit Beach
Beit Yannai Beach
WEST BANK
Jenin
Hadera
Mikhmoret Beach
Mikhmoret
Baqa el Gharbiya
Qabatiyah
Sironit Beach
Attil
Ajjah
Netanya
Tubas
Tulkarem

Mediterranean Sea

0   5 mi
0   5 km

SPORTS AND THE OUTDOORS

Fodor'sChoice **Dor Beach.** Part of a coastal nature reserve, Dor Beach, also known as
★ Tantura Beach, is a dreamy stretch of beige sand. Rocky islets form
breakwaters and jetties provide calm seas for happy bathers. Amenities
are ample: lifeguards in season, chair and umbrella rentals, a first-aid
station, a restaurant, parking, and changing rooms and showers. The
beach, beside Nahsholim Hotel, gets crowded on summer weekends
and holidays. ⊠ *Off Rte. 4.*

Paradive. Paradive offers thrills and chills with tandem skydives 12,000
feet over the Mediterranean. No experience is required. It's about 3
km (2 miles) north of Nahsholim Hotel. ⊠ *Habonim Beach, off Rte. 4*
☎ *04/639–1068* ⊕ *www.paradive.co.il.*

Underwater Archaeological Center. Kurt Raveh, a marine archaeologist
and resident of Nahsholim Hotel, runs the Underwater Archaeological
Center. Raveh conducts underwater expeditions and "dives into history" where divers (even those without experience) get to tour ancient
shipwrecks (many of which he discovered) and explore reefs under his
experienced eye. You can also arrange kayaking trips along the coast.
⊠ *Nahsholim Hotel* ☎ *052/516–2795* ⊕ *www.northern-wind.com.*

EN
ROUTE
Atlit Detention Camp. Atlit is a peninsula with the jagged remains of an
important Crusader castle. Of more recent vintage, to the west (about
1,500 feet from the highway) is the Atlit detention camp used by the
British to house refugees smuggled in during and after World War II.
The reconstructed barracks, fences, and watchtowers stand as remind-
ers of how Jewish immigration was outlawed under the British Mandate
after the publication of the infamous White Paper in 1939. More than
a third of the 120,000 illegal immigrants to Palestine passed through
the camp from 1934 to 1948. In 1945, Yitzhak Rabin, then a young
officer in the Palmach, planned a raid that freed 200 detainees. The
authenticity of the exhibit is striking: it was re-created from accounts of
actual detainees and their contemporaries; you'll see the living quarters,
complete with laundry hanging from the rafters. The camp is 15 km
(9 miles) south of Haifa. ⊠ *Rte. 2* ☎ *04/984–1980* 🎫 *NIS 18* ⊗ *Sun.–*
Thurs. 9–2, Fri. 9–1, Sat. by prior arrangement.

CAESAREA

49 km (29½ miles) south of Haifa.

The Phoenicians discovered it, and the Romans fell in love with it: Caesarea is most famous for its intriguing Roman, Byzantine, and Crusader
ruins, but also offers a stroll through artists' galleries, an underwater
archaeological park, and culinary delights. Modern-day Caesarea is a
popular tourist center that juxtaposes a vibrant past and bustling present. Near the archaeological site is the well-to-do community of Caesarea, a group of homes on the sea. Here you'll find the Ralli Museum
and the famed Roman aqueduct.

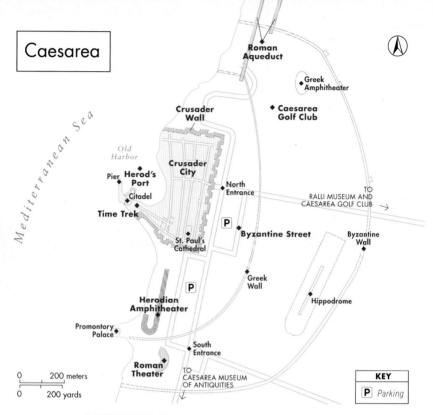

Caesarea

Mediterranean Sea

Roman Aqueduct

Greek Amphitheater

Caesarea Golf Club

Crusader Wall

Old Harbor

Crusader City

Pier

Herod's Port

Citadel

Time Trek

North Entrance

TO RALLI MUSEUM AND CAESAREA GOLF CLUB →

Byzantine Street

Byzantine Wall

St. Paul's Cathedral

Greek Wall

Hippodrome

Herodian Amphitheater

Promontory Palace

South Entrance

Roman Theater

TO CAESAREA MUSEUM OF ANTIQUITIES

0   200 meters
0   200 yards

KEY

P *Parking*

GETTING HERE AND AROUND

A car is your best option for reaching Caesarea. It's off Route 2, about one hour by car from Tel Aviv or Haifa. You can also opt for a guided bus tour with Egged Tours or United Tours, two well-regarded companies.

ESSENTIALS

Tour Contacts Egged Tours ☎ *03/920–3992* ⊕ *www.eggedtours.com.*
United Tours ☎ *03/617–3333* ⊕ *www.unitedtours.co.il.*

EXPLORING

Fodor's Choice
★

Caesarea. By turns an ancient Roman port city, Byzantine capital, and Crusader stronghold, Caesarea is one of the country's major archaeological sites—and a delightful place to spend a day of leisurely sightseeing among the fascinating ruins. You can browse in souvenir shops and art galleries, take a dip at the beach, snorkel or dive around a submerged port, or enjoy a seaside meal. Caesarea is an easy day trip from Tel Aviv and Haifa or even Jerusalem.

There are two entrances to this intriguing site. A good strategy is to start at the Roman Theater, at the southern entrance. After exploring, you can then leave through the northern entrance. If you're short on time, enter through the northern entrance and take a quicker tour of the site. At either entrance, pick up the free brochure and map.

Entry to the **Roman Theater** is through one of the vomitoria (arched tunnels that served as entrances for the public). Herod's theaters—here as elsewhere in Israel—were the first of their kind in the ancient Near East. The theater today seats 3,600 and is a spectacular venue for summer concerts and performances. What you see today is largely a reconstruction. Only a few of the seats of the *cavea* (where the audience sat) near the orchestra are original, in addition to some of the stairs and the decorative wall at the front of the stage.

The huge **Herodian Amphitheater** is a horseshoe-shaped stadium with sloping sides filled with rows of stone seats. It's most likely the one mentioned by 1st-century AD historian Josephus Flavius in *The Jewish War*. A crowd of 10,000 watched horse and chariot races and various sporting events here some 2,000 years ago. Up the wooden steps, you'll see the street's beautiful and imaginative mosaic floors in the bathhouse complex of the Roman-Byzantine administrative area.

King Louis IX of France built the walls that surround the **Crusader City.** The bulk of what you see today—the moat, escarpment, citadel, and walls, which once contained 16 towers—dates from 1251, when the French monarch spent a year pitching in with his own two hands to help restore the existing fortifications. As you enter the southern wall gate of the Crusader city, you'll see the remains of an unfinished cathedral with its three graceful apses.

At the observation point, you can gaze out over the remains of **Herod's Port,** once a magnificent sight that writers of the day compared to Athens' Port of Piraeus. An earthquake devastated the harbor in AD 130, which is why the Crusaders utilized only a small section of it when they conquered the city in 1101.

East of the northern entrance to the site, a fenced-in area encloses Caesarea's **Byzantine Street.** During the Byzantine period and late Roman times, Caesarea thrived as a center of Christian scholarship. In the 7th century, Caesarea boasted a famous library of some 30,000 volumes that originated with the collection of the Christian philosopher Origen (185–254), who lived here for two decades. Towering over the street are two headless marble statues, probably carted here from nearby Roman temples. The provenance of the milky white statue is unknown; Emperor Hadrian might have commissioned the reddish figure facing it when he visited Caesarea.

A wonderful finale to your trip to Caesarea, especially at sunset, is the beachfront **Roman Aqueduct.** The chain of arches tumbling northward until they disappear beneath the sand is a captivating sight. During Roman times, the demand for a steady water supply was considerable, but the source was a spring about 13 km (8 miles) away in the foothills of Mt. Carmel. Workers cut a channel approximately 6½ km (4 miles) long through solid rock before the water was piped into the aqueduct. In the 2nd century, Hadrian doubled its capacity by adding a new channel. Today you can walk along the aqueduct and see marble plaques dedicated to the troops of various legions who toiled here. ✉ *Off Route 2, near Kibbutz Sdot Yam* ☎ *04/626-7080* ⊕ *www.parks.org.il* ✆ *NIS 38* ☉ *Oct.–Mar., daily 8–4; Apr.–Sept., daily 8–6.*

Herod's Amazing Port at Caesarea

The port's construction at Caesarea was an unprecedented challenge—there was no artificial harbor of this size anywhere in the world. But Herod wasn't one to avoid a challenge and spent twelve years building a port for the luxury-goods trade (including spices, textiles, and precious stones) that would make Caesarea the economic capital of the country and the most modern harbor in the whole Roman Empire.

During underwater research in the 1970s, archaeologists were stunned to discover concrete blocks near the breakwater offshore, indicating the sophisticated use of hydraulic concrete (which hardens underwater).

Historians knew that the Romans had developed such techniques, but before the discoveries at Caesarea, they never knew hydraulic concrete to have been used on such a massive scale. The main ingredient in the concrete, volcanic ash, was probably imported from Italy's Mt. Vesuvius, as were the wooden forms. Teams of professional divers actually did much of the trickiest work, laying the foundations hundreds of yards offshore.

Once finished, two massive breakwaters—one stretching west and then north from the Citadel restaurant some 1,800 feet and the other 600 feet long, both now submerged—sheltered an area of about 3½ acres from the waves and tides.

Two towers, each mounted by three colossal statues, marked the entrance to the port; and although neither the towers nor the statues have been found, a tiny medal bearing their image was discovered in the first underwater excavations here in 1960. The finished harbor also contained the dominating temple to Emperor Augustus and cavernous storage facilities along the shore.

Time Trek. When you're exploring the harbor area, don't miss the Time Trek. Inside, you'll meet twelve of Caesarea's fascinating historic personages—among them Herod the Great, Rabbi Akiva, and St. Paul. These realistic-looking, larger-than-life figures can answer all kinds of questions you might have about their long-ago lives in Caesarea. If you climb the stairs of the nearby squarish stone tower of the recreated fortress on the pier, you can view an intriguing three-dimensional animation on giant screens that explains the amazing construction of the port. ☎ *6550 ⊕ *www.caesarea.com.*

Caesarea Museum of Antiquities. In Kibbutz Sdot Yam just outside Caesarea, this excellent museum houses many of the artifacts found by kibbutz members as they plowed their fields in the 1940s. The small museum has arguably the best collection of late-Roman sculpture and figurines in Israel; impressive holdings of rare Roman and Byzantine gemstones; and a large variety of coins minted in Caesarea over the ages, as well as oil lamps, urns excavated from the sea floor, and fragments of jewelry. ⊠ *Kibbutz Sdot Yam, near southern entrance to Caesarea* ☎ *04/636–4367* 💲 *NIS 13* ⊗ *Tues.–Thurs. 10–4, Fri. 10–1.*

Caesarea. "We stumbled upon this field of flowers by the ruins." —photo by mgplessner, Fodors.com member

Ralli Museum. Once you've entered Caesarea's villa area, you can't miss the two Spanish colonial-style buildings of the Ralli Museum, with their red tiled roofs and expansive terraces. One of these dazzling white buildings houses an exhibit on the ancient city's history. The second building, in a Moorish style, examines the golden age of Spanish Jewry in the Middle Ages. It's a pleasure to wander along the walls of the courtyard and gaze at the sculptures of various dignitaries such as Maimonides and Spinoza. Inside are paintings with biblical themes by European artists of the 16th to 18th centuries. Rotating exhibitions feature contemporary Latin American art. ✉ *Rothschild Blvd., next to water tower* ☎ *04/626–1013* 🌐 *www.rallimuseums.com* 🎟 *Free* 🕒 *Mar.–Dec., Mon., Tues., Thurs., and Fri. 10:30–3; Jan. and Feb., Fri. and Sat. 10:30–3.*

WHERE TO EAT

$$ ECLECTIC FAMILY 🍴 **Agenda.** If you're one of those people who could eat breakfast three times a day, Agenda is for you. Try the *shakshuka*, a local dish in which eggs are poached in a sharp tomato sauce. For lunch and dinner there are also pizzas, sushi, and other light fare, plus cocktails and wine. The staff is friendly, the atmosphere casual. [$] *Average main: NIS 60* ✉ *Off Rte. 2, Caesarea Junction* ☎ *04/626–2092* 🕒 *No dinner Fri. No breakfast or lunch Sat.*

$$$ MEDITERRANEAN FAMILY 🍴 **Crusaders' Restaurant (HaTzalbanim).** You can depend on savory fare at this cavernous seaside restaurant. Expect the menu to include plenty of fresh seafood, caught right from the sea below, as well as juicy steaks and kebabs. An excellent starter is the salad of grilled eggplant, hummus, and fried cauliflower, with crunchy pita rounds toasted with olive oil and local spices served alongside. House specialties include baked

Caesarea: Roman City

Herod the Great gave Caesarea its name, dedicating the magnificent Roman city he built to his patron, Augustus Caesar. It was the Roman emperor who had crowned Herod—born to an Idumean family that had converted to Judaism—King of the Jews around 30 BC.

Construction began in 22 BC; Herod spared nothing in his elaborate designs for the port and the city itself, which included palaces, temples, a theater, a marketplace, a hippodrome, and water and sewage systems. When Caesarea was completed 12 years later, only Jerusalem outshined it. Its population under Herod grew to around 100,000, and the city covered some 164 acres.

In AD 6, a decade after Herod died, Caesarea became the seat of the Roman procurators, one of whom was Pontius Pilate, governor of Judea when Jesus was crucified. With Jerusalem predominantly Jewish, the

Romans preferred the Hellenistic Caesarea, with its Jewish minority, as the seat of their administration.

But religious harmony didn't prevail. The mixed population of Jews and Gentiles (mainly Greeks and Syrians) repeatedly clashed, with hostilities exploding during the Jewish revolt of AD 66. Vespasian, proclaimed emperor by his legions in AD 69, squelched the first Jewish rebellion. A year later, his son Titus razed Jerusalem and celebrated his suppression of the Jewish revolt.

Henceforth, Caesarea was a Roman colony and the local Roman capital of Palestine for nearly 600 years. It was here that Peter converted the Roman centurion Cornelius to Christianity—a milestone in the spread of the new faith—and Paul preached and was imprisoned for two years. In the 2nd century, Rabbi Akiva, the spiritual mentor of the Bar Kochba revolt, was tortured to death here.

---

red snapper topped with chopped vegetables or black mussels sautéed in garlic, butter, and wine. Still hungry? Creamy cheesecake or warm apple pie with ice cream will do the trick. $ *Average main: NIS 80* ✉ *Northern end of the port* ☎ *04/636–1679.*

$$$ ✗ **Helena.** Two of Israel's best-known culinary personalities, Amos Sion
MEDITERRANEAN   and Uri Buri, opened this restaurant to create a first-rate yet affordable
Fodor'sChoice   dining experience. It occupies a beautifully restored stone building in
★   the ancient harbor. Large windows everywhere maximize the sea view under a wooden pergola. The chef puts an Israeli spin on Mediterranean-style cooking, turning out such tantalizing appetizers as calamari with lemon and hyssop leaves on sheep's milk yogurt, and sliced sirloin in aged balsamic vinegar with Cambozola cheese and pistachios. Main dishes include an aromatic fish stew made of red mullet, spinach, and Swiss chard, and grilled *barbuni* (sardine-sized fish). The wine room holds the chef's private collection. A children's menu is available. $ *Average main: NIS 95* ✉ *Southern end of the port* ☎ *04/610–1018.*

$$ ✗ **Minato.** With a name that means "port" in Japanese, Minato is per-
JAPANESE   fect for beachgoers craving sushi. The restaurant does a brisk take-out business, serving sashimi and nigiri as well as a variety of tempura dishes. You can also eat at the long sushi bar and watch the knives

flash in front of you. Try the *temaki*, a cone of seaweed filled with rice, vegetables, and the fish of your choice. [$] *Average main: NIS 60* ✉ *Rte. 2* ☎ *04/636–0812* 🌐 *www.minato.co.il* ⏲ *No dinner Fri. No lunch Sat.*

WHERE TO STAY

$$ HOTEL FAMILY 🏨 **Dan Caesarea.** Equidistant from Tel Aviv and Haifa, this chain hotel suits business executives and vacationers alike. **Pros:** beautiful grounds; family-friendly vibe; helpful staff. **Cons:** no public transportation; far from restaurants. [$] *Rooms from: $290* ✉ *1 Rothschild St.* ☎ *04/626–9111* 🌐 *www.danhotels.com* 🛏 *111 rooms, 3 suites* 🍴 *Breakfast.*

SPORTS AND THE OUTDOORS

BEACHES

Caesarea Beach Club. In a calm cove in Caesarea's ancient harbor, the Caesarea Beach Club has chairs, umbrellas, and showers. A lifeguard is on duty in season, and the restaurant sells sandwiches and other light fare. Admission is NIS 25. ✉ *Northern entrance to archaeological site.*

Hof Shonit. The largest and most popular beach in the area is the exceptionally well-kept Hof Shonit (Reef Beach). There are lifeguards in season, a refreshment stand, and a restaurant, as well as restrooms and cold showers. Parking is NIS 15. ✉ *South of archaeological site.*

Roman Aqueduct. Caesarea's Roman aqueduct frames a spacious beach with the dramatic backdrop of arches disappearing into the sand. There's no entrance fee, and there's plenty of parking, but few amenities— no restaurants and no promenade. The beach and swimming areas have been cleared of rocks and debris, but swimming outside the designated area is prohibited. Never swim unless the seasonal lifeguard is on duty. ✉ *North of archaeological site.*

GOLF

Caesarea Golf Club. The country's only 18-hole golf course is the Caesarea Golf Club, adjacent to the Dan Caesarea. Although it was first established by the Rothschilds in the 1960s, noted golf course architect Pete Dye remodeled the course to high standards in 2009. Greens fees are NIS 480 on weekdays, NIS 540 on weekends. There's also a pro shop and the Albatross restaurant. ✉ *Off Rte. 2* ☎ *04/610–9600* 🌐 *www.caesarea.com.*

Ga'ash Golf Club. At the nine-hole Ga'ash Golf Club, you can play a second time from alternative tees to make for an 18-hole experience. Greens fees are NIS 300 for nine holes on weekdays and NIS 375 on weekends. There's a shop and a restaurant here, too. ✉ *Off Rte. 2* ☎ *09/951–5111* 🌐 *www.golfgaash.co.il.*

SCUBA DIVING

Old Caesarea Diving Center. Located inside the National Park, this diving center runs a full range of diving courses for novices, experts, and everyone in between. Snorkelers are welcome, and divers can use a plastic map and four underwater trails marked by ropes to follow a route of numbered artifacts in the submerged port built by King Herod 2,000 years ago. Half-hour introductory dives to a depth of six meters range from NIS 230 to NIS 350. You can also explore the nocturnal marine life on a night dive. ✉ *Caesarea Harbor, behind Time Trek* ☎ *04/626–5898* 🌐 *www.caesarea-diving.com.*

NETANYA

65 km (43 miles) south of Haifa, 30 km (18 miles) north of Tel Aviv.

The lively resort city of Netanya (literally, "gift of God") has a pretty seaside promenade along the cliffs, endless sandy beaches, a pleasant town square, and plenty of cafés and restaurants. Once a sleepy place surrounded by orange groves, the town—named after Jewish philanthropist Nathan Strauss—has steadily grown from a few settlers in 1929 to some 200,000 residents today. Since the 1930s, it has also been a center for the diamond-cutting industry.

Just south of the city are several nature reserves: the Irises Reserve, where purple irises flower in February and March; the Nahal Poleg Reserve, with fauna unique to the area; and the Udim Reserve, which includes a pool with turtles, fish, and waterbirds.

Though citrus farming is still evident on Netanya's outskirts, there are few traces of small-town charm. Tracts of residential development during the past five years or so can be seen all along the southern approach to the city following the shoreline, with high-rise towers dotting the landscape, many of the apartment units bought by vacationers from abroad.

GETTING HERE AND AROUND

To get here by car from Tel Aviv or Haifa, take coastal Route 2. Trains from Haifa depart on the hour and take about 25 minutes. Egged buses from Haifa leave at least every 30 minutes and take 1 hour 40 minutes.

ESSENTIALS

Vistor Information Netanya Tourist Information Office ⊠ *12 Ha'atzmaut Sq.* ☎ *09/882–7286* ⊕ *www.gonetanya.com.*

EXPLORING

Ha'atzmaut Square. Benches set among the palm trees surround a large fountain at this lively central square. Its open-air cafés and restaurants are crowded from the morning until late into the evening. Netanya attracts droves of French visitors, and in summer their lilting tones float above the café au lait and croissants. Saturday nights are often enlivened by folk dancing, and the amphitheater hosts free concerts in summer and an arts-and-crafts fair on Friday morning.

NEED A BREAK?

Tony Ice Café. Cool off at Tony Ice Café with divine, authentic gelati in a huge array of flavors, all made by hand by a family of immigrants from Italy. The ice-cream parlor also offers a wide selection of coffees, milkshakes, and pastries. ⊠ *Ha'atzmaut Sq., 5 Herzl St.* ☎ *09/834–0406.*

FAMILY **Seaside Promenade.** Also known as "the boulevard," the seaside promenade extends north and south of the city for about 6 km (4 miles). Its beautifully landscaped walkways wind around the contours of the sandstone cliffs overlooking the sea; every angle affords a gorgeous view. It's dotted with pergola-shaded benches, wooden bridges, colorful playground areas, and waving palm trees. An elevator at the center of the promenade eases the climb up and down the seaside cliff.

During the Jewish holiday of Purim, revelers in Netanya and around the country dress up in costume.

WHERE TO EAT

$$$$
STEAKHOUSE

✗ **El Gaucho.** Tucked into the Carmel Hotel, El Gaucho is one of Israel's best kosher steak houses. Decorated in a rustic style, the restaurant is dominated by a dramatic view of the sea. South American–style meat specialties, among them thick slabs of entrecote steaks and veal asado, are cooked over embers on a giant grill. The kitchen also offers grilled sea bream and skewered chicken, and the wine list is extensive. $ *Average main: NIS 130* ✉ *Carmel Hotel, Oved Ben Ami St.* ☎ *09/884–1264* ⊕ *www.elgaucho.co.il* ⌚ *Reservations essential* ⊗ *No dinner Fri. No lunch Sat.*

$$$
FRENCH

✗ **Mul Hayam.** Perched on a cliff overlooking the sea, this eatery has a wonderful view from every table. Its menu has a French accent: trout amandine in butter and herbs, for example, and mushroom or spinach quiches. There's also an extensive wine menu. Seating is available in an outdoor plaza, with its pleasant sea breeze, or in the dining room with its comfortable upholstered banquettes. $ *Average main: NIS 90* ✉ *1 King David Plaza, Gan Hamelech* ☎ *09/884–5885* ⊗ *No dinner Fri. Closed Sat.*

$$
MEDITERRANEAN

✗ **Miriam's Grill (Shipudei Miriam).** A stone's throw from the main approach to the beach, this well-known eatery on Ha'atzmaut Square faces a bubbling fountain. Moroccan-style grilled fish and lamb dishes are served both indoors and outdoors. Appetites sharpened by sea breezes and splashes in the surf will be rewarded with appetizers like creamy hummus, tasty couscous, or shakshuka. Main dishes are served with crispy fries or green salads. Wine and beer are available. $ *Average main: NIS 60* ✉ *7 Ha'atzmaut Sq.* ☎ *09/834–1376* ⊗ *No dinner Fri. No lunch Sat.*

$$
SEAFOOD
✕ **Rosemarine.** At this unpretentious heaven for fish lovers, you can enjoy fresh and tasty fare as you sit indoors or on the terrace overlooking the famous promenade. The kitchen serves a wide range of excellent fish dishes, such as tilapia, cod, and gray mullet, grilled, baked, or sautéed. Entrées come with salad or roasted potatoes. $ *Average main: NIS 75* ⊠ *8 Nitza Blvd.* ☎ *09/832–3322* ⊘ *Closed weekends.*

WHERE TO STAY

$
HOTEL
⬚ **Mizpe Yam.** Don't expect luxury at this family-owned five-story hotel; what you can count on is good value and a warm welcome. **Pros:** near the promenade and beach; nice fifth-floor sun roof. **Cons:** no sea views; no-frills decor. $ *Rooms from: $125* ⊠ *1 Jabotinsky St.* ☎ *09/862–3730* ⊕ *www.mizpe-yam.co.il* ⤴ *35 rooms* ⦶ *Breakfast.*

$$$
HOTEL
⬚ **Seasons Netanya.** Consistently good service is the hallmark of this hotel; guest rooms are spacious, with private terraces and sea views, and the bathrooms are luxurious. **Pros:** free Wi-Fi; sea views. **Cons:** not for those seeking peace and quiet. $ *Rooms from: $350* ⊠ *1 Nice Blvd.* ☎ *09/860–1555* ⊕ *www.seasons.co.il* ⤴ *103 rooms, 45 suites* ⦶ *Breakfast.*

SPORTS AND THE OUTDOORS

BEACHES

Showers, restrooms and changing rooms, lifeguards, and first-aid stations are available free at all of Netanya's beaches, which cover 14 km (8½ miles) of soft, sandy coastline. Most beaches rent beach chairs and umbrellas.

Beit Yannai. About 5 km (3 miles) north of Netanya is lovely Beit Yannai, named after ancient Judean king Alexander Yannai. Amenities include barbecue grills, picnic tables, restrooms with showers, chair and umbrella rentals, and seasonal lifeguards. There's a seafood restaurant right on the beach, and you can stroll along the Alexander Stream, shaded by eucalyptus trees. Parking is NIS 20 on weekdays and NIS 30 on Saturday. ☎ *09/866–6230.*

Herzl. Netanya's most popular beach, Herzl, has a broad staircase that leads down to the waterfront. For fitness nuts there's a shaded exercise area with all sorts of equipment, volleyball nets, and a paved basketball court. You can rent kayaks and windsurfing gear in the summer. The beach is handicap accessible. There are also a café and two lifeguard stations. ⊠ *Ha'atzmaut Square.*

Kiryat Sanz. North of town is the Orthodox beach Kiryat Sanz, where men and women have different bathing days and hours. ⊠ *Nitza Blvd.*

Mikhmoret. The beach at Mikhmoret, a tiny *moshav* 7½ km (4½ miles) north of Netanya, is popular with swimmers as well as those who laze away the day under an umbrella. The huge dirt parking lot, which charges NIS 30 per car, is 1 km (½ miles) after the turnoff from Route 2. There are three lifeguard stations, a restaurant, a café, and chair and umbrella rentals.

Sironit. The main beach, Sironit, is the largest stretch of sand on the Netanya coast. An elevator takes you down the sandstone cliff to this beach. There are two cafés and two drink kiosks with seating inside and out. Fridays are filled with salsa and folk dancing. The parking lot is on the beach, just south of Ha'atzmaut Square. It costs NIS 15 per car, NIS 25 on Saturday. ⊠ *Gad Machness St.*

HORSEBACK RIDING

The Ranch (Hachava). In northern Netanya, The Ranch offers horseback riding for NIS 120 per hour. It's wise to reserve well ahead for weekend trips or for sunset rides along the beach. ⊠ *Havatzelet Hasharon St.* ☎ *09/866–3525* ⊕ *www.the-ranch.co.il.*

PARAGLIDING

Netanya's cliffs make for exciting paragliding. Under the guidance of experienced instructors, you take off from a specially designed field along the promenade about half a mile south of the city center.

Dvir Paragliding. Dvir Paragliding is an established company that offers thrilling adventures throughout the year, but the ideal time is from May to October. Make reservations at least two days in advance. ☎ *054/655–4466* ⊕ *www.dvirparagliding.co.il.*

Paragliding Israel. Paragliding Israel offers paragliding instruction as well as a video of you soaring through the air. ☎ *052/803–3824* ⊕ *www.paraglidingisrael.ning.com.*

Sky Paragliding School. Sky Paragliding School, founded in 1998, offers a one-time guided experience as well as two-day introductory courses. ☎ *09/954–9788* ⊕ *www.paragliding.co.il.*

THE WINE COUNTRY AND MT. CARMEL

Wine has been produced in this fertile region for thousands of years. In the book of Deuteronomy, the fruit of the vine was listed as one of the seven blessed species of fruit found in the land of Israel. The Sharon plain near the Mediterranean coast south of Haifa, including the towns of Zichron Ya'akov and Benyamina, is the largest grape growing area in Israel. Though the Rothschilds updated viniculture around Zichron Ya'akov some 120 years ago, truly world-class wines began to appear only in the 1990s. After a tour of a winery, it's delightful to sit under the grapevines and sample the vintages along with fresh salad, warm bread, and good local cheese.

The Druze villages high in the Carmel offer traditional confections like *knafeh* and baklava as well as excellent olive oil and homemade *labaneh* cheese. A meal in one of the towns won't only be a tasty experience, but also a warmly welcoming one.

Route 4, which runs north to south parallel to Route 2, is a more scenic drive, with Mt. Carmel looming to the east beyond cultivated fields and banana plantations (though you may not see the bananas, as they're usually bagged in blue or gray plastic to protect them from bugs). The road leads through undulating countryside dotted with cypresses, palms, and vineyards.

In 2010, a forest fire—the most severe in Israel's history—raged for several days on Mt. Carmel. It was all the more devastating due to dry conditions following many years of drought. The area damaged was estimated at about one third of the entire forested area of the Carmel mountain range. As a result, you may notice bare swathes along the mountainside when traveling along Route 2 or Route 4. In the aftermath of the fire replanting was initiated, and many areas will show bright green new growth, along with the gradual natural regeneration of oak, pistachio, and pine trees.

EIN HOD

Fodor's Choice
★
15 km (10 miles) south of Haifa, 5 km (3 miles) west of Isfiya.

A charming village nestled in ancient olive groves on the western slope of Mt. Carmel, Ein Hod is home to some 500 residents, most of them sculptors, painters, ceramicists, architects, jewelers, and other types of artists. The setting is an idyllic one, with rough-hewn stone houses built on the hillside and sweeping views down to the Mediterranean. The Dadaist painter Marcel Janco (1895–1984) wrote upon his first visit in 1950: "The beauty of the place was staggering."

Parking is across the road, opposite the entrance to the village. Climbing up the hill, you soon come to a winding street on the left that starts a lovely walk through the small village. Signs along the way indicate studios and workshops where artists paint, sculpt, and make jewelry, pottery, silkscreen prints, and clothing. You can continue straight to the town square, bordered by a restaurant and a large gallery where works by Ein Hod artists are exhibited.

GETTING HERE AND AROUND

Your best option is to get here by car via Route 4, since buses are few and far between. The village itself is small and quite walkable.

EXPLORING

Janco-Dada Museum. On the village square is this museum dedicated to one of the founders of the Dada movement. The Romanian-born Marcel Janco had already established a considerable professional reputation by the time he moved here in 1941. The museum houses a permanent collection of the artist's work in various media, reflecting Janco's 70-year output both in Europe and Israel. A 20-minute slide show chronicles the life of the artist and the Dada movement, and the DadaLab offers hands-on activities for children. Don't miss the view from the roof. ⊠ *Near the village square* ☎ *04/984–2350* ⊕ *www.jancodada.co.il* ☐ *NIS 20* ⊗ *Sun.–Thurs. 9:30–3:30, Fri. 9:30–2, Sat. 10–4.*

FAMILY **Nahal Me'arot Nature Reserve.** The prehistoric Carmel Caves, recognized in 2012 as a UNESCO World Heritage Site, are a highlight of the Nahal Me'arot Nature Reserve, 3 km (2 miles) south of Ein Hod. They form a key site for the study of human evolution in general and the prehistory of the Levant in particular.

The three excavated caves are up a steep flight of stairs, on a fossil reef that was covered by the sea 100 million years ago. The first discoveries of prehistoric remains were made when this area was being scoured for stones to build the Haifa port. In the late 1920s, Dorothy Garrod of England headed the first archaeological expedition, receiving assistance from a British feminist group on condition that exclusively women carry out the dig.

In the Tannur cave, the first on the tour, the strata Garrod's team excavated are clearly marked, spanning about 150,000 years in the life of early humans. The most exciting discovery made in the area was that of both Homo sapiens and Neanderthal skeletons; evidence that both lived here has raised fascinating questions about the relationship between the two and whether they lived side by side. A display on the daily life of early man as hunter and food gatherer occupies the Gamal cave. The last cave you'll visit, called the Nahal, is the largest—it cuts deep into the mountain—and was actually the first discovered. A burial place with 84 skeletons was found outside the mouth of the cave.

The bone artifacts and stone tools discovered in the Nahal cave suggest that people who settled here, about 12,000 years ago, were the forebears of early farmers, with a social structure more developed than that of hunters and gatherers. There is also evidence that the Crusaders once used the cave to guard the coastal road. There's a snack bar at this site. ✉ *Off Rte. 4* ☎ *04/984–1750* 🌐 *www.parks.org.il* 🎟 *NIS 20* 🕒 *Oct.–Mar., Sat.–Thurs. and holidays 8–4, Fri. and Jewish holiday eves 8–1; Apr.–Sept., Sat.–Thurs. 8–5, Fri. 8–3.*

FAMILY **Nisco Museum of Mechanical Music.** When was the last time you saw a hurdy-gurdy? Nisan Cohen, a colorful and charming character who knows everything there is to know about old mechanical musical instruments, has amassed 150 music boxes, hand-operated automatic pianos, manivelles, antique gramophones on which to play his collection of old Yiddish records, and more antique musical marvels. Cohen, who renovated the museum after it was damaged in the 2010 Carmel Forest fire, will be pleased to give you a guided tour, then treat you to a personal concert. His sense of humor and gift of the gab make for a touching and intriguing experience. Before the entrance to Ein Hod, watch for a brown wooden sign with yellow letters. ✉ *Off Rte. 7111* ☎ *052/475–5313* 🌐 *ein-hod.info/nisco* 🎟 *NIS 30* 🕒 *daily 10–5.*

NEED A BREAK?

ArtBar. Enjoy a homemade beer or a slice of delicious pizza (call ahead to order) in the garden at Danny and Analia's alternative-style ArtBar. While you're here, have a look at Analia's unusual sculptures and paintings. ✉ ***South of Ein Hod village square*** ☎ ***052/836–2498*** 🌐 ***ein-hod.info/rest/artbar/.***

WHERE TO EAT

$ ISRAELI 🍴 **Abu Yakov.** You reach Abu Yakov's by climbing the stone seats of Ein Hod's amphitheater, or through nearby Café Ein Hod. There are a few seats inside—most people head outside to the blue plastic chairs beneath a ragged plastic tarp. It feels a bit makeshift, but the fresh food counts for everything. Dine on what locals often called "Oriental" (meaning Middle Eastern) food: hummus, fluffy pita bread, chopped vegetable salad, and grilled meat on skewers. Call ahead for oven-roasted lamb. [$] *Average main: NIS 50* ✉ *Near village square* ☎ *04/984–3377* 💳 *No credit cards* 🕒 *Closed Sun.*

$ CAFÉ 🍴 **Café Ein Hod.** Climb up the stairs beside the Doña Rosa restaurant and keep an eye out for this favorite of the locals: a two-level collection of mismatched chairs and odd tables surrounded by potted plants—there's often a cat sunning itself on a stool. Inside the old stone building, handmade clothes and handbags are for sale. You can sit outside to sip coffee or fruit smoothies or chow down on homemade *bourekas* (filled pastry triangles), *shakshuka* (eggs in tomato sauce), carrot cake, or apple pie.

If you're hungry, nosh on grilled cheese sandwiches with salad. You can stop for a beer or a glass of wine, too. Indian cuisine is served every Thursday night. [$] *Average main: NIS 45* ✉ *Near the village square* ☎ *054/667–6089* ▭ *No credit cards* ⏲ *Closed Mon.*

$$$ ARGENTINE 🍴 **Doña Rosa.** If you can't read the restaurant's sign in Hebrew, just follow the tantalizing aroma up the steps of this wooden building on the town square. Doña Rosa's grandsons, Uri and Doron, import meat and special charcoal from Argentina and roast the food in the true Argentinean style. The bar is decorated with a drawing of a hefty cow that illustrates each cut of meat. Highlights include grilled pork spareribs; seafood simmered with fragrant yellow rice; and *asado,* delicious, chunky ribs (available only on Saturday). There's beer and Chilean and Argentinean wine, too, and live music on Friday nights. [$] *Average main: NIS 90* ✉ *Near the village square* ☎ *04/954–3777, 057/934–5520* 🌐 *doniarosa.rest.co.il* ⏲ *Closed Sun.*

WHERE TO STAY

$ B&B/INN 🏨 **Jancourt B&B.** Batia's and Claude's bed-and-breakfast is quiet and private, hidden behind masses of hot pink bougainvillea. **Pros:** pretty, private building; fun shop. **Cons:** often gets booked well in advance. [$] *Rooms from: $130* ✉ *Second (east) entrance to Ein Hod* ☎ *04/984–1648* 🌐 *www.eisenwasser-jancourt.co.il* 🛏 *2 rooms* ▭ *No credit cards* 🍽 *Breakfast.*

$ B&B/INN 🏨 **Yakir Ein Hod.** Care for a dip in a pool ringed by olive trees while you gaze at the blue Mediterranean? **Pros:** quiet location; private pool; lovely sea views. **Cons:** minimum stay required on weekends. [$] *Rooms from: $190* ✉ *Second (east) entrance to Ein Hod* ☎ *050/554–3982* 🌐 *www.yakireinhod.co.il* 🛏 *3 suites.*

NIGHTLIFE AND THE ARTS

Gertrud Kraus House. Just off the main square, Gertrud Kraus House (named after a pioneer of modern dance in Israel) features chamber music concerts. Admission is NIS 50, which often includes coffee and cake. ✉ *Village square* ☎ *04/984–1058.*

SHOPPING

Many of the artists who live in the winding lanes of Ein Hod throw open their workshops to visitors, who are welcome to browse and buy. Between the olive trees and behind painted gates, look for signs on homes that indicate the sale of jewelry, gold metalwork, sculptures, paintings, ceramics, stained glass, hand-painted clothing, and artistic photography. Either start at the entrance to the village where signs point to the left or head for the village square straight ahead.

Central Gallery. The Ein Hod Central Gallery, an integral part of the artistic community here since 1953, carries a wide selection of handicrafts and art by resident artists at its space on the main square. Displayed in the front room are ceramics, enamel, and silver and gold jewelry, while through the arch into another room are paintings, sculptures, and graphic works. ✉ *Village square* ☎ *04/984–2548* 🌐 *www.ein-hod.org/en/maingallery.asp* ⏲ *Sun., Tues., Wed., and Thurs. 10–5; Fri. 10–2; and Sat. 11–4.*

Silver Print. Silver Print is a lovely little studio holding Vivienne Silver-Brody's collection of vintage works by Israel's best photographers. The emphasis is on the building of the State of Israel. There's also a wide range of 19th-century photos of the Holy Land. A digital print costs NIS 150. Call or email ahead for hours. ⊠ *Ein Hod* ☎ *04/954–1673* ✉ *vivroy@netvision.net.il.*

DALIYAT EL CARMEL AND ISFIYA

16 km (11 miles) south of Haifa.

Daliyat el Carmel (Vine of the Carmel) is Israel's largest Druze village, and its weekend market, oil press, and *hilweh* (house of worship) are well worth exploring. Though most of the younger generation wears jeans and T-shirts, most older people wear traditional garb. Head coverings indicate the degree of religious belief, from the high white turban resembling a fez to the white kerchief covering the head and shoulders. Many men sport a bushy moustache, a hallmark of the Druze, and some older ones wear dark robes and black pantaloons.

Very similar to neighboring Daliyat el Carmel, Isfiya is a village of flat-roof homes built closely together into the hillside, many of them raised on pillars and cut with arched windows. It stands on the remains of a Jewish village dating back to Roman times. Hospitality is second nature to the Druze who live here; you may be able to visit a village home and eat pita bread with yogurt cheese and spices while hearing about Druze life. The village is about 1 km (½ mile) from Daliyat el Carmel.

GETTING HERE AND AROUND
Coming from Haifa, drive south on Route 672.

TOURS
To really get to know Isfiya, arrange a tour through Druze Hospitality in Isfiya. Your guide will take you to visit their place of prayer, an olive oil press, and then to a private home where the matriarch bakes pita bread in a *tabun* (oven). You'll hear about the distinctive Druze way of life. It's best to call a few days ahead. The price is NIS 120 per person.

ESSENTIALS
Tour Information **Druze Hospitality** ☎ *04/839–0125.*

EXPLORING
Daliyat el Carmel Marketplace. About 1 km (½ mile) inside town, take a right turn into the marketplace, a colorful jumble of shops lining the street. You can be assured of finding excellent falafel and fresh produce at any of the roadside stands or restaurants.

WHERE TO EAT
$ ✕ **Halabi Brothers.** At this storefront eatery, brothers Fouad and Ahmad
MIDDLE EASTERN Halabi greet you with a handshake and a "Hello, my cousin!" The delicious falafel and shawarma, wrapped in thin, lightly browned Druze-style pitas, are a nice change from the fluffy ones served at most other places in the country. A refreshing splash of lemon tips the platter of salads. Watch everything being prepared in the glass-front kitchen that

The Druze

The Druze are an Arabic-speaking minority whose remarkable cohesion and esoteric faith have enabled them to maintain their close-knit identity through almost a thousand years of turbulent history. In Israel, they number about 125,000 and live in 17 villages in the Carmel, the Galilee, and the Golan Heights. Larger kindred communities exist in Syria and Lebanon.

So exclusive is this sect that only a fraction of the community is initiated into its religious doctrine, one tenet of which is a belief in continuous reincarnation. The Druze broke away from Islam about 1,000 years ago, incorporating other traditions and also believing in the divinity of their founder, al-Hâkim bi-Amr Allâh, the Caliph of the Egyptian Fatimid dynasty from AD 996 to 1021. They don't permit gambling or the use of alcohol.

The Druze who live in the two existing villages on Mt. Carmel (Daliyat el Carmel and Isfiya) serve in the Israeli army, a mark of their loyalty to Israel.

opens onto a series of tile-floor dining rooms. The adjoining gift shop, also run by the siblings, displays locally woven tablecloths and pillowcases. $ *Average main: NIS 45* ⊠ *14 Commercial Center Str., Daliyat el Carmel* ☎ *052/477–6048.*

$$
MIDDLE EASTERN
✕ **House of Druze Heritage.** The Druze are justly famous for their hospitality. Here you get not only a warm welcome from Fadal, the congenial owner, but if you call ahead you can enjoy a traditional meal in his own home. The house formerly belonged to the British traveler and diplomat Laurence Oliphant. Fadal explains the Druze way of life and shows you displays of Druze farm implements, household objects, and handicrafts. If you choose to dine à la Druze, the meal may include skewers of grilled lamb or steak and big, flat pita bread. Baklava and Turkish coffee provide the finishing touch. $ *Average main: NIS 50* ⊠ *4 Ahat St.* ☎ *04/839–3242.*

$$$
MIDDLE EASTERN
✕ **Nof HaCarmel.** To find this excellent Druze restaurant, drive to the northern edge of the village. The eatery is on your left; look for a few tables outside under the trees. People come from all over the Carmel for the fine Middle Eastern fare, especially the homemade hummus with pine nuts, olive oil, garlic, and lemon juice, and the well-seasoned kebab on skewers. Those with a sweet tooth should sample the *sahlab* (a warm, custard-like pudding of crushed orchid bulb with thickened milk and sugar). $ *Average main: NIS 80* ⊠ *Rte. 672, Isfiya* ☎ *04/839–1718* ⌿ *Reservations not accepted.*

SHOPPING
Along a brief stretch of the main road that winds through Daliyat el Carmel are shops selling lightweight throw rugs, handwoven baskets, brightly colored pottery, brass dishes, characteristic woven wall hangings, and embroidered skullcaps worn by men. Bargaining is expected. Some shops close on Friday; the strip is crowded on Saturday.

Shorashim. The trunks of olive trees outside mark the place where Shachar Amasha and his workers fashion art out of gnarled pieces of olive wood. He will offer you strong Druze coffee and show you around the workshop and the beautiful benches, chairs, and decorative pieces fashioned there. The store fronts on the main street running through Isfiya. ⊠ *Rte. 672, Isfiya* ☎ *04/839–2279.*

MUKHRAKA

18 km (12 miles) south of Haifa, 2 km (1 mile) west of Daliyat el Carmel.

You can't miss Mukhraka, marked by a tall white statue of Elijah the Prophet with his sword raised on high. Just beyond is the graceful Carmelite monastery with a sweeping rooftop view of the Jezreel Valley. The site offers well-marked hiking trails.

GETTING HERE AND AROUND

Mukhraka is an interesting stop if you're on the way to Isfiya and Daliyat el Carmel on Route 70. It's not accessible for those without a car.

EXPLORING

Carmelite Monastery. Past open, uncultivated fields and a goatherd's rickety shack, Mukhraka's Carmelite monastery stands on the spur of the Carmel range, at an altitude of 1,580 feet, on the site where the struggle between the prophet Elijah and the priests of Ba'al is believed to have taken place. Climb to the roof for an unforgettable panorama: to the east stretches the Jezreel Valley and the hills of Nazareth, Moreh, and Gilboa. On a clear day, you can even see Jordan's Gilead Mountains beyond the Jordan River and Mt. Hermon.

Mukhraka is the Arabic word for a place of burning, referring to the fire that consumed the offering on Elijah's altar. The conflict developed because the people of Israel had been seduced by the pagan cults introduced by King Ahab's wife, Jezebel. Elijah demanded a contest with the priests of Ba'al in which each would erect an altar with a butchered ox as an offering and see which divinity sent down fire. Elijah drenched his altar with water, yet it burst into flames. On his orders, the pagan priests were taken down to the Kishon ravine and slain, an event depicted by the impressive statue of Elijah inscribed in Hebrew, Arabic, and Latin.

The stark stone monastery was built in 1883 over Byzantine ruins. There's a small gift shop in the monastery, but no place to buy drinks or snacks. ☉ *Mon.–Sat. 8 am–noon and 2:30 pm–4:30 pm.*

ZICHRON YA'AKOV

Fodor'sChoice
★

35 km (22 miles) south of Haifa, 61 km (40 miles) north of Tel Aviv.

Zichron Ya'akov, the country's first moshava, or cooperative farming community, was founded in 1882 with the help of Baron Edmond de Rothschild. From the beginning, it centered on its vineyards and large winery. A visit to the charming town should start on its main street, Hameyasdim, a cobblestone pedestrian mall lined with small, restored, red-roofed, 19th-century homes. Pick up a town map in the tourist office at the entrance to the town.

Continued on page 329

In a land where grapes have been grown and enjoyed since biblical times, a modern winemaking revolution has taken hold. Whether the vintage is from big producers or boutique up-and-comers, the improved quality of Israeli wine has catapulted all things oenological into the spotlight. This tiny country is now home to over 200 wineries large and small. It was Baron Edmond de Rothschild—the proprietor of France's prestigious Château Lafite winery and an early Zionist—who jumpstarted the modern Israeli wine industry by providing money to found wineries in the 1880s. After a few false starts, Carmel Mizrachi, which his funds helped support, flourished; to this day it is Israel's most prolific wine producer.

by Adeena Sussman

(top) Ancient floor mosaic depicting wine vase at Eretz Israel Museum, Tel Aviv. (right) Golan Heights Winery

The
Wines
of
Israel

WINEMAKING IN ISRAEL

(top left) Winemaking barrel shop in Zichron Ya'akov, 1890s. (bottom left) Golan Heights Winery. (right) Wine fair in Tel Aviv.

Israel manufactured mostly mediocre wines until the late 1970s, when the first *moshavim* and *kibbutzim* (living cooperatives) planted vines in the Golan Heights on the advice of scientists from California, who saw a grape-growing diamond in the rough amid the mountain ranges of this northern region. Soon thereafter Golan Heights Winery was born, and awards and accolades were uncorked almost immediately.

GROWTH AND CHALLENGE

Besides two dozen or so larger operations, more than 150 smaller wineries now operate, many less than 15 years old and some producing just a few thousand bottles per year. Five large wineries account for 75 percent of production. Winemaking is a relatively young industry, sparked by a new crop of winemakers with experience at outstanding wineries. Though top wine writers have given some Israeli wines high marks, confirming internationally that these are vintages worth seeking out, there is still room for improvement in the ongoing, so-called "quality revolution."

Per capita wine consumption in Israel has nearly doubled since the late 1990s but remains low. A culture of wine appreciation is gradually fomenting, although the lion's share of bottles are exported to the United States and Europe. Despite challenges, winemakers continue to experiment: up-and-coming regions include the Judean Hills outside Jerusalem and even the Negev desert.

KOSHER & MEVUSHAL: MESSAGE ON A BOTTLE

For a wine to be certified kosher, as many Israeli wines are, a religious supervisor must oversee the process to ensure that no non-kosher tools or ingredients are used. Only rigorously observant Jews can handle equipment. Critics agree that these regulations don't affect the quality of wine. *Mevushal* wines, with more stringent kosher requirements, are flash-pasteurized, and then rapidly chilled; this can affect quality. However, many top-tier Israeli wines today are non-Mevushal, or are unsupervised altogether.

WINE REGIONS AND GRAPES

Sea Horse winery

GRAPE EXPECTATIONS

After commercial vines were first planted in the 19th century, Israeli winemakers focused on a small group of grape varietals that seemed to take well to Israeli terrain. The country has no indigenous grapes. With the help of technology, experience, and trial and error, a wide range of grapes are now raised with success.

Some of Israel's red wines are world-class, notably those that blend Cabernet Sauvignon grapes with Merlot, Cabernet Franc, and Petit Verdot. Chardonnays also do well here—the warm days and cool nights of the northern region seem particularly advantageous for this varietal.

Winemakers consistently push the envelope, introducing exciting new wines into the market. Two recent examples? Viognier, which has been one of the darlings of the current Israeli wine market, and Syrah, a grape that flourishes amid the country's hot days and cool, breezy nights.

Israel's wine-growing areas are typically divided into five regions, although no official, European-style government-regulated classification system exists. Since the country is so small—about the size of New Jersey—grapes are often shared among the regions. This is especially true of the northern plains, which provide grapes to many of the country's best wineries. Still, each area is geographically unique.

GALILEE Actually two regions, this area covers a lot of geographical ground in the north. The Galilee is a rocky area, and the Golan Heights, which borders Syria, sees winter snowfall at its highest altitudes. With cool climes and rich soil, the Galilee and Golan still claim bragging rights as home to many of the country's premier grapes.

SHOMRON/CARMEL The advantageous growing conditions of the lush Carmel Mountains make this coastal plain south of Haifa the most prolific grape-growing region in Israel, if not the most prestigious. The climate and soil variety make it the most traditionally Mediterranean of the regions.

SAMSON/CENTRAL COAST Situated west of Jerusalem and stretching north toward Tel Aviv and south toward Ashkelon, this region has hot, humid summers and mellow winters that make for good growing conditions. If you're in Tel Aviv, this is an easy region for accessing great wineries.

JUDEAN HILLS Ten years ago, barely a winery or tasting room existed here, though ancient winemaking equipment has been unearthed. Thin limey or rocky soil, sunny days, and breezy nights have helped this region's wines shine. With its winding roads, and lush, shallow mountainsides, the region west and south of Jerusalem is day-trip perfect from Jerusalem and Tel Aviv.

THE NEGEV Thanks to drip-irrigation technology and an influx of talented winemakers, grapes are thriving in the desert. Since there are relatively few wineries in the southern part of the Negev, they're best included in a trip to Eilat or Mitzpe Ramon; call to schedule a visit.

Clos de Gat Winery in the Judean Hills

WINE TOURING AND TASTING

Visiting wineries in Israel can require a different approach from touring vineyards in California, and your touring strategy may depend on the size of the winery.

Most of the **bigger players**, including Golan Heights, Carmel, and Barkan/Segal, offer tasting rooms. You can simply stop by and visit to sample and purchase wines, though generally it's good to call in advance if you want to include a winery tour. Many **medium- and smaller-sized wineries** are often happy to accommodate visitors, but always call ahead to ensure that English-speaking staff will be on hand and to confirm hours.

Many **boutique** wineries welcome tourists, but some of the best aren't equipped for a regular onslaught of visitors. While you can call yourself, this is where private tour guides come in handy. Often, these individuals have the connections to get you inside wineries you'd otherwise never see—not to mention the knowledge of the back roads in some of the harder-to-find locales.

Through **Israel Wine Experience** (☎ 054/052–0604, ✍ facebook.com/IsraelWineExperience), wine expert Oded Shoham and his staff offer customized half- and full-day tours and tastings. Fees vary, but a half-day tour of three wineries is about $400 for a group of up to 5 people.

PICK OF THE VINEYARDS

These wineries either have open tasting rooms, or visits can be arranged with an advance phone call. Note: most kosher wineries are open only a half-day on Friday, and are closed on Saturdays and Jewish holidays. Small tastes are usually free, but at most wineries a guided tasting costs between $10 and $18 per person for three to five wines.

Carmel Winery

GALILEE

1 Golan Heights Winery Still the standard bearer for Israeli wines, this large producer has a welcoming visitor center and tours. Wines are made under the Yarden, Gamla, and Golan labels. Kosher. *Try: Single-vineyard Odem Organic Chardonnay; Yarden Syrah.* ✉ Rte. 87, Industrial Zone, Katzrin ☎ 04/696–8420 ⊕ www.golanwines.com.

2 Chateau Golan A French-style chateau houses an art-filled tasting room. It's open daily; call in advance. Not kosher. *Try: Plummy, balanced-tannin Eliad Cabernet blends.* ✉ Moshav Eliad, Ramat Hagolan ☎ 04/660–0026 ⊕ www.chateaugolan.com.

3 Galil Mountain Winery A sleek, modern low-lying stone-and-wood building offers views of the

WINES IN RESTAURANTS AND SHOPS

Look for vintages from these superior regional producers in restaurants or shops in Israel. **Galilee:** Golan Heights, Pelter and Chateau Golan in the Golan; Clos de Gat

Dalton and Galil Mountain in the Galilee **Shomron/Carmel:** Recanati, Margalit, Amphorae **Samson/Central Coast:** Carmel, Barkan, Soreq

Judean Hills: Sea Horse, Domaine du Castel, Clos de Gat **The Negev:** Yatir, La Terra Promessa, Rota, Kadesh Barnea

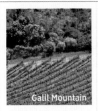
Galil Mountain

vineyards and the wine-making facilities. These are great-value wines for the money. Kosher. *Try: Fruity, mineral-tinged Sauvignon Blanc.* ✉ Kibbutz Merom, Yiron ☎ 04/686–8740 ⊕ www.galilmountain. co.il.

4 Tabor Winery Set amid almond groves near Mt. Tabor in the Galilee, this intimate visitor center offers tastings and tours, plus a restaurant called Bordeaux. Kosher. *Try: Full-bodied, oaky Mas'ha, a Caber-net-Shiraz-Merlot blend that is the winery's calling card.* ✉ Kfar Tavor, ☎ 04/676–0444 ⊕ www.taborwinery. com.

SHOMRON/ CARMEL

5 Tishbi Winery The vistor center at this fourth-generation winery offers harvest activities August–October. Kosher. *Try: Woodsy, berry-rich Pinot Noir.* ✉ 33 Hameyasdim St., Zichron Ya'akov ☎ 04/638–0435 ⊕ www.tishbi.com.

6 Amphorae Winery This boutique winery is set in a series of rustic, Tuscan-style stone build-

ings. Call in advance to arrange a visit. Not kosher. *Try: Balanced, full-bodied Cabernet Sauvignon.* ✉ Makura Farm, Kerem Maharal ☎ 04/984–0702 ⊕ www.amphorae-v. com.

SAMSON/ CENTRAL COAST

7 Carmel Winery One of two visitor centers for Carmel (the other is in Zichron Ya'akov near Haifa), this facility at the country's largest winery offers tours of the original underground cellars built by Baron Edmond de Rothschild, as well as the facility's original barrel room. Kosher. ✉ 25 Hacarmel St. Rishon LeZion ☎ 03/948–8851 ⊕ www.carmelwines. com.

JUDEAN HILLS

8 Ella Valley For about $16 groups of 10 or more can tour the winery and sample four vintages in a wood-bar tast-ing room. Kosher. *Try: Fruity Sauvignon Blanc.* ✉ Rte. 475, off Rte. 38, Netiv Halamed Heh ☎ 02/999–4885 ⊕ www.ellavalley.com.

9 Flam Winery Two dynamic brothers, the sons of a former chief winemaker for Carmel Mizrachi, run this well-regarded pro-ducer. Call to arrange a cheese and wine

tasting. *Try: Woodsy, berry-rich Flam Reserve Merlot.* ✉ Eshtal Junction, Ya'ar Ha'kodshim ☎ 02/992–9923 ⊕ www.flamwinery. com.

THE NEGEV

10 Yatir Winery Gen-erating great excite-ment, Yatir is a desert

Mediterranean Sea

Haifa
3 GOLAN HEIGHTS
1
GALILEE **2**
4
6
5
SHOMRON/ CARMEL
Tel Aviv
7
Jerusalem
SAMSON/ **9**
CENTRAL **8**
COAST **JUDEAN HILLS**
GAZA
10
Beersheva

THE NEGEV

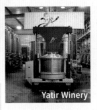
Yatir Winery

gem with promise. Call in advance. Kosher. *Try: Yatir Forest, whose grape blend varies from year to year; fruity, light Viognier.* ✉ Off Rte. 80, Tel Arad ☎ 08/995–9090 ⊕ www.yatir.net.

5

IN FOCUS THE WINES OF ISRAEL

MORE ISRAELI WINE RESOURCES

Pina BaRosh Wine Bar

WINE FESTIVALS

Annual wine festivals offer the opportunity to meet winemakers and taste their products, often in beautiful surroundings. Every July, Jerusalem's **Israel Museum** (☎ 02/670–8811 ✉ info@imj.org.il for dates) turns over its outdoor space at night for a weeklong wine festival featuring more than 150 wineries, food from local restaurants, and various other vendors. This Jerusalem tradition is highly recommended.

Up north, the **Golan Heights Winery** stages harvest festivals in September or October at their Katzrin headquarters (☎ 04/696–8420 ✉ ghwinery@golanwines.co.il).

The **Yoav Yehuda Wine Festival** (☎ 08/850–2240 ⊕ www.goisrael.com) occurs every year during wine season (fall) and celebrates the more than two dozen wineries operating near Jerusalem in the Judean Hills and the surrounding area.

TASTING IN SHOPS AND BARS

Avi Ben, Jerusalem. This chain of retail wine shops offers free wine tastings every Friday from 11 to 2:30. On Thursday evenings look for winemaker-hosted tastings (NIS 20—NIS 50 per glass). ✉ 22 Rivlin St. ☎ 02/625–9703 ⊕ www.avibenwine.com.

Methusaleh, Tel Aviv. Of the 160 selections at this wine bar in the hipster Florentine neighborhood, nearly half are local, with many available by the glass. A custom-crafted flight of three Israeli wines ranges from NIS 28 to NIS 56. There's great food, too, from cheese and tapas to a full dinner menu. ✉ 16 Uriel Acosta St., ☎ 03/510–2923.

Pina BaRosh Wine Bar, Rosh Pina. This wine bar near Tzfat features more than 300 mostly northern Israeli wines. Wines by the glass are available every day from 8:30 AM to midnight, as are tastings, which range from NIS 74 to NIS 134. ✉ 8 Ha Chalutzim St. ☎ 04/693–7028 ⊕ www.pinabarosh.com.

BRINGING IT HOME

Although you can ship wines home for personal enjoyment, the prices are prohibitively high, and your wines may get held up in U.S. Customs. A better bet is to save suitcase space for a few boutique bottles. Then, at the larger wineries, take notes on favorites and purchase them back home. **Skyview Wines & Spirits** in New York has the largest selection (⊕ www.skyviewwine.com ☎ 888/759–8466) from conventional wineries.

Wine clubs like **Israeli Wine Direct** (⊕ www.israeliwinedirect.com) are a source for smaller producers like Margalit, Pelter, Flam, and Clos de Gat. Wines are shipped to your home (not available in all states).

Avi Ben (⊕ www.avibenwine.com) ships wine overseas.

READING & PLANNING

An increasing number of resources are available for vino-tourists in Israel. The Web site **Wines Israel** (⊕ www.wines-israel.co.il), a great place to start, has an easy-to-read English-language section including information about the industry, wine-making history, wine routes, places to visit, and more.

GETTING HERE AND AROUND

If you're driving from Haifa or Tel Aviv, take Route 2 to the Zichron Ya'akov exit. Buses run from Haifa and Tel Aviv.

ESSENTIALS

Vistor Information **Zichron Ya'akov Tourist Office** ⊠ *Southern entrance to town, opposite the cemetery, HaMeyasdim St.* ☎ *04/639–8811.*

EXPLORING

TOP ATTRACTIONS

Fodor'sChoice
★
Carmel Winery. Rare among Israel's many wineries are Carmel Winery's underground vaulted-ceiling wine cellars. Dating from 1892, the huge old, chilly rooms are a contrast to the state-of-the art facility aboveground, where the winery's top wines are produced. Founder Baron Edmond de Rothschild, owner of France's famous Château Lafite, would be pleased at the success of his viniculture venture, now the country's largest winery. At the new Center for Wine Culture, a guided 45-minute tour outlines the stages of local wine production. Included in the tour are a tasting of some four varieties and a seven-minute audiovisual presentation screened in the original wine cellar. Tours depart between 9 and 4 and must be reserved in advance. ⊠ *2 Winery St.* ☎ *04/639–1788* ⊕ *www.carmelwines.co.il* 💲 *NIS 30* ⊗ *Sun.–Thurs. 9:30–5, Fri. 9–2.*

Ramat Hanadiv. In the hills near Zichron Ya'akov, this sprawling garden is a fitting tribute to Baron Edmond de Rothschild. (*Hanadiv* means "the benefactor.") At its center is the dignified tomb where Rothschild and his wife Ada lie buried. A 20-minute film in the welcoming Visitors Pavilion tells of his legacy in Israel. Outside, curving paths are framed by rolling green lawns, abundant patches of flowers, carob trees, waving palms, and 42 rare plant species. Clearly marked trails lead to a 2,000-year old Roman farmhouse and a hidden spring. After all that legwork, the terraces of the on-site café beckon. A children's playground is set off to one side. ⊠ *Southern end of Mt. Carmel, south of Zichron Ya'akov, Rte. 652* ☎ *04/629–8111* ⊕ *www.ramat-hanadiv. org.il* 💲 *Free* ⊗ *Sun.–Thurs. 8–4, Fri. 8–2, Sat. 8–4.*

WORTH NOTING

Bet Aaronson (*Aaronson House*). About halfway down Hameyasdim Street is Bet Aaronson, whose late-19th-century architecture successfully combines art nouveau and Middle Eastern traditions. This museum was once the home of the agronomist Aaron Aaronson (1876–1919), who gained international fame for his discovery of an ancestor of modern wheat. The house remains as it looked after World War I, with family photographs and French and Turkish furniture, as well as Aaronson's library, diaries, and letters.

Aaronson and his two sisters became local heroes as leaders of an underground group called NILI dedicated to ousting the Turks from Palestine. Both sisters were in love with Aaron's assistant, Absalom Feinberg, who was killed in an ambush in the Gaza Strip. His remains were recovered some 50 years later from a grave marked simply by a date tree, the tree having sprouted from some dates in Feinberg's pockets. A tour in English is provided; the last one takes place at 1:30

pm. ✉ *40 Hameyasdim St.* ☎ *04/639–0120* 🎟 *NIS 15* 🕒 *Sun., Mon., Wed., and Thurs. 8:30–3, Tues. 8:30–4, Fri. 8:30–1.*

Binyamin Pool. On Hameyasdim Street, near Bet Aaronson, is Binyamin Pool, a misnomer because it's actually the town's original water tower, built in 1891. Zichron Ya'akov was the first village in Israel to have water piped to its houses; Meir Dizengoff, the first mayor of Tel Aviv, came here to see how it was done. The facade, with its inscription honoring Baron de Rothschild, resembles that of an ancient synagogue. ✉ *Hameyasdim St.*

First Aliya Museum. Commissioned by Baron de Rothschild, this three-floor building is a fine example of late-19th-century Ottoman-style architecture, built of white stone with a central pediment capped by a tile roof. During World War I, the Turks used it as a military hospital. The museum is dedicated to the lives of the 30,000 immigrants who came to Palestine with the First Aliya (a period of settlement from 1882 until 1904). Life-size model displays of local immigrants (like Zachariya, the seed vendor, and Izer, the cobbler) illustrate how life was lived at that time. A film traces the struggles of a family who came from Europe in this difficult period of Israel's modern history. ✉ *2 Hanadiv St.* ☎ *04/629–4777* 🎟 *NIS 15* 🕒 *Mon. and Wed.–Fri., 9–2, Tues. 9–3.*

Ohel Ya'akov. On a prominent corner stands the old synagogue, Ohel Ya'akov, built by Baron de Rothschild in 1886 to serve immigrants from Romania. It's only occasionally open to visitors. ✉ *Hameyasdim St. and Hanadiv St.* 🌐 *www.ohelyaakov.com.*

WHERE TO EAT

$$$ MEDITERRANEAN 🍴 **Haneshika.** The restaurant's huge courtyard with dark orange umbrellas is usually packed with diners. Inside, the restaurant—run since 1999 by the husband and wife team Keren and Ronen Raviv—is small and elegant. For country-style eating, you might start with mozzarella gnocchi with sautéed mushrooms, or a zucchini and feta cheese terrine. Main courses include baked crabs in a sweet-and-hot chili sauce, lamb casserole with eggplant and pine nuts, and seafood and fennel salad. Apple crumble with a cinnamon-flavored sauce is a delightful dessert. [$] *Average main: NIS 90* ✉ *37 Hameyasdim St.* ☎ *04/639–0133* 🌐 *www.haneshika.com* ✍ *Reservations essential* 🕒 *Closed Sun.*

$$$ MIDDLE EASTERN 🍴 **Hatemaniya shel Santo.** Grab a table in the courtyard if you want an authentic Yemenite meal. There's no menu—the waiter brings you soft pita bread, country black bread, a fresh vegetable salad, and a rugged hummus drizzled with olive oil. You can order stuffed vegetables or chicken, but make sure you also try the potato cakes and a plate of the small meat patties flavored with cilantro. It's all delicious and nicely washed down with Yemenite coffee or cold water with lemon and mint. [$] *Average main: NIS 85* ✉ *52 Hameyasdim St.* ☎ *04/639–8762* 🕒 *Closed Sat.*

$$$ MEDITERRANEAN 🍴 **Kashtunyo Wine Cellar.** A 140 year-old underground wine cellar is an auspicious place to hear about wines from owner Amos Meroz, whose hat is always rakishly tilted to one side. Eight tables covered with checkered cloths fill a small space defined by curving stone walls.

Dishes of olives glisten on a tiny wooden bar in the dimly lighted room. Scores of wine bottles line the back wall, where you'll find vintages from Israel, Italy, Australia, California, France, and South Africa. You can enjoy cheese and stuffed grape leaves while learning from an expert. Or just sit quietly with your glass while French songs fill the air. $ *Average main: NIS 80* ⊠ *56 Hameyasdim St.* ☎ *04/629–1244* ⚱ *Reservations essential.*

$$$ ✕ **Picciotto.** Pots of geraniums and rosemary and lavender bushes grace
ECLECTIC the entrance of this charming, eclectic eatery. The original settlers peer out sternly from photos on the vanilla-colored walls. A wood stove in the middle keeps the restored 19th-century space cozy. The gourmet chef's lemon-cured salmon with cucumber dressing merits mention, as does the goat-cheese soufflé and the roasted eggplant with tomatoes and mint leaves. Each makes a fine introduction to main courses such as seafood pasta in white wine and wild herbs, and lemony chicken breast with capers. For dessert, try the phyllo leaves filled with crème anglaise and seasonal fresh fruit. $ *Average main: NIS 90* ⊠ *41 Hameyasdim St.* ☎ *04/629–0646* ⚱ *Reservations essential.*

WHERE TO STAY

$$ 🏨 **Bet Maimon.** On the western slopes of Zichron Ya'akov, a ten-minute
HOTEL walk from the center of town, this family-run hotel has a spectacular view of the coastal valley and the sea. **Pros:** city's best lodging; superb views. **Cons:** lots of steps to climb; old-fashioned feel. $ *Rooms from: $200* ⊠ *4 Zahal St.* ☎ *04/629–0390* ⊕ *www.maimon.com* ⤴ *25 rooms* ❖| *Breakfast.*

BENYAMINA

5 km (3 miles) south of Zichron Ya'akov, 55 km (34 miles) north of Tel Aviv.

Picturesque Benyamina, the youngest settlement in the area, was founded in 1922 and has several wineries. It was named after Baron Edmond de Rothschild, the head of the French branch of the famous family, who took a keen interest in the welfare of his fellow Jews in Palestine. (His Hebrew name was Benyamin.)

The advice of the viniculture experts Rothschild hired in the 1880s paid off handsomely, at least in this region—the fruit of the vines flourished in the 1890s. Rothschild's paternalistic system was not without its pitfalls, however; some of his administrators ruled his colonies like petty despots, trying, for instance, to impose the use of the French language on the local settlers, who wished to speak Hebrew. Language notwithstanding, the Binyamina Winery, the fourth largest in Israel, was founded in 1952; you can find it at the end of the village by following the Hebrew signs that show a bunch of grapes.

GETTING HERE AND AROUND
You can easily reach Benyamina by train. If you're driving, take Route 4. Either option makes for a very pretty ride. Once you're here, you'll need a car to get around because public transport is uneven.

EXPLORING

Binyamina Winery. The large visitor center at the country's fourth-largest winery is housed in a former perfume factory built by Baron de Rothschild in 1925. (As of this writing, it's undergoing extensive renovations.) It hasn't changed as much as you'd think, as cosmetics made from grape seeds are some of the products for sale here. You can also find olive oil, vinegar, and yes, even wine. The production facilities are next door in buildings surrounded by towering palm trees. Reservations are required for the 45-minute tour of the winery and barrel rooms, including a sampling of four or five wines. You can also do your tasting while having lunch or dinner in the restaurant that was once an orange packing facility. Or, you can simply drop in for coffee and cake. ⊠ *17 Hanassi St.* ☎ *04/610–7535* ⊕ *www.binyaminawines.com* ☜ *Free* ☉ *Sun.–Thurs. 9–5; Fri. 9–noon.*

Tishbi Estate Winery. Set among the hills and valleys of this pastoral area is one of the country's most esteemed wineries. The first vines were planted here 120 years ago. Tishbi Estate is the premier label (the Sauvignon Blanc and Chardonnay are among the best in Israel). At the new country-style visitor center, you can pair a French Valrhona chocolate with a Tishbi wine, or enjoy breakfast, brunch, or lunch under the grapevines in the courtyard. Apart from wine, you'll also find local cheeses, olive oil, honey, and wine jellies at the shop. Call ahead to arrange a one-hour tour, which includes tastings and a visit to the old alembic distillery where their prized brandy is made. It's about 3 km (1½ miles) north of Benyamina. ⊠ *Rte. 652* ☎ *04/638–8635* ⊕ *www.tishbi.com* ☜ *Free* ☉ *Sun.–Thurs. 8–5, Fri. 8–3.*

AKKO TO ROSH HANIKRA

One of the oldest and most entrancing port cities in the world, Akko's rampart-ringed Old City encloses an 18th-century mosque, underground Crusader halls, an extraordinary Templer tunnel, and winding lanes through a bazaar to restaurants at the water's edge. North of Akko, wide beaches, two of them within nature reserves, follow one after the other up the coast. The *moshavim* and *kibbutzim* (cooperative agricultural settlements) offer unusual settings for gourmet restaurants and upscale bed-and-breakfasts. Rosh Hanikra, at the top of the northern coast, has a cable car that carries you down a 210-foot cliff to caves hollowed out by wildly crashing waves.

AKKO

Fodor's Choice ★ *22 km (13½ miles) north of Haifa.*

The Old City of Akko, a UNESCO World Heritage Site, is an enchanting mix of mosques, markets, and vaulted Crusader ruins (many of them underground). A walk through the cobbled alleys and outdoor market stalls brings you to a small port filled with fishing boats. When viewed from the surrounding ramparts, it's one of the country's prettiest views. On the way, sample fresh halva, nougat-filled pralines, whole-wheat pita, or homemade *kibbeh* (a ground lamb and bulgur wheat dish), a specialty of the city's small Greek Orthodox community.

Akko's History

History clings to the stones in the Old City of Akko, which bear the marks of the many civilizations that have inhabited and built it. The city's history begins 4,000 years ago, when Akko was first mentioned in Egyptian writings that refer to the mound northeast of its walls. The Old Testament describes in Judges 1 that after the death of Joshua the tribe of Asher was unable to drive the Canaanites from Akko, so they lived among them.

With its well-protected harbor, fertile hinterland, and a strategic position, Akko has always proved worth fighting for. Alexander the Great had such regard for Akko that he set up a mint here. Akko was Phoenician for long periods, but the Hellenistic king Ptolemy II gained control in the 2nd century BC and renamed it Ptolemais.

King Baldwin I led the Crusaders who conquered Akko in 1104, and the port city was the Crusaders' principal link to home. Commerce thrived, and the European maritime powers—Genoa, Pisa, Venice, and Marseilles—developed separate quarters here. After the disastrous defeat of the Crusader armies in 1187, Akko surrendered to Saladin, but Richard the Lionheart soon recaptured the European stronghold. In its Crusader heyday, Akko had about 40 churches and monasteries and a population of 50,000.

In the 13th century, after the conquest of Jerusalem by the Muslims, Akko became the effective capital of a shrunken Latin kingdom; it fell to the Mamluks in 1291 and lay in ruins for centuries. In 1749 Dahr el-Omar, the Bedouin sheikh, moved his capital from Tiberias to Akko and rebuilt the walls of the city.

Napoléon's attempt to conquer the city in 1799 was repulsed, but the British captured it in 1918. With the founding of the State of Israel in 1948, many Arab inhabitants left Akko, though a good number remain. Akko's population now numbers about 46,000, with people living inside the Old City itself and in new developments pushing the city limits to the north.

To reach the historic parts of Akko, you'll be driving through a modern city: a bustling metropolis of about 46,000. It's rather plain, so reserve judgment until you've seen the Old City.

GETTING HERE AND AROUND

From Haifa, you can get here via Route 4. A much slower but far prettier inland route takes you north on Route 70, passing through rolling hills and avoiding the drab satellite towns north of Haifa. There are direct buses from Haifa, and trains from Jerusalem and Tel Aviv (you may have to change trains). Once you're here, a car is the best way to get around.

From Akko's port, the *Queen of Akko* (Malkat Akko, in Hebrew), a 200-passenger ferry, makes a 40-minute jaunt around the bay. The cost is NIS 22. Two well-known companies, Egged Tours and United Tours, offer one-day trips to Akko from Haifa.

TIMING AND PRECAUTIONS

Plan on spending the better part of a day if you want to see everything, including the excellent presentation in the Turkish bathhouse. Women should exercise caution walking around alone at night.

ESSENTIALS

Vistor and Tour Information

Akko Visitor Center ⊠ At the town entrance, just inside the stone arch, 1 Weizmann St. ☎ 04/995–6706 ⊕ www.akko.org.il/en/. **Egged Tours** ☎ 03/920–3992 ⊕ www.eggedtours.com. **Queen of Akko** ☎ 050/555–1136. **United Tours** ☎ 03/617-3333 ⊕ www.unitedtours.co.il.

EXPLORING AKKO

The walled city of Old Akko is relatively small and the well-signed sights are close to one another, making it easy to tour. You approach the Old City on Weizmann Street (watch for signs that say Old Akko), proceeding through a breach in the walls. If you're driving, park in the large lot.

OLD CITY

Start your tour at the Akko Visitor Center, just inside the main entrance to the Old City. This is where you purchase tickets. A combination ticket that includes all sights in the Old City is NIS 27. A combination ticket that includes all the sights along with the Turkish bath is NIS 46.

Once you've bought your ticket, take the time to get a map of the area and see the seven-minute film on the history of the region. Before you enter the Old City, you might want to walk along the Ramparts and visit the Ethnography Center. To get there, ascend the steps at the opening in the city walls. The El-Jazzar Mosque, south of the main entrance, also makes a good stop. Deeper in the Old City are the fascinating Hospitaller Fortress, as well as many other sights. You'll end up at the seaside walls of the Pisan Harbor.

TOP ATTRACTIONS

Fodor's Choice ★ **El-Jazzar Mosque.** This house of worship, the largest mosque in the country outside of Jerusalem, is also considered one of the most beautiful in Israel. Ahmed el-Jazzar, who succeeded Dahr el-Omar after having him assassinated, ruled Akko from 1775 to 1804. During his reign he built this mosque along with other public structures. His cruelty was so legendary that he earned the epithet "the Butcher." (He's buried next to his adopted son in a small white building to the right of the mosque.)

Just beyond the entrance is a pedestal engraved with graceful calligraphy; it re-creates the seal of a 19th-century Ottoman sultan. Some of the marble and granite columns that adorn the mosque and courtyard were plundered from the ruins of Caesarea. In front of the mosque, known in Arabic as Jama el-Basha, or the Pasha's Mosque, is an ornate fountain used by the faithful for ritual washings of hands and feet before prayer. Inside the mosque, enshrined in the gallery reserved for women, is a reliquary containing a hair believed to be from the beard of the prophet Muhammad; it's removed only once a year, on the 27th day of Ramadan.

Akko–Old City

HOSPITALLERS' QUARTER

Mediterranean Sea

Napoleon Bonaparte St.

Weizmann St.

El-Jazzar Wall

El-Jazzar Wall

Moat Garden

Visitor Center

Mausoleum

Parking

Akkotel Hotel

Salahaddin St.

Yonatan Hachashmonai

Majdala Mosque

El-Jazzar

Shazalia Mosque

Parchi Sq.

TO PALM BEACH CLUB HOTEL →

Efendi Hotel

El-Zituneh Mosque

A-Ramal Mosque

Marco Polo

Baha'i House

St. George's Church

Binyamin Mitudela

Ramchal Synagogue

Zalman Hatzoref

Sha'ar Nikanor

Akko Bay

Hagana St.

Uri Buri Restaurant

Maronite Church

Mu'allek Mosque

Sinan Basha Mosque

Venezia Sq.

Parking

St. Andrew's Church

Khan A-Shuna

Pisa Sq.

Akko Port

Church of St. John

Abu Christo Restaurant

Southern Promenade

Lighthouse

0   100 yards

0   100 meters

El-Jazzar Mosque 3
Ethnography Museum 2
Hospitaller Fortress
(Knights' Halls) 4
Khan el-Umdan 8
Pisan Harbor 9

Ramparts 1
Refectory 6
Souk 7
Turkish bathhouse 5
Underground Prisoners
Museum 10

The mosque closes five times a day for prayers, so you might have a short wait. Dress modestly. ⊠ *Off El-Jazzar St.* ☎ *04/991–3039* ⊠ *NIS 6* ☺ *Sat.–Thurs. 8–5, Fri. 8–11 and 1–5.*

NEED A BREAK?

In the plaza outside the El-Jazzar Mosque are outdoor restaurants where you can enjoy a falafel, fresh-squeezed orange or pomegranate juice, or coffee while watching the world go by.

Fodor's Choice
★
Hospitaller Fortress (Knights' Halls). This remarkable 12th-century fortress was once known as the Crypt of St. John—before excavation, it was erroneously thought to have been an underground chamber. The dimensions of the colossal pillars that support the roof (girded with metal bands for extra support) make this one of Israel's most monumental examples of Crusader architecture. It's also one of the oldest Gothic structures in the world. In the right-hand corner opposite the entrance is a fleur-de-lis carved in stone, the crest of the French house of Bourbon, which has led some scholars to suggest that this was the chamber in which Louis VII convened the knights of the realm.

Just outside this room is an entrance to an extremely narrow subterranean passageway. Cut from stone, this was a secret tunnel that the Crusaders probably used to reach the harbor when besieged by Muslim forces. (Those who are claustrophobic can take an alternate route, which goes back to the entrance of the Turkish bathhouse and continues from there.) You'll emerge to find yourself in the cavernous vaulted halls of the fortress guard post, with a 13th-century marble Crusader tombstone at the exit.

Here you'll find a series of barrel-vaulted rooms known as the Knights' Halls. Six such halls have been discovered thus far. Arrows point the way through vast rooms filled with ongoing reconstruction work, huge marble columns, and myriad archaeological pieces from the past. Above this part of the Crusader city stands the Ottoman citadel, which you can glimpse from the courtyard. Built by Dahr el-Omar in the 18th century on the rubble-filled Crusader ruins, the citadel was the highest structure in Akko.

The different factions within Akko's walls probably sowed the seeds of the Crusaders' downfall here. By the mid-13th century, open fighting had broken out between the Venetians and Genoese. When the Mamluks attacked with a vengeance in 1291, the Crusaders' resistance crumbled, and the city's devastation was complete. It remained a subdued place for centuries, and even today Akko retains a medieval cast. ⊠ *1 Weizmann St.* ☎ *04/995–6706* ⊕ *www.akko.org.il* ⊠ *Combination ticket NIS 27* ☺ *Nov.–Mar., Sat.–Thurs. 8:30–5, Fri. 8:30–4; Apr.–Oct., Sat.–Thurs. 8:30–6, Fri. 8:30–5.*

Pisan Harbor. Climbing the stone steps at the water's edge, you can walk along the sea walls at the Pisan Harbor, so named after an Italian Pisa commune here in Crusader times. Start at the café perched on high— a great lookout—and head west in the direction of the 18th-century Church of St. John. You'll end up at the southwestern extremity of Akko, next to the lighthouse. Head north along Haganah Street, which runs parallel to the crenellated western sea wall. After five minutes

Now a museum, the 18th-century Turkish bathhouse in Akko is illuminated through a dome with glass bubbles.

you'll reach the whitewashed, blue-trimmed Baha'i house (not open to the public), where the prophet of the Baha'i religion, Baha'u'llah, spent 12 years of his exile. His burial site is just north of Akko at the Baha'i Founder's Shrine and Gardens. ⊠ *Southern tip of Akko.*

FAMILY **Turkish Bathhouse.** Built for Pasha el-Jazzar in 1781, Akko's remarkable Turkish bathhouse (*Hamam al-Basha*, in Arabic) was in use until 1947. Don't miss the sound-and-light show called *The Story of the Last Bath Attendant*, set in the beautiful bathhouse itself. You follow the story, with visual and audio effects, from the dressing room decorated with Turkish tiles and topped with a cupola, through the rooms with colored-glass bubbles protruding from the roof domes, sending a filtered green light to the steam rooms below. ⊠ *1 Weizmann St.* ☎ *04/991–1764* ⊕ *www.akko.org.il* ✉ *Combination ticket NIS 46* ☺ *Nov.–Mar., Sat.–Thurs. 9–5, Fri. and Jewish holiday eves 9–4; Apr.–Oct., Sat.–Thurs. 8:30–6, Fri. and Jewish holiday eves 9–5.*

WORTH NOTING

Khan el-Umdan. In Venezia Square, in front of the port, is the two-tiered Inn of the Pillars. Before you visit this Ottoman *khan*—the largest of the four in Akko—and the Pisan Quarter beyond, take a stroll around the port, with its small flotilla of fishing boats, yachts, and sailboats. Then walk through the khan's gate beneath a square clock tower, built at the turn of the 20th century. The khan served vast numbers of merchants and travelers during Akko's golden age of commerce, in the late 18th century. The 32 pink-and-gray granite pillars that give it its name are compliments of Ahmed el-Jazzar's raids on Roman Caesarea. There was once a market at the center of the colonnaded courtyard. ⊠ *Venezia Sq.*

Ramparts. As you enter the Old City, climb the blue-railing stairway on your right for a stroll along the city walls. Walking to the right, you can see the stunted remains of the 12th-century walls built by the Crusaders, under whose brief rule—just less than two centuries—Akko flourished as never before or since. The indelible signs of the Crusaders, who made Akko the main port of their Christian empire, are much more evident inside the Old City itself.

The wall girding the northern part of the town was built by Ahmed el-Jazzar, the Pasha of Akko, who added these fortifications following his victory over Napoléon's army in 1799. With the help of the British fleet, el-Jazzar turned Napoléon's attempted conquest into a humiliating rout. Napoléon had dreamed of founding a new Eastern empire, thrusting northward from Akko to Turkey and then seizing India from Great Britain. His defeat at Akko hastened his retreat to France, thus changing the course of history. Walk around to the guard towers and up an incline just opposite; there's a view of the moat below and Haifa across the bay. Turn around and let your gaze settle on the exotic skyline of Old Akko, the sea green dome of the great mosque its dominating feature. Walk down the ramp, crossing the rather messy Moat Garden at the base of the walls; straight ahead is the El-Jazzar Mosque.

Souk. At this outdoor market, stalls heaped with fresh produce and seafood alternate with specialty stores: a pastry shop with an astonishing variety of exotic Middle Eastern delicacies; a spice shop filled with the aromas of the East; a bakery with steaming fresh pita. You'll often see fishermen sitting on doorsteps, intently repairing their lines and nets to the sounds of Arabic music blaring from the open windows above. The loosely defined area twists and turns through the center of the Old City, but Marco Polo Street is a good place to begin your exploration.

"Treasures in the Walls" Ethnography Museum. There are two sections to this small but charming museum: one re-creates a 19th-century marketplace, including craftsmen's workshops such as a hatmaker and a blacksmith, filled with every last tool they'd need to make hats and horseshoes; the other room displays a traditional Damascene living room, complete with an astounding collection of furniture and accoutrements. To get here once you're up the steps to the Ramparts, keep an eye out for the short flight of stairs heading down to the left. ⊠ *On the ramparts* ☎ *04/991–1004* ⊠ *NIS 15* ⊗ *Sat.-Thu. 10–5; Fri. 10-3.*

NEED A BREAK?

Oudah Brothers Cafe. In the souk, duck into the Oudah Brothers Cafe and enjoy a coffee, hummus, or kebab in the courtyard of the 16th-century Khan el-Faranj, or Franks' Inn. Note the 18th-century Franciscan monastery and tower to your left. ⊠ *Khan Ha-Frankim St.* ☎ *04/991–2013.*

Underground Prisoners Museum. Located at the sea's edge, this museum run by the Ministry of Defense is housed in several wings of the citadel built by Dahr el-Omar and then modified by Ahmed el-Jazzar in 1785. It served as a major prison during the British Mandate. On the way in, you pass the citadel's outer wall; the difference between the large Crusader building stones and the smaller Turkish ones above is easy to spot. The original cells and their meager contents, supplemented by photographs and documents that reconstruct the history of the Jewish resistance to British rule in the '30s and '40s, illustrate prison life. During the Mandate, the citadel became a high-security prison whose inmates included top members of Jewish resistance organizations, among them Ze'ev Jabotinsky and, later, Moshe Dayan. In 1947 a dramatic prison breakout by leaders of the Irgun captured headlines around the world and provided Leon Uris's novel *Exodus* with one of its most dramatic moments. ☒ *Hahagana St.* ☎ *04/991–1375* ☜ *NIS 10* ☉ *Sun.–Thurs. 8:30–4:30, Fri. 8:30–1:30.*

NEAR THE CITY

Baha'i Founder's Shrine and Gardens. For the Baha'is, this is the holiest place on earth, the site of the tomb of the faith's prophet and founder, Baha'u'llah. First you'll pass the gardens' west gate, open only to Baha'is. Take the first right (no sign) and continue to the unobtrusive turn, 500 yards up, to the north (main) gate. Baha'u'llah lived in the red-tile mansion here after he was released from jail in Akko, and was buried in the small building next door, now the Shrine of Baha'u'llah. It's best to go on weekends, when the inner gardens and shrine are open. Going through the black-iron gate, follow a white gravel path in the exquisitely landscaped gardens, with a fern-covered fountain and an observation point along the way, until you reach the shrine. Visitors are asked to dress modestly. The shrine is on Route 4, about 1 km (½ mile) north of the gas station at Akko's northern edge. ☒ *Rte. 4* ☎ *04/835–8845* ⊕ *www.bahaigardens.org.il* ☜ *Free* ☉ *Gardens daily 9–4; Shrine Fri.–Mon. 9–noon.*

Ghetto Fighters' House Museum (Lochamei Hageta'ot). Kibbutz Lochamei Hageta'ot was founded in 1949 by survivors of the German, Polish, and Lithuanian Jewish ghettos set up by the Nazis. To commemorate their compatriots who perished in the Holocaust, the kibbutz members set up the **Ghetto Fighters' House Museum,** which you enter to the right of the main gate. Exhibits include photographs documenting the Warsaw Ghetto and the famous uprising, and halls devoted to different themes, among them that of the Jewish communities before their destruction in the Holocaust; the death camps; and deportations at the hands of the Nazis. You can also see the booth in which Adolf Eichmann, architect of the "Final Solution," sat during his Jerusalem trial.

In a cone-shaped building, the adjacent **Yad Layeled** (Children's Memorial) is dedicated to the memory of the 1½ million children who perished in the Holocaust. It's designed for young visitors, who can begin to comprehend the events of the Holocaust through a series of tableaux and images accompanied by recorded voices, allowing them to identify with individual victims without seeing shocking details. There's a small cafeteria on the premises. The site is 2 km (1 mile) north of Akko on Route 4. ☒ *Kibbutz Lochamei Hageta'ot, Rte. 4* ☎ *04/995–8080* ⊕ *www.gfh.org.il/eng* ☜ *30 NIS* ☉ *Sun.–Thurs. 9–4; Fri. 9–1 (by reservation).*

Despite modern boats, the old harbor in Akko retains echoes of past eras.

WHERE TO EAT

$$$ SEAFOOD

🍴 **Abu Christo.** In the Old City, this popular waterfront fish restaurant stands at one of the original 18th-century gates built by Pasha Ahmed el-Jazzar when he fortified the city after his victory over Napoléon. It's a Greek family business that's been passed from father to son since 1948. The covered patio is an idyllic place to dig into earthy hummus with pine nuts, eggplant salad spiced with sumac, and other mezze salads. Abu Christo serves the daily catch—often grouper, red snapper, or sea bass—prepared simply, either grilled or deep-fried. Shellfish such as jumbo shrimp and crabs, and grilled meats or beef Stroganoff are also available. [$] *Average main: NIS 100* ✉ *Crusader Port* ☎ *04/991–0065* 🌐 *www.abu-christo.co.il* ✍ *Reservations essential.*

$$$$ SEAFOOD Fodor's Choice ★

🍴 **Uri Buri.** Justly known far and wide for its excellent fish and seafood, this Akko institution is housed in an old Turkish building. One room is furnished with sofas, copper dishes, and *nargillas* (water pipes). Everything on the menu is seasonal, and the fresh fish is steamed, baked, or grilled. Allow time to linger here—it's not your everyday fish fry. Two house specialties are gravlax and Thai-style fish; delicious seafood soup is another fixture. Or try the baby calamari with kumquats and pink grapefruit or Creole shrimp with five spices. Uri Buri is near the lighthouse, on one edge of the parking lot. [$] *Average main: NIS 110* ✉ *On the promenade near the lighthouse, 11 Ha-haganah St.* ☎ *04/955–2212* ✍ *Reservations essential.*

WHERE TO STAY

$ **Akkotel.** This three-story hostelry, a former Turkish police station, is
HOTEL built into the city wall. **Pros:** family run; unusual lodging; warm service.
Cons: no pool; small rooms. $ *Rooms from: $180* ✉ *1 Salahaddin St.*
☎ *04/987–7100* ⊕ *www.akkotel.com* ⌁ *16 rooms, 2 suites* ⧖*Breakfast.*

$$$$ **Efendi Hotel.** Uniquely charming, this boutique hotel opened in 2012
Fodor'sChoice by chef-entrepreneur Uri Jeremias is housed in two adjoining Otto-
★ man palaces erected over a Crusader vault, lovingly restored over eight
HOTEL years by a joint team of Venetian and Israeli artisans with great attention to detail. **Pros:** superb staff; perfect Old City location. **Cons:** not
a lively nighttime neighborhood. $ *Rooms from: $450* ✉ *Louis IX St.*
☎ *074/729–9799* ⊕ *www.efendi-hotel.com* ⌁ *12 rooms* ⧖*Breakfast.*

$ **Nes Ammim Hotel.** Founded fifty years ago, Nes Ammim is an ecu-
HOTEL menical Christian settlement between Akko and Nahariya focusing on
mutual respect and tolerance. **Pros:** good for families; outdoor swimming pool in summertime. **Cons:** basic rooms; few activities. $ *Rooms
from: $115* ✉ *Rd. 8611, off Rte. 4* ☎ *04/995–0000* ⊕ *www.nesammim.
com/en/* ⌁ *48 rooms, 13 apartments* ⧖*Breakfast.*

$ **Palm Beach Club.** A private beach with exceptional views and a coun-
HOTEL try club with state-of-the-art facilities make this hotel a great deal, espe-
FAMILY cially for families. **Pros:** attentive staff; private beach; tennis and squash
courts. **Cons:** small rooms. $ *Rooms from: $170* ✉ *Rte. 4* ☎ *04/987–
7777* ⊕ *eng.palmbeach.co.il* ⌁ *97 rooms, 27 suites* ⧖*Breakfast.*

SPORTS AND THE OUTDOORS

Just south of the Old City on the Haifa–Akko road is a sandy stretch of
municipal beach in **Akko Bay,** with parking, showers, toilets, and chair
rentals. Admission is NIS 10.

SHOPPING

David Miro. Iraq-born artist David Miro sells a range of handmade products. The jewelry that combines silver and gold is especially interesting;
some incorporates Roman glass, some uses turquoise Eilat stone, and
there's also hand-worked copperware and silver pieces. ✉ *1 Weizmann
St.* ☎ *04/991–3735* ⊕ *www.davidmiroarts.com.*

EN
ROUTE
To the west of Route 4, as you travel north from Akko, stands a segment of the multitiered **aqueduct** built by Ahmed el-Jazzar in the late
18th century to carry the sweet waters of the Kabri springs to Akko.

NAHARIYA

8 km (5 miles) north of Akko.

This vibrant seaside recreation spot, Israel's northernmost coastal
town, was built along the banks of a river lined with eucalyptus trees.
(The town's name comes from *nahar,* Hebrew for "river.") The town
is popular with vacationing Israelis who throng the small shops and
cafés along the main street, Haga'aton Boulevard. European visitors,
too, appreciate the lively atmosphere and the white-sand beaches. One
of the region's most beautiful stretches of sand is just at the end of
the main street. Achziv Beach, just 4 km north of town, is one of the
country's finest.

Although German was once the most common language here, these days you're just as likely to hear Russian or Amharic (spoken by Ethiopians). In July and August, there's dancing in the amphitheater at the mouth of the river, and Israeli stars perform on the beach and in the town square.

GETTING HERE AND AROUND

There are direct buses from Haifa. Trains from Tel Aviv travel several times a day to Nahariya. By car, take Route 4 north of Akko. From a location 5 km (3 miles) north of Nahariya, Trek Yam takes you on an exciting 30-minute ride up the coast to Rosh Hanikra in a high-speed Tornado motorboat. The cost is NIS 800 per trip, maximum 10 passengers.

ESSENTIALS

Tour Information **Trek Yam** ☎ *04/982–3671.*

EXPLORING

Byzantine Church. This church dedicated to St. Lazarus features an elaborate, 17-color mosaic floor, discovered in 1964, that depicts peacocks, other birds, hunting scenes, and plants. It was part of what experts consider one of the largest and most beautiful Byzantine churches in the Western Galilee, where Christianity spread from the 4th to the 7th century. To get here, head east on Haga'aton to Route 4, making a left at the stoplight and then the first right onto Yechi'am Street. From here take the third left and then an immediate right onto Bielefeld Street. ✉ *Bielefeld St.* 🎟 *NIS 2.*

WHERE TO EAT

$$$$ MEDITERRANEAN Fodor's Choice ★

🍴 **Adelina.** When dining at this stellar restaurant, you may wonder how you got so lucky. There's the knockout view of the Mediterranean from the stone terrace, the olive tree–shaded setting, and the wonderful Catalonian-accented dishes prepared by Adelina. Cooking is done in the huge silver tabun oven as Spanish music drifts across the dark wooden tables. Try the paella marinara packed with shellfish, roast sirloin with bacon and tarragon, or broccoli cannelloni in a creamy pepper sauce. Move on to *knafe* (a local pastry) with pistachio ice cream. The eatery is about 8 km (5 miles) east of Nahariya. [$] *Average main: NIS 130* ✉ *Kibbutz Kabri, Rte. 89* ☎ *04/952–3707* ✍ *Reservations essential* 🕑 *Closed Sun.*

$$$ MEDITERRANEAN

🍴 **BaNahala.** Be prepared for taste-bud overload at this lovely restaurant surrounded by pecan trees. Inside the old building, part of a family estate, wood tables are set with fresh flowers, chairs are made from woven rope, and one wall displays the charming faces of the owners as children. Outside, market umbrellas shade the tables on the huge wood-plank terrace. When the kids are finished choosing from their own menu, they can frolic on the lawn. For grown-ups there's everything from lamb kebabs with tahini to sweet red peppers stuffed with tangy cheese and risotto to tuna steak marinated in ginger. Top off the meal with baked cheesecake and berry sorbet. The comprehensive list of Israeli wines gives you a chance to sample local vintages. [$] *Average main: NIS 85* ✉ *17 Yitzhak Sadeh, Rasco* ☎ *04/951–2074* 🌐 *www.banahala.co.il* ✍ *Reservations essential* 🕑 *Closed Sun.*

$$$$
MODERN ISRAELI

✕ **Ida.** On the main street, you'll recognize Ida by the white stucco building topped by a sign in big blue letters. Ida was the wife of the town's first mayor, and the couple lived here in the 1950s. The mood is relaxed and the service excellent. Gold roses are stenciled on several walls, and wood screens divide the interior into cozy areas. It's an impressive modern Israeli dining experience: start with duck confit with cranberry sauce or pickled sirloin carpaccio, then move on to shellfish risotto with a creamy shrimp sauce or the pan-fried trout with a coconut-and-carrot sauce. It'll be hard to say no to chocolate cheesecake as a finale. $ *Average main: NIS 120* ✉ *48 Haga'aton Blvd.* ☎ *04/951–3444.*

WORD OF MOUTH

"I second the recommendation of Nahariya. Nahariya is right next to the fabulous Achziv Beach, and it's a couple of miles from Rosh Hanikra. It's a much quieter experience than Haifa."
—judyinjerusalem

$$
FRENCH

✕ **La Crepe Jacob.** This tiny but popular place is in a small cottage with blue window frames and a flower-filled garden. A wood-burning stove keeps things cozy inside. Locally made goat cheeses from the Teva Ez dairy next door cram the counter. The hefty crepes, lovingly prepared by Betty and Jacob, come with fillings such as feta, ham, and mushrooms; smoked salmon and cheese; and tomato, onion, olives, cheese, and mushrooms. The banana and chocolate crepe is a delicious wrap-up. In addition, the menu includes heartier dishes like veal fillet with shrimp. It's about 3 km (2 miles) east of the city. $ *Average main: NIS 70* ✉ *Moshav Ben Ami, Rte. 89* ☎ *04/952–0299.*

$$
ECLECTIC

✕ **Penguin.** The doors to this legendary institution opened in 1940—it's probably the oldest restaurant in the country. Three generations of the Oppenheimer family work here, and the walls carry enlarged photographs of how the place looked when it was just a hut. Stop off for coffee and cake, or make a meal of spinach blintzes with melted cheese, hamburger platters, or Chinese dishes. The management swears that the schnitzel gets accolades from Viennese visitors. Kids will enjoy the enclosed playground. $ *Average main: NIS 70* ✉ *31 Haga'aton Blvd.* ☎ *04/992–8855.*

WHERE TO STAY

$
B&B/INN

⌂ **Aromantica.** Varda, who makes every effort to provide a relaxing stay for guests, runs these comfortable country cottages in the rural farming settlement of Moshav Ben Ami. **Pros:** personal service; landscaped garden. **Cons:** not for families; a bit hard to find. $ *Rooms from: $150* ✉ *Rte. 89* ☎ *04/982–0484, 053/809–5058* ⊕ *www.aromantica.co.il* ⤳ *3 cabins* ⦿l *Breakfast.*

$$$$
B&B/INN

⌂ **Pinhas & Gaston (Moshav Liman Estate).** Billed as a "holiday estate," this heavenly retreat offers four delightful guesthouses, each featuring carved-wood beds, down quilts, and well-equipped kitchens. **Pros:** exquisite setting; romantic getaway. **Cons:** expensive rates; no Internet. $ *Rooms from: $590* ✉ *Moshav Liman, Rte. 4* ☎ *057/728–2828, 04/952–6000* ⊕ *www.gaston.co.il* ⤳ *4 houses* ⦿l *Breakfast.*

At Rosh Hanikra, take a cable car down the cliffs for an up-close look at the sea grottoes.

$
B&B/INN
 **Pivko Village.** Nestled among the trees on the grounds of a kibbutz, these roomy log cabins hold up to five people, making them a good bet for families. **Pros:** lots of activities; good restaurant. **Cons:** a bit hard to find. *$ Rooms from: $160* ⊠ *Kibbutz Kabri, Rte. 89* ☎ *04/995–2711* ⊕ *www.weekend.co.il/galilwest/pivko_village/* ⤳ *6 cabins* ¶⊙¶ *Breakfast.*

$$$
B&B/INN
Villa Provence. Hidden away in a rural settlement 10 km (6 miles) from the city, this out-of-the-ordinary lodging founded by a French couple who came here in 2006 looks as though it was plucked from a French hillside. **Pros:** gorgeous setting; pretty pool. **Cons:** expensive; no restaurants nearby. *$ Rooms from: $335* ⊠ *Moshav Manot, Rte. 8911* ☎ *04/980–6246* ⊕ *www.villaprovence.co.il* ⤳ *6 rooms* ¶⊙¶ *Breakfast.*

NIGHTLIFE AND THE ARTS
La Scala. La Scala, Nahariya's flashiest disco, draws the over-30 crowd for standard dance tunes with a throbbing beat. It's in the passageway just west of the Carlton Hotel. The cover charge on Friday is NIS 50; doors open at 10 pm. ⊠ *23 Haga'aton St.* ☎ *04/900–5555.*

SPORTS AND THE OUTDOORS
BEACHES
FAMILY
Fodor's Choice
★
Achziv Beach. This beautifully maintained stretch of sand in the Achziv National Park is just north of Nahariya, on the road to Rosh Hanikra. Beside the ruins of the ancient settlement of Achziv, there are two huge lagoons along the shore, one shallow, the other deep. There are also watchful lifeguards and playground facilities. In July and August, turtles lay their eggs on the beach. You can picnic on the

grassy slopes or make use of the restaurant. Enter at the second sign for Achziv Beach, not the first. Admission, which is NIS 35, includes the use of showers and toilets. For NIS 60 per person, you can camp here overnight. ⊠ *Rte. 2* ☎ *04/982–3263.*

Betzet Beach. Betzet Beach, a bit farther north of Achziv Beach, is part of a nature reserve and offers abundant vegetation, shade-giving trees, and the ruins of an ancient olive press. There's a lifeguard on duty in season, but few frills. Admission is free. ⊠ *Rte. 2.*

FAMILY **Galei Galil Beach.** Nahariya's public bathing facilities at Galei Galil Beach are ideal for families. Apart from the lovely beach, facilities include an outdoor Olympic-size pool, a heated indoor pool, a wading pool, a playground for children, clean changing rooms and showers, plus a snack bar. In peak season, the beach offers exercise classes early in the morning. The entrance fee is NIS 30. ⊠ *North of Haga'aton Blvd.*

SCUBA DIVING

Trek Yam. Trek Yam takes scuba divers to explore the caves at Rosh Hanikra along the coast. The price of each trip is NIS 75. The company also offers Jeep trips and boating excursions. Reserve several days in advance. ☎ *04/982–3671.*

> ### WORD OF MOUTH
>
> "If you are limiting yourself to coastal sites, then I would make sure to drive a bit farther north to Rosh Hanikra—there is a beautiful view and interesting caves; it's well worth the trip. Caesarea and Akko will occupy a full day."
> —Oreet

ROSH HANIKRA

Fodor's Choice ★ *7 km (4½ miles) north of Nahariya and 38 km (24 miles) north of Haifa.*

GETTING HERE AND AROUND

It's a short drive from Nahariya to Rosh Hanikra, the last destination on the country's northern coast. You'll need your own car, as there's no public transportation.

EXPLORING

Rosh Hanikra. The dramatic white cliffs on the coast signal both Israel's border with Lebanon and the sea grottoes of Rosh Hanikra. Even before you get in line for the steep two-minute ride down to the grottoes on the Austrian-made cable car, take a moment to absorb the stunning view back down the coast. Bring binoculars. Still clearly visible is the route of the railway line, now mostly a dirt road, built by the British through the hillside in 1943 to extend the Cairo–Tel Aviv–Haifa line to Beirut. (You're now much closer to Beirut than to Jerusalem.) After the descent, you can see the 12-minute audiovisual presentation called *The Sea and the Cliff.*

The incredible caves beneath the cliff have been carved out by relentless waves pounding away at the white chalky rock for countless centuries. Footpaths inside the cliff itself lead from one huge cave to another, while the sound of waves—and the squealing of fruit bats—echoes off the water-sprayed walls. Huge bursts of seawater plunge into pools at your feet (behind protective rails). It's slippery, so hang on to the children. ✉ *End of Rte. 4* ☎ *073/271–0100* 🌐 *www.rosh-hanikra.com* 🎟 *NIS 45* 🕓 *Winter weekdays, 9–4; summer weekdays 9–6, Fri. 9–4, Sat. 9–6. Call to verify hrs.*

WHERE TO EAT

$$$ ISRAELI 🍴 **Diners Ba-Rosh.** This bright and breezy spot for Israeli fare offers a fabulous view of the sea swirling and crashing below. The selection of beers on tap—all produced in the Golan Heights—range from pale ale to a tangy red lager. Starters include a bagel with corned beef and a baked potato with garlic sauce and fried onions. As a main course, the appealing casserole of beef and root vegetables simmered in beer is a sure hit, as are franks and sauerkraut, steaks, and burgers. Every other Wednesday evening features live jazz. [$] *Average main: NIS 80* ✉ *End of Rte. 4* ☎ *04/952–0159* 🕓 *Closed Sat.*

6

LOWER GALILEE

With Nazareth, Tiberias, and
the Sea of Galilee

WELCOME TO LOWER GALILEE

TOP REASONS TO GO

★ **Sunset on the Sea of Galilee:** The lake at sundown is always evocative, often beautiful, and occasionally spectacular. Walk a beach, sip a drink, or take a sail as dusk slowly settles.

★ **Zippori:** The distant past is palpable at this archaeological site, once a worldly Jewish and Hellenistic city. Set amid woods, it has the loveliest ancient mosaics in the land.

★ **Nazareth:** Tradition and modernity collide in the town where Jesus grew up. Today it's a city of baklava and BMWs, new politics and ancient passions. Talk to a local as you sample Middle Eastern delicacies.

★ **Mt. Gilboa:** This little-visited region offers local beauty and grand views for the independent traveler who has a bit of time and no checklist of must-see famous sites.

★ **A spiritual source:** Tune your ear to the Galilee's spiritual reverberations. Listen as pilgrims chant a Mass at the Mt. of Beatitudes or sit meditatively on Tabgha's shore.

1 Jezreel and Jordan Valleys. Crisscrossed by ancient highways that once linked Egypt and Mesopotamia, the scenic Jezreel and Jordan valleys are studded with major archaeological and historical sites. Megiddo, corrupted in Greek as "Armageddon," is known for a biblical battle and is prophesied to be the site of a future one. Zippori, also called Sepphoris, is a site with Jewish and Christian links. The Roman ruins at Beit She'an evoke the glory of one of the richest cities in the eastern Mediterranean.

2 Nazareth and the Galilee Hills. The once-sleepy town of Nazareth, the site of Jesus' boyhood, has boomed in recent decades to become a regional center. The nearby hills, such as Mt. Tabor and Mt. Gilboa, are both biblical byways and part of the reforested landscape many find so entrancing.

Map labels

Kafar Manda
Shefar'am
784
79
70
Zippori National Park
77
Cana
Hamovil Junction
Zippori
754
77
Nazerat 'Illit (Upper Nazareth)
75
Ramat Yishay
Nazareth
◆ Beit She'arim
75
2
Shibli
Nahalal
Migdal Ha'emek
Mt. Tabor
70
73
Mizrav
Dovrat
66
60
65
Nain
JEZREEL VALLEY
Afula
65
Kibbutz Ein Harod (Me'uchad)
Megiddo
Megiddo Junction
1
Yehezkel
Tel Yizre'el
Ma'ayan Harod
60
WEST BANK

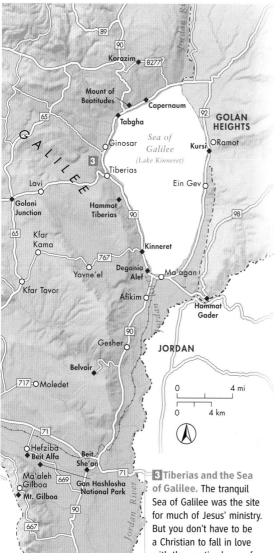

GETTING ORIENTED

The Hebrew word *gal* means "wave," and the Lower Galilee is indeed a hilly country, with deep valleys framed by mountain ridges. Not much more than a creek, the Jordan River cuts through the topography on the eastern border, first draining into the freshwater Sea of Galilee and then flowing south toward the Dead Sea. The Galilee is the storied land where King Saul lost his life fighting the Philistines; where the Romans built cities such as Beit She'an; where Jesus, who grew up in Nazareth, carried out much of his ministry; and where the Crusaders built and lost a kingdom. The lakeside resort city of Tiberias beckons with its hot springs and history.

3 Tiberias and the Sea of Galilee. The tranquil Sea of Galilee was the site for much of Jesus' ministry. But you don't have to be a Christian to fall in love with the mystic charm of this harp-shaped lake. A number of historic hotels, inns, ranches, and private villas ring the lake. The hot springs at Tiberias and Hammat Gader have been attracting guests since the time of Augustus Caesar.

Updated by
Shari Giddens
Helmer

The Lower Galilee is a history-soaked region where scores of events in the Hebrew Bible and the New Testament took place. Blessed with forested hills, fertile valleys, gushing springs, and the Sea of Galilee, it has strong appeal. The graves of Jewish, Christian, Muslim, and Druze holy men attract those seeking spiritual solace, but the region is also the scene of earthly delights, including fine restaurants and spas.

To most Israelis, the Galilee is synonymous with "the North," a land of nature reserves and national parks. In short, they would claim, it's a great place to visit, but they wouldn't want to live there: it's provincial and remote. Still, the Lower Galilee has its own quiet beauty and varied landscape. Whatever your agenda is—spiritual, historical, recreational, or restful—savor your time here. Follow a hiking trail above the Sea of Galilee. Wade through fields of irises in the spring. Bathe in a warm mineral spa. Buy some good goat cheese. Nazareth, the region's administrative center, has character and deserves some time.

Farming and tourism form the economic base. The region's kibbutzim and a smaller number of *moshavim* (Jewish family-farm villages) are concentrated in the Jezreel and Jordan valleys and around the Sea of Galilee. The rockier hill country is predominantly Arab (*Israeli* Arab; this isn't disputed territory) and Israeli Druze. For the last half a century, the communities—Jewish, Druze, and Arab—have been attempting neighborly relations despite the ethnic tensions that swirl around them. By and large, they've succeeded.

Culture and entertainment aren't this region's strong suits. A number of annual festivals and events are the highlights. Tiberias's pubs and restaurants probably come closest to providing lively nightlife, but there are worse ways to spend an evening than sitting by a moonlit lake washing down a good St. Peter's fish or a lamb kebab with an excellent Israeli wine.

LOWER GALILEE PLANNER

WHEN TO GO

The Galilee is prettiest in the spring months of March and April when it's covered with wildflowers, and its hills are draped in green. Summer can be torrid. Avoid the Sea of Galilee during Passover (March–April) and the High Holidays and Sukkot (September–October): although the weather is great at these times, half the country vacations here and rates soar.

Some hotels charge high-season rates during July and August; this is also true the week of Christmas. Weekends in general (Thursday night through Saturday night) are more crowded; some hotels hike rates substantially.

PLANNING YOUR TIME

It's possible to get a feeling for this region in a few days, but you can expand your trip to include some highlights of the Upper Galilee and the Golan including Tzfat (Safed). Tiberias, with its many accommodations, or the Sea of Galilee region are good bases for exploring archaeological sites—Beit She'an is impressive—as well as sites associated with the ministry of Jesus. Nazareth is worth a trip, either from Tiberias or en route to it from other areas. The Galilee is a low-key area with some lovely national parks and natural sites, including Mt. Tabor, if you choose to linger.

Ein Gev, on the eastern shore of the Sea of Galilee, has an Israeli-music festival in the spring. Beit She'an revives its ancient Roman theater for a short series of events in October, and in May and December, Jacob's Ladder—the twice-annual folk festival—fills the air above Nof Ginosar, on the Sea of Galilee, with traditional folk and country music of the British Isles and North America.

GETTING HERE AND AROUND

BUS TRAVEL

The Egged bus cooperative provides regular service from Jerusalem, Tel Aviv, and Haifa to Nazareth, Beit She'an, Afula, and Tiberias. There's no direct service from Ben Gurion International Airport; change in Tel Aviv or Haifa. There are several buses an hour from Tel Aviv to Afula (1½ hours). Bus 842 (*yashir*, or "direct") is quickest; Buses 829, 830, and 835 are express, stopping at major stations en route. Bus 823 from Afula to Nazareth (20 minutes) is infrequent. The 830 and 835 continue from Afula to Tiberias (about an hour). The 829 and 843 link Afula to Beit She'an (20 minutes) three times a day.

To get from Haifa to Tiberias, take the slow Bus 430 (about an hour), which leaves hourly from Merkazit Hamifratz. From the same Haifa station, the slow Bus 301 leaves two or three times an hour for Afula. Buses from Jerusalem to Beit She'an and Tiberias (Buses 961, 963, 966, and the slower 948) depart roughly hourly; change in Beit She'an for Afula, where you change again for Nazareth. Buses 961 and 963 continue to Tiberias. The ride to Beit She'an is about two hours, to Tiberias another 25 minutes. Bus 431 connects Nazareth and Tiberias once every two hours.

CAR TRAVEL

Driving is the best way to explore the Lower Galilee. Driving time from Tel Aviv or Jerusalem to Tiberias is two hours. Some newer four-lane highways are excellent, but some secondary roads may be in need of repair.

Signposting is clear (and usually in English), with route numbers clearly marked. Brown signs indicate most sights. The Lower Galilee is served by a number of highways. Route 90, going up the Jordan Valley to Tiberias and on to Metulla on the Lebanese border, is the most convenient road from Jerusalem. Routes 2 and 4, both multilane expressways, lead north from Tel Aviv. Turn east onto Route 65, then north onto Route 60 to get to Nazareth. Stay on Route 65 and turn east on Route 77 to reach Tiberias. While Route 6 is a modern superhighway, it's also an electronic toll road. If you're driving a rental car, you'll be charged for using it.

For more information about getting here and around, see Travel Smart Israel.

DINING

Tiberias in particular and the Sea of Galilee in general have far livelier culinary options than other parts of Lower Galilee. Some places in the countryside are worth going out of your way for. Restaurant attire is casual. The local specialty is the native St. Peter's fish (tilapia), though most restaurants serve the (still excellent) pond-bred variety. Meat dishes tend to be Middle Eastern: *shashlik* and kebabs (ground meat grilled on skewers) accompanied by hummus, pickles, and french fries. Most economical are *shawarma* (slices of spit-grilled turkey meat served in pita bread) and falafel. The cheapest eats are always at the stands at a town's central bus station.

Prices in the reviews are the average cost of a main course at dinner, or, if dinner isn't served, at lunch.

LODGING

Tiberias, the region's tourist center, has hotels for budgets from deluxe to economy. Within a 20- to 30-minute drive are excellent guesthouses, some run by kibbutz residents and some on the Sea of Galilee. Nazareth has a couple of deluxe hotels and several older inexpensive ones that cater primarily to Christian pilgrim groups but also attract individual travelers and Israelis. Also in Nazareth, and to a lesser extent around Tiberias, are hospices run by Christian orders.

Bed-and-breakfasts have sprung up in profusion. Many are in or adjacent to private homes in rural farming communities; others are within kibbutzim. These are a good value, especially for families. Many "guesthouses," as upgraded youth hostels are now called, are suitable for families; these are generally the cheapest deals and are useful.

Prices in the reviews are the lowest cost of a standard double room in high season.

TOUR OPTIONS

Both Egged Tours and United Tours have one-day tours around the region from Jerusalem and Tel Aviv that take in Nazareth, the Sea of Galilee, and other highlights.

Visitor and Tour Information Egged Tours ☎ *03/694–8888* ⊕ *www.egged.co.il/Eng.* **United Tours** ☎ *03/617–3315* ⊕ *www.unitedtours.co.il.*

JEZREEL AND JORDAN VALLEYS

"Highways of the world cross Galilee in all directions," wrote the eminent Victorian scholar George Adam Smith in 1898. The great international highway of antiquity, the *Via Maris* (Way of the Sea), swept up the Mediterranean coast from Egypt and broke inland along three separate passes through the hills to emerge in the Jezreel Valley before continuing northeast to Damascus and Mesopotamia. It made the Jezreel Valley a convenient and frequent battleground. In fact, the Jezreel Valley heard the clash of arms so often that the very name of its most commanding tell—Har Megiddo (Mt. Megiddo), or Armageddon—became a New Testament synonym for the final apocalyptic battle of all time. Today, this and other ancient sites such as Beit She'an remain highlights here.

On a topographical map, the Jezreel Valley appears as an equilateral triangle with sides about 40 km (25 miles) long, edged by low mountains and with a narrow extension east to Beit She'an in the Jordan Rift. From there, the Jordan Valley stretches like a ribbon north to the Sea of Galilee. Your first impression will be one of lush farmland as far as the eye can see. But as recently as the 1960s, malarial swamps still blighted the area; some pioneering settlements had cemeteries before their first buildings were completed.

With a few exceptions, restaurants in this rustic area are confined to roadside cafeterias, lunchtime diners at or near parks, and small restaurants and snack bars in the towns of Afula and Beit She'an.

BEIT SHE'ARIM

20 km (12½ miles) southeast of Haifa, 25 km (15½ miles) west of Nazareth.

GETTING HERE AND AROUND

Driving from Tel Aviv, take Route 4 (the old Tel Aviv–Haifa Highway) to Furadis Junction, then turn east on Route 70. Continue to Yokneam Junction, then take Route 722 to Hashomrim Junction. Take the first left, and continue until you reach the national park.

EXPLORING

Beit She'arim. Chalk slopes are honeycombed with catacombs around this attractively landscaped ancient site—today called Beit She'arim National Park. Orthodox Jews pilgrimage here to the Tomb of Judah HaNasi, chief editor and redactor of the Mishnah, the seminal text of rabbinic Judaism, but you don't need to be religious to appreciate the role this vast necropolis has played in the development of modern

Judaism. The landscape is soothing, there are pleasant walking paths, and some of the caves have an *Indiana Jones*–style intrigue. Equipped with a flashlight, a free park brochure, and a map, you'll discover ornately carved sarcophagi that attest to the complex intercultural relations in the Roman world.

A Jewish town flourished here after the eclipse of Jerusalem brought about by Titus's legions in AD 70 and its reconstruction as a pagan town by Hadrian in AD 135. For generations, Jews were denied access to their holy city and its venerated burial ground on the Mt. of Olives, so the center of Jewish life and religious authority shifted first to Yavne, in the southern coastal plain, and then northward to the Lower Galilee.

By around AD 200 Beit She'arim had become the unofficial Jewish capital, owing its brief preeminence to the enormous stature of a native son. Rabbi Yehuda (or Judah) "HaNasi" (the Patriarch: a title conferred on the nominal leader of the Jewish community) was responsible for the city's inner workings and for its relations with its Roman masters. Alone among his contemporaries, Yehuda HaNasi combined worldly diplomatic skills with scholarly authority and spiritual leadership.

The rabbi eventually moved east to Zippori because of its more salubrious climate, and there gathered the great Jewish sages of his day and compiled the Mishnah, which remains the definitive interpretation of biblical precepts for religious Jews. Nonetheless, it was in his hometown of Beit She'arim that Yehuda HaNasi was finally laid to rest. If Beit She'arim was a magnet for scholars and petitioners in his lifetime, it became a virtual shrine after his death. With Jerusalem still off-limits, the town became the most prestigious burial site in the Jewish world for almost 150 years.

Two major expeditions in the 1930s and '50s uncovered a vast series of 20 **catacombs.** The largest of these is open to the public, with 24 chambers containing more than 200 sarcophagi. A wide range of carved Jewish and Roman symbols and more than 250 funerary inscriptions in Greek, Hebrew, Aramaic, and Palmyrene throughout the site testify to the great distances people traveled—from Yemen and Mesopotamia, for instance—to be buried here. Without exception, the sarcophagi were plundered over the centuries by grave robbers seeking the possessions with which the dead were often interred. ⊠ *Off Rte. 75 or 722, Beit She'arim National Park* ☎ *04/983–1643* ⊕ *www.parks.org.il* ⊠ *NIS 22* ☉ *Apr.–Sept., daily 8–5; Oct.–Mar., daily 8–4.*

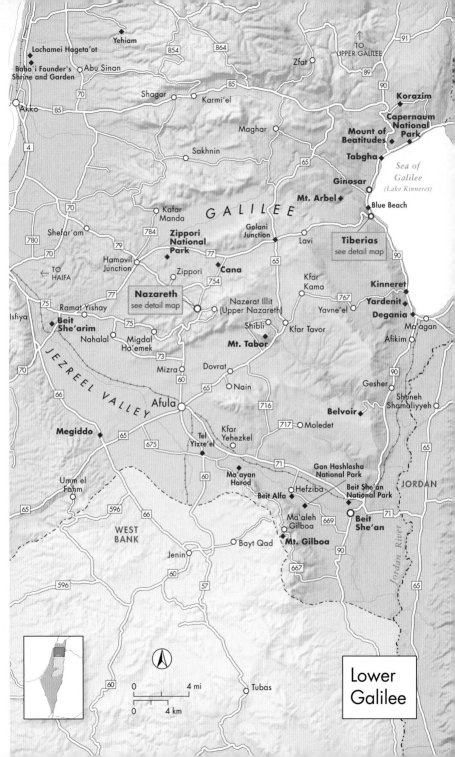

The archaeological layers at Megiddo include prehistoric remains and an ingenious biblical-era water system.

MEGIDDO

GETTING HERE AND AROUND

A car is the best way to get here, as the site is poorly served by public transportation. You can reach the site by taxi from Afula.

ESSENTIALS

Taxi Contact **Yizre'el** ⊠ *Afula* ☎ *04/652-3111.*

EXPLORING

Fodor's Choice
★

Tel Megiddo National Park. A UNESCO World Heritage Site, this ancient city was built on foundations dating back to the biblical era. Today called Tel Megiddo National Park, it's one of the region's most impressive ruins. Allocate about 90 minutes to see the park.

Most people are fascinated by the ancient water system. In a masterful stroke, King Ahab's engineers dug a deep shaft and a horizontal tunnel through solid rock to reach the vital subterranean spring outside the city walls. With access secure, the spring's original opening was permanently blocked. There's nothing more than a trickle today, though, the flow perhaps choked by subsequent earthquakes. As you descend 180 steps through the shaft, traverse the 65-yard-long tunnel under the ancient city wall, and climb up 83 steps at the other end, look for the ancient chisel marks and hewn steps. A visit to the water system at noon offers a reprieve from the summer heat.

Apart from the ancient water system, don't miss the partially restored Late Bronze Age gate, perhaps the very one stormed by Egyptian troops circa 1468 BC, as described in the victory stela of Pharaoh Thutmose III. A larger gate farther up the mound was long identified with King

Solomon (10th century BC)—Megiddo was one of his regional military centers—but has been redated by some scholars to the time of Ahab, a half century later. There's consensus, however, on the ruined stables at the summit of the tell: they were certainly built by Ahab, whose large chariot army is recorded in an Assyrian inscription.

Evidence indicates prehistoric habitation here as well, but among the earliest remains of the *city* of Megiddo are a round altar dating from the Early Bronze Age and the outlines of several Early Bronze Age temples, almost five thousand years old, visible in the trench between the two fine lookout points.

A tiny museum at the site's entrance offers good visual aids, including maps, a video, and a model of the tell. A small gift shop alongside the museum sells handsome silver and gold jewelry, some incorporating pieces of ancient Roman glass. There's also a restaurant. ⊠ *Rte. 66, Tel Megiddo National Park* ☎ *04/659–0316* ⊕ *www.parks.org.il* ✉ *NIS 29* ⊙ *Apr.–Sept., daily 8–5; Oct.–Mar., daily 8–4.*

MT. GILBOA AND ENVIRONS

24 km (15 miles) southeast of Megiddo via Rtes. 675 and 667, 10 km (7 miles) east of Afula.

Fodor's Choice ★

Visit Mt. Gilboa in February or March, and you'll find yourself surrounded by people enraptured with the delicate purple iris native to these slopes. The views of the valley below and the hills of Galilee beyond are great year-round, but on a clear winter or spring day they're amazing, reaching as far as the snowcapped Mt. Hermon, far to the north. Afternoon is the best time to come.

Mt. Gilboa—actually a steep mountain range rather than a single peak—is geographically a spur of the far greater Samaria Range (the biblical Mt. Ephraim, today the West Bank) to the southwest. Half the mountain has been reforested with evergreens, while the other half has been left in pristine rockiness. Environmentalists prefer the latter, as it protects the wildflowers that splatter the slopes with color every spring. From the gravel parking area off Route 667, easy and well-marked trails wind through the natural habitat of the rare black (actually deep purple) iris, which draws hordes of Israelis every spring.

Three thousand years ago, the Philistines rerouted the Israelites on Mt. Gilboa. Saul, the nation's first king, was wounded and took his own life on the battlefield. The next day, the Bible relates, when the Philistines came to plunder their fallen foes, they discovered the bodies of Saul and his sons. Seeking trophies, "they cut off his head and stripped off his armor, and they fastened his body to the wall of [Beit She'an]" (I Samuel 31). In his eulogy for Saul and his son Jonathan, king-to-be David cursed the battlefield where "thy glory, O Israel" was slain: "Let there be no dew or rain upon you" (II Samuel 1).

GETTING HERE AND AROUND

Driving from Afula, follow Route 71 east, turn right on Route 675, then left on Route 667. There's no reliable public transportation.

EXPLORING

Beit Alfa. In 1928, members of Kibbutz Hefziba who were digging an irrigation trench discovered this ancient synagogue, now part of Beit Alfa Synagogue National Park. Their tools hit a hard surface, and excavation uncovered a multicolored mosaic floor, almost entirely preserved. The art is somewhat childlike, but that, too, is part of its charm. An Aramaic inscription dates the building to the reign of Byzantine emperor Justinian in the second quarter of the 6th century AD; a Greek inscription credits the workmanship to one Marianos and his son, Aninas. In keeping with Jewish tradition, the synagogue faces Jerusalem, with an apse at the far end to hold the ark. The building faithfully copies the architecture of the Byzantine basilicas of the day, with a nave and two side aisles, and the doors lead to a small narthex and a onetime outdoor atrium. Stairs indicate there was once an upper story.

Classic Jewish symbols in the top mosaic panel leave no doubt that the building was a synagogue: a holy ark flanked by lions, a menorah, and a shofar (ram's horn). The middle panel, however, is the most intriguing: it's filled with human figures depicting the seasons, the zodiac, and—even more incredible for a Jewish house of worship—the Greek sun god, Helios, driving his chariot across the sky. These images indicate more liberal times theologically, when the prohibition against making graven images was perhaps not applied to two-dimensional art. The last panel tells the story of Abraham's near-sacrifice of his son Isaac, captioned in Hebrew. Take time to watch the lighthearted but informative film. Allocate 45 minutes for a visit here. ⊠ *Kibbutz Hefziba, Rte. 669* ☎ *04/653–2004* ⊕ *www.parks.org.il* ⊠ *NIS 22* ◷ *Apr.–Sept., daily 8–5; Oct.–Mar., daily 8–4.*

FAMILY **Gan Hashlosha National Park.** Commonly known as Sahne, this park is considered one of the most beautiful places in the world—and not only by Israelis. The park was developed around a warm spring (28°C, or 82°F, most of the year) and a wide, still stream deep enough to dive into at spots, with artificial cascades in others. Lifeguards are on duty. Facilities include changing rooms for bathers, two snack bars, and a restaurant. Apart from swimming, this is also a very popular picnic spot. ⊠ *Off Rte. 669* ☎ *04/658–6219* ⊕ *www.parks.org.il* ⊠ *NIS 40* ◷ *Apr.–Sept., Sat.–Thurs. 8–5, Fri 8–4; Oct.–Mar., Sat.–Thurs. 8–4, Fri. 8–3. Last entrance 1 hr before closing.*

FAMILY **Ma'ayan Harod** (*Spring of Harod*). At the foot of Mt. Gilboa is this small national park with huge eucalyptus trees and a big swimming pool fed by a spring. Today it's a bucolic picnic spot, but almost 3,200 years ago, Gideon, the reluctant hero of the biblical book of Judges, organized his troops to fight a Midianite army that had invaded from the desert. At God's command—in order to emphasize the miraculous nature of the coming victory—Gideon dismissed more than two-thirds of the warriors and then, to reduce the force still more, selected only those who lapped water from the spring. Equipped with swords, ram's horns, and flaming torches concealed in clay jars, this tiny army of three hundred divided into three companies and surrounded the Midianite camp across the valley in the middle of the night. At a prearranged

Panoramic views of the Galilee draw hikers to explore Mt. Gilboa.

signal, the attackers shouted, blew their horns, and smashed the jars, revealing the flaming torches, whereupon the Midianites panicked and fled, resulting in an Israelite victory.

The spring has seen other armies in other ages. It was here in 1260 that the Egypt-based Mamluks stopped the invasion of the hitherto invincible Mongols. And in the 1930s, the woods above the spring hid Jewish self-defense squads training in defiance of British military law. ✉ *Off Rte. 71* ☎ *04/653–2211* 🌐 *www.parks.org.il* 🎟 *NIS 29* 🕘 *Apr.–Sept., Sun.–Thurs. 8–5, Fri. 8–2; Oct.–Mar., Sun.–Thurs. 8–4, Fri. 8–2.*

NEED A BREAK?

Barkanit Dairy. At Michal and Avinoam Barkin's goat farm, you can sample excellent cheeses over wine or coffee in the wooden reception room or enjoy a light meal of salads, toasted sandwiches, or hot stuffed pastries. The farm is open Fridays, 2 pm to 10 pm, and Saturdays, 4 pm to 10 pm. ✉ ***Rtes. 71 and 675, 1 km (½ mile) east of Navot Junction, Kfar Yehezkel*** ☎ ***050/449–2799.***

WHERE TO EAT AND STAY

$$$ MIDDLE EASTERN

🍴 **Al-Noor Restaurant.** A short drive from the Gilboa region, this restaurant specializes in grilled meats, and locals come for the take-out containers of hummus and grilled cauliflower. Traditional favorites like kebabs, steaks, and chicken come plated or in giant *laffe* sandwiches. The adjacent deli is the perfect place to stock up for your picnic. [$] *Average main: NIS 100* ✉ *Rte. 60, entrance to Mizra, Mt. Gilboa* ☎ *04/642–9214.*

Kibbutz Life Then and Now

The founding fathers and mothers would probably be bewildered by life on a 21st-century kibbutz (a collective settlement, but literally translated as "a gathering"). Many of Israel's founders came from Russia in the early 20th century, inspired by Zionist ideals of returning to their ancestral homeland and a work ethic that regarded manual labor as an almost spiritual value. They were socialists who believed "from each according to his ability, to each according to his need."

EARLY DAYS

Degania, the first kibbutz, was founded in 1909 on the shores of the Sea of Galilee, where 10 men and two women began to work the land. The utopian ideology, in which individual desires were subordinated to the needs of the community, was wedded to the need for a close-knit communal structure, in order to cope with forbidding terrain and a hostile neighborhood. Life was arduous, but their numbers grew.

Kibbutzim played a considerable role in molding the fledgling state, absorbing immigrants, and developing agriculture. By 1950, two years after Israel's independence, there were more than 200 kibbutzim. Their egalitarian ethos meant that all shared chores and responsibility—but also ownership of the means of production. The kibbutz movement became the world's largest communitarian movement.

GROWTH AND CHALLENGE

With time, many kibbutzim introduced light industry or tourism enterprises, and some became successful businesses. The standard of living improved, and kibbutzim took advantage of easy bank loans. When Israel's hyperinflation reached 454% during the mid-1980s, many communities found themselves bankrupt. Change became inevitable, and the movement peaked around 1990, when the almost 270 kibbutzim across the country reached 130,000 members. (An individual kibbutz can range from fewer than 100 to more than 1,000 members.)

THE KIBBUTZ TODAY

In today's Israel, many young "kibbutzniks," after compulsory military service or university studies, have found the kibbutz ethos stifling and have opted for the individualism and material attractions of city life. Despite the changes, city folk, volunteers, and tourists are still drawn to this rural environment, which offers a slower pace.

Only some 15% of kibbutz members now work in agriculture, though they account for a significant proportion of the national production. Industry, services, and tourism—including kibbutz guesthouses and hotels—are the real sources of income. Differential wage systems have been introduced, unemployment is growing, and foreign laborers often provide menial labor in fields and factories. All kibbutzim have abandoned children's dormitories, instead allowing parents to raise their children in a family home.

Many members of the older generation have become distressed by what they see as the contamination of pioneering principles. But reality bites hard, and ironically, only those kibbutzim that succeed economically can afford to remain socialist.

$$$$ MODERN ISRAELI 🍴 **Herb Farm on Mount Gilboa.** The sweeping panorama from the wooden deck and picture windows is attraction enough, but this family restaurant—operated by Yossi Mass, his wife Penina, and their son Oren—is also known for its greens. Homemade bread and a "salad basket" of antipasti are fine starters, but try one of the imaginative salads. Tempting entrées might include a tart of shallots, forest mushrooms, and goat cheese, or a colorful pie of beef, lamb, goose breast, tomatoes, pine nuts, and basil. Desserts make for an agonizing decision, so share. [$] *Average main: NIS 120* ✉ *Rte. 667, 3 km (2 miles) off Rte. 675, Gan Nir* ☎ *04/653–1093* ✍ *Reservations essential* 🕓 *Closed Sun.*

$ B&B/INN FAMILY 🏨 **Ein Harod Country Suites and Guest Houses.** Set in a lovely landscape, this 90-year-old kibbutz has beautiful cabins and suites to meet every need. **Pros:** serene atmosphere; pretty views; options for both families and couples. **Cons:** luxury suites are pricey on weekends. [$] *Rooms from: $160* ✉ *Kibbutz Ein Harod* ☎ *052/830–9737* 🌐 *www.ein-harod.co.il/en* 🛏 *26 rooms, 10 cabins, 6 suites* 🍽 *Breakfast.*

SPORTS AND THE OUTDOORS

Two annual *Tza'adot* (Big Walks) take place in March or April: one along the shore of the Sea of Galilee (2½ km [1½ miles] and 9 km [5½ miles]), the other along the trails of Mt. Gilboa (routes range from 6 km [4 miles] to 40 km [25 miles] over two days). These mass rambles attract folks from all over the country and abroad. For information, contact Israeli Sports for All Association.

Israeli Sport for All Association ☎ *03/562–1441* 🌐 *www.isfa.co.il.*

BEIT SHE'AN

23 km (14 miles) southeast of Afula, 39 km (24 miles) south of Tiberias.

The modern town of Beit She'an has little to offer visitors, but the past beckons. Unlike some archaeological sites that appear to be just piles of rocks, ancient Beit She'an is a gloriously rich ruin, complete with bathhouses, pagan temples, and public theaters. It's one of the country's most notable sites.

GETTING HERE AND AROUND

The national park is northeast of modern Beit She'an. From Route 90, turn west on Sha'ul Hamelech Street, and right after Bank Leumi.

EXPLORING

Fodor's Choice ★ **Beit She'an National Park.** At the intersection of the Jordan and Jezreel valleys, this town has one spectacular site, Beit She'an National Park. A Roman theater was excavated in the 1960s, but the rest of Scythopolis, as this great Late Roman and Byzantine (2nd–6th centuries AD) city was known, came to light only in more recent excavations. The enormous haul of marble statuary and friezes says much about the opulence of Scythopolis in its heyday—especially when you remember that there are no marble quarries in Israel, and all that stone was imported from what is today Turkey, Greece, or even Italy.

6

The remains of the wealthy late Roman and Byzantine city of Beit She'an include a large public bathhouse.

A free site map available at the visitor center gives a good layout. In summer, it's best to arrive early in the morning, as the heat quickly becomes insufferable. Better yet, consider returning in the evening for the engaging **sound-and-light spectacle,** presented Monday, Wednesday, and Thursday from 7 pm to 9:30 pm and Saturday from 7:30 pm to 9:30 pm. Tickets cost NIS 40; reserve in advance and check times. Scythopolis's **downtown area,** now exposed, has masterfully engineered, colonnaded main streets converging on a central plaza that once boasted a pagan temple, a decorative fountain, and a monument. An elaborate Byzantine bathhouse covered more than 1¼ acres. On the main thoroughfare are the remains of Scythopolis's amphitheater, where gladiatorial combats were once the order of the day.

The high tell dominating the site to the north was the location of Old Testament **Canaanite/Israelite Beit She'an** 2,500 to 3,500 years ago. Don't climb to the top for the meager archaeological remains, but rather for the fine panoramic view of the surrounding valleys and the superb bird's-eye view of the main excavations.

The semicircular **Roman theater** was built of contrasting black basalt and white limestone blocks around AD 200, when Scythopolis was at its height. Although the upper *cavea*, or tier, hasn't survived, the theater is the largest and best preserved in Israel, with an estimated original capacity of seven to ten thousand people. The large stage and part of the *scaena frons* (backdrop) behind it have been restored, and Beit She'an hosts autumn performances as in days of yore. ⊠ *Off Sha'ul Hamelech St.* ☎ *04/658–7189* ⊕ *www.parks.org.il* 🎫 *NIS 29* ☉ *Apr.–Sept., Sat.–Thurs. 8–5; Oct.–Mar., Sun.–Fri. 8–4, Sat. 8–5.*

NEED A BREAK?

Migfash HaEsh. Nestled next to the Egged Bus Station, this casual eatery in the commercial center of Beit She'an is the place to stop for a quick shawarma or falafel. Opt for freshly baked pita bread or upsize your sandwich and put it in a baguette. If you're on your way to Jerusalem, this may be your last chance for a decent snack. The refreshing air-conditioning is another draw. ✉ *24 Merkaz Rasco* ☎ *04/658-7278.*

WHERE TO STAY

$ HOTEL **Beit She'an Guest House.** A cross between a guest house and a hostel, this modern limestone and basalt building is wrapped around a courtyard shaded by palm trees. **Pros:** convenient to the national park; pretty pool area. **Cons:** sometimes noisy with teenage groups; no evening entertainment. [$] *Rooms from: $98* ✉ *126 Menachem Begin Blvd.* ☎ *02/594-5644* 🌐 *www.youth-hostels.org.il/english.html* 🛏 *62 rooms, 2 suites* 🍴 *Breakfast.*

NIGHTLIFE AND THE ARTS

Roman Theater. This marvelous theater hosts concerts, mostly by Israeli artists, every October. ✉ *King Shaul St.* ☎ *04/658-7189.*

6

BELVOIR

On Route 717; turn off 12 km (7½ miles) north of Beit She'an, then continue 5 km (3 miles) to site.

GETTING HERE AND AROUND

Driving north on Route 90 from Beit She'an, turn west on Route 717. While any bus traversing Route 90 will let off at the road, the fortress is high above the valley. It's a long hike, and don't count on getting a ride. The road from Ein Harod via Moledet is passable in dry weather but in very bad condition in places.

EXPLORING

Belvoir. The Crusaders chose their site well: they called it Belvoir—"beautiful view"—and it was the most invincible fortress in the land. The Hebrew name *Kochav Hayarden* (the Star of the Jordan) and the Arabic *Kaukab el Hauwa* (the Star of the Wind) underscore its splendid isolation. Today it's part of **Kochav Hayarden National Park.** The breathtaking view of the Jordan River Valley and southern Sea of Galilee, some 1,800 feet below, is best in the afternoon. You don't need to be a military historian to marvel at the never-breached concentric walls.

The Hospitallers (the Knights of St. John) completed the mighty castle in 1173. In the summer of 1187, the Crusader armies were crushed by the Arabs under Saladin at the Horns of Hittin, west of Tiberias, bringing an end to the Latin Kingdom of Jerusalem with one decisive battle. Their remnants struggled on to Tyre (in modern Lebanon), but Belvoir alone refused to yield; 18 months of siege got the Muslims no farther than undermining the outer eastern rampart. The Crusaders, for their part, sallied out from time to time to battle the enemy, but their lone resistance had become pointless. They struck a deal with Saladin and surrendered the stronghold in exchange for free passage, flags flying, to Tyre.

Don't follow the arrows from the parking lot; instead, take the wide gravel path to the right of the fortress. This brings you to the panoramic view and the best spot from which to appreciate the strength of the stronghold, with its deep, dry moat, massive rock and cut-stone ramparts, and gates. Once inside the main courtyard, you're unexpectedly faced with a fortress within a fortress, a scaled-down replica of the outer defenses. Not much remains of the upper stories; in 1220, the Muslims systematically dismantled Belvoir, fearing another Crusade. Once you've explored the modest buildings, exit over the western bridge (once a drawbridge) and spy on the postern gates, the protected and sometimes secret back doors of medieval castles. ⊠ *Rte. 717, 5 km (3 miles) west of Rte. 90, Belvoir National Park* ☎ *04/658–1766* ⊕ *www. parks.org.il* 🖻 *NIS 22* ☉ *Apr.–Sept., daily 8–5; Oct.–Mar., daily 8–4.*

NAZARETH AND THE GALILEE HILLS

Remove the modern roads and power lines, and the landscape of this region becomes a biblical illustration. Villages are scattered haphazardly on the hillsides, and small farm-holdings crowd the valleys. Olive groves, the region's ancient resource, are everywhere. Hilltop views and modern pine forests, white-and-red houses, and decorative trees that dab the countryside provide visually arresting moments.

There are several New Testament settings here—Nazareth, where Jesus grew up; the Cana wedding feast; and Mt. Tabor, identified with the Transfiguration—but Jewish history resonates strongly, too. Tabor and Yodefat were fortifications in the Great Revolt against the Romans; Shefar'am, Beit She'arim (in a nearby valley), and Zippori were in turn the national centers of Jewish life (2nd–4th centuries AD); and latter-day Jewish pioneers, attracted to the region's untamed scenery, put down roots where their ancestors had farmed.

NAZARETH

25 km (15½ miles) east of Beit She'arim, 56 km (35 miles) east of Haifa, 15 km (9½ miles) north of Afula.

Fodor's Choice The Nazareth where Jesus grew up was an insignificant village nestled
★ in a hollow in the Galilean hills, but today's city of 65,000 pulses with energy. Apart from the occasional donkey plying traffic-clogged Paulus VI Street, there's little that evokes the Bible in contemporary Nazareth, unless you know where to look—and indeed, droves of Christian pilgrims come to pray at the awe-inspiring Basilica of the Annunciation or seek quiet contemplation at one of Nazareth's many smaller churches.

For nonbelievers, Nazareth is a fascinating day or half-day stop; the Christian devout will want to spend a full day, if not two. If your goal is to experience Nazareth as Jesus did, plan a tour at Nazareth Village. The calmest days to visit are Wednesday, when many businesses close for a midweek sabbatical, and Sunday, the day of rest for the Christians who make up a third of the town. If you're looking for local color (and traffic jams), come on Saturday, when Arab villagers come to the big city to sell produce and buy goods.

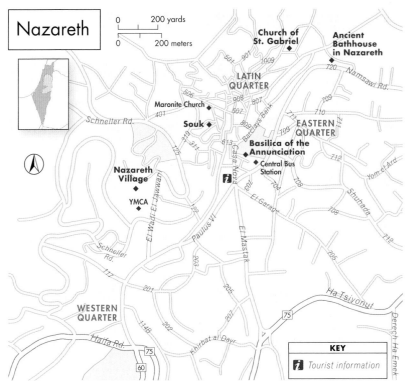

GETTING HERE AND AROUND

If you're driving from Beit She'arim or Haifa on Route 75, Route 77 breaks off to the north—to Zippori, the Golani Junction, and Tiberias. Route 75 continues to skirt the north side of the picturesque Jezreel Valley as it climbs into the hills toward Nazareth; at the crest of the hill, Route 60 from Afula joins it. A turn to the left takes you down to Paulus VI, Nazareth's main drag. If you pick up Route 77 from the opposite side, from Tiberias and points north, a left turn onto Route 764 takes you into Nazareth's Paulus VI Street. Nazareth's Central Bus Station is downtown on Paulus VI Street, near the Basilica of the Annunciation.

Nazareth itself is mired in traffic but the historic and religious sites are all close together, so it's best to park and walk.

TOURS

Tours run by Fauzi Azar Inn are unique because they skip religious sites almost entirely (except on Sundays, when shops are closed) and focus instead on the colorful sights, sounds, and smells of daily life in Nazareth. You can also see St. George Greek Orthodox Monastery, not normally open to the public. Tours depart daily at 9:30 am and cost NIS 35 to NIS 40.

Both Egged Tours and United Tours run one-day tours that take in Nazareth, Capernaum, Tabgha, the Sea of Galilee, Tiberias, and the Jordan River. Current prices are NIS 320 from Tel Aviv, NIS 340 from Jerusalem.

ESSENTIALS

Taxi Contacts Abu el-Assal ☎ 04/655–4745. **Diana** ☎ 04/655-5554.

Visitor and Tour Information Fauzi Azar Tour ✉ *Fauzi Azar Inn, off the Souk* ☎ *04/602–0469* ⊕ *www.fauziazarinn.com.* **Nazareth Tourist Information Office** ✉ *Casa Nova St.* ☎ *04/657–3003, 04/657-0555.*

EXPLORING

TOP ATTRACTIONS

Ancient Bathhouse in Nazareth. In 1993, Elias and Martina Shama-Sostar were renovating their crafts shop when they discovered ancient steam pipes under the store. Further excavation revealed a huge, wonderfully preserved Roman-style bathhouse. Israel's Antiquities Authority has not made any official announcements about the site, but several historians who have visited speculate that the bathhouse might date from the 1st century AD. A one-hour tour takes you to the hot room, the heating tunnels, and the furnace. Coffee is served in the arched hall where wood and ashes were once kept. ✉ *Mary's Well Square* ☎ *04/657–8539* ⊕ *www.nazarethbathhouse.org* ☞ *NIS 120 for up to 4 visitors* ☉ *Mon.–Sat. 9:30–7.*

Fodor's Choice ★ **Basilica of the Annunciation.** Casa Nova Street climbs steeply to the entrance of the Roman Catholic Basilica of the Annunciation, the largest church in the Middle East, consecrated in 1969. It enshrines a small ancient cave dwelling or grotto, identified by many Catholics as the home of Mary. Here, they believe, the angel Gabriel appeared to her and announced that she would conceive "and bear a son" and "call his name Jesus" (Luke 1). Pilgrim devotions suffuse the site throughout the day. Crusader-era walls and some restored Byzantine mosaics near the grotto bear witness to the antiquity of the tradition. The grotto is in the so-called lower church. Look up through the "well," or opening over the grotto, that connects with the upper church to the grand cupola, soaring 195 feet above you.

A spiral staircase leads to the vast upper church, the parish church of Nazareth's Roman Catholic community. Italian ceramic reliefs on the huge concrete pillars represent the Stations of the Cross, captioned in the Arabic vernacular. You now have a closer view of the cupola, its ribs representing the petals of an upside-down lily—a symbol of Mary's purity—rooted in heaven.

The large panels on the walls of the upper church, touching on the theme of mother and child, include a vivid offering from the United States, a fine Canadian terra-cotta, and mosaics from England and Australia. Particularly interesting are the gifts from Japan (with gold leaf and pearls), Venezuela (a carved-wood statue), and Cameroon (a stylized painting in black, white, and red).

In the exit courtyard, a glass-enclosed baptistery is built over what is thought to have been an ancient *mikvah*, a Jewish ritual bath. The adjacent small Church of St. Joseph, just past Terra Sancta College, is

Nazareth's Basilica of the Annunciation has a venerable cave many Catholics believe was the home of Mary.

built over a complex of rock-hewn chambers traditionally identified as the workshop of Joseph the Carpenter. Note that parking is hard to find; try Paulus VI Street or the side streets below it. ⊠ *Casa Nova St.* ☎ *04/657–2501* 🖅 *Free* ☉ *Grotto: daily 5:45 am–9 pm. Basilica: Apr.– Oct., daily 8–11:45 and 2–6, Sun. 2–5:30; Nov.–Mar., daily 8–11:45 and 2–5, Sun. 2–4:30.*

NEED A BREAK?

Mahroum Sweets. Try the unbeatable Arab pastries at this bakeshop. The place serves wonderful *bourma* (cylindrical pastries filled with whole pistachio nuts), cashew baklava, and great halvah. Don't confuse this spot with Mahroum Bakery: look for the Arab pastries, not gooey Western cakes. ⊠ *Casa Nova and Paulus VI Sts.* ☎ *04/656–0214.*

Souk. Bathed in the aromas of herbs and spices, this market in the Old City has something for everyone, from coffee sets to antiques to freshly baked pastries. The old lanes are narrow and the shops are tiny, with goods spilling into the street, but this souk is more orderly than those in many other Israeli cities. If it does get overwhelming, take a coffee break. ⊠ *Casa Nova St.*

WORTH NOTING

Church of St. Gabriel. This Greek Orthodox church is built over Nazareth's only natural water source, a spring dubbed Mary's Well. The Greek Orthodox, citing the noncanonical Gospel of St. James, believe it to be the place where the angel Gabriel appeared to Mary to announce the coming birth of Jesus.

The ornate church was built in 1750 and contains a stunning carved-wood pulpit and iconostasis (chancel screen) with painted New Testament scenes and silver-haloed saints. The walls are adorned with frescoes of figures from the Bible and the Greek Orthodox hagiography. A tiny "well" stands over the running water, and a modern aluminum cup gives a satisfying plop as it drops in. (The water is clean; the cup is more suspect.) ✉ *2 Salezian, off Paulus VI St.* ☎ *04/657–6437* 🎫 *Free* 🕐 *Mon.–Sat. 7–7, Sun. 7–2.*

FAMILY **Nazareth Village.** The shepherds, weavers, and other characters in this reconstructed Jesus-era community will delight children and adults alike. Using information gained from archaeological work done in the area, this attraction aims to reconstruct Jewish rural life as Jesus would've known it more than two thousand years ago. Workshops, farms, and houses have been created with techniques that would've been used at the time. Interpreters in period costume cook and work at winepresses and looms, giving a sense of daily life. Reservations are required for guided tours, which meet on the second floor of the Nazareth YMCA. ✉ *Nazareth YMCA, 5105 St., 2nd fl* ☎ *04/645–6042* 🌐 *www.nazarethvillage.com* 🎫 *NIS 50* 🕐 *Mon.–Sat. 9–5.*

WHERE TO EAT

After a full day of visiting Nazareth's shrines, you can quench your thirst with the locals at one of the little Arab restaurants along Paulus VI Street. Dinner here usually means hummus, shish kebab, baklava, and the like. Decor is incidental, atmosphere a function of the clientele of the moment, and dinnertime early. Needless to say, reservations aren't necessary, and dress is casual. If you're looking for more upscale dining, several high-end restaurants have opened in the past few years, serving both traditional Arab foods and fusion fare.

$$$ MIDDLE EASTERN 🍴 **Al-Reda.** In a magnificent 19th-century mansion with a *Thousand and One Nights* atmosphere, this eatery matches its magical setting with excellent Arab cuisine, from interesting salads (eggplant with cheese) and roasted lamb neck to kebabs and shashlik, as well as dishes with Indian or European influences. Pesto and grilled vegetables stuffed in a chicken breast is a good option, as are the many vegetarian choices. Don't pass up dessert. [$] *Average main: NIS 100* ✉ *23 Al Bishara St., next to the Basilica of the Annunciation* ☎ *04/608–4404* 🕐 *No lunch Sun.*

$ ECLECTIC Fodor's Choice ★ 🍴 **Annai.** In a 200-year-old mansion, this restaurant is perhaps the most elegant in Nazareth—although there's not much competition. The eclectic menu includes a salad of baby shrimp and calamari in a chili-mayonnaise sauce, appetizers like seasonal vegetables with grilled goat cheese and a date vinaigrette, and the house specialty, goose liver in cream sauce. There are three choices for seating: an outdoor terrace, a dining room with traditional Middle Eastern accoutrements, and a second indoor area with sleeker, more modern decor. [$] *Average main: NIS 45* ✉ *604 Bank Barclays St., at Al-Bishara Rd., Old City* ☎ *077/789–0064.*

$$$$ MIDDLE EASTERN 🍴 **Diana.** Ranked among the region's best Arab restaurants, Diana doesn't fail to impress. Owner Duhul Safadi is most famous for his kebabs and lamb chops, but the fish and seafood dishes are all equally

Shopping in Nazareth's popular market is a good introduction to this growing, largely Arab city.

wonderful. There's a plant-filled terrace and a sophisticated dining room that wouldn't be out of place in Tel Aviv. $ *Average main: NIS 150* ⊠ *51 Paulus VI St.* ☎ *04/657–2919* ⊙ *Closed Mon.*

$$
MIDDLE EASTERN
✕ **Tishreen.** The tile floors, stone walls, and dim lighting at this restaurant and bar named after a month on the Muslim calendar are the perfect setting for the Middle Eastern menu. Known for the wood-burning oven from which fresh breads emerge, try any of the popular kebabs, meat and cheeses wrapped in bread, or the eggplant stuffed with pesto and cheese. Alcohol is served, too. $ *Average main: NIS 75* ⊠ *56 El-Bishara St., near Mary's Well St.* ☎ *04/608–4666.*

WHERE TO STAY

$
B&B/INN
🏨 **Fauzi Azar Inn.** In a handsomely restored 200-year-old mansion in the heart of the Old City, this inn offers private rooms with soaring ceilings that are perfect for couples or families. **Pros:** historic building; reasonable rates; friendly staff. **Cons:** no elevator; not much parking; hard to find. $ *Rooms from: $85* ⊠ *Off the Souk, Old City* ☎ *04/602–0469* ⊕ *www.fauziazarinn.com* ⇨ *10 rooms* ❖ *Breakfast.*

$
HOTEL
🏨 **Nazareth Plaza.** The imposing stone facade of the Nazareth Plaza is the first hint that the city has finally acquired an upscale hotel. **Pros:** sweeping views; pretty swimming pool; air-conditioned rooms. **Cons:** no evening entertainment; far from Nazareth's shrines. $ *Rooms from: $180* ⊠ *2 Hermon St., Upper Nazareth* ☎ *04/602–8200* ⇨ *177 rooms, 7 suites* ❖ *Breakfast.*

$
HOTEL
🏨 **Rimonim Hotel Nazareth.** Most of the action here is underground, where the adjoining bar, lounge, and dining room add a bit of buzz. **Pros:** convenient to the sights; air-conditioned rooms. **Cons:** street

noise; no evening entertainment. [$] *Rooms from: $130* ✉ *1 Paulus VI St.* ☎ *04/650–0000* 🌐 *www.rimonim.com* 🛏 *226 rooms* 🍴 *Breakfast.*

$ HOTEL 🏨 **St. Gabriel.** High on the ridge that overlooks Nazareth, this hotel began life as a convent—hence the charming neo-Gothic church still in use today. **Pros:** near the shrines; memorable views; plenty of character. **Cons:** no evening entertainment. [$] *Rooms from: $120* ✉ *2 Salesian St.* ☎ *04/657–2133, 04/645–4448* 🌐 *www.stgabrielhotel.com* 🛏 *60 rooms* 🍴 *Breakfast.*

SHOPPING

Shababik. If you're looking for handmade souvenirs, you should check out this shop, whose name means "windows" in Arabic. Local women make the pottery, clothing, and other items, and the prices are reasonable. ✉ *Almutran St., Old City* ☎ *04/608–0747.*

ZIPPORI NATIONAL PARK

Village 5 km (3 miles) northwest of Nazareth off Rte. 79; site 3 km (2 miles) from village via bypass; 47 km (29 miles) east of Haifa.

GETTING HERE AND AROUND

Driving to this national park from Nazareth, follow Route 79 west and turn north at the signs. No buses service this route. If you don't have a car, take a taxi from Nazareth (agree on the price in advance, and consider asking the driver to wait).

EXPLORING

Fodor's Choice ★ **Zippori National Park.** The lush beauty and fantastic archaeological finds make this place well worth a visit, especially if you have an interest in Roman culture or the beginnings of Talmudic thought. Like many places during the Roman era, Zippori—known in the classical world as Sepphoris—was a prosperous city where Jews and gentiles coexisted fairly peaceably. The extensive ruins at the much-visited park include Israel's finest Roman-era mosaics. The ancient city, situated on a high ridge with commanding views, can be visited in two hours. The key sites are relatively close together.

Zippori's multiple narratives begin with a Jewish town that stood here from at least the 1st century BC. Christian tradition reveres the town as the birthplace of the Virgin Mary. Zippori's refusal to join the Great Revolt of the Jews against the Romans (AD 66–73) left a serious gap in the rebel defenses in the Galilee, angering its compatriots but sparing the town the usual Roman vengeance when the uprising failed. The real significance of Zippori for Jewish tradition, however, is that in the late 2nd or early 3rd century AD, the legendary sage Rabbi Yehuda HaNasi, head of the country's Jewish community at the time, moved here from Beit She'arim, whereupon the Sanhedrin (the Jewish high court) soon followed. Rabbi Yehuda summoned the greatest rabbis in the land to pool their experiences. The result was the encyclopedic work known as the Mishnah. Further commentary was added in later centuries to produce the Talmud, the primary guide to Orthodox Jewish practice to this day.

By the 3rd century AD, Zippori had acquired a mixed population of Jews, pagans, and Christians. The most celebrated find on the site is the mosaic floor of a Roman villa, perhaps the governor's residence, depicting a series of Dionysian drinking scenes. Its most stunning detail is the exquisite face of a woman, by far the finest mosaic ever discovered in Israel, which the media dubbed "the Mona Lisa of the Galilee." The restored mosaics are housed in an air-conditioned structure with helpful explanations. In other parts of the park, the so-called Nile Mosaic displays Egyptian motifs, and a mosaic synagogue floor (below the parking lot) is decorated with the signs of the zodiac, like those found in Beit Alfa and Hammat Tiberias.

If the mosaic floors bespeak the opulence of Roman Sepphoris, the relatively small Roman theater is mute evidence of the cultural life the wealth could support. Take a few minutes to climb the watchtower of Dahr al-Omar's 18th-century castle for the panoramic view and the museum of archaeological artifacts. About 1 km (½ mile) east of the main site—near the park entrance—is a huge section of ancient Zippori's water system, once fed by springs just north of Nazareth. The ancient aqueduct-reservoir is in fact a deep, man-made, plastered canyon, and the effect is extraordinary. ⊠ *Off Rte. 79* ☎ *04/656–8272* ⊕ *www.parks.org.il* ✆ *NIS 28* ☉ *Daily 8–4.*

6

CANA

8 km (5 miles) north of Nazareth on Rte. 754, 1 km (½ miles) south of junction of Rtes. 77 and 754; 50 km (31 miles) east of Haifa.

Near the large, modern Arab village of Kfar Kanna is the site of the ancient Jewish village of Cana, mentioned in the New Testament. Here Jesus performed his first miracle, turning water into wine at a wedding feast, thereby emerging from his "hidden years" to begin a three-year ministry in the Galilee.

Within the village, red signs lead to rival churches—one Roman Catholic, the other Greek Orthodox—that enshrine the scriptural tradition. (The alley to these churches is just wide enough for cars, and you can sometimes park in the courtyard of a souvenir store. If the street is blocked, park on the main road.)

The plaza of the Greek Orthodox St. George Convent is a peaceful spot. The First Miracle Church, on the grounds, is rarely open to visitors, but you can wander the landscape freely. On a lower plaza is a handsome statue of Jesus (surrounded, perhaps predictably, by souvenir shops).

GETTING HERE AND AROUND
Part of the sprawling suburbs of Nazareth, Kfar Kanna sits astride Route 754, linking Route 77 to the north and Route 79 to the south.

EXPLORING
Cana Wedding Church. This quaint church was built in 1881 where Catholics believe Jesus performed his first miracle (John 2:1–11). Check out the basement, where stones and mosaics bear witness to the ancient building that was once on this site. ⊠ *Churches St.* ☎ *04/651–7011* ✆ *Free* ☉ *Apr.–Sept., Mon.–Sat. 8–noon and 2–6, Sun. 8–noon; Oct.– Mar., Mon.–Sat. 8–noon and 2–5, Sun. 8–noon.*

Golani Junction Tree Planting Center. Around the Golani Junction are groves of evergreens planted by visitors as part of the Plant a Tree with Your Own Hands project of the Jewish National Fund. Since the early 1900s, more than 250 million trees have been restored to barren hillsides across Israel. At the Golani Junction Tree Planting Center, you can choose a sapling, dedicate it to someone, and plant it yourself; the cost is $18. ✉ *Off Rte. 77, east of Golani Junction, Givat Avni* ☎ *05/546–9069* ⊕ *www.jnf.org* ⊗ *Sun.–Thurs. 8–3, Fri. 8–noon.*

MT. TABOR

16 km (10 miles) south of the Golani Junction, off Rtes. 65 and 7266, 17 km (10½ miles) northeast of Afula.

Now covered with pine trees, Mt. Tabor has a serene look that belies its strategic and historical importance. Here you'll find the Church of the Transfiguration marks the place where tradition says Jesus began to radiate light and was seen conversing with Moses and Elijah. Christian pilgrims have venerated this site for centuries: Napoleon brought 3,000 French soldiers here to battle the Ottomans in 1799. Today Mt. Tabor is popular with hang-gliding enthusiasts, and there's a marathon around the mountain in April.

GETTING HERE AND AROUND

If you're driving, take Route 7266 through Shibli, a village of Bedouins who abandoned their nomadic life a few generations ago. A narrow switchback road starts in a clearing between Shibli and the next village, Dabouriya. Nazareth-based taxis often wait at the bottom of the mountain to provide shuttle service to the top. Watch out for them if you're driving your own car up; they come down in overdrive like the lords of the mountain they almost are.

EXPLORING

Church of the Transfiguration. As far back as the Byzantine period, Christian tradition identified Mt. Tabor as the "high mountain apart" that Jesus ascended with his disciples Peter, James, and John. There, report the Gospels, "he was transfigured before them" (Matthew 17:2) as a radiant white figure, flanked by Moses and Elijah. The altar of the present imposing church, which was consecrated in 1924, represents the tabernacle of Jesus that Peter suggested they build; those of Moses and Elijah appear as small chapels at the back of the church. Step up to the terrace to the right of the church doors for a great view of the Jezreel Valley to the west and south. From a platform on the Byzantine and Crusader ruins to the left of the modern church (watch your step), there's a panorama east and north over the Galilean hills. A nearby Franciscan pilgrim rest stop has refreshments and restrooms. 🖼 *Free* ⊗ *Daily 8–noon and 2–7.*

Kfar Tavor. Jewish pioneers founded this veteran farming village in 1901 in the shadow of the domed mountain from which it took its name. Not everyone farms today, and the village side streets, with single-family homes and well-tended gardens, feel like a nice piece of suburbia. ✉ *Off Rte. 767, Kfar Tavor.*

FAMILY **Marzipan Museum.** In the same compound as the Tabor Winery, this charming museum contains explanations of delectable products made from locally grown almonds. If you have kids in tow, don't think twice about signing up for the fun marzipan-making workshop. (There's also a chocolate workshop.) Best of all, you get to take your creations home. ⊠ *Kfar Tabor Visitor Center, Keren Kayemet L'Yisrael Ave., Kfar Tavor* ☎ *04/677–2111* ⊕ *www.shakedtavor.co.il* 🖾 *NIS 15* ⊙ *Sun.–Thurs. 9–6, Fri. 9–4, Sat. 10–6. Closes 1 hr earlier in winter.*

Mt. Tabor. The dome-like mountain, the region's highest, looms over one of the prettiest stretches of the Lower Galilee. Quilts of farmland kaleidoscope through the seasons as different crops grow, ripen, and are harvested. Modern woods of evergreens cover the hillsides.

Apart from the natural beauty, Mt. Tabor and its immediate surroundings have considerable biblical history. About 32 centuries ago, Israelite warriors of the prophetess-judge Deborah and her general, Barak, routed a Canaanite chariot army that had gotten bogged down in the mud. The modern kibbutz of Ein Dor, south of the mountain, is the site of ancient Endor, where King Saul unsuccessfully beseeched the spirit of the prophet Samuel for help before his fateful (and fatal) battle against the Philistines (I Samuel 28:3–25).

Tabor Winery. An excellent time-out from historical sights, this winery was founded in 1997. The quality of its wines has risen steeply in the last decade. A 12-minute film and wine tasting are free. From late July through September, you can pay to stomp grapes the traditional way—a great family activity. ⊠ *Kfar Tavor Visitor Center, Keren Kayemet L'Yisrael Ave., Kfar Tavor* ☎ *04/676–0444* ⊕ *www.taborwinery. com* 🖾 *NIS 19* ⊙ *Sun.–Thurs. 9–5, Fri. 10–4.*

WHERE TO EAT

$ ✕ **Sahara.** The menu at this Middle Eastern restaurant is a bit more
MIDDLE EASTERN sophisticated than that of its neighbors. Within the stone building with its landmark round tower is a spacious interior with stone floors and arches, wooden tables, and a centerpiece water cascade. Follow the excellent *mezze* (local salads) with traditional skewers of grilled meat, baked lamb, or one of the fish or chicken dishes. The Jordanian *mansaf* (a mix of rice, pine nuts, and pieces of lamb cooked with aromatic herbs) is an interesting discovery. 🖫 *Average main: NIS 25* ⊠ *Off Rte. 65, next to gas station in Kfar Nin, Kfar Nin* ☎ *04/642–5959* ⌂ *Reservations essential.*

EN
ROUTE   If you're heading to the Sea of Galilee, take Route 767, which breaks off Route 65 at Kfar Tavor. It's a beautiful drive of about 25 minutes. The first village, **Kfar Kama,** is one of two in Israel of the Circassian (*Cherkessi*) community, Sunni Muslim non-Arabs from Russia's Caucasus Mountains who settled here in 1876. The unusually decorative minaret of the mosque is just one element of the tradition the community vigorously continues to preserve. On the descent to the lake, there's a **parking area** precisely at sea level. The Sea of Galilee is still more than 700 feet below, and the view is superb, especially in the afternoon. You meet Route 90 at the bottom of the road.

Continued on page 381

Jesus in the
Galilee

Galilee beckons shyly. As in days of old, there is little of the frenetic pace and charged emotions of Jerusalem. For many Christians, the evocative, soft landscapes breathe new life into old familiar stories, and brush black-and-white scriptures with color. But curious visitors with less religious motivation will be drawn into Galilee's gentle charm. This tour of selected sights will speak to both.

"And passing along by the **Sea of Galilee**, he saw Simon and Andrew the brother of Simon casting a net into the sea, for they were fishermen. And Jesus said to them,

'Follow me and I will make you become fishers of men.'"

(Mark 1: 16–17)

Hills ring the Sea of Galilee, a freshwater lake.

Jesus was born in Bethlehem and died in Jerusalem, but it was in the Galilee that his ministry was forged. Over time, archaeologists and historians have unearthed many sites referred to in the New Testament. Today you can walk the hillsides, sail the Sea of Galilee, explore the ruins, and touch the churches of this beautiful region. Or you can sit under a tree and read scripture in the place where its narrative unfolded. If you have an eye for the contours of the land and an ear for echoes of the past, the experience can be unforgettable.

The activity and teachings of Jesus gain meaning and resonance from the landscape and social setting in which they emerged. Understand their context, and you will enhance your understanding of the events that have so shaped Western civilization.

By Mike Rogoff

RESTLESS SOCIETY, TURBULENT TIMES

Christ in the Storm on the Sea of Galilee by Jan Brueghel the Elder

The Romans came for the weekend in 63 BC and stayed for four centuries. Herod (later "the Great"), scion of a powerful political family, began his brutal reign as King of the Jews, courtesy of Rome, in 37 BC. He died in 4 BC, only a short time after the birth of Jesus (Matt. 2:1).

Herod's kingdom was divided among his three surviving sons: Archelaus, Herod Antipas (who got Galilee, and Perea beyond the Jordan River), and Philip. It was Herod Antipas who executed John the Baptist (Matt. 14:10), and was in Jerusalem at the time of the crucifixion (Luke 23:7).

RIVAL THEOLOGIES

Jewish society in the land of Israel was anything but unified and placid 2,000 years ago. Two ideological streams dominated: the Sadducees were the establishment, many of them wealthy, led by the priestly class that controlled the Temple-based cult of Yahweh, the One God, in Jerusalem. They took religious texts literally, and rejected the idea of resurrection and an afterlife (Acts 23:6-9).

The Pharisees, on the other hand, drew their strength from the common people, offering a comforting belief in resurrection and an afterlife in a better world.

Their rabbis, or teachers, would interpret biblical law, a practice that laid the groundwork for post-Temple Judaism as practiced until today.

Jesus himself came from the Pharisaic tradition, and "taught in their synagogues" (Luke 4:15). He was critical of the Pharisees' behavior, but not of their theology: They "sit on Moses' seat," he told his followers, "so practice and observe whatever they tell you" (Matt. 23:2).

SECTS AND CATACLYSM

Theological differences and domestic politics gave rise to numerous Jewish sects with strong religious agendas: the followers of Jesus, and of John the Baptist before him, were just two. One of the best known at the time were the Essenes, widely identified today as the monastic Jewish community that wrote the Dead Sea Scrolls.

There were other, less spiritual types like the Zealots—extreme nationalists who spearheaded the Great Revolt against Rome in AD 66. The cataclysm was not long in coming: Jerusalem and the Temple were razed in AD 70, four decades after Jesus' prediction that "there will not be left here one stone upon another" (Matt. 24:2).

Marriage Feast at Cana by Hieronymus Bosch

FACT, FAITH, AND TRADITION

The church on the Mount of Beatitudes has sweeping views of the Sea of Galilee.

Finding evidence of events or personalities in the distant past, the New Testament era included, is a kind of treasure hunt; and there is rarely an "X" to mark the spot. But when you do strike gold, through archaeological discoveries or ancient writings, for example, it thrills scholars and laypeople alike.

POPULATING ANCIENT MAPS

There are Galilean towns, like Nazareth and Tiberias, that have survived the centuries and are obviously genuine. Others, like Cana, are still debated. A lot of rocks have been turned over in the last three-quarters of a century, however, and archaeologists have exposed and identified Capernaum, Bethsaida, Chorazin (Korazim), Caesarea Philippi (Banias) in the Upper Galilee, and, to the satisfaction of many, Gennasaret (Ginosar) and Nain as well.

"TRADITIONAL" SITES:
WHERE MEMORIES ENDURE

Other sites have been linked to events over time, though no real evidence exists. Scriptural descriptions don't exactly offer geographical coordinates, and some locations that are still much visited by pilgrims are conjecture that has jelled into tradition. Visitors in the distant past often took local hearsay for hard fact when tour guides and other opportunists pointed out the very rock or glade or spring where this or that happened. It's not surprising that many traditional holy places are found so close to each other. Guides were often paid by the site—why should they journey unnecessary distances?

Events like the Sermon on the Mount, the Transfiguration, the feeding of the multitudes, the "feed my sheep" encounter of John 21, and the swine of the Gadarenes are all in this category. But for the faithful, the personal spiritual experience is more than a search for "the very stone" on which a particular event actually took place. Centuries of prayers and tears will sanctify a site, making it a remembrance place in the region where it all began.

TOURING THE CRADLE OF CHRISTIANITY

An astonishing three-quarters of the activity of Jesus recorded in the New Testament took place on, around, or within sight of the "Sea" of Galilee. The lake provided the largely Jewish towns and villages on its shores with a source of fresh water, a fishing industry, and a means of transportation.

Base yourself in Tiberias and head north, or clockwise, around the lake. The sights are close enough to see in a day. To visit Nazareth, Cana, and Mt. Tabor, 25 miles west of Tiberias, allot another day or be selective. Below are key places associated with Jesus, and scriptural references to them.

❶ TIBERIAS "…boats from Tiberias came near the place…" (John 6:23). Herod Antipas, son of Herod the Great, built the city as the capital of the Galilee in AD 20. The town never lost its importance, and is today the region's urban center.

❷ GINOSAR/GENNESARET Eight kms (5 mi) north of Tiberias, modern Ginosar is a kibbutz, with a museum that houses the extraordinary 1st-century-AD wooden boat found nearby. "…they came to land at Gennesaret…immediately the people recognized him…and as many as touched [the fringe of his garment] were made well" (Mark 6:53–56).

❸ MT. OF BEATITUDES "Seeing the crowds, he went up on the mountain, and when he sat down his disciples came to him…'Blessed are the poor in spirit…'" (Matt. 5–7). The traditional site of Jesus' Sermon on the Mount is set in hilltop gardens, with a church and a superb view of the lake.

❹ TABGHA Two events in the life of Jesus are recalled in two churches here. The Multiplication was one: a famous 5th-century mosaic records the event. Crowds followed Jesus and evening came. What about food? "'You give them something to eat'… 'We have only five

loaves here and two fish'… 'Bring them…' He looked up to heaven, and blessed…And they all ate and were satisfied…about 5,000 men, besides women and children" (Matt. 14: 15–21).

The primacy of Peter is another. The beach and an attractively simple chapel recall the appearance of Jesus on the shore: "'Have you any fish?'… 'No'… 'Cast the net'… 'It is the Lord!'… 'Simon [Peter]… Do you love me?… Feed my sheep'" (John 21:1–19).

❺ CAPERNAUM Jesus made this thriving Jewish town, now an archaeological site, the center of his ministry: "He went and dwelt in Capernaum…" (Matt. 4:13). Here he preached—"…and immediately on the sabbath he entered the synagogue and taught" (Mark 1:21).

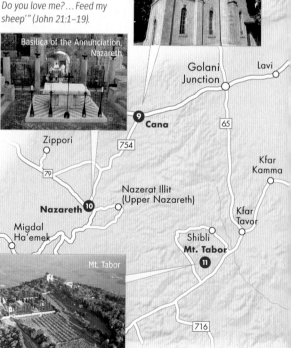

Greek Orthodox church, Cana

Basilica of the Annunciation, Nazareth

Golani Junction

Lavi

❾ Cana

65

Zippori

754

Kfar Kamma

79

Nazerat Illit (Upper Nazareth)

Nazareth ❿

Kfar Tavor

Migdal Ha'emek

Shibli

Mt. Tabor ⓫

Mt. Tabor

716

6 BETHSAIDA This was the hometown of the disciples Philip, Andrew, and Peter (John 1:44), and the place where Jesus cured a blind man (Mark 8:22–25). The town was left stranded when its lagoon dried out, and eluded identification until recently.

7 KURSI Jesus cured two madmen on the Golan Heights slopes, *"the country of the Gadarenes": "…a herd of swine was feeding… [the demons] came out [of the demoniacs] and went into the swine…" (Matt. 8:28–34).*

8 JORDAN RIVER Today people come to be baptized in the Jordan in this northern region, but the New Testament story almost certainly refers to the river's southern reaches, near Jericho: *"Then Jesus came from the Galilee to the Jordan to John, to be baptized by him" (Matt. 3:13).*

9 CANA When the wine ran out at a wedding feast, Jesus (after some persuasion) turned six stone jars-full of water into superior wine. *"This, the first of his signs, Jesus did in Cana of Galilee…" (John 2:1–11).*

Synagogue at Capernaum

Mount of Beatitudes
3
5 Capernaum
6 Bethsaida
4 Tabgha
87
92
2 Ginosar
Sea of Galilee (Lake Kinneret)
Kursi **7**
1 Tiberias
90
Ein Gev

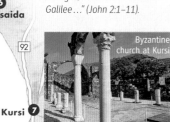

Byzantine church at Kursi

10 NAZARETH Here, the New Testament relates, an angel appeared to Mary to announce the coming birth of Jesus (Luke 1:26–38). It was here he grew up (his so-called "hidden years") and to Nazareth he returned as a teacher: *"…he went to the synagogue…on the sabbath…he stood up to read…the prophet Isaiah…"(Luke 4:16–30).*

Ancient boat at Ginosar
767
Kinneret
Jordan River
8
Yavne'el
Degania Alef

Baptism in the Jordan River
90

11 MT. TABOR In the event called "the Transfiguration," Jesus took three of his disciples *"up a high mountain apart,"* where they had a vision of him as a radiant white figure flanked by Moses and Elijah (Mark 9:2–8). Mt. Tabor has long been identified as the place, though some prefer Mt. Hermon in the far north.

TIPS FOR EXPLORING THE GALILEE

Greek Orthodox church at Capernaum

GETTING AROUND

Buses may be the cheapest way to see Israel, but they are not time-effective in the Galilee. Nazareth and Tiberias are easy to get to (and are 45 minutes apart), and a few less-frequent lines stop at Cana, Ginosar, and near Tabgha. Other Christian sites in the area are a fair hike from the highway or only doable by car.

HOLIDAYS, SERVICES, AND MORE

The Christmas and Easter celebrations that are so much part of the culture in many places are absent in Israel, where only 2% of its citizens are Christian. In the Galilee, the exception is Nazareth, with its lights and Christmas trees, and a traditional procession downtown at 3 PM on Christmas Eve. Many denominations are represented here, but Nazareth has no scheduled services in English.

In Tiberias, English-speakers can attend Catholic mass in St. Peter's Church (daily at 6:30 PM, Sundays at 8:30 AM) and occasional Protestant services at YMCA Penuel (just north of town) and St. Andrew's (opposite the Scots Hotel). A good source of information is the Web site of the Christian Information Center: ⊕ www.cicts.org

■ TIP→ For information about Nazareth Village, which re-creates the town as it was 2,000 years ago, and Yardenit, a group baptismal site, see the listings elsewhere in this chapter.

VISITING SUGGESTIONS

Christian sites demand respectful behavior and conservative dress (no shorts, short skirts, or sleeveless tops). Photography is usually permitted, but professionals may require prior permission. Pay attention to advertised opening times and allow time for unexpected delays in getting there.

HIKING THE LANDSCAPE

Hikers can consider the Jesus Trail. Its primary route is 65 kms (40 mi) long, but you can select sections for a shorter hike. Organized tours are available. Visit ⊕ www.jesustrail.com.

You can also walk or cycle along the footpaths of the new 60-km (37-mi) Gospel Trail, which traces the path that Jesus took along the Sea of Galilee. Visit ⊕ www.goisrael.com.

CREATING SPECIAL MOMENTS IN THE GALILEE

■ Carry a Bible and a good map.

■ In fine weather, the Mount of Beatitudes is best in the afternoon, when the light is gentler on the lake and the hills.

■ If you are unencumbered by luggage, and don't have a car to retrieve, stroll the easy trail from Mount of Beatitudes down to Tabgha (cross the highway with care), visit the two sites there, and then walk the 2-mi promenade that follows the highway east to Capernaum.

■ The little beach of volcanic pebbles at Tabgha (the Primacy site) can be magical.

■ Bethsaida is evocative—pure 1st century: no Byzantine, Crusader, or modern structures. It's never crowded, and offers a great place to sit with a view of the lake and read your favorite verses.

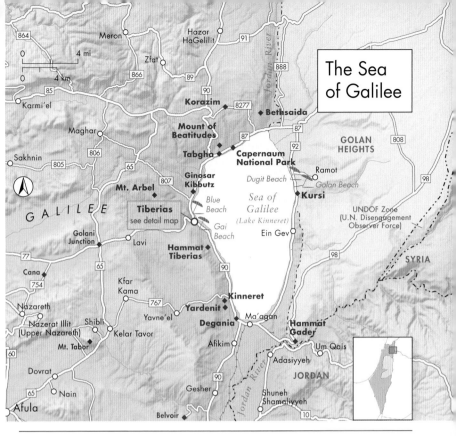

TIBERIAS AND THE SEA OF GALILEE

The Sea of Galilee is, in fact, a freshwater lake, measuring 21 km (13 miles) long from north to south and 11 km (7 miles) wide from east to west. Almost completely ringed by cliffs and steep hills, the lake lies in a hollow about 700 feet below sea level, which accounts for its warm climate and subtropical vegetation. This is Israel's Riviera-on-a-lake, replete with beaches and outdoor recreation facilities. Its shores are also dotted with sites hallowed by Christian tradition (note that several of these sites demand modest dress) as well as some important ancient synagogues. Tiberias itself is one of Judaism's four holy cities, along with Jerusalem, Hebron, and Tzfat.

The city of Tiberias is the logical starting base for exploration. One sightseeing strategy is to circle the Sea of Galilee clockwise from Tiberias (via Routes 90, 87, 92, and 98).

TIBERIAS

38 km (23½ miles) north of Beit She'an, 36 km (23 miles) east of Nazareth, 70 km (43 miles) east of Haifa.

As the only city on the Sea of Galilee, Tiberias, with a population of 40,000, has become the region's hub. The city spreads up a steep hillside, from 700 feet below sea level at the lake, to about 80 feet above sea level in its highest neighborhoods—a differential big enough to create significant variations in comfort levels during midsummer.

The splendid panoramic views of both the lake and the Golan Heights on the far shore deserved a better sort of development. Tiberias has little beauty and less charm, and although almost 2,000 years old, it still has the atmosphere of a place neglected for decades, if not centuries. It's at once brash and sleepy, with a reputation as a resort town based more on its location than its attractions. Travelers tend to see little of the town itself, sticking to the restaurants and hotels along the lake, and the boardwalk, which comes alive at night with vendors hawking clothes, jewelry, and knickknacks. Those traveling by car often skip the town altogether, opting for the numerous bed-and-breakfasts that dot the region.

GETTING HERE AND AROUND

The city sits astride the junction of Routes 90 and 77. Egged buses regularly serve Tiberias from Haifa, Nazareth, Tel Aviv, and Jerusalem. Haifa is one hour away, while Tel Aviv and Jerusalem are both two hours distant. Tiberias is small enough to walk to most locations, though given the punishing summer heat you may wish to have a taxi take you for even short jaunts.

Both Egged Tours and United Tours run one-day tours three times a week that take in Nazareth, Capernaum, Tabgha, the Sea of Galilee, Tiberias, and the Jordan River. Current prices are NIS 245 from Tel Aviv, NIS 260 from Jerusalem.

ESSENTIALS

Taxi Contacts HaEmek ☎ *04/604–4888*. **Hagalil** ☎ *04/672–0353*.

EXPLORING

Hammat Tiberias. This is where you'll find Israel's hottest spring gushing out of the earth at 60°C (140°F) due to cracks in the earth's crust along the Syrian–African Rift. Alas, this is an archaeological site, so you don't get to dip you toes into the waters here. (You can do that at the more impressive hot springs at Hammat Gader.)

Legend says that Solomon, the great king of Israel, wanted a hot bath and used his awesome authority to force some young devils belowground to heat the water. Seeing that the springs brought great happiness to his subjects, Solomon worried about what would happen when he died and the devils stopped their labors. Solomon made the hapless devils deaf, so to this day they continue to heat the water for fear of his wrath.

By the end of the Second Temple period (the 1st century AD), when settlement in the Sea of Galilee region was at its height, a Jewish town

The god Helios occupies the center of a spectacular 4th-century mosaic of the zodiac at Hammat Tiberias.

called Hammat (Hot Springs) stood here. With time, Hammat was overshadowed by its newer neighbor, Tiberias. The benefits of the mineral hot springs were already legendary: a coin minted in Tiberias during the rule of Emperor Trajan, around AD 100, shows Hygeia, the goddess of health, sitting on a rock with a spring gushing out beneath it.

Parts of ancient Hammat have been uncovered, bringing to light a number of ruined synagogues. The most dramatic dates from the 4th century AD, with an elaborate mosaic floor that uses motifs almost identical to those at Beit Alfa: classical Jewish symbols, human figures representing the four seasons and the signs of the zodiac, and the Greek god Helios at the center. They're among the finest ever found in Israel. ⊠ *Rechov HaMerchatzaot, 2 km (1 mile) south of Tiberias* ☎ *04/672–5287* ⊕ *www.parks.org.il* ⊠ *NIS 15* ⊘ *Apr.–Sept., Sat.–Thurs. 8–5, Fri. 8–4; Oct.–Mar., Sat.–Thurs. 8–4, Fri. 8–3.*

Promenade. A promenade follows the lakeshore for about 5 km (3 miles) south of Tiberias, offering nice views of the lake and Golan Heights. As you leave the hotels behind, you appreciate the Sea of Galilee's mystic beauty. At this writing the promenade is being extended north of the city.

Tiberias Hot Springs. In addition to sophisticated therapeutic services and facilities, this modern spa has a large, warm indoor mineral pool (35°C, or 95°F) and a small outdoor one right near the lake's edge. A restaurant serves lunch. ⊠ *Rte. 90, HaMarchatzaot Rd.* ☎ *04/672–8500* ⊠ *NIS 70* ⊘ *Sun., Mon., and Wed. 8–8, Tues. and Thurs. 8–10, Fri. 8–4, Sat. 8:30–6.*

Tiberias Through Time

Tiberias was founded in AD 18 by Herod Antipas, son of Herod the Great, and dedicated to Tiberius, then emperor of Rome. The Tiberians had little stomach for the Jewish war against Rome that broke out in AD 66. They soon surrendered, preventing the vengeful destruction visited on other Galilean towns.

With Jerusalem laid waste in AD 70, the center of Jewish life gravitated to the Galilee. By the 4th century, the Sanhedrin had settled in Tiberias. Here Jewish oral law was compiled into what became known as the Jerusalem Talmud, and Tiberias's status as one of Judaism's holy cities was assured.

Tiberias knew hard times under the Byzantines, and further declined under the hostile Crusaders. Starting in the 1700s, newcomers from Turkey and Eastern Europe swelled the Jewish population, but an 1837 earthquake left Tiberias in ruins.

Relations between Jews and Arabs were generally cordial until the Arab riots of 1936, when some 30 Jews were massacred. During the 1948 War of Independence, an attack by local Arabs brought a counterattack from Jewish forces, and the Arabs abandoned the town. Today the citizenry is entirely Jewish, and abandoned mosques stand as silent monuments.

Tomb of Moses Maimonides. Foremost among Tiberias's many venerated resting places is this tomb. Born in Córdoba, Spain, Moses Maimonides (1135–1204)—widely known by his Hebrew acronym, the "Rambam" (for Rabbi Moshe Ben Maimon)—was the greatest Jewish scholar and spiritual authority of the Middle Ages. To his profound knowledge of the Talmud, Maimonides brought an incisive intellect honed by his study of Aristotelian philosophy and the physical sciences. The result was a rationalism unusual in Jewish scholarship and a lucidity of analysis and style admired by Jewish and non-Jewish scholars alike.

Maimonides never lived in Tiberias, but after his death in Egypt, his remains were brought to this Jewish holy city for interment. His whitewashed tomb has become a shrine, dripping with candle wax and tears. To get here, walk two blocks up HaYarden Street, and turn right onto Ben Zakkai Street. The tomb is on your right, topped by a soaring spire of red steel girders. ⊠ *Ben Zakkai St.* ▨ *Free* ⊙ *Sun.–Thurs. dawn–dusk, Fri. and Jewish holiday eves dawn–2 pm.*

WHERE TO EAT

At a right angle to the waterside promenade, the *midrachov* (pedestrian mall) has a wide range of affordable dining options. If you're into local color, look for the tiny, modest restaurants (where English really *is* a foreign language) on Hagalil Street and in the little streets that connect it to Habanim Street, like the pedestrian-only Kishon Street.

Use the coordinates at the end of each listing (✛ 2A) to locate a site on the corresponding map.

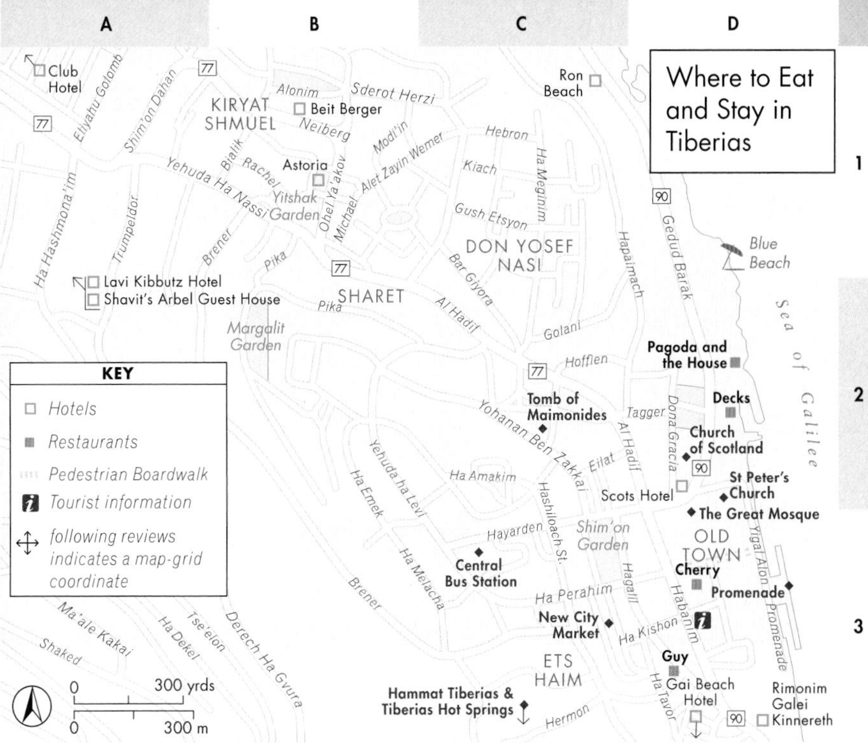
A
B
C
D
1
2
3
Where to Eat and Stay in Tiberias
KEY
Hotels
Restaurants
Pedestrian Boardwalk
Tourist information
following reviews indicates a map-grid coordinate
Club Hotel
Beit Berger
Astoria
Lavi Kibbutz Hotel
Shavit's Arbel Guest House
Ron Beach
Blue Beach
Pagoda and the House
Decks
Church of Scotland
Scots Hotel
St Peter's Church
The Great Mosque
Cherry
Promenade
Guy
Gai Beach Hotel
Rimonim Galei Kinnereth
Tomb of Maimonides
Central Bus Station
New City Market
Hammat Tiberias & Tiberias Hot Springs
KIRYAT SHMUEL
DON YOSEF NASI
SHARET
OLD TOWN
ETS HAIM
Sea of Galilee
Margalit Garden
Yitshak Garden
Shim'on Garden
Alonim
Sderot Herzl
Neiberg
Hebron
Kiach
Gush Etsyon
Ha Meginim
Modi'in
Alet Zayin Werner
Ohel Ya'akov
Michael
Bialik
Rachel
Yehuda Ha Nassi
Eliyahu Golomb
Shim'on Dahan
Ha Hashmona'im
Trumpeldor
Brener
Pika
Bar Giyora
Al Hadif
Golani
Hoffien
Hapalmach
Gedud Barak
Tagger
Dona Gracia
Yohanan Ben Zakkai
Eilat
Ha Amakim
Hashiloach St.
Hayarden
Yehuda ha Levi
Ha Emek
Ha Melacha
Ha Perahim
Hagalil
Habanim
Ha Kishon
Yigal Alon Promenade
Ha Tavor
Hermon
Ma'ale Kakai
Shaked
Ha Dekel
Tse'elon
Derech Ha Gvura
77
90
0
300 yrds
300 m

$ ISRAELI

🍴 **Cherry.** On the Tiberias boardwalk, this eatery has become an institution for budget travelers. The menu, simple and familiar to Western visitors (bagel melts, pasta dishes, omelets, and the like), offers satisfying and generous helpings at reasonable prices. The St. Peter's fish fillet, which is oven-baked in olive oil with herbs and garlic and served with antipasti, is a good choice. For a refreshing and healthy summer dessert, try the watermelon served with salty Bulgarian cheese, or treat yourself to a chocolate crepe. [$] *Average main: NIS 25* ✉ *4 Habanim St.* ☎ *04/679–0051* 🕓 *No dinner Fri. No lunch Sat.* ✥ *D3.*

$$ MODERN ISRAELI

🍴 **Decks.** Built on a pier extending into the Sea of Galilee, this family-run restaurant has breathtaking views. It's something of an institution, and locals keep coming back for the delicious meats—sizzling steaks, succulent goose liver, or long skewers of veal and vegetables—grilled slowly over hickory wood. The bluefin tuna carpaccio, caught by the manager's brother, is a delicacy. An apple tart pan-baked at your table is the house dessert. [$] *Average main: NIS 50* ✉ *Rte. 90* ☎ *04/672–1538* 🌐 *www.lido.co.il* 🕓 *Sun.–Thurs. noon–midnight, Fri. noon–6, Sat. ½ hr after sundown–midnight* ✥ *D2.*

$ MIDDLE EASTERN

🍴 **Guy.** Stuffed vegetables are the calling card at this kosher eatery, whose name means "ravine" in Hebrew. The cook-matriarch Geula comes from a Tiberias family, but her Moroccan ancestry shines through in delicious dishes like eggplant stuffed with seasoned ground beef. There are good, if more conventional, Middle Eastern options, but go for the excellent soups, and try some *kibbeh* (a Kurdish-Iraqi

To escape the heat or just to have fun, take a ride on the Sea of Galilee.

specialty of seasoned ground meat and bulgur). Ask your waiter to recommend the tastiest treats, such as apricots or dates stuffed with rice. The restaurant faces the lake and is slightly set back from the sidewalk; keep your eyes open or you'll miss it. It gets quite busy at lunchtime but is quieter at dinner. $ *Average main: NIS 20* ✉ *63 Hagalil St.* ☎ *04/672–3036* ▬ *No credit cards* ☉ *Closed Sat. and 1 hr before sundown on Fri.* ✛ *D3.*

$$ ✕ **Pagoda and the House.** This faux-Chinese temple has an outdoor patio
ASIAN overlooking the lake, and across the road you'll find a maze of more intimate rooms entered through a garden. The kosher menu is identical at both places, so pick your favorite and try the Thai soups (such as the tasty hot-and-sour soup), the goose spareribs, or strips of beef with peanut sauce. There's a sushi bar, too. Note that Pagoda is closed for the Sabbath, but the House remains open. $ *Average main: NIS 75* ✉ *Gedud Barak St.* ☎ *04/672–5513, 04/672–5514* ✍ *Reservations essential* ☉ *Pagoda: no dinner Fri. No lunch Sat. The House: no dinner Sat.–Thurs. No lunch Sun.–Fri.* ✛ *D2.*

WHERE TO STAY
Use the coordinates at the end of each listing (✛ 2A) to locate a site on the corresponding map.

$ 🏨 **Astoria.** One of Tiberias's better moderately priced hotels, the Asto-
HOTEL ria is set away from the lake. **Pros:** good value; great views of the water. **Cons:** too far to walk downtown; basic decor. $ *Rooms from: $100* ✉ *13 Ohel Ya'akov St.* ☎ *04/672–2351* ⊕ *www.astoria.co.il* ⤷ *88 rooms* ❍❘ *Breakfast* ✛ *B1.*

$ 🏨 **Beit Berger.** This family-run hotel has spacious rooms, most with bal-
HOTEL   conies. **Pros:** reasonable rates; hillside views; handy kitchens. **Cons:** too
far to walk downtown; no swimming pool. $ *Rooms from: $80* ✉ *27
Neiberg St.* ☎ *04/671–5151* 🛏 *45 rooms, 2 apartments* ✛ *B1.*

$$$ 🏨 **Club Hotel.** Cascading down a hillside, this all-suites hotel offers
HOTEL   an unimpeded view of the lake. **Pros:** spectacular views; spacious
FAMILY   rooms; resort feel. **Cons:** crowded on weekends; away from down-
town. $ *Rooms from: $300* ✉ *HaBanim St.* ☎ *04/671–4444* ⊕ *www.
leonardo-hotels.com* 🛏 *398 suites* ❖ *Breakfast* ✛ *A1.*

$$ 🏨 **Gai Beach Hotel.** The rare lakeshore location is a big plus, and for
RESORT   some, so is the distance from the noisy downtown promenade. **Pros:**
FAMILY   on the lake; gorgeous spa; far from the hubbub. **Cons:** a bit isolated;
crowded on weekends. $ *Rooms from: $220* ✉ *Rte. 90* ☎ *04/670–0700*
⊕ *www.gaibeachhotel.com* 🛏 *198 rooms, 2 suites* ❖ *Breakfast* ✛ *D3.*

$ 🏨 **Lavi Kibbutz Hotel.** The atmosphere here is welcoming for all, and wak-
HOTEL   ing up in peaceful rural surroundings has much to recommend it. **Pros:**
opportunity to experience kibbutz life; central location; good children's
programs. **Cons:** no evening entertainment; the kibbutz is religious so
there's no checking in or out Friday and Saturday evening. $ *Rooms
from: $175* ✉ *Rte. 77, 11 km (7 miles) west of Tiberias, Lavi* ☎ *04/679–
9450* ⊕ *hotel.lavi.co.il* 🛏 *184 rooms, 4 suites* ❖ *Breakfast* ✛ *A1.*

$$$$ 🏨 **Rimonim Galei Kinnereth.** It's easy to understand why this grande dame
HOTEL   was a personal favorite of Israel's founding prime minister, David Ben-
Gurion: its location right on the lake is unbeatable, and its spa is a
soothing complex suffused with incense and candles. **Pros:** convenient
to Tiberias; lakeside swimming pool; quiet atmosphere. **Cons:** can
be crowded on weekends and in summer. $ *Rooms from: $560* ✉ *1
Eliezer Kaplan St.* ☎ *04/672–8888* ⊕ *www.rimonim.com* 🛏 *114 rooms,
7 suites* ❖ *Some meals* ✛ *D3.*

$ 🏨 **Ron Beach.** The family-run Ron Beach is the northernmost hotel in
HOTEL   Tiberias and has rare private lake frontage, though no beach. **Pros:**
lakeside location; pretty pool. **Cons:** too far to walk to downtown;
no beach. $ *Rooms from: $165* ✉ *Gedud Barak St.* ☎ *04/679–1350*
⊕ *www.ronbeachhotel.com* 🛏 *123 rooms, 4 suites* ❖ *Breakfast* ✛ *C1.*

$$$ 🏨 **Scots Hotel.** This upscale hotel, with a contemporary structure linking
HOTEL   two older ones, has a pleasingly asymmetrical design filled with pleasant
Fodor's Choice   surprises, such as a roof terrace, where you can enjoy a drink or light
★   meal, and an inviting courtyard with a waterfall. **Pros:** boutique-hotel
feel; historic setting; central location. **Cons:** no nightly entertainment.
$ *Rooms from: $380* ✉ *1 Gedud Barak St., at Hayarden St.* ☎ *04/671–
0710* ⊕ *www.scotshotels.co.il* 🛏 *69 rooms* ❖ *Breakfast* ✛ *D2.*

$ 🏨 **Shavit's Arbel Guest House.** Israel and Sarah Shavit make congenial
B&B/INN   hosts, with the added bonus that he's a licensed tour guide and a chef.
Pros: warm hospitality; delicious food; pretty grounds. **Cons:** far from
downtown Tiberias. $ *Rooms from: $150* ✉ *Rte. 7717, off Rte. 77,
Arbel Village* ☎ *04/679–4919* ⊕ *www.4shavit.com* 🛏 *1 room, 5 apart-
ments* ❖ *Breakfast* ✛ *A2.*

6

NIGHTLIFE AND THE ARTS

Much of the entertainment, especially in the larger hotels in Tiberias, is of the live lounge-music variety: piano bars, one-man dance bands, and crooners. Generally speaking, the younger set wouldn't be caught dead here, preferring to hang out at one of the few pubs, where the recorded rock music is good and loud and the beer is on tap.

Bet Gabriel. This cultural center is located on the southern shores of the Sea of Galilee, a 10-minute drive from Tiberias. Its fine architecture, beautiful garden setting, and concert facilities have established its popularity in the area. ⊠ *Rte. 92, east of Tzemach Junction* ☎ *04/675–1175* ✐ *www.betgabriel.co.il.*

SPORTS AND THE OUTDOORS

BEACHES

The Sea of Galilee—a freshwater lake—is a refreshing but rocky place for a swim. You can recline on pleasant commercial beaches with amenities ranging from cafeterias to water parks, or on free beaches with minimal facilities. Note that after several years of drought conditions in the region, the water level remains low.

September's Kinneret Swim, a tradition since 1953, has both amateur (3½ km [2 miles] and 1½ km [1 mile]) and competitive (1½ km [1 mile]) categories.

Blue Beach. Blue Beach on the north shore of the Sea of Galilee is a well-kept private beach. Picnic areas and raft rentals are available. It's open May to October, and admission is NIS 50. **Amenities:** food and drink; lifeguards; parking (fee); showers; toilets; water sports. **Best for:** swimming. ⊠ *Rte. 90* ☎ *04/672–0105.*

Gai Beach. Open May to October, Gai Beach has a private bathing beach and one of the country's most attractive water parks. Admission is NIS 80. **Amenities:** food and drink; lifeguards; parking (fee); showers; toilets; water sports. **Best for:** swimming. ⊠ *Rte. 90* ☎ *04/670–0713* ☉ *Daily 9:30–5.*

WATER SPORTS

At several locations around the Sea of Galilee, you can hire pedal boats, rowboats, and motorboats and arrange to water-ski. Serious kayakers convene for an annual international competition in March.

Holyland Sailing. This company has five wooden boats that are replicas of those in use during the time of Jesus. The 45-minute cruises include historical commentary and concerts of traditional music. Sunset cruises are especially popular. ⊠ *Tiberias Marina* ☎ *04/672–3006* ⊕ *www.jesusboats.com.*

SHOPPING

Tiberias relies heavily on tourism yet has little particularly interesting in the way of shopping. The exception is jewelry. There are a few jewelry stores near the intersection of Habanim and Hayarden streets and in some of the better hotels.

MT. ARBEL

8 km (5 miles) northwest of Tiberias.

GETTING HERE AND AROUND

To get here from the Tiberias-Golani junction road (Route 77), turn at the Kfar Hittim junction to Route 7717. Turn right at the turnoff for Moshav Arbel, then turn left.

Arbel National Park and Nature Reserve. This 2,600-acre park sits on a plateau that slopes from the Arbel Valley to a cliff at the top of Mt. Arbel, above Lake Kinneret; the views are of the Sea of Galilee and the Golan Heights. The reserve has few trees but, depending on the season, there are a variety of flowers and small fauna. Jesus is said to have preached and performed miracles at the foot of the mountain.

Ancient texts indicate that the Seleucid Greeks conquered the Biblical-era Jews of Arbel as the Seleucids made their way to Jerusalem. Roman historian Flavius Josephus describes a battle here in 37 BC between the Jews and Marc Antony, who had been sent by Herod the Great to suppress the Jewish rebellion. According to Josephus, the Jews were "lurking in caves . . . opening up onto mountain precipices that were inaccessible from any quarter except by torturous and narrow paths." Antony eventually crushed the rebels by lowering his soldiers into the caves from above, but the bravery and rashness of the rebels may be the source of the tradition saying that after the coming of the Messiah, the battle of the End of Days will take place at Arbel. ⊠ *Rte. 7717* ☏ *04/673–2904* ⊕ *www.parks.org.il* ✉ *NIS 22* ⊗ *Apr.–Oct., daily 8–5; Nov.–Mar., daily 8–4. Last entrance 1 hr before closing.*

GINOSAR

10 km (6 miles) north of Tiberias.

Many Israelis know Ginosar, a kibbutz founded in 1937, as the home of the late Yigal Allon (1918–80), commander of the crack Palmach battalions in the War of Independence and deputy prime minister of Israel in the 1970s under Golda Meir and Yitzhak Rabin. Travelers, however, come here to see the ancient fishing boat.

GETTING HERE AND AROUND

Egged buses frequently make the short trip here from the Tiberias Central Bus Station. Ask the driver to tell you where to get off.

EXPLORING

Yigal Alon Museum. Kibbutz Ginosar's premier tourist attraction is a wooden fishing boat from the 1st century AD, found on the shore by two amateur archaeologists in 1986. Three years of drought had lowered the level of Lake Kinneret, and bits of the ancient wood were suddenly exposed in the mud. Excavated in a frenetic 11 days, the 28-foot-long boat became an instant media sensation. Given the frequency of New Testament references to Jesus and his disciples boating on the Sea of Galilee—including coming ashore at Gennesaret, perhaps today's Ginosar—the press immediately dubbed it the "Jesus Boat."

6

On the other hand, the startlingly vivid relic might have been a victim of the Roman naval victory over the rebellious Jewish townspeople of nearby Magdala in AD 67, as described by the historian Flavius Josephus. Whatever its unknown history, it's the most complete boat this old ever found in an inland waterway anywhere in the world. Today it's beautifully exhibited in all its modest but remarkably evocative glory in a specially built pavilion in the Yigal Alon Museum. A short video tells the story. ✉ *Nof Ginosar, off Rte. 90* ☎ *04/672–7700* 🎫 *NIS 20* 🕐 *Sat.–Thurs. 8–5, Fri. 8–4; last entry 1 hr before closing.*

KIBBUTZ MUSIC

Nof Ginosar hosts the twice-annual **Jacob's Ladder Festival** (🌐 *www.jlfestival.com*), a perennial favorite for folk-music fans. The music is eclectic, with international artists performing anything from Celtic to country classics. The crowd is equally diverse, coming from the United States, Canada, Britain, and around the world.

WHERE TO STAY

$ B&B/INN 🏨 **Ginosar Village.** Its grand location—with a private beach right on the Sea of Galilee—makes this kibbutz guesthouse especially popular. **Pros:** convenient location; opportunity to experience kibbutz life; beautiful gardens. **Cons:** too far to walk to town; no evening entertainment. [$] *Rooms from: $125* ✉ *Rte. 90* ☎ *04/670–0300* 🌐 *www.ginosar.co.il* 🛏 *162 rooms* 🍴 *Breakfast.*

TABGHA

4 km (2½ miles) north of Ginosar, 14 km (8 miles) north of Tiberias, at Capernaum Junction (Rtes. 90 and 87).

With a name that's an Arabic corruption of the Greek *Heptaegon* (Seven Springs), Tabgha is a cluster of serene holy places associated with Jesus' ministry in the Galilee. A promenade and hiking trails connect the shrines.

GETTING HERE AND AROUND

Tabgha is located off Route 87, a few hundred meters from the junction with Route 90. A promenade connects the Church of the Multiplication with the Church of the Primacy of St. Peter. A trail leads up to the Mt. of Beatitudes, but the hike is best enjoyed going downhill, with the glorious views of the lake in front of you.

EXPLORING

Church of the Multiplication. The German Benedictines dedicated this large, orange-roofed Roman Catholic church in 1936 on the scanty remains of earlier shrines. The site has long been venerated as the "deserted place" (Mark 6:30–6:34) where Jesus miraculously multiplied two fishes and five loaves of bread to feed the crowds. The present airy limestone building with the wooden-truss ceiling was built in the style of a Byzantine basilica to give a fitting context to the beautifully wrought 5th-century mosaic floor depicting the loaves and fishes in front of the altar. The nave is covered with geometric designs, but the front of the aisles is filled with flora and birds and, curiously,

Churches are among the sights along the peaceful shores of the Sea of Galilee.

a Nilometer, a graded column once used to measure the flood level of the Nile for the purpose of assessing that year's collectible taxes. ✉ *Rte. 87* ☎ *04/670–0180* 🎫 *Free* 🕐 *Sun. 10–5, Mon.–Sat. 8:30–5.*

Church of the Primacy of St. Peter. The austere, black basalt church, just east of the Church of the Multiplication, is built on the water's edge, over a flat rock known as *Mensa Christi* (the Table of Christ). After his resurrection, the New Testament relates, Jesus appeared to his disciples by the Sea of Galilee and presented them a miraculous catch of fish. Three times Jesus asked the disciple Peter if he loved him, and after his reply of "You know that I love you," Jesus commanded him to "Feed my sheep." Some scholars see this affirmation as Peter's atonement for having thrice denied Jesus in Jerusalem. The episode is seen as establishing Peter's "primacy" (Matthew 16:18). ✉ *Rte. 87* ☎ *04/672–4767* 🎫 *Free* 🕐 *Daily 8–noon and 2–5.*

MT. OF BEATITUDES

8 km (5 miles) north of Ginosar, 3 km (2 miles) north of Capernaum Junction.

Fodor'sChoice
★ Tradition identifies this tranquil hillside as the site of Jesus' most comprehensive teaching, recorded in the New Testament as the Sermon on the Mount: "And seeing the multitudes, he went up into a mountain; and when he was set, his disciples came unto him. And he opened his mouth, and taught them, saying: 'Blessed are the poor in spirit, for theirs is the kingdom of Heaven.'" (Matthew 5:3).

GETTING HERE AND AROUND
It's best to drive here. Lots of tourist buses make the journey, but there's no public transportation. It's on a spur road off the main lake road, atop a hill.

EXPLORING
Church of the Beatitudes. This domed Roman Catholic Church, run by the Franciscan Sisters, was designed by the famous architect and monk Antonio Barluzzi. Commissioned by Fascist leader Benito Mussolini while he was dictator of Italy, the church was completed in 1938. The windows are inscribed with the opening words of the Sermon on the Mount. The terrace surrounding the church offers a superb view of the Sea of Galilee, best enjoyed in the afternoon when the diffused western sun softens the light and heightens colors. Keep in mind this is a pilgrimage site, so dress modestly and respect the silence. ✉ *Rte. 8177, off Rte. 90* ☎ *04/679–0978* 🎟 *NIS 5 per vehicle* ⏲ *Apr.–Sept., daily 8–noon and 2:30–5; Oct.–Mar., daily 8–noon and 2:30–4.*

KORAZIM

Rte. 8277 at Rte. 90, 6 km (4 miles) north of Capernaum Junction.

Built on a basalt bluff a few miles north of the Sea of Galilee, the town of Korazim has long been renowned for its high-quality wheat. It's famous as the home of Korazim National Park.

GETTING HERE AND AROUND
Scenic Route 8277 offers some breathtaking views of the Sea of Galilee far below, but you'll need a car to enjoy them. There's no public transit to Korazim. Consider saddling up a horse from the stables at Vered Hagalil and riding here.

EXPLORING
Korazim National Park. These extensive and often remarkable ruins, dating from the 4th or 5th century AD, are on the site of the ancient Jewish village that Jesus condemned for rejecting him (Matthew 11:21), and include a monumental basalt **synagogue** adorned with the stone carvings of plants and animals. One remarkable artifact, a decorated and inscribed stone "armchair" dubbed the Throne of Moses, is thought to have been used by the worthies of the community during the reading of the Torah. The lake views from the site are also impressive. ✉ *Rte. 8277* ☎ *04/693–4982* 🌐 *www.parks.org.il* 🎟 *NIS 20* ⏲ *Apr.–Sept., Sat.–Thurs. 8–5, Fri. 8–3; Oct.–Mar., Sat.–Thurs. 8–4, Fri. 8–3.*

WHERE TO STAY
$ B&B/INN 🏨 **The Frenkels Bed-and-Breakfast.** Americans Etha and Irwin Frenkel retired to this rustic village on the border between the Lower and Upper Galilee and have made gracious hospitality a second career. **Pros:** convenient to national parks; charming rooms; pleasant hosts. **Cons:** no evening entertainment; no telephones in rooms. [$] *Rooms from: $150* ✉ *Rte. 8277* ☎ *04/680–1686* 🌐 *www.thefrenkels.com* 🛏 *3 suites* 💳 *No credit cards* 🍴 *Breakfast.*

$$ RESORT 🏨 **Vered Hagalil Guest Farm.** Yehuda Avni and his Jerusalem-born wife Yonah have created something unique in Israel: a ranch where guests

can ride horses during the day and retire to luxurious rooms at night. **Pros:** best stables in the area; convenient to national parks; panoramic views. **Cons:** no evening entertainment. $ *Rooms from: $200* ⊠ *Rtes. 8277 and 90* ☎ *04/693–5785* ⊕ *www.veredhagalil.co.il* ⟿ *6 cabins, 25 cottages* †○| *No meals.*

CAPERNAUM

3 km (2 miles) east of Tabgha and the Capernaum Junction, 17 km (10½ miles) northeast of Tiberias.

GETTING HERE AND AROUND

Capernaum is on Route 87, east of the intersection with Route 90. Since buses leave you a few miles from the site, it's best to drive.

EXPLORING

Fodor'sChoice ★ **Capernaum National Park.** For Christians, this park is among the most moving places in Israel, because it's where Jesus established his base for three years and recruited some of his disciples ("Follow me, and I will make you fishers of men" [Matthew 4:19]). It's also the site of the House of St. Peter, the ruins of an actual home where Jesus is believed to have lodged. Astride the ruins is an ultramodern Franciscan church, looking a bit like a spaceship.

Capernaum is also a site of interest to Jews, and the prosperity of the ancient Jewish community (it's *Kfar Nahum* in Hebrew) is immediately apparent from the remains of its **synagogue,** which dominates the complex. Once thought to date to the 2nd or 3rd century AD, the synagogue is now regarded by many scholars as belonging to the later Byzantine period (4th–5th centuries AD).

Limestone reliefs that once graced the synagogue exterior represent a typical range of Jewish artistic motifs: the native fruits of the land, the biblical Ark of the Covenant, a seven-branched menorah, a shofar, and an incense shovel (to preserve the memory of the Temple in Jerusalem, where they were used prior to the city's destruction). A small 1st-century mosaic from Magdala shows a contemporary boat, complete with oars and sails—a dramatic illustration of the many New Testament and Jewish references to fishing on the lake.

Jesus eventually cursed the people of Capernaum for failing to heed his message, saying "And you, Capernaum, will you be lifted up to the skies? No, you will go down to the depths" (Matthew 11:23–24). If you're visiting Capernaum, dress appropriately: you won't be allowed in if you're wearing shorts or a sleeveless shirt. ⊠ *Rte. 87* ☎ *04/672–1059* ⟿ *NIS 3* ⊘ *Daily 8:30–11:30 and 3:30–4:45.*

SPORTS AND THE OUTDOORS

Abukayak. Northeast of Capernaum, this outfitter's so-called kayaks are really inflated rubber canoes. They offer a serene one-hour paddle down the lower Jordan River, from March through November; a truck picks you up at the end. Life jackets are provided, and the trip is appropriate for young children. ⊠ *Jordan River Park, Rte. 888* ☎ *04/692–2245, 04/692–1078* ⊕ *www.abukayak.co.il.*

Capernaum was the base of Jesus' Galilean ministry, but the synagogue remains date from a later era.

EN ROUTE Route 87 continues east past Capernaum and crosses the **Jordan River**—somewhat muddy at this point—at the Arik Bridge. Those raised on spirituals extolling the Jordan's width and depth are often surprised to find how small a stream it really is: seldom wider than 30 feet. The Jordan enters the Sea of Galilee just a few hundred yards downstream.

BETHSAIDA

6 km (4 miles) north of Capernaum.

GETTING HERE AND AROUND
Route 87 provides an easy drive around the Sea of Galilee for Christian pilgrims visiting the major Galilean sites related to the life of Jesus. At the north side of the lake, where Route 87 ends, turn at Bet Tzida junction onto Route 888; Jordan River Park and Bethsaida will be on your left. There's a parking fee of NIS 50 per vehicle.

EXPLORING
Jordan River Park. On this spot, archaeologists have partially excavated an ancient fishing village, including the remains of several homes that, while now only rubble, provide an idea of how communal life was once lived here. Now, as then, the village affords a view of the Sea of Galilee (though the shore moved drastically, relative to the town, in an earthquake in AD 363). A shaded and serene sitting area includes arrows pointing to other Christian sites around the lake. Other than the sitting area, shade is limited here, so bring a hat and plenty of water. ✉ *Rte. 888* ☎ *04/692–3422.*

KURSI AND THE EASTERN SHORE

Kursi is 17 km (10½ miles) southeast of Capernaum on Rte. 92, 5 km (3 miles) north of Ein Gev.

Kursi, where Jesus healed two men possessed by demons (Matthew 8:28–32), is today a park incorporating the ruins of a Byzantine monastery. The eastern shore of the Sea of Galilee is far less developed than the western and northern sides, and the relatively rural character remains today, even as negotiations sputter along between Israel and Syria about returning this area to the control of Damascus.

GETTING HERE AND AROUND

Route 92 follows the eastern shore of the Sea of Galilee while Route 87 circles to the north of the lake. You can reach Kursi either by driving north or south from Tiberias. Whether you circle the lake clockwise or counterclockwise, the views are often breathtaking.

EXPLORING

Kursi National Park. Huddling under the imposing cliffs of the Golan Heights, where Route 789 climbs away from 92, this place is linked with the New Testament story of a man possessed by demons. Jesus exorcised the spirits, causing them to enter a herd of swine grazing nearby, which then "rushed down the steep bank into the lake, and perished in the waters" (Matthew 8:32). Fifth-century Byzantine Christians identified the event with this spot and built a monastery. It was an era in which earnest pilgrims inundated the holy places, true and new, and the monastery prospered from their gifts. The partly restored ruins of a fine Byzantine church are a classic example of the basilica style common at the time; the ruined monastery is higher up the hillside. ✉ *Rte. 92* ☎ *04/673–1983* 🌐 *www.parks.org.il* 🎟 *NIS 15* 🕒 *Apr.–Sept., Sat.–Thurs. 8–5, Fri. 8–4; Oct.–Mar., daily 8–4.*

6

WHERE TO EAT

$ MIDDLE EASTERN 🍴 **Ein Gev Fish Restaurant.** At lunchtime this popular establishment on the eastern shore bustles with tour groups, but it's a fine dinner option, too. Famous for St. Peter's fish, it has added sea bream, trout, and gray mullet to the menu, as well as entrées such as quiche, pizza, pasta, salads, and omelets. In fine weather, sit on the large outdoor terrace, and take in the view across the lake to Tiberias. Watch for the signs for "Kibbutz Inn Ein Gev." [$] *Average main: NIS 30* ✉ *Kibbutz Ein Gev* ☎ *04/665–8136* 🕒 *No dinner Fri., closed Sat.*

$$ ISRAELI 🍴 **HaBikta.** With a name that literally means "the cabin," HaBikta evokes the smoked meats for which it's best known. The chicken and steaks, smoked over cherrywood and grape vines, come with access to the generous salad buffet. Try the whole chickpeas coated in cumin and green onions, or the coriander tossed with slivered almonds and lentils. [$] *Average main: NIS 50* ✉ *Moshav Ramot* ☎ *04/679–4016* 🕒 *Closed Fri. and Sat.*

WHERE TO STAY

$$ B&B/INN FAMILY 🏨 **Beit Ram Sheraf.** The four suites owned by Judit Sheraf and Avi Ram are the perfect place for a family weekend: each cottage has a double bedroom, a living room that sleeps three, a kitchenette, a whirlpool tub, and a private yard with a barbecue grill and a hammock or swing set.

Pros: heated pool; child-friendly atmosphere. **Cons:** relatively expensive. [$] *Rooms from: $200* ✉ *32 Zevitan, Golan Heights, Moshav Ramot* ☎ *052/284–4013* 🌐 *www.beit-ram.co.il* 🛏 *4 cottages* 🍴 *No meals.*

$$ B&B/INN **Ein Gev Holiday Village.** Located on the palm-shaded eastern shore of the Sea of Galilee, this complex has everything from waterfront units with sunset-watching patios to spacious apartments with room for the whole family. **Pros:** convenient to national parks; beachfront setting. **Cons:** no evening entertainment. [$] *Rooms from: $201* ✉ *Rte. 92, 12 km (7½ miles) north of Tzemach Junction, Ein Gev* ☎ *04/665–9800* 🌐 *www.eingev.com* 🛏 *184 rooms* 🍴 *Breakfast.*

$ RESORT FAMILY **Ma'agan.** At the southern tip of the Sea of Galilee, this kibbutz has arguably the most enchanting view of all the properties around the lake. **Pros:** pretty beach; gorgeous lake views; convenient location. **Cons:** no evening entertainment. [$] *Rooms from: $150* ✉ *Rte. 92, 1 km (½ mile) east of Tzemach Junction* ☎ *04/665–4411* 🌐 *www.maagan.com* 🛏 *36 rooms, 112 suites* 🍴 *Breakfast.*

$$ B&B/INN **Ramot Resort Hotel.** High in the foothills of the Golan Heights, this hotel is only a few minutes from good beaches and a water park. **Pros:** convenient to national parks; cooler temperatures than at the lake; beautiful vistas. **Cons:** no evening entertainment. [$] *Rooms from: $220* ✉ *East of Rte. 92* ☎ *04/673–2636* 🌐 *www.ramot-nofesh.co.il* 🛏 *80 rooms, 25 chalets, 18 cabins* 🍴 *Breakfast.*

NIGHTLIFE AND THE ARTS

Ein Gev Spring Festival. This festival's focus is Israeli vocal music, from traditional to contemporary. It's held at Kibbutz Ein Gev during Passover. ☎ *04/675–1195.*

SPORTS AND THE OUTDOORS

The shoreline of the Sea of Galilee has receded somewhat with the low level of the water, and the bottom now drops precipitously. Keep a close eye on children.

BEACHES

Dugit Beach. With lifeguards on duty, this beach offers boating, sailing, and rafting, as well as rock climbing and other activities. **Amenities:** food and drink; lifeguards; parking (fee); showers; toilets; water sports. **Best for:** swimming. ✉ *Rte. 92, 8 km (5 miles) north of Ein Gev* ☎ *04/667–8015, 04/667–8009* 🎟 *NIS 60 per car.*

Golan Beach. The best-known beach on the lake's northeastern shore has powerboat, rowboat, kayak, and pedal-boat rentals, as well as waterskiing and other water sports. **Amenities:** food and drink; lifeguards; parking (fee); showers; toilets; water sports. **Best for:** swimming. ✉ *Moshav Ramot, Rte. 92, 7 km (4½ miles) north of Ein Gev* ☎ *04/667–8015, 04/667–8009* 🕒 *June, Sept., and Oct., Fri. and Sat. 10–4; July and Aug., Fri. and Sat. 9:30–5, Mon. and Thurs. 9:30–8.*

WATER PARK

FAMILY **Lunagal.** This popular water park has pools, waterslides, and other diversions for kids. ✉ *Golan Beach, Rte. 92, 7 km (4½ miles) north of Ein Gev* ☎ *04/667–8000* 🌐 *www.dugal.co.il* 🎟 *NIS 96* 🕒 *May, June, and Sept., Fri. and Sat. 10–4; July and Aug., daily 9:30–5.*

HAMMAT GADER

10 km (6 miles) east of Tzemach Junction on Rte. 98, 22 km (14 miles) southeast of Tiberias, 36 km (22½ miles) northeast of Beit She'an.

GETTING HERE AND AROUND

Whether you're driving via Tiberias (Route 90) or the Golan Heights (Route 98), this highway is one of the most captivating in Israel, with expansive views across the Yarmuk River into Jordan. Don't leave the roadway. The minefield signs mean exactly what they say.

EXPLORING

FAMILY **Hammat Gader.** Popular with Israelis—who come for the freshwater and mineral pools, giant waterslide, alligator farm, performing parrots, petting zoo, and restaurants—this place has history, too: in its heyday, it was the second-largest spa in the Roman Empire (after Baiae, near Naples). Built around three hot springs, the impressive complex of baths and pools attests to its opulence. The large number of ancient clay oil lamps found in one small pool is proof of nighttime bathing. ⊠ *Rte. 98* ☎ *04/665–9964, 04/665-9966* ⊕ *www.hamat-gader.com* ⊠ *NIS 80– NIS 100* ⊗ *Jun.–Sept., daily 7–5; Oct.–May, weekdays 7 am–11 am, Sat. 7 am–9 pm, Sun. 7 am–5 pm.*

WHERE TO STAY

$$$$ ☷ **Spa Village.** In a Thai-style complex that's a world apart from any-
RESORT thing else in this region, these superbly outfitted cabins have hot tubs that use thermal mineral water from the nearby springs. **Pros:** sybaritic experience; tropical gardens; pampering staff. **Cons:** no evening enter-tainment. Ⓢ *Rooms from: $450* ⊠ *Rte. 98* ☎ *04/665–5555* ⊕ *www. spavillage.co.il* ⤳ *29 suites* ⦿ *Breakfast.*

DEGANIA, KINNERET, AND YARDENIT

Degania Aleph: 10 km (6 miles) south of Tiberias; Kinneret: 2 km (1 mile) northwest of Degania Aleph.

Degania and Kinneret, two historic kibbutzim founded in the early 20th century, contain museums and historic graveyards worth a visit. Also nearby is Yardenit, a baptism site for Christians.

GETTING HERE AND AROUND

Both Degania Aleph and Kinneret are south of Tiberias along Route 90. If you take a bus, ask the driver in advance about stopping.

EXPLORING

Degania Aleph. The first kibbutz, the collective village of Degania Aleph was founded by Jewish pioneers from Eastern Europe in 1909. (Aleph is the *A* of the Hebrew alphabet; don't confuse the kibbutz with its younger neighbor, Degania Bet.) Near the entrance is a small Syrian tank of World War II vintage. On May 15, 1948, the day after Israel declared its independence, Arab armies invaded it from all sides. Syr-ian forces came down the Yarmuk Valley from the east, overran two other kibbutz complexes en route, and were only stopped here, at the gates of Degania. A teenager with a Molotov cocktail set alight the lead tank. On the grounds is the museum of Beit Gordon, named for the

6

spiritual mentor of the early pioneers. It houses two collections: one devoted to the region's natural history, the other examining the history and archaeology of human settlement in the surrounding valleys. ⊠ *Near Rte. 90* ☎ *04/675–0040* ⊕ *www.beitgordon.museumline.co.il* 💷 *Museum: NIS 15.*

FAMILY **Galita Chocolate Farm.** A short drive from Degania Aleph is Degania Bet, where you can smell the chocolate long before you get to the farm. In addition to the "bar" serving hot- and cold-chocolate drinks, and a tempting gift shop, Galita has eight different chocolate-making workshops. Reservations aren't required, but advance notice will ensure you can enjoy the activities in English. ⊠ *Kibbutz Degania Bet, off Rte. 90* ☎ *04/675–5608* ⊕ *www.galita.co.il* 💷 *Free; workshops NIS 40–180* ⊙ *Sun.–Thurs. 10–6, Fri. 10–5, Sat. and holidays 10–6.*

Kinneret. Across the Jordan River from Degania, Kinneret was founded in 1911 as the country's second kibbutz, taking its name from the Hebrew word for the Sea of Galilee. The serene **Kibbutz Kinneret Cemetery** includes the grave of Rachel *HaMeshoreret* (Rachel the Poetess), a secular shrine for many Israelis. The pebbles left on her grave by visitors (a token of respect in the Jewish tradition) are a tribute to Rachel's renown and to the romantic hold she has on the national imagination. Born in Russia in 1890, she became a poet of national stature in the Hebrew language; she died in 1931. The cemetery offers a superb view of the lake, the Golan Heights, and majestic Mt. Hermon. ⊠ *Off Rte. 90, south of junction with Rte. 767* ☎ *04/675–9500.*

Yardenit. On a picturesque bend of the Jordan River where huge eucalyptus trees droop into the quiet water, this spot was developed as a baptism site for Christian pilgrims. The baptism of Jesus by John the Baptist (John 1:28) is traditionally identified with the southern reaches of the Jordan River, near Jericho. But when the area became a hostile frontier between Israel and Jordan, pilgrims began to seek out accessible spots beyond the conflict zone. You'll often see groups of pilgrims being immersed in the river amid prayers and hymns and expressions of joy. The white robes required to enter the water become transparent when wet, so bring a bathing suit or large towel. Snacks and souvenirs are available. ⊠ *Off Rte. 90* ☎ *04/675–9111* ⊕ *www.yardenit.com* 💷 *Free* ⊙ *Sun.–Thurs. 8–6, Fri. 8–4.*

UPPER GALILEE AND THE GOLAN

with Tzfat (Safed)

WELCOME TO UPPER GALILEE AND THE GOLAN

TOP REASONS TO GO

★ **The Old City of Tzfat:** While the tiny historic synagogues offer a rare taste of Jewish houses of worship from bygone days, the galleries are saturated with contemporary colors and shapes.

★ **Kayaking on the Jordan River:** A cool ride downriver can be a strenuous adventure or a tame family float; either way, it adds an interesting accent to a trip to the northern Galilee.

★ **The Hula Lake Nature Reserve:** The Hula Reserve provides shelter for birds, some 500 million of which fly over the Hula Valley twice a year on migrations between Europe and Africa.

★ **Hermon River Nature Reserve:** Hike to the Banias Waterfall and the Crusader ruins, and pick up a freshly baked pita from the Druze mill along the way.

★ **Gamla:** This is the site of the Jews' heroic last stand following a siege by the Romans in AD 67. Aside from its history, it offers a challenging hike or an easy amble, all with glimpses of wildlife.

1 Tzfat (Safed) and Environs. At 3,000 feet above sea level, Tzfat is Israel's highest city, known for being the center of Kabbalah, or Jewish mysticism. Although it's one of several holy sites in Israel, this city north of the Sea of Galilee has a spiritual dimension found nowhere else. Its twisting passageways, vestiges of the Ottomans and the Crusaders, caught the attention of artists, who make this one of the country's most enchanting destinations every spring and summer.

2 Upper Hula Valley. Situated between the Golan Heights, Naftali Ridge, and the Beqaa Valley, the Upper Hula Valley is best known for the Tel Dan Nature Preserve. Spread out over 800 acres, it's a prime spot for hiking, cycling, or picnicking. Bustling Kiryat Shmona and sleepy Metulla are the region's largest communities.

3 Golan Heights. This region's main geographic feature is the Sea of Galilee, the country's main water reservoir. This is the northernmost part of the country, and from Mt. Hermon you can gaze out over Lebanon and Syria.

The Golan Heights draws visitors throughout the year to its relaxing countryside, inventive restaurants, and leading wineries.

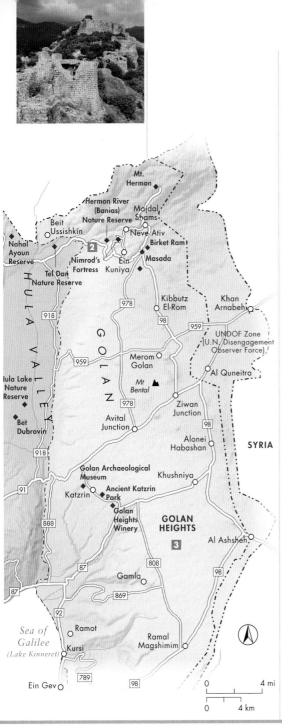

GETTING ORIENTED

The undulating hills of Western Galilee push upward into sharp limestone and basalt formations, bordered on the north by Lebanon and on the east by the volcanic, mountainous Golan Heights, beyond which lies Syria. The major cities—Tzfat in the rugged Galilee mountains and Katzrin in the Golan Heights—are a study in contrasts. The former is immersed in Jewish mysticism, and the latter is the result of a hardheaded determination to secure Israel's border with Syria by establishing a modern town in what was once a battlefield.

7

Updated by
Noya Kohavi

"Israel's Little Tuscany" has long been a nickname for the Upper Galilee. The green countryside, the growing numbers of both large-scale and boutique wineries, and the laid-back atmosphere have attracted urbanites on weekend jaunts as well as adventurous travelers.

The mountain air is redolent with the fragrance of spice plants; visitors can hike, cycle, or ride horses along trails that range from easy to challenging; and opportunities for kayaking, bird-watching, and other outdoor pursuits abound. These are the best vacation treats, all in a fascinating historical setting.

The main geographical feature of this region is towering Mt. Hermon, known as Israel's "sponge." Huge volumes of water from winter snow and rainfall soak into its limestone, emerging at the base of the mountain in an abundance of springs that feed the Jordan River and its tributaries and provide half of Israel's water supply. The water also sustains lush vegetation that thrives year-round and is home to wildcats, hyraxes, gazelles, and hundreds of species of birds.

This water and the strategic vantage points of the Galilee mountaintops and the Golan Heights have made the region a source of political contention since time immemorial. Over the centuries, Egyptians, Canaanites, Israelites, Romans, Byzantines, Muslims, Crusaders, and Ottomans locked horns here; in the 20th century alone, the borders have been changed by Britain, France, and of course, Israel, Lebanon, and Syria.

Borders aren't the only things that have shifted here. A geological fault line, the Syrian–African Rift, cuts straight through the 30-km (19-mile) Hula Valley; in 1837 an earthquake razed Tzfat and Tiberias, though no significant rumbles have been heard since. Extinct volcanic cones give the Golan its unusual topographic profile.

With all this water and fertile soil, the region has long been an agricultural center and is today studded with apple and cherry orchards, fishponds, and vineyards. The pastoral beauty and variety of outdoor activities attract visitors from elsewhere in Israel and the world, supplying the region's other main industry: tourism.

Proximity to Lebanon and Syria doesn't ordinarily deter people from visiting the Upper Galilee and the Golan. On the contrary, the combination of an exciting past with a gorgeous natural setting is precisely the draw here.

Over the last century, both Jews and non-Jews have faced hardships and hurdles in this region. Yet the tenacious Galileans will say there's no better place to live. Although the area is only a four-hours drive from Tel Aviv and Jerusalem, visitors find this is another world.

UPPER GALILEE PLANNER

WHEN TO GO

Unlike other parts of the country, there's no best time of the year to tour the Upper Galilee and the Golan. The range of colors is wonderful in spring, when hillsides are covered with wildflowers. Summer brings families traveling with children, as well as music and culinary festivals; days can be hot, but the low humidity makes it manageable. Wine fans appreciate the area in autumn during harvest time at the vineyards. Nights can be cold year-round. In winter, more precipitation means gushing streams and gray skies.

PLANNING YOUR TIME

A day trip to the Golan Heights from Tiberias is doable, but there's something about the lush foliage of the forests and the mountain air of the Golan that makes you want to linger. Three or four days is ideal to explore the region, including wine tasting, hiking a piece of wilderness, kayaking, or just kicking back in a room with a stunning view. The ideal way to see this area is by car, though local buses will get you almost anywhere you want to go if you have time. Note that touring the Upper Galilee and Golan is usually very safe but if security demands unusual caution, certain areas may be temporarily inaccessible.

GETTING HERE

Only one airline flies from Tel Aviv to the small airport of Mahanayim, near Rosh Pina: Ayit operates two 35-minute flights each day.

There's no transportation at the airport except for taxis. Nevertheless, you can arrange for a rental car to be waiting at the airport. From the airport, it's 10 km (6 miles) to Tzfat and 30 km (19 miles) to Kiryat Shmona.

GETTING AROUND

BUS TRAVEL

Local Egged buses stop at all major sights in this region (there's always a kibbutz, a town, or some other small residential settlement nearby). Avoid buses if you're on a tight schedule, as they tend to be infrequent.

CAR TRAVEL

The Upper Galilee and the Golan are a 1½-hour, 60-km (37-mile) drive from both Akko and Nahariya; a three-hour, 180-km (112-mile) drive from Tel Aviv; and four hours from Jerusalem, which is 200 km (124 miles) to the south.

There are a few different ways to get here. From Tiberias and the Sea of Galilee, Route 90 runs north between the Hula Valley, on the east, and the hills of Naftali, on the west. The more rugged Route 98 runs from the eastern side of the Sea of Galilee up through the Golan Heights to Mt. Hermon. Near the top of Route 98 you can pick up Route 91, which heads west into the Upper Galilee.

From the Mediterranean coast there are several options, but the main one is Route 85 from Akko. Route 89 runs parallel to Route 85 a little farther north, from Nahariya, and has some gorgeous scenery.

From Haifa take Route 75 to Route 77, turning onto Route 90 at Tiberias, or Route 70 north onto Route 85 east. If you're starting from Tel Aviv, drive north on Route 4 or 2 to Hadera; from there you'll head northwest on Route 65, exiting onto Route 85 east.

The state of Israel's roads is generally fair to good, but in the Upper Galilee in particular, some roads are still two-lane. Drive cautiously. Try to avoid driving during peak hours (usually late Thursday and Saturday afternoons), when city folk crowd the roads back to Jerusalem and Tel Aviv after a day out in the country.

RESTAURANTS

The Upper Galilee and the Golan's crisp, appetite-whetting air is an exquisite backdrop for some excellent restaurants. Fresh grilled Dan River trout, Middle Eastern fare prepared by Druze villagers, or home-style Jewish cooking in Tzfat are all regional fare. Excellent local wines enhance any meal: try the Mt. Hermon red, Gamla Cabernet Sauvignon, and Yarden Cabernet Blanc and Merlot. In a few places (such as Tzfat), it can be hard to find a restaurant open on Shabbat (sundown Friday to sundown Saturday). *Prices in the reviews are the average cost of a main course at dinner or, if dinner isn't served, at lunch.*

HOTELS

There are few grand hotels here, but the ample selection of guesthouses and inns ranges from ranch-style to home-style. As the tourist industry has developed, many kibbutzim and moshavim have added hotels (or guest wings attached to homes); some also arrange tours, from rafting to Jeep excursions. Rooms in kibbutz guesthouses can be reserved directly or through the Israel Kibbutz Hotels chain, a central reservation service based in Tel Aviv, although not all the kibbutzim are represented. *Prices in the reviews are the lowest cost of a standard double room in high season.*

VISITOR INFORMATION

Beit Ussishkin Nature Museum has information about area nature reserves, natural history, and bird-watching. The Israel Nature and Parks Authority staff is a good resource for planning itineraries that include national parks in other parts of the country. The visitor information service at Moshav Beit Hillel is especially helpful, with a wide selection of bed-and-breakfast accommodations in the *moshav*, which is in the heart of the Hula Valley tourist region. The Tourist Information Center–Upper Galilee can also provide information.

Contacts Beit Ussishkin Nature Museum ✉ *Kibbutz Dan, Rte. 99, Kiryat Shmona* ☎ *04/694–1704* ☉ *Sun.–Thurs. 8–4.* **Israel Kibbutz Hotels** ☎ *03/560-8118* ⊕ *www.kibbutz.co.il.* **Israel Nature and Parks Authority Northern District** ☎ *04/659-0316* ⊕ *www.parks.org.il.* **Tourist Information Center–Upper Galilee** ✉ *Gome Junction, Rte. 90 and Rte. 977, Kiryat Shmona* ☎ *04/681-7152* ⊕ *www.gogalil.org* ☉ *Sun.–Thurs. 9–5.*

TZFAT (SAFED) AND ENVIRONS

In the southern part of the Upper Galilee, attractions range from the narrow streets and historic synagogues of Tzfat to the wilderness of the Hula Nature Reserve. Other sites, like Mt. Meron, pair scenic appeal with spiritual importance. In Rosh Pina, you can shop and dine where the Galilee's first Zionist pioneers labored, or you can just relax at an inn or a kibbutz guesthouse and enjoy the wooded scenery.

TZFAT

33 km (20 miles) north of Tiberias, 72 km (45 miles) northeast of Haifa.

Fodor's Choice
★

Tzfat attracts artists who look for inspiration, travelers charmed by its cobbled alleys, and religious people in search of meaning—a rare example of harmony between the secular and the spiritual. The city is known for its spiritual, even sacred, vibe and its breathtaking views.

It doesn't take long to walk all of Tzfat's Old City, but allow plenty of time to poke around the little cobbled passages that seem to lead nowhere, to linger over some minute architectural detail on a building from another time, or to browse through shops filled to overflowing with locally made art. It's almost impossible to get lost; Yerushalayim (Jerusalem) Street is a good orientation point—it runs through the heart of the Old City, encircles the Citadel, and from there, steps lead down to the two main areas of interest, the Old Jewish Quarter and the adjacent Artists' Colony. There's no way to avoid the hilly topography, so remember to wear comfortable walking shoes. As the town is largely Orthodox, modest dress is recommended when visiting synagogues. For women, this means a below-the-knee skirt or long pants and at least a short-sleeve top; for men, long pants are appropriate. In the hot summer days, dress lightly and carry around a shawl or cover up for visiting holy places.

Tzfat hibernates from October through June, when the city's artists move to their galleries in warmer parts of the country. This doesn't mean you should leave Tzfat out of your itinerary during those months; there's enough to occupy the curious wanderer for at least a few hours, and much of it is free. In summer, especially during July and August, Tzfat is abuzz with activity: galleries and shops stay open late, *klezmer* music (Eastern European Jewish "soul music") dances around corners, and the city extends a warm welcome to everyone.

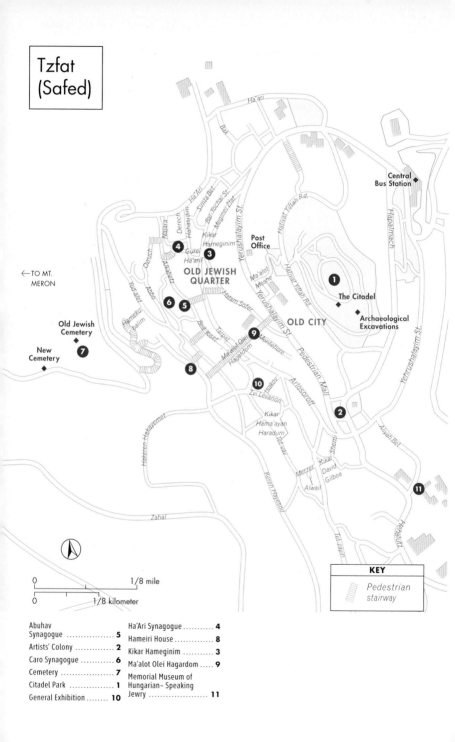

Tzfat (Safed)

← TO MT. MERON

Central Bus Station

Ha'ari

Bat

Hapalmach

Hatzvi Yiflah Rd.

Najara

Derech Hehasidim

Simta Bet

Bar-Yochai St.

Meginei Tzfat

Kikar Hameginim

Post Office

Yerushalayim St.

Ohrach

Alkabetz

4 Gurei Ha'ari

3

OLD JEWISH QUARTER

Ma'alot Moshe

Hatzvi Yiflah Rd.

1

The Citadel

Hamekubalim

Abbo

Yud Alef

6 **5**

Haram Sofer

Yerushalayim St.

OLD CITY

Archaeological Excavations

Old Jewish Cemetery

Berl Yosef

Tarpat

7

New Cemetery

8

Mifraot Olei Hagardom

9

Montefiore

Pedestrian Mall

Yerushalayim St.

10

Tzvi Levanon

Yslakov

2

Aliyah Bet

Hateren Hakayemet

Kikar Hama'ayan Haradum

Tel-Haivav

Merzer

Kikar David Gilboa

Sherri

11

Keren Hayesod

Alwail

Hatnuitz

Tel-Zaivin

Zahal

N

| 0 | 1/8 mile |

| 0 | 1/8 kilometer |

KEY

Pedestrian stairway

Abuhav Synagogue **5**

Artists' Colony **2**

Caro Synagogue **6**

Cemetery **7**

Citadel Park **1**

General Exhibition **10**

Ha'Ari Synagogue **4**

Hameiri House **8**

Kikar Hameginim **3**

Ma'alot Olei Hagardom **9**

Memorial Museum of Hungarian– Speaking Jewry **11**

GETTING HERE AND AROUND

If you're driving to Tzfat from Jerusalem, take Route 6 north. If you're starting in Tel Aviv, head north on Route 2. Either way, you'll want to turn east on Route 65, then north on Route 90, then west on Route 89 to Tzfat. If your journey starts in Haifa, head north on Route 4, then east on Route 89 to Tzfat. Egged runs at least two buses daily to Tzfat from Tel Aviv, at least seven from Jerusalem, and at least 30 from Haifa.

In Tzfat the private company Nativ Express runs 13 local bus lines. The Hamavreek taxi company in Tzfat will pick up incoming travelers at the Mahanayim Airport and take them to various destinations in the region. Buses from Tzfat's central station, at the entrance to the city, head to most towns in the region.

Both of Israel's major bus companies, Egged Tours and United Tours, offer one- and two-day guided tours of the region, departing from Tel Aviv and Jerusalem.

Within the Old City, the many streets closed to traffic make it difficult to drive. You may have to drive around the perimeter of the city rather than through it. The best way to get around is on foot.

ESSENTIALS

Bus Contacts Egged ☎ *2800 ⊕ www.egged.co.il.
Nativ Express ☎ 1/599–559–5599 ⊕ www.nateevexpress.com.

EXPLORING

TOP ATTRACTIONS

Abuhav Synagogue. This large Sephardic synagogue is named for a 14th-century Spanish scribe, one of whose Torah scrolls found its way here with the Spanish Jewish exiles 200 years later. A look around reveals several differences between this synagogue and its Ashkenazi counterparts, such as the Ha'Ari; for example, the walls are painted the lively blue typical of Sephardic tradition, and the benches run along the walls instead of in rows (so that no man turns his back on his neighbor).

Every detail is loaded with significance: there are three arks—for the three forefathers, Abraham, Isaac, and Jacob (the one on the right is said to be the Abuhav original)—and 10 windows in the dome, referring to the Commandments. The charmingly naive illustrations on the squinches include pomegranate trees, whose seed-filled fruit symbolizes the 613 Torah Commandments. The original building was destroyed in the 1837 earthquake, but locals swear that the southern wall—in which the Abuhav Torah scroll is set—was spared. ⊠ *Abuhav St.* ☎ *04/692–3885* ⊗ *Open Sun.–Thurs. 9–5, Fri. 9–1.*

Artists' Colony. The colony, set in Tzfat's old Arab Quarter, was established in 1951 by six Israeli artists who saw the promise hidden in Tzfat's war-torn condition; for them, the old buildings, the fertile landscape, and the cool mountain air fused into the magic ingredients of creativity. Others soon followed until, at its peak, the colony was home to more than 50 artists. Many galleries host workshops as well as exhibits, and many are open only in the spring and summer, from about 10 am to 6 pm. ⊠ *Old City of Tzfat.*

What Is Kabbalah?

Kabbalah, which means "receiving," is an ancient study of Jewish mysticism that gained popularity in the 13th century. Tzfat has been the main center for Kabbalah scholarship since the 16th century, making it one of Judaism's four holiest cities (along with Jerusalem, Tiberias, and Hebron).

Kabbalah, as opposed to formal rabbinical Judaism, is about reading between, behind, and all around the lines. Each letter and accent of every word in the holy books has a numerical value with particular significance, offering added meaning to the literal word. One of the most popular Kabbalistic concepts is that of *tikkun olam*, or "fixing the world." According to Jewish mystics, the universe was "broken" by God in order to make room for the physical realm. Thus the quest of humankind is to repair the universe through good works and service to God.

Although classical Kabbalah studies are intertwined with those of the Bible and the Talmud, not all religious Jews study Kabbalah. In fact, tradition holds that a person studying Kabbalah must be at least 40 years old and have a thorough knowledge of other Jewish texts. Outside of Hasidic Judaism, which has incorporated some Kabbalah into its worldview, many mainstream Orthodox Jews don't study Kabbalah at all, preferring to focus on matters of the perceivable world.

Caro Synagogue. Tucked among art galleries, the Caro appears quite run-down, but it's considered one of the Old City's most interesting and charming synagogues by those who feel a deep spiritual connection to the great scholar after whom it was named. Rabbi Yosef Caro arrived in Tzfat in 1535 and led its Jewish community for many years. He's the author of Shulchan Aruch, the code of law that remains a foundation of Jewish religious interpretation to the present day, and this synagogue is said to have been Caro's study hall. It was rebuilt in the mid-19th century. If you ask, the attendant might open the ark containing the Torah scrolls, one of which is at least 400 years old. A glass-faced cabinet at the back of the synagogue is the *geniza*, where damaged scrolls or prayer books are stored (because they carry the name of God, they can't be destroyed). The turquoise paint here—considered the "color of heaven"—is believed to help keep away the evil eye. ⊠ *Alkabetz St.* ☎ *04/692–3284* 🎫 *Free* ☉ *Sun.–Thurs. 9–5, Fri. 9–1.*

General Exhibition. An important stop in a tour of the Artists' Colony, the works inside this large space are a representative sample of the work of Tzfat's artists, ranging from oils and watercolors to silk screens and sculptures, in traditional and avant-garde styles. The permission of the Muslim authorities was required to organize the exhibition, as it's housed in the old mosque, easily identified from afar by its minaret. The Artists' Colony has recognized artists from the former Soviet Union, and the adjacent building holds the **Immigrant Artists' Exhibition.** In either facility, if any works catch your fancy, just ask directions to the artist's gallery for a more in-depth look at his or her work. ✉ *Leon Isakov and Zvi Levanon Sts.* ☎ *04/692–0087* ⊕ *www.artistcolony.co.il* ✉ *Free* ☉ *Sun.–Thurs. 9–5; Fri., Sat., and Jewish holidays 10–2.*

Ha'Ari Synagogue. This Ashkenazi synagogue has associations going back to the 16th century. It's named for a rabbi who left an indelible mark on Tzfat and on Judaism: Isaac Luria, known to all as the Ari, Hebrew for "lion" and an acronym for Adoneinu Rabbeinu Itzhak ("our master and teacher Isaac"). In his mere three years in Tzfat, he evolved his own system of the Kabbalah, which drew a huge following that would influence Jewish teaching the world over. Even more astounding is that he died in his 30s; it's generally said that one should not even consider study of the Kabbalah before the age of 40, when one reaches the requisite level of intellectual and emotional maturity.

The pale colors of this tiny Ashkenazi synagogue contrast sharply with its olive-wood Holy Ark, a dazzlingly carved tour de force with two tiers of spiral columns and vibrant plant reliefs. (The Sephardic Ari Synagogue, where the rabbi prayed, is farther down the quarter, by the cemetery. The oldest of Tzfat's synagogues, this 16th-century structure has especially fine, carved, wooden doors.) ✉ *Najara St.* ✉ *Free* ☉ *Sun.–Thurs. 9:30 until afternoon prayer service (about 20 mins. before sunset), Fri. 9:30–1.*

Hameiri House. This centuries-old three-story stone building, located at the northern end of Keren Ha'yesod Street, houses a historical museum that offers great insight into the daily life of Jews in Tzfat over the past 200 years. Textiles, tableware, and Judaica like ornate menorahs are displayed with notations in Hebrew and English. Guided tours are available by appointment. ✉ *158 Keren Ha'yesod St.* ☎ *04/697–1307* ✉ *NIS 20* ☉ *Sun.–Thurs. 8:30–2:30, Fri. and holidays 8:30–1:30.*

WORTH NOTING

Cemetery. Old and new cemeteries are set into the hillside below the Old Jewish Quarter. The old plots resonate with the names and fame of the Kabbalists of yore, as their graves are identifiable by sky-blue markers. The new cemetery holds the graves of members of the pre-State underground Stern Gang and Irgun forces, who were executed by the British in Akko's prison. In a separate plot, bordered by cypresses, lie the 21 Tzfat teenagers killed by terrorists in 1974—they were taken hostage while on a field trip in the northern Galilee town of Ma'alot. ✉ *Below Keren Hayesod St.* ✉ *Free.*

Citadel Park. In Talmudic times, 1,600 years ago, hilltop bonfires here served as a beacon to surrounding communities heralding the beginning of the lunar month, the basis for the Jewish calendar. In the 12th century, the Crusaders grasped the strategic value of this setting and built the Citadel. The Muslim sultan Baybars conquered it in 1266, leaving only the scattered pieces you see today. The Jewish settlement outside the Citadel's walls grew and prospered during and after the Crusader era, becoming a center of Kabbalah studies. When the departing British Mandate forces left the town's strategic positions to the Arab forces, the remains of the Citadel again became a battleground between Jews and Arabs. ✉ *Derech Hativat Yiftach.*

Tzfat is an artsy village in the northern Galilee known for being the birthplace of Kabbalah (Jewish mysticism).

Kikar Hameginim. "Defenders' Square," in the Old Jewish Quarter, was once its heart. A sign points to a two-story house that served as the command post of the neighborhood's defense in 1948—hence the plaza's name. ⊠ *Bar Yochai St., at Ma'alot Gore Ha'Ari.*

Ma'alot Olei Hagardom. Part of Tzfat's charm is its setting, on the slope of a hill. This *ma'alot,* or stairway, which extends from Yerushalayim Street to Keren HaYesod Street, forms the boundary between the Old Jewish Quarter and the Artists' Colony. It's named for Tzfat freedom fighters executed by the British during the mandate. ⊠ *Off Yerushalayim St.*

Memorial Museum of Hungarian-Speaking Jewry. The founders of this museum are Tzfat residents and Holocaust survivors Hava and Yosef Lustig. The exhibits in the museum's three small rooms, including letters, children's books, drawings, items of clothing, and more, tell of the everyday life of communities and individuals in the Hungarian-speaking Jewish pre-Holocaust world. The computer database has information about 1,700 Jewish communities in Hungary, Transylvania, Slovakia, and other countries. Guided tours can be arranged in advance. ⊠ *Old Ottoman Government Center, Independence Sq.* ☎ *04/692–5881* ⊕ *www.hjm.org.il* ⊡ *NIS 15* ⊘ *Sun.–Fri. 9–1.*

WHERE TO EAT

$$$$
STEAKHOUSE

✕ **Bat Ya'ar.** Its wooded-mountaintop setting enhances this timbered restaurant's delicious food. A meaty bowl of bean stew, eaten by the fireplace, is a pleasure any time of year. Outside is a playground for children. Hour-long family nature-activity packages are offered, as well as horseback-riding excursions. Bat Ya'ar is 5 km (3 miles) north of Tzfat.

It's best to call for directions. $ *Average main: NIS 110* ⊠ *Birya Forest* ☎ *04/692–1788* ⊕ *www.batyaar. co.il* ⌲ *Reservations essential.*

$$$
ISRAELI
FAMILY
Fodor'sChoice
★

✗ **Ein Camonim.** The Galilee Hills make perfect pastureland for livestock—in this case, goats—and here you can taste the fresh output

of Ein Camonim's dairy, one of the best in Israel. The all-you-can-eat menu includes a platter of about three-dozen goat cheeses, a selection of home-baked breads, a variety of fresh salads, and house wine. There's a half-price menu for kids. The specialty shop next door sells the dairy's cheeses, olives, and other homemade products. The eatery is 20 km (12½ miles) southwest of Tzfat, 5 km (3 miles) west of Kadarim Junction. $ *Average main: NIS 88* ⊠ *Rte. 85* ☎ *04/698–9894.*

$$
ECLECTIC

✗ **Gan Eden.** The setting, a charming stone house with both indoor and outdoor seating, lends great atmosphere to this family-run kosher eatery. Taking in the view of Mt. Meron (the restaurant's name means "paradise"), the place is best known for its fish, especially its fillets of sea bass and sea bream. What they call calzones are actually dumplings stuffed with salty Tzfat cheese and served with a delicious salad of lettuce, cranberries, and walnuts. Gan Eden serves no meat or chicken. $ *Average main: NIS 70* ⊠ *Mt. Canaan Promenade, 33 HaGedud Hashlishi St.* ☎ *057/944–3471* ⊘ *Closed Sat.*

$
MIDDLE EASTERN

✗ **Lachuch Original.** This popular local eatery's upstairs dining room has benches and tables inlaid with Middle Eastern designs, walls painted the soft shade of blue found inside local synagogues, and colorful carpets from all over the region. The strikingly dressed owner and chef, Ronen Jarufi, makes each meal to order. Choose from a variety of Yemenite breads—*lachuch*, *malawa*, or *jachnun* are all good picks—and he'll top it with homemade cheese and his own hot sauce. The place also stocks books on Kabbalah and CDs of evocative Jewish music. $ *Average main: NIS 40* ⊠ *18 Elkabetz St.* ☎ *050/225–4148* ⊘ *Closed Sat. No dinner Fri.*

WHERE TO STAY

$$$
HOTEL

▥ **Canaan Spa.** This elegant hotel on the outskirts of Tzfat knows how to pamper its guests. **Pros:** truly relaxing atmosphere; great pool; fabulous brunch. **Cons:** remote location; not for families. $ *Rooms from: $396* ⊠ *Mt. Canaan Promenade, Gdud Hashlishi St.* ☎ *04/699–3000* ⊕ *www. canaanspa.com* ⧉ *116 rooms, 8 suites* ⧖ *Some meals.*

$
B&B/INN
FAMILY

▥ **Joseph's Well.** At Kibbutz Amiad, 10 km (6 miles) south of Tzfat, this lodging has clusters of rooms sharing private patios. **Pros:** informal vibe; terrific for children; a peek into kibbutz life. **Cons:** plain decor; don't expect sophisticated breakfast. $ *Rooms from: $199* ⊠ *Kibbutz Amiad, off Route 90* ☎ *04/690–9829* ⊕ *www.amiad-inn.com* ⧉ *27 rooms* ⧖ *Breakfast.*

$$
HOTEL

▥ **Ruth Rimonim.** Built 200 years ago for a Turkish sultan, this spectacular castle was transformed into a hotel in 1961. **Pros:** romantic; nice pool; central location. **Cons:** pool is open only in summer; some older rooms are small. $ *Rooms from: $273* ⊠ *45 HaNasi St., off Tet Zayin St.* ☎ *04/699–4666* ⊕ *www.rimonim.com* ⧉ *77 rooms* ⧖ *Breakfast.*

7

Getting on horseback is a popular activity in the Galilee, with its verdant hills, quiet forests, and gentle paths.

$
B&B/INN
⌂ **Safed Inn.** On the outskirts of Tzfat, the budget-minded Safed Inn caters especially well to families. **Pros:** very good value; family-friendly atmosphere. **Cons:** owner can be a bit brusque; no kids in deluxe rooms. $ *Rooms from: $87* ⊠ *Mt. Canann Promenade, off HaGdud Hashlishi St.* ☏ *04/697–1007* ⊕ *www.safedinn.com* ⇥ *20 rooms* ⦿ *No meals.*

NIGHTLIFE AND THE ARTS

Klezmer Festival. Every July or August, Tzfat hosts the Klezmer Festival, and there could be no better setting for three days of "Jewish soul music" than this mystical, cobbled-lane city. Many events are street performances and therefore free. Tzfat practically bursts at the seams at this time, with revelers both religious and secular. ☏ *04/692–7484* ⊕ *www.klezmerf.com.*

SPORTS AND THE OUTDOORS

FAMILY **Bat Ya'ar Ranch.** In the Birya Forest, 5 km (3 miles) from Tzfat, the Bat Ya'ar Ranch offers outdoor fun for the whole family including pony rides, rope bridges between trees, and outdoor bowling with wooden lanes and balls. Horseback riding is NIS 130 for kids 10 and under. ☏ *04/692–1788* ⊕ *www.batyaar.co.il.*

SHOPPING

Daniel Flatauer. Creative stoneware, porcelain, and ceramics can be found in Daniel Flatauer's studio and shop. His salt-fire glazes are especially worth noting. The artist, who came to Tzfat from England, is welcoming and helpful. ⊠ *63 Yud Alef St., Artists' Colony, Tzfat* ☏ *04/697–5970* .

Safed Candles. This place has grown from a one-room workshop to a huge space filled with the pleasant aroma of beeswax and the bright colors of hand-decorated Sabbath, Havdalah, and Hanukkah candles. ⊠ *42 HaAri St.* ☎ *04/692–1093.*

Sheva Haya. Colorado-born Sheva Haya's blown-glass sculptures and vibrant watercolors are meant to evoke the beauty of the Jewish people and land. The artist offers demonstrations of her work and explains how it relates to Kabbalah, but you can also just poke around her studio. ⊠ *7 Tet Vav St.* ☎ *050/430–5107* ⊙ *Sun.–Thurs. 9–6, Fri. 9–2.*

MT. MERON

21 km (13 miles) west of Tzfat on Route 89.

GETTING HERE AND AROUND
From Tzfat, take Route 89 west, following signs to "Tomb of Rashbi," which is an abbreviation for the Tomb of Rabbi Shimon Bar Yochai. A security guard will check the trunk of your car before you ascend to the parking lot.

EXPLORING
Mt. Meron. The spiritual importance of Tzfat extends beyond the city limits to Mt. Meron, a pilgrimage site both for ultra-Orthodox Jews and for nature lovers. Meron has for centuries drawn thousands upon thousands of Orthodox Jews to pay homage to the great rabbis of the Roman era who are buried at the eastern foot of the mount. The most important site on Mt. Meron—and one of the holiest places in Israel—is the **Tomb of Rabbi Shimon Bar Yochai,** survivor of the Bar Kochba Revolt of almost 2,000 years ago. The simple building that houses the tomb is a place for quiet reflection and prayer, though you may encounter a bar mitzvah or other festive event in the courtyard outside. Women and men have separate prayer areas, and all are expected to dress modestly (coverups are available for those who don't have them).

Bar Yochai is said to have fled from the Romans with his son Elazar after the fall of Jerusalem to a cave at Peki'in, not far from here, where he remained for 13 years. The faithful, beginning with the 16th-century mystics who settled in Tzfat, believe that from his cave-hideout Bar Yochai penned the *Zohar* (*The Book of Splendor*), his commentary on the first five books of the Hebrew Bible. Others claim that the Zohar dates from 13th-century Spain. Nevertheless, the constant flow of visitors is evidence of the pilgrims' devotion to the great rabbi and rebel.

The pilgrimage is still celebrated en masse on Lag Ba'Omer, the festive 33rd day of the seven solemn weeks that begin with Passover and end with *Shavuot* (Pentecost). At this time Mt. Meron comes alive as a grand procession arrives on foot from Tzfat, carrying Torah scrolls and singing fervently. Bonfires are lighted, with celebrations lasting days. Many ultra-Orthodox Jews still uphold the tradition of bringing their three-year-old sons here on Lag Ba'Omer for their first haircuts. ▓TIP➔ Signs point to the Tomb of Rashbi, which is the Hebrew acronym of the rabbi's name. ⊠ *Off Rte. 89.*

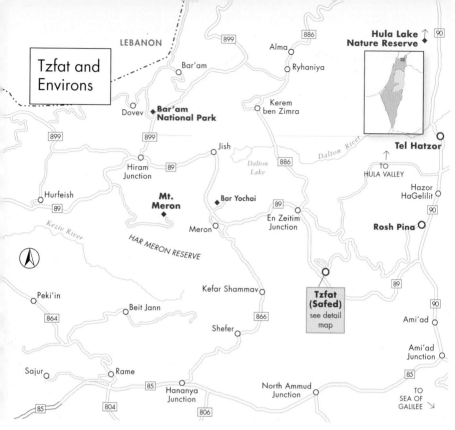

WHERE TO EAT

$$
VEGETARIAN

✕ **Dalia's.** The cheerful chef at this restaurant, the oldest dining establishment in Moshav Amirim, is a former nutritionist, so you know everything on the menu is wholesome as well as toothsome. The set menu includes, among other items, almond and peanut patties in onion sauce and tomatoes stuffed with wheat and barley, as well as a beautiful array of salads and soups. Dessert, consisting of yogurt with fresh fruit, is served with a big helping of fresh air and scenery. It's a bit hard to find, so call for directions. $ *Average main: NIS 50* ⊠ *Moshav Amirim, main road into the village* ☎ *04/698–9349* ⌚ *Reservations essential.*

WHERE TO STAY

$$$
B&B/INN

 Hase'uda Ha'aharona. This lodging's peculiar choice of name (it means "The Last Supper") shouldn't stop you from enjoying its magnificent views of the Golan Heights, the Sea of Galilee, and the Galilee mountains. **Pros:** pretty pool; cozy atmosphere; tasty food. **Cons:** not much for nonvegetarians; need a car to get around. $ *Rooms from: $300* ⊠ *Moshav Amirim, main road into the village* ☎ *04/698–9788* ⊕ *www. haseudah-haacharonah.com* ⤴ *7 rooms* ⦿ *Breakfast.*

SPORTS AND THE OUTDOORS

Eretz Hagalil Jeeps. Yoram Zarchi takes off-road aficionados on two-hour excursions through the Galilee and the Golan, taking in sites of natural beauty and historical significance along the way. Trips cost NIS 650 to NIS 750 per vehicle. ⊠ *Moshav Amirim, Amirim* ☎ *04/698–0434, 050/531–6140* ⊕ *www.eretz-hagalil.co.il.*

Malkiya Stables. This kibbutz offers spectacular mountain views on its rides. Ask about trail rides of one to four hours for ages seven and up. Rides are NIS 125 per hour. The stables are about 29 km (18 miles) north of Khiram Junction. ⊠ *Rte. 899, Kibbutz Malkiya* ☎ *052/281–6293.*

BAR'AM NATIONAL PARK

15 km (9 miles) northwest of Meron, 22 km (14 miles) northwest of Tzfat.

GETTING HERE AND AROUND

From Tzfat, head west on Route 89, then north on Route 899. After 2 km (1 mile), turn right onto a dirt road. There's no bus service to Bar'am.

EXPLORING

Bar'am National Park. In an otherwise deserted spot lie the ruins of Bar'am, one of the best-preserved ancient synagogues anywhere. Like most other synagogues uncovered in this area, this structure dating from the 3rd century faces south, toward Jerusalem; unlike any other, however, this one has lavish architectural elements, such as an entrance with a segmental pediment and freestanding giant columns in front. The interior, which resembles that of other Galilean synagogues of the Talmudic period (3rd to 8th centuries AD), is less well preserved. Rows of pillars in the prayer hall apparently served as supports for the ceiling, and the building may have had a second story. Allow at least an hour to wander around or bring a picnic; tables are available. ⊠ *Off Rte. 899, 3 km (2 miles) east of Khiram Junction, Tzivon* ☎ *04/698–9301* ⊕ *www.parks.org.il* ☑ *NIS 15* ⊗ *Apr.–Sept. Mon.–Thurs. 8–5, Fri. 8–3; Oct.–Mar. Mon.–Thurs. 8–4, Fri. 8–3.*

ROSH PINA

Fodor's Choice
★
10 km (6 miles) east of Tzfat, 25 km (15½ miles) north of Tiberias.

The restored village of Rosh Pina is a gift-shop-and-gallery-browser's delight, and the dilapidated wooden doors and stonework of some still-abandoned premises are part of the charm.

Rosh Pina—literally "cornerstone"—gets its name from Psalm 118:22: "The stone that the builders rejected has become the chief cornerstone." This verse inspired the Galilee's first Zionist pioneers, who came from Romania in 1882, determined to build a village in the malaria-infested area. They bought this land, at the foot of the mountain ridge east of Tzfat, from the neighboring Arab villagers of Ja'uni.

The pioneers, who had little experience in agriculture, struggled to survive until Jewish philanthropist Edmund de Rothschild bought the land. He provided them with tools, workers, and a new industry: the

7

production of silk by silkworms. By the turn of the 20th century, Rosh Pina had grown into the country's fourth-largest Jewish farming community. Today it's a vacation destination and a year-round residence for 2,500 people.

GETTING HERE AND AROUND

From Tel Aviv, you can fly into the small airport of Mahanayim, near Rosh Pina. There are also daily buses from Tzfat, Tiberias, and Haifa. If you're driving from Tzfat, head east on Route 89, then north on Route 90.

ESSENTIALS

Taxi Contacts Meir Taxi ☎ *04/693–5735.*

EXPLORING

HaBaron Garden. Unveiled in 1886, this public park was created at the request of philanthropist Edmund de Rothschild. Olive and almond trees and fragrant herbs like rosemary are planted in terraces on the hillside so that you can enjoy shade and a tree-framed view of the valley below. ✉ *HaChalutzim St.*

Old Rosh Pina Office. The office occupies the house that belonged to Professor Gideon Mer, a leading expert on malaria in the 1930s. Legend has it that Mer used to inject his wife and children with experimental remedies in his efforts to combat malaria in this region. (Happily, all survived.) The British were so impressed with Mer's work that they sent him to Burma to fight malaria epidemics there. Implements and household items from the early days of Rosh Pina are on display. Next door, a colorful audiovisual presentation showcases the founding of this pioneering community. ✉ *HaChalutzim St.* ☎ *04/693–6603* 🎫 *NIS 15* ⏲ *Sun.–Thurs. 8:30–5, Fri. and Sat. 8:30–1.*

Schwartz Hotel. Built in 1890, the two-story hotel was the first guesthouse in the Galilee. Today it's a mere shadow of the original, but try to imagine what it was like to check in here after a long, tiring journey and enjoy the tranquil view of the Sea of Galilee and white-capped Mt. Hermon. ✉ *HaElyon St.*

Synagogue. The old synagogue's interior remains pretty much as it was when it was built in the mid-1880s. The dark pews, made of the timber brought from Romania, have aged gracefully. The painted ceiling has depictions of palm trees and biblical motifs. The building is usually locked, but ask around and you might find someone to open it for you. ✉ *HaElyon St.*

WHERE TO EAT

$$$$ CONTEMPORARY Fodor's Choice ★

🍴 **Auberge Shulamit.** This charming inn takes its name from the original Hotel Shulamit, where the 1948 Armistice Treaty was signed. Among the menu's delectables—along with the home-smoked meats—are seasonal chestnut soup, shrimp with wild rice, and an elegant array of desserts. If you can't bear to leave, the inn has three French country-style guest rooms. [$] *Average main: NIS 160* ✉ *34 David Shub St.* ☎ *04/693–1485* 🌐 *www.shulamit.co.il* ✍ *Reservations essential.*

$$$$ ARGENTINE

🍴 **Babayit Shel Rafa.** The sizzling steaks of his native Argentina figure prominently on Rafa's menu. The best starters are the pickled tongue and the meat or corn empanadas. Entrées include roast beef and a sausage and lamb casserole with rice and green beans. Vegetarians

Visit Rosh Pina for its charming streets, shops, and galleries.

shouldn't despair, as the rich vegetable, mozzarella, prune, and almond stew is delicious. Business lunches, served daily from noon to 5 pm, are tasty and economical at NIS 90 to NIS 110. $ *Average main: NIS 120* ⊠ *HaChalutzim St., next to the Old Rosh Pina Office* ☎ 04/693–6192 ⚭ *Reservations essential.*

$$
ISRAELI
✕ **Chocolata.** The original arched stone basement of the old synagogue is the setting of this romantic restaurant. In addition to the usual fresh salads, pastas, and sandwiches, there are unusual dishes like artichokes filled with cheese. True to its name, the kitchen serves a host of chocolate delights, including 37 different kinds of pralines made by the house chocolatier. $ *Average main: NIS 60* ⊠ *Ha'elyon St., lower entrance to the Synagogue* ☎ 04/686–0219 ⚭ *Reservations essential.*

$$$
ECLECTIC
✕ **Ja'uni.** Named after the Palestinian village that stood on this spot until 1948, this hippie-chic bistro serves salads, pasta, fish, and meat dishes with Italian flair. While the dishes aren't the most sophisticated, the atmosphere defines the relaxed, casual vibe of Rosh Pina. During the day, this is a perfect spot for a coffee break or a light lunch. The outdoor seating is pleasant, especially when there's live music on summer evenings. $ *Average main: NIS 80* ⊠ *30 David Shub St.* ☎ 04/693–1881.

$$$$
STEAKHOUSE
Fodor's Choice
★
✕ **Meat-balim.** Go easy on the appetizers here, as you'll want to save room for this sleek, modern kosher eatery's savory meat dishes. Those in the know recommend the generous veal entrecote and the lamb chops in a flavorful sauce of caramel, oranges, mint, and ginger. Avoid the creamy desserts, which don't contain real dairy. The extensive wine list is a pleasure, however. $ *Average main: NIS 130* ⊠ *Hagalil St.* ☎ 04/686–0107 ⊗ *Apr.–Sept., no dinner Fri., no lunch Sat.; Oct.–Mar., closed Fri. and Sat.*

WHERE TO STAY

Rosh Pina is a budding center of tourism for this region, and many residents are now opening their homes as bed-and-breakfasts.

$$$ B&B/INN Fodor's Choice ★ 🏨 **Ahuzat Hameiri.** This stunning mansion has been in the Hameiri family since it was built in the late 1880s. **Pros:** breathtaking views; nice grounds; family-friendly atmosphere. **Cons:** no pool; many steps to rooms. [$] *Rooms from: $325* ✉ *1 HaChalutzim St.* ☎ *04/6938707* 🌐 *www.hrp.co.il* 🛏 *9 rooms* 🍴 *Breakfast.*

$$$$ HOTEL 🏨 **Mizpe Hayamim.** With a splendid view of the Sea of Galilee, this hotel specializes in pampering its clients. **Pros:** great food; enchanting walking paths; pretty pool. **Cons:** need a car to get around; not a place for families. [$] *Rooms from: $580* ✉ *Off Rte. 8900* ☎ *04/699–4555* 🌐 *www.mizpe-hayamim.com* 🛏 *100 rooms* 🍴 *Some meals.*

$$ HOTEL 🏨 **Pina Barosh.** With its stained glass windows, handsome wooden furniture, and handwoven rugs, you'd never guess that this charming boutique hotel used to house livestock. **Pros:** romantic restaurant; relaxing atmosphere. **Cons:** no view from rooms; not for families. [$] *Rooms from: $210* ✉ *8 HaChalotzim St.* ☎ *04/693–6582* 🛏 *7 rooms* 🍴 *Breakfast.*

$$ B&B/INN FAMILY 🏨 **Villa Tehila.** Amichai and Tehila Yisraeli bought what was a run-down 19th-century farm in Rosh Pina and started converting the stables, storehouse, and dairy into a charming guesthouse. **Pros:** child-friendly vibe; friendly owners; pool open year-round. **Cons:** some rooms very small; courtyard dimly lit at night. [$] *Rooms from: $220* ✉ *7 HaChalutzim St.* ☎ *04/693–7788* 🌐 *www.villa-tehila.co.il* 🛏 *11 rooms* 🍴 *Breakfast.*

NIGHTLIFE AND THE ARTS

Pina Barosh Wine Bar. A must for wine lovers, this pleasant spot isn't only a good place to sample local varietals, but also a great source of information, if you're interested in learning more about the local wine industry. The staff can connect you with specialized tour guides, and flyers advertise seasonal events. The bar stocks local wines from both well-known and up-and-coming vineyards, all at reasonable prices. ✉ *8 HaChalutzim St.* ☎ *04/693–6582* .

SHOPPING

The Well. Sigal Eshet-Shafat and her husband Inbar used to sell typical handicrafts, but it turned out that their jams, dressings, and liqueurs were what attracted customers. The on-site coffee shop lets you sample the store's delights and sign up for the occasional cooking class. The onion jam is a favorite for both dairy and meat dishes. ✉ *HaElyon St.* ☎ *04/693–0020* 🕒 *Sun.–Thurs. 10:30–1, Fri. 10:30–3.*

TEL HATZOR

8 km (5 miles) north of Rosh Pina, 14 km (9 miles) east of Tzfat.

GETTING HERE AND AROUND

From Tzfat, head east on Route 89, then north on Route 90.

EXPLORING

Tel Hatzor. This site is a good stop for archaeology buffs—its massive mound is made up of the remnants of 21 cities. The excavation and restoration of some of these antiquities have produced fascinating results. On the Via Maris—the major trade route linking Egypt and Mesopotamia—Hatzor is referred to several times in documents from ancient archives in both lands, and scholars believe a huge archive may someday be found here. The book of Joshua (11:13) notes that Joshua destroyed Canaanite Hatzor in the 13th century BC, and Israelites resettled it. Its next heyday came three centuries later, when King Solomon decided it would serve him well as a regional military and administrative center, like Megiddo and Gezer. In 732 BC, Hatzor met its end when invading Assyrian king Tiglath Pileser III conquered the Galilee and forced its Israelite inhabitants off the land in chains and into exile.

The huge site is divided into two areas: the **Upper City,** which comprised the most ancient settlements, and the **Lower City,** first settled in the 18th century BC. Only the Upper City, covering less than a fifth of the total excavation site, is open to the public. The **Hatzor Museum** (on the grounds of Kibbutz Ayelet Hashachar, across the highway) houses figurines, weapons, stone pots, and other artifacts unearthed in the two areas; others are at the Israel Museum in Jerusalem. It's open by appointment. ⊠ *Tel Hatzor National Park, Rte. 90* ☎ *04/693–7290* 🔁 *NIS 18* ☉ *Apr.–Sept., Sat.–Thurs. 8–5, Fri. 8–4; Oct.–Mar., Sat.–Thurs. 8–4, Fri. 8–3.*

7

HULA LAKE NATURE RESERVE

14 km (8½ miles) north of Tel Hatzor, 35 km (22 miles) northeast of Tzfat.

GETTING HERE AND AROUND

From Tzfat, head east on Route 89 and north on Route 90.

EXPLORING

Hula Lake Nature Reserve. More than 390 avian species flock to the Hula Lake during the migration season, which makes this nature preserve a prime spot for bird-watching. These wetlands were drained during the 1950s after a malaria outbreak, which drove away the unique wildlife. In recent years, the lake was reflooded and birds, especially cranes, once again make it their winter homes. About a half-million birds pass through each year. The park offers an 8.5-km (5.2-mile) trail with bird-watching huts along the way. Bicycles and golf carts are available for rent. ⊠ *Off Rte. 90, Kiryat Shmona* ☎ *04/681–7137* ⊕ *www.agamon-hula.co.il* 🔁 *NIS 4* ☉ *Sun.–Thurs. 9–6, Fri. and Sat. 6:30–6.*

NEED A BREAK?

Ahuzat Dubrovin. For a rest stop with a bit of history, try Ahuzat Dubrovin, near the entrance to the Hula Lake Nature Reserve. The Dubrovin family, Russian immigrants who moved here in 1909, once owned this reconstructed farmhouse. The property was donated to the Jewish National Fund and opened to the public in 1986. An exhibit in the former family home highlights the old days of the Hula Valley, and a short video provides context. A pleasant garden surrounds the property. ⊠ *East of Rte. 90, Yesod Hama'ala* ☎ *04/693–7371* ⧄ *NIS 10* ⊙ *Mon.–Thurs. 10:30–4, Fri. 10:30–2.*

UPPER HULA VALLEY

The sights that hug the border with Lebanon show contrasting sides of Israel. The bustling town of Kiryat Shmona and sleepy Metulla bear eloquent witness to the varying fortunes of Israel's relationships with its Arab neighbors. Tel Dan Nature Reserve, on the other hand, draws visitors with its antiquities, surging river, and lush, wild beauty.

KIRYAT SHMONA

55 km (34 miles) north of Tiberias, 42 km (26 miles) north of Tzfat.

The major urban center in the Upper Hula Valley, Kiryat Shmona is known for the cable car up Manara Cliff. For years, the instability in neighboring Lebanon profoundly affected life in the town, and by 1982 the spate of terrorist attacks had reached such proportions that Israel responded by invading Lebanon, the first stage of what would become the First Lebanon War. Kiryat Shmona was again in the news in 1996 when Hezbollah terrorists launched a focused and continued rocket attack on the town. The Israel Defense Forces responded by targeting Hezbollah's bases in southern Lebanon in a campaign that became known as the Grapes of Wrath. In 2006, Hezbollah again lobbed rockets into northern Israel, sparking the Second Lebanon War.

GETTING HERE AND AROUND

From Tzfat, head east on Route 89, then north on Route 90. There are at least 20 buses daily from Tel Aviv, at least 19 from Haifa, and 3 from Jerusalem.

ESSENTIALS

Taxi Contacts **Hatzafon Taxi** ☎ *04/694–2333.*

EXPLORING

FAMILY **Manara Cliff.** The Kiryat Shmona–Kibbutz Manara cable car at Manara Cliff gives you a bird's-eye view of the Hula Valley. It has one station midway on the 1,890-yard trip, where the adventurous can step out and do some rappelling and dry sliding (a roller-coaster-like activity) or try the climbing wall. Another option is to ride a mountain bike down or experience a 600-foot zip line. If you opt to remain in the cable car, the trip takes eight minutes each way, overlooking cliffs and green hills. At the bottom are a trampoline and other attractions for kids.

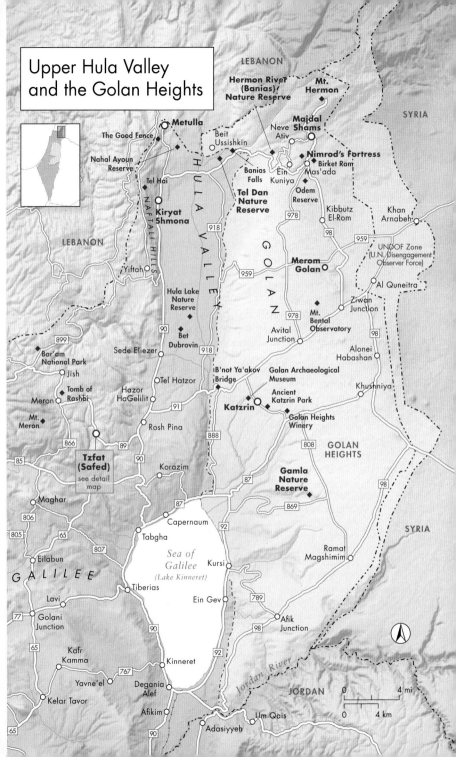

There's wheelchair access to the cable car and upper station. ✉ *Kibbutz Manara, Rte. 90* ☎ *04/690–5830* 🎟 *NIS 59 weekdays; NIS 69 weekends* ⏲ *Mar.–Jul. and Sept.–Oct., daily 9:30–5; Aug., daily 9:30–7; Nov.–Feb., daily 11–4. Last cable car leaves 30 mins before closing.*

Tel Hai. Perched on the northern edge of Kiryat Shmona is Tel Hai, meaning "hill of life," which played an important role in Israel's history. In the aftermath of World War I, while Britain and France bickered over control of the upper Hula Valley, bands of Arabs often harassed the Jewish farms, and finally overran Tel Hai in 1920. Only Kibbutz Kfar Giladi was successful in defending itself. Following this incident, Tel Hai resident Josef Trumpeldor and seven comrades were called on to protect the place. Trumpeldor already had a reputation as a leader in the czar's army in his native Russia. Fired by Zionist ideals, he'd moved to Palestine in 1912 at the age of 32. During the final battle in 1920, Trumpeldor and his comrades were killed and it's for them that Kiryat Shmona—City of the Eight—is named. It's said that Trumpeldor's last words were: "It is good to die for our country." He is buried up the road from the museum, beneath the statue of a lion.

The heroic last stand at Tel Hai was important not only because it was the first modern instance of Jewish armed self-defense, but also because the survival of at least two of the Jewish settlements meant that when the final borders were drawn by the League of Nations in 1922, these settlements were included in the British-mandated territory of Palestine and thus, after 1948, in the State of Israel. ✉ *Off Rte. 90.*

Tel Hai Courtyard Museum. The Tel Hai Courtyard Museum displays agricultural tools used in Trumpeldor's time. A moving audiovisual show highlights the history of the place. Call ahead for reservations. ✉ *Off Rte. 886* ☎ *04/695–1333* ⏲ *Tours on Fri. at 11, noon, and 1.*

WHERE TO EAT

$$ BURGER 🍴 **Arburger.** Unlike many local eateries, this western-inspired burger joint is open on weekends. Arburger offers 12-ounce burgers, steaks, and seafood, as well as some vegetarian options. The cozy interior offers a nice break after a long drive or hike, and the menu is varied enough to suit most tastes. [$] *Average main: NIS 55* ✉ *Gome Junction, off Rte. 90, behind the gas station* ☎ *057/ 944–3587.*

$$$ SEAFOOD 🍴 **Dag al Hadan.** Fresh trout and a glass of wine, in a shady copse by the gurgling Dan River—it's as good as it sounds, which is why Dag al Hadan draws crowds on weekends. This was the first restaurant in the region to specialize in the fish the Dan yields in abundance; you can see the trout ponds in a small installation on the grounds. The same management also runs a café next door serving light, tasty vegetarian fare. The restaurant, opposite Kibbutz Hagoshrim, is tucked away behind the main road, but it's large and well signposted. [$] *Average main: NIS 100* ✉ *Beit Hillel, off Rte. 99* ☎ *04/695–0225* ✍ *Reservations essential.*

$$ ECLECTIC 🍴 **Focaccia Bar.** This family restaurant serves a good selection of pastas and pizzas, as well as meat dishes with a Middle Eastern touch. It sits opposite Kibbutz Ma'ayan Baruch. Reservations are recommended on weekends. [$] *Average main: NIS 75* ✉ *Gan Hatzfon, off Rte. 99* ☎ *04/690–4474.*

In the Upper Hula Valley, you'll find the Tel Dan Nature Reserve and the Hermon River (Banais) Nature Reserve.

WHERE TO STAY

$$$ HOTEL **Hagoshrim Kibbutz Hotel.** The waters of the Hermon River flow right through Hagoshrim—under a glass-topped channel set in the ceramic tile of the lobby and then through the property. **Pros:** wide selection of activities; nice common areas; good selection of tours. **Cons:** basic decor; can get loud in summer. [$] *Rooms from: $309* ✉ *Rte. 99* ☎ *04/681–6000* 🌐 *www.hagoshrim-hotel.co.il* 🛏 *164 rooms* 🍴 *Breakfast.*

$$ HOTEL **Kibbutz Hotel Kfar Giladi.** Atop a hill behind Tel Hai is one of the country's oldest and largest kibbutz hotels. **Pros:** good value; lovely indoor and outdoor swimming pools; good place for souvenirs. **Cons:** basic decor; uninspired food. [$] *Rooms from: $250* ✉ *Rte. 90* ☎ *04/690–0000* 🌐 *www.kfar-giladi.co.il* 🛏 *170 rooms* 🍴 *Breakfast.*

$ HOTEL FAMILY **Pastoral Kfar Blum Hotel.** Part of Kibbutz Kfar Blum, this deluxe hotel in the northern Hula Valley has spacious and elegantly appointed rooms. **Pros:** excellent amenities; lovely spa; variety of programs for children. **Cons:** rooms are spread around property, so check location. [$] *Rooms from: $154* ✉ *Off Rte. 90, Kfar Blum* ☎ *04/683–6611* 🌐 *www.kfarblum-hotel.co.il* 🛏 *120 rooms* 🍴 *Breakfast.*

THE ARTS

Chamber Music Days. For the classically minded, the Upper Galilee Regional Council hosts Chamber Music Days each year in late July and early August, a nationally renowned festival of chamber music in a pastoral setting. ✉ *Kibbutz Kfar Blum, off Rte. 90* ☎ *04/681–6640.*

SPORTS AND THE OUTDOORS

A plethora of outfits organize water-sports trips in this region, and almost all hotels can make reservations for you. The minimum age for kayaks and other water "vehicles" is usually six.

KAYAKING

Hagoshrim Kayaks. Hagoshrim Kayaks has a 5-km (3-mile) family course that takes about 90 minutes and a 6-km (4-mile) "stormy" course that lasts almost two hours. The family course costs NIS 89 per person, the stormy course NIS 109 per person. ✉ *Kibbutz Hagoshrim, off Rte. 99* ☎ *077/271–7500* 🌐 *www.kayak.co.il.*

OFF-ROAD VEHICLES

Easy Track. Based in the northern Hula Valley, Easy Track offers wind-in-your-hair ways to explore the countryside, including self-drive dune buggies and 1½-hour guided Jeep trips. ✉ *Moshav She'ar Yashuv, near Rte. 99* ☎ *04/690–4440* 🌐 *www.mbez.co.il.*

METULLA

9 km (6 miles) north of Kiryat Shmona, 50 km (31 miles) north of Tzfat.

Israel's northernmost town, Metulla, is so picturesque that it's hard to believe this tranquil spot is just a stone's throw from a contentious border. The tensions of the Middle East dissipate here in the charm of the European-style limestone buildings that line Metulla's quaint main street, and the city itself seems to have changed little since its founding as a farming settlement in 1896. The signs offering *zimmer* (German for "room") for rent enhance the Continental atmosphere. Even the weather is un-Mediterranean, with refreshingly cool mountain breezes carrying whiffs of cypress and spice plants in summer, and snow in winter.

GETTING HERE AND AROUND

From Tzfat, head east on Route 89, then north on Route 90.

EXPLORING

Nahal Ayoun Nature Reserve. In summer, the stream that gives this nature reserve its name slows to a trickle because the water is channeled away to irrigate crops. In winter, though, the water gushes, becoming a beautiful backdrop for hiking trips. Two trails meander through the reserve; the shorter one, taking about half an hour, begins and ends in the lower parking lot and goes to Oven Falls, the most famous of the reserve's four waterfalls. The longer one, taking 1½ hours, begins in the upper parking lot and leads downstream. ✉ *East of Rte. 90* ☎ *04/695–1519* 🎫 *NIS 29* 🕒 *Apr.–Sept., Sat.–Thurs. 8–5, Fri. 8–3; Oct.–Mar., Sat.–Thurs 8–4, Fri. 8–3.*

WHERE TO EAT

$$$$ STEAKHOUSE

🍴 **HaTachana.** This ranch-style steak house, whose name means "The Mill," uses only meat from local cattle, so you're assured of the finest T-bones, as well as tasty sausages, lamb chops, and hamburgers. Each entrée comes with grilled vegetables and either fries or a baked potato, so you won't go away hungry. The place gets crowded, so reservations are a good idea. [$] *Average main: NIS 140* ✉ *1 Harishonim St.* ☎ *04/694–4810* 🌐 *www.ha-tachana.co.il.*

SPORTS AND THE OUTDOORS

FAMILY **Canada Centre.** The multistory Canada Centre has just about everything a sports complex can offer. You can spend the whole day here, playing basketball, ice-skating, swimming, or taking aim on the shooting range. ⌧ *1 Harishonim St.* ☎ *04/695–0370* ⊕ *www.canada-centre.co.il* ☾ *Closed Sun.*

TEL DAN NATURE RESERVE

15 km (9½ miles) southeast of Metulla, 10 km (6 miles) northeast of Kiryat Shmona, 50 km (31 miles) northeast of Tzfat.

GETTING HERE AND AROUND

From Tzfat, head east on Route 89, then turn north on Route 90. Once you pass Kiryat Shmona, turn east on Route 99. The reserve is near Kibbutz Dan.

EXPLORING

FAMILY **Beit Ussishkin Museum.** Adjacent to the Tel Dan Nature Reserve, the Beit Ussishkin Museum has interesting exhibits about the flora, fauna, and geology of the Hula Valley, the Golan Heights, and the Jordan River. The audiovisual presentations are concise and informative. ⌧ *Kibbutz Dan, off Rte. 99* ☎ *04/694–1704* ✉ *NIS 18* ☾ *Sun.–Thurs. 8–4, Fri. and Jewish holiday eves 8–2, Sat. 10–3.*

Fodor'sChoice **Tel Dan Nature Reserve.** This wildlife sanctuary is hard to beat for sheer
★ natural beauty. A river surges through it, and luxuriant trees provide shade. A host of small mammals lives here—many partial to water, such as the otter and the mongoose—as well as the biblical coney, also known as the hyrax. This is home to Israel's largest rodent, the nocturnal Indian crested porcupine, and its smallest predator, the marbled polecat. The reserve has several hiking trails; a short segment, on a raised wooden walkway, is wheelchair accessible.

Dan was a majestic city in biblical times. According to Genesis, Abraham came here to rescue his nephew Lot and, five centuries later, Joshua led the Israelites through the area to victory. Fine ruins from several epochs lie here. Among them are the 9th-century-BC city gate and the cultic site where King Jeroboam set up a golden calf to rival the Jerusalem Temple. Just inside the city gate is the platform for a throne, where the city's king pronounced judgment. One of the site's most extraordinary finds is an arched gateway dating from the 18th-century BC Canaanite period, more than a millennium earlier than scholars had previously thought. ⌧ *North of Rte. 99, near Kibbutz Dan* ☎ *04/695–1579* ✉ *NIS 29* ☾ *Apr.–Sept., Sat.–Thurs. 8–5, Fri. 8–3; Oct.–Mar., Sat.–Thurs. 8–4, Fri. 8–3; last entrance 1 hr before closing.*

WHERE TO STAY

$$ 🏠 **Pausa-Gourmet Galilee Inn.** Leaders in Israel's Slow Food movement
B&B/INN own this beautiful boutique hotel, and their minimalist taste is reflected in the lovely and warm setting. **Pros:** unforgettable meals; lovely decor; outdoor hot tub. **Cons:** remote location; small rooms; no pool. $ *Rooms from: $205* ⌧ *Moshav She'ar Yashuv, Rte. 99* ☎ *054/690–4434* ⊕ *www. pausa-inn.co.il* ⤵ *8 rooms* ⦿ *Breakfast.*

7

THE GOLAN HEIGHTS

Considered the most fertile land in Israel, the Golan Heights is known for its many fine wineries. As you drive through these verdant hills, covered with wildflowers in the spring, you'll also see abundant olive groves and apple and cherry orchards. Fruit picking is a popular tourist activity: cherries from mid-May through June and figs in August and September. You can explore the area by joining a guided tour, perhaps galloping away on a horse or zipping by in a four-wheel-drive vehicle.

The region was once volcanic, and many symmetrical volcanic cones and pronounced reliefs dominate the landscape, particularly in the Upper Golan. The gentle terrain and climate of the rest of the region have historically attracted far more settlement than the less hospitable northern Upper Galilee. Today it's home to Jewish, Druze, and Alawite communities.

HERMON RIVER (BANIAS) NATURE RESERVE

20 km (12½ miles) east of Kiryat Shmona, 50 km (31 miles) northeast of Tzfat.

GETTING HERE AND AROUND

From Tzfat, head east on Route 89, then turn north on Route 90. Once you pass Kiryat Shmona, go east on Route 99.

EXPLORING

Fodor's Choice ★ **Hermon River (Banias) Nature Reserve.** One of the most stunning parts of Israel, this reserve contains gushing waterfalls, dense foliage along riverbanks, and the remains of a temple dedicated to the god Pan. There are two entrances, each with a parking lot: the sign for the first reads "Banias Waterfall"; the other is 1 km (½ mile) farther along the same road and is marked "Banias."

The **Banias Spring** emerges at the foot of mostly limestone Mt. Hermon, just where it meets the basalt layers of the Golan Heights. The most popular short route in the reserve is up to the **Banias Cave,** via the path that crosses the spring. Excavations have revealed the five niches hewed out of the rock to the right of the cave; these are what remain of Hellenistic and Roman temples, depicted in interesting artist renderings. Three of the niches bear inscriptions in Greek, mentioning Pan, the lover of tunes, Echo, the mountain nymph, and Galerius, one of Pan's priests. All early references to the cave identify it as the source of the spring, but earthquakes over the years have changed the landscape, and the water now emerges at the foot of the cave rather than from within it.

The reserve offers three interconnected hiking trails—ask for the English-language trail map and advice at the cashier's booth. One, which passes a Crusader gate, walls, and moat, takes about 45 minutes. The second, also about 45 minutes, explores the magnificent 1,613-square-foot palace complex dating to the reign of Herod's grandson, Agrippa II, on top of which are the ruins of what's thought to have been the

The City of Pan

The name *Banias* is an Arabic corruption of the Greek *Panias* (Arabic has no *p*), the original name given to the area that, in the early 4th century BC, was dedicated to the colorful Greek god Pan, the half-goat, half-human deity of herdsmen, music, and wild nature—and of homosexuals and nymphs. The Banias Reserve encompasses the ruins of this ancient city.

Herod the Great ruled the city in the 1st century AD; his son Philip inherited it and changed the city's name to Caesarea Philippi, to distinguish it from the Caesarea his father had founded on the Mediterranean coast. The city continued to flourish until after the Muslim conquest in the 7th century AD, when it declined

into little more than a village. In the 10th century AD, Muslim immigration brought renewed settlement and Jews also came to Banias (as it became known sometime during the 7th century).

In the early 12th century, Crusaders held Banias, who saw it as a natural border between their kingdom and the neighboring Muslim realm, whose center was Damascus. The Muslims recaptured Banias in 1132, but the city declined in importance and was taken over by Bedouin chieftains. It became a small village, which it remained until the Israel Defense Forces (IDF) conquered the area in the 1967 Six Days' War.

7

marketplace of the day: a string of single chambers along a well-preserved section of wall might well have been shops. The third is a 90-minute trail leading past the **Officers' Pool,** built by the Syrians, and a water-operated flour mill, to the thundering 33-meter-high **Banias Waterfall.** The trails are spiced with the pungent aroma of mint and figs, and studded with blackberry bushes. If time is short, you may prefer to take a brief walk to the falls, return to your car, then drive on to the second entrance to see the caves and the spring where the Hermon River originates. The cost of admission covers entry to both sites.

If you're ready for a real hiking challenge and can have a car waiting at the other end, a long, very steep trail leads from the parking lot at the Banias Nature Reserve through the oak and thorny broom forest up to Nimrod's Fortress, a 40- to 60-minute climb. ⊠ *Off Rte. 99* ☎ *04/695–0272* ✒ *NIS 27* ⊙ *Apr.–Sept., Sat.–Thurs. 8–5, Fri. 8–4; Oct.–Mar., Sat.–Thurs. 8–4, Fri. 8–3; last entry 1 hr before closing.*

QUICK
BITES

Stall. A few minutes' walk along the trail leading to the Banias Waterfall is the ancient flour mill and a stall where Druze villagers make their traditional pita bread (bigger and flatter than the commercial version), which isn't only baked on the premises but also milled here. Pull up a rock, and for a few shekels you'll be served a large rolled-up pita with *labaneh* (white goat's cheese) and Turkish coffee. ⊠ *Off Rte. 99.*

Golani Lookout. The large number of monuments to fallen soldiers in the Golan is a reminder of the region's strategic importance—and the price paid to secure it. Among the easily accessible sites, where pre-1967 Syrian bunkers give a gunner's-eye view of the valley below, is the Golani Lookout, known in Arabic as Tel Faher, in the northern Golan. Here you can explore the trenches and bunkers that now stand silent. ⊠ *Off Rte. 98.*

NIMROD'S FORTRESS

5 km (3 miles) east of Hermon River (Banias) Nature Reserve, 58 km (36 miles) northeast Tzfat.

GETTING HERE AND AROUND

From Tzfat, head east on Route 89, then turn north on Route 90. Once you pass Kiryat Shmona, go east on Route 99. Once you pass the Hermon River Nature Reserve, turn north on Route 989. The fortress is on the left.

EXPLORING

FAMILY **Nimrod's Fortress.** The dramatic views of this towering, burly fortress, appearing and disappearing behind each curve of the narrow road that leads to it, are part of the treat of a visit to Nimrod's Fortress (Kal'at Namrud). Once you're there, the fortress commands superb vistas, especially through the frames of its arched windows and the narrow archers' slits in its walls. Nimrod's Fortress is a highlight for kids, with a ladder down to a vaulted cistern, a shadowy spiral staircase, and unexpected nooks and crannies. A path leads up to the fortress's central tower, or keep, where the feudal lord would've lived.

In 1218, the Mameluke warlord al-Malik al-Aziz Othman built this fortress to guard the vital route against a Crusader *reconquista* after their 1187 defeat. It changed hands between Muslims and Christians in the succeeding centuries, as both vied for control of the region. ⊠ *Nimrod's Fortress National Park, Rte. 989* ☏ *04/694–9277* ⊡ *NIS 21* ⊙ *Apr.–Sept., daily 8–5; Oct.–Mar., daily 8–4; last entrance 1 hr before closing.*

MT. HERMON

25 km (15½ miles) northeast of Kiryat Shmona, 66 km (41 miles) northeast of Tzfat.

GETTING HERE AND AROUND

From Tzfat, head east on Route 89, then turn north on Route 90. Once you pass Kiryat Shmona, go east on Route 99. At Mahanayim Junction turn east on Route 91, then north on Route 98.

EXPLORING

Mt. Hermon. The summit of Mt. Hermon—famous as Israel's highest mountain, at 9,230 feet above sea level—is actually in Syrian territory. Its lower slopes attract Israelis to the country's only ski resort. Summer is arguably the most interesting time on the Hermon, though: after the winter snows melt, hikers can discover chasms and hidden valleys here, the long-term result of extremes in temperature. A powerful array of

Israel's highest mountain—Mt. Hermon, at 9,230 feet—gets plenty of snow in winter and spring.

colors and scents emerges from the earth as the summer sun draws out cockscomb, chamomile, and scores of other flowers and wild herbs. Approaching from Nimrod's Fortress, you'll pass **Moshav Neve Ativ,** designed to look like a little piece of the Alps in the Middle East, complete with A-frame chalet-style houses, a handful of which have guest rooms. A detour through the old Druze village of **Majdal Shams** offers a number of good eateries.

EN
ROUTE

Ein Kiniya. This Druze village, which appears across a valley on your left as you head east into the Golan on Route 99, is the most picturesque in the area. The houses are built from the black basalt typical of the Golan. ⊠ *Off Rte. 99, Ein Kiniya.*

MAJDAL SHAMS

25 km east of Kiryat Shemona; 35 km north of Katzrin.

Majdal Shams may not look like much, but the Druze town is a hub for skiers in the winter and berry pickers in the fall. It's also a year-round destination for wine lovers because of the local vineyards, and foodies, as Druze cuisine is renowned in the region.

Unlike their counterparts in the Galilee, the Druze of the Golan Heights are not, for the most part, Israeli citizens. They do, however, consider themselves an important part of the country's cultural landscape.

GETTING HERE AND AROUND

From Kiryat Shmona, head east on Route 99, then turn north at Masadeh onto Route 98, which will take you into Majdal Shams. The streets aren't signed, so call ahead for directions to your hotel.

EXPLORING

Bahat Winery. Made using traditional methods, 5,000 bottles of wine are sold each year from the shop at Bahat Winery. The grapes—mostly Cabernet Sauvignon, Pinot Noir, and Chardonnay—are grown in basalt soil 1,000 meters (3,280 feet) above sea level. Their distinctive flavor comes from being aged in French oak barrels. Owner Ofer Bahat is happy to divulge information and offer tastings. ✉ *Kibbutz Ein Zivan, off Rte. 91, Golan Hights* ☎ *050/877–1770* 🕒 *Sun.–Thurs. 9–5, Fri. 9–3.*

De Karina Artisan Gourmet Chocolates. Selling treats for the young and young at heart, De Karina Artisan Gourmet Chocolates was founded by a third-generation chocolatier from Argentina. Try the Mt. Hermon Chocolates—milk chocolate cones topped by white chocolate "snow." Call in advance for factory tours and chocolate-making workshops. ✉ *Kibbutz Ein Zivan, off Rte. 91, Golan Heights* ☎ *04/699–3622* 🌐 *www.de-karina.co.il* 🎫 *Tour NIS 22, workshop NIS 65* 🕒 *Sun.–Thurs. 9–5, Fri. 9–3.*

Odem Mountain Winery. This family-owned boutique winery, located between Majdal Shams and Merom Golan, produces 80,000 bottles a year, mostly dry reds but also a crisp Chardonnay. There are also lovely fortified wines and cherry wines. Drop in for an impromptu tasting; local cheese and ceramic tableware are also for sale. Thirty-minute tours of the vineyards are available by appointment. ✉ *Moshav Odem, off Rte. 978, Odem* ☎ *04/687–1122* 🌐 *www.harodem.co.il* 🎫 *Free* 🕒 *Sun.–Thurs. 10–5, Fri. 10–2.*

WHERE TO EAT AND STAY

$ MIDDLE EASTERN 🍴 **Abu Zaid Candies.** The main street in Majdal Shams is speckled with pita stands where the popular street wrap is served warm and filled with tangy yogurt cheese. For dessert, stop by Abu Zaid, which sells a type of orange-hued pastry called *knafeh*. Similar to baklava, it's delicious here: layers of gooey goat's cheese covered in a flaky crust and peppered with pistachios. The to-go delicacy loses its charm when it cools down, so eat it while it's warm. [$] *Average main: NIS 10* ✉ *Northern end of main street* ☎ *052/698–3190* 💳 *No credit cards.*

$$$$ ECLECTIC 🍴 **The Milkman and the Witch.** Located in Nimrod, a short drive from Majdal Shams, this whimsical restaurant is decorated with smiling witch dolls and boasts a magnificent view of volcanic lakes and cherry fields. The staff is attentive and friendly, and the food is hearty. The chef specializes in casseroles, such as salmon cooked with coconut milk, ginger, and oranges. [$] *Average main: NIS 125* ✉ *Off Rte. 98, Nimrod* ☎ *04/687–0049* 🌐 *www.the-witch.co.il* ✍ *Reservations essential.*

$ B&B/INN 🏨 **Toskana in the Hermon.** Owner Shoky Ayob has channeled the spirit of Italy in his beautiful bed-and-breakfast, which has a castle-like exterior faced with golden-hued Jerusalem stone and an interior bathed in soothing browns, tans, and maroons. **Pros:** lovely accommodations; great views; bargain price. **Cons:** no elevator. [$] *Rooms from: $137* ✉ *Rtes. 98 and 99, Mas'ada* ☎ *050/752–8623* 🌐 *www.toskana.co.il* 🛏 *9 rooms* 🍽 *Breakfast.*

MEROM GOLAN

20 km (12½ miles) south of Mt. Hermon, 46 km (28 miles) northeast of Tzfat.

Kibbutz Merom Golan was the first settlement built in the Golan after the Six Days' War. Its fields and orchards are typical of local kibbutzim. Apples and cherries are especially good in these parts. Another popular attraction is the nearby Mt. Bental Observatory.

GETTING HERE AND AROUND

From Tzfat, head east on Route 89, then north on Route 90. At Mahanayim Junction, turn east on Route 91, then north on Route 98. Merom Golan is on the left.

EXPLORING

Mt. Bental Observatory. From the top of this volcanic cone, once a military outpost, Mt. Hermon rises majestically to the north and the Syrian side of the Golan stretches eastward. Opposite is the ruined town of Kuneitra, captured by Israel in 1967, lost and regained in the 1973 Yom Kippur War, and returned to Syria in the subsequent disengagement agreement—it's now a demilitarized zone. Modern Kuneitra is in the distance. The cluster of white buildings south of old Kuneitra houses the United Nations Disengagement Observer Force. A pine-cabin shop serving delicious herb teas and snacks is the perfect place to get out of the wind that often sweeps this peak. The observatory is near Kibbutz Merom Golan; signs along the rural roads point the way. ⊠ *Off Rte. 98 and Rte. 959.*

WHERE TO EAT

$$$
STEAKHOUSE

✕ **Cowboys' Restaurant.** This is the best corral this side of the Israel-Syria disengagement zone. Saddle-shaped stools at the bar and cattle hides on the walls contribute to the frontier atmosphere. But it's the grub—specifically the hearty steaks and the house specialty, chicken breast stuffed with smoked meat—that packs 'em in. $ *Average main: NIS 90* ⊠ *Kibbutz Merom Golan, off Rte. 959* ☎ *04/696–0206.*

KATZRIN

20 km (12½ miles) south of Merom Golan, 38 km (23½ miles) northeast of Tiberias, 35 km (22 miles) northeast of Tzfat.

Katzrin, founded in 1977 near the site of a 3rd-century town of the same name, has a suburban feel, despite its strategic location and attendant sensitivity. The water here, which comes straight from the basalt bedrock, is delicious and makes your skin feel like silk.

GETTING HERE AND AROUND

From Tzfat, head east on Route 89, then north on Route 90. At Mahanayim Junction turn east on Route 91, then south on Route 9088.

Rolling green hills and rocky terrain surround the ancient ruins of the synagogue at Gamla.

ESSENTIALS

Visitor Information Tourist Information Center—Golan ⊠ Hutzot HaGolan Center, Derech HaHermon ☎ 04/696–2885 ⊕ tour.golan.org.il ⊘ Sun.–Thurs. 9–4.

EXPLORING

FAMILY **Ancient Katzrin Park.** About 2 km (1 mile) east of downtown Katzrin, this park is a partially restored 3rd-century Jewish village. The Katzrin synagogue has decorative architectural details, such as a wreath of pomegranates and amphorae in relief on the lintel above the entrance. The complexity of its ornamentation reflects the importance of the city. Built of basalt, the synagogue was used for 400 years until it was partly destroyed, possibly by an earthquake, in AD 749. Two reconstructed buildings, the so-called House of Uzi and House of Rabbi Abun, are attractively decorated with rope baskets, weavings, baking vessels, and pottery (based on remnants of the originals), and lighted with little clay oil lamps. ⊠ Rte. 87 ☎ 04/696–2412 ⊠ NIS 28, includes Golan Archaeological Museum ⊘ Sun.–Thurs. 9–4, Fri. 9–2, Sat. 10–2.

Golan Archaeological Museum. This museum has a fascinating collection of animal bones, stones, and artifacts that put the region into historical and geographical perspective. Among the exhibits is a Bronze Age dwelling reconstructed from materials excavated nearby. Don't miss the moving film on the last stand at Gamla, the "Masada of the North," during the Great Revolt against Rome in AD 66. The museum reveals how it was rediscovered by archaeologists 1,900 years later. ⊠ Near corner of Shayon and Daliyot Sts. ☎ 04/696–1350 ⊕ www.museum.golan.org.il ⊠ NIS 28, includes Ancient Katzrin Park ⊘ Sun.–Thurs. 9–4, Fri. 9–2.

Golan Heights Winery. This winery caught the world's attention with its award-winning Yarden, Gamla, and Golan labels. The area's volcanic soil, cold winters, and cool summers, together with state-of-the-art winemaking, have proven a recipe for success. The shop sells the full line of wines, including the Katzrin Chardonnay, the Yarden Gewürztraminer, and the Yarden Cabernet Sauvignon, as well as sophisticated accessories for the oenophile. Call in advance about a tour of the winery and a tasting for NIS 20. ✉ *Southern entrance to town* ☎ *04/696–8435* 🌐 *www.golanwines.co.il* 🕒 *Sun.–Thurs. 9–5:30, Fri. 9–2:30.*

WHERE TO EAT

The commercial center of Katzrin, the "capital" of the Golan Heights, has a number of falafel stands, a couple of restaurants, and a pizzeria, making it a perfect midday stop for travelers.

$ ISRAELI 🍴 **Hummus'illa.** Hilla Ben Yosef, the second generation in the family to run this tiny and unassuming eatery, offers fresh hummus and home-style cooking. Dishes arrive with fluffy pitas and crushed garlic—not for the faint of heart. Middle Eastern salads and other local favorites are also on offer. [$] *Average main: NIS 30* ✉ *Off Derech Habermon and Daliyot Sts.* ☎ *04/696–2120* 💳 *No credit cards* 🕒 *Closed Fri. and Sat. No dinner Sun.–Wed.*

GAMLA NATURE RESERVE

20 km (12 miles) southeast of Katzrin.

GETTING HERE AND AROUND

From Tzfat, head east on Route 89, then south on Route 90. Turn east on Route 87, then south on Route 808. Watch for the Gamla signpost.

EXPLORING

Gamla Nature Reserve. Aside from the inspiring history of "the Masada of the North," the beauty of Gamla's rugged terrain, softened in spring by greenery and wildflowers, is truly breathtaking. Griffon vultures soar above, and you can often see gazelles bounding through the grasses. The main story of the camel-shaped Gamla (the name *Gamla* comes from *gamal,* the Hebrew word for "camel") goes back to the year AD 67, when at the beginning of the Great Revolt, Vespasian launched a bloody attack here that ended seven months later, when the 9,000 surviving Jews flung themselves to their deaths in the abyss below the town. The vivid descriptions of the battle, as written by Flavius Josephus in *The Jewish War,* are engraved in stones along the trail site: "Built against the almost vertical flank, the town seemed to be hung in the air"—exactly the impression visitors still have as they approach the site.

Because Gamla was never rebuilt, the relics of the battlefield still eerily match the ancient sources, among them the fortifications, 2,000 "missile stones," and a large number of arrowheads. From a much earlier period (probably the 2nd millennium BC), there are about 200 dolmens scattered in the area—strange basalt structures shaped like the Greek letter pi, probably used for burial. There's an excellent film on the story of Gamla at the Golan Archaeological Museum in Katzrin. ✉ Off Rte. 808 ☎ 04/682–2282 [$] NIS 29 🕒 Apr.–Sept. daily 8–5, Oct.–Mar. 8–4; last entry 1 hr before closing.

EILAT AND THE NEGEV

With a Side Trip to Petra

WELCOME TO EILAT AND THE NEGEV

TOP REASONS TO GO

★ **Coral Reserve, Eilat:** Put on a snorkel and marvel at the brilliant-colored fish and entrancing corals at one of the world's finest protected coral reefs.

★ **Hiking the desert:** Explore the splendid scenery, deep wadis, rugged heights, and steep cliff faces of the Negev. The mountains of Eilat and the desert craters offer spectacular hikes.

★ **Makhtesh Ramon:** This giant crater is an utterly unique geological phenomenon, with hundreds of rock formations and multihued cliffs.

★ **Side trip to Petra:** Just over the border in Jordan, Petra's awe-inspiring Treasury (the Khazneh), carved into a rose-red cliff, is one of many archeological treats at this UNESCO World Heritage Site.

★ **Timna Park:** A half hour from Eilat, trek across the lunar-like landscape, making sure to see this desert park's famous red-hued Solomon's Pillars and its 20-foot mushroom-shaped rock formation.

1 Eilat and Environs. Sun-drenched Eilat, a resort town on the shores of the Red Sea, brims with hotels, restaurants, duty-free shopping, and the lion's share of the Negev's nightlife. It's just south of Timna Park, which isn't to be missed.

2 The Heart of the Negev. In the very center of the upside-down triangle that makes up the Negev, you'll find several of the region's top sites, including the Ramon Crater and Ben-Gurion's desert home and grave, as well as the ancient Nabatean city of Avdat.

3 Beersheva. Beersheva, a World Heritage Site, is Israel's fourth-largest city and makes a great jumping-off point for trips around the Negev.

4 Side Trip to Petra. Nearby in Jordan are the amazing ruins of the ancient city of Petra.

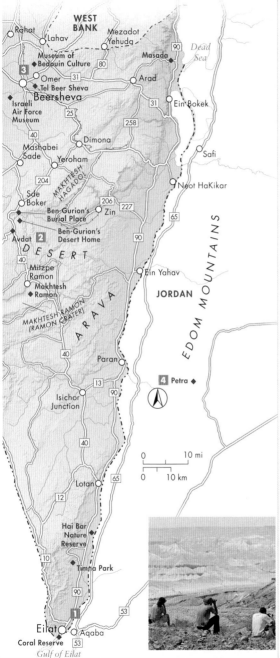

GETTING ORIENTED

Three basic areas in the inverted triangle of the Negev, Israel's southern desert, make up the southern part of the country. The first, and farthest south, is carefree Eilat, with the Underwater Observatory at Coral Beach, and Timna Park. Eilat is also a convenient jumping-off point for a trip to Jordan and the splendid ruins of the ancient city of Petra. Next is the Negev's heart, with sites such as Ben-Gurion's desert home and grave, the ancient Nabatean-Roman-Byzantine ruins at Tel Avdat, and the amazing Makhtesh Ramon (Ramon Crater). The third, in the north, includes the regional capital city of Beersheva.

Updated
by Adeena
Sussman

With its stark mountains, dramatic wadis, archaeological treasures, colorful Bedouin encampments, and the spectacular Ramon Crater, the Negev—a word meaning "dry" in Hebrew—is much more than simply "a desert." The Negev contains Israel's most dramatic natural scenery, with its rugged highlands, as well as Eilat, a resort town set on the Red Sea, with luxury hotels, good restaurants and bars, and duty-free shopping. There's even a growing winery scene here that will intrigue oenophiles.

The region can satisfy both history buffs and adventure lovers. You can visit the kibbutz home and grave of Israel's founding father and first prime minister—David Ben-Gurion, the man who first dreamed of settling the desert—and on the same day, you can tour the millennia-old ruins at Tel Beersheva, visited by the biblical patriarch Abraham. For those seeking adventure, the Negev is the place to take camel treks and Jeep tours, spend the afternoon hiking, or scuba dive in the Red Sea. If all this isn't enough, the Negev offers the ideal base for a day trip or overnight visit to Petra in Jordan. The rose red remains of this ancient city of the Nabateans, who controlled a spice route that stretched from Arabia to the Mediterranean, are carved into towering sandstone cliffs. Petra's gigantic monuments and royal tombs, 2,000 years old, are exceptional, even in a region filled with antiquities.

The Negev makes up about half the country's land area, yet is home to only about 8% of its population. The ancient Israelites had fortifications here, as did the merchant Nabateans and the Romans after them. The region's first kibbutzim were established in the early 1940s, with new immigrants sent south after the War of Independence, in 1948. Two years later, people started trickling into Eilat, which was nothing but a few rickety huts. The desert itself was made to bloom, and the semiarid areas between Tel Aviv and Beersheva became fertile farmland. Today, agricultural settlements throughout the Negev make use of advanced irrigation to raise tomatoes, melons, olives, and dates that are exported to winter markets in Europe.

EILAT AND THE NEGEV PLANNER

WHEN TO GO

October through May is the best time to explore the Negev. In early March, scarlet, bright yellow, white, and hot pink desert flowers burst out against the brown desert earth; March is also when Eilat's International Bird-watchers' Festival takes place. In January and February, it's dry and cold, especially at night. Scorching-hot conditions prevail in the summer, from June through September, though it's very dry, and locals claim this is the "sleeper season" to be here: no humidity, cool nights, less crowds, and easier availability at desirable hotels, restaurants, and venues.

DESERT PRECAUTIONS

To remain comfortable and safe, respect certain rules of the desert. Drink two quarts of water a day in winter and one quart per hour in summer. Keep a jerrican (which holds five gallons) of water in your car, plus extra bottles. Water fountains found along the way don't always work. Flash floods pose an occasional danger from September through March, especially after rainfall farther north. If even a small amount of water is flowing across the road, wait for it to stop (it can take a while); it can be a sign of imminent flooding. Driving at night isn't recommended; plan to reach your destination by 5 pm in winter and by 8 pm in summer. Make sure to have a car charger for your cell phone; service is spotty, and phones seeking available networks eat up battery life.

PLANNING YOUR TIME

As you drive along the Negev's scenic roads, you'll pass stretches of flat, uninhabited countryside under hot, blue skies punctuated by the odd acacia tree, twisting wadi, ancient ruin, or craggy mountain. In winter, desert flowers decorate the landscape. If you want to skip the desert-driving experience, you might limit your trip to Eilat. In Eilat, you can stay at a luxurious hotel, relax on the sunny shore, take a cruise on the bay, visit the underwater observatory, and dive or snorkel.

Most Negev sites open at 8:30 am and close by 4 pm in winter and 5 pm in summer. Keep in mind that outside Eilat restaurants close early on Friday for the Jewish Sabbath, and since the main meal of the day is served at noon in the desert, lunch may be history if you arrive after 1:30; roadside diners close at around 1:30 pm.

GETTING HERE AND AROUND

AIR TRAVEL

Flights to Eilat take off from Ben Gurion Airport (about halfway between Jerusalem and Tel Aviv), Sde Dov Airport in north Tel Aviv, and Haifa Airport. Two domestic airlines serve Eilat: Arkia (☎ 09/8644444 ⊕ www.arkia.com) and Israir (☎ 03/7954038 ⊕ www.israirairlines.com). Plane fares vary wildly, often cheapest for crack-of-dawn flights or off-hours. In Eilat, the airport is actually in the middle of the city. From there, it's about a five-minute cab ride to hotels and a ten-minute walk to the center of town.

BUS TRAVEL

The national bus company, Egged (☎ *03/694–8888 or *2800 ⊕ www. egged.co.il*) provides frequent bus service to Beersheva from Tel Aviv and Jerusalem; each takes about 1½ hours. Buses run from Tel Aviv to Eilat at least four times a day and twice at night and take 4½ to 5 hours. Service from Jerusalem to Eilat takes about 4½ hours. You can reserve Eilat bus tickets up to two weeks in advance, recommended for weekend travel. Within Eilat, Bus 15 starts at the Central Bus Station (entrance to town) and runs through the hotel area to pick up passengers and take them to points south, ending at the Taba border with Egypt. Bus 16 follows the same route, only in reverse.

CAR TRAVEL

The only way to see the Negev Desert comfortably and efficiently is to drive (air-conditioning in summer is a must). Beersheva is 113 km (70 miles) southeast of Tel Aviv and 83 km (52 miles) south of Jerusalem. To get to Eilat from Tel Aviv, the most direct way is Route 40 south to Beersheva, which takes about five hours.

TAXI TRAVEL

In Eilat, the preferred way of hopping from one place to another is by taxi. Rides don't usually cost much more than NIS 35, and you can hail a cab on the street.

TRAIN TRAVEL

Israel Railways (☎ *03/6117000 or *5770 ⊕ www.rail.co.il/EN*) provides service only between Tel Aviv and Beersheva. There's frequent service (except on Saturday, when just two trains run, and both late in the evening) from the north to Beersheva all day; new high-speed trains have shaved time off the trip, allowing you to get from Tel Aviv to Beersheva in 50 minutes.

For more information on getting here and around, see Travel Smart Israel.

RESTAURANTS

Although Eilat is nestled at the southern tip of a desert, there are all sorts of cuisines to choose from when you're dining out: Italian, Indian, French, Argentinean, Yemenite, and Thai among them. There's excellent fish here, including delicacies such as *denis* (sea bream). In the rest of the Negev, with the notable exception of the Mitzpe Ramon Inn, meals often reflect the cook's ethnic background, though the restaurant scene in Beersheva has added a host of tasty options in recent years. Visitors who keep kosher should note that while most hotels serve kosher meals, few of the restaurants in Eilat are kosher, including chains with kosher branches elsewhere. *Prices in the reviews are the average cost of a main course at dinner or, if dinner isn't served, at lunch.*

HOTELS

Hotels in sunny Eilat run from family-style to huge, lush, and luxurious. Pleasure comes first: business facilities on a modest scale are available in larger hotels, whereas a beautiful and luxurious spa with a wide range of facilities is an important feature of each large hotel. Even many of the smaller hotels have installed spas. In Eilat, a few hotels operate on an all-inclusive basis. High season is Hanukkah/Christmas, Passover/Easter, and July and August, though Eilat is Israel's number-one destination for families—so expect lots of kids at the pool, restaurants, attractions, and malls. *Prices in the reviews are the lowest cost of a standard double room in high season.*

TOURS AND VISITOR INFORMATION
For tour operators for outdoor activities in Eilat, check the listings in the Sports and the Outdoors section of Eilat.

Though Eilat's visitor center *(see Eilat, below)* is highly organized, hours vary at the region's tourist information offices and visitor centers—so phone ahead. In Eilat, pick up the useful "Events in Eilat" brochure from the tourist information office.

EILAT AND ENVIRONS

The Arava Plain comes to an abrupt end where it meets the Bay of Eilat, home to Israel's southernmost town: the sun-drenched resort of Eilat. The Gulf of Eilat gives way to the Red Sea, which lies between the Sinai Mountains to the west and Jordan's Edom Mountains to the east. The Jordanian port of Aqaba is directly across the bay, so close you can see the distinctive flag flapping on its pole. Eilat residents will eagerly point out the Jordanian royals' yacht and vacation villa. To the southeast is Saudi Arabia, and the Sinai Desert is just over the Egyptian border.

Most travelers fly down to Eilat to flop down on its beaches and snorkel or scuba dive among its tropical reefs. But if you have time, explore the vast desert landscape to the north of Eilat. You'll find cliffs, canyons, and unique geological formations at Timna Park and indigenous animals at Hai Bar Nature Reserve. Both make good side trips from Eilat. Another option is to explore ancient Petra, over the border in Jordan.

8

EILAT

307 km (190 miles) south of Jerusalem, 356 km (221 miles) south of Tel Aviv.

A legend says that after the Creation, the angels painted the earth and when they got tired, they spilled their paints: the blue became the waters of Eilat, and the other colors became its fish and coral. Whether or not this is true, add to this rainbow of colors Eilat's year-round warm weather, its superb natural surroundings of sculptural red-orange mountains, and its prime location on the sparkling Red Sea—whose coral reefs attract divers from all over the world—and you've got a first-rate resort.

Eilat, a city of about 50,000, is now Israel's prototypical "sun-and-fun" destination, with over 60 hotels to choose from, and its relaxed cadences depart from the usual Israeli bustle. But its strategic location as a crossroads between Asia and Africa has given it a long place in history. According to the Bible, the Children of Israel stopped here as they fled from Egypt into the Promised Land, and King Solomon kept his fleet in the area. Later, because of its position on a main trade and travel route, Eilat was conquered by every major power: the Romans, Byzantines, Arabs, Crusaders, Mamluks, Ottoman Turks, and, most recently, the British, whose isolated police station, called Umm Rash

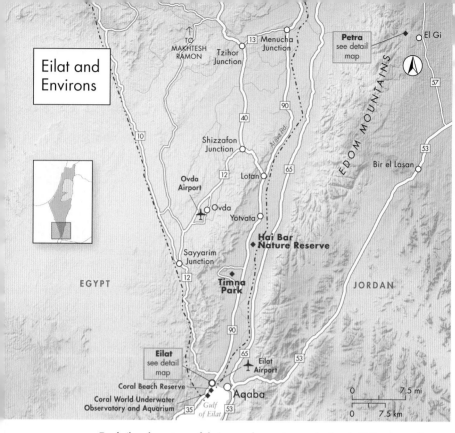

Eilat and Environs

TO MAKHTESH RAMON

Tzihor Junction

13 Menucha Junction

Petra see detail map

El Gi

57

90

40

10

Shizzafon Junction

12 Lotan

65

53

Bir el Lasan

Ovda Airport

Ovda

Yotvata

Hai Bar Nature Reserve

Sayyarim Junction

12

Timna Park

JORDAN

EGYPT

90

Eilat see detail map

65

Eilat Airport

53

Coral Beach Reserve

Coral World Underwater Observatory and Aquarium

35

Aqaba

Gulf of Eilat

53

EDOM MOUNTAINS

Arava Rd.

0   7.5 mi

0   7.5 km

Rash (headquarters of their camel corps), was the first building in modern-day Eilat. When David Ben-Gurion visited in 1935, he envisioned an international port here, and in 1945 Shimon Peres, today president of Israel, led a camel trek to the area. "Shards of coral and beautiful large seashells are scattered on the shore," he reported. "A gulf with a natural port pleads for life."

The Israelis took the area in March 1949, the last action of the War of Independence. The modern town was founded in 1951 and developed as a port in 1956 after the Egyptian blockade of the Tiran Straits was lifted.

Most travelers are persuaded that Eilat's natural assets more than make up for its undistinguished architecture and overdevelopment. For wherever you are in Eilat, a glance eastward presents you with the dramatic sight of the granite mountain range of Edom, whose shades of red intensify toward evening, culminating in a crimson sunset blaze over the Red Sea. This incongruous name for a body of water that's brilliantly turquoise along the shore is the result of a 17th-century typographical error by an English printer: in setting the type for an English translation of a Latin version of the Bible, the printer left out an *e* and thus *Reed Sea* became *Red Sea*. The name was easily accepted because of the sea's red appearance at sunset.

GETTING HERE AND AROUND

The most direct way to Eilat from both Tel Aviv and Jerusalem is via Beersheva. From Tel Aviv, Route 40 south runs directly to Beersheva. To reach Beersheva from Jerusalem, take Route 1 west to the Route 6 turnoff. Follow Route 6 southbound; after Kiryat Gat it turns into Route 40 south, which leads into Beersheva. Leave Beersheva via Route 25 (marked "Dimona—Eilat"), driving 69 km (43 miles) to the Arava Junction. Turn right (south) onto Route 90 (Arava Road), and travel straight to Eilat. The trip takes about five hours. For bus travel between Eilat, Tel Aviv, Jerusalem, and points in between, the national bus company, Egged, provides widespread service.

WORD OF MOUTH

"August is very hot, and the end of August or beginning of September will still be hot, especially in Eilat and Petra. I was once in Eilat in August where it was 113 degrees in the shade. It's a dry heat but you still bake. If you can go to Eilat and Petra in the early part of June, the weather should not be as hot as later toward the summer."
—maxima

VISITOR INFORMATION

Eilat Central Bus Station. Eilat Central Bus Station ✉ *Ha-Tmarim Blvd. 12, next to Shalom Mall* ☎ *03/914-3711.*

Eilat Tourist Information Office. This modest, one-room office packs lots of information into a little space. Accommodating employees happily connect tourists with outfitters, guides, and restaurants, writing down numbers and even making calls when they can. ✉ *Bridge House, North Shore Promenade* ☎ *08/630-9111* ⊕ *www.goisrael.com* ☺ *Sun.–Thurs. 8–5, Fri. and Jewish holiday eves 8–1.*

EXPLORING

TOP ATTRACTIONS

FAMILY
Fodor's Choice
★
Coral Beach Reserve. Less than 1 km (½ mile) south of Eilat, this is one of the finest and most densely populated coral reefs in the world. Close to the shoreline, the reef is 1¼ km (¾ mile) long and is zealously guarded by the Israel Nature and Parks Authority. The most northern reef in the world, it contains over 100 types of coral and 650 species of fish. In the lagoon, divers and snorkelers take two bridges, or a trail marked by buoys, to get to the reef wall. Stunning multicolored fish and soft and hard corals are your rich reward. There are hot showers, snorkel rental (NIS 19 for a mask and snorkel, NIS 11 for a float vest), and a snack bar on the premises. Kids should be over five to snorkel—younger ones can play on the beach. ✉ *Rte. 90 (Eilat–Taba Rd.) opposite the Eilat Field School* ☎ *08/637-6829* ⊕ *www.parks.org. il* ☞ *NIS 33* ☺ *Apr.–Sept. 9–6; Oct.–Mar. 9–5.*

FAMILY
Fodor's Choice
★
Coral World Underwater Observatory and Aquarium. One of Eilat's star attractions can be recognized by its tall space needle–like structure punctuating the waves just offshore. Located 8 km (5 miles) south of the city center, this is the largest aquarium complex in the Middle East. Plan to spend several hours here (there's a cafeteria for lunch on the premises). The **Aquarium's** 12 windows provide views of rare fish so

8

magnificent and so Day-Glo colorful that it's hard to believe they're real; there's an unlighted room where phosphorescent fish and other sea creatures glow in the dark. And there are turtle and stingray pools, too. Don't miss feeding time (11 am daily) in the 650,000-liter **Shark Pool.** The anaconda snakes, poisonous frogs, and piranha are fed in the **Amazonas** exhibit at 3 pm. Captain Jaws takes you on a sea journey during an audiovisual show presented in a simulated-motion theater with moving seats at the **Oceanarium.**

A 300-foot wooden bridge leads to the **Underwater Observatory**. Head down the spiral staircase and into the sea—you're now 15 feet underwater, where two round, glass-windowed halls, connected by a tunnel, offer stunning views of the surrounding coral reef, home to exotic tropical fish. The **Observatory Tower**—reached by stairs—gives coastal views of Israel's neighboring countries. There's a café up here. You can also take a ride on the Coral 200 glass-bottom boat or on a 100-ton yellow submarine that dives to 60 meters. Bus 15 runs to and from downtown Eilat every half hour. ⊠ *Rte. 90 (Eilat–Taba Rd.)* ☎ *08/636–4200* ⊕ *www.coralworld. com/eilat* ⊠ *NIS 99, including Oceanarium; glass-bottom boat additional* ⊙ *Sat.–Thurs. 8:30–5, Fri. and Jewish holiday eves 8:30–4.*

Promenade. Depending on which part you stroll, a walk on Eilat's *tayelet*, or promenade, can seem like a luxurious foray or a far more pedestrian (pardon the pun) experience. Start at the quieter, northernmost end, at the Herods Hotel, near the Jordanian border. The 3-km (2-mile) promenade is also known as the Peace Walk, since it's hoped that one day it will continue to Aqaba, Jordan. As you head south, purple and pink bougainvillea pour down from the Royal Beach Hotel's terrace above. Add to your enjoyment by stopping for an ice cream from one of the stands. If you're here at sunset, sit and savor the show-stopping view of the Red Sea turning red, with the dark, reddish gray shapes of the Edom Mountains to the east and the rugged Eilat Mountains to the west. On a clear day, you can see as far as Saudi Arabia and Egypt.

A stroll past swanky hotels and loads of shops, coffee bars, and restaurants, with palm-lined beaches on the other side, brings you to the Dutch Bridge, which opens for tall-masted vessels. On one side is the lagoon, or inner marina, where yachts are anchored and various small craft are for hire; on the other side is the marina, where cruise boats of all types wait to sally forth. The promenade winds along beside more beaches covered with sunbathers. The scene includes sophisticated promenaders, the backpack crowd, artists doing quick portraits, vendors selling all sorts of knickknacks, and tattoo artists, all accompanied by meandering street performers. At the intersection of Durban and Arava streets (at the roundabout), you can continue along the waterfront—with the Mul Yam shopping mall on your right—until you reach a small palm-filled plaza with a tiny, cement block–shaped building with a statue of four fighters raising a comrade aloft while a flag "flies" above. This is Umm Rash Rash, where the Israelis first took control of the Gulf of Eilat in March 1949, as determined by the United Nation's partition plan. The small building—the only one that existed then—is a far cry from today's luxury resorts. The promenade effectively ends right before Le Meridien hotel.

The Red Sea, just off the coast of Eilat, offers spectacular snorkeling and scuba diving.

NEED A BREAK? On the promenade underneath the Royal Beach hotel sits Aldo, one of Israel's better ice-cream chains. Queue up for a luscious cup or cone topped with a generous lashing of halvah or seasonal fruit.

Fodor's Choice ★ **The Relaxation Pools at Dolphin Reef.** Above the Dolphin Reef beach, a planked walkway leads to a hideaway consisting of a warren of open spaces designed for pure relaxation. Blink and you might miss it—and trust us, you won't want to. Three pools—a deep seawater pool, a soft rainwater pool, and a saltwater pool that'll have you floating Dead Sea–style—offer 2 hours of sybaritic rest that you've likely never experienced. Admission to the pools is strictly capped, ensuring a lack of overcrowding. During the day, the pools offer stunning views of the water beyond tented-plastic windows; at night, candles and heaters enhance the atmosphere. Cell phones aren't allowed—a rarity in Israel. For an additional fee, an instructor will float you around the pool in a 30-minute "relaxation technique," a series of undulating exercises that further enhance the experience. Once you're done floating, you can spend the rest of the day reading, walking on the raised outdoor plank to watch the dolphins, sleeping, or ordering drinks from the small bar/snack counter in the front room. For the price of admission, you get to stay as long as you want. Admission also includes entrance to the Dolphin Reef. The pools offer a true one-of-a-kind experience. ⊠ *South Beach* ☎ *08/630–0010* ⊕ *dolphinreef.co.il* ⊠ *Weekdays NIS 160, holidays NIS 190; treatments extra* ⊙ *Daily 9 am–1 am.*

WORTH NOTING

FAMILY **Dolphin Reef.** At this beach-cum-observation point very popular with families, the price of entry may be high but the perks make it worthwhile. The highlight is clearly the opportunity to walk by foot on the wooden paths that extend into the water. There, you may see a dolphin leap from the water, but more likely, you can watch groups as they snorkel with dolphins right before your eyes (prices for adults or children run NIS 280 per person). In addition to a spacious sandy beach punctuated with billowing palms and bright tropical flowers, chairs and umbrellas are free of charge, but get there early to avoid crowds. There's an indoor café-bar to escape the sun, a great gift shop, and even a video you can watch to learn the story of the dolphins. ⊠ *South Beach* ☎ *08/630–0100* ⊕ *dolphinreef.co.il* ⊡ *NIS 64* ☼ *Sun.–Thurs. 9–5, Fri. and holidays 9–4:30.*

FAMILY **Kings City.** This gigantic fairy-tale castle looms behind the hotels on North Beach. Kings City, a biblical theme park on three levels, offers three distinct sections of sophisticated entertainment, and there's a high-flying water ride to boot. The **Cave of Illusions** has, among other interactive diversions, hands-on games that test your mental acuity, a jail to test your ability to escape, a huge maze, and a large, endless kaleidoscope. Next, you reach the **Bible Cave** in an elevator that descends almost 200 feet underground to an immense cavern where human-like robots reenact Bible stories about King Solomon and other tales. In the **Journey to the Past** you see 3-D films of pharaohs in ancient Egypt, and then there's the thrilling 10-minute waterfall ride that ends in a huge splash (you're in a boat). **David's Spiral** includes two slides, one of them 150 feet long. There's a kid-friendly restaurant, a café, a bar, and a gift shop, too. You'll need three to four hours to do this park justice. It's located at the end of the promenade, next to the eastern lagoon. Note that children less than 1 meter tall (about 3 feet) are not admitted, and the park is handicapped accessible. If your hotel has free Wi-Fi, order tickets in advance for a 20% discount. ⊠ *East Lagoon, next to Herods Hotel* ☎ *08/630–4444* ⊕ *www.kingscity.co.il* ⊡ *NIS 125* ☼ *Sun.–Thurs. 9–10, Fri. 9–3 hrs before Shabbat.*

WHERE TO EAT

Eilat has so many restaurants that you can easily dine on a different cuisine each night over a long holiday. Savor fine local seafood and fresh fish; charcoal-grilled meats of every kind; or Chinese, Indian, Thai, and Italian cuisine and other ethnic meals, reflecting Israel's many waves of immigration. Many restaurants offer outdoor seating, often near the water or amid pots of pink bougainvillea. Outdoor cafés serve café *hafuch* (strong coffee with a frothy, hot-milk topping) and light food, such as cheese toast (grilled-cheese sandwiches) and salads, as well as rich cakes, ice cream, iced drinks, and various other coffee concoctions. In recent years, several chain restaurants have opened in Eilat, so you may see some names you recognize from Tel Aviv and elsewhere.

Use the coordinate (✛ B2) at the end of each listing to locate a site on the corresponding map.

Where to Eat and Stay in Eilat

KEY
- □ Hotels
- ■ Restaurants
- ▦ Restaurants in Hotels
- ✛ following reviews indicates a map-grid coordinate

INDUSTRIAL AREA

Hativat Golani

90

A   B   C   D

1

Shderot Ayalot

Ha Tmarim

Arava Road

Kampen

Kamen

Isrotel Agamim □

2

Hativat Ha Negev

Central Bus Station ◆

Eilat Airport ✈

Agadir ■

Eddie's Hideaway ■

Central Park

Derech Yotam

Durban

Tarshish

Lagoon

New Marina

Isrotel King Solomon □

3

Ginger Asian Kitchen and Bar ■

Horev

Olla ▦

Antib

Kings City ■ ◆

Smolin

Hilton Queen of Sheba □

Shderot Eilot

Lalo ■

90

Leonardo Plaza □

Tourist Police ◆

Ranch House ▦
□ Royal Beach

Ha Yam

Promenade ◆

□ Dan Eilat

4

Argaman

North Beach

Herods Palace □

Le Meridien □

Dekel Beach

TO TABA BORDER CROSSING ↙

Eilat-Taba Road

Eilat Port

Gulf of Eilat

5

Coral Beach
Last Refuge ■

↙ □ The Orchid Reef
□ Isrotel Princess
□ Isrotel Yam Suf

6

0   300 yrds
0   300 meters

A   B   C   D

$$ BURGER FAMILY 🍴 **Agadir.** This offshoot of the Tel Aviv chain is known for juicy burgers and a copious selection of beers on tap. Located in a small complex of restaurants and bars, Agadir's slightly off-the-beaten-track locale makes it feel more intimate and cozy than your average (albeit upscale) burger joint. The restaurant draws a lively nighttime crowd seeking solid food and drink, the main draw being good-quality beef (or veggie) patties in a variety of sizes, topped to order with condiments ranging from goose breast to a sunny-side-up egg and caramelized onions. If you're in the mood for something else, appetizers including juicy merguez sausage and house-made, meat-filled Moroccan "cigars," full-sized entrée salads, and main courses including garlicky sautéed shrimps and tender roast-beef sandwiches hit the spot. [$] *Average main: NIS 57* ✉ *Kamen 10* ☎ *08/633–3777* 🌐 *www.agadir.co.il* ✍ *Reservations not accepted* ✣ *C2.*

$$$ ECLECTIC 🍴 **Eddie's Hideaway.** As the name suggests, Eddie's is slightly hard to find and not within walking distance of the hotel strip, but tucked into a residential neighborhood best reached by car or taxicab. Decor is more French countryside than beach resort, and the affable Eddie ("I consider each guest a visitor in my own home—a friend," he says) prepares straightforward but delicious food, which makes it easy to understand why his restaurant—one of the oldest in Eilat—is worth seeking out and earns such stellar reviews, especially for its steaks and seafood. Devotees also appreciate the shrimp and fish dishes. Savor the filet Dijon (filet mignon graced with mustard and brown sugar), seafood gratinée, the schnitzel Cordon Bleu, or Shanghai fish with hot soybean paste. Inquire if Eddie has prepared a "daily"—a dish he particularly likes to cook. [$] *Average main: NIS 90* ✉ *68 Almogim St. (enter from Elot St.)* ☎ *08/637–1137* ✍ *Reservations essential* 🕓 *Closed Sun. Lunch only on Sat.* ✣ *A2.*

$$ ASIAN 🍴 **Ginger Asian Kitchen and Bar.** A duo of Thai chefs presents an Asian-fusion and sushi cuisine of delicate spiciness at this spiffy New York look-alike. It's small, but the menu is huge. Recessed lighting contributes to the chic vibe, as do the off-white walls and black leather chairs. Start with plump *gyoza* dumplings stuffed with chicken, goose, and vegetables, or shrimp tempura on avocado with miso sauce, or the full sushi menu; then try the Jakarta (chicken or beef with eggplant and zucchini with an Indonesian sweet sauce) or Exotica (chicken or seafood dressed with coconut milk and chili paste and scattered with basil leaves). Finish off with a light-as-air pavlova topped with berries and whipped cream. [$] *Average main: NIS 60* ✉ *Yotam St. across from the IMAX* ☎ *08/637–2517* 🌐 *www.gingereilat.com* ✣ *A3.*

$ MOROCCAN 🍴 **Lalo.** This kosher, unpretentious lunch restaurant, one of the most established in Eilat, is a top-drawer example of Moroccan-Israeli ethnic cooking, by a mother-and-son team. Upon your arrival, five different salads (including cauliflower, tahini, eggplant, and hot peppers) are set quickly upon the table. The menu may confront you with foods you've never eaten before, but it rewards any adventuresome choices you make. Consider such delicacies as beef cooked with hummus (a house specialty); tongue; calves' brains served straight up with Moroccan spices; spicy beef meatballs; succulent couscous with vegetables, chickpeas, and tender chicken; and spicy-hot fish. No fancy pitas here—just plain bread. Dessert is specially prepared fruit, such as oranges or plums cooked until thick and soft, accompanied by fresh mint tea. $ *Average main: NIS 40* ⊠ *259 Horev St., Shkunat Alef* ☎ *08/633–0578* ⌂ *Reservations not accepted* ⊘ *Closed Fri. and Sat. No dinner* ⊹ *B4.*

$$$

SEAFOOD

✕ **Last Refuge.** Locals hold this fish and seafood restaurant (known in Hebrew as *Hamiflat Ha'acharon*) in high regard and take their guests from "up north" here as a real treat. The dining room, with dark-wood paneling and nautical motifs, spills onto a spacious balcony, where diners eat beside the water, looking at Jordan across the way. Presented with a flourish are fish or crab soups, freshly caught charcoal-grilled Red Sea fish, lobster (order in advance), jumbo shrimp, and creamed seafood served in a seashell. A Refuge specialty is stir-fried, small, spicy sea crabs, prepared in olive oil and garlic. Start with the *coquille* (shell) of seafood. Weekends tend to be extra busy, so it's smart to reserve several days ahead (and to ask for balcony seating). $ *Average main: NIS 85* ⊠ *Rte. 90, across from the Isrotel Yam Suf Hotel, Coral Beach* ☎ *08/637–3627* ⌂ *Reservations essential* ⊹ *A5.*

$$$

SPANISH

Fodor's Choice

★

✕ **Olla.** For several years now the best tapas bar in Eilat, this restaurant has leather-backed booths and tastefully subdued lighting. The bar level, extraordinarily lively on weekends, offers some of the best bartending in the city. As for the tapas, try the goose-liver slices on fig confit, the shrimp coated in *kadaif* (a honey-drizzled, shredded phyllo pastry), and the Cornish game hen lavished with honey and served with charred onions. Ask the manager for special recommendations. Downstairs, and under the same management, is an enticing meat restaurant, Rak Bsarim, where you can choose your cut of meat, butcher-style, or try the 300-gram (two-thirds of a pound), locally raised lamb ribs or foie gras marinated in red wine sauce with chili pepper confiture. $ *Average main: NIS 95* ⊠ *Tarshish 17, Bell Hotel* ☎ *08/632–5566* ⊕ *www.olla-tapas.co.il* ⌂ *Reservations essential* ⊹ *C3.*

$$$$

STEAKHOUSE

✕ **Ranch House.** Accessed either from the lower level of the Royal Beach Hotel or via the promenade directly outside the property, this large, comfortable, and kosher steak house distinguishes itself from the pack with service as solicitous as its steaks are juicy. Wooden tables, carpeted floors, and comfy chairs set the stage for a megameal that will have you begging for a doggy bag. Appetizers are named after American states: "Texas" is a serving of crispy, honey-barbecued chicken wings. Steaks, including a copious rib eye, are cooked to order and arrive with a tangle of crispy fried onions and a side of spinach that isn't quite creamed, American-style but delicious nonetheless. The wine list is diverse and offers several reasonably priced selections. $ *Average main: NIS 110* ⊠ *Shvil Hayam 3* ⊹ *Under Royal Beach Hotel promenade* ☎ *08/636–8989* ⊕ *www.isrotelexclusivecollection. com/restaurants* ⌂ *Reservations essential* ⊘ *No lunch. closed Fri., open Sat. after sunset until 11 pm* ⊹ *C4.*

WHERE TO STAY

Use the coordinate (✛ B2) at the end of each listing to locate a site on the corresponding map.

$$$ HOTEL FAMILY Fodor's Choice ★

🏨 **Dan Eilat.** The glitzy 14-floor, U-shaped Dan is on the North Beach promenade near the Jordanian border. **Pros:** great location on the beach; excellent breakfasts (marked with nutritional symbols to highlight low sodium and no added sugar offerings) and superb buffet dinners. **Cons:** sometimes noisy; crowded dining room. [$] *Rooms from: $320* ✉ *North Beach Promenade* ☎ *08/636–2222* 🌐 *www.danhotels.co.il* 🛏 *374 rooms, 48 suites* 🍴 *Breakfast* ✛ *D4.*

$$$$ HOTEL

🏨 **Herods Palace.** Herods—designed with the legendary king in mind—is all about over-the-top opulence and palatial, Vegas-style pizzazz. **Pros:** widest, northernmost, and quietest beach in Eilat; no cell phones in public areas; largest hotel in Eilat. **Cons:** public areas could use a refresh; furniture worn in some rooms. [$] *Rooms from: $400* ✉ *North Beach* ☎ *08/638–0000* 🌐 *www.herodshotels.com* 🛏 *Palace: 296 rooms, 33 suites. Vitalis: 52 rooms, 4 suites. Forum: 104 rooms, 20 suites* 🍴 *Breakfast* ✛ *D4.*

$$$ HOTEL

🏨 **Hilton Queen of Sheba.** The imaginary palace King Solomon built for the queen is what Hilton International set out to construct with this imposing example of grandeur: a palatial entrance capped with a pillared dome rises between two turrets, with a wing of more than 200 rooms on either side. **Pros:** prime location, close to both seafront and shops; stunning views of the Eilat Bay and mountains. **Cons:** late-night music from the boardwalk can be disturbing to rooms on lower floors; lines for the dining room at dinner are sometimes annoyingly long. [$] *Rooms from: $360* ✉ *8 Antib Rd., North Beach* ☎ *08/630–6666* 🌐 *www.hilton.com* 🛏 *479 rooms, 20 suites* 🍴 *Breakfast* ✛ *C4.*

$$ HOTEL

🏨 **Isrotel Agamim.** With a name that means "lakes," this water-garden hotel, also part of the Isrotel chain, was designed with pure relaxation in mind. **Pros:** one of Eilat's more laid-back hotels; great pool area. **Cons:** a 10- to 15-minute walk to the beach; not convenient for strollers or wheelchairs. [$] *Rooms from: $295* ✉ *Kampan St., North Beach* ☎ *08/630–0300* 🌐 *www.isrotel.co.il* 🛏 *288 rooms* 🍴 *Breakfast* ✛ *D2.*

$$$$ HOTEL FAMILY

🏨 **Isrotel King Solomon.** Solomon's entire court could easily have been accommodated at the oldest member of Isrotel's chain. **Pros:** perhaps Eilat's most child-friendly hotel, with a jamboree, arts-and-crafts workshops, computer rooms, games, and supervised activities; rooftop lounge with free Internet access. **Cons:** not on the beachfront; noisy; food is uninspired. [$] *Rooms from: $420* ✉ *The King's Wharf, North Beach* ☎ *08/636–3444* 🌐 *www.isrotel.co.il* 🛏 *398 rooms, 22 suites* 🍴 *Breakfast* ✛ *C3.*

$$$$ HOTEL Fodor's Choice ★

🏨 **Isrotel Princess.** The southernmost hotel in Israel (it's five minutes from the Egyptian border), the Princess, which completed a total renovation about five years ago, is one of Eilat's most luxurious hotels. **Pros:** elegant business lounge on the 15th floor; chic Moscow–New York nightclub downstairs (open during certain periods); free shuttles every hour into town for sightseeing. **Cons:** far from the action in Eilat; mobbed with kids during summer vacation. [$] *Rooms from: $415* ✉ *Taba Beach* ☎ *08/636–5555* 🌐 *www.isrotel.co.il* 🛏 *338 rooms,*

CLOSE UP

Kids in the Negev

Think of the Negev as a huge sandbox for kids. There's lots to do and enjoy: alpaca rides, camel trips, Jeep excursions, dolphin rides snorkeling, floating in the Dead Sea, boat rides on the Red Sea, smearing on mud. And children like the kind of food prevalent in the Negev, such as french fries, schnitzel (fried, breaded chicken cutlets) and ice cream. Even fancy restaurants have these on their menus to please the young ones. Many hotels in Eilat go out of their way to cater to kids, trying to outdo one another with their children's programs and playrooms. These are separate facilities on the hotel grounds, filled with every imaginable distraction, from toys and crafts to PlayStations, and there are qualified supervisors on hand. Many hotels employ staff trained to keep kids entertained, allowing parents some much-needed R&R. Even in upscale restaurants at night, it's not unusual to see baby strollers parked beside the candlelit tables.

---

64 suites (including 7 "theme suites" and 8 "club suites," each with an outdoor Jacuzzi) |O| *Breakfast* ✛ *A6.*

$$$
HOTEL

🖼 **Isrotel Yam Suf.** Just across from Coral Beach, this charming property, formerly known as the Ambassador, is made up of three wings: an L-shaped, three-floor wing where all rooms have balconies and face the sea; the Garden Wing, comprising two three-floor buildings with rooms and suites that have private gardens; and the Diver's Wing, which faces the Manta Dive Center (offering five- and two-day certification courses) and has nine rooms that can each accommodate four guests. **Pros:** great beach for snorkeling; very close to the aquarium and the Last Refuge fish restaurant. **Cons:** bland food; not within walking distance to central Eilat. $ *Rooms from: $350* ⊠ *Rte. 90 (Eilat–Taba Rd.), South Beach* 🕾 *08/638-2222* ⊕ *www.isrotel.co.il* ⤴ *237 rooms, 14 suites* |O| *Breakfast* ✛ *A6.*

$$
HOTEL
FAMILY
Fodor'sChoice
★

🖼 **Le Meridien.** Enter this hotel, and the first thing you'll see through its glass walls is a breathtaking view of the shimmering sea and Jordanian mountains beyond. **Pros:** lovely views; a short walk from the Mul Hayam shopping area; feels separated from the boardwalk hubbub. **Cons:** pool can be cold in winter months; late-night music from the hotel's club may disturb some guests; not much of a beachfront; pool closes early. $ *Rooms from: $300* ⊠ *Arava Rd.* 🕾 *08/638-3333* ⊕ *www.fattal.co.il* ⤴ *246 suites* |O| *Breakfast* ✛ *B4.*

$$$
HOTEL

🖼 **Leonardo Plaza.** This hotel, formerly known as the Sheraton, faces the beach from the promenade near the marina, and everything is within walking distance. **Pros:** well-situated beachfront location, in the middle of the promenade; extensive kids' activities. **Cons:** within earshot of the beachfront discos; Internet is expensive. $ *Rooms from: $331* ⊠ *North Beach Promenade* 🕾 *08/636-1111* ⊕ *www.leonardo-hotels.com* ⤴ *301 rooms, 7 suites* |O| *Breakfast* ✛ *C4.*

8

After a day at the beach, secure a seat with a waterside view at one of Eilat's many restaurants.

$$$
HOTEL
FAMILY
Fodor'sChoice
★

Orchid Reef. Formerly the Reef Hotel, this recently renovated, beach-combing property is one of South Beach's newest stars. **Pros:** freshly renovated; lots of complimentary amenities; great beach proximity. **Cons:** limited dining options; South Beach not for everyone. $ *Rooms from: $350* ⊠ *Almog Beach* ☎ *08/636–4444* ⊕ *www.orchidreef.co.il* ⤳ *74 rooms, 5 suites* ⦿ *Breakfast* ✛ *A6.*

$$$$
HOTEL

Royal Beach. At the jewel in the Isrotel chain's crown, guests discover a blend of comfort, glamour, and sophistication. **Pros:** pleasant pool area graced by palm trees and waterfalls; excellent seaside location. **Cons:** laissez-faire staff; apart from the suites, the rooms can be small; some in-room fixtures in rooms could use a refresh; Internet is exorbitantly expensive, especially with rooms this eye-poppingly pricey. $ *Rooms from: $630* ⊠ *North Beach* ☎ *08/636–8888* ⊕ *www.isrotel.co.il* ⤳ *363 rooms, 19 suites* ⦿ *Breakfast* ✛ *D4.*

NIGHTLIFE AND THE ARTS

For an overview of local events, pick up a copy of the detailed leaflet "Events and Places of Interest," available at the tourist information office. For the coming week's arts and entertainment information, check out Friday's *Jerusalem Post* magazine, or the *Herald Tribune*'s *Haaretz Guide*, both of which carry listings for Eilat.

BARS AND CLUBS

Most hotels in Eilat have a piano bar (some with space for cutting loose), and many have dance clubs; all are open to the public. Pubs abound; top bands perform at several, and at many you can even get a decent meal. Other dancing options are beach parties, where bronzed bodies groove to recorded music (often the local favorite genre, trance, or house) all night; keep an eye out in town for English-language posters listing times and places. Admission is free. On Friday night, join Eilatis who gather at the Aqua Sport beach at sunset.

Mezach (Pier) 99. This fun, laid-back pub, as popular with locals as it is with visitors, manages to be both cozy and sceney at the same time. Inside, the spacious U-shaped bar is manned by skilled bartenders pulling beers on tap and shaking cocktails. Outside on the deck, comfortable outdoor seating offers great views of the boats moored in the lagoon below. Get there early if you'd like to play a round of pool on the outdoor table, or prepare for a queue. Food, in the bar-snack vein, is surprisingly tasty if you stick to basics like fries, burgers, wings, and sandwiches. There's often live music; ask your hotel concierge to check the roster for you. ⊠ *Hamayim No. 99* ☏ *08/866–5477.*

Three Monkeys Pub. Good bands are the claim to fame at this very popular pub, where live music begins most nights at 11 pm. A great place for mature crowds; it's not unusual to find older patrons hanging around outside, drinks in hand, or dancing until last call. ⊠ *Royal Beach Promenade* ☏ *08/636–8888* ◷ *7 pm–last customer.*

ISRAELI FOLK DANCING

Etzion Gaver School. In keeping with a time-honored Israeli tradition, everyone's welcome at the Etzion Gaver School to learn how to folk dance. Though it's best to come in a *ben zug* (couple), teacher Ilana Bar El will pair you up with a willing partner for the evening. Beginners come at 8:30 to learn basic moves before the action begins at nine. ⊠ *Sheshet Hayimim St., entrance on Argaman St.* ☏ *052/866–3218* ⤶ *NIS 27* ◷ *8:30 pm–last song.*

MUSIC FESTIVALS

The Red Sea International Music Festival. This classical-music festival, a series of concerts curated and often conducted by visiting maestro Valery Gergiev, takes place at different venues in and around Eilat every January. ⊕ *redsea-classic.co.il.*

Fodor's Choice ★ **Red Sea Jazz Festival.** Many Israelis and foreign visitors plan their trips to coincide with this world-class event, which draws top-notch musicians from all over the world, twice a year in January and August. Now that the festival is sponsored by the omnipresent Isrotel, many performances take place at their hotel properties. ⊕ *redseajazzeilat.com.*

THEATER

FAMILY **WOW.** This 1½-hour show (performances are daily 11 am to 9 pm) combines vaudeville sketches, magicians, jugglers, and gravity-defying circus acrobatics—all in a 3-D video-art setting. New shows, produced by a top Israeli choreographer, debut every year or two. ⊠ *Isrotel Royal Garden, North Beach* ☏ *08/638–6701* ⊕ *www.isrotel.co.il* ⤶ *NIS 120; discounts for Isrotel guests.*

SPORTS AND THE OUTDOORS

Many activities outlined can be arranged through your hotel or a travel agency. Several tour operators maintain desks in hotel lobbies and will take reservations there.

8

BEACHES

At its heart, Eilat is one long, laid-back oceanfront resort, and the town takes pride in its beaches; it's not unusual to hear locals bragging about the clarity of the water and the quality of the snorkeling, diving, and water sports. City-employed beach managers ensure the cleanliness of their sections, provide open-air showers and (for a fee, usually somewhere between NIS 20 to NIS 30) deck chairs. It's only 10 kilometers from the Jordanian border at the north to the southern crossing, but Eilat packs a lot into the beach zone, which everyone refers to as North and South beaches. Look for beaches with the large white sign that indicate public authorized-swimming zones, along with the wooden lifeguard huts on stilts; lifeguards are usually on duty until 4 or 5 in the afternoon. Some beaches are unguarded; at those, swimming is prohibited. Beaches themselves are free, and many turn into clubs after nightfall, with thatched-roof restaurants and pubs, contemporary music, and dancing.

Families and luxury travelers favor North Beach, which fronts most of Eilat's high-end hotels and generally has a sleeker, more organized look and feel. North Beach, which begins by the Herods Hotel just before the closed-in "religious" beach, runs northeast from the intersection of Durban and Arava streets up to the marina and the bridge. This part of the beach is extra convenient if food and drink are important; most beaches have kiosks selling drinks, ice cream, and french fries; just behind you, the promenade has a bevy of options for more involved meals. Here you can go paragliding or rent a paddleboat or a "banana" (a plastic boat towed by a motorboat). Farther along, after the bridge and opposite the Queen of Sheba, Royal Beach, Dan, and Herods hotels, lies a beautifully landscaped series of beaches. Young people tend to hang out at the southernmost beaches, near the dive centers (south of the port, along the Eilat–Taba road). The southern beaches share the coast with the Underwater Observatory and the Coral Reserve.

The Eilat municipality has in recent years made a number of beaches wheelchair accessible. The best is opposite the Neptune Hotel, where a wheelchair path leads from the promenade to the water's edge.

North Beach. Although North Beach actually begins with the "religious" beach (a walled area with segregated swimming hours for men and women) and a rocky area dotted with thatch-covered tables, you'll want to start your stroll just over a small footbridge in front of the Herods Hotel, where a series of primary-colored, floor-mounted exercise structures host a bevy of fitness-minded strollers. Walking south, you'll pass several mellow beaches, including Kochav Hayam and HaZahav, before you come to Royal Beach where white-shirted attendants rent space on oversized, white-cushioned platforms. Drinks (very expensive) can be ordered from the Royal Beach Hotel just behind it. Pass the marina, where you can reserve glass-bottomed boats and other boat rides (you'll be grouped with dozens, or even hundreds, of other patrons unless you choose to reserve a private ride). Heading south, beaches with names like Tarshish, Leonardo, Rimonim, and HaPnina are filled with families and hard-core sunbathers oiling themselves for maximum exposure. These beaches are more self-service with only vendors selling popsicles and sodas; you'll have to walk a few feet behind you on the boardwalk for lunch. North Beach comes to a natural end by the Meridien Hotel, whose beach is the only private one. ⊠ *Begins near Herods Hotel.*

South Beach. Think of North Beach as the grown-up, settled-down parent and South Beach as the laid-back surfer child just ready to hang loose. In safer days, Israelis used to flock across the border to Egypt's Sinai region to snorkel and chill out, and South Beach still retains a bit of that funky vibe, with more spacious beaches displaying a unique character and a more spirited energy. South Beach is actually a much longer (almost 7 miles) stretch than its northern sibling, but a long length of it is cannibalized by the Eilat Port (look for the gaudy gambling boats moored there) and a large refinery. Before the port sits Dekel Beach, with a shaded Bedouin tent, tanning raft, snorkeling station, and beach bar; it's great for families during the day and often hosts private parties in the evening. Past Dolphin Reef sits Almog (Coral) Beach, a relaxation haven with a full bar and restaurant, low-slung tables, and ample parking. Farther down, Aquasport Beach is a standout; local scuba divers and water-sports enthusiasts know this is the laid-back alternative to better-trodden coves, and the vibe is free-spirited and decidedly chilled-out. Chairs rent for NIS 10, and there's a scuba school suitable for all levels of skill and experience. ⊠ *South Beach, Rte. 90.*

BIRD-WATCHING

International Birding and Research Center. More than a billion birds migrate annually through these skies to and from Africa along the Rift Valley, and bird-watching enthusiasts increasingly come for the spectacle, at its height from late February through mid-May. The nonprofit birding center seeks to create a safe haven for the species whose natural habitats in and around Eilat have degraded due to development, pollution, and other environmental factors. The center offers daytime Jeep bird-watching tours (must be arranged in advance) as well as night tours to experience the nocturnal life of the Arava Desert. ⊕ *At entrance to Eilat, turn off Route 90 at the sign to the Rabin Border Crossing (the Eilat interchange) and follow the signs* ☎ *057/776–9103, 050/767–1290* ⊕ *eilatbirding.blogspot.com* ✉ *Free.*

BOATING AND WATER SPORTS

You've got to get out on the water if you're in Eilat; choose from an array of water-ski, Jet-ski, banana-ride, or parasailing adventures. There are boat-rental and water-sports facilities at both Eilat's marina (near the bridge) and Coral Beach, south of the port on the Eilat–Taba road, and every hotel has a desk where representatives can help you arrange the aquatic adventure of your choice.

DESERT TOURS

FAMILY **Camel Ranch.** This family-friendly venue, a 10-minute drive from the center of Eilat, offers free admission to its Adventure Park and a variety of paid options for experiencing a camel adventure. You can take a 90-minute or half-day excursion (four hours) or a sunset tour (two hours). Longer trips end with Bedouin-style tent hospitality complete with food and drink. Reserve the desert camel excursions in advance. ⊠ *Nachal Shlomo, South Beach* ✛ *Take Eilat-Taba road, turn right at Nachal Shlomo, and follow signs to the ranch* ☎ *08/637–0022* ⊕ *www. camel-ranch.co.il* ☉ *Closed 1–3:30 pm and Sun.*

RAPPELLING

Glitch. This company, which specializes in desert tourism, runs customized Jeep tours and rappelling (known in Israel as snappelling) trips for both novices and more seasoned adventurers, and also runs desert archery courses. Call ahead to reserve. ☎ *08/637–3330* ⊕ *www.glitch.co.il.*

SCUBA DIVING AND SNORKELING

In Eilat you'll find everything from beginner's courses to expert PADI (Professional Association of Diving Instructors) five-star dive centers; snorkeling and scuba diving are extremely popular activities here. Eilat Bay is located at the northern tip of a coral reef that extends from the equator.

Fodor's Choice
★
Aqua Sport International Red Sea Diving Center. For more than 50 years, this dive center has been operating PADI-certified diving courses in Eilat, as well as snorkeling cruises to the most magnificent sections of the reef. There are special Bubblemaker introductory courses for kids and courses ranging from a few hours to multiday lessons resulting in accreditation. ⊠ *Coral Beach, South Beach* ☎ *08/633–4404* ✎ *info@ aqua-sport.com* ⊕ *www.aqua-sport.com.*

FAMILY
Caves Reef. Families (kids ages eight and older) have fun "snuba" diving at Caves Reef, south of the Underwater Observatory on South Beach. In this snorkeling-diving hybrid, you breathe through tubes connected to tanks carried in an inflatable raft on the surface. The price, NIS 200 per person, includes instruction, a practice session, and a guided underwater tour that goes no deeper than 20 feet. Reserve in advance. ⊠ *South Beach* ✛ *Between the Underwater Observatory and the Princess Hotel* ☎ *08/637–2722* ⊕ *www.snuba.co.il.*

Coral Beach Nature Reserve. One of Eilat's star attractions, this nature reserve is a veritable utopia for qualified divers who want to get close to the region's indigenous fish and corals. Facilities include hot showers, equipment rental, lockers, and a small restaurant. ⊠ *Eilat–Taba Rd., Coral Beach* ☎ *08/637–6829* ⊕ */www.parks.org.il* ✎ *NIS 35; rental equipment extra* ☉ *Apr.–Sept. 9–6; Oct.–Mar. 9–5.*

Lucky Divers. For 30 years, Eilat's only PADI Gold Palm five-star diving center has been offering all manner of dive courses from two-hour introductory dives (NIS 220) to a five-day, open-water certification course (NIS 1,100 plus mandatory NIS 220 fee for PADI manual). ⊠ *Near the Orchid Reef Hotel, Coral Beach* ✛ *On foot, cross hotel parking lot onto Veranda Beach and turn right.* ☎ *08/632–3466* ✎ *luckysue@ luckydivers.com* ⊕ *www.luckydivers.com.*

Manta Diving Club. At the Isrotel Yam Suf hotel, this diving club is known for incredibly supportive staff. They offer the full range of equipment and courses. ⊠ *Eilat–Taba Rd., Coral Beach* ☎ *08/633–3666* ⊕ *www. divemanta.co.il.*

SHOPPING

Eilat is a duty-free zone; all items are exempt from V.A.T. (value-added tax) and/or purchase tax. Articles such as bathing suits and jewelry sold in chain stores are less expensive in Eilat branches, as are items that are price-controlled, like gas, cigarettes, and alcohol.

SHOPPING CENTERS AND MALLS

Kanion Adom and Shalom Plaza. The two sections of Kanion Adom and Shalom Plaza are connected by a café-filled passage. You'll find a variety of shops, but this is on a smaller scale than Mul Yam. There's a notable absence of tacky souvenir and gift shops. ⊠ *HaTmarim Blvd., across from the entrance to the airport.*

Mul Yam. One of Eilat's two shopping malls, Mul Yam is at the entrance to town and is noted for made-in-Israel products. Here you can stroll along with the chattering crowd, stop for a drink of freshly squeezed orange or carrot juice, and perhaps pick up a lottery ticket at the stand outside the Israel Jewelry Exchange shop. Then check out such stores as **Intima** for women's soft and sexy lingerie; **Gottex** for famous swimwear; **Honigman** for women's sweaters, shirts, and skirts; and **Fox** for cheeky casual clothing for adults and children. There are also a bookstore, drugstore, and several coffee shops. Outside the mall, on the promenade going west, are one-after-the-other tacky but fun stalls selling hats, T-shirts, and earrings. Also, a branch of **Rockport** sells Teva sandals and other shoes. ⊠ *Arava Rd. and Yotam St.* ⊙ *Closed Fri. at sunset and Sat. until sundown.*

HOTEL BOUTIQUES

Along the beachside promenade, on the ground level of each hotel, you'll pass one boutique shop after another. You'll find at least 40 stores and lots of restaurants, pubs, and coffeehouses—Cafe Aroma, which is open 24/7, is a good bet for a chocolate croissant, Greek salad, orange cake, or fresh-squeezed carrot juice, even at 3 am. If you'd rather sun and play during the day, you'll still have plenty of time to shop at night—these places are open until 9 pm or later (except Friday night). Here's a sampling of some of the best.

Cardo. At Herods Palace Hotel, the Cardo is an intriguing series of shops carrying unusual paintings, sculptures, Judaica, old-style objets d'art, Moroccan furnishings such as painted and inlaid mirrors, boxes and frames, gifts, and wall hangings. ⊠ *North Beach* ☎ *08/638–0000.*

H. Stern. With five Eilat locations, this shop has an excellent reputation for high-quality gold and diamond pieces, pearls, and other quality jewelry. The location at the Royal Beach Hotel has an especially good selection. ⊠ *Royal Beach Hotel* ☎ *08/633–0674.*

Laline. This large chain specializes in Israeli-made soap, body-care products, and candles. Their salt scrubs, infused with mineral oils, are especially luxurious, and a slathering of verbena-coconut body lotion is an apt salve for sunburned skin. ⊠ *Promenade near Queen of Sheba Hotel* ☎ *08/633–5713* ⊕ *www.laline.co.il.*

Padani. Look for Breitling and Cartier timepieces at this shop, considered one of Israel's premiere sources for watches. Both locations are located at the Royal Beach—one inside the hotel and one on the promenade below. ⊠ *Royal Beach Hotel* ☎ *08/633–6625* ⊕ *padani.co.il.*

8

HAI BAR NATURE RESERVE

35 km (21½ miles) north of Eilat on Route 90, between Kibbutz Yot-vata and Kibbutz Samar.

GETTING HERE AND AROUND

The reserve is located on the Dead Sea–Eilat (Route 90) road, between Kibbutzim Yotvata and Samar. Look for the sign for Hai Bar and Predator Center, opposite the entrance to Kibbutz Samar. Drive 1½ km (1 mile) to the entrance. The reserve is also accessible via Egged Bus 390 from Tel Aviv, Bus 397 from Beersheva, or Bus 444 from Jerusalem.

EXPLORING

Hai Bar Nature Reserve. This reserve consists of a 12-square-km (4½-square-mile) natural habitat for biblical-era animals and birds and the Predator Center. It makes a good day trip from Eilat and can be combined with a visit to the Timna Park. The reserve was created not only as a refuge for animals that were almost extinct in the region but also as a breeding ground for animals set free in the Negev. Opened to the public in 1977, the area re-creates the ancient savanna landscape of acacia groves and includes a salt marsh. Roaming around are stripe-legged wild asses, addaxes, gazelles and ibex, the Arabian oryx (antelope), and other desert herbivores. Ostriches come prancing over, ready to stick their heads into your car windows. Try to be here in the morning, when the animals are most active. You need a car and a CD player if you want a "guided tour"; you rent the CD for a few shekels and off you go. It takes about 45 minutes.

The 20-square-km (7¾-square-mile) **Predators Center** houses local birds and beasts of prey: foxes, wolves, spotted leopards, and striped hyenas. As you watch a hyena, notice that its front legs are stronger than its rear legs, enabling it to carry heavy prey a long distance. The birds of prey hang out in gigantic cages, where you'll see, among other species, the only lappet-face vultures left in Israel, with average wingspans of about 10 feet. In the pitch-black **Nightlife Room,** watch nocturnal animals that are active when we sleep: owls, desert hedgehogs, scorpions, and Egyptian fruit bats. ⊠ *Rte. 90, 35 km (21 miles) north of Eilat* ☎ *08/637–6018* ⊕ *www.parks.org.il* ⊠ *NIS 46 for combined ticket (Predator Center only, NIS 29)* ☉ *Sun.–Thurs. 8:30–5, Fri. and Sat. 8:30–4.*

NEED A
BREAK?

Yotvata Rest Inn. If you're looking for fantastic kibbutz-made ice cream (try the *pitaya*, or dragonfruit, flavor), stop by this inn, an Israeli institution next to a gas station on Route 90 between the Hai Bar Reserve and Timna Park, 40 km (25 miles) north of Eilat. The kibbutz of the same name is across the way, and their dairy products are much loved by locals: cheeses, flavored milks, yogurt, and puddings. Hot dishes (chicken or beef) and sandwiches are available as well. There's also a tourist information center at the entrance. Open 24 hours, but late-night food menu is more limited. ☎ *08/635–7229.*

TIMNA PARK

25 km (15 miles) north of Eilat; 15 km (9 miles) south of Hai Bar Nature Reserve.

GETTING HERE AND AROUND

From Hai Bar Nature Reserve, return to Route 90 south toward Eilat. Turn right after 15 km (9 miles) at the sign for Timna Park and Timna Lake. A 3-km (2-mile) access road (which passes Kibbutz Elifaz) leads to the entrance booth. The reserve is also accessible via Egged Bus 390 from Tel Aviv, Bus 397 from Beersheva, or Bus 444 from Jerusalem.

EXPLORING

Fodor'sChoice ★ **Timna Park.** Timna Park is a lunar-like desert landscape interspersed with amazing geological shapes and ancient archaeological sites, surrounded by beautifully colored cliffs in a range of shades from sandy beige to rich red and dusky black. The granite Timna Mountains (whose highest peak is 2,550 feet) encompass the park's spectacular collection of rock formations and canyons. Millions of years of erosion have sculpted shapes of amazing beauty, such as the red-hued Solomon's Pillars (sandstone columns created by rare patterns of erosion, not by the biblical king) and the 20-foot-high freestanding Mushroom. The late-afternoon hours provide unusual light for spectators and photographers alike.

People have also left their mark here. South of the pillars are the remains of a small **temple** built in white sandstone by Egyptians who worked the mines 3,400 years ago, during the Egyptian New Kingdom (the time of Moses); the temple was dedicated to the cow-eared goddess Hathor. This "Lady of the Rock" was the patroness of miners, as you can discover at the multimedia presentation *Mines of Time.* In the temple, archaeologists have discovered a snake made of copper (*nehushtan* in Hebrew)—according to Numbers 21:4–9, Moses made a serpent in the wilderness to heal people suffering from snake bites, and the snake remains a symbol of healing to this day. Near the temple, a path and stairway lead up to the observation platform overlooking the valley. Above the platform is a rock-cut inscription whose hieroglyph you can see clearly with the aid of a sighting telescope. It shows Ramses III offering a sacrifice to Hathor. You can also explore a life-size replica of the biblical tabernacle.

When you arrive, ask for the explanatory pamphlet, which shows the driving route in red. Because of the park's size (60 square km [23 square miles]), we suggest driving from sight to sight and exploring each on foot; some of the sights are several kilometers apart. A small building just inside the entrance screens a multimedia video (with a revolving stage and 360-degree screen) detailing humanity's 6,000-year-old relationship with the Timna area, starting with the ancient Egyptians who established the world's oldest-known copper mines here. Take note of the 8,000 stone circles discovered in the park: they once led to mine shafts, one of which you can explore. The bright teal rock known as Eilat stone, a byproduct of copper mining, is today a trademark of Israeli jewelry. Wall panels explain the valley's fascinating geological makeup.

Experienced hikers can pick up a map detailing various serious hikes that take from 7 to 10 hours to complete. They're best done in winter (summer daytime heat exceeds 100 degrees). Watch out for old mine shafts, take adequate water, and *be sure* to let the staff at the gate know you're going, and when you plan to return. You can also rent bikes and paddleboats near the small lake. Multimedia sunset stargazing tours, accompanied by actors and darbooka-playing musicians, run through July and August. ⊠ *Rte. 90* ☎ *08/631–6756* ⊕ *www.timna-park.co.il* ⊠ *NIS 49; night entrance NIS 69* ☾ *Sat.–Thurs. 8–4, Fri. 8–3; Jul. and Aug. 8–1.*

NEED A BREAK?

Solomon's Khan. Here's a surprise in the desert landscape, right in Timna Park: a lake (man-made), where you can take out a paddleboat. Nearby is Solomon's Khan, a restaurant serving *pliant*, charred bread cooked in a *taboon* (traditional oven) with goodies and refreshing drinks for the worn-out traveler. ⊠ *Timna Park* ☎ *08/631–7850.*

THE HEART OF THE NEGEV

The area extending from the Negev Highlands to Eilat offers a wide range of sights: Mitzpe Revivim, a reconstructed desert outpost; David Ben-Gurion's kibbutz home and grave site; an icy desert pool at Ein Avdat; the 2,000-year-old Nabatean hilltop stronghold of Avdat; and the immense Makhtesh Ramon (Ramon Crater). You'll also have the opportunity to meet the Negev's indigenous people, the Bedouin.

MITZPE RAMON AND MAKHTESH RAMON

On Route 40, between Beersheva and Eilat, 21 km (13 miles) south of Avdat, 80 km (50 miles) south of Beersheva.

The raison d'être of **Mitzpe Ramon,** a town of 5,500 people on the northern edge of the crater, founded in 1951 by workers building the road to Eilat, is to serve as an access point to the magnificent giant crater, and as a center of ecotourism and hiking. Visitors love the area because of its pure air and natural beauty, and slowly but surely, commerce and culture are beginning to catch up with the area's unparalleled scenic and adventure offerings The local main road runs through the crater on its way to Eilat, a promenade winds along its edge, and a huge sculpture park sits on its rim. Outdoor enthusiasts will enjoy exploring the geology, nature (note the metal fences around the trees to keep the ibex from eating the leaves), and stunning scenery by foot, mountain bike, or Jeep. The winter weather here is cool and pleasant.

Israel's most spectacular natural sight, and one of the largest craters in the world, the **Makhtesh Ramon (Ramon Crater)** in the heart of the Negev is a place of unparalleled serenity and breathtaking views. The crater's walls are made from layers of different-color rock beds containing fossils of shells, plants, and trees. Under the sea, the *makhtesh* floor is today covered with heaps of black basalt, the peaks of ancient volcanoes, jagged chunks of quartzite, natural prism rock, and beds of multicolor clays.

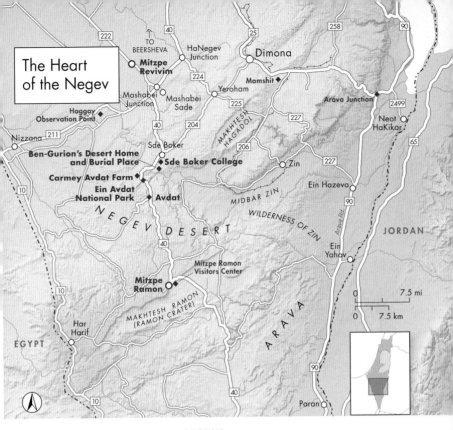

The Heart of the Negev

GETTING HERE AND AROUND

On Route 40, between Beersheva and Eilat, the crater is 21 km (13 miles) south of Avdat and 80 km (50 miles) south of Beersheva. Egged Bus 392 runs four times a day from Beersheva to Mitzpe Ramon (a 1¾-hour drive); there are no direct buses from Jerusalem.

If you're continuing south to Eilat, you can still see the crater, as Route 40 goes right through it; just try to plan your day so that you won't be driving to Eilat after dark. There are no gas stations between Mitzpe Ramon and Yotvata, a distance of more than 100 km (62 miles).

VISITOR INFORMATION

Mitzpe Ramon Visitor Center. The visitor center, perched at the very edge of the makhtesh, reopened in spring 2013. Offering majestic views and relevant information about how to best experience the crater, the center is also now dedicated to Israeli astronaut Haim Ramon, who perished in the 2003 Columbia Space mission. There's also a restaurant and a branch of the Pharan beauty products store located in the Industrial Zone. ✉ *Top of main street* ☎ 08/658–8691, 08/658–8698 ⊕ *www.goisrael.com.*

EXPLORING

FAMILY   **Alpaca Farm.** Just to the west of Mitzpe Ramon near the rim of the Ramon Crater is this farm, with its herd of 600 sweet-faced alpacas and llamas. Young and old get a kick out of feeding the animals, even if they receive the occasional spit in the face from these long-lashed creatures. Children weighing less than about 50 pounds can take a llama ride; horseback rides (some at night) and tours are available to all. You can also weave wool on a loom, purchase items at the local factory, and the shearing festival, which takes place around Passover, is worth catching if you're here. ⌖ *Turn off main road onto Ben Gurion Boulevard, opposite the town's main gas station at the town's main roundabout* ☎ *08/658–8047* ⊕ *www.alpaca.co.il* ✉ *NIS 25; 1½-hour horse ride along the crater rim, NIS 150, weekends and holidays NIS 190* ⊙ *Daily 8:30–6:30 (8:30–4:30 in winter).*

Ammonite Wall. One of nature's works is the Ammonite Wall, which is on the right just as you finish the descent on route 40 from Mitzpe Ramon into the crater itself (on its northeastern edge). A sign indicates a distance of 5 km (3 miles), which applies to the marked hike in the crater (for fit walkers only—take water). The rock face, which is actually part of the crater wall, contains hundreds of ammonite fossils, which look like spiraled rams' horns and are indeed named for the Egyptian god Ammon, who had the head of a ram.

Goat Cheese Farms. En route to Mitzpe Ramon, you can get an authentic sampling of local goat cheeses that have become cult favorites around the country. At Na'ot Goat Farm (⊕ *www.naotfarm.co.il* ✉ *Route 40* ☎ *054/421–8789*), the Gadi and Lea Nachimov craft soft and hard goat cheeses, yogurt and other products) from a herd of 150 goats who clamber over their land. Just down the road, Kornmehl Dairy (✉ *Route 40* ☎ *052/278–8051*) offers the opportunity to watch the adorable goats being fed and milked daily, as well as the opportunity to sample (and purchase) the dairy's superb (and quite stinky) cheeses at their charming restaurant just below. Perched on a hillside, the wooden restaurant offers indoor or outdoor seating and a menu that includes goat cheese pizza, bruschettas, pasta, toasted sandwiches—even a tender goat-cheese cheesecake lavished in fruit sauce.

Fodor's Choice   **Makhtesh Ramon (Ramon Crater).** Words simply can't do this natural wonder justice; it must be seen to be appreciated. This immense depression is 40 km (25 miles) long, 10 km (6 miles) wide, and at its deepest, measuring 2,400 feet. Because it's a phenomenon known only in this country (there are two others in the Negev), the Hebrew term *makhtesh* is now accepted usage. By definition, a makhtesh is an erosion valley walled with steep cliffs on all sides and drained by a single watercourse.

You can take a walk (about 1 km, or ½ mile) along the Albert Promenade, which winds east to west along the edge of the crater from the visitor center to the cantilevered observation platform hanging over the rim. This isn't the time to forget a camera—the view is overwhelming. The promenade is fashioned from local stone, as is the huge sculpture by Israel Hadani, the back of which faces the town and represents the crater's geological layers.

Makhtesh Ramon (Ramon Crater), shown in the valley below, is one of the Negev's top sites.

With the crater as a magnificent backdrop, the Desert Sculpture Park exhibits a far-flung collection of 19 huge contemporary stone sculptures. The park took shape in 1962 with the work of a group of prominent Israeli and foreign sculptors under the direction of Negev artist Ezra Orion. Their idea was to add to the natural stone "sculptures" with geometrical rock formations of similar design. The sculptors brought their chosen rocks and formed their desert works of art with minimal hand shaping. Ibex often wander through. To get there, turn off the main road near the gas station at the sign marked "Ma'ale Noah."

For a look at one of the crater's geological subphenomena, drive into the makhtesh by Jeep to see the Carpentry, a hill of black prismatic rock that appears to be neatly sawed. A path goes up to a wooden walkway, built to protect nature's artwork from travelers' feet. Long ago, the sandstone was probably hardened and slightly warmed by volcanic steam, and the rocks split into prisms. ✉ *Rte. 40, going south* ⊕ *www. parks.org.il* ☉ *Daily 8 am–sunset.*

EN ROUTE It's a **scenic drive** through the Ramon Crater on Route 40, heading south. The Negev wadis increase in size from their source in the Sinai, and cut through the Negev on their way to the Arava Valley, to the east. The sight of the Edom Mountains on the eastern horizon is beautiful, especially in the light of late afternoon. South of the crater on Route 40, near the Shizafon Junction, stop at Kibbutz Neot Smadar, home both to an arts center with stained glass, ceramics, and textile workshops, and to a farm shop that sells dates, cheeses, almonds, olive oil, and herbal creams.

After the Tzichor Junction with Route 13 (which connects Route 40 with the parallel north–south highway Route 90), you'll see limestone strata that have "folded" over the millennia. After the Ketura Junction (where Route 40 ends), there are breathtaking views of the Arava Valley (on your left), which marks the Israel–Jordan border and is part of the Great Syrian-African Rift, a fault line formed millions of years ago. From here, Route 90 leads straight to Eilat (52 km [33 miles]). It's not advisable to take Route 12 to Eilat if you're finishing this tour after a long day's drive or toward dark; Route 90 is the more direct and safer road.

WHERE TO EAT

$ ✕ **Cafeneto.** Ah, the taste of a flaky croissant and the enticing scent of
CAFÉ cappuccino—in the desert! You can get a full Israeli breakfast here (including local cheese, omelets, and vegetables) as well as sandwiches such as the Baghdadi (hard-boiled egg, roasted eggplant, tomato, cucumbers, scallions, parsley, and tahini). Or you might try a salad of finely chopped vegetables with mint, coriander, lemon, and olive oil. Sip an iced chai, fresh juice, espresso, *sachlav* (a custardy, spiced hot beverage), or a latte with shredded chocolate on the terrace. $ *Average main: NIS 20* ✉ *Chachmov Center, Nahal Tziya 5* ☎ *08/658–7777* ⌲ *Reservations not accepted.*

$ ✕ **Hadassar.** The brainchild of recent arrivals to the area, Hadass and
ISRAELI Sa'ar Badash, this inviting store-cum-community center is bringing new life to the morbund Spice Quarter. The large space features a funky secondhand thrift shop, an area selling hard-to-find organic ingredients, and several cases of fetching jewelry. Most excitingly, in a town with surprisingly few unique dining options, Hadassar's sweet little café counter sells coffee made with house-roasted beans; sandwiches featuring local cheeses, breads from a local bakery, and house-made spreads; and some of the best tahini cookies in Israel. A half hour spent in the sunny garden or roaming around browsing local products including Argan oil, goat's milk soaps, and wine will leave you wanting more. $ *Average main: NIS 30* ✉ *6 Har Boker St., Spice Quarter* ☎ *08/940–8473* ⌲ *Reservations not accepted* ⊙ *Closed Fri. and Sat.*

$$ ✕ **HaHavit.** At this pub-restaurant frequented by everyone from teen-
ECLECTIC agers to octogenarians, you can choose from fairly predictable fare including juicy burgers, onion soup, pasta, meatballs, chicken, schnitzel, hummus, and stuffed mushrooms. What's unusual is the copious selection of local and Israeli beers, which reflects the explosion of the microbrew trend. On Tuesday nights, the restaurant morphs into a disco, and soldiers stationed in the area come to dance the night away. $ *Average main: NIS 50* ✉ *Chachmov Center, Nachal Tziya 10* ☎ *08/658–8226* ⌲ *Reservations not accepted* ⊙ *No lunch.*

WHERE TO STAY

$$$$ 🏨 **Beresheet.** For sheer natural magnificence, few venues can top the
HOTEL splendor of the newest, most luxurious feather in the Isrotel cap.
Fodor's Choice **Pros:** unmatched setting; access to natural wonders; gorgeous pools.
★ **Cons:** extremely pricey; amenities could be spiffier for a five-star hotel. $ *Rooms from: $650* ✉ *Derech Beresheet 1* ☎ *08/638–7797* ⊕ *http://www.isrotelexclusivecollection.com/beresheet* ⌁ *111 rooms* ❑ *Breakfast.*

$$ \text{HOTEL} $$

$$ **Chez Eugene.** Set in the slowly developing industrial zone, this unpretentious boutique restaurant-hotel has only six high-ceilinged suites. **Pros:** ideal for couples looking for a haven of serenity. **Cons:** no views; no bathtubs; situated in the still-developing old industrial area, which can feel very remote for single travelers. $ *Rooms from: $250* ⌂ *Har Hardon 8/1, Spice Quarter* ✛ *Make first left into Spice Quarter and drive 100 meters; hotel will be on your right, marked by a sign on the street* ☎ *08/653–9595* ⊕ *mitzperamonhotel.co.il* ⤴ *6 suites, some with private patio and Jacuzzi* ❤ *Breakfast.*

$ **Desert Home.** Here's a little piece of heaven on the outskirts of B&B/INN Mitzpe Ramon: a building with five lovely guest rooms designed for couples, each with a covered terrace facing the surrounding desert hills. **Pros:** lots of privacy; breakfast of local delicacies delivered to your room each morning. **Cons:** remote location; not geared toward children. $ *Rooms from: $175* ⌂ *70 Ein Shaviv* ☎ *052/322–9496* ⊕ *www.baitbamidbar.com/default_en.html* ⤴ *5 rooms* ▭ *No credit cards* ❤ *Breakfast.*

$$ **Ramon Inn.** There's nothing rugged about a stay at this charming HOTEL desert hotel. **Pros:** ideal for mountain bikers looking to take advantage of the craters many trails; ask staff about "cyclists' packages." **Cons:** no elevator; no views to speak of; other than the crater, which is a daytime activity, not much to do nearby at night. $ *Rooms from: $210* ⌂ *1 Ein Akev St.* ☎ *08/658–8822* ⊕ *www.isrotel.co.il* ⤴ *96 rooms* ❤ *Breakfast.*

$ **Succah in the Desert.** In the middle of nowhere (but accessible by B&B/INN unpaved road) is this out-of-the-ordinary encampment of huts (like the portable dwellings used by the Children of Israel when they wandered into this desert). **Pros:** homemade vegetarian breakfasts and dinners included in the price; great for stargazing. **Cons:** can be cold during the desert nights; difficult to reach without a car; must arrive before nightfall; bathrooms are shared, which isn't for everyone. $ *Rooms from: $130* ⌂ *On road to Alpaca Farm, 7 km (4½ miles) west of Mitzpe Ramon* ☎ *08/658–6280* ⊕ *www.succah.co.il/en* ⤴ *8 units sleep 2, 1 unit sleeps 10, all with shared bath* ❤ *Multiple meal plans.*

SPORTS AND THE OUTDOORS

ARCHERY

Desert Archery. Desert Archery offers trips where you hike through a desert course while shooting arrows at targets—a kind of cross between archery and golf. ☎ *050/534–4598* ⊕ *www.desertarchery.co.il.*

JEEP AND HIKING TOURS

A hike, or a ride in a Jeep, is an unforgettable way to immerse yourself in the landscape.

Adam Sela Tours. Camel-supported hikes, rappelling excursions, camping trips and Jeep and mountain-bike trips are run by Adam Sela Tours, which offers ecological tours and Bedouin visits as well. ☎ *050/530–8272* ⊕ *www.adamsela.com.*

Fodor'sChoice **NegevJeep.** If you're looking for a one-stop guiding company in and ★ around Mitzpe Ramon, look no further than Negev Jeep. Though the name refers to the wonderful Jeep tours they offer—you'll get a firsthand education on the flora, fauna, animal life, and anthropological history of the region—there's so much more. Owner Haim Berger, a longtime area resident and excellent Engligh speaker, is an animal scientist by training but a general expert in everything about Mitzpe Ramon and the environs. He and his friendly staff can coordinate many activities, from night safaris to tours highlighting prehistoric rock art, forays to hidden wells and cisterns, to hikes to the top of Mount Karkom. ☎ 054/534–3797 ⊕ negevjeep.co.il.

Society for the Protection of Nature in Israel (*SPNI*). This nature society often includes the Negev heartland in its guided trips. ☎ 03/638–8666 ⊕ www.teva.org.il/english/about.

MOUNTAIN BIKING AND RAPPELLING

Negev Land (Tiyulei Eretz Negev). Treat yourself to a thrilling bike ride: Veteran tour guide Alan Gafni's Negev Land Tours (*Tiyulei Eretz Negev*) rents mountain bikes for the day, offers Jeep tours, and leads rappelling adventures with instructors. ☎ 050/998–8144 ⊕ www.negevland.co.il ⊗ Closed Sat.

STARGAZING

Fodor's Choice
★
Astronomy Israel. Due to its generally sleepy small-town nature, Mitzpe Ramon turns pitch-black at night—one of the factors Astronomy Israel guide Ira Machefsky claims makes the city a stargazer's paradise. A serious amateur who can take you on a stargazing adventure you'll not soon forget, American transplant Machevsky will either pick you up from your hotel or lead you in a two-car caravan to a secret desert plateau where his telescopes have been expertly situated for maximum viewing pleasure (if you've never seen the surface of the Moon up close, you're in for a treat). What's more, to counteract Mitzpe Ramon's chilly nights, he supplies blankets, hot-water bottles, and a double dose of good cheer. ☎ 052/544–9789 ✉ machefsky@gmail.com ⊕ www.astronomyisrael.com.

SHOPPING

FAMILY **Alpaca Farm.** Alpaca Farm sells skeins of alpaca wool—light as a feather, soft as down, and warm as toast. There are cozy hats, sweaters, and other accessories, too. ☎ 08/658–8047.

Faran. For all-natural, environmentally friendly, handmade, deliciously scented cosmetics, soaps, and body-care products that make ideal gifts, visit this shop. They use local herbs and make specialty soaps and beauty products featuring goat and camel milk. ⊠ Har Ardon 22, Spice Quarter ☎ 08/653–9333 ⊕ www.faran-cosmetic.com ⊗ Sun.–Thurs. 8 am–9 pm, Fri. 8–4 ⊗ Closed Sat.

AVDAT

On Route 40, 21 km (13 miles) north of Mitzpe Ramon, 101 km (63 miles) south of Beersheva.

GETTING HERE AND AROUND

On the Beersheva–Mitzpe Ramon road (Route 40), a 15-minute drive south of Sde Boker.

EXPLORING

Avdat. The remains of the Nabatean city of Avdat, a 12-acre acropolis, looms on a hilltop over the spice route between Petra and Gaza. The Nabateans were seminomadic pagans who came here from northern Arabia in the 3rd century BC. With their prosperous caravan routes connecting the desert hinterland to the port city of Gaza, on the Mediterranean coast, they soon rose to glory with a vast kingdom whose capital was Petra (in present-day Jordan). Strongholds to protect the caravans were established along these routes, usually a day's journey apart.

The name Avdat is the Hebrew version of Oboda (30 BC–9 BC), a deified Nabatean king who may have been buried here. Another king of Avdat, Aretes, is mentioned in the New Testament. The prominent local dynasty intermarried with the family of Herod the Great, and in AD 106 the Romans finally abolished the Nabatean kingdom. The Nabatean temple on Avdat's acropolis left almost no remains, but its magnificence can be imagined from its restored gateway. Most of the remains on the acropolis date from the 3rd, 4th, and 5th centuries— the Christian Byzantine period. The city continued to flourish until it was sacked by the Persians in AD 620 and was rediscovered only in the 20th century.

Start at the **visitor center,** where you can learn about the Nabateans in a 10-minute video, see examples of what these ancient traders actually transported across the desert, and examine archaeological artifacts found in the excavations. Be sure to pick up the Israel Nature and Parks Authority's excellent explanatory brochure and map of the site. Drive up the road (save your energy for walking around the site itself), stopping first at the sign for the **Roman burial cave.** Park, and walk the 300 feet for a quick peek. The 21 double catacombs cut into the rock date from the 3rd century BC.

Back in your car, drive up to the lookout point at the restored Roman building (note the watchtower with an inscription dating to the late 3rd century). The cultivated fields below were re-created in 1959 in order to see if the ancient Nabatean and Byzantine methods of conserving the meager rainfall (measured in millimeters) for desert farming would still work. The proof is in the cultivated crops and orchards before you.

Using the Israel Nature and Parks Authority's map, you can trace the lifestyle of these former locals at sites that include a reconstructed three-story Roman tower, a rare Nabatean pottery workshop, a Byzantine winepress, cisterns, two Byzantine churches, and a large baptismal font (to accommodate the converted). Near the baptismal font, you can walk down the steps to see 6th-century AD Byzantine dwellings, each consisting of a cave (possibly used as a wine cellar) with a stone house in front of it. At the bottom of the hill, north of the gas station, is a Byzantine bathhouse. There's an eatery that serves light meals at the visitor center. ⊠ *Rte. 40, Avdat* ⊕ *About 20 minutes north of Mitzpe Ramon* ☎ *08/655–1511* ⊕ *www.parks.org.il* ⊠ *NIS 29* ☉ *Apr.–Sept., Sat.–Thurs. 8–5, Fri. and Jewish holiday eves 8–4; Oct.–Mar., Sat.–Thurs. 8–4, Fri. and Jewish holiday eves 8–3.*

8

Continued on page 476

ADVENTURES

The Negev—a word that means "dry" in Hebrew—is a desert that
covers more than half of Israel's land area, yet remains a wilderness
waiting to be explored.

At first glance, the Negev appears to
be a monolithically desolate landscape.
But take a closer look and you'll find an
impressive variety of sights: stark ridges,

enormous erosion craters, serpentine
wadis (dry riverbeds) and gorges, sun-
scorched mesas, burnt cliffs, sculptured
sandstone, treeless plains and sand dunes,

The Negev Desert

IN THE NEGEV

Since the days of the biblical patriarchs, the Negev has played host to ancient Egyptian miners, Bedouin herders, and Nabatean spice merchants who made the Negev the trade crossroads of Asia, Africa, and Europe.

With its sense of remoteness, the Negev is unusually—almost eerily—still and silent. But it's also an excellent activity base that invites fast-paced adventures. Whether you choose to explore it by jeep or camel, or experience its Bedouin culture, or take a stargazing or bird-watching trip, time spent in this giant desert wonderland won't disappoint.

by Benjamin Balint

ACTIVE ADVENTURES

There are several ways to explore the Negev. Popular choices include hiking in craters and near the Dead Sea, perching yourself atop a camel, or taking a Jeep excursion across the desert.

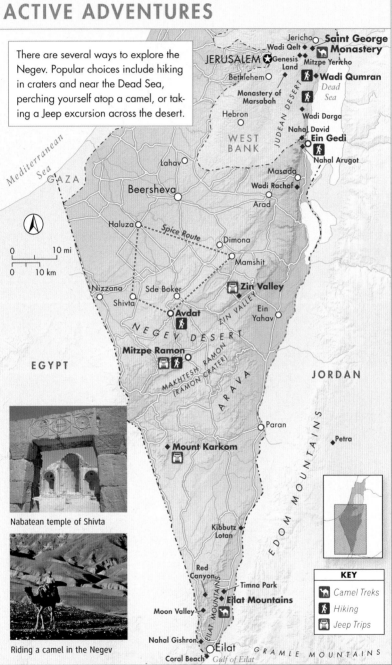

Jericho
Wadi Qelt
Saint George Monastery
JERUSALEM Genesis Land
Mitzpe Yericho
Bethlehem
Wadi Qumran
Dead Sea
Monastery of Marsabah
JUDEAN DESERT
Hebron
Wadi Darga
Nahal David
Ein Gedi
WEST BANK
Nahal Arugot
Lahav
Masada
Beersheva
Wadi Rachaf
Arad
GAZA
Mediterranean Sea
Haluza
Spice Route
Dimona
Mamshit
0   10 mi
0   10 km
Nizzana
Sde Boker
Zin Valley
Shivta
Ein Yahav
Avdat
ZIN VALLEY
Mitzpe Ramon
NEGEV DESERT
EGYPT
MAKHTESH RAMON (RAMON CRATER)
ARAVA
JORDAN
Paran
Petra
Mount Karkom
EDOM MOUNTAINS
Nabatean temple of Shivta
Kibbutz Lotan
Red Canyons
Timna Park
Eilat Mountains
Moon Valley
EILAT MOUNTAINS
Riding a camel in the Negev
Nahal Gishron
Eilat
Coral Beach Gulf of Eilat GRAMLE MOUNTAINS

KEY

🐫 Camel Treks
🚶 Hiking
🏛 Jeep Trips

Nabatean temple of Shivta

Riding a camel in the Negev

HIKING TRIPS

Hiking in the Negev

Israel's trails are excellently marked, and well signposted in both English and Hebrew. Although some guided one-day hikes are in English, don't dismiss hikes in Hebrew; English-speakers in the group are often glad to translate.

THE DEAD SEA

The labyrinth of rocky, brush-covered canyons and wadis found here are eminently hikable. Spend the day exploring one of several in the region, such as **Wadi Qumran**, where the Dead Sea Scrolls were discovered. The most accessible hikes are in **Ein Gedi**, a lush oasis with waterfalls, springs, and shade. The **Ein Gedi National Park** encompasses two wadis, Nahal David and Nahal Arugot, and has the area's best maintained trails.

THE SPICE ROUTE

Many of the ancient towns found in the heart of the Negev were once part of the Spice Route, which stretched from south Arabia to the Mediterranean, and flourished from the 3rd century BC to the 2nd century AD. One of the most spectacular of these towns, all of which are in complete ruin, is **Avdat**.

These cities, now in ruins, reflect the rich trade in frankincense and myrrh from south Arabia to the Mediterranean, which flourished from the 3rd century BC until the 2nd century AD. You'll see remains of the fortresses, irrigation systems, and caravanserai.

THE CRATERS

The Negev has three stunning craters: the Large Crater, the Small Crater, and Makhtesh Ramon (Ramon Crater), said to be the largest erosion crater on earth, at about 24 miles (40km) long, 5 miles (8 km) wide, and 1,600 feet (500 m) deep. Each has well-marked trails that lead past dizzying cliffs of multi-hued stratified rock.

HOW TO GO A **visitors' center** on the edge of Makhtesh has maps and helpful rangers. A safe, interesting, alternative is a guided, off-the-beaten-track hike. If you are planning a multi-day hike and prefer having gear and food provided, you can easily arrange a private tour. ■■ TIP➔ Summer temperatures can easily reach 100 degrees, so drink a liter of water every hour.

CAMEL TREKS

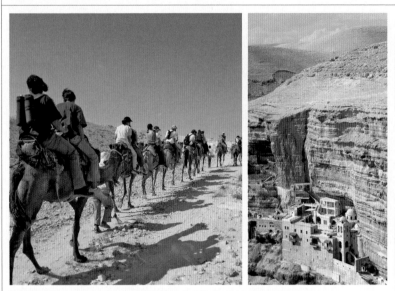

(left) A camel trip through the Negev. (right) Greek Orthodox Saint George Monastery

If you'd like to give your feet a rest, but still experience the desert up close, a camel ride is just the thing.

The local Bedouin name for camels is Ata Allah, or God's gift. The animal has traditionally provided both transport—a camel can go 5–7 days with little or no food and water—and milk. And meat from young male camels is a delicacy of the Arabian diet.

After you mount, the camel lurches forward rump first, which means you should lean back to avoid getting "camelpulted." Once you get going, however, riding is surprisingly comfortable. A walking camel moves both feet on one side of its body, then both feet on the other. This long-strided gait suggests the rolling motion of a boat, which explains the camel's other nickname in this part of the world:

"ship of the desert." The reins used to steer a camel, unlike a horse's reins, are attached to a bit inserted in the nose, so be gentle. Since camels travel in single-file, however, you won't have to worry too much about steering your beast.

Common routes, which can run up to half-day, take you through the **Eilat Mountains**, or to the lip of **Wadi Qelt** (known in Hebrew as Nahal Prat), home to the beautiful **Greek Orthodox Saint George Monastery**, often stopping at a shady oasis along the way.

HOW TO GO Eilat's Camel Ranch (☎ 08/637–0022; enter just after the Texas Ranch opposite Coral Beach) is one place that offers tours for every taste: a daily tour at 4:30 ventures into the desert mountains and canyons (affording fabulous sunset views). Or try the two-hour tour on which you ride for an hour, then savor a desert meal including vegetables and goat cheese. The ranch is closed Sunday.

A Nubian ibex, often seen in the Ramon Crater.

JEEP TRIPS

"Mushroom Rock," one of the many sandstone formations found in Timna Park.

After visiting the Negev, Mark Twain described it as "a desolation that not even imagination can grace with the pomp of life and action." Had he roared through the desert on the back of a 4x4, the American writer might have taken a different view.

Many jeep tours whisk you through the **Ramon Crater**, the **Zin Valley** (a desert moonscape punctuated by natural springs), or **Mount Karkom** (an ancient sacred mountain where you can see rock art, stone circles, geoglyphs, and cultic altars).

Other than the lurching off-road excitement, one of the advantages of jeep tours is the high standard of guiding. Licensed Israeli guides undergo rigorous training, and most have developed an amazing feel for the contours of the landscape. Guides will introduce you to the desert's geologic past and present habitat, and describe Israel's sophisticated water and soil conservation programs.

HOW TO GO From Eilat, the well-established **Red Sea Sports Club** leads jeep safaris through the **Granite Mountains** around Eilat to lookout points above **Moon Valley**, with a descent into the **Red Canyon** where you walk for an hour and take in the natural beauty. The cost is NIS 140 per person. Another experienced company, **Jeep Sea**, offers a 1½-hour "Desert Glimpse" tour, with a view of the hot-pink flamingos near Eilat; the cost is NIS 65. Jeep Sea also provides a four-hour trip to the Red Canyon (including hiking) for NIS 140 per person.

SPECIAL-INTEREST ACTIVITIES

Hiking, trekking, and zooming across the desert in a jeep aren't the only ways to experience the Negev. Try spending an overnight in a Bedouin tent, joining an archaeological dig, or bird-watching.

A Bedouin hospitality tent

THE BEDOUIN EXPERIENCE

Spending a day with Bedouins usually involves making a meal. You'll sit on beautiful woven mats and dine on *labane* (thick, tangy yogurt), *taboun* (Bedouin bread) with hummus, fresh-baked pita with zatar, goat cheese, and skewered meat. The feast is then washed down with sweet mint tea or black cardamom-spiced coffee. Sometimes there's belly dancing and music played on traditional instruments like the shabbaba, a kind of flute, and the rababa, a one-string violin. As you're soaking it in, smoke a *nargilla* (water pipe) with your host, and ask him about the herbal expertise and plant lore that are so intrinsic to Bedouin culture.

STAYING OVERNIGHT Staying overnight in a Bedouin tent is a worthwhile experience as part of your time in the Negev. The two best Bedouin outfitters are **Chan Shayarot** (☎ 08/653–5777), on route 40, about 20 minutes north of Mitzpe Ramon, and **Kashkhar** (☎ 050/668–9743), which is a family-run and organizes night-tracking tours, located a little more than a mile north of Avdat, also on route 40.

THE BIBLICAL EXPERIENCE

Visit **Genesis Land**, (Eretz Breishit) (☎ 02-9974477), where Israeli actors bring Biblical stories to life in the landscape in which they took place. You might be greeted by Eliezer, who'll lead you to Abraham's tent to enjoy meats, shepherd casseroles, and pita with zatar. Activities can include letter-writing with a quill on parchment, baking bread, or making pottery. Or, you can take a camel ride to the Monastery of Marsabah or the nearby Ein Mabua oasis.

STAYING OVERNIGHT Stay the night (Genesis Land offers accommodation either in Abraham's tent or a cabin), allows you to watch the sun set and the moon rise over the stark Judean hills, and put yourself into the rhythms of an ancient and simpler way of life.

ASTRONOMY

If stargazing is your thing, the Negev offers an awesome nightly spectacle, completely free of light pollution.

HOW TO DO IT To peer at some constellations and nebulae, visit Tel Aviv University's world-class **Wise Observatory** (☎ 08/6588133), located on a high plateau in the central Negev, 5 km west of the town of Mitzpe Ramon. Astronomers here recently discovered a planetary system–a star and two giant planets. The best—most cloudless—season to visit is June through August.

ECOTOURISM

Over the past decade, the Negev has incubated the development of ecotourism for the naturalistically minded. You can visit one of several kibbutzim and farms, which have traditionally engaged in environmentally friendly practices.

Visitors can learn how the kibbutz or farm deals ecologically with waste disposal, grows organic agriculture, reuses solid waste for alternative building, composts, and recycles.

Sifting for artifacts on an archaeological dig

Working on a kibbutz

HOW TO DO IT A good place to start is **Kibbutz Lotan** (☎ 08/635–6811), 55 km (33 mi) north of Eilat. The kibbutz, which was awarded a prize for ecological villages, also conducts tours to familiarize visitors with organic gardening and more. (Tours leave daily at 9 AM from the parking lot in front of the holiday village.) The kibbutz also offers tours that introduce visitors to birds' migratory paths and local agriculture. (These tours depart at 10 AM from the parking lot.)

Another recommended Negev company with expert guides is **Beerotayim Ecotourism Center** (☎ 08/655–4369), which offers everything from 3-hour donkey rides to 8-day combined camel and 4 x 4 excursions. Wadi Beerotayim itself lies in the western Negev Highland, near the Sinai–Negev border, and offers an excellent base for exploring the Ramon Crater.

DESERT DIGS

In late 2008, a British tourist visiting Israel discovered almost 300 24-carat gold coins dating from the 7th century at a dig where she had been volunteering. If you fancy working in the dust under a blazing sun in the hopes of finding treasure, take part in one of several ongoing archaeological digs.

HOW TO DO IT The best resource to volunteer for digs that appeal to you is the **Israel Ministry of Foreign Affairs** Web site (⊕ www.israel-mfa.gov.il).

BIRD-WATCHING

Millions of birds fly over Eilat and the Negev on their journey between winter grounds in Africa and summer breeding grounds in Eurasia. Migration takes place between mid-February and the end of May, and between early September to late November (spring is the larger of the two migrations). Lanner falcons, imperial eagles, long-legged buzzards, oriental skylarks, white storks, Egyptian vultures, and desert eagle owls—all these and many more come to visit.

HOW TO DO IT The **International Birding and Research Center** (050/767–1290), just north of Eilat, is aflutter year-round (except August, when it closes); it's open Sunday–Thursday 8:30–5. The center conducts half- and full-day trips with names like "Morning Birder," "Desert Birding Trip," and "The Grouser." Binoculars are provided.

Blackstart

EIN AVDAT AND SDE BOKER

14 km (9 miles) north of Avdat on Route 40.

Ein Avdat (Avdat Spring) lies at the foot of the narrow canyon dividing the plateau between the ancient Nabatean city of Avdat and Kibbutz Sde Boker, in Ein Avdat National Park. The park encompasses the remains of one of the famed ancient Nabatean cities along the Incense Route, the road over which precious incense, perfumes, and spices were brought from Arabia across the Negev and to the Mediterranean ports. Ask for the explanatory leaflet when you pay. Lock your car, taking valuables with you. On the way, it's worth taking a reflective pause in Sde Boker, where Israel's first prime minister, dedicated to the dream of making the Negev flourish, lived and is now buried.

GETTING HERE AND AROUND

Ein Avdat National Park is located off the Beersheva–Mitzpe Ramon road (Route 40). To get to the lower entrance, head down the curving road from Ben-Gurion's grave. The upper entrance is about 5 km (3 miles) to the south.

Ben-Gurion's home and grave is also along Route 40; driving north, you'll see the sign for Ben-Gurion's home directing you to turn right immediately after Kibbutz Sde Boker. Egged Bus 392 runs to Sde Boker from Beersheva four times a day (a 45-minute ride).

The Sde Boker College is just next door to Ben-Gurion's home and grave. Enter through the gate with the traffic arm, next to the "Ben-Gurion's Memorial" sign.

EXPLORING

Ben-Gurion's Desert Home. Thousands of people make their way to this pilgrimage site every year. David Ben-Gurion (1886–1973), Israel's first prime minister, was one of the 20th century's great statesmen. He regarded the Negev as Israel's frontier and hoped that tens of thousands would settle there. When Ben-Gurion resigned from government in 1953 (later to return), he and his wife, Paula, moved to the isolated, brand-new **Kibbutz Sde Boker** to provide an example for others. "Neither money nor propaganda builds a country," he announced. "Only the man who lives and creates in the country can build it." And so, the George Washington of Israel took up his new role in the kibbutz sheepfold. In February 1955, he became prime minister once more, but he returned here to live when he retired in 1963. (He moved back to his Tel Aviv residence some months before his death, at the age of 87, in 1973.)

Set amid the waving eucalyptus trees is Paula and David Ben-Gurion's simple dwelling, a testament to their typically Israeli brand of modesty and frugality. Ben-Gurion's small Negev home is commonly known as "the hut," owing to its humble appearance. It's a one-story wooden home with a small kitchen, an eating corner with a table and two chairs, and simple furniture throughout. Visitors such as United Nations Secretary-General Dag Hammarskjöld drank tea with Ben-Gurion in the modest living room. Ben-Gurion's library shelves contain 5,000 books (there are 20,000 more in his Tel Aviv home, on Ben Gurion Boulevard).

These ruins in the ancient Nabatean city of Avdat are perched more than 2,000 feet above sea level.

His bedroom, with its single picture of Mahatma Gandhi, holds the iron cot on which he slept (often only three hours a night) and his slippers on the floor beside it. The house is exactly as he left it.

Next door, in another painted-wood building, is an exhibition whose themes are the story of Ben-Gurion's extraordinary life, original documents that show the leader's strong ties to the Negev, and the Negev today in light of Ben-Gurion's dream. A film showing the footage of kibbutz members actually voting on his acceptance into their community is shown in the **visitor center**; the shop here sells gifts, jewelry, and books about the "Old Man," as he was known locally. ⊠ *Avdat* ☎ *08/656–0469* ⊕ *www.bgh.org.il* ⊠ *NIS 12* ⊙ *Sun.–Thurs. 8:30–4, Fri. and Jewish holiday eves 8:30–2, Sat. and Jewish holidays 10–4; last admission ½ hr before closing.*

Fodor's Choice ★ **Ben-Gurion's Grave.** The revered prime minister's grave, just 2 miles south of his desert home, is often visited at the same time. Walk through the beautiful garden until you reach the quiet, windswept plaza; in the center are the simple raised stone slabs marking the graves of David and Paula Ben-Gurion (she died five years before her husband). The couple's final resting place commands a view of Zin Valley's geological finery: a vast, undulating drape of stone that changes hue as the daylight shifts. The cluster of greenery and palm trees to the right on the valley floor marks Ein Avdat (Avdat Spring). ⊠ *Sde Boker* ☎ *08/655–0954* ⊠ *Free* ⊙ *Daily.*

NEED A
BREAK? **Menta.** By the gas station just to the south of the entrance to Ben-Gurion's Desert Home on Route 40 at Sde Boker is a small café called Menta, which is open 24 hours, and offers tasty cappuccino, espresso, muffins, and sandwiches. ⊠ *Avdat* ☎ *08/657–9938.*

Fodor'sChoice ★ **Carmey Avdat Farm Winery.** Set on an ancient riverbed and vineyard site, this winery-guesthouse-gift shop complex is the labor of love of Hannah and Eyal Israel, who moved here in 1998. Pick up a handy map and self-tour the property; you'll pass six well-appointed guesthouses *(see Where to Stay)*, ancient archaeological remnants including stone terraces and rock drawings, a small olive grove, and assorted fruit trees and herb bushes. Then ask Eyal to show you around the winery, where he'll share the story of how he came to plant new vines on an ancient terrace with a 1,500-year legacy. You can then sample the delicious (kosher) wines and learn about Eyal's fascinating journey to winemaking—even create your own customized wine label (bottling and labeling costs NIS 75, takes 4 hours, and makes great gifts). At the farm store buy wines, products make with fruit harvested on the farm, souvenirs, and local pottery. ⊠ *Route 40, just south of Tziporim Junction, Midreshet Ben Gurion* ☎ *08/653–5177* ✐ *farm@carmey-avdat.co.il* ⊕ *www.carmeyavdat.com* ⌧ *Free.*

FAMILY **Ein Avdat National Park.** Water flowing from Ein Avdat has cut a beautiful, narrow canyon through the area's soft white chalk forming a marvelous oasis that offers the ideal respite from your arduous Negev travels. Walk toward the thickets of rushes, and look for ibex tracks, made with pointed hoofs that enable these agile creatures to climb sheer rock faces. It's not easy to spot an ibex—their coats have striped markings that resemble the rock's strata. Rock pigeons, Egyptian vultures (black-and-white feathers, bright yellow beak, and long, pinkish legs), and sooty falcons nest in the natural holes in the soft rock and in cliff ledges.

The big surprise at Ein Avdat is the Ein Marif pools of ice-cold, spring-fed water, complete with splashing waterfall. To reach this cool oasis, shaded by the surrounding cliffs, walk carefully along the spring and across the dam toward the waterfall. Swimming and drinking the water aren't allowed (you'll not be *sorely* tempted, though—the water is swarming with tadpoles), but enjoying the sight and sound of water in the arid Negev certainly is. The trail leads through stands of Euphrates poplars, and by caves inhabited by monks during Byzantine days, and then continues up the cliff side (using ladders and stone steps), but you can't follow it unless your party has two cars and leaves one at the destination. The easier and more common option is to walk along the streambed from the lower entrance to the Ein Marif pools at the foot of the waterfall, return along the same path. ⊠ *Ein Avdat National Park, Advat, Route 40, Avdat* ☎ *08/655–5684* ⊕ *www.parks.org.il* ⌧ *NIS 29* ☉ *Apr.–Sept., Sun.–Thurs. 8–5, Fri. and Jewish holiday eves 8–4; Oct.–Mar., Sun.–Thurs. 8–4, Fri. and Jewish holiday eves 8–3; last admission 1 hr before closing.*

Sde Boker College. Ben-Gurion envisioned a place of learning in the desert. Sde Boker College, which specializes in environmental studies, became part of Ben-Gurion University of the Negev, whose main campus is in Beersheva. For the traveler, the college, just 2 miles south of Sde Boker proper, is primarily a place to eat and possibly spend the night. The commercial center in the middle of the campus has several restaurants including a new cheese-and-sandwich shop, a supermarket open until 8 pm, a post office, an outdoor-adventure company, and the field school (among the largest in Israel) of the **Society for the Protection of Nature in Israel.** The new neighborhoods cropping up just outside the commercial center, Neve Boker and Neve Ziv, are worth a drive-by; modern desert architecture embellished with multihued paint jobs and smart landscaping add up to some spiffy residences. ⊠ *Sde Boker College, Sde Boker* ☎ *08/653–2016* ⊕ *www.boker.org.il/english.*

National Solar Energy Center. Although there isn't a great deal to see, the National Education Facility, where a research program investigates new ideas for harnessing solar energy and alternative energy technologies, offers one-hour guided tours. ⊠ *Ben-Gurion University of the Negev, Sde Boker Campus, Sde Boker* ☎ *08/659–6934*

EN ROUTE

Ein Avdat Observation Point. For an eagle's-eye view of the waterfall and spring below, turn off Route 40 at the orange sign for Ein Avdat to get to the Ein Avdat Observation Point. Below you is the white canyon carved out by the Zin River, with its waterfall (most of the year) tumbling into a pool surrounded by greenery. From the lookout, a path leads around the top of the cliff (be very careful), enabling you to see the rope marks in the rock; these have been created over the years by Bedouin pulling up water buckets. For information on the hike from here to ancient Avdat, consult the Field School at Sde Boker College. ⊠ *Avdat* ⊕ *boker.org.il/english.*

WHERE TO STAY

$
B&B/INN

⌂ **Carmey Avdat Farm.** Set on the site of an ancient winery, these six cabins are designed for anyone craving an authentic Negev experience. **Pros:** unique experience; quiet; private. **Cons:** very quiet; paths to rooms could be better lit. ⓢ *Rooms from: $170* ⊠ *Rte. 40, just south of Tziporim Junction, Midreshet Ben Gurion* ☎ *08/653–5177* ✎ *farm@carmey-avdat.co.il* ⊕ *www.carmeyavdat.com* ⇴ *6 cabins* ⦿ *Breakfast.*

MITZPE REVIVIM

36 km (22 miles) southeast of Beersheva.

GETTING HERE AND AROUND

On Route 40, the Beersheva–Mitzpe Ramon road, turn onto Route 222 at Mashabim Junction after Kibbutz Mashabei Sade, then drive 9 km (6 miles) to the turnoff to Retamim on your left, following signs to the Mitzpe.

Mitzpe Revivim. Mitzpe Revivim, the southernmost Jewish outpost during the early settlement of the country, played a strategic role in the defense of the Negev. It's now essentially a museum on a tiny kibbutz. In 1943, in a desolate and empty Negev, three such outposts were set up to gauge the feasibility of Jewish settlement in the southernmost part of the country; one of these was Mitzpe Revivim (*mitzpe* means "lookout," and *revivim* means "rain showers"). Revivim's very presence, along with a handful of other Negev settlements, influenced the

United Nation's decision to include the Negev as part of the State of Israel in the 1947 partition plan. During the War of Independence, Egyptian soldiers besieged isolated Mitzpe Revivim, and a hard battle was won by a small band of pioneers and Palmach soldiers. You can enter its Byzantine caves, which once served as command bunker (the radio crackles original messages) and field hospital; climb the lookout tower; and see WWII-era Dakota C-47 and Piper Cub planes used to bring supplies and evacuate the wounded. A one-page "self guide" brings the rooms to life. Snacks, drinks, and Revivim's fine Halutza olive oil are available at the visitor center. ⊠ *Kibbutz Revivim, Rte. 222, Avdat* ✛ *Turn right at Mashabim Junction onto Route 222, then left to Retamim.* ☎ *08/656–2570* ⊕ *mitzpe-revivim.net* ⌑ *NIS 18* ☼ *Sun.– Thurs. 8–4, Fri. and Jewish holiday eves 8–noon.*

EN ROUTE

Driving north along Route 40 to Beersheva, you'll see a sign on the left for the **Haggay Observation Point,** which offers a glorious first glimpse of the **Wilderness of Zin**—stark, flat, beige terrain—and **Kibbutz Sde Boker.** Except for the greenery of the kibbutz, the area looks just as it did to the wandering Children of Israel making their way from Egypt to the Land of Canaan more than 3,000 years ago, no doubt complaining all the while about the lack of figs, vines, and water. (Along this stretch of Route 40, you'll pass through areas where signs announce "firing zone." The signs indicate closed military areas, which you may not enter without proper authorization. It's perfectly safe to travel on the main roads; just don't wander off them.) Continue north along Route 40 and just before passing the turnoff to Golda Park (featuring a lake filled by the floodwaters of the Revivim River), you'll come to the gas station at **Mashabim Junction,** which also serves as a roadside café (good for stocking up on bottled water and, as usual, great coffee).

BEERSHEVA

Beersheva's emblem depicts a tamarisk tree, representing the biblical past, and a pipe through which water flows, symbolizing the city's modern revival. Four thousand years ago, the patriarch Abraham dug wells (*be'er* in Hebrew) here and swore an oath (*shevua*) over seven (*sheva*) ewes with the king of Gerar, who vowed to prevent his men from seizing the well. And it was here that Abraham planted a grove of tamarisk trees. Isaac built an altar here, the prophet Elijah found refuge here from Jezebel, and King Saul constructed a fort here. It's easy to envision these scenes today thanks to the cloaked figures of Bedouin shepherds with their sheep and goats on the hillsides surrounding the city.

With a population of some 200,000, Beersheva has often been overlooked in spite of its size. But in recent years a young and ambitious mayor, Ruvik Danilovich, has pushed to raise the profile of Israel's fourth-largest city by introducing or renewing public spaces, museums, and attractions and encouraging investment in infrastructure and the arts. Beersheva houses a major university, named after David Ben-Gurion, an Israel Aircrafts Industries complex, a high-tech center, a sparkling performance hall, and a regional hospital serving Bedouin shepherds, kibbutzniks, and other desert dwellers.

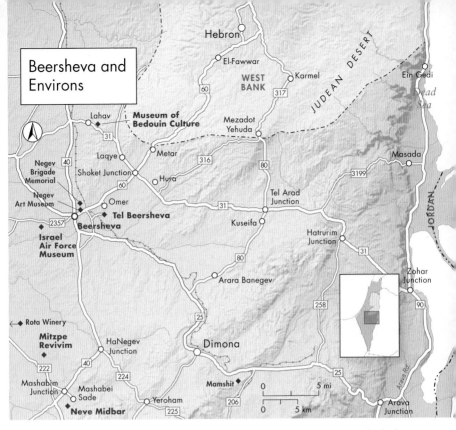

Beersheva and Environs

New additions to the city are an expansive river-flanking park, the largest shopping mall in the Middle East (currently under construction), and the revival of biblical sites like a well believed to have been used by Abraham (at this writing, the project was scheduled to open sometime in 2014). The city is also home to thousands of more recent immigrants, many from Ethiopia and the former Soviet Union.

The Old City, anchored by Smilansky Street and dotted with handsome stone structures and the lion's share of Beersheva's better restaurants, continues to evolve. Many structures are boarded up, awaiting purchase and renovation by enterprising entrepreneurs. The famed Bedouin market, once a source of some of Israel's best ethnic handicrafts, has been hit hard by modern times (especially the competition of cheap imports from the Far East), and isn't what it used to be. But it now has a permanent location, and you might still find something authentic. Most intriguing are the Bedouin themselves, sitting cross-legged with their goods spread out on the ground.

Tel Beersheva, just outside the city, is the site of biblical Beersheva and could easily be the site of Abraham's well. An expression from the book of Judges, "from Dan to Beersheva," once indicated the northern and southern boundaries of the land of Israel. UNESCO declared it a World Heritage Site in July 2005.

Romans and Byzantines built garrisons in Beersheva, but in subsequent centuries the city was abandoned. In 1900 the Ottoman Turks, who had ruled Palestine since 1517, rebuilt Beersheva as their Negev district center (the present Old City). They set aside an area for a Bedouin market, which still takes place every Thursday. During World War I, when the British took Beersheva from the Turks, the city rapidly expanded; in October 1948 it was conquered by Israel.

From time immemorial, Beersheva has acted as a crossroads. In antiquity, the city straddled the intersection of two ancient, important, international road junctions: The "Way of the Sea" (Via Maris), which extended along the shoreline in the west, and the King's Highway (the Valley Route) in the east. Today, because it's quite close to Tel Aviv and Jerusalem, this unpretentious city serves as a jumping-off point for Negev travel—main roads branch out from here; buses serving the Negev depart from here; and trains from the north end up in Beersheva. If your schedule permits, stay overnight in Beersheva for a glimpse of a growing desert city with an interesting citizenry and a gentrifying population.

GETTING HERE AND AROUND

Beersheva is 113 km (70 miles) southeast of Tel Aviv and 120 km (75 miles) southwest of Jerusalem. The drive from either Tel Aviv or Jerusalem takes about 1½ hours. To get to Beersheva from Tel Aviv, take Route 2 (the Ayalon Highway) south until the turnoff marked "Beersheva–Ashdod." After this you'll be on Route 41, which runs into Route 40 after 6 km (4 miles). Continue on Route 40 to Beersheva; there are clear signs all the way.

To reach Beersheva from Jerusalem, take Route 1 west to the Route 6 turnoff. Follow Route 6 southbound; after Kiryat Gat it turns into Route 40 south, which leads into Beersheva.

The Israel Air Force Museum is 7 km (4½ miles) west of Beersheva on a narrow desert road that pushes past the city's drab outskirts.

For the Museum of Bedouin Culture, at the Lehavim Junction on Route 40, turn east onto Route 31, and turn in at the brown sign for the Joe Alon Center. It's 95 km (57 miles) south of Tel Aviv, 24 km (14 miles) north of Beersheva.

Tel Beersheva is 2 km (1¼ miles) east of Beersheva, on the road between Beersheva and Shoket Junction (Route 60), near the Bedouin town of Tel Sheva.

VISITOR INFORMATION AND TOURS

Beer Sheva Art Experience. This organization, founded by enterprising British immigrant Hannah Rendell, organizes a variety of art-focused tours around town—but can show you around any aspect of burgeoning Beersheva. If you bring your camera, Rendell and her staff can direct you on a personal photography tour of the city's many photogenic sights, with stops for lunch along the way. ☎ *054/654–6811* ⊕ *www.b7artexperience.co.il.*

EXPLORING
TOP ATTRACTIONS

FAMILY **Israel Air Force Museum.** For plane lovers, this is a field of dreams. The open-air museum (housed on the active Hatzerim Air Force Base) is a gigantic concrete field with more than a hundred airplanes and helicopters parked in rows. The fighter, transport, and training (plus a few enemy) aircraft tell the story of Israel's aeronautic history, from the Messerschmitt—obtained in 1948 from Czechoslovakia, and one of four such planes to help halt the Egyptian advance in the War of Independence—to the Kfir, the first fighter plane built in Israel. The young air force personnel who staff the museum lead tours that take about 1½ hours and include a movie shown in an air-conditioned Boeing 707 used in the 1977 rescue of Israeli passengers held hostage in a hijacked Air France plane in Entebbe, Uganda. Another attention-getting display is a shiny, black Supermarine Spitfire with a red lightning bolt on its side, flown by Ezer Weizmann, the IAF's first pilot and later president of Israel. The museum also houses an antiaircraft exhibit and a rare collection of historical and instructive films. Tours are available in English, French, and Russian. ⊠ *Rte. 2357* ⊹ *Follow Joe Alon Rd. due west out of Beersheva* ☎ *08/990–6855* ⊕ *www.iaf.org.il* ✉ *NIS 30* ⊙ *Sun.–Thurs. 8–5, Fri. 8–1 pm.*

FAMILY
Fodor's Choice
★ **Museum of Bedouin Culture.** Once off the main road, you'll drive through the Lahav pine forest adjacent to Kibbutz Lahav to reach the Joe Alon Center, whose centerpiece is this one-of-a-kind museum focusing on the Bedouin people, who have long populated the Negev. The study center (marked with an orange sign) is named for the late Colonel Joe Alon, a pilot who took a great interest in this area and its people. Housed in a circular, tent-like building designed by Israeli architect Tzvi Lissar, the museum tells the story of the Bedouin's rapid change from a nomadic to a modern lifestyle through tableaux of life-size mannequins. The tableaux are grouped by subject: wool spinning and carpet weaving, bread baking, the Bedouin coffee ceremony, wedding finery (including a camel elaborately decorated for the event), donkeys and camels at work, and toys made from found objects such as pieces of wire and wood. The tools and artifacts—most handmade, and many already out of use in modern Bedouin life—form an outstanding collection. Admission includes a cup of thick coffee in a real Bedouin tent, where the sheikh performs the coffee ceremony over an open fire. ⊠ *Rte. 325 off Rte. 31* ☎ *08/991–3322* ⊕ *www.joealon. org.il* ✉ *NIS 20* ⊙ *Sun.–Thurs. 9–4, Fri. and holiday eves, 9–2, Sat. and holidays 9–4.*

Tel Beersheva. Tel Beersheva, biblical Beersheva—traditionally associated with the patriarch Abraham—is a mound of ruins created by nine successive settlements. Archaeologists have uncovered two-thirds of a city dating from the early Israelite period (10th century BC). Because of the site's significance for the study of biblical-period urban planning, UNESCO has recognized Tel Beersheva as a World Heritage Site. At the top of the tell is the only planned Israelite city uncovered in its entirety, which includes sophisticated waterworks and a fascinating reconstructed horned altar. A fine example of a circular layout typical

DID YOU KNOW?

Dromedary camels, such as this one, have been used in the Negev for thousands of years, and are particularly well suited for transporting heavy loads through the desert.

of the Iron Age, the city is believed to have been destroyed around 706 BC by Sennacherib of Assyria. At the northeastern end, outside the 3,000-year-old city gate, is a huge well (the deepest in Israel, and more than 6 feet in diameter) which apparently once reached groundwater 90 feet below. This ancient well served the city from its earliest times, and scholars speculate that it could be the well that is documented in the Bible as Abraham's Well (Genesis 21:22–32). The observation tower is rather ugly, but it does afford beautiful views. ⊠ *Rte. 60* ☎ *08/646–7286* ⊕ *www.parks.org.il* ▭ *NIS 15* ⊙ *Apr.–Sept., Sun.–Thurs. 8–5, Fri. and Jewish holiday eves 8–3; Oct.–Mar., Sun.–Thurs. 8–4, Fri. and Jewish holiday eves 8–2.*

WORTH NOTING

Negev Art Museum. Fresh off a multiyear renovation, this handsome structure—once home to a British Mandate–era governor—houses a rotating display of classic and modern Israeli art near the center of town. For a while the source of an unfortunate turf war, the museum, housed in a former mosque, has now arrived at a compromise seemingly all parties Arab can seem to agree on; a permanent display of Islamic art is set to open some time in late 2013. ⊠ *60 HaAtzma'ut Street* ☎ *08/699–3535* ⊕ *www.negev-museum.org.il.*

OFF THE BEATEN PATH

Neve Midbar. This spacious health spa (for daytime visits) centers on a pool of natural thermomineral waters pumped up from deep underground, at a temperature of 39°C (around 102°F). Neve Midbar also has two freshwater pools, a shallow pool for babies, a large outdoor pool and relaxation area, and a new spa-within-the-spa offering a full range of beauty treatments. A hot tub, sauna, various massages, and aromatherapy treatments make for an unusual desert experience. A gift shop, kosher restaurant, and coffee shop share the premises. ⊠ *Rte. 222, 20 mins. drive south of Beersheva* ✛ *Heading south on Rte. 40, turn right at Mashabei Sadeh junction, spa on left* ☎ *08/657–9666* ⊕ *neve-midbar.ilbiz.co.il* ▭ *Sun.–Fri. NIS 70, Sat. and holidays NIS 80* ⊙ *Sun., Mon., Wed., and Sat. 9–6, Tues. and Thurs. 9 am–10 pm; Fri. 9–4.*

Rota Winery. One of the pioneers of the Negev winemaking scene, Erez Rota lives and works on a secluded ranch that's worth a stop. Since beginning to make wines over a decade ago, Rota's wines have gained recognition for their complexity and sophistication—all made in an incredibly rustic, mildly hippie-dippie setting. Call in advance to arrange a tasting (try the Yael, a nuanced Cabernet-Merlot fusion) accompanied by a selection of local Negev cheeses. An accomplished artist, Rota has created a free-form sculpture garden around the property, punctuated by his metal creations. He'll tour you around the property and tell you the story of how a Tel Aviv artist became one of the Negev's winemakers to watch. ⊠ *Rte. 222, north of Kibbutz Revivim* ✛ *From Mashabim junction, go 3 km past Kibbutz Revivim. Follow the second of two small handmarked signs up a dirt road for 1 km. Turn left before the large stone statue with the hole in the middle.* ☎ *054/496–8703.*

8

WHERE TO EAT

$$ EUROPEAN 🍴 **Ahuzat Smilansky.** On a tree-lined street with old-fashioned streetlights, you'll find this perfect venue for a laid-back, gourmet dining experience. Located in a renovated Ottoman-era building in Beersheva's Old City, the rustic restaurant and tapas bar has an outdoor balcony, high ceilings, floors enhanced with arabesque tiles, and an inner courtyard. Candle boxes hang from the walls, and dark-wood padded chairs and beautifully set tables give serene elegance to the lovely setting. The chef and owner, Yariv Eitani, apprenticed in Provence before returning to his hometown, but has changed the menu's focus to creatively prepared tapas-style dishes that don't disappoint. The menu is organized by type of protein, and filled with luxurious choices like house-made chorizo, glazed lamb spareribs, and Thai shrimp, but there are also plenty of prosaic—and delicious—meat skewers, salads, and vegetable dishes. [$] *Average main: NIS 65* ✉ *23 Smilansky, Old City* ☎ *08/665–4854* 🌐 *www.rol.co.il/sites/smilanski* ✍ *Reservations essential* 🕒 *Sun.–Thurs. 5 pm–last customer, Fri.–Sat. noon–last customer.*

$ MODERN ISRAELI 🍴 **Cafe Lola.** This whimsically decorated café in the Old City is a breath of fresh air in every respect. Eclectic, funky decor with wooden tables and splashes of color all around are the backdrop for a menu serving tasty dishes at breakfast, lunch, and dinner. Of course, there's a smashing Israeli breakfast-for-two featuring house-made bread, smoked salmon, and a mind-boggling array of condiments, and trays of citrus fruit behind the bar hint at the quality of the fresh-squeezed juices. Lunch is equally fetching, with a delicious *haloumi* cheese salad as a star choice. At night the vibe changes, and the small bar mixes up basic cocktails with flair-to-go with tapas-style dishes like bruschetta with juicy, thinly sliced steak and preserved lemon. Try one of their thick shakes, like an indulgent combination of dates, candied pecans, and coconut milk. [$] *Average main: NIS 40* ✉ *Smilansky Street 13, Old City* ☎ *08/628–8937* 🌐 *www.rol.co.il/sites/cafe-lola* ✍ *Reservations not accepted* 🕒 *Mon.–Thurs. 9 am–11 pm, Fri. 8 am–2 pm, Sat. 10 am–midnight.*

$ MODERN ISRAELI 🍴 **Saba Gepetto.** If you need a break from traditional Middle Eastern food, head to Saba (Grandpa) Gepetto, tucked into an alleyway of a small shopping mall. The dark, cavelike room features gourmet sandwiches served on fresh focaccia bread, with fillings ranging from stir-fried goose breast to chicken breast with pesto—and whimsical names like Mad Cow and Chicken Little. There are also serviceable salads and soups. The restaurant offers English-language menus and an excellent beer selection. For an after-dinner drink, make like a local and ask the hostess about Bar Basaba (Grandpa's Bar). She'll take you around the corner, unlock an unmarked door, and lead you into the coolest bar in Beersheva, hidden in the courtyard between office buildings. There you'll find local Negev beers on tap and, for the homesick, select American beers in bottles—and you can order a sandwich from the restaurant. [$] *Average main: NIS 45* ✉ *109 Rager Street* ✣ *In the alleyway of the small shopping mall in front of the Leonardo Negev hotel* ☎ *08/627–2829* 🕒 *No lunch Sat.*

$$$ MOROCCAN 🍴 **Yakota.** On a sleepy corner in the Old City sits this classic Moroccan restaurant, run by the same family since the 1960s. Though Yakota—decorated sumptuously in Moroccan textiles with accents of ornate pottery and hammered metal—often seems empty, the food is exceedingly fresh, creative, and delicious. Just say the word and chef Bebe will order for you, starting with a course of delicious house-made salads featuring seasonal ingredients like fennel, dates, and candied oranges, followed by simmering tagines of tender meat and vegetables (even local specialties like *kmehin*, a tuber-like desert root) simmered in delicate sauces. For dessert, a local baker prepares a host of delicate French Moroccan petits fours, delivered to the table on a tiered metal tower alongside steaming mint tea. [$] *Average main: NIS 80* ✉ *27 Mordai Hagettaíot St, Old City* ☎ *08/623–2689* ⏲ *No lunch Sat.*

WHERE TO STAY

$$ HOTEL 🏨 **Leonardo Negev.** Formerly the Golden Tulip, this hotel is the only game in town, and feels a bit like it's fallen prey to captive-audience syndrome. **Pros:** decent rates for what you get; nice gym; for those using Beersheva as a base for a Negev road trip, easy location at the entrance to the city. **Cons:** dull, nondescript setting; listless service; Internet costs extra. [$] *Rooms from: $245* ✉ *4 Henrietta Szold St., near City Hall* ☎ *08/640–5444* 🌐 *www.fattal.co.il* 🛏 *210 rooms, 48 suites* 🍽 *Breakfast.*

NIGHTLIFE AND THE ARTS

BARS

Coca Bar. Join Ben-Gurion University students for a beer, pizza, and burgers at Coca Bar, behind the Gimmel student dorms on Arlozorov Street. ✉ *Arlozorov 50* ☎ *050/773–7772.*

MUSIC

The Israel Sinfonietta Beer Sheva. This well-regarded symphonic group was founded in 1973 under the conduction of Doron Salomon as an outlet for immigrant musicians. Its concert hall seats more than 400 and features state-of-the-art acoustics. ✉ *Center for Performing Arts, Rager Boulevard 41* ☎ *08/626–6422* 🌐 *english.isb7.co.il.*

THEATER

Light Opera Group of the Negev. Once a year, in March or April, this opera company, a nonprofit group of amateur singers, presents performances of Gilbert and Sullivan and other light operas and musicals in English like *My Fair Lady, South Pacific,* and *Beauty and the Beast.* ☎ *08/641–4081* ✉ *negevlightopera@gmail.com* 🌐 *www.negevlightopera.com.*

SHOPPING

Bedouin Market. Although the Negev is still home to the Bedouin, many of today's Bedouin women are less inclined than yesterday's to stay home weaving. An eagle's eye and a saint's patience will guide your search through the bundles and stacks of rather ordinary stuff at the Bedouin market, where you can find goods made by elder generations. The market starts at daybreak each Thursday and lasts until early afternoon; south of the Old City, it's on the eastern side of the huge outdoor market site near the bridge. (A goat and sheep sale takes place once in a while.)

CLOSE UP

Bedouin Culture

Bedu, the Arabic word from which the name Bedouin derives, simply means "inhabitant of the desert." Some 160,000 Bedouin, seminomadic Arab tribesmen and full citizens of Israel, live in the Negev. The present-day Bedouin of the Negev (and the Sinai) trace their origins to nomads of the Arabian Peninsula who wandered west 400 to 600 years ago. The exceptions are members of the Jebeliya tribe, descendants of East European slaves sent by Emperor Justinian to serve Greek monks at St. Catherine's Monastery at Mt. Sinai. The slaves slowly adopted the Bedouin way of life, and they still serve the monks from their desert nearby.

Since Israel gained independence in 1948, the Bedouin's urbanization and integration into Israeli society has been difficult. The Negev's Bedouin men have loyally served in the Israeli army, and some have lost their lives doing so. Starting in the late 1960s, however, the Israeli government built seven Bedouin towns, the largest of which is Rahat (a settlement of over 40,000 residents, ten minutes north of Beersheva), and encouraged resettlement. Their simple, nomadic way of life becomes more difficult to maintain each year as they resist these policies.

EARNING A LIVING
The Bedouin's main livelihood is the raising of livestock, camels, and black goats in particular. The animals supply milk, meat, hair for weaving, and dung for burning as fuel. The wanderings of the Bedouin are driven by the unending search for grazing land and water for their flocks. Marriages are arranged, taking family interests into account. It is not uncommon today

for a man to have two wives, the first wife and a younger one to help her. The Bedouin boast one of the highest birth rates in the world.

The family is structured as a business. Men, who work as herders, make decisions about buying and selling livestock as well as finding new pastures. Women and children do the cooking, weaving, searching for firewood, and often caring for the flocks.

HOSPITALITY AND HERITAGE
A Bedouin proverb says, "He who shares my bread and salt is not my enemy." Bedouin are known for their warm hospitality. It is not only a pleasure to extend hospitality but the Bedouin see it as a duty. A Bedouin host would never fail to invite a stranger into his tent. And refusing a Bedouin's invitation would be unthinkable because it would deny the host an opportunity to display his kindness. Having the honor of being invited by a Bedouin host to drink sweet tea or coffee, made over an open fire in his tent, is an unforgettable experience. A Bedouin tent is customarily divided into two sections by a woven curtain known as a *ma'nad*. Having been welcomed into a tent, guests are honored, respected, and nourished, frequently with cardamom-spiced coffee, and music played on a traditional instrument called the *rababa*, a one-string violin.

A rich heritage of poetry has been passed down through the generations by word of mouth. Only in the past few years have these words been recorded, written in their original Arabic, and preserved by scholars who recognize that the Bedouin way of life is rapidly slipping away.

The best time to visit is 6 am, an hour or so later in winter. Walk to the back, passing coffee and tea sellers. For sale, if you can find them, are embroidered dresses, yokes, and side panels from dresses, woven camel bags, bales of wool, rugs, earrings, bracelets, amulets, and nose rings, coin headbands (used as dowry gifts), tassels, copperware, and *finjans* (Bedouin coffee pots). ⊠ *Corner of Derech Eilat and Derech Hevron Sts.* ⊕ *www.goisrael.coim* ⊙ *Open Thurs. early morning–sunset.*

Wine Aficionado (Inyanei Ha-Yayin). State-of-the-art design, a stock of imported and local wines, and well-informed staff (including owner Oded Arnat) distinguish this nearly-20-year-old shop. They also sell a well-curated selection of chocolate, olive oil, and coffee—great for gift-giving if you're visiting locals. ⊠ *117 Trumpeldor St., across the street from the Muslim cemetery* ☎ *08/628–9444* ⊕ *www.wine4you. co.il* ⊙ *Sun.–Thurs. 8:30–7:30, Fri. 8:30–3:30* ⊙ *Closed Sat.*

EN ROUTE **Monument to the Negev Brigade.** On Route 40 northeast from Beersheva to Arad is the large and impressive Monument to the Negev Brigade, designed by renowned Israeli artist Danny Karavan and built during the 1960s. The monument's 18 symbolic parts and Hebrew text tell the story of the Palmach's Negev Brigade, which halted the Egyptian attack during the War of Independence after the birth of the State of Israel in 1948. Framed by two acacia trees, the tower offers a great view of Beersheva and the surrounding desert. ▬ *Free.*

SIDE TRIP TO PETRA

Fodor'sChoice
★ Poet Dean Burgon called Petra, the ancient city of dazzling facades tucked into the mountains of southern Jordan, the "rose red city, half as old as time." Situated between the Red Sea and the Dead Sea, Petra is about two hours north of Eilat and four hours south of the Jordanian capital Amman. Its boulevards, temples, and splendid tombs (800 in all) secreted among the high cliffs, evoke incomparable mystery and grandeur. Once inaccessible to all but an intrepid few, this fabulous archaeological site is now easier to reach and has become an increasingly popular destination.

Petra (called Rekem in the Dead Sea Scrolls) lies in the biblical region of Edom. According to Genesis, the Edomites were descendants of Esau, Jacob's brother and rival. Edom's fertile land was a magnet that desert dwellers couldn't ignore, but the Edomites were careful to keep it exclusive. When Moses led the Israelites to the Promised Land and asked to pass through Edom, he was denied.

By the 7th century BC, a new group had swept in from Arabia: the Nabateans. Their spectacular tombs and carved monuments draw travelers to Petra today. With a wealthy empire that at its height reached from Damascus to the Sinai, the Nabateans controlled the region's trade routes, their caravans bearing frankincense and myrrh, Indian silks, and African ivory.

Most of Petra's famous tombs—which fuse Greco-Roman, Egyptian, and Mesopotamian styles—were carved during the 1st century AD, before the Nabatean kingdom was subsumed into the Roman Empire.

Although the combination of a necropolis and a capital city may seem strange today, this custom was common among ancient peoples, who established cemeteries at the entrances to many of their capitals. The presence of tombs of the rich and powerful near the city's major monuments was perhaps part of a cult of the dead. When travelers came to the city, they would leave offerings at the tombs to ensure the success of their journeys.

Gradually, Christianity replaced the old religion, and churches were built in Petra. Around the same time, the rise of sea trade began to precipitate Petra's decline, as ancient traders learned that they could use prevailing winds to hasten ships across the sea. Some Arabian goods began to come to Egypt and its Mediterranean ports via the Red Sea. It didn't help that a series of earthquakes left a ruinous mark on the city.

After Petra's takeover by the Muslims in 633, alliances and crossroads changed and the rest of the world lost interest in the area. The Crusaders built fortifications among the ruins in the 11th century, but after their 1189 surrender to the Muslim warrior Saladin, the city sank into oblivion. Only the local Bedouin knew its treasures. It wasn't until 1812 that Swiss explorer Johann Ludwig Burckhardt rediscovered Petra, providing the Western world with its first contemporary description of the marvels of this Nabatean caravan-city. It's now justly recognized as a UNESCO World Heritage Site.

PETRA PLANNER

WHEN TO GO

Summer temperatures hit 100 degrees, but it can get chilly and rainy in January and February. In all seasons, sturdy shoes are essential for negotiating the rocky, uneven terrain. If traveling during the Muslim holy month of Ramadan, some services may not be operating or operating at reduced hours; however, all tourist sites and services are open for regular business. Check with your hotel or the tourist office ahead of time.

PLANNING YOUR TIME

An overnight (two-day) trip to Petra is optimal. Be prepared for a lot of walking: it's about 2 miles from the entry to the Basin restaurant.

Begin at the Horse Square and walk through the narrow, mysterious Siq to the Treasury, Petra's most magnificent facade. From there, continue along what was once the city's main street, lined with monuments from Petra's glory days. Walk along the colonnaded street to the Basin for lunch. The route back is the same, but the sun striking the rocks at different angles reveals new dimensions of the site's beauty; note that the way back is uphill. The horse-drawn carriages you'll see are meant only for the infirm, but they can be hired, gypsy-cab style, by tired pedestrians. Expect to pay about JD 40 from the entry to the Treasury or JD 40 from the Basin to the entry. In the evening, enjoy the sunset from a hotel balcony or rooftop terrace. Check at the visitor center to see if the Petra by Night tour is on.

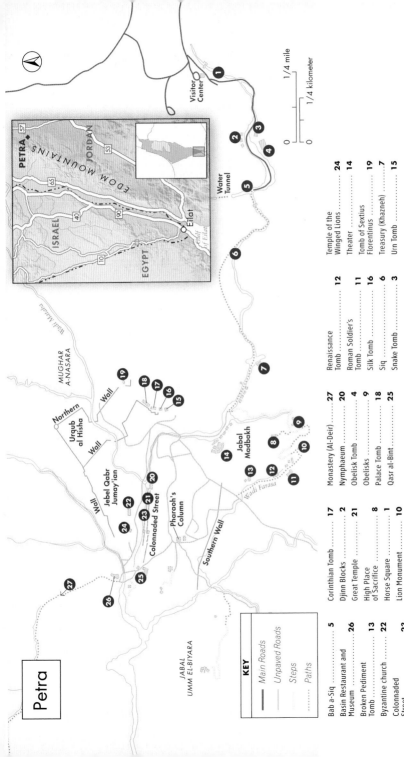

Petra

KEY

━━━	*Main Roads*
───	*Unpaved Roads*
	Steps
·······	*Paths*

Bab a-Siq	5
Basin Restaurant and Museum	26
Broken Pediment Tomb	13
Byzantine church	22
Colonnaded Street	23

Corinthian Tomb	17
Djinn Blocks	2
Great Temple	21
High Place of Sacrifice	8
Horse Square	1
Lion Monument	10

Monastery (Al-Deir)	27
Nymphaeum	20
Obelisk Tomb	4
Obelisks	9
Palace Tomb	18
Qasr al-Bint	25

Renaissance Tomb	12
Roman Soldier's Tomb	11
Silk Tomb	16
Siq	6
Snake Tomb	3

Temple of the Winged Lions	24
Theater	14
Tomb of Sextius Florentinus	19
Treasury (Khazneh)	7
Urn Tomb	15

1/4 mile

1/4 kilometer

Visitor Center

Water Tunnel

ISRAEL

JORDAN

EGYPT

EDOM MOUNTAINS

PETRA

Eilat

Gulf of Eilat

Wadi Mataha

MUGHAR A-NASARA

Northern Wall

Urqub al Hisha

Wall

Jebel Qabr Jumay'ian

Wall

Colonnaded Street

Pharaoh's Column

Southern Wall

Jabal Madbakh

Wadi Farasa

JABAL UMM EL-BIYARA

On the second day, you can return to the Treasury and explore other sites, perhaps making the climb up to the Monastery. There are lots of well-stocked souvenir shops by the visitor center if you want some souvenirs or gifts.

GETTING HERE AND AROUND
AIR TRAVEL

El Al and Royal Jordanian Airlines both fly to Amman, Jordan's capital, from Tel Aviv's Ben Gurion Airport. This option has limited appeal, as you must be at the airport two hours before flight time for the 15-minute flight, then drive three hours from Amman to Petra.

Twice a week, Arkia Airlines offers one-day guided tours in which you fly from Tel Aviv to Eilat at 6:30 am, drive to Petra in an air-conditioned bus, spend three hours walking through Petra, and take a return flight arriving in Tel Aviv at 9 pm. The rate per person is about $300 (⊕ *www.arkia.com*).

BUS TRAVEL

To get to Petra from Aqaba—the Jordanian town just across the border that shares the Red Sea shore with Eilat—two buses a day run at a cost of JD 5, but there's no specific timetable.

To get to Petra from Amman, public buses run from Amman's Mujema Al Janoub, or the South Bus Station. They depart when full. Three private bus companies offer air-conditioned service between Petra and Amman.

CAR TRAVEL

A parking area on the Israeli side of the border makes it possible to drive a rental car here, but only cars registered to their drivers can be taken into Jordan. For those taking longer trips, rental cars are available in Aqaba and Petra. Hidab Hotel can book rental cars from local agencies. There's an Avis agency in the Moevenpick Hotel in Petra and in Aqaba. The Hertz office in Petra is located next to the Palace Hotel on the main street of Wadi Musa.

TAXI TRAVEL

Once you cross into Jordan from Eilat, shared taxis are available on the Jordanian side of the border to take you into Aqaba, where you can rent a car or take the bus to Petra if the scheduling is right. A shared taxi to Aqaba costs about JD 10, which is divided among the passengers. If your time in Petra is limited, consider taking the faster but costlier private taxi, which will run you JD 45 to JD 50; be prepared to negotiate.

CROSSING THE BORDER

The closest border crossing to Petra is just north of Eilat at what's called the Arava crossing. Cross the border early in the morning to avoid waiting in line behind large tour groups and aim to be in Petra before noon. When crossing back from Jordan to Israel, bring JD 6 for the Jordanian exit tax.

Americans need a visa to enter Jordan. It can be bought on the spot for about NIS 88.

Most visitors take a taxi to the Jordan border from Eilat (10 minutes, NIS 35), walk across, and catch a taxi to Petra on the other side (about JD 45). The Arava border crossing, just north of Eilat, is open Sunday to Thursday 6:30 am to 10 pm, Friday and Saturday 8 to 8. The crossing is closed on the religious holidays Yom Kippur and Id el Fitr. Two other border crossings might be convenient under certain circumstances. The Allenby Bridge crossing (known in Jordan as the King Hussein crossing, four hours' drive from Petra) is about 45 minutes from Jerusalem. Remember to bring a passport photo. The northern Beit She'an border crossing (five hours' drive from Petra) is approximately 40 minutes from Tiberias.

MONEY MATTERS

The Jordanian unit of currency is the dinar, abbreviated JD. The exchange rate at this writing was approximately JD 0.71 to the U.S. dollar. You can change money at the Moevenpick, next to the entrance to Petra.

TOURS

A number of operators run tours to Petra that you can reserve in advance from Eilat. They're a good option if you want to see the highlights without worrying about logistics. (⊕ *www.petraisrael.com* offers tips on arranging tours to Petra from Israel.)

VISITOR INFORMATION

Visitor Center. Petra's visitor center, next to the site entrance, has brochures and you can arrange local guides for a basic two-hour Petra tour for a flat fee of JD 15. ☎ *03/215–6029* ⊕ *www.petrapark.com* 🖃 *1-day pass JD 50; 2-day pass JD 55* ☉ *Summer 6–6; winter 6–4.*

EXPLORING PETRA

TOP ATTRACTIONS

Colonnaded Street. The Romans built the main street of Petra in the early 1st century BC. In typical Roman style, it became the city's major thoroughfare, suitable for both commerce and grand ceremonial processions. After the Roman annexation of the Nabatean kingdom, the street was restored, as noted in an inscription dated AD 114, and dedicated to Emperor Trajan. The original marble paving stones as well as remains of statues of deities still stand, including those depicting Hermes (messenger of the gods) and Tyche (goddess of fortune). In AD 363 an earthquake devastated Petra and the surrounding region, and the street never returned to its former glory.

Great Temple. No one can say for sure who was worshipped at this temple, or if it was the seat of the city's government. But the dozens of columns that adorn its courtyards, beautifully restored in recent years by archaeologists from Brown University, attest to its ancient grandeur; it even boasted its own theater, which some scholars believe may have been a meeting hall for Petra's rulers.

Qasr al-Bint. This structure's full name, which translates as the "Palace of the Daughter of Pharaoh," derives from a legend that the pharaoh's daughter promised she would marry the man who could channel water to the city where she lived. When she had to choose between two winners, she asked each how he'd managed his appointed task. The one whose answer she preferred won her hand. In fact, the structure was the most important temple in Petra, built in the early 1st century AD. As in the Temple of the Winged Lions, the identity of the deity worshipped here isn't known, but a statue depicting him or her—perhaps Dushara,

8

DID YOU KNOW?

The Treasury, Petra's most famous facade, was featured in the movie *Indiana Jones and the Last Crusade* and was the location where the Holy Grail was found.

the greatest deity of the Nabatean pantheon—certainly stood in the temple's inner sanctum. A giant marble hand, part of a colossal statue, was discovered here in 1959.

Fodor's Choice
★

Siq. The main entrance to Petra, in ancient times as in ours, is through the Siq (meaning "cleft"), a narrow, 1200-meter long canyon between towering walls of astonishing red and purple-hued stone. Bands of Nabatean paving stones are still visible along the way. Votive niches, some of which contain inscriptions dating from the 2nd and 3rd centuries AD, show that this road served as much as a ceremonial path as a passageway. Your first glimpse of the magnificent Treasury, after you've walked a hundred meters or so through the narrow Siq, will take your breath away. Film buffs may recall Harrison Ford galloping through this area in *Indiana Jones and the Last Crusade*.

Theater. This semicircular amphitheater is a clear sign of the extent to which the Nabateans, like most other peoples of this region, had adopted Roman culture. The Nabateans apparently had no qualms about building a theater in a cemetery; their stonemasons even cut into some of the existing tombs (the remains of which you can see at the back of the rock-cut theater) to do so. The capacity of the theater has been estimated at 7,000.

Fodor's Choice
★

Treasury. The Siq opens suddenly onto Petra's most famous monument, known locally as the Khazneh. This 130-foot-high structure displays a splendid frontage graced by a number of mythological figures adopted by the Nabateans from Greek and Roman worship. Castor and Pollux (who after their deaths became the two brightest stars in the constellation Gemini), Amazons, Gorgons, eagles, and other creatures march across the Khazneh's rosy facade. Between the columns of the *tholos* (the rounded section above the tympanum) are the remains of a female deity holding a cornucopia; she's believed to be al-Uzza, the patroness of Petra and the Nabatean version of Aphrodite, goddess of love.

The full Arabic name for this monument is Khazneh Fara'un, or Pharaoh's Treasury. It was assumed by archaeologists to be a royal tomb, and legends of treasures allegedly secreted within have drawn grave robbers to this place for centuries. The urn carved at the top of the tholos was thought to be the hiding place for the hoard. The Bedouin have been taking potshots at it for generations in the hopes of dislodging its contents, a practice whose results are still visible.

WORTH NOTING

Bab a-Siq. The Gate of the Cleft opens onto the Siq, the canyon-lined passageway leading to the main sights. From here you can spot the remains of a Nabatean water tunnel, built to divert flood waters from coursing through the narrow cleft and flooding the necropolis. A dam, constructed for the same purpose in the second half of the 1st century AD, was restored by the Jordanians after particularly serious flooding some years ago.

Broken Pediment Tomb. One of a series of facades carved into the western face of Jabal Madhbah, or the Mount of the Altar, this tomb is characterized by the broken-off gable of its roof, supported by four pilasters topped with Nabatean capitals.

Byzantine Church. Richly decorated with mosaics in the characteristic style of the period, this church (discovered by the American archaeologist Kenneth Russell, and excavated in the 1990s) appears to have been destroyed by fire soon after its construction, perhaps in a severe earthquake that took place in AD 551. The remains, including a spectacular mosaic floor, have undergone only partial conservation. One hundred and forty papyrus scrolls were found here.

Corinthian Tomb. Set among some of Petra's finest tombs is one named for the large number of Corinthian capitals, now badly deteriorated, that once decorated its facade.

Djinn Blocks. The function of these three large structures is unclear; they may have been connected to Nabatean worship, perhaps symbolizing one of their deities. In Arabic, *djinn* refers to malevolent spirits, a common theme in Arab folklore.

High Place of Sacrifice. An ancient flight of stairs cut into the rock—and restored by the Jordanian Department of Antiquities—leads to the summit of Jabal Madhbah, or the Mount of the Altar. Its peak, besides offering spectacular views of Petra below, contains a rectangular court surrounded on three sides by benches in the triclinium style of the Roman dining room; in the center of the court is a raised block of stone, on which the priest may have stood. To the west are two altars accessed by steps, in front of which is a channel into which the blood of the sacrificial animal drained.

Horse Square. Horses used to be the conveyance of choice for the approximately 1-km (½-mile) trip to Petra's main antiquities. Your entry ticket currently entitles you to a horseback ride (no carriage) along the first 800 yards of the path before it narrows to become the Siq; you'll still be expected to tip though (about 5 JD), and many people skip this.

Lion Monument. Surface runoff fed this fountain on the path to the High Place via a channel leading to the lion's mouth, from which water once streamed.

Monastery (Al-Deir). Second only to the Treasury in its magnificence, the Monastery is reached at the end of a winding uphill 4-km (2½-mile) trail. It's larger than the Treasury (it stands 170 feet wide), but less impressively ornate. An inscription was discovered nearby referring to "the symposium of Obodas the God." From this inscription, archeologists deduced that the Monastery was built 2,000 years ago as a meeting place for members of the cult of Obodas. Either tomb or temple, it holds a spacious chamber cut deep into the mountainside, and offers sweeping views of the adjacent gorges.

Museum. Petra's museum, which has restrooms, is in the same building as The Basin restaurant. Displays include a small number of Nabatean artifacts, such as jewelry and pottery.

Nymphaeum. Dedicated to the water nymphs, this fountain was used for both refreshment and worship. The fountains of the two-story structure were fed by a water channel that continued along Petra's main street.

Obelisk Tomb. This upper story of a two-story tomb is named for the four freestanding obelisks that decorate its facade. The lower story, the Triclinium Tomb, was so named because three walls of the empty room are lined with *triclinia*, a Latin word for this kind of bench. Sacred memorial feasts to honor the dead were held here.

Obelisks. On the terrace below the High Place stand two obelisks hewed from the bedrock, examples of a common method of representing deities in the ancient Near East. Some scholars believe them to be representations of Dushara and al-Uzza; others believe they're simply the remains of quarries.

Palace Tomb. This unfinished tomb is one of the few in Petra not carved entirely out of the rock. Many of the tomb's constructed segments have fallen away, so it's hard to ascertain its original dimensions. At the base of the Palace Tomb are the remains of the northern city wall, built after the 1st century BC.

Renaissance Tomb. This tomb, bearing a pediment with three urns, bears a close resemblance to the Tomb of Sextius Florentinus, in the main part of the city. It may have been created around the same time, the first third of the 1st century AD.

Roman Soldier's Tomb. The headless figure in the niche of this unusual tomb's facade is dressed in typical Roman military garb, while the friezes and floral capitals appear more typical of Nabatean architecture before the Roman annexation. Directly opposite the Roman Soldier's Tomb is a triclinium; the rubble in between was probably once a colonnaded courtyard connecting the two edifices.

Silk Tomb. The striations of natural color in the Silk Tomb's rock make it one of Petra's finest and certainly the easiest to spot. The ribbons of rock flow across the facade like a multicolored silk scarf blowing in the wind.

Snake Tomb. No outward decoration marks this tomb, but 12 burial niches are carved into the floor inside. The name comes from a rough wall relief that shows two snakes attacking what may be a dog. Notice also the horse-and-rider relief above it.

Temple of the Winged Lions. This impressive building overlooking the Colonnaded Street takes its name from the sculptures that serve as capitals for its columns. The identity of the deity worshipped within is unknown, but votive figurines suggest that it may have been Isis, Egyptian goddess of the heavens and patroness of fertility. An inscription dates the construction of the temple to around AD 27, during the reign of Aretas IV.

8

Tomb of Sextius Florentinus. This is one of the few Petra monuments that can be dated with certainty: the name of this Roman governor of Arabia who died in office in AD 128 appears in the Latin inscription over the tomb's doorway.

Urn Tomb. Named for the vaselike decoration at the top of its pediment, this is the largest of Petra's royal tombs. It's supported by a series of vaults at its lower level, dubbed *al makhamah* (the law court) by the locals for some long-lost reason; the upper level was called *a-sijn* (the prison). Although originally carved around AD 70, according to an inscription within, Petra's Byzantine Christians turned the Urn Tomb into a church in AD 446.

WHERE TO EAT

Dining in the town closest to the antiquities site of Petra—Wadi Musa—ranges from simple, inexpensive fare to the elegant and pricey, with little in between. Both dining experiences, however, have one thing in common: courteous service and a welcoming spirit. Don't be put off by the plainness of center-village eateries. The locals enjoying their meal at the next table will remind you that the best fare is often to be had at such unostentatious restaurants.

$$ MIDDLE EASTERN
🍴 **Al-Arabi.** This is a reliable place for a quick, inexpensive lunch, where diners can get a substantial meal, including mixed grill (their specialty), shawarma, barbecued meats, and hummus. The interior is very simple but bright. Look for the red sign on the left as you walk uphill. [$] *Average main: JD 5* ✉ *Main St., Wadi Musa* ☎ *03/215–7661.*

$$$$ MIDDLE EASTERN
🍴 **Petra Kitchen.** If you're up for a hands-on dinner, this spot is an enticing choice. Here, Jordanian chefs take you through your paces as you chop, slice, cook, and assemble Jordanian specialties like *maqlouba* (a layered meat-and-vegetable dish served at festive meals) and *fattoush* (moistened bread salad) before sitting down to dinner. Market tours and multiday tours can be arranged with advance notice. [$] *Average main: JD 24* ✉ *Wadi Musa,* ☎ *03/215–7900* ✍ *Reservations essential.*

WHERE TO STAY

Petra has many lodging options. You can choose from luxurious to money-saving accommodations; both can be found adjacent to or near the site. The hotels closest to the site obviously provide the most convenient access to Petra and save you taxi money. A short car drive away in Wadi Musa are several good hotels, with some on the ridge above Wadi Musa. Taybet Zeman, in the village of Taybeh 9 km (5½ miles) from Petra, is the farthest from the site, but its uniquely authentic flavor is well worth the ride. All rooms have a private bath unless otherwise indicated.

$$$$ HOTEL
🏨 **Marriott Petra.** This excellent three-floor hotel is located on the ridge above Petra, somewhat farther away than the other hotels, though free shuttle service to the Petra entrance is available. **Pros:** stunning sunset views; Petra's best Italian restaurant, L'Affresco. **Cons:** 15-minute drive to Petra entrance; doesn't change Israeli currency. [$] *Rooms from: $210*

✉ *Queen Rania Al Abdallah St., Wadi Musa* ☎ *03/215–6407* 🌐 *www.marriott.com/hotels* 🛏 *99 rooms, 1 suite* 🍴 *No meals.*

$$$$ HOTEL Fodor's Choice ★ 🏨 **Moevenpick.** One good reason to stay here is the unmatched location: just steps from the entrance to Petra, this five-floor, Swiss-run hotel has comfortable rooms with blond-wood furnishings and gold-framed mirrors, some with balconies.**Pros:** the hotel's sumptuous Al Iwan restaurant is the best in Wadi Musa; the breakfast buffet is excellent; quiet. **Cons:** slow Internet. [$] *Rooms from: $250* ✉ *Tourism Street, Wadi Musa* ☎ *03/215–7111* 🌐 *www.moevenpick-petra.com* 🛏 *183 rooms* 🍴 *Multiple meal plans.*

$$$$ HOTEL Fodor's Choice ★ 🏨 **Petra Moon.** This 52-room hotel has rapidly become a favorite with visitors to Petra. **Pros:** convenient location; great service; good restaurant. **Cons:** no views; expensive restaurant. [$] *Rooms from: $142* ✉ *Visitor Center Street, Wadi Musa* ☎ *03/215–6220* ✉ *info@petramoonhotel.com* 🌐 *www.petramoonhotel.com* 🛏 *52 rooms* 🍴 *Breakfast.*

$$$$ HOTEL FAMILY 🏨 **Taybet Zeman.** On the outskirts of the town of Taybeh, 9 km (5½ miles) from Petra, this charming lodging was once a Bedouin village. **Pros:** on a ridge high above Petra, the hotel offers views of the mountains of Edom, especially from the Diwan, its garden terrace; excellent service. **Cons:** not within walking distance to the entrance to Petra. [$] *Rooms from: $175* ✉ *Queen Rania St., Wadi Musa* ☎ *03/215–0111* 🌐 *www.taybetzaman.jordantourismresorts.com/* 🛏 *105 rooms* 🍴 *Breakfast.*

NIGHTLIFE AND THE ARTS

Petra by Night. The two-hour Petra by Night candlelit walk of Petra is atmospheric. Strolling through the Siq as shadows play on the canyon walls allows you to appreciate another side of the magnificent carved city. Music is played on traditional instruments such as the *rababa*. Check for availability at the Petra visitor center. It's recommended to do this first, if you arrive in the evening, and then go back and do a thorough visit the next day; it can seem anticlimactic if you already know what to expect. Keep in mind that the walk through the Siq to the Treasury is about 1 km (½ mile), downhill on the way in, and back up the same route out; there are no carriage rides at night. ☎ *03/215–6029* 🎫 *JD 12* ⏲ *Mon., Wed., and Thurs. 8:30–10:30 pm.*

SHOPPING

Petra's handicraft specialty is the work of its "sand artists"—artisans who fill bottles with sand in a variety of hues and complex designs. They can customize the purchase by writing a name or other text in the sand. The artists work and sell their unique wares in shops in Wadi Musa, as well as in the Siq.

HEBREW VOCABULARY

Many people in Israel speak at least one other language, in addition to Hebrew, and most can get by in English. So the chances of getting too lost for words are slim. At the same time, your traveling experience can be enriched by having at least a few words to share in conversation or to use while touring and shopping, even at the local grocery store. Here are some basic words and expressions that may be of use during your stay. Please note that the letters "kh" in this glossary are pronounced like the "ch" in chanuka or the Scottish loch.

ENGLISH	HEBREW TRANSLITERATION	PRONUNCIATION
GREETINGS AND BASICS		
Hello/good-bye/peace	Shalom	shah-**lohm**
Nice to meet you	Na'im me'od	nah-**eem** meh-**ohd**
Good morning	Boker tov	boh-ker **tohv**
Good evening	Erev tov	eh-rev **tohv**
Good night	Layla tov	lahy-lah tohv
How are you?	Ma shlomekh?	mah shloh-**maykh**
How are you? (to a man)	Ma shlomkha?	mah shlohm-**khah**
How are you?	Ma nishma?	mah-nee-**shmah**
Fine	Beseder	beh-**say-dehr**
Everything is fine	Hakol beseder	hah-kohl beh-**say-dehr**
Is everything okay?	Hakol beseder?	hah-kohl beh-**say-dehr**
Very well	Tov me'od	tohv-meh-**ohd**
Excellent/terrific	Metzuyan	meh-tzoo-**yahn**
Send regards!	Timsor dash!	teem-sohr **dahsh**
Thank you	Toda	toh-**dah**
Thank you very much	Toda raba	toh-dah rah-**bah**
See you again	Lehitra'ot	leh-heet-rah-**oht**
Yes	Ken	kehn
No	Lo	lo
Maybe	Oolai	**oo**-ligh
Excuse me/Sorry	Slicha	slee-**khah**
Again/Could you repeat that?	Od pa'am	ohd pah-**ahm**

	ENGLISH	HEBREW TRANSLITERATION	PRONUNCIATION
DAYS			
	Today	Hayom	hah-**yohm**
	Tomorrow	Machar	mah-**khahr**
	Yesterday	Etmol	eht-**mohl**
	Sunday	Yom Rishon	yohm ree-**shohn**
	Monday	Yom Sheni	yohm sheh-**nee**
	Tuesday	Yom Shlishi	yohm sh-**leeshee**
	Wednesday	Yom Revi'i	yohm reh-**vee**
	Thursday	Yom Chamishi	yohm kha-mee-**shee**
	Friday	Yom Shishi	yohm shee-**shee**
	Saturday, Sabbath	Shabbat	yohm shah-**bat**
NUMBERS			
	1	Echad	eh-**khad**
	2	Shtayim	shtah-**yeem**
	3	Shalosh	shah-**lohsh**
	4	Arba	ah-**rbah**
	5	Chamesh	chah-**maysh**
	6	Shesh	shehsh
	7	Sheva	**sheh**-vah
	8	Shmoneh	**shmoh**-neh
	9	Teisha	**tay**-shah
	10	Esser	**eh**-sehr
	11	Achad esreh	ah-**chahd** eh-**sreh**
	12	Shteim esreh	sh**taym** eh-**sreh**
	20	Esrim	eh-**sreem**
	50	Chamishim	khah-mee-**sheem**
	100	Me'a	may-**ah**
	200	Ma'tayim	mah-**tah**-yeem

ENGLISH	HEBREW TRANSLITERATION	PRONUNCIATION

USEFUL PHRASES

Do you speak English?	Ata medaber anglit?	ah-ta meh-dah-ber ahng-**leet**
I don't understand (man)	Ani lo mevin	a-**nee** loh meh-**veen**
I don't understand (woman)	Ani lo m'vina	a-**nee** m'veena
I don't know (man)	Ani lo yodea	a-nee loh yoh-**day**-ah
I don't know (woman)	Ani lo yodaat	a-nee loh yoh-**dah**-aht
I am lost (man)	Ani avud	a-nee ah-**vood**
I am lost (woman)	Ani avuda	a-nee ahvoo-**dah**
I am American	Ani Amerika'i	ah-nee ah-mer-ee-**kah**-ee
I am British	Ani Briti	ah-**nee bree**-tee
I am Canadian	Ani Canadi	ah-**nee** kah-**nah**-dee
What is the time?	Ma hasha'a?	mah hah-shah-**ah**
Just a minute	Rak rega	rahk **reh**-gah
Minute, moment	Rega	**reh**-gah
Now	Achshav	ahkh-**shahv**
Not yet	Od lo	ohd loh
Later	Achar kach	ah-**khahr** kahkh
I would like	Hayiti mevakesh	hah-**yee**-tee m-vah-**kehsh**
Where is…?	Eifo…?	**ay**foh
The central bus station	Hatachana hamerkazit	hah-tah-khah-**nah** hah-mehr-kah-**zeet**
The bus stop	Tachanat ha'autobus	tah-khah-**naht** hah-oh-toh-**boos**
The train station	Tachanat harakevet	tah-khah-**naht** hah-rah-**keh-veht**
The city center	Merkaz ha'ir	mehr kahz hah-**eer**
The post office	Hado'ar	hah-**doh**-ahr
A pharmacy	Beit mirkachat	bayt meer-**kah**-khaht

ENGLISH	HEBREW TRANSLITERATION	PRONUNCIATION
A public telephone	Telefon tziburi	teh-leh-**fohn** tzee-boo-**ree**
A good restaurant	Mis'ada tova	mee-sah-**dah toh-vah**
The rest rooms	Hasherutim	hah-shay-roo-**teem**
Right	Yemina	yeh-**mee**-nah
Left	Smola	s-**moh**-lah
Straight ahead	Yashar	yah-**shar**
Here	Kan	kahn
There	Sham	shahm
Do you have a (vacant) room?	Yesh lachem cheder (panui)?	yehsh lah-**chehm khed**-ehr (pah-**nooy**)
Is it possible to order a taxi?	Efshar lehazmin monit?	ehf-**shahr** leh-hahz-**meen** moh-**neet**
Taxi	Monit	moh-**neet**
A little	k'tzat	keh-**tzaht**
A lot	harbe	hahr-**beh**
Enough	maspik	Mah-**speek**
I have a problem	Yesh li ba'aya	yehsh lee bah-**yah**
I don't feel well (man)	Ani lo margish tov	ah-**nee** loh mahr-**geesh** tohv
I don't feel well (woman)	Ani lo margisha tov	ah-**nee** loh mahr-**gee-shah** tohv
I need a doctor (man)	Ani tzarich rofe	ah-**nee** tzah-**reech** roh-**feh**
I need a doctor (woman)	Ani tzricha rofe	ah-**nee** tzree-**khah** roh-**feh**
Help	Ezra	Eh-**zrah**
Fire	Dleika	duh-leh-**kah**

DINING

I would like	Hayiti mevakesh	hah-**yee**-tee m-vah-**kehsh**
Some water, please	Mayim, bevakasha	mah-**yeem** beh-vah-kah-**shah**
Bread	Lechem	leh-khehm

ENGLISH	HEBREW TRANSLITERATION	PRONUNCIATION
Soup	Marak	mah-**rahk**
Meat	Bassar	bah-**ssahr**
Chicken	Off	ohf
Vegetables	Yerakot	yeh-rah-**koht**
Dessert	Kinuach	kee-**noo**-ahkh
Cake	Ooga	**oo**-gah
Fruit	Perot	peh-**roht**
Coffee	Cafe	kah-**feh**
Tea	Te	teh
fork	Mazleg	mahz-**lehg**
spoon	Kapit	kah-**peet**
knife	Sakin	sah-**keen**
plate	Tzalachat	tzah-**lah**-chaht
Napkin	Mapit	mah-**peet**
Food	Ochel	**oh**-khehl
Meal	Arucha	ah-roo-**khah**
Breakfast	Aruchat boker	ah-roo-**khaht boh**-ker
Lunch	Aruchat tzaharayim	ah-roo-khaht tzah-hah-**rah**-yeem
Dinner	Aruchat erev	Ahroo-**khaht eh**-rehv
Do you have a menu in English?	Yesh tafrit be'anglit?	yehsh tahf-**reet** beh- ahng-**leet**
A pita filled with falafel	Manat felafel	mah-naht feh-**lah**-fehl
Without hot sauce	Bli charif	blee khah-**reef**
It's tasty, delicious	Zeh ta'im	zeh tah-**eem**
I don't like the taste	Zeh lo ta'im li	zeh loh tah-**eem** lee
The check, please	Cheshbon, bevakasha	Khehsh-bohn beh-vah-kah-**shah**

ENGLISH	HEBREW TRANSLITERATION	PRONUNCIATION

SHOPPING

ENGLISH	HEBREW TRANSLITERATION	PRONUNCIATION
Do you have…?	Yesh lecha…?	yesh leh-khah
Milk	Chalav	khah-**lahv**
(Orange) Juice	Mitz (tapuzim)	meetz (tah-poo-**zeem**)
Butter	Chem'a	khem-**ah**
Cream cheese	Gevina levana	geh-vee-**nah** leh-vah-**nah**
Hard cheese	Gevina tzehuba	gevee-**nah** tzeh-**hoo**-bah
Sausage	Naknik	Nahk-**neek**
Jelly	Riba	**ree**-bah
Sugar	Sukar	**soo**-kahr
Ice cream	Glida	**glee**-da
Map	Mapa	**mah**-pa
Cigarettes	Sigariyot	see-gahr-ee-**yoht**
Telephone card (for public phones)	Telecart	teh-leh-**kahrt**
That one, please	Et zeh, bevakasha	eht zeh, beh-vah-kah-**shah**
May I see it?	Efshar lir'ot?	ehf-**shahr** leer-**oht**
How much does it cost?	Kama zeh oleh?	**kah**-ma zeh **ohleh**
That's expensive!	Yakar!	yah-**kahr**
No, it's too expensive	Lo, zeh yakar midai	loh, zeh yah-**kahr** meed-**igh**
Too big	Gadol midai	gah-dohl meed-**igh**
Too small	Katan midai	kah-tan meed-**igh**
Perhaps there is a discount ?	Yesh hanacha oolai	Yehsh hah-na-**khah** oo-ligh oo-**ligh**
I'll take it	Ani ekach et zeh	ah-nee eh-**kakh** eht zeh

PALESTINIAN ARABIC VOCABULARY

Arabic is spoken by all Arab citizens of Israel (about 20% of the Israeli population) and in the West Bank and Gaza. The areas where you're most likely to hear Arabic are East Jerusalem, Jaffa, and Nazareth, and in the popular sites of the West Bank, Bethlehem and Jericho (when these are open to travelers). Many people in these areas speak some English, but a little Arabic will come in handy with some vendors and taxi drivers or when you are in more rural areas and villages. It helps to have a written address for a taxi ride as well. You may run into small differences in dialect and accent between villages and cities, but for the most part Palestinians dialects are similar.

Some letters in Arabic do not have English equivalents. This glossary tries to approximate Arabic sounds. The letter 'r' is always rolled. When you see 'gh' at the start of a word, pronounce it like a French 'r', lightly gargled at the back of the throat. Any double letters should be extended: 'aa' is pronounced as an extended 'ah'; 'hh' is an extended 'h' sound; 'ss' is an extended hiss.

ENGLISH	ARABIC TRANSLITERATION	PRONUNCIATION
GREETINGS AND BASICS		
Hello/ peace be upon you	salamou alaikom	sah-**lah**-moo aah-**lay**-kom
(reply) Hello/ and peace be upon you	wa aalaikom essalaam	wah aah-**lay**-kom **ehss**-sah-**ahm**
Good-bye	maa issalameh	**maah** is-**ah-lah**-meh
Mr./ Sir	sayyed	**sigh**-yed
Mrs./ Madam	sayyida	**sigh**-yee-dah
Miss	anisseh	**ah**-niss-say
How are you? (man speaking)	keif hhalak	kayf **hah**-luck
How are you? (woman speaking)	keif hhalik	kayf **hah**-lik
Fine, thank you	bi kheir elhhamdilla	bee **khayr** el-**ham**-dihl-lah
Pleased to meet you	tsharrafna	tshahr-**ruhf**-nah
Please (man)	min fadlak	min **fahd**-lahk
Please (woman)	min fadlik	min **fahd**-lik
Thank you	shokran	shohk-rahn
God willing	Inshallah	ihn-**shahl**-lah
Yes	aah or naam	aah or naahm
No	la	lah

ENGLISH	ARABIC TRANSLITERATION	PRONUNCIATION
I'm Sorry (man)	mit assif	miht **ass**-sef
I'm Sorry (woman)	mit assfeh	miht **ass**-feh

DAYS

Today	eliom	el-**yohm**
Tomorrow	bokra	bok-rah
Yesterday	embarehh	ehm-**bah**-rehh
Sunday	il ahhad	**il ah**-had
Monday	Ittinein	it-tee-**nayn**
Tuesday	ittalata	it-tah-**lah**-tah
Wednesday	il 'arbaa	il **ahr**-bah-**aah**
Thursday	il khamees	il khah-**mees**
Friday	iljumaa	il zhum-**aah**
Saturday	issabet	**iss-sah**-bet

NUMBERS

1	wahed	**wah**-hed
2	tinein	tee-**nayn**
3	talati	tah-**lah**-tee
4	arbaa	**ahr**-bah-aah
5	khamseh	**khahm**-seh
6	sitteh	**sit**-teh
7	sabaa	sub-**aah**
8	tamanyeh	tah-**mah**-nee-**yeh**
9	tisaa	**tiss**-aah
10	aashara	**aah**-shah-rah
11	ihhdaaesh	ihh-**dah**-ehsh
12	itnaaesh	it-**nah**-ehsh
20	ishreen	iish-**reen**
50	khamseen	khahm-**seen**
100	meyyeh	**may**-yeh
200	mitein	**mee**-tain

ENGLISH	ARABIC TRANSLITERATION	PRONUNCIATION

USEFUL PHRASES

ENGLISH	ARABIC TRANSLITERATION	PRONUNCIATION
Do you speak English?	btihki inglizi?	btih-**kee** in-**glee**-zee?
I don't understand (man)	mish fahem	mish **fah**-him
I don't understand (woman)	mish fahmi	mish **fah**-meh
I don't know (man)	mish aarif	mish **aah**-ref
I don't know (woman)	mish aarfi	mish **aahr**-fee
I'm lost (man)	ana dayih	ah-nah **dah-yeh**
I'm lost (woman)	ana dayaa	ah-nah **dah**-ye-aah
I am American (man)	ana amriki	ah-nah ahm-**ree-kee**
I am American (woman)	ana amrikiyya	ah-nah ahm-**ree-key**-yah
I am British (man)	ana baritani	ah-nah bah-**ree-tah-nee**
I am British (woman)	ana baritaniya	ah-nah bah-**ree-tah-nay**-yah
What is this?	eish hada?	aysh **hah**-dah?
What time is it?	Addeish el wa'ed?	Ahd-**daysh**-el **wah**-ed
Where is?	wein?	wayn?
The train station	mahattit iltrain	mah-huht-**tit il-train**
The bus station	mahattit el buss	mah-**huht**-tit el **buhss**
The intracity bus station	mahattit el bus eddakheli	mah-huht-**tit el** buhss **ed**-dah-**khe-lee**
The taxi station	mujammaa el takasi	moo-**jam**-maah el tah-**kah**-see
The airport	el matar	el mah-**tahr**
The hotel	el oteil	el **ooh**-tayl
The cafe	el ahwi	el ah-**weh**
The restaurant	el mataam	el **matt-aahm**
The telephone	el tiliphon	el tih-lih-**fohn**
The hospital	el mostashfa	el moos-**tash**-fah

ENGLISH	ARABIC TRANSLITERATION	PRONUNCIATION
The post office	el bareed	el bah-**reed**
The rest room	el hammam	el huhm-**mahm**
The pharmacy	el saydaleyyeh	el sigh-dah-**lay-yeh**
The bank	el bank	el bahnk
The embassy	el safara	el sah-fah-**rah**
Right	yameen	yah-meen
Left	shmal	shmahl
Straight ahead	doughri	doo-ghree
I would like a room	beddi ghorfi	bed-dee **ghor-fih**
A little	shway or aleel	shway or ah-leel
A lot	kteer	kteer
Enough	bikaffi	bee-kaf-fee
I have a problem	aandi moshkili	aahn-dee **moosh**-keh-lee
I am ill	ana mareed	ah-nah mah-reed
I need a doctor	beddi daktor	bed-**dee** dac-**tor**
Help	saadoonee	**saah-doo**-nee
Fire	naar or harika	naahr or hah-**ree**-kah
Caution/ look out	entebeh or owaa	in-teh-beh or ohw-**aah**

DINING

ENGLISH	ARABIC TRANSLITERATION	PRONUNCIATION
I would like	beddi	behd-dee
Water	mayy	muhyy
Bread	khobez	kho-bihz
Vegetables	khodra	khod-rah
Meat	lahhmi	**lahh**-meh
Fruits	fawakeh	fah-**wah**-keh
Cakes/ Sweets	helou/ halaweyyat	**heh**-loo/ hah-lah-**way-yaht**
Tea	shay	shahy
Coffee	ahwi	ah-weh
A fork	shokeh	show-keh

ENGLISH	ARABIC TRANSLITERATION	PRONUNCIATION
A spoon	maala a	**maah**-lah ah
A knife	sikkeen	sick-**keen**
A plate	sahin	sah-hin

SHOPPING

I would like to buy	beddi ashtri	bed-**dee** ahsh-tree
cigarettes	sagayer or dokhkhan	sah-**gah**-yer or dokh-**khahn**
a city map	khareeta lal madeeni	khah-**ree**-tah lahl mah-**dee**-nee
a road map	khareeta lal tareek	khah-**ree**-tah lahl tah-**reek**
How much is it?	addaish ha o	**ad**-daysh **ha** oh
It's expensive	ghali	**ghah**-lee

TRAVEL SMART
ISRAEL

GETTING HERE AND AROUND

▮ AIR TRAVEL

The least expensive airfares to Israel are often priced for round-trip travel and must be purchased well in advance. Airlines generally allow you to change your return date for a fee; most low-fare tickets, however, are nonrefundable.

Flights to Israel tend to be least expensive from November through March, except for the holiday season at the end of December. Prices are higher during the Jewish High Holiday period (usually in September or October) and during Passover (usually in April).

Flying time from New York to Israel is approximately 11 hours; from Los Angeles, it's about 20 hours (including the usual stopover in Europe or New York). International passengers are asked to arrive at the airport three hours prior to their flight time in order to allow for security checks.

From North America, the New York City area's international airports offer the highest number of nonstop flights, with El Al Airlines, United, and Delta providing nonstop service. Direct flights are also available on El Al from Los Angeles and Toronto and on US Airways from Philadelphia. Major European carriers—including Air France, Alitalia, British Airways, Brussels Airlines, Czech Airlines, Iberia, KLM, Lot, Lufthansa, Swissair, Turkish Airways, and Virgin Atlantic—have daily flights from the United States and on to Israel with stopovers in their domestic hub airports.

Because Israel is slightly smaller than New Jersey, it's often more efficient to drive within the country than fly. The exception is the resort city of Eilat, which is 360 km (224 miles) south of Tel Aviv on the Gulf of Eilat. There are flights several times a day from Tel Aviv and daily from Haifa.

Reconfirmation obligations differ from airline to airline (and change from time to time); be certain to check with your carrier for all legs of your journey.

Airline Security Issues Transportation Security Administration ⊕ *www.tsa.gov.*

AIRPORTS

Israel's main airport, Ben Gurion International Airport (TLV) is a few miles southeast of Tel Aviv. The airport has towering interior walls of Jerusalem stone adorned with 6th-century Byzantine mosaics that were discovered during construction. A soothing fountain lies in the center of the departure hall, which has plenty of comfortable seating and two cafés. Free Wi-Fi means you can stay connected while waiting for your flight. The spacious food court serves Middle Eastern cuisine and fast-food favorites. From Sde Dov Airport (SDV), about 4 km (2½ miles) north of the city center, domestic airlines fly to Eilat in the south and to Haifa or Rosh Pina in the north.

Charter flights between Europe or Russia and the southern resort town of Eilat land either at Ovda Airport (VDA) or Eilat Airport (ETH).

Airport Information Ben Gurion International Airport ☏ *03/975–5555* ⊕ *www.iaa.gov.il/rashat/en-US/airports/ bengurion.* Eilat Airport ☏ *1-700/705–022* ⊕ *www.iaa.gov.il/rashat/en-US/airports/eilat.* Ovda Airport ☏ *1-700/705–022* ⊕ *www.iaa. gov.il/rashat/en-US/airports/ovda.* Sde Dov Airport ☏ *03/698–4500* ⊕ *www.iaa.gov.il/ rashat/en-US/airports/sdedov.*

GROUND TRANSPORTATION

The quickest and most convenient way to get to and from the airport is by taxi. Taxis are always available outside the arrivals hall. Fares are approximately NIS 185 to Tel Aviv and NIS 300 to Jerusalem.

From the airport, trains depart for Tel Aviv every 25 minutes. They'll take you to the city in 25 minutes for NIS 15. Trains continue on to Herzliya, Netanya, Haifa, Akko, and Nahariya. Direct train service to Jerusalem won't commence until 2017.

The Nesher shuttle service takes you to Jerusalem for NIS 62. The 10-passenger *sherut* taxis (limo-vans) depart whenever they fill up. The main disadvantage is that if you're the last passenger to be dropped off, you may tour the city for an hour while the driver discharges the other passengers. To get to Ben Gurion Airport from Jerusalem the same way, call Nesher a day in advance. A "special" taxi (as opposed to a shared sherut) costs about NIS 350, with a 25% surcharge after 9 pm and on Saturday and holidays.

If you depart for the airport from central Tel Aviv by car or taxi at rush hour (7 to 9 am, 5 to 7 pm), note that the roads can get clogged. Allow 45 minutes for a trip that would otherwise take only about 20 minutes.

Taking the bus from Ben Gurion Airport to Jerusalem is tedious. Board the Egged local shuttle (line 5, NIS 5.50) for the 10-minute ride to the El Al Junction, and wait there for a Jerusalem-bound Egged bus (line 947, NIS 24). It runs to Jerusalem's Central Bus Station about every 30 minutes during the day, less frequently in the evening.

Contacts Egged ☎ 03/694–8888 ⊕ www.egged.co.il/eng. **Nesher** ☎ 02/625–7227 ⊕ www.neshertours.co.il.

FLIGHTS

The national carrier, El Al Israel Airlines, is known for maintaining some of the world's strictest security standards. It's not necessarily the cheapest carrier, especially from the United States. United, Delta, and US Airways often have cheaper nonstop fares, and some European airlines have better prices if you don't mind a stopover in their hub cities. Within Israel, Arkia Israeli Airlines and Israir Airlines have flights from Tel Aviv to Eilat and Haifa. Royal Jordanian Airlines flies the 45-minute route between Tel Aviv and Amman.

To Israel Delta Airlines ✉ *Israel* ☎ *800/221–1212 for U.S. reservations, 800/241–4141 for international reservations* ⊕ *www.delta.com.* **El Al Israel Airlines** ☎ *800/223–6700 in the U.S., 03/977–1111 in Israel* ⊕ *www.elal.co.il.* **Royal Jordanian Airlines** ☎ *03/516–5566* ⊕ *www.rj.com.* **United Airlines** ☎ *800/864–8331* ⊕ *www.united.com.* **US Airways** ☎ *800/428–4322 for international reservations* ⊕ *www.usairways.com.*

Within Israel Arkia Israeli Airlines ☎ *03/690–3712* ⊕ *www.arkia.com.* **Israir Airlines** ☎ *03/510–9589* ⊕ *www.israirairlines.com.*

▌ BIKE TRAVEL

Biking has really taken off in Israel, with tens of thousands of avid cyclists hitting the trails every year. With mountains, deserts, and wooded hills, this small country is ideal for two-wheel adventures. Off-road tours take you to remote archeological sites and other places not reachable by car. The Keren Kayemeth LeIsrael—Jewish National Fund has information about trails through some beautiful areas. Keep in mind that the going can get rough due to the summer's extreme heat and there are winding and hilly roads and aggressive drivers. The weather is best from September to June.

Urban biking is also becoming more popular. Tel Aviv has 70 km (43 miles) of designated bike lanes and a user-friendly bike rental system. Look for the bright green Tel-O-Fun signs throughout the city, pay the daily fee of NIS 17, and pedal away for a few hours. In Jerusalem, a bicycle path network is under construction. In 2012, a 10-km (7-mile) circular bike trail opened in Jerusalem's Metropolitan Park, and there are plans to expand it in the coming years. Bikes are welcome on intercity buses with luggage holds. Except for Friday, trains accept bikes during nonpeak hours (between 9 and 3 and after 7).

Bike maps in English can be hard to find, but Israel Bike Trails has comprehensive trail information listing elevations and level of difficulty on its website. Several companies offer organized guided tours throughout the country, including Israel Cycling.

Bike Contacts Israel Bike Trails ⊕ *www.israelbiketrails.com.* **Israel Cycling** ☎ *052/247–8821* ⊕ *www.israelcycling.com.* **Keren Kayemeth LeIsrael—Jewish National Fund** ⊕ *www.kkl.org.il.* **Tel-O-Fun** ⊕ *www.tel-o-fun.co.il/en.*

▌ BOAT TRAVEL

Many large cruise companies, including Celebrity, Costa, Holland America, Oceania, and Regent Seven Seas have Mediterranean itineraries that include stops at the Israeli ports of Ashdod and Haifa. In addition, the Israeli company Mano sails from Haifa to many points in the Mediterranean between April and November.

FERRY CONTACTS

Cruise Lines Celebrity Cruise ☎ *800/647–2251* ⊕ *www.celebritycruise.com.* **Costa Cruises** ☎ *800/462–6782* ⊕ *www.costacruise.com.* **Holland America** ☎ *877/932–4259* ⊕ *www.hollandamerica.com.* **Mano Maritime** ☎ *700/700–666* ⊕ *www.mano.co.il.* **Oceania Cruises** ☎ *800/531–5619* ⊕ *www.oceaniacruises.com.* **Princess Cruises** ☎ *800/774–6237* ⊕ *www.princess.com.* **Regent Seven Seas** ☎ *877/505–5370* ⊕ *www.rssc.com.*

▌ BUS TRAVEL

Buses can take you almost anywhere in Israel. City bus routes are run exclusively by Egged, except in metropolitan Tel Aviv, where Dan operates. Buses in Israel are clean, comfortable, and air-conditioned. Intercity bus fares vary according to the distance traveled. During weekday rush hours, allow time for long lines at the obligatory security checks to enter the bus station. Buses are often overcrowded on Saturday nights after Shabbat and always on Sunday mornings when it looks like the entire Israeli army is returning to base after a weekend at home.

The Central Bus Station in Tel Aviv resembles the work of a mad scientist. The stark concrete building has multiple entrances on several levels, endless corridors, and a confusing array of platforms. It's all topped off by dozens of kiosks selling fast food and cheap merchandise. By contrast, Jerusalem's Central Bus Station is clean, well organized, and easy to navigate. There's a pleasant food court, an ATM, an efficient information desk, and branches of some of the country's best-known stores.

Although the buses resemble those in most other countries, there are a few quirks. When you're in Jerusalem, remember that the ultra-Orthodox population primarily uses Buses 1 and 2, which service the Western Wall area. It's generally accepted that women sit separately in the rear of the bus. A woman should never sit in an empty seat next to an ultra-Orthodox man and shouldn't be offended if a man would rather stand than sit beside her in an empty seat. (And in case you're wondering, ultra-Orthodox women generally accept this arrangement.)

Frequent bus service is available between Jerusalem and Tel Aviv. Egged Bus 405 runs from the Tel Aviv Central Bus Station, and Bus 480 from the Arlozorov Street terminal, each with two to five departures per hour, depending on the time of day (NIS 18). There's a similar service to Jerusalem from most major cities, terminating at the Central Bus Station. The two small bus stations in East Jerusalem are for private, Palestinian-operated bus lines, with daily service to West Bank towns such as Bethlehem and Jericho.

FARES

For both local and long-distance travel, drivers accept payment in shekels. Drivers on the long-distance buses will grumble when they have to make change for a bill over NIS 100, so make sure to have smaller denominations. Unless you're running to catch a bus, it's almost always faster to buy your ticket at the office in the bus station. On city buses you don't need exact change. Children under age five ride free whether or not they occupy their own seat.

The fare on all city routes is NIS 6.60. If you'll be taking another bus within 90 minutes, ask for a free *ma'avar*, or transfer ticket. Intercity fares are based on distance traveled. The one-hour trip between Tel Aviv and Jerusalem will cost you about NIS 18, while the 2½-hour journey between Tel Aviv and Tiberias runs about NIS 42. There are no advance reservations except to Eilat or the Dead Sea area.

SCHEDULES

All bus service is available Sunday to Thursday from 5:30 am to 12:30 am. Keep in mind that public transportation in all cities except Haifa ceases to run on Jewish holidays and on Shabbat, which lasts from sundown Friday afternoon to an hour after sundown Saturday evening. Be sure to give yourself extra time if traveling just before Shabbat.

Every large bus station has an information booth where you'll generally be able to find schedule and platform information in English. The Egged website has an easy-to-use trip planner that includes timetables, routes, and fares.

TOURS

Egged operates Route 99, a two-hour circle tour of Jerusalem for visitors. Its distinctive red double-decker buses are equipped with audio explanations in eight languages. The route begins at the Central Bus Station and includes stops at the Machaneh Yehuda market, Mt. Scopus, the City of David, the Dung Gate, Mt. Zion, the Jaffa Gate, Safra Square, the King David Hotel, Haas Promenade, Jerusalem Mall, the railway station at the Biblical Zoo, Mt. Herzl, Yad Vashem, Israel Museum, the Knesset, and the Supreme Court. Departures are Sunday to Thursday at 9, 11, 1:30, and 3:45 (with an additional 6 pm departure between March and October). On Friday and on Jewish holidays, the last bus leaves at 1:30 pm. The cost is NIS 60 for one trip, NIS 80 for an all-day ticket with unlimited transfers, and NIS 130 for a two-day ticket.

In Tel Aviv, Dan operates the hop-on, hop-off Route 100. The two-hour circuit, which begins at the Reading Terminal in north Tel Aviv, departs Sunday to Thursday at 9, 11, noon, 1, 2, 3, and 4. On Friday, the last bus is at noon. The fare is NIS 45. There are 28 stops along the way, including Tel Aviv University, Dizengoff Center, and Carmel Market.

Bus Information Dan ☏ *03/639–4444* ⊕ *www.dan.co.il/english.* **East Jerusalem Bus Station** ⊠ *Sultan Suleiman St., opposite Damascus Gate, East Jerusalem* ☏ *02/627–2881.* **Egged** ☏ *03/694–8888* ⊕ *www.egged. co.il/eng.* **Jerusalem Central Bus Station** ⊠ *224 Jaffa Rd., Romema* ☏ *054/797–1147.*

▌ CAR TRAVEL

The Hebrew word for a native-born Israeli is *sabra,* which literally refers to a prickly cactus with a sweet inside. You'll meet sweet Israelis if you get lost or have automotive difficulties—helping hands are quick to arrive—but behind the wheel, Israelis are aggressive and honk their horns far more than their Western counterparts.

Some travelers feel more comfortable hiring a driver, and there are plenty of ways to find someone reliable. Ask for recommendations at your hotel. Every hotel has taxi drivers that serve their guests and most are familiar with all parts of the country and will be happy to quote you a daily rate. It should be around NIS 800.

Israel's highways are numbered, but most people still know them simply by the towns they connect: the Tiberias–Nazareth Road, for example. Intersections and turnoffs are similarly indicated, as in "the Eilat Junction." Orange signs indicate tourist sites; national parks signs are on brown wood.

ADDRESSES

In Israel, streets are generally named after famous people or events, meaning that almost every community has a Herzl Street and a Six-Day War Street. Don't worry about the "boulevard" or "alley" attached to many street names—Israelis just use the proper name. You won't find a Jabotinsky Street and a Jabotinsky Alley in the same city. What you might encounter is a street that will change names after a couple of blocks. Street numbers follow the standard format, with odd numbers on one side and even numbers on the other.

If you know history, you'll have an easier time finding your way around Jerusalem's neighborhoods. In Baka the streets are named after the biblical tribes, in Rehavia they're medieval Jewish scholars, and in Old Katamon the brigades who fought in Israel's War of Independence are honored with street names.

There are four towns in Israel that have functioning Old Cities dating from either biblical times (Jerusalem), the Crusader period (Akko and Jaffa), or the Middle Ages (Tzfat). Streets and alleys in these areas have names, but often not numbers.

GASOLINE

Gas stations are to be found at regular intervals along the country's major highways, except in the Negev. On highways they're generally always open, while those in the city tend to close at midnight. Prices are standardized, so it doesn't matter which station you choose. Most offer both full- and self-service pumps. If you go the full-service route, ask for a *kabbalah* (receipt). Attendants don't expect to be tipped. Most rental cars take unleaded

gas, which at the time of this writing costs NIS 7.85 per liter. Most stations accept international credit cards.

PARKING

In Tel Aviv, Jerusalem, and Haifa, parking laws are stringently enforced. Expect a ticket of NIS 150 on your windshield if you've overstayed your welcome at a paid parking spot. Cars will be towed if parked in a no-parking zone. Pay attention to the curb, as parking is forbidden where it's painted red. In downtown areas, parking is permitted only where there are blue and white stripes on the curb or where there are meters. Meters cost NIS 5.50 per hour and accept 5, 2, and 1 shekel coins. Pay-and-display cards may also be used and are for sale at post offices, kiosks, and lottery booths. Read the signs carefully: in some areas free evening parking begins at 6, in others at 7 or 8.

Sound complicated? Stick to parking lots. Covered and open parking lots are plentiful in the major cities, and cost around NIS 15 per hour or NIS 70 per day.

RENTAL CARS

If you plan on heading north to the Golan or Upper Galilee, a rental car will be a significant time-saver. But if you're sticking to the cities, a rental car is often more of a bother than a boon. In Jerusalem, a combination of walking and taking cabs is your best bet.

Rental rates in Israel start at around $50 per day and $200 per week for an economy car with unlimited mileage. Minivans and four-wheel-drive vehicles are very popular and should be reserved well in advance, especially during high season. Allow plenty of time to pick up and drop off your vehicle if you're renting from a city office.

Drivers must be at least 24. Your driver's license is acceptable in Israel, but an International Driver's Permit is still a good idea. This international permit is universally recognized, so having one in your wallet is extra insurance against problems with the local authorities.

RENTAL CARS IN THE WEST BANK

There are no restrictions on driving Israeli rental cars into West Bank areas under Israeli control (known as Area B). However, your rental-car insurance coverage doesn't extend to West Bank areas under Palestinian control (known as Area A). If you rent from companies at the airport, in Tel Aviv, or in West Jerusalem, you won't be able to drive the car to Bethlehem, Jericho, and other towns under the Palestinian Authority. If you plan on visiting these areas by car, use Green Peace or one of the other Palestinian-operated companies in East Jerusalem. Passing through the checkpoints within Israel is usually stress free, as tourist vans and rental cars are routinely waved through with no need to show identification.

If your rental car comes with a GPS system, check to see if it includes or excludes West Bank routes. If the West Bank is excluded, the GPS will route your journey from Jerusalem to the Dead Sea along a circuitous three-hour route instead of a more direct one that takes less than an hour. Even if you're using GPS, it's always a good idea to discuss possible routes with your rental-car company if you plan on passing through the West Bank.

Rental Agencies Avis ☎ *800/638–4016* ⊕ *www.avis.co.il.* **Best** ☎ *800/220–015* ⊕ *www.best-car.co.il.* **Budget** ☎ *800/828–9975* ⊕ *www.budget.co.il.* **Eldan** ☎ *03/977–3400* ⊕ *www.eldan.co.il/en.* **Green Peace Car Rental** ☎ *02/585-9756* ⊕ *www.greenpeace.co.il.* **Sixt** ☎ *700/50-1502* ⊕ *en.shlomo.co.il.*

ROAD CONDITIONS

Israel's highway system is very modern and has signs in English as well as Hebrew and Arabic. Route 6, the main north–south toll road, can save significant time on longer journeys. The highway starts at the Maahaz Junction south of Kiryat Gat and ends about 87 km (54 miles) north at the Ein Tut Junction near Yokneam. Electronic sensors read your license plate number and transmit the bill according to the distance you travel, to your rental-car company. Expect to pay around NIS 60 to drive the length of the highway.

Route 1 is the chief route to Jerusalem from both the west (Tel Aviv, Ben Gurion Airport, Mediterranean coast) and the east (Galilee via Jordan Valley, Dead Sea area, Eilat). The road from Tel Aviv is a divided highway that presents no problems except at morning rush hour (7 am to 9:30 am), when traffic backs up at the entrance to the city. For this reason, some drivers prefer Route 443—via Modi'in—which leaves Route 1 just east of the Ben Gurion Airport, and enters Jerusalem from the north (most convenient for East Jerusalem locations). Route 1, which enters Jerusalem under the Bridge of Strings, is more convenient for Givat Ram, West Jerusalem, downtown, and Talbieh.

Jerusalem, Haifa, and Tel Aviv are all clogged with traffic during the workday. In Jerusalem, the Old City and Jaffa Road are closed to private vehicles, with traffic routed around the periphery. Don't consider driving in Jerusalem if you're not comfortable negotiating narrow spaces or parking in tight spots.

If you're driving through the Negev, watch out for camels that can come loping out of the desert and onto the road. In the winter rainy season, sudden flash floods sometimes cascade through the desert *wadis* (streambeds that are usually dry) with little warning, washing out roads. It's best to postpone your desert trip if there's heavy rain in the forecast.

The desert can be unbelievably hot, sometimes even in the winter. It's a good idea to carry extra water—both for yourself and for your car—while driving at any time of year.

ROADSIDE EMERGENCIES

In case of an accident or roadside emergency, call the police. English-speaking assistance is generally available.

The local representative of AAA is Memsi. Should anything happen to your rental car, call your rental company for roadside repair or replacement of the vehicle.

Automobile Associations Memsi ☎ *03/564-1111 in Tel Aviv, 02/625-0661 in Jerusalem* ⊕ *www.memsi.co.il.*

Emergency Services Police ☎ *100.*

RULES OF THE ROAD

By law, drivers and all passengers must wear seat belts at all times. Police crack down on drunk driving; the legal blood-alcohol limit is .05%. It's against the law to use a cell phone while driving.

Speed limits vary little across Israel: motorways (represented with blue signs) have speed limits of either 100 or 110 kph (62 or 68 mph). The exception is Route 6, where the limit is 120 kph (74 mph). Highways with green signs have speed limits of 80 or 90 kph (50 or 56 mph). Urban roads are 50 or 60 kph (31 or 37 mph).

Headlights must be turned on in daylight when driving on intercity roads from November through April 1. A flashing green traffic light indicates that the red stoplight is about three seconds away and you should come to a halt.

Children under 10 must be seated in age-appropriate car seats, and children under 14 aren't allowed in the front seat.

▌ TAXI TRAVEL

Taxis are an affordable way to get around. If you need to get somewhere fast or are unfamiliar with the area, a taxi is your best bet, and you can hail one on the street or request one by phone. On the whole, drivers are knowledgeable, cheerful, and like to practice their English with tourists.

Taxis are white sedans with a yellow sign on the roof. The sign lights up to indicate availability. According to law, taxi drivers must use the meter (be firm when you request this) unless you hire them for the day or for a trip out of town, for which there are set rates. Agree on the price before you begin the journey and assume that the driver has built in a tip. In the event of a serious problem with the driver, report his cab number (on the illuminated plastic sign on the roof) or license plate number to the Ministry of Tourism or the Ministry of Transport.

Certain shared taxis or minivans have fixed rates and run fixed routes, such as from Tel Aviv to Haifa or from the airport to Jerusalem; such a taxi is called a *sherut* (as opposed to a "*special,*" the term used for a private cab). Some sheruts can be booked in advance.

Sheruts are an option if you're traveling between Jerusalem and Tel Aviv. They operate from the parking lot of Tel Aviv's Central Bus Station seven days a week, departing when they fill up (NIS 24 on weekdays; NIS 35 on Saturday). They end their journey with stops near the Jerusalem Central Bus Station and Zion Square. A "special" cab on this route costs about NIS 270, with a 25% surcharge after 9 pm and on Saturday and holidays.

Taxi Contact Nesher ☎ *599/500-205, 02/625-7227* ⊕ *www.neshertours.co.il.*

Jerusalem Taxi Contacts Hapalmach ☎ *02/679-3333.* **Hapisgah** ☎ *02/642-1111.* **Ha'ooma/Habira** ✉ *1 Harav Kook St., near Zion Sq., Downtown* ☎ *02/538-9999.* **Rehavia** ☎ *02/625-4444.* **Smadar** ☎ *02/566-4444.*

Eilat Taxi Contacts London ☎ *08/996-3789.* **Massada Taxis** ☎ *08/642-2222.* **aba** ☎ *08/633-3339.*

▌TRAIN TRAVEL

Until new tracks are completed in 2016, train travel between Jerusalem and Tel Aviv is more a pleasant and scenic excursion than an efficient way to travel between the two cities. The journey currently takes 1 hour and 45 minutes, compared to 45 minutes by bus. It's a comfortable ride, and many just do it for the attractive scenery. The train, which departs every hour, runs between Jerusalem's Malcha Station and Tel Aviv's Savidor Station. There are connections to Haifa and other destinations to the north. Service ends midafternoon on Friday and resumes about two hours after dark on Saturday. The fare to or from Tel Aviv is NIS 22.50 one-way, NIS 40.50 round-trip.

Other cities—including Ashkelon, Beersheva, Beit Shemesh, Haifa, Herzliya, Akko, and Nahariya—are easily reachable by train from Tel Aviv. There are no different classes of service. All carriages are clean, spacious, and comfortable with well-upholstered seats. They're often crowded, however.

All train stations post up-to-date schedules in English. Complete schedules are also available on the website of the Israel Railway Authority. Tickets may be purchased at the ticket office in the station. Reserved seats are available Monday to Wednesday and may be bought up to a week in advance.

Information Israel Railways ☎ *03/577–4000* ⊕ *www.rail.co.il.*

ESSENTIALS

▊ ACCOMMODATIONS

Between 2009 and 2012, Israel added almost 4,000 new hotel rooms—good news for travelers looking for more amenities than those offered by many older hotels. Today you'll find every possible type of lodging, including luxury spa resorts, chic boutique hotels, country inns, and rural bed-and-breakfasts. There are also some more unusual offerings, including Christian hospices (meaning hotels, rather than hospitals) and kibbutz hotels (lodgings on the grounds of collective communities). *For more information, see the Israel Lodging Primer in Chapter 1.*

Throughout Israel, lodging prices often include breakfast. Prices in the reviews are the lowest cost of a standard double room in high season.

Apartment and House Rental Contacts Good Morning Jerusalem ☎ 02/623-3459 ⊕ www.accommodation.co.il. **Israel Holiday Apartments** ☎ 09/772-7163 ⊕ www.holidayapartments.co.il. **Kleiman Real Estate** ☎ 052/238-0638 ⊕ www.kleimanrealestate.com. **Vacation Rental By Owner** ⊕ www.vrbo.com/vacation-rentals/asia/israel.

Bed-and-Breakfast Contacts Bed and Breakfast in Israel ⊕ www.b-and-b.co.il. **Home Accommodation Association of Jerusalem** ☎ 02/645-2198 ⊕ www.bnb.co.il. **ural Tourism in Israel** ⊕ www.zimmeril.com.

Christian Hospice Contacts GoIsrael ☎ 888/7747-7235 ⊕ www.goisrael.com. **Guided Tours Israel** ☎ 646/807-0111 ⊕ www.guidedtoursisrael.com/christian-accommodation-israel.html.

Home Exchange and Vacation Rental Contacts Sabbatical Homes ⊕ www.sabbaticalhomes.com.

Kibbutz Hotel Contact Kibbutz Hotels Chain ☎ 03/560-8118 ⊕ www.kibbutz.co.il.

▊ COMMUNICATIONS

INTERNET

Most hotels in Israel have connections for laptops, and almost every hotel offers wireless access. Ask about the price, as some charge as much as $20 per day for the privilege. You can also find Internet access at the Tel Aviv and Jerusalem Central Bus Stations and in most cafés. Large swaths of Tel Aviv have free Wi-Fi, and Jerusalem has free Wi-Fi in the downtown area, on Emek Refaim Street, and at Safra Square. Ben Gurion Aiport and the Eilat Airport also offer free Wi-Fi.

Contacts Cybercafes. Cybercafes lists over 4,000 Internet cafés worldwide. ⊕ www.cybercafes.com.

PHONES

Israel's phone numbers have seven digits, except for certain special numbers that have four to six digits. Toll-free numbers in Israel begin with 177, 1800, 1700, or 1888. Many toll-free customer service numbers begin with an asterisk followed by three or four digits. When calling an out-of-town number within Israel, be sure to dial the zero that begins every area code.

The country code for Israel is 972. When dialing an Israeli number from abroad, drop the initial 0 from the local area code. The country code for Jordan is 962. When dialing from Israel, dial 00962 and the area code 3 before landline numbers in Petra; for Amman, use 00962 and the area code 6. When dialing within Jordan, add a 0 before the area code.

CALLING WITHIN ISRAEL

Making a local call in Israel is quite simple. All public telephones use phone cards that may be purchased at newspaper kiosks and post offices. Pick up the receiver, insert the card in the slot, dial the number when you hear the tone, and the number of units remaining on the card will appear on the screen. One unit equals two minutes.

The area codes for dialing between cities within Israel are Jerusalem (02); Tel Aviv (03); Netanya and Herzliya (09); Haifa, Galilee, Tiberias, Tzfat, and Nazareth (04); Eilat and the Negev (08).

Dial 144 for directory or operator assistance. Operators all speak English. Dial 188 for an international operator.

CALLING OUTSIDE ISRAEL

When calling internationally direct from Israel, first dial the international access code and then the country code. The international access code for the United States and Canada is 001, and the country code for each is 1.

You can make international calls using a telecard from a public phone. A call from Israel to most countries costs about 25¢ per minute.

By dialing Israel's toll-free numbers (1800 or 177) and the number of your long-distance service, you can link up directly to an operator in your home country. This service works from all public phones and most hotel rooms.

Access Codes AT&T Direct ☎ *180/949–4949* ⊕ *www.att.com.* **MCI WorldPhone** ☎ *180/940–2727* ⊕ *www.mci.com.* **Sprint International Access** ☎ *180/938–7000* ⊕ *www.sprint.com.*

MOBILE PHONES

If you have a multiband phone and your service provider uses the world-standard GSM network (as do T-Mobile, Cingular, and Verizon), you can probably use your phone abroad. Roaming fees can be steep, however: 99¢ a minute is considered reasonable. And overseas you normally pay the toll charges for incoming calls. It's almost always cheaper to send a text message than to make a call, since text messages have a very low set fee (often less than 5¢).

If you just want to make local calls, consider buying a new SIM card (note that your provider may have to unlock your phone for you to use a different SIM card) and a prepaid service plan in the destination. You'll then have a local number and can make local calls at local rates.

▌▌▌TIP➡ If you travel internationally frequently, save one of your old mobile phones or buy a cheap one on the Internet; ask your cell-phone company to unlock it for you, and take it with you as a travel phone, buying a new SIM card with pay-as-you-go service in each destination.

It's significantly cheaper to rent a cell phone at Ben Gurion Airport than to use your cell phone from abroad. Rental booths are in the arrivals hall.

Several Israeli cell-phone rental companies offer tourists a phone for 65¢ per day. ATS offers free incoming calls, local calls inside Israel at 24¢ per minute, and 29¢ per minute to the United States. SMS messages are billed at 12¢ per minute. If you order the phone in advance, it'll be waiting for you on the day of your arrival.

Contacts ATS ☎ *718/838–1511 from abroad, 050/571–2972 from Israel* ⊕ *www.atsisrael.com.* **Cellular Abroad** ☎ *800/287–5072* ⊕ *www.cellularabroad.com.* **Mobal** ☎ *888/888–9162* ⊕ *www.mobalrental. com.* **Planet Fone** ☎ *888/988–4777* ⊕ *www.planetfone.com.*

▍ CUSTOMS AND DUTIES

For visitors with nothing to declare, clearing customs at Ben Gurion Airport requires simply following the clearly marked green line in the baggage claims hall. There are generally no lines and customs inspectors rarely examine luggage. The red line for those with items to declare is next to the green line. Those over 17 may import into Israel duty-free: 250 cigarettes or 250 grams of tobacco products; 2 liters of wine and 1 liter of spirits; ¼ liter of eau de cologne or perfume; and gifts totaling no more than $125 in value. You may also import up to 15 kg of food products, but no fresh meat.

Pets are not quarantined if you bring a general health certificate issued by a government veterinary officer in your country of origin issued within seven days prior to travel. The certificate must state that you've owned the pet for more than 90 days and that the animal has been vaccinated against rabies not more than a year and not less than one month prior to travel. Dogs and cats less than three months old won't be admitted. At least 48 hours prior to arrival, pet owners must send a fax to the Ramla Quarantine Section stating the name of the owner, animal species, age, flight number, and approximate arrival time.

Information in Israel Israel Customs Authority ☎ 800/345–6541 ⊕ www.israel. visahq.com/customs. **Ramla Quarantine Station** ☎ 03/968–8963 🖶 03/960–5194.

U.S. Information U.S. Customs and Border Protection ☎ 877/227–5511 ⊕ www.cbp.gov.

▍ EATING OUT

Israeli restaurants are sophisticated and varied, as one would expect from a country with immigrants from dozens of countries and a well-traveled population. Be sure to sample the culinary traditions of the Middle East at neighborhood restaurants known as *steakiya*. Here you'll fill up on dishes such as hummus and warmed pita bread accompanied by a variety of skewered grilled meats, mounds of french fries, and an astonishing array of fresh salads. Visitors might be surprised to find plates of falafel and shawarma on the menu in steakiyas, too. Unlike the street version, pita is served on the side and portions tend to be very generous. Restaurants in Eilat, Haifa, and Tel Aviv take advantage of their seaside location to serve the best in seafood dishes, and in any major city it's not difficult to find authentic Thai, Italian, Indian, Latin American, Chinese, French, Indonesian, Japanese, even American food

While "kosher" once meant "boring," the number of inventive and sophisticated kosher restaurants is growing. Restaurants certified as kosher by the local rabbinate in every city are required to display a dated and signed Hebrew certificate. All the major hotels throughout the country are kosher and their restaurants and cafés welcome nonguests. The Friday editions of the *Jerusalem Post* and *Haaretz* newspapers both carry extensive restaurant listings and note kosher restaurants. The website eLuna is a good source for listings, reviews, and discount coupons for kosher eateries.

Prices in the reviews are the average cost of a main course at dinner or, if dinner isn't served, at lunch. For more information on Israeli cuisine, see Flavors of Israel in Chapter 1.

Kosher restaurant resource eLuna ⊕ www.eluna.com.

MEALS AND MEALTIMES

Hotels serve a huge, buffet-style breakfast called *arukhat boker,* comprising a variety of breads and rolls, eggs, oatmeal, excellent yogurt, a huge variety of local cheeses, olives, vegetable and fish salads, and such American-style breakfast foods as pancakes and granola. You can find the same spread at many cafés. Outdoor coffee shops serving salads, sandwiches, cakes, and delicious coffee abound. Every city and small town has modestly priced restaurants that open in midmorning and serve soup, salad, and grilled meats.

Many restaurants offer business lunch specials or fixed-price menus, but à la carte menus are most common. A service charge (*sherut*) of 10% to 15% is sometimes levied and should be noted separately on your bill.

Because Friday isn't a workday for most Israelis, Thursday night is the big night out at the start of the weekend, when cafés and restaurants fill up quickly. Friday mornings at Israeli cafés are the equivalent of the U.S.–style Sunday brunch.

PAYING
Credit cards are widely accepted in restaurants, but always check first. Tips of between 12% and 15% can be paid in cash only. If you're dining in a smaller town or village, make sure you have sufficient cash with you, as credit cards are sometimes not accepted.

RESERVATIONS AND DRESS
Dress in all but the most expensive Israeli restaurants is generally casual. Apart from the restaurants in five-star hotels, men won't need a jacket and tie, and anything goes for women. Israeli restaurants in the larger cities fill up in the evening. Unless you're dining early—before 7 pm—reservations are advised for all except the smallest neighborhood restaurants.

WINES, BEER, AND SPIRITS
Wine has deep roots in Israeli culture. Israel is one of the earliest wine-producing areas in the world, and the symbol of Israel's Ministry of Tourism is a cluster of grapes borne on a pole by two men. Wineries built during the 19th century are still producing wine today, and a plethora of boutique wineries have sprung up in the past decade. Dalton, Castel, Ben Ami, Golan, and Carmel's Rothschild Series are good bets and are found on many Israeli wine lists. As for spirits, those with a taste for Greek *ouzo* may enjoy the comparable local *arak*. Sabra is a locally produced chocolate- and orange-flavored liqueur.

The commercially produced brews in Israel are Maccabee (lager) and Goldstar (bitter), and Carlsberg, Heineken, and Tuborg

WORD OF MOUTH

Was the service stellar or not up to snuff? Did the food give you shivers of delight or leave you cold? Did the prices and portions make you happy or sad? Rate restaurants and write your own reviews in Travel Ratings or start a discussion about your favorite places in Travel Talk on ⊕ *www.fodors.com*. Your comments might even appear in our books. Yes, you, too, can be a correspondent!

are popular imports. Beer is most commonly available by the bottle, but some bars serve it on draught. In recent years, the microbrew trend has hit Israel, with more than 20 boutique breweries producing beer that's winning awards in international competitions. Ask for Dancing Camel or Malka, if you're adventurous.

▌ ELECTRICITY

The electrical current in Israel is 220 volts, 50 cycles alternating current (AC); wall outlets take Continental-type plugs, with two round prongs.

If your appliances are dual-voltage, you'll need only an adapter. Don't use 110-volt outlets marked for shavers only for high-wattage appliances such as blow-dryers. Most laptops operate equally well on 110 and 220 volts and so require only an adapter.

▌ EMERGENCIES

Israel has an extremely sophisticated emergency response system and a high percentage of citizens who are trained medics. If you find yourself in any kind of medical or security emergency in a public place, the professional and citizen response will be instantaneous.

To obtain police assistance at any time, dial 100. For emergency ambulance service, run by Magen David Adom, dial 101. To report a fire, dial 102. Emergency calls are free at public phones.

MEDICAL CENTERS

Emergency rooms in major hospitals are on duty 24 hours a day in rotation; the schedule is published in the daily press. In an emergency, call Magen David Adom to find out which hospital is on duty that day for your specific need (orthopedic or gastric, for example). Be sure to take your passport with you. There will be a fee.

EILAT AND THE NEGEV

Three hospitals serve the Negev: Soroka in Beersheva, Barzilai in Ashkelon, and Yoseftal in Eilat. All have English speakers on staff and 24-hour emergency rooms (bring your insurance documents).

JERUSALEM

The privately run Terem Emergency Care Center in Jerusalem offers first aid and full medical attention, 24 hours a day, at its Romema clinic, and more limited hours at its other two Jerusalem locations.

A private dental clinic offers emergency service Sunday and Monday 8 to 6, Tuesday to Thursday 8 to 8, and Friday 8 to 1. Call first: when the office is closed, the call is automatically transferred to an on-call dentist.

The major hospitals in Jerusalem are Hadassah Ein Kerem, Sha'arei Zedek near Mt. Herzl, and Hadassah Mt. Scopus.

TEL AVIV

Tel Aviv Sourasky Medical Center (also known as Ichilov Hospital) is in north Tel Aviv, about a 10-minute drive (depending on traffic) from the heart of downtown. There's a 24-hour emergency room. Be sure to bring your passport with you. You'll be provided with all records in English for your insurance providers at home. If you need an ambulance, you can call 101 to reach Magen David Adom.

Foreign Embassies U.S. Embassy ⊠ 71 Hayarkon St., Tel Aviv, Israel ☎ 03/519–7575 ⊕ www.israel.usembassy.gov.

General Emergency Contacts Magen David Adom ⊠ 2 Alkalai St., Tel Aviv, Israel ☎ 101 for emergencies, 02/652–3133 in Jerusalem, 03/546–0111 in Tel Aviv.

Eilat and the Negev Hospital Contacts Barzilai Medical Center ⊠ 2 Hahistadrout St., Ashkelon, Israel ☎ 08/674–5100 ⊕ www.barzilaimc.org.il/eng.

Soroka Hospital ⊠ Hanessi'im St., Beersheva, Israel ☎ 08/640–0111. **Yoseftal Hospital** ⊠ Yotam St., Eilat, Israel ☎ 08/635–8011.

Jerusalem Hospital Contacts adassah Ein Kerem Hospital ⊠ Derech Kalman Mann, Ein Kerem, Jerusalem, Israel ☎ 02/677–7111, 02/677–9444 children's emergency room ⊕ www.hadassah-med.com. **Hadassah Mt. Scopus Hospital** ⊠ Sderot Churchill, Jerusalem, Israel ☎ 02/584–4111, 02/584–4333 emergency Room ⊕ www.hadassah-med.com. **Sha'arei Zedek** ⊠ 12 Bayit St., Mt. Herzl, Jerusalem, Israel ☎ 02/655–5111, 02/655–5509 emergency room ⊕ www.szmc.org.il/en. **Terem Emergency Care Center** ⊠ Bet Yahav, 80 Yirmiyahu St., Romema, Jerusalem, Israel ☎ 599/520–520 ⊕ www.terem.com/en.

Tel Aviv Hospital Contact Tel Aviv Sourasky Medical Center ⊠ 6 Weizmann St., Center City, Tel Aviv, Israel ☎ 03/697–4444 ⊕ www.tasmc.org.il/sites/en.

▌ HEALTH

No vaccinations are required to visit Israel. The country has one of the world's most advanced healthcare systems. Most doctors at emergency clinics and hospitals in Israel speak English. Emergency and trauma care is among the best in the world.

It's safe to drink tap water and eat fresh produce after it's been washed, but take care when buying food from outdoor stands; make sure the food is hot and cooked in front of you. Heat stroke and dehydration are real dangers if you're going to be outdoors for any length of time: a sun hat and sunblock are musts, as is plenty of bottled water (available even in the most remote places) to guard against dehydration. Take at least 1 liter per person for every hour you plan to be outside. Use sunscreen with SPF 30 or higher. Most supermarkets and pharmacies carry sunscreen in a wide range of SPFs, but it's much more expensive than in the United States.

U.S. brands of mosquito repellent with DEET are available in pharmacies and supermarkets. Wear light, long-sleeved clothing and long pants particularly at dusk when mosquitoes like to attack.

Yad Sarah is a nationwide voluntary organization that lends medical equipment and accessories such as wheelchairs, crutches, and canes. There's no charge, but a contribution is expected. It's open Sunday to Thursday 8 to 7 and Friday 8 to noon. Equipment can be returned elsewhere in the country.

OVER-THE-COUNTER REMEDIES

At the pharmacy (*beit mirkachat*), it's easy to find many of the same over-the-counter remedies as you would at home. Imodium and Pepto-Bismol are available over the counter at every pharmacy. Everyday pain relievers such as Tylenol and Advil are also widely available. Medication can be obtained from pharmacies, which are plentiful. English is spoken in the majority of pharmacies. Locally produced medication is fairly inexpensive, but expect to pay more for drugs that are imported.

The daily press publishes the addresses of pharmacies on duty at night, on Saturday, and on holidays. This information is also available from Magen David Adom. In Jerusalem, Super-Pharm Nayot is open Sunday to Thursday 8:30 am to midnight, Friday 8:30 am to 3 pm, and Saturday one hour after the Sabbath ends until midnight. Its downtown location has slightly shorter hours.

In Eilat, the Michlin Pharmacy will deliver to your hotel and is open Sunday to Thursday 8 am to 9 pm and Friday 8 to 3. Super-Pharm City Gate is open daily 8 am to 10 pm. There are also pharmacies in Arad, Beersheva, and Mitzpe Ramon.

Health Contacts **Michlin Pharmacy** ⊠ *11 Hatmarim St., opposite Central Bus Station, Eilat, Israel* ☎ *08/637–2434.* **Super-Pharm** ⊠ *5 Burla St., Nayot, Jerusalem, Israel* ☎ *02/649–7555* ⊠ *3 Hahistadrut St., Downtown, Jerusalem, Israel* ☎ *02/624–6244* ⊠ *Kanion Mul Yam, Eilat, Israel* ☎ *08/634–0880.* **Yad Sarah** ⊠ *124 Herzl Blvd., Bet Hakerem, Jerusalem, Israel* ☎ *02/644–4444* ⊕ *www.yadsarah.org.*

∎ HOURS OF OPERATION

Sunday is a regular workday in Israel. All government offices and most private offices and travel agencies are closed on Friday and Saturday as well as for all Jewish religious holidays. Businesses are generally open by 8:30 am in Israel.

Although hours can differ among banks, almost all open by 8:30 Sunday to Thursday. Most close at 12:30 and then reopen from 4 to 7 pm. Banks are closed on Jewish religious holidays and on Friday and Saturday except in Muslim areas, where they're closed Friday. In Christian areas they're open Saturday morning and closed Sunday.

Museums don't have a fixed closing day, so although they're usually open 10 to 6, and often on Saturday mornings, confirm the schedule before you go.

Most local pharmacies close at 7 pm. Large chain stores, such as Super-Pharm and NewPharm, are usually open until 10 pm. In most cities a few drugstores are open all night, on a rotating basis. Daily listings can be found in English-language newspapers.

Shops generally open at 9 or 9:30; neighborhood grocery stores usually open around 7. A few shops still close for a two- or three-hour siesta between 1 and 4. Most stores don't close before 7 pm; supermarkets are often open later, and in large cities, there are all-night supermarkets. Arab-owned stores usually open at 8 and close in late afternoon. Mall hours are 9:30 to 9:30 Sunday to Thursday. In Jerusalem, malls shut down about two hours before sundown on Friday and reopen two hours after sunset on Saturday evening. Outside Jerusalem, some malls keep regular hours on Saturday, while others stay closed.

▌ MAIL

The post office does it all: handles regular and express letters, sends and receives faxes, accepts bill payments, sells phone cards and parking cards, handles money transfers, and offers quick-delivery service. Nearly every neighborhood has a post office, identified by a white racing deer on a red background. English is almost always spoken. The main branches are usually open from 8 until 6 or 7, and small offices are usually open Sunday to Tuesday and Thursday 8 to 12:30 and 3:30 to 6, Wednesday 8 to 1:30, and Friday 8 to noon. In Muslim cities the post office is closed Friday, and in Christian areas it's closed Sunday.

It takes 7 to 12 days for mail to reach the United States from Israel. Mail delivery from Israel is reliable.

Israel changed from using postal codes with five digits to codes with seven in 2013. In mailing addresses, the abbreviation M. P. stands for Mobile Post (M. P. Gilboa, for example). You'll see this as part of the address in more-rural areas. Tourists who want to receive mail at a local post office should have it addressed to "Poste Restante" along with the name of the town. Such mail will be held for pick-up free of charge for up to three months.

SHIPPING PACKAGES

Most stores offer shipping to international destinations. If you choose to send your purchases home yourself, you'll find all the supplies you need at any local post office, but be prepared to wait in a long line. Bring picture ID with you. To Canada and the United States, packages take approximately two weeks by air. Quicker, more expensive alternatives are FedEx and UPS.

Express Services EMS Service ☎ 76/887–0007 ⊕ www.israelpost.co.il. **FedEx** ☎ 1700/700–339 ⊕ www.fedex.com/il. **UPS** ☎ 1800/834–834 ⊕ www.ups.com.

▌ MONEY

Israel is a moderately priced country compared to Western Europe, but it's more expensive than many of its Mediterranean neighbors. Prices are much the same throughout the country. To save money, try the excellent prepared food from supermarkets, take public transportation, eat your main meal at lunch, eat inexpensive local foods such as falafel, and stay at hotels with kitchen facilities and guesthouses. Airfares are lowest from late October to early December and from late January to early March.

Sample prices: cup of coffee, NIS 12; falafel, NIS 12; beer at a bar, NIS 20; canned soft drink, NIS 12; hamburger at a fast-food restaurant, NIS 30; short taxi ride, about NIS 35 to NIS 45; museum admission, NIS 32; movie, NIS 35.

Prices throughout this guide are given for adults. Substantially reduced fees are almost always available for children, students, and senior citizens.

▌▌▌**TIP➜** Banks never have every foreign currency on hand, and it may take as long as a week to order. If you're planning to exchange funds before leaving home, don't wait till the last minute.

Currency Conversion Google ⊕ www. google.com. **Oanda.com** ⊕ www.oanda.com/ currency/converter. **XE.com** ⊕ www.xe.com.

ATMS AND BANKS

ATMs—called *kaspomats* in Hebrew— are ubiquitous all over Israel. Look for machines that have stickers stating that they accept foreign credit cards or that have a PLUS, NYCE, or CIRRUS sign. All have instructions in English. Almost all ATMs now have protective shields around the keypad to prevent anyone seeing your PIN.

With a debit card, the ATM will give you the desired amount of shekels and your home account will be debited at the current exchange rate. Note that there may be a limit on how much money you are allowed to withdraw each day and that service charges are usually applied. Make sure you have enough cash in rural areas, villages, and small towns where ATMs may be harder to find.

The main branches of all the banks—Hapoalim, Leumi, Discount, First International—are in Jerusalem's downtown area, but they're arguably the last resort for changing money. Several times a week they have morning hours only (different banks, different days), they give relatively low rates of exchange, and it usually involves waiting in line and having the clerk fill out paperwork.

Your own bank will probably charge a fee for using ATMs abroad; the foreign bank you use may also charge a fee. Nevertheless, you'll usually get a better rate of exchange at an ATM than you will when changing money in a bank. And extracting funds as you need them is a safer option than carrying around a large amount of cash.

▉TIP➜ PIN codes with more than four digits aren't recognized at ATMs in Israel. If yours has five or more, remember to change it before you leave.

CREDIT CARDS

It's a good idea to inform your credit-card company before you travel, especially if you're going abroad and don't travel internationally very often. Otherwise, the credit-card company might put a hold on your card owing to unusual activity. Record all your credit-card numbers—as well as the phone numbers to call if your cards are lost or stolen—in a safe place. Both MasterCard and Visa have general numbers you can call (collect if you're abroad) if your card is lost, but you're better off calling the number of your issuing bank, since MasterCard and Visa usually just transfer you to your bank; your bank's number is usually printed on your card.

All hotels, restaurants, and shops accept major credit cards. Israelis use credit cards even for $5 purchases. Plastic is also accepted at banks for cash advances, although some banks will accept one card but none of the others. For cash advances using a Visa card, go to the Israel Discount Bank or Bank Leumi; with a MasterCard go to Bank Hapoalim or the United Mizrahi Branch.

Most credit cards offer additional services, such as emergency assistance and insurance. Call and find out what additional coverage you have.

Reporting Lost Cards American Express ☎ 800/528–4800 in the U.S., 336/393–1111 collect from abroad ⊕ www.americanexpress. com. **Diners Club** ☎ 800/234–6377 in the U.S., 303/799–1504 collect from abroad ⊕ www.dinersclub.com. **MasterCard** ☎ 800/627–8372 in the U.S., 636/722–7111 collect from abroad ⊕ www.mastercard.com. **Visa** ☎ 800/847–2911 in the U.S., 180/941–1605 in Israel ⊕ www.usa.visa.com.

CURRENCY AND EXCHANGE

Israel's monetary unit is the new Israeli shekel, abbreviated NIS. There are 100 agorot to the shekel. The silver one-shekel coin is the size and shape of an American dime, but thicker. Smaller-value bronze coins are the half-shekel and the 10-agorot coin (both of which are larger than the shekel). There's also a 2-shekel round coin (silver), a 5-shekel hexagonal coin (silver), and a similar-size 10-shekel coin (bronze center, silver rim). Paper bills come in 20-, 50-, 100-, and 200-shekel denominations.

Dollars are widely accepted at hotels and shops, less so at restaurants. As of this writing, the exchange rate was about 3.60 shekels to the U.S. dollar.

In Israel, the best rates are at ATMs or at the myriad of currency-exchange shops (typically marked "Change") in and around the central areas of the large cities. In Jerusalem you'll find these around Zion Square and the Ben Yehuda Street pedestrian mall, and at a few strategic locations elsewhere in the city (Jerusalem Mall, German Colony neighborhood, Jewish Quarter).

▮ PACKING

Israel is a very casual country, and comfort comes first. For touring in the hot summer months, wear cool, easy-care clothing. If you're coming between May and September, you won't need a coat, but you should bring a sun hat that completely shades your face and neck. Take one sweater for cool nights, particularly in the hilly areas (including in and around Jerusalem) and the desert. Also take long pants to protect your legs and a spare pair of walking shoes for adventure travel. A raincoat with a zip-out lining is ideal for October to April, when the weather can get cold enough for snow (and is as likely to be warm enough in the south for outdoor swimming). Rain boots may also be a useful accessory in winter. Pack a bathing suit for all seasons.

Note that many religious sites forbid shorts and sleeveless shirts for both sexes—a light scarf comes in handy to throw over the shoulders. Women should bring modest dress for general touring in religious neighborhoods.

Along with the sun hat, take plenty of sunscreen, insect repellent, and sunglasses in summer. Essentials such as contact-lens solution and feminine hygiene supplies are available everywhere, but are more costly than in North America.

▮ PASSPORTS AND VISAS

Israel issues three-month tourist visas free of charge at the point of entry when a valid passport is presented. Make sure your passport is valid for at least six months after your travel date or you won't be permitted entry. No health certificate or inoculations are required.

Some countries, particularly those in the Middle East, refuse to admit travelers whose passports carry an Israeli visa entry stamp. If you're concerned about regional mobility, you can ask the customs officer at your point of entry to issue a tourist visa on a separate piece of paper; you can also apply for a second passport and include a letter with the application explaining that you need the passport for travel to Israel. Be advised that it's not unheard of for Israeli customs officers to stamp passports despite requests not to do so; if you plan to travel repeatedly between Israel and those Arab states still hostile to Israel, a second passport is advisable.

Notarized consent from parents is required for children under 18 traveling alone, with one parent, or in someone else's custody.

▮ RESTROOMS

Public restrooms are plentiful in Israel and similar in facilities and cleanliness to those in the United States. At gas stations and some parks, toilet paper is sometimes in short supply, so you might want to carry some with you. Few public sinks, except those at hotels, have hot water, but most dispense liquid soap. Occasionally you may be asked to pay one shekel at some facilities.

▮ SAFETY

For the latest governmental travel advisories regarding travel to and within Israel, check with the U.S. State Department. The Israel Ministry of Tourism includes a section on its website with a nonalarmist perspective on visiting Israel during periods of unrest. For the latest local news, check the English-language papers *Haaretz* or the *Jerusalem Post*, available online.

General Information and Warnings
Israel Ministry of Tourism ⊕ www.goisrael. com. **U.S. Department of State** ⊕ www.travel.state.gov.

Online News *Haaretz* ⊕ www.haaretzdaily. com. *Jerusalem Post* ⊕ www.jpost.com.

▌ TAXES

A value-added tax (V.A.T.) of 18% is charged on all purchases and transactions except tourists' hotel bills and car rentals paid in foreign currency (cash, traveler's checks, or foreign credit cards). Upon departure, you're entitled to a refund of this tax on purchases made in foreign currency of more than $100 on one invoice; but the refund isn't mandatory, and not all stores provide V.A.T. return forms. Stores so organized display "taxvat" signs and give 5% discounts, or you can inquire.

Keep your receipts and ask for a cash refund at Ben Gurion Airport. Change Place Ltd. has a special desk for this purpose in the duty-free area. If you leave from another departure point, the V.A.T. refund will be sent to your home address.

▌ TIME

Israel is two hours ahead of Greenwich Mean Time. Normally, New York and Montréal are seven hours behind; California is 10 behind. From late March until early September, Israel operates on Daylight Saving Time. When the Daylight Saving Times don't match, the time difference is reduced by one hour.

Time Zones Timeanddate.com
⊕ *www.timeanddate.com/worldclock.*

▌ TIPPING

There are no hard-and-fast rules for tipping in Israel. Taxi drivers do not expect tips, but a gratuity for good service is in order. If you've negotiated a price, assume the tip has been built in. If a restaurant bill doesn't include service, 15% is expected—round up if the service was particularly good, down if it was dismal. Hotel bellboys should be tipped a lump sum of NIS 10 to NIS 20, not per bag. Tipping is customary for tour guides, tour-bus drivers, and chauffeurs. Bus groups normally tip their guide NIS 30 to NIS 40 per person per day, and half

that for the driver. Private guides normally get tipped NIS 100 to NIS 120 a day from the whole party. Both the person who washes your hair and the stylist expect a small tip—except if one of them owns the salon. Leave NIS 10 per day for your hotel's housekeeping staff, and the same for spa personnel.

TIPPING GUIDELINES FOR ISRAEL	
Bartender	NIS 10–NIS 20 per round, depending on the number of drinks.
Bellhop	NIS 10–NIS 20, not per bag.
Hotel Concierge	NIS 20 or more, if he or she performs a special service for you.
Hotel Doorman	NIS 10 if he helps you get a cab.
Hotel Maid	NIS 10 per day.
Hotel Room-Service Waiter	If service isn't already added to the bill, tip 10%–15.
Taxi Driver	No tip expected.
Tour Guide	NIS 30–NIS 40 per day.
Waiter	If service isn't already added to the bill, tip 10%–15%, with 15% being the norm. Tips in cash only.
Other	Hairdressers and barbers get 10%–15%.

▌ TOURS

Although Israel is a very small country, its wealth of different terrains, climate zones, and historical periods can make it overwhelming to tackle on your own. But should you join an organized tour? That depends on whether this is your first visit to Israel, if you have friends or family in the country, and how much local color you want to take in.

If it's your first time in the Middle East and you're looking for a general overview of the main historic, religious, and natural sites, an escorted tour can be both efficient and cost effective.

They're led by licensed tour guides and usually include visits to Jerusalem, Tel Aviv, Masada, and the Dead Sea. It's not difficult to find itineraries tailored to your religious affiliation or areas of interest.

If an organized trip isn't for you, a private tour with a licensed guide is another option. But all tours aren't equal—be sure to check out the itinerary to make sure it matches your pace, and whether the accommodations and restaurants are up to snuff.

SIGHTSEEING GUIDES

Licensed tour guides must undergo a rigorous two-year training program with annual continuing education required to maintain their credentials. Licensed guides can put together a complete customized itinerary for your group or take you for a couple of days on a private guided tour. Many are native English speakers and have fascinating backgrounds they're happy to share with you.

Freelance guides may approach unaccompanied travelers near the Jaffa Gate in the Old City of Jerusalem and other places on the beaten path. These guides aren't licensed, so it's impossible to know whether the tour they're offering is worthwhile or if they're planning on taking you to their best friend's souvenir stall. It's best to ignore them and walk on.

Contacts Israel Tour Guides ☎ 054/465–3762 ⊕ www.israel-guides.net.

GUIDE-DRIVEN VEHICLES

Modern, air-conditioned limousines and minibuses driven by expert, licensed guides are a great way to see the country for anyone whose budget can bear it. At this writing, the cost was $450 to $550 per day; add another $100 for bigger vans. An additional $150 to $200 per night is charged for the driver's expenses if he or she sleeps away from home. Half-day tours are also available, and you may hire a guide without a car.

Guided Limousine Tours and Superb Limousine Services offer good vehicles and knowledgeable guides. Haifa-based Abboud Tours, run by Israeli Christian Abboud Maroun, specializes in private minibus tours of Jerusalem and the Dead Sea, Nazareth and the Galilee, and the fascinating walled city of Akko. Consolidated Tour Operation is an experienced tour agency founded by Moshe Eshed, a former president of the International Association of Tour Managers. The company arranges everything from day trips to Nazareth and the Galilee to a few days in Petra.

Contacts Abboud Tours ☎ 04/852–5077 ⊕ www.abboudtours.com. **Consolidated Tour Operation** ✉ Tel Aviv, Israel ☎ 03/522–5253 ⊕ www.highlightstoursofisrael.com. **Guided Limousine Tours** ☎ 03/642–1649 ⊕ www.glt. co.il. **Superb Limousine Services** ☎ 03/973–1780 ⊕ www.superb.co.il.

GENERAL-INTEREST TOURS

Several major international tour companies offer all-inclusive trips geared to the general traveler. D. D. Travel, Globus Tours, Isram, and Trafalgar Tours all have one-to-two-week trips that are perfect for first-time visitors to Israel. British-based Longwood Holidays is another well-established company offering week-long tours, with optional extensions in Eilat or Tel Aviv, at very competitive prices.

On a smaller scale, two Israeli-based companies—Egged Tours and United Tours—offer one- or two-day bus tours to many parts of Israel and the Palestinian Authority, including Bethlehem and Jericho. Prices start at $100 per person for one-day tours and $260 per person for two-day tours. These tours are good options for solo travelers or for people who don't want to be part of a tour for their entire trip.

Contacts **D. D. Travel** ☎ 866/403–8457 ⊕ www.ddtravel-acc.com/tours.htm. **Egged Tours** ☎ 03/920–3992 ⊕ www.eggedtours. com. **Globus Tours** ☎ 800/942–3301 ⊕ www. escortedglobustours.com. **Isram** ☎ 800/223–7460 ⊕ www.isram.com. **Longwood Holidays** ☎ 20/8418–2516 ⊕ www.longwoodholidays. co.uk. **Trafalgar Tours** ☎ 866/544–4434 ⊕ www.trafalgartours.com. **United Tours** ☎ 03/617–3333 ⊕ www.unitedtours.co.il.

SPECIAL-INTEREST TOURS
ART
Haifa-based Israel My Way offers exciting five-day "Art Lover" tours that include the latest exhibits at the country's top museums, studio visits with local artists, and a chance to take in the best of Israeli music, opera, and dance.

Contacts **Israel My Way** ☎ 77/300–5717 ⊕ www.israelmyway.co.il.

BIKING
Israel's EcoBike Cycling Vacations offers a selection of countrywide bike tours as well as one-day Tel Aviv and Jerusalem trips. Genesis Cycling organizes four signature bike tours, including the Tour de Israel. For half-day tours through Tel Aviv and Jaffa, try Tourist Israel. Walkways runs countrywide one-to-two-week trips with professional guides. These tours combine cycling and hiking along biblical paths around the Carmel area, the coastal plain, the Galilee, the Red Sea, the Sinai Desert, as well as Petra in Jordan.

▐▌▐TIP→ Most airlines accommodate bikes as luggage, provided they're dismantled and boxed.

Contacts **EcoBike** ☎ 077/450–1650 ⊕ www.ecobike.co.il. **Tourist Israel** ⊕ www.touristisrael.com/interest/bike-tours-israel. **Walkways** ☎ 02/534–4452 ⊕ www.walk-ways.com.

BIRD-WATCHING
The Kibbutz Lotan Center for Bird-watching offers bird-watching tours for small groups during the winter and spring around Eilat and Lotan. Carmel Birding Tours is run by Dr. Carmel

Zitronblat, an experienced birder. Her single- or multiday tours include well-known birding destinations in the Beit She'an and Hula Valleys.

Contacts **Carmel Birding Tours** ☎ 054/800–1212 www.carmelbirdingtours.com. **Kibbutz Lotan Center for Birdwatching** ☎ 800/200–075 ⊕ www.birdingisrael.com.

HIKING
Israel is a hiker's paradise, with terrains ranging from desert to forest to mountains. Try a segment or two of the nearly 1,000-km (620-mile) Israel National Trail if you want to experience the diversity of the landscape. For hiking the Galilee, the 65-km (36-mile) Jesus Trail combines rugged scenery with historic and religious sites.

Israel Extreme and Hi Road Adventures can create an itinerary for you. The Society for the Protection of Nature in Israel runs "field schools" across the country. It also conducts city walks and nature hikes. The Israel Trails Committee has provided maps for hikers since 1960.

Contacts **Hi Road Adventures** ☎ 614/581–4251 ⊕ www.hiroadadventures.com. **Israel Extreme** ☎ 052/647–8474 ⊕ www.israelextreme.com. **Israel National Trail** ☎ 03/638–8719 ⊕ www. israelnationaltrail.com. **Israel Trails Committee** ✉ Israel ⊕ www.teva.org.il/english/itc. **Jesus Trail** ⊕ www.jesustrail.com.

JEWISH EDUCATIONAL TOURS
Keshet and Da'at Educational Expeditions run customized guided tours from one to ten days, focusing on Judaism and Jewish history. Both are staffed by experienced teams of Jewish educators and guides.

Contact **Da'at Educational Expeditions** ☎ 888/811–2812 ⊕ www.daattravel.com. **Keshet** ☎ 646/358–4058 ⊕ www.keshetisrael.co.il.

WINE
Amiel Tours offers a 10-day tour that focuses on Israel's best boutique wineries.

Contact **Amiel Tours** ☎ 03/538–8444 ⊕ www.amiel.com.

▌ TRIP INSURANCE

Comprehensive trip insurance is valuable if you're booking a very expensive or complicated trip (particularly to an isolated region) or if you're booking far in advance. Comprehensive policies typically cover trip cancellation and interruption, letting you cancel or cut your trip short because of illness, or, in some cases, acts of terrorism in your destination. Such policies cover evacuation and medical care. Some also cover you for trip delays because of bad weather or mechanical problems as well as for lost or delayed luggage.

Another type of coverage to consider is financial default—that is, when your trip is disrupted because a tour operator, airline, or cruise line goes out of business. Generally you must buy this when you book your trip or shortly thereafter, and it's available to you only if your operator isn't on a list of excluded companies.

Always read the fine print of your policy to make sure that you're covered for the risks that most concern you. Compare several policies to be sure you're getting the best price and range of coverage available.

Insurance Comparison Information Insure My Trip ☎ *800/487–4722* ⊕ *www.insuremytrip.com.* **Square Mouth** ☎ *800/240–0369* ⊕ *www.squaremouth.com.*

Comprehensive Insurers Access America ☎ *800/284–8300* ⊕ *www.accessamerica.com.* **AIG Travel Guard** ☎ *800/826–4919* ⊕ *www.travelguard.com.* **CSA Travel Protection** ☎ *800/873–9855* ⊕ *www. csatravelprotection.com.* **Travelex Insurance** ☎ *888/228–9792* ⊕ *www.travelex-insurance.com.* **Travel Insured International** ☎ *800/243–3174* ⊕ *www.travelinsured.com.*

▌ VISITOR INFORMATION

The Israel Ministry of Tourism has a toll-free information line and information-packed website. It also has an iPhone and iPad app, available on iTunes.

Contacts Israel Government Tourism Office ⊕ *www.goisrael.com.*

ONLINE TRAVEL TOOLS

Drive Israel provides comprehensive coverage if you're going to rent a car and seek out your own accommodations. The Israel Nature and Parks Authority has info about the country's outdoor attractions, including where to buy discounted admission cards. The Index Tourism site has a good roundup of useful tips about Israel.

Contacts Drive Israel ⊕ *www.drive-israel. com.* **Israel Nature and Parks Authority** ⊕ *www.parks.org.il.* **Index Tourism Israel Tourism Guide** ⊕ *www.index.co.il/tourism.*

INDEX

A

Aaronson, Aaron, *329–330*
Abeer Haela, *197*
Abouhav Synagogue, *407*
Absalom's Pillar, *102*
Abu Gosh, *192*
Accommodations, *520*
Achziv Beach, *344–345*
Acre.⇨ *See* Akko
Addresses, *516*
Adelina ✕, *342*
Afteem ✕, *208*
Ahuzat Dubrovin, *420*
Ahuzat Hameiri ☕, *418*
Ain as-Sultan, *173*
Air travel, *512–513*
Akko, *19, 278, 332–341*
Al-Aqsa Mosque, *82–85*
Al-Deir, *496*
Alpaca Farm, *462*
American Colony Hotel ☕, *144*
Ammonite Wall, *462*
Ancient Bathhouse in Nazareth, *366*
Ancient Katzrin Park, *433*
Andromeda's Rock, *231*
Annai ✕, *368*
Apartment and house rentals, *29, 520*
Aqua Sport International Red Sea Diving Center, *456*
Aquariums, *443–444*
Aqueduct (Akko region), *341*
Arad, *181, 188–189*
Arava Road, *190*
Arbel National Park and Nature Reserve, *389*
Archaeology sites, *22*
Akko, 332, 336
Avdat, 467
Beit Guvrin, 200–202
Beit She'an, 361–362
Beit She'arim, 354
Bethsaida, 394
Caesarea, 305–311
digs, 201–202, 475
Eilat and the Negev, 483, 485
Ein Hod, 316–317
Haifa and the Northern Coast, 305, 306–307, 316–317, 336
Hammat Tiberias, 382–383
Jericho, 173
Jerusalem, 66, 77, 90, 101–102, 116–117
Jerusalem and the Dead Sea region, 184, 185, 188, 198, 200–202
Katzrin, 433
Korazim, 392
lower Galilee, 348, 354, 356–357, 361–362, 366, 370–371, 394
Megiddo, 356–357
Nahal Me'arot Nature Reserve, 316–317
Nazareth, 366
Qumran, 176–177
Tel Arad, 188
Tel Aviv, 231
Tel Beersheva, 483, 485
Tel Bet Shemesh, 198
Tel Dan, 425
Tel Hatzor, 419
Tel Maresha, 200–202
upper Galilee and the Golan, 419, 425
Zippori, 348, 370–371
Archery, *465*
Art galleries and museums
Ein Hod, 316
Eilat and the Negev, 485
Haifa and the Northern Coast, 287, 292, 293–294, 309, 316
Jerusalem, 107, 112, 116, 155, 157
Tel Aviv, 223, 226, 228, 232, 234–235
Tzfat (Safed) and environs, 408–409
upper Galilee and the Golan, 408–409
Art tours, *531*
Artists' Colony, *407*
Artists' retreats
Ein Hod, 316–317
Tzfat (Safed) and environs, 407
ArtPlus Hotel Tel Aviv ☕, *252*
Arts.⇨ *See* Nightlife and the arts
Astronomy tours, *466, 474*
Atlit detention camp, *305*
ATMs, *526–527*
Auberge Shulamit ✕, *416*
Auja Eco Center, *173, 175*
Avdat, *466–467*
Avenue of the Righteous, *111*
Azrieli Towers, *224*

B

Bab a-Siq, *495*
Baha'i Founder's Shrine and Gardens (Akko), *339*
Baha'i Shrine and Gardens (Haifa), *19, 278, 286*
Bahat Winery, *430*
Banana Land (water park), *175*
Banias Nature Reserve, *426–427*
Banias Spring, *426*
Banias Cave, *426*
Banias Waterfall, *427*
Banking hours, *525*
Banks, *526–527*
Bar Yochai, Rabbi Shimon, tomb of, *413*
Bar'am National Park, *415*

Barbunia (bar), *265*
Bars and lounges
Eilat and the Negev, 452–453, 487
Haifa and the Northern Coast, 301
Jerusalem, 144–147
Tel Aviv, 259–260, 262, 263, 264, 265–267
Basilica of the Agony, *97*
Basilica of the Annunciation, *366–367*
Bat Ya'ar Ranch, *412*
Bauhaus buildings, *212, 214–215*
Bauhaus Center, *274*
Bauhaus Foundation Museum, *230*
Beaches and pools, *35*
Eilat and the Negev, 454–455
Jerusalem and the Dead Sea region, 172, 177, 178, 180–181
Haifa and the Northern Coast, 278, 301–302, 311, 314, 341, 344–345
lower Galilee, 388, 396
Tel Aviv, 212, 269–272
Bed-and-breakfasts, *29, 520*
Bedouin culture, *474, 483, 488*
Bedouin market, *487, 489*
Bedouin life tours, *474*
Beersheva and the northern Negev, *436, 480–489*
Beit Alfa, *358*
Beit Bialik, *224*
Beit Guvrin, *200–202*
Beit Ha'ir, *220*
Beit She'an, *361–363*
Beit She'an National Park, *361–362*
Beit She'arim, *353–354*
Beit Shemesh, *196–198*
Beit Ussishkin Museum, *425*
Beit Yannai beach, *314*
Belvoir fortress, *363–364*
Ben-Gurion, David
desert home, 476–477
grave site, 477
Benyamina, *331–332*
Ben-Yehuda Street (Jerusalem), *113–114*
Beresheet ☕, *464*
Bet Aaronson, *329–330*
Bet Ticho, *116*
Bethlehem, *160, 202–210*
Bethsaida, *379, 394*
Betzet Beach, *345*
Bialik, Chaim Nachman, *224–225*
Bialik Street (Tel Aviv), *224–225*
Biankini Beach, *177*
Bible Lands Museum, *103–104*

Biblical life tours, *474*
Bicycling, *513–514*
Eilat and the Negev, 466
Jerusalem, 61
mountain, 466
Tel Aviv, 217, 271
tours, 61, 531
Big Walks (Tza'adot), *361*
Binyamin Pool, *330*
Binyamina Winery, *332*
Bird-watching
Eilat and the Negev, 455, 475
Hula Lake Reserve, 419
tours, 455, 531
Bloomfield Science Museum, *112*
Blue Beach, *388*
Boat and ferry travel, *514*
Boating and sailing
Eilat and the Negev, 455
Kiryat Shmona, 424
lower Galilee, 388, 393
Tel Aviv, 271–272
upper Galilee and the Golan, 400
Breweries, *194, 197, 198, 199*
Bridge of Strings, *104*
Broad Wall, *90*
Broken Pediment Tomb, *495*
Brown TLV 🏨, *252*
Burnt House, *88*
Bus tours, *515*
Bus travel, *514–515*
Business hours, *525–526*
Byzantine Church (Nahariya), *342*
Byzantine Church (Petra), *496*
Byzantine street (Caesarea), *307*

C

Cable car, *167, 184, 420, 422*
Caesarea, *19, 278, 305–311*
Caesarea Beach Club, *311*
Caesarea Museum of Antiquities, *308*
Café Mizrachi ✕, *119, 121*
Camel tours, *455–456, 465, 472*
Cameri Theatre of Tel Aviv, *268*
Cana, *371–372, 379*
Cana Wedding Church, *371*
Capernaum, *378, 393–394*
Capernaum National Park, *393*
Car rentals, *15, 516–517*
Car travel, *14, 515–518*
Cardo, *90–91*
Carmel Beach, *301*
Carmel Forest Spa Resort 🏨, *298*
Carmel Market, *220, 275*
Carmel Winery, *329*
Carmelite Monastery (Haifa), *291*
Carmelite Monastery (Mukhraka), *321*

Carmey Avdat Farm Winery, *478*
Caro Synagogue, *408*
Casemate Wall (Masada), *185*
Castles.⇨ *See Fortresses*
Catacombs (Beit She'arim), *353, 354*
Caverns
Haifa and the Northern Coast, 316–317, 345–346
Jerusalem and the Dead Sea region, 179–180, 195, 200–202
upper Galilee and the Golan, 426
Caves Reef, *456*
Cemeteries
Jerusalem, 113
Kibbutz Kinneret, 398
Tzfat (Safed) and environs, 409
Chagall, Marc, *104*
Chagall Windows, *104*
Chakra ✕, *121*
Chamber of the Holocaust, *95*
Children, activities for, *32–33.*
⇨ *See also under cities and areas*
Children's Memorial, *111, 339*
Christian hospices, *29, 520*
Christmas, *207*
Church of All Nations, *97*
Church of Mary Magdalene, *101*
Church of St. Anne, *86*
Church of St. Catherine, *204*
Church of St. Gabriel, *367–368*
Church of St. John the Baptist, *112*
Church of the Beatitudes, *392*
Church of the Holy Sepulcher, *66, 78–81*
Church of the Multiplication, *390–391*
Church of the Nativity, *204–205*
Church of the Primacy of St. Peter, *391*
Church of the Transfiguration, *372*
Church of the Visitation, *112*
Churches.⇨ *See also Convents;*
Monasteries and abbeys
Bethlehem, 204–205
Cana, 371
Haifa and the Northern Coast, 291, 321, 342
Jerusalem, 78–81, 86, 95, 97, 101, 102, 112
Jerusalem and the Dead Sea region, 185, 204–205
Latrun, 194
lower Galilee, 366–367, 368, 371, 372, 390–391, 392
Masada, 185
Mount of Beatitudes, 392
Mt. Tabor, 372
music in, 150
Nahariya, 342

Nazareth, 366–367, 368
Petra, 496
Tabgha, 390–391
Tel Aviv, 230, 232
Citadel Park (Tzfat), *409*
City of David, *88–90*
Clandestine Immigration and Naval Museum, *292*
Cliff rappelling.⇨ *See Rappelling*
Clock Tower Square (Jaffa), *231*
Colleges and universities, *478–479*
Colonnaded Street (Petra), *493*
Communications, *520–521*
Convents, *69, 102*
Coral Beach Reserve, *436, 443, 456*
Coral World Underwater Observatory and Aquarium, *443–444*
Corinthian Tomb, *496*
Credit cards, *7, 527*
Crusader City, *307*
Currency exchange, *527–528*
Customs, *522*

D

Dado Beach, *301*
Daliyat el Carmel, *319–321*
Dan Eilat 🏨, *450*
Dance
folk, 453
Jerusalem, 148
Tel Aviv, 268
Dance clubs
Jerusalem, 146, 147
Tel Aviv, 265, 266, 267
David, King, tomb of, *95*
David Citadel 🏨, *138*
David Intercontinental 🏨, *258*
Davidson Visitors Center, *66*
De Karina Artisan Gourmet Chocolates, *430*
Dead Sea, bathing in, *169–172*
Dead Sea region.⇨ *See Jerusalem and the Dead Sea region*
Dead Sea Scrolls, *106*
Degania, *397–398*
Degania Aleph, *397–398*
Desert precautions, *439*
Desert tours, *455–456*
Design Museum Holon, *232*
Detention camp, *305*
Diaspora Museum, *234*
Dining, *7, 15, 16, 30–31, 522–523.*⇨ *See also Restaurants; Under cities and areas*
Diving.⇨ *See Scuba diving and snorkeling*
Djinn Blocks, *496*
Dolphin Reef, *446*
Dolphinarum Beach, *269*
Domaine du Castel, *197*
Dome of the Rock, *66, 82–85*
Dominus Flevit Church, *101*

Dor Beach, *305*
Dormition Abbey, *95*
Druze people, *320*
Dudim (Lovers') Cave, *179–180*
Dugit Beach, *396*
Duties, *522*

E

Ecce Homo Convent of the Sisters of Zion, *69*
Ecotourism, *475*
Efendi Hotel ⛾ , *341*
Eilat and the Negev, *12, 19, 435–499*
  beaches, *454–455*
  Beersheva and the northern Negev, *436, 480–489*
  border crossings, *492–493*
  children, activities for, *443–444, 446, 448, 450, 451, 452, 455–456, 462*
  desert precautions, *439*
  Eilat and environs, *441–460*
  emergencies, *524*
  festivals, *453*
  guided tours, *441, 471, 482, 493*
  heart of the Negev, *436, 460–480*
  hotels, *440–441, 450–452, 464–465, 479, 487, 498–499*
  money matters, *493*
  nightlife and the arts, *452–453, 487, 499*
  orientation, *437*
  outdoor activities and sports, *436, 453–456, 465–466, 471–473, 475*
  Petra and environs, *436, 489–499*
  prices *440, 441*
  restaurants, *440, 446, 448–449, 464, 486–487, 498*
  shopping, *457, 466, 487, 489, 499*
  timing the visit, *439, 490*
  transportation, *439–440, 458, 459, 476, 482, 492*
  visitor information, *441, 443, 461, 482, 493*
Ein Avdat, *476–479*
Ein Avdat National Park, *478*
Ein Avdat Observation Point, *479*
Ein Bokek, *189–191*
Ein Camonim ✕, *411*
Ein Gedi, *160, 178–181*
Ein Gedi Nature Reserve, *178–179*
Ein Gedi Public Beach, *180*
Ein Gedi Spa, *180–181*
Ein Hod, *316–319*
Ein Kerem, *104*
Ein Kiniya, *429*
Ein Tamar, *190*
Einot Zukim, *177*
Electoral system of Israel, *109*

El-Jazzar Mosque, *334*
Electricity, *523*
Elijah's Cave, *292*
Ella Valley, *198–199*
Ella Valley Vineyards, *197*
El-Mahmoudiye Mosque, *232*
Emergencies, *523–524*
  and car travel, *518*
Eretz Israel Museum, *234–235*
Ethiopian Monastery, *69, 86*
Etiquette for visitors, *16–17*
Etzion Gaver School, *453*
Eucalyptus ✕, *124*

F

Festivals and seasonal events
  Eilat and the Negev, *453*
  Ginosar, *390*
  Haifa, *328*
  Jerusalem, *148*
  lower Galilee, *351, 363, 390, 396*
  Tel Aviv, *228*
  Tzfat (Safed) and environs, *412*
  upper Galilee and the Golan, *412*
Film, *37*
  Jerusalem, *149*
First Aliya Museum, *330*
Folk dancing, *453*
Folk music, *390*
Fortresses
  Akko, *336*
  lower Galilee, *363–364*
  upper Galilee and the Golan, *428*
Founders' Monument and Fountain, *225*
Frischman Beach, *270*

G

Gai Beach, *388*
Galei Galil Beach, *345*
Galilee region.⇨ See Lower Galilee; Upper Galilee and the Golan
Galita Chocolate Farm, *398*
Gamla Nature Reserve, *400, 434*
Gan Hashelosha National Park, *358*
Gan Meir (Tel Aviv), *225*
Ganei Yehoshua (Hayarkon Park), *235*
Garden of Gethsemane, *97*
Garden Tomb, *99*
Gardens
  Akko, *339*
  Haifa and the Northern Coast, *19, 278, 286, 294, 329*
  Jericho, *173*
  Jerusalem, *97, 99, 109–110*
  upper Galilee, *416*
Gas stations, *516*
General Exhibition (Tzfat), *408–409*

Genesis Land, *165*
German Colony (Haifa), *287*
German Colony (Jerusalem), *115, 129–131, 142–143*
Ghetto Fighters Museum, *339*
Ginosar, *378, 389–390*
Glass Art Museum, *188*
Goat Cheese Farms, *462*
Golan Archaeological Museum, *433*
Golan Beach, *396*
Golan Heights, *400, 426–434.* ⇨ See also Upper Galilee and the Golan
Golan Heights Winery, *326, 434*
Golani Junction Tree Planting Center, *372*
Golani Lookout, *428*
Golf, *311*
Golgotha, *79*
Gordon Beach, *270*
Great Temple, *493*
Grotto of the Nativity, *205*
Guided tours, *529–531*
Gutmann, Nahum, *227*
Gutmann Museum, *227*

H

Ha'Ari Synagogue, *409*
Haas Promenade (Jerusalem), *116*
Ha'atzmaut Square (Netanya), *312*
HaBaron Garden, *416*
Ha'Basta ✕, *242–243*
HaChazer ✕, *130*
Hadassah Hospital, *104*
Haggay Observation Point, *480*
Hai Bar Nature Reserve, *458*
Haifa and the Northern Coast, *12, 277–346*
  Akko to Rosh Hanikra, *278, 279, 332–346*
  beaches, *278, 301–302, 311, 314, 341, 344–345*
  children, activities for, *292–293, 294, 303, 312, 316–317, 337, 344–345*
  festivals, *326*
  guided tours, *284, 306, 319, 326–327, 342*
  history, *290, 333*
  hotels, *283, 298, 300, 303, 311, 314, 318, 341, 343–344*
  nightlife and the arts, *300–301, 318, 344*
  orientation, *279*
  outdoor activities and sports, *301–302, 305, 311, 314–315, 341, 344–345*
  prices, *283*
  restaurants, *282–283, 295–298, 309–311, 313–314, 317–318, 319–320, 340, 342–343, 346*
  safety and precautions, *334*

shopping, 302, 318–319, 320–321, 341

timing the visit, 281

transportation, 282, 284–284, 303, 306, 312, 321, 329, 333, 341, 345

visitor information, 284, 312, 329, 334

Wine Country and Mt. Carmel, 278, 279, 315–332

Haifa Museum of Art, 292

Haifa Zoo, 292–293

Hall of Remembrance, 111

HaMaoz (bar), 265

Hameiri House, 409

Hammat Gader, 397

Hammat Tiberias, 382–383

Hanamal 24 ✕, 296

Hans Sternbach Vineyards ✕, 199

Haram Esh-Sharif, 76–77

Harmony Hotel ⬚, 136

HaTachana, 226–227

Hatzor Museum, 419

Health concerns, 524–525

Hebrew language, 500–505

Hecht Museum, 293

Helena ✕, 310

Helena Rubinstein Pavilion, 225

Herbert Samuel ✕, 247

Hermon River (Banias) Nature Reserve, 400, 426–427

Herod, King, 90, 183

Herodian amphitheater, 307

Herodian Quarter, 90

Herod's port, 307, 308

Herzl, Theodor, 108, 109

Herzl Beach, 314

Herzl Museum, 109

Herzliya Pituach Beach, 270

Hidden Waterfall, 180

High Place of Sacrifice, 496

Hiking

Eilat and the Negev Desert, 436, 465, 471

lower Galilee, 380

tours, 531

Hilton Beach, 270–271

Hinnom Valley, 116–117

Hisham's Palace, 167

History, 24–27, 47–52

of Haifa and the Northern Coast, 290, 310, 333

of Jerusalem, 91

of Tiberias, 384

Hof HaShaket Beach, 302

Hof Shonit Beach, 311

Holidays, 38–40

Christian, 380

cuisine for, 56–57

Holocaust History Museum, 111

Holocaust memorials, 95, 111

Holy Sepulcher Church, 66, 78–81

Home exchanges, 29, 520

Horse Square (Petra), 496

Horseback riding

Heifa and the Northern Coast, 315

upper Galilee and the Golan, 412, 415

Hospitaller Fortress (Knights' Hall), 336

Hot springs

Hammat Gader, 397

Hammat Tiberias, 382–383

Hotel Montefiore ⬚, 253

Hotels, 7, 15, 29, 520

prices, 15, 136, 165, 252, 283, 352, 404, 441

House rentals, 29, 520

Hula Lake Nature Reserve, 400, 419–420

Hutzot Hayotzer Arts and Crafts Festival, 148

I

Ilana Goor Museum, 232

Ima ✕, 125–126

Immigrant Artists' Exhibition, 408–409

Inbal ⬚, 139

Independence Hall Museum, 222–223

Independence Park, 117

Inn of the Good Samaritan, 165–166

Insurance, 532

International Birding and Research Center, 455, 475

Internet, 520, 533

Isfiya, 319–321

Israel Air Force Museum, 483

Israel Festival, 148

Israel Museum, 18, 104, 106–107

Isrotel Dead Sea ⬚, 190

Isrotel Princess ⬚, 450

Itineraries, 41–46

J

Jacir Palace InterContinental Bethlehem ⬚, 210

Jacob's Ladder Festival, 390

Jaffa, 213, 228–233, 248, 250–251, 262, 267, 275–276

Jaffa Flea Market, 230, 276

Jaffa Port, 230

Janco-Dada Museum, 316

Jazz clubs, 147

Jeep tours, 415, 465–466, 473

Jericho, 166–167, 173, 175

Jeiicho Cable Car, 167

Jerusalem, 12, 53–158

cafés, 133

Center City, 55, 113–117, 119, 121, 124–129, 136, 145–147, 151–154

children, activities for, 104, 106–107, 112, 119, 121, 125, 126, 127, 128–129, 130, 131–132, 138, 139, 142, 143

City of David, 54, 88–91

East Jerusalem, 144–145, 147

emergencies, 524

exploring, 62–117

festivals, 148

German Colony, 115, 129–131, 142–143

guided tours, 61–62

history, 72–73, 91, 96

holy places, 70–85

hotels, 61, 135–145

Jewish Quarter, 54, 86–91

Mount of Olives and East Jerusalem, 54, 55, 97–102

nightlife and the arts, 145–150

Old City, 18, 54, 63–69, 86, 131–132, 143, 154–156

orientation, 55

prices, 118, 136

Rehavia, Talbieh, King David Street and Yemin Moshe, 132, 134, 138–139, 156–157

restaurants, 61, 118–135

safety and precautions, 60

Seam Line, 144–145

shopping, 150–158

street markets, 151, 155

timing the visit, 59

Tower of David and Mt. Zion, 54, 91–95

transportation, 60–61

visitor information, 62

West Jerusalem, 55, 102–113, 134, 140, 142, 147, 157–158

Jerusalem and the Dead Sea region, 12, 159–210

beaches and pools, 177–178, 180–181

Bethlehem, 160, 202–210

children, activities for, 165, 173, 175, 177, 179, 192–193, 200–202

guided tours, 165, 186, 203

hotels, 164, 175, 181, 189, 190–191, 196, 210

Masada and the Dead Sea, 160, 165–191

orientation, 161

outdoor activities and sports, 180–181, 191

prices, 164, 165

restaurants, 164, 175, 181, 189, 194–195, 199, 208

safety and precautions, 176, 178, 203

shopping, 191, 196, 210

timing the visit, 163, 187

transportation, 163–164, 172, 186

visitor information, 187, 188, 203

West Bank, 206

West of Jerusalem, 160, 192–202

Jerusalem Archaeological Park, 66, 77

Jerusalem Beach, 271

Jerusalem Cinematheque, 149

Jesus in Galilee, *374–380*
Jewish educational tours, *531*
Jewish shrines. *See also*
  Synagogues
Bethlehem, 207–208
Haifa and the Northern Coast,
  292
Jerusalem, 66–67, 68, 74–75,
  76–77, 104
lower Galilee, 384, 398
Mt. Meron, 413
upper Galilee and the Golan,
  413
Jezreel and Jordan Valleys,
  348, 353–354, 356–364
Jordan River, *18, 379, 394*
Jordan River Park, *394*
Judean Hills, *160, 197*

K

Kabbalah, *408*
Kadma Wines, *198*
Kalamata ✕, *250*
Kalia Beach, *178*
Katzrin, *432–434*
Kayaking
lower Galilee, 388, 393
upper Galilee and the Golan,
  400, 424
Kedumim Square (Tel Aviv),
  230
Kfar Kama, *373*
Kfar Tavor, *372*
Khan el-Umdan, *337*
Khazneh monument, *495*
Kibbutz guest houses, *29, 520*
Kibbutz Kinneret Cemetery, *398*
Kibbutz life, *360*
Kibbutz Mitzpe Shalem, *178*
Kibbutz music, *390*
Kibbutz Sde Boker, *476*
Kibbutz Tzora, *198*
Kibbutzim, history of, *360*
Kidron Valley, *101–102*
Kikar Hameginim, *410*
Kikar Magen David (Tel Aviv),
  225
King Albert Square (Tel Aviv),
  225
Kings City, *446*
Kinneret, *397, 398*
Kiryat Sanz Beach, *314*
Kiryat Shmona, *420, 422–424*
Klezmer Festival, *412*
Knesset, *108*
Kochav Hayarden National
  Park, *363*
Korazim, *392–393*
Korazim National Park, *392*
Kursi, *379, 395–396*
Kursi National Park, *395*

L

L.A. Mayer Museum for Islamic
  Art, *112*
Language, *16–17*

Hebrew vocabulary, 500–505
Palestinian Arabic vocabulary,
  506–510
Last Supper, Room of, *93*
Latrun, *192–195*
Latrun Armored Corps Museum,
  192
Le Meridien (Eilat) 🛏, *451*
Le Meridien (Ein Bokek) 🛏, *190*
Limonah ✕, *175*
Lion Monument, *496*
Little Jerusalem ✕, *126*
Lodging, *7, 15, 29, 520.* *See*
  also Hotels
Lovers' Cave, *179–180*
Lower Galilee, *12, 347–398*
beaches, 388, 396
children, activities for, 358–359,
  361, 368, 373, 387, 395–396,
  397, 398
festivals and seasonal events,
  351, 363, 390, 396
guided tours, 353, 365–366
hotels, 352, 361, 363, 369–370,
  386–387, 390, 392–393,
  395–396, 397
Jezreel and Jordan Valleys, 348,
  353–354, 356–364
Nazareth and the Galilee Hills,
  348, 364–373
nightlife and the arts, 363, 388,
  396
orientation, 349
outdoor activities and sports,
  361, 388, 393
prices, 352
restaurants, 352, 359, 361,
  368–369, 373, 384–386, 395
shopping, 370, 388
Tiberias and the Sea of Galilee,
  349, 381–398
timing the visit, 351
transportation, 351–352, 365,
  380, 382
visitor information, 366
Lunagal (water park), *396*

M

Ma'alot Olei Hagardom, *410*
Ma'ayan Harod, *358–359*
Machaneh Yehuda, *114, 151*
Mahneyuda ✕, *126*
Mail and shipping, *526*
Maimonides, Moses, *384*
Majdal Shams, *429–430*
Makhtesh Ramon, *19, 436, 460,*
  462–466
Mamilla Hotel 🛏, *139*
Manara Cable Car, *420, 422*
Mané Katz Museum, *293–294*
Manger Square, *207*
Markets, *34*
Akko, 338
Jerusalem, 151, 155
Nazareth, 367
Tel Aviv, 275, 276
Mary, Virgin, tomb, *102*

Marzipan Museum, *373*
Masada, *18, 183–187*
Mashabim Junction, *480*
Me'a She'arim, *117*
Meat-balim ✕, *417*
Megiddo, *357–358*
Memorial Museum of
  Hungarian-Speaking Jewry,
  410
Merom Golan, *432*
Messa ✕, *244*
Metulla, *424–425*
Metzizim Beach, *271*
Midnight Biking Through
  Jerusalem, *61*
Mikhmoret beach, *314*
Mikveh (Masada), *185*
Military Cemetery, *113*
Milk Grotto, *207*
Mineral Beach, *178*
Mini Israel, *193*
Mizgaga Museum, *303*
Mitzpe Ramon, *460–466*
Mitzpe Revivim, *479–480*
Moevenpick 🛏, *499*
Mona ✕, *127*
Monasteries and abbeys
Haifa and the Northern Coast,
  291, 321
Jerusalem, 69, 86
Jerusalem and the Dead Sea
  region, 194
Latrun, 194
lower Galilee, 395
Mukhraka, 321
Petra, 496
Tel Aviv, 230
Monastery (Al-Deir), *496*
Money matters, *17, 526–528*
Mony Wines, *198*
Montefiore ✕, *244*
Montefiore's Windmill,
  114–115
Monument to the Negev Bri-
  gade, *489*
Moshav Neve Ativ, *429*
Mosques
Akko, 334, 336
Jerusalem, 82–84
Tel Aviv, 232
Mt. Arbel, *389*
Mt. Bental Observatory, *432*
Mt. Gilboa, *348, 357–359, 361*
Mt. Hermon, *428–429*
Mt. Herzl Military Cemetery,
  113
Mt. Herzl National Memorial
  Park, *108–109*
Mt. Meron, *413–415*
Mount of Beatitudes, *378,*
  391–392
Mount of Olives, *97, 99,*
  101–102
Mount of Olives Observation
  Point, *99, 101*
Mt. Tabor, *372–373, 379*
Mt. Zion, *91–95*

Mount Zion ⛰, *143*
Mountain biking, *466*
Mukhraka, *321*
Museum of Bedouin Culture, *483*
Museum of the Good Samaritin, *166*
Museum of the Underground Prisoners, *338–339*
Museums.⇨ *See also* Art galleries and museums
Aaronson, 329
architecture, 220
Air Force, 33, 483
in Akko, 338–339
archaeology, 90, 101, 103–104, 105–106, 166, 184, 234–235, 293, 303, 308, 309, 357, 419, 433
Bedouin culture, 483
in Caesarea, 308
design, 232
Diaspora, 234
in Eilat and the Negev, 483, 485
in Ein Hod, 316, 317
ethnography, 338
farming, 424
Ginosar, 389–390
glass, 188
in Haifa and the Northern Coast, 33, 287, 292, 293–294, 303, 308, 309, 316, 317, 329, 338–339, 340
Herzl, 109
Holocaust, 95, 110–111, 339
hours, 525
Hungarian Jewry, 410
immigrants to Palestine, 292, 330
Israeli history, 220, 222–223, 234–235, 409
Israeli independence, 222–223
in Jerusalem, 18, 32, 90, 94–95, 101, 103–104, 106–107, 109, 110–111, 112
in Jerusalem and the Dead Sea region, 166, 173, 184, 188, 192
Jerusalem history, 94–95, 101
in Katzrin, 432
in Kiryat Shmona, 422
in lower Galilee, 357, 373, 389–390
maritime history, 294
marzipan, 373
military, 192, 292
in Mt. Tabor, 373
music, 317
in Nahsholim-Dor, 303
natural history, 397–398, 425
in Petra, 496
prison, 338–339
Roman artifacts, 308
in Rosh Pina, 416
Russian, 173
science, 112, 232, 294

in Tel Aviv, 220, 222–223, 227, 228, 232, 232, 234–235
in Tel Hatzor, 419
in Tzfat (Safed) and environs, 409, 410
Tzfat (Safed) history, 409
in upper Galilee and the Golan, 409, 410, 419, 422, 425, 433
Warsaw Ghetto uprising, 339
in Zichron Ya'akov, 329
Music, classical
Eilat and the Negev, 453, 487
Haifa and the Northern Coast, 301, 318
Jerusalem, 149–150
lower Galilee, 363, 396
Tel Aviv, 268
upper Galilee and the Golan, 423
Music, popular.⇨ *See* Dance clubs; Folk-music clubs; Jazz clubs

N

Nahal Arugot, *180*
Nahal Ayoun Nature Reserve, *424*
Nahal David, *179*
Nahal Me'arot Nature Reserve, *316–317*
Nahalat Binyamin Pedestrian Mall, *212, 223, 275*
Nahalat Shiva, *115*
Nahariya, *341–345*
Nahsholim-Dor, *303, 305*
Nanutchka (bar), *265*
National Maritime Museum, *294*
National Museum of Science, Technology and Space, *294*
National Solar Energy Center, *479*
Nature reserves
Eilat and the Negev, 436, 443, 456, 458
Haifa and the Northern Coast, 316–317
Jerusalem and the Dead Sea region, 179–180
lower Galilee, 389
upper Galilee and the Golan, 400, 419–420, 414, 425, 426–427, 434
Nazareth and the Galilee Hills, *348, 364–373, 379*
Nazareth Village, *368*
Negev Brigade Memorial, *489*
Negev Desert.⇨ *See* Eilat and the Negev
Neot HaKikar, *190*
Neot Kedumim, *194*
Netanya, *312–315*
Neve Midbar Beach, *178*
Neve Midbar spa, *485*
Neveh Tzedek, *213, 226–228, 247, 258, 263, 266, 276*

Nightlife and the arts, *36–37*
Nimrod's Fortress, *428*
Nisco Museum of Mechanical Music, *317*
North Beach, *454–455*
Northern Coast.⇨ *See* Haifa and the Northern Coast
Number 7 Simtat Plonit, *226*
Nymphaeum fountain, *496*

O

Obelisk Tomb, *497*
Obelisks, *497*
Observatory Tower, *444*
Odem Mountain Winery, *430*
Off-road vehicles, *424*
Ohel Ya'akov, *330*
Old Rosh Pina office, *416*
Olla ✕, *449*
Opera, *268, 487*
Orchid Reef ⛰, *452*
Orna and Ella ✕, *245*
Oud Fesival, *148*
Outdoor activities and sports.
⇨ *See* specific sports; under cities and areas

P

Packing for the trip, *528*
Palace Tomb, *497*
Palaces
Jericho, 167
Masada, 183, 185
Palestinian Arabic language, *506–510*
Palmach Museum, *235*
Pan, *427*
Paragliding, *315*
Parks, national
Eilat and the Negev, 478
Jerusalem, 108
lower Galilee, 348, 356–357, 358–359, 361–362, 363, 370–371, 389, 392, 393, 395
Tel Aviv, 231, 235
upper Galilee and the Golan, 415
Passports, *528*
Pater Noster Convent, *102*
Peace Center Restaurant ✕, *208*
Pepo Beer, *194*
Performing arts, *36–37*
Petra and environs, *436, 489–499*
Petra Moon ⛰, *499*
Pisan Harbor, *336–337*
Pools of Bethesda, *86*
Precautions.⇨ *See* Desert precautions; Safety and precautions
Predator Center, *458*
Prehistoric cultures
Carmel Caves, 316
Megiddo, 357–358

Index > **539**

Prices
dining, 15, 118, 164, 236, 284, 352, 404, 440
Eilat and the Negev, 440, 441
Haifa and the Northern Coast, 283
Jerusalem, 118, 136
Jerusalem and the Dead Sea region, 164, 165
lodging, 15, 136, 165, 252, 283, 352, 404, 441
lower Galilee, 352
Tel Aviv, 236, 252
upper Galilee and the Golan, 404
Promenade (Eilat), 444
Pubs
Jerusalem, 145–147

Q

Qasr al-Bint, 493, 495
Qasr Al Yahud, 167
Qumran, 176–178

R

Rabin, Yitzhak, 225
Rabin Square (Tel Aviv), 225
Rachel's Tomb, 207–208
Ralli Museum, 309
Rama's Kitchen ✕, 194–195
Ramat Hanadiv, 329
Ramat Rachel ▨, 143
Ramparts, The (Akko), 338
Ramparts Walk (Jerusalem), 92–93
Rappelling, 456, 466
Red Sea International Music Festival, 453
Red Sea Jazz Festival, 453
Relaxation Pools at Dolphin Reef, 445
Renaissance Tomb, 497
Restaurants, 7, 15, 30–31, 522–523.⇨ *See under cities and areas*
prices, 15, 118, 164, 236, 284, 352, 404, 440
street food, 240–241
Restrooms, 528
Robinson's Arch, 66
Rockefeller Museum of Archaeology, 101
Rokach House, 228
Roman aqueduct (Caesarea), 307, 311
Roman Catholic church, 390–391
Roman sites and artifacts
Avdat, 467
Beit She'an, 361, 362, 363
Beit She'arim, 354
Caesarea, 305–311
Eilat and the Negev, 467
Gamla, 400, 434
Ginosar, 389–390
Haifa and the Northern Coast, 305, 306–309, 310, 332

Jerusalem, 88, 90
Jerusalem and the Dead Sea region, 173, 176–177, 183–187, 200–202
lower Galilee, 348, 361, 362, 363, 366, 370–371
Masada, 184, 185
Nazareth, 366
Petra, 497, 498
upper Galilee and the Golan, 400, 434
Zippori, 348, 370–371
Roman Camps, 184
Roman Soldier's Tomb, 497
Roman theater (Beit She'an), 362, 363
Roman theater (Caesarea), 307
Roman theater (Petra), 495
Room of the Last Supper, 93
Rosh Hanikra, 345–346
Rosh Pina, 415–418
Rota Winery, 485
Rothschild Boulevard (Tel Aviv), 223
Rothschild 71, *The* ▨, 257
Rubin Museum, 223
Rubin, Reuven, 223
Russian Museum, 173

S

Safed. ⇨ *See Tzfat (Safed) and environs*
Safety and precautions, 17, 528
Eilat and the Negev, 439
Haifa and the Northern Coast, 334
Jerusalem, 60
Jerusalem and the Dead Sea region, 176, 178, 203
Sailing. ⇨ *See Boating and sailing*
Saloona (bar), 267
St. Peter's Monastery, 230
San Antonio Roman Catholic Church, 232
Sarona, 223
Sataf, 193
Schwartz Hotel, 416
Scots Hotel ▨, 387
Scuba diving and snorkeling
Caesorea, 311
Eilat and the Negev, 456
Ein Bokek, 191
Haifa and the Northern Coast, 302, 311, 345
Nahariya, 345
Tel Aviv, 272
Sde Boker College, 478–479
Sea of Galilee, 19, 388
Seaside Promenade (Netanya), 312
Sermon on the Mount, site of, 391
Shai Seltzer, 193
Shalom & Relax ▨, 257
Shapiro Beer, 198

Sheinkin Street (Tel Aviv), 225
Shepards' Fields, 207
Shopping, 17.⇨ *See also under cities and areas*
hours, 525–526
Sidonian Burial Caves, 201
Silk Tomb, 497
Simtat Plonit (Tel Aviv), 226
Siq, 495
Sironit Beach, 314
Skydiving, 305
Skiing, 428–429
Snake Path, 184
Snake Tomb, 497
Snorkeling. ⇨ *See Scuba diving and snorkeling*
Soreq Cave, 195–196
Souk (market; Akko), 338
Souk (market; Jerusalem), 155
Souk (market; Nazareth), 367
South Beach, 455
Southern Steps, 66
Spas
Eilat and the Negev, 485
Jerusalem and the Dead Sea region, 172
Sports. ⇨ *See specific sport; Under cities and areas*
Spring of Gihon, 89
Srigim Brewery, 198
Stations of the Cross, 66–67
Stella Maris Church, 291
Stone of Unction, 79
Summit Park, 231
Suzanne Dellal Center for Dance and Theater, 227, 268
Swimming
Jerusalem and the Dead Sea region, 171
Tel Aviv, 272
Surfing, 272
Swimming, 272
Symbols, 7
Synagogues
Bar'am, 415
Beit Alfa, 358
Capernaum, 393
Ein Gedi, 180
Hammat Tiberias, 383
Jerusalem and the Dead Sea region, 180, 185
Katzrin, 433
Korazim, 392
lower Galilee, 358, 383, 392, 393
Masada, 185
Rosh Pina, 416
Tzfat (Safed) and environs, 407, 408, 409
upper Galilee and the Golan, 407, 408, 409, 416
Zichron Ya'akov, 330

T

Tabgha, 378, 390–391
Tabor Winery, 327, 373
Taxes, 529

Taxis, *518*
Technion (research center), *294*
Tel Arad, *188*
Tel Aviv, *12, 18, 211–276*
 beaches, *212, 269–272*
 Center City, *213, 220, 222–226,
  236–237, 242–247, 252–253,
  257, 258–259, 265–266,
  273–275*
 children, activities for, *222, 225,
  235, 244*
 emergencies, *524*
 festivals, *228*
 Florentine, *248, 267, 276*
 guided tours, *219*
 Herzliya Pituach, *258*
 hotels, *218, 252–258*
 Jaffa, *213, 228–233, 248,
  250–251, 262, 267, 275–276*
 Neveh Tzedek, *213, 226–228,
  247, 258, 263, 266, 276*
 nightlife and the arts, *259–269*
 orientation, *213*
 outdoor activities and sports,
  269–272
 prices, *236, 252*
 restaurants, *212, 218, 235–252*
 shopping, *272–276*
 Tel Aviv Port and Northern Tel
  Aviv, *213, 233–235, 251–252,
  264–265, 267, 276*
 timing the visit, *216*
 transportation, *217–218*
 visitor information, *219*
 walking tours, *219*
Tel Aviv Museum of Art, *223*
Tel Baruch Beach, *271*
Tel Beersheva, *483, 485*
Tel Beit Shemesh, *198*
Tel Dan Nature Reserve, *425*
Tel Hai, *422*
Tel Hai Courtyard Museum, *424*
Tel Hatzor, *419*
Tel Jericho, *173*
Tel Maresha, *200*
Tel Megiddo National Park,
 356–357
Telephones, *520–521*
Tel-O-Fun (bike-sharing), *271*
Telul Abu'Alayiq, *173*
Temple Mount, *76–77*
Temple of the Winged Lions,
 497
Theater, *36–37*
 Eilat and the Negev, *453, 487*
 Jerusalem, *150*
 Tel Aviv, *268–269*
Tiberias and the Sea of Galilee,
 349, 381–398
Tiberias Hot Springs, *383*
Tikotin Museum of Japanese
 Art, *287*
Time, *529*
Time Trek, *308*
Timing the visit, *15*
Timna Park, *436, 459–460*
Tipping, *529*

Tisch Family Zoological
 Gardens, *109–110*
Tishbi Estate Winery, *332*
Tomb of David, *95*
Tomb of Moses Maimonides,
 384
Tomb of Rabbi Shimon Bar
 Yochai, *413*
Tomb of Sextius Florentinus,
 498
Tomb of the Virgin, *102*
Tour operators, *529–531*
Tower of David, *91–95*
Tower of David Museum, *94–95*
Train travel, *519*
Transportation, *14, 512–519*.
 ⇨ See also under cities and
 areas
Trappist Abbey of Latrun, *194*
"Treasures in the Walls" Eth-
 nography Museum, *330*
Treasury, *495*
Tree-planting projects, *372*
Turkish Bathhouse, *337*
Tza'adot (Big Walks), *361*
Tzfat (Safed) and environs,
 400, 405–413
Tzuba Vineyard, *195*

U

Underground Prisoners
 Museum, *338–339*
Underwater Archaeological
 Center, *305*
Underwater Observatory, *444*
Upper Galilee and the Golan,
 12, 399–434
 children, activities for, *420, 422,
  425, 428, 433*
 festivals, *412*
 Golan Heights, *400, 426–434*
 guided tours, *415*
 hotels, *404, 411–412, 414, 418,
  423, 425, 430*
 nightlife and the arts, *412, 418,
  423*
 orientation, *401*
 outdoor activities and sports,
  400, 412, 415, 424, 425
 prices, *404*
 restaurants, *404, 410–411, 414,
  416–417, 422, 424, 430,
  432, 434*
 shopping, *412–413, 418*
 timing the visit, *403*
 transportation, *403–404, 407,
  416*
 Tzfat (Safed) and environs, *400,
  405–413*
 Upper Hula Valley, *400,
  420–426*
 visitor information, *404–405*
Upper Hula Valley, *400,
 420–426*
Uri Buri ✕, *340*
Urn Tomb, *498*

V

Valley of the Communities, *111*
Value-added tax, *529*
Via Dolorosa, *66–67, 68*
Visas, *528*
Visitor information, *532*.⇨ See
 also under cities and areas
Vista of Peace Sculpture
 Garden, *294*

W

Walking
 Tel Aviv, *219*
Water Cistern (Masada), *185*
Water sports
 Eilat and the Negev, *455*
 lower Galilee, *388, 393, 396*
 Tel Aviv, *271–272*
 upper Galilee, *424*
Waterfalls
 Jerusalem and the Dead Sea
  region, *180*
 upper Galilee and the Golan,
  427
Way of Suffering (Way of the
 Cross), *66–67*
Weather, *15*
Websites, *532*
Weizmann Institute of Science,
 232
West Bank, *206*
Western Palace (Masada), *185*
Western Wall, *69, 74–75*
Western Wall Tunnel, *69*
Wildlife preserves.⇨ See
 Nature reserves
Wine festivals, *148, 328*
Wine touring and tastings,
 322–328, 329, 332, 531
Wineries, *322–328*
 Eilat and the Negev, *478, 485*
 Haifa and the Northern Coast,
  278, 315, 329, 332
 Jerusalem and the Dead Sea
  region, *189, 194, 195,
  197–198, 199*
 lower Galilee, *373*
 upper Galilee and the Golan,
  430, 434
Wohl Archaeological Museum,
 90
Wooden fishing boat, *389–390*

Y

Yad Layeled, *339*
Yad Vashem, *110–111*
Yardenit, *397, 398*
Yatir Winery, *189*
Yefe Nof Street (Haifa), *287*
Yefet Street (Jaffa), *233*
Yehelim Boutique Hotel 🖬 , *189*
Yemin Moshe, *117*
Yigal Alon Museum, *389–390*
YMCA, *115*

Z

Zachariah's Tomb, *102*
Zamire Beach, *302*
Zichron Ya'akov, *321, 329–331*
Zippori National Park, *348, 370–371*
Zoological Gardens, *109–110*
Zoos
Haifa and the Northern Coast, 292–293
Jerusalem, 109–110

PHOTO CREDITS

ABOUT OUR WRITERS

Benjamin Balint, a writer based in Jerusalem, writes for the *Wall Street Journal, Haaretz, the Weekly Standard, Die Zeit,* and the *Claremont Review of Books.* His book *Running Commentary* came out in 2010. Benjamin updated the "Haifa and the Northern Coast" chapter. Contact him at benjamin.balint@gmail.com.

Judy Lash Balint, updater of "Travel Smart Israel," is the author of two books about Jerusalem and is the social media coordinator at the Jerusalem Center for Public Affairs. She blogs at jerusalemdiaries. blogspot.com and contributes to several U.S.-based news services and magazines. Judy shares her passion for Jerusalem through her writing as well as by leading private briefing seminars for visitors. Contact her at judy.balint@gmail.com.

Inbal Baum, who updated Tel Aviv, is the founder of Delicious Israel, a company she created to reveal local and insider aspects of Israel. Passionate about lifestyle and culture, Inbal left her career as an attorney and immigrated to Israel in 2009. Based in Tel Aviv, she spends her free time as an amateur chef and yoga instructor. Contact Inbal at www.deliciousisrael.com and inbal@deliciousisrael.com.

Daniella Cheslow is a print and radio journalist based in Tel Aviv. She has reported on Israeli culture and politics for the Associated Press, *Tablet* magazine, PRI's *The World, Deutsche Welle,* and the *Christian Science Monitor.* Daniella updated the "Around Jerusalem and the Dead Sea" chapter and added, among other things, the microbreweries in the Ella Valley. Daniella's website is daniellacheslow.com; e-mail her at daniella.cheslow@gmail.com.

Shari Giddens Helmer, a Tel Aviv–based writer for the Start-up Nation, is an avid QR Code blogger and travel enthusiast. A native Chicagoan, she has made Israel her home since 2006. Shari updated the "Lower Galilee" chapter. Contact her at shari.helmer@gmail.com.

Matthew Kalman is a writer and filmmaker based in Jerusalem, reporting for *Technology Review, The Guardian, Channel 4 News,* and other world media. He is the author of *The Murder of Yasser Arafat* and *Psychobibi* and director of *Circumcise Me: The Comedy of Yisrael Campbell.* His Fodor's assignment included parts of the chapter on Jerusalem.

Noya Kohavi is a Tel Aviv-based writer and reporter who covers culture, music, food, and politics. Her work has appeared in *Haaretz,* the *New York Observer* and the *Telluride Daily Planet,* among other places. She updated the "Upper Galilee and the Golan" chapter.

Mike Rogoff, a professional tour guide and writer, has been exploring the byways of Israel with visitors of all persuasions since the early 1970s. South African–born and Jerusalem-based, Mike is a recipient of the Israel government's Guide of the Year award, and has contributed to Fodor's Israel since 1985. He updated "Experience Israel" as well as "Jerusalem Exploring," and the "Jesus in the Galilee" and "Jerusalem: Keeping the Faith" features. Contact Mike at rogoff@netvision.net.il.

Adeena Sussman is a food writer, recipe developer, and cooking instructor who has written about Israeli food and wine and created Israeli-inspired recipes for publications including *Food and Wine, Sunset,* and *Hadassah.* Based in New York, she updated the Eilat and the Negev chapter as well as the feature on "The Wines of Israel." Adeena's website is adeenasussman.com.